# Communications
# in Computer and Information Science  278

Miltiadis D. Lytras   Da Ruan
Robert D. Tennyson   Patricia Ordonez De Pablos
Francisco José García Peñalvo   Lazar Rusu   (Eds.)

# Information Systems, E-learning, and Knowledge Management Research

4th World Summit on the Knowledge Society
WSKS 2011
Mykonos, Greece, September 21-23, 2011
Revised Selected Papers

 Springer

Volume Editors

Miltiadis D. Lytras
The American College of Greece
Agia Paraskevi, Athens, Greece
E-mail: mlytras@acg.edu

Da Ruan †
Ghent University, Belgium

Robert D. Tennyson
University of Minnesota
Minneapolis, MN, USA
E-mail: rtenny@umn.edu

Patricia Ordonez De Pablos
University of Oviedo
Oviedo-Asturias, Spain
E-mail: patrio@uniovi.es

Francisco José García Peñalvo
Universidad de Salamanca, Spain
E-mail: fgarcia@usal.es

Lazar Rusu
Stockholm University, Kista, Sweden
email: lrusu@dsv.su.se

ISSN 1865-0929                          e-ISSN 1865-0937
ISBN 978-3-642-35878-4                  e-ISBN 978-3-642-35879-1
DOI 10.1007/978-3-642-35879-1
Springer Heidelberg Dordrecht London New York

Library of Congress Control Number: 2012954790

CR Subject Classification (1998): J.1, K.5.2, H.4, H.3, H.5, C.2, K.4

*Typesetting:* Camera-ready by author, data conversion by Scientific Publishing Services, Chennai, India

Printed on acid-free paper

Springer is part of Springer Science+Business Media (www.springer.com)

# Preface

It is a great pleasure to share with you the Springer CCIS proceedings of the 4th World Summit on the Knowledge Society—WSKS 2011—that was organized by the International Academic Council for the Knowledge Society, during September 21–23, 2011, in Mykonos, Greece.

The 4th World Summit on the Knowledge Society (WSKS 2011) was an international attempt to promote dialogue on the main aspects of the knowledge society toward a better world for all.

This annual summit brings together key stakeholders of the knowledge society development worldwide, from academia, industry, government, policy makers, and active citizens, to look at the impact and prospects of information technology, and the knowledge-based era it is creating, on key facets of living, working, learning, innovating and collaborating in today's hyper-complex world. The summit provides a distinct, unique forum for cross-disciplinary fertilization of research, favoring the dissemination of new scientific ideas relevant to international research agendas such as the EU (FP7), OECD or UNESCO.

Eleven general scientific pillars provided the constitutional elements of the summit:

1. Information Technologies – Knowledge Management Systems – E-business and Business, Organizational and Inter-organizational Information Systems for the Knowledge Society
2. Knowledge, Learning, Education, Learning Technologies and E-learning for the Knowledge Society
3. Social and Humanistic Computing for the Knowledge Society – Emerging Technologies for Society and Humanity
4. Culture and Cultural Heritage – Technology for Culture Management – Management of Tourism and Entertainment – Tourism Networks in the Knowledge Society
5. Government and Democracy in the Knowledge Society
6. Innovation, Sustainable Development and Strategic Management for the Knowledge Society
7. Service Science, Management, Engineering, and Technology
8. Intellectual and Human Capital Development in the Knowledge Society
9. Advanced Applications for Environmental Protection and Green Economy Management
10. Future Prospects for the Knowledge Society: From Foresight Studies to Projects and Public Policies
11. Technologies and Business Models for the Creative Industries

In the fourth event of the series, WSKS 2011, five main tracks were organized. Springer's *Communications on Computer and Information Sciences,*

Volume 278, summarizes 90 articles that were selected after a double-blind review process from 198 submissions, contributed by 432 co-authors.

We are confident that in this volume of CCIS you will find excellent quality research that summarizes sound propositions for advanced systems toward the knowledge society.

I would like to thank the more than 400 co-authors, from 32 countries, for their submissions; the Program Committee members and their subreviewers for the thoroughness of their reviews; and all the colleagues for the great support they offered in the organization of the event in Mykonos, Greece.

We are honored for the support and encouragement of the Editors-in-Chief of the eight ISI SCI/SSCI listed journals that agreed to publish special issues from extended versions of papers presented at the summit:

- Robert Tennyson, Editor-in-Chief of *Computers in Human Behaviour*
- Amit Sheth, Editor-in-Chief of *International Journal of Semantic Web and Information Systems*
- Patricia Ordonez De Pablos, Editor-in-Chief of *International Journal of Learning and Intellectual Capital*

A great thank you also to Alfred Hofmann, Springer, and his staff for the excellent support in all the phases of publishing the CCIS 278 proceedings.

We need a better world. We contribute with our sound voices to the agenda, policies, and actions. We invite you to join your voice with ours and all together to shape a new deal for our world. Education, sustainable development, health, opportunities for well-being, culture, collaboration, peace, democracy, technology for all.

We look forward to seeing you at the fifth event of the series, for which you can find more information at: http://www.wsks.org.

With 11 special issues already agreed for WSKS 2012, and six main tracks, we want to ask for your involvement and we would be happy to see you joining us.

Miltiadis D. Lytras

# Organization

WSKS 2011 was organized by the International Scientific Council for the Knowledge Society, and supported by the *International Journal of the Knowledge Society Research* (http://www.igi-global.com/ijksr).

## Executive Committee

## General Chair

**Miltiadis D. Lytras**
Research Faculty, The American College of Greece, Deree College, Greece

## Co-chairs

### Prof. Da Ruan[†] (in memorial)

With great sadness and disbelief we inform you that our colleague Da Ruan passed away unexpectedly deceased on July 31. The Board of Directors, the management and staff of SCK·CEN express their condolences and deepest sympathy to his family.

Da Ruan began his career at SCK·CEN in 1991, after obtaining his PhD in mathematics from Ghent University. As a postdoc, Da completed the TRANSFUSION project successfully by developing a fast algorithm for the analysis of well-logging signals for the oil industry. Subsequently he took the initiative in the FLINS (Fuzzy Logic In Nuclear Science) project and the FLINS conferences, which grew to become the leading conference in this specialized field.

Da Ruan searched tirelessly for applications of fuzzy logic and related theories and found them, for example, in reactor control, cost estimates including uncertainties of large projects, decision support systems and the analysis of large data sets for safety culture and the non-proliferation of nuclear weapons. He published more than 90 peer-reviewed journal articles, two textbooks and 20 research books. His international recognition is also shown by numerous invitations to act as a keynote speaker at international conferences, as well as by the award of an honorary doctorate from the Nuclear Power Institute of China.

Da Ruan served as member of the editorial board of *Fuzzy Sets and Systems*, as regional editor for Europe of the *International Journal of Intelligent Automation and Soft Computing*, co-editor-in-chief of the *International Journal of Nuclear Knowledge Management*, editor-in-chief of the *International Journal of Computational Intelligence Systems*, editor of the book series *Intelligent Information Systems* and editor of the proceedings series *Computer Engineering and Information Science*.

Da Ruan was guest professor at the Department of Applied Mathematics and Computer Science at Ghent University and at the Department of Applied Economics at Hasselt University. At the Faculty of Information Technology at the University of Technology in Sydney, Australia, he was assistant professor.

His colleagues will remember Da as a motivated scientist with an indefatigable but also very congenial personality. With the passing away of Da, SCK·CEN has lost one of its most outstanding and productive scientists. He is survived by his wife, Greet, and two sons, Alexander and Nicolas.

**Robert D. Tennyson**
University of Minnesota
College of Education and Human Development, USA

**Patricia Ordonez De Pablos**
University of Oviedo, Spain

**Francisco José García Peñalvo**
Universidad de Salamanca, Spain

**Lazar Rusu**, Stockholm University, Kista, Sweden

## Program Chairs

| | |
|---|---|
| Miltiadis D. Lytras | American College of Greece, Greece |
| Ambjorn Naeve | Royal Institute of Technology, Sweden |
| Patricia Ordonez De Pablos | University of Oviedo, Spain |

## Knowledge Management and E-Learning Symposium Chair

| | |
|---|---|
| Miguel Angel Sicilia | University of Alcala, Spain |

## Workshops and Tutorials Chairs

| | |
|---|---|
| Ambjorn Naeve | Royal Institute of Technology, Sweeden |
| Miguel Angel Sicilia | University of Alcala, Spain |

## Publicity Chair

| | |
|---|---|
| Ekaterini Pitsa | Open Research Society, Greece |

## Exhibition Chair

| | |
|---|---|
| Efstathia Pitsa | University of Cambridge, UK |

# Program and Scientific Committee Members Senior Advisors – World Summit on the Knowledge Society / IJ of Knowledge Society Research Council

| | |
|---|---|
| Horatiu Dragomirescu | Bucharest University of Economics, Romania |
| Michel Grundstein | Paris Dauphine University, France |
| Ott Michela | National Research Council, Italy |
| Matthew K.O. Lee | University of Hong Kong , Hong Kong |
| Ravi S. Sharma | Nanyang Technological University, Singapore |
| Toyohide Watanabe | Nagoya University, Japan |
| Carel S. De Beer | University of Pretoria, South Africa |
| Sean Siqueira | Federal University of the State of Rio de Janeiro, Brazil |
| Saad Haj Bakry | King Saud University, Saudi Arabia |
| Nitham Hindi | Qatar University, Qatar |
| Maria Braz | Technical University of Lisbon, Portugal |
| Przemysław Kazienko | Wrocław University of Technology, Poland |
| Jose Maria Moreno-Jimenez | University of Zaragoza, Spain |
| Marco Temperini | Sapienza University of Rome, Italy |
| Michal Žemlika | Charles University, Czech Republic |

## International Review Board

| | |
|---|---|
| Marie-Helene | Abel University of Technology of Compiegne, France |
| Turon Alberto | University of Zaragoza, Spain |
| Adriano Albuquerque | University of Fortaleza, Brazil |
| Luis Alvarez Sabucedo | University of Vigo, Spain |
| Heli Aramo-Immonen | Tampere University of Technology, Finland |
| Patricia Almeida | University of Aveiro, Portugal |
| Jose Enrique Armendariz-Inigo | Public University of Navarra, Spain |
| Ozlem (Gokkurt) Bayram | Ankara University, Turkey |
| Ana Maria Beltran Pavani | Pontifical Catholic University of Rio de Janeiro, Brazil |
| Sambit Bhattacharya | Fayetteville State University, USA |
| John Biggam | Glasgow Caledonian University, UK |
| Constanta Nicoleta Bodea | The Academy of Economic Studies, Romania |
| Philip Bonanno | University of Malta, Malta |
| Helen Bond | Howard University, USA |
| Maria Braz | Technical University of Lisbon, Portugal |
| Miguel A. Brito | University of Minho, Portugal |
| Berta Buttarazzi | University of Rome Tor Vergata, Italy |
| Carlos Cabanero-Pisa | Open University of Catalonia, Spain |

| | |
|---|---|
| Gerassimos Kekkeris | Democtius University of Thrace, Greece |
| Georgiadou Keratso | DUTH, Greece |
| Kathy Kikis-Papadakis | FORTH/IACM, Greece |
| George M. Korres | University of the Aegean, Greece |
| Kornelia Kozovska | Joint Research Center, Italy |
| Panagiotis Kyriazopoulos | Graduate Technological Education Institute of Piraeus, Greece |
| Habin Lee | Brunel University, UK |
| Jean-Marc Lezcano | Sogeti, France |
| Carla Limongelli | Università degli Studi Roma Tre, Italy |
| Alessandro Longheu | University of Catania, Italy |
| Margarida Lucas | University of Aveiro, Portugal |
| Aristomenis Macris | University of Piraeus, Greece |
| Giuseppe Mangioni | University of Catania, Italy |
| Davide Mazza | Politecnico di Milano, Italy |
| Miroslav Minovic | University of Belgrade, Serbia |
| El-Mekawy Mohamed | Royal Institute of Technology (KTH), Sweden |
| Olmo Moreno | Modelo University, Mexico |
| Beniamino Murgante | University of Basilicata, Italy |
| Rita C. Nienaber | University of South Africa, South Africa |
| Nicolae Nistor | Ludwig Maximilians University Munich, Germany |
| Angela Paleologou | University of Ioannina, Greece |
| Placido Pinheiro | University of Fortaleza, Brazil |
| Yossi Raanan | College of Management, Israel |
| Liana Razmerita | Copenhagen Business School, Denmark |
| Eva Rimbau-Gilabert | Open University of Catalonia, Spain |
| Lorayne Robertson | University of Ontario Institute of Technology, Canada |
| Marco Ronchetti | Università Di Trento, Italy |
| Elisabet Ruiz-Dotras | Open University of Catalonia, Spain |
| Lazar Rusu | Stockholm University, Sweden |
| Luis Alvarez Sabucedo | University of Vigo, Spain |
| Saqib Saeed | University of Siegem, Germany |
| Irene Samanta | Graduate Technological Education Institute of Piraeus, Greece |
| Jesus David Sanchez De Pablo Gonzalez Del Campo | University of Castilla-La Mancha, Spain |
| Juan M. Santos | University of Vigo, Spain |
| Akila Sarirete | Effat University, Saudi Arabia |
| Fabio Sartori | University of Milan-Bicocca, Italy |
| Chaudhary Imran Sarwar | Creative Researcher, Pakistan |
| Filippo Sciarrone | Università degli Studi Roma Tre, Italy |

# Table of Contents

# Bypassing School Disenchantment: Strategies to Promote School Attainment

Margarida Lucas, Jaime Ribeiro, and António Moreira

Research Centre for Didactics and Technology in Teacher Education,
3810-193 Campus de Santiago, University of Aveiro
{mlucas,jaimeribeiro,moreira}@ua.pt

**Abstract.** Special Education Needs refers to more than just to students with learning disabilities that impair their access to and participation in education. Many others struggle each day just to stay in school, focus on lessons or make sense about what is taught. Several students face underachievement and dropout because they feel that school is outdated, uninteresting and does not fulfil their learning needs. Here we offer a proposal, often talked about but rarely put into action to bring back struggling students to school: using multiple forms of presenting information and expression, we can attract students that need more dynamic and broader learning strategies.

**Keywords:** Social Web, Special Educational Needs, underachievement, inclusion.

## 1 Introduction

Web-based environments for communicating, networking and collaborating, often referred to as Web 2.0 or social Web have become pervasive in educational settings. Understanding how such technologies can be used for educational purposes has become a focus of research in various fields of Education. Research suggests that the use of communication technologies (CT) fosters students' development and enhancement on a number of aspects, including collaboration [1][2]; knowledge construction [3][4]; critical thinking [5], socialization [6]; satisfaction [7], or inclusion [8][9].

Students' inclusion has been one of the major challenges for school systems in the past decades. It is safeguarded by the Inclusive Education Framework (IEF) [10], which poses that inclusion rejects exclusion and that Education is for all "regardless of their physical, intellectual, emotional, social, linguistic or other conditions" [10]. But inclusive education is not the mere implementation of policies. In order for inclusive practices to be achieved, teachers and other educational agents should receive adequate training, so that the different circumstances and needs of all learners can be addressed and an inclusive education through inclusive schools/environments can be set.

Inclusive education may comprehend a variety of initiatives, including the ones with students with disabilities, living in poor conditions, belonging to ethnic or

M.D. Lytras et al. (Eds.): WSKS 2011, CCIS 278, pp. 1–6, 2013.

linguistic minorities, experiencing exploitation, discrimination or segregation, among others. In the case of the present article, it relates only to students with special educational needs (SEN). More specifically, to those who, due to a series of reasons, experience academic underachievement, drop out or leave school with no appropriate qualifications. These may include children that either because of behavioural or social problems, feel detached from the school's environment, neglected or rejected by their peers or excluded from mainstream educational experiences. These students often possess interests and abilities that remain unveiled merely because conventional pedagogical practices and strategies do not fulfil or address their interests.

In Portugal, guidelines for Special Education are covered by the IEF and although the framework dates back to 1994, what has been done does not seem innovative or inclusive enough to attract those who do not "fit" the traditional educational setting. Within the European Union, Portugal continues to present one of the highest dropout rates [11]. Though the number of students finishing basic, secondary and higher education has increased in the past few years, the country's dropout rate still doubles European average rates, suggesting that there is still a long way to be covered.

In the present work, we suggest that the use of CT, namely the ones that belong to the so called social Web era, can help meet the challenges posed by academic underachievement and leveraging inclusive policies and practices in education.

## 2     Some Considerations about underachievement

Academic underachievement may be caused by various factors. SEN related to sensory, motor and cognitive impairments usually appear at the top of the array of causes that lead limitations on learning. Many others may be mentioned, though they are usually given less visibility and are often misinterpreted. For example, contrary to popular belief, gifted children are amongst those who tend to underachieve [12]. Also, children from disadvantaged or marginalized areas or groups are likely to do so due to a variety of characteristics that may range from functional limitations to social misfit and inconsistent school performance [13].

By definition, underachievement is a discrepancy between intellectual potential or ability and academic achievement. It is primarily caused by a combination of personal attributes and environmental factors. Personal attributes can include an undetermined learning disability, an individual's lack of self-confidence to successfully accomplish a task or goal or a limited ability to self-regulate behaviour. Environmental variables may involve factors such as social and family related issues, and a mismatch between a student's learning style, the peers' learning styles or a teacher's instructional style. Variables may also be related to a conjuncture of problems and limitations of a typical classroom and of the educational system itself. Some students may be disruptive to other students and teachers may not be able to dedicate the necessary time to them due to a high number of students per class, the need to comply with the lesson plan or even the time ascribed to each lesson.

Often students that underperform may be highly creative or have special abilities that lead them to lose interest in traditional text-based instruction, rote memory learning tasks, or teacher-directed activities [14]. When combined with uninteresting, undifferentiated and disengaging curriculum, these factors often lead to underachievement and the development of adverse feelings towards school [15], which may result in further reluctance to pursue academic success and even rejection behaviours. It must be noted, however, that the fact that the school environment does not meet the needs of students who need special support, is not the sole factor for school failure, but it is one that can be addressed through innovative strategies that appeal to the current interests of young people today. In this matter, we believe emerging technologies can play an important role. Web based tools and environments have brought about new ways to access and manipulate information and have redesigned interaction dynamics. When merged with appropriate pedagogical strategies these technologies and environments can have a significant impact in the way students exchange knowledge, engage and learn.

## 3 The Social Web as an Inclusive Platform

The social web, as we know it today, relies heavily on user-generated content, communities, networking and social interaction. It offers innumerable free-easy-to-use tools and applications that give users a high level of control to sort, manage, use and recreate knowledge in many different ways and for many different purposes. The great force beyond the surface of the social web is driven by people's attitudes towards wanting to know, participate and engage in sharing, creating and interacting.

Several authors refer to "this new web" as a social platform where individuals can interact, (re)create, share and redefine ways of learning [16][17]. Social web tools, such as wikis, blogs, social networking or sharing sites, enable users to explore different paths, connect to others and learn through the exploration of knowledge areas, on the basis of individual choices. Users are prompted to engage, interact and participate and, at the same time, develop the necessary competences required to actively participate and interact with others.

When integrated into teaching practices and explored as an extension of the classroom, social web tools can become a means to distribute different learning environments and contexts, in which students' interests or particular abilities can be brought into play. Students are given new opportunities that afford them the power to be knowledge producers and transmitters, form learning networks, jump outside classroom walls and look for relevant aspects related to their lives [18]. When applied as pedagogical tools, they can also foster the transfer of responsibility to students, autonomous learning, real life problem based learning and collaborative work. Students benefit from developing adequate attitudes to participate in the tools and benefit from a more equitable environment, in which one becomes "uno inter pares" as hierarchies and individual differences tend to dilute [19].

Assumptions made so far are in line with conclusions gathered by Walker and Logan [9]. They state that students with SEN can "benefit from social interactions with people of all backgrounds" in at least three different areas: i) learning, ii) emotional and iii) behavioural. Benefits reported include: "enhanced skill acquisition and generalization", "greater academic outcomes", "sense of belonging", "peer role models for academic, social and behavioural skills", "increased inclusion in future environments" or "increased appreciation and acceptance of individual differences and diversity" [9]. According to the same authors, when extending learning environments into the web, students cultivate feelings of belonging, improve motivation, self-confidence, behaviour, attitudes to learning, attendance and achievement. Achievement is fostered when students experience support and sense that their opinions and insights are trusted and valued by others. Moreover, it benefits from the development of student centred approaches and individualized education paths that these tools afford.

The integration of social web tools into teaching practices also gives teachers new opportunities to rethink their teaching and learning practices. As change driven agents, educators and teachers, are demanded new roles and skills that can facilitate learning and make it more meaningful to all of their students. Without proper training or without practical examples through trial and error, inclusive practices may be hard to accomplish.

## 4       The Portuguese Case

Although the education of students with SEN has been assured as a right and a duty under European and Portuguese law for a long time, effective action to move educational policies and practices towards a more inclusive direction is only now starting to take its course. Nevertheless, recent legislation has somehow left a void and narrowed the possibilities for some students with special education needs, especially for those who cannot make proof of a diagnosed need. Furthermore, it has diminished the number of teachers for these students and the number of hours per week assigned to them. This has resulted in students with SEN being taught in regular classes according to regular standards or being relegated to professional courses in order to receive certification of compulsory education.

Including these students in regular classes may increase rates of inclusion, but it implies that all teachers are prepared to work with them in their regular classes and this is not often the case. During the last year, due to the implementation of the Technological Plan for Education (TPE) more attention has been given to the training of teachers in SEN, namely in the use of CT as promoters of inclusion and facilitators of learning for students with special needs. Although results of the TPE initiative are not yet available, studies being conducted in the field of SEN highlight various requirements in initial and continuous training programs. For instance, a study conducted in a Master's degree course in Special Education [20] reveals that the majority of students agree that CT offers significant educational benefits and that it can help students with SEN to overcome some of the obstacles imposed by their needs. They also agree that it is a factor of increased motivation and participation for students with learning problems. However, further research indicates that in the specific case of using CT with children with SEN, most teachers refer that they were never offered or attended any training in the area and that their knowledge about it is reduced and outdated. [20][21].

Studies on the use of the social web as a platform for the inclusion of students with special needs in Portugal are inexistent and when initiatives of such use occur, they are usually the result of individual initiatives rather than institutional ones.

Students with learning problems want to learn, but their constraints pose significant barriers to such endeavour and to positive results in academic settings. This may also fuel a sense of personal failure with the emergence of feelings of anger, frustration and disillusionment with the education system. Progressive withdrawal from classes, underachievement, periods of disaffection, reluctance to engage positively with the learning process, emotional outbursts or episodes of inappropriate behaviour are all symptoms that, generally, remain unattended and unaddressed.

## 5      Final Considerations

The social Web can afford unimagined possibilities to motivate and encourage students with SEN. Apart from the aforementioned benefits, it is considered to promote the increase of students' self-esteem, the overcoming of feelings related to failure, inadequacy and isolation. For students that face learning problems and underachievement, these aspects are of critical importance, as emotional well-being is often the difference between being or not being predisposed to learn.

In the present work we suggest that social web tools and other CT can be used and explored as a means to meet students' special needs and motivate them to the learning process. The integration of such tools with innovative and appealing pedagogical strategies may result in more equitable learning environments where knowledge can be shared and constructed and where limitations or specific needs are diluted.

Nevertheless, we concur with the idea that change in traditional practices is never a matter of simply using new tools – it is a matter of using them with particular purposes and attitudes. Therefore, much needs to be done, especially nationwide, to encourage the use of the social Web at all levels of education in order to promote a learning environment that meets the needs of students that simply do not cope with traditional teaching and learning methods.

## References

1. Schellens, T., Valcke, M.: Collaborative learning in asynchronous discussion groups: What about the impact on cognitive processing? Computers in Human Behavior 21(6), 957–975 (2005)
2. Persico, D., Pozzi, F., Sarti, L.: Design patterns for monitoring and evaluating CSCL processes. Computers in Human Behaviour 25(5), 1020–1027 (2009)
3. Yap, K.C., Chia, K.P.: Knowledge construction and misconstruction: A case study approach in asynchronous discussion using Knowledge Construction - Message Map (KCMM) and Knowledge Construction - Message Graph (KCMG). Comput. Educ. 55(4), 1589–1613 (2010)
4. Lucas, M., Moreira, A.: Knowledge Construction with Social Web Tools. In: Lytras, M.D., Ordonez De Pablos, P., Avison, D., Sipior, J., Jin, Q., Leal, W., Uden, L., Thomas, M., Cervai, S., Horner, D. (eds.) TECH-EDUCATION 2010. CCIS, vol. 73, pp. 278–284. Springer, Heidelberg (2010)

5. Garrison, D.R., Anderson, T., Archer, W.: Critical thinking, cognitive presence, and computer conferencing in distance education. American Journal of Distance Education 15(1), 7–23 (2001)
6. Richardson, J., Swan, K.: Examining social presence in online courses in relation to students' perceived learning and satisfaction. Journal of Asynchronous Learning Networks 7, 68–88 (2003)
7. Hostetter, C., Busch, M.: Measuring up Online: The Relationship between Social Presence and Student Learning Satisfaction. Journal of Scholarship of Teaching and Learning 6(2), 1–12 (2006)
8. Ware, D.: Spike the bear and an on-line special school. In: Abbott, C. (ed.) Special Educational Needs and the Internet: Issues for the Inclusive Classroom, pp. 58–63. RoutledgeFalmer, London (2002)
9. Walker, L., Logan, A.: Using digital technologies to promote inclusive practices in education (2009),
   http://archive.futurelab.org.uk/resources/documents/handbook s/digital_inclusion3.pdf (retrieved January 11, 2011)
10. UNESCO: The Salamanca Statement and Framework for Action on Special Needs Education. Salamanca (1994)
11. OECD: Education at a Glance 2010: OECD Indicators (2010)
12. Emerick, L.J.: Academic Underachievement Among the Gifted: Students' Perceptions of Factors that Reverse the Pattern. Gifted Child Quarterly 36(3), 140–146 (1992)
13. Westminster Institute of Education: Underachievement. Oxford Brookes University (2006),
   http://www.brookes.ac.uk/schools/education/rescon/cpdgifted/ docs/secondarylaunchpads/4underachievement.pdf
   (retrieved January 11, 2011)
14. Worrel, F.: Gifted Education: Traditional and Emerging Approaches. In: Bursztyn, A. (ed.) The Praeger Handbook of Special Education, pp. 122–124. Praeger, London (2007)
15. Rimm, S.: Underachievement. In: Kerr, B. (ed.) Encyclopedia of Giftedness, Creativity, and Talent, pp. 911–914. Sage Publications, Los Angeles (2009)
16. Selwyn, N.: Web 2.0 applications as alternative environments for informal learning: a critical review. Paper presented at the OECD-KERIS Expert Meeting (2007)
17. Klamma, R., Chatti, M.A., Duval, E., Hummel, H., Thora, E., Kravcik, M., et al.: Social Software for Lifelong Learning. Educational Technology & Society 10(3), 72–83 (2007)
18. Ribeiro, J., Casanova, D., Nogueira, F., Moreira, A., Almeida, A.M.: Personal Learning Environments - Meeting the Special Needs of Gifted Students. In: Zhao, J., De Pablos, P., Tenysson, R. (eds.) Technology Enhanced Learning for People with Disabilities: Approaches And Applications. IGI Global, Hershey (2011)
19. Lucas, M., Moreira, A.: Bridging Formal and Informal Learning – A Case Study on Students' Perceptions of the Use of Social Networking Tools. In: Cress, U., Dimitrova, V., Specht, M. (eds.) EC-TEL 2009. LNCS, vol. 5794, pp. 325–337. Springer, Heidelberg (2009)
20. Ribeiro, J., Moreira, A.: ICT Training for Special Education Frontline Professionals: A Perspective from Students of a Master's Degree on Special Education. International Journal of Emerging Technologies in Learning 5 (2010)
21. Ribeiro, J., Moreira, A., Almeida, A.M.: ICT in the Education of Students with SEN: Perceptions of Stakeholders. In: Lytras, M.D., Ordonez De Pablos, P., Avison, D., Sipior, J., Jin, Q., Leal, W., Uden, L., Thomas, M., Cervai, S., Horner, D. (eds.) TECH-EDUCATION 2010. CCIS, vol. 73, pp. 331–337. Springer, Heidelberg (2010)

# Paper Wrapping, Based on Knowledge about Face Connectivity among Paper Fragments

Toyohide Watanabe and Kenta Matsushima

Department of Systems and Social Informatics,
Graduate School of Information Science, Nagoya University
Furo-cho, Chikusa-ku, Nagoya 464-8603, Japan
watanabe@is.nagoya-u.ac.jp

**Abstract.** The purpose of paper wrapping is to protect goods from external shocks, decorate goods beautifully, carry out materials/goods safely, etc. Also, the paper wrapping is intelligent and creative work. The knowledge about paper wrapping is dependent on the features of target-objects, paper sheets and wrapping purposes. This article addresses a method to design the wrapping process. We introduce the knowledge about paper wrapping and then construct a stage tree, which represents various kinds of wrapping means successfully. We propose a framework for designing the wrapping process appropriate to target-objects, and also describe an interactive support interface in the wrapping process.

## 1    Introduction

The paper wrapping takes various kinds of roles to protect goods from external shocks, decorate goods beautifully, carry out materials easily, etc.    The make-up procedures are different from object shapes, sheet sizes or wrapping purposes.    In order to wrap target-objects by paper sheets successfully the skills or experiences are necessary, and in many cases the heuristics about paper wrapping has been inherited repeatedly by hand-in-hand.    However, it is not always easy for beginners to wrap various shapes of target-objects by appropriate paper sheets compactly.    In this article, we address a method to support paper wrapping operations for beginners, based on the knowledge about relationships among wrapping-side faces.    Though the instruction textbook is useful as a typical support means for paper wrapping, the existing textbook cannot show individual wrapping shapes in 3-dimensional view.

The researches about paper folding have been popular in comparison with those about paper wrapping [1].    Many of these researches are related to computer geometry, and aimed to make the mathematical features clear [2, 3].    For example, H.Shimanuki, et al. proposed an advanced folding method which can transform 2-dimensional paper sheet, designed creatively with folding lines, into 3-dimensional Origami directly, and visualized the folding procedure explicitly by using the computer animation [4].    S.Miyazaki, et al. proposed an interactive system of operating paper folding, which instructs the folding procedure based on stepwise interactions [5].    In these systems, users operate interactively computer-generated

M.D. Lytras et al. (Eds.): WSKS 2011, CCIS 278, pp. 7–15, 2013.

Origami in 3-dimensional display window, and the system validates the operations of user in Origami model and then displays the correctly-operated folding shape or replies "wrong operation".   In this case, Origami model takes an important role to check up whether individual operations are correctly indicated in accordance with the successive folding procedure.

However, the paper wrapping is inherently different from the paper folding: the basic wrapping operation, "wrapping-in" which attaches closely a wrapping sheet to the side-faces of corresponding materials, is not observed in the paper folding, and also the wrapping-specific textbooks are not usually published.

## 2    Approach

### 2.1    Modeling Paper Wrapping

The wrapping procedure must be absolutely different according to the wrapping purpose [6]: the wrapping for peculiar gifts in department stores is always different from that for daily foods in super-markets.   In order to make our basic framework explicit [7], we focus on only the wrapping process for ⌐⌐-polyhedron.

In our research, we represent the paper wrapping process by using a stage tree, and manage several wrapping procedures effectually in this stage tree.   The node in the stage tree is called "stage" and corresponds to a stepwise state, specified by vertices, edges and faces in wrapping sheet.   The path from root node to leaf node corresponds to one wrapping procedure.   The edge is a wrapping operation from a stage to another stage.   Figure 1 shows an example of stage tree for caramel wrapping.   $S_l$ is an initial stage, while $S_m$ and $S_{m-l}$ are final stages, which indicate respectively different wrapping shapes.

### 2.2    Knowledge about Paper Wrapping

In order to support paper wrapping operations successfully, the heuristics are useful to design the connective relationship between stages.   Experts with rich heuristics and critical skills can make up the successive wrapping procedure to be adaptable to object feature and wrapping purpose.   Our knowledge consists of two different types:

1)    knowledge about object shape;
2)    knowledge about evaluation criterion for procedure design.

The feature and correlation about object shapes describe the information about evaluation criterion to indicate whether the designed wrapping procedure can cover the corresponding object shape completely.   Figure 2 is our framework.   First, our system selects the adaptable wrapping knowledge from object shapes, and then indicates it to user.   Second, the user chooses one from the proposed knowledge. Finally, the system analyzes the feature of object shape, corresponding to the chosen knowledge, and then designs an adjustable procedure on the basis of the evaluation criterion.

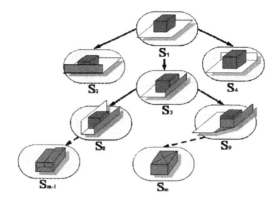

**Fig. 1.** Stage tree

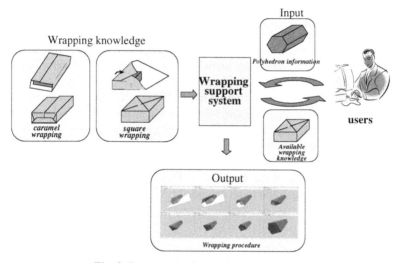

**Fig. 2.** Framework of wrapping support system

## 3    Paper Wrapping Model

### 3.1    Basic Structure

The paper wrapping model in the stepwise process takes an important role to design the wrapping procedure based on the physical features about target-object and wrapping sheet.    Our wrapping model is basically derived from Origami folding model, proposed by S.Miyazaki, et al.[5], and consists constructively of vertex **V**, edge **E** and face **F**.    Our model keeps a best structure which can indicate the overlapping order when two different faces overlap on the same plane.    The wrapping sheet and target-object are manipulated on this basic representation structure, and various wrapping operations can be supported on this model: "wrapping-in" which pushes a part of wrapping sheets into the inside along the object surface.    Figure 3 shows an example of overlapping among faces, and its management structure.    In this example a face group $f_{gl}$ keeps by overlapped order list $\{f_2, f_3\}$, $fg_2$ does by $\{f_1\}$, and $fg_3$ does by $\{f_4\}$, respectively.

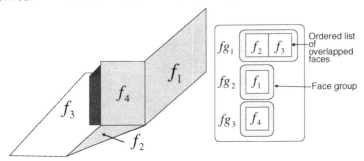

**Fig. 3.** Overlapped faces and management structure

## 3.2    Wrapping Graph

Our objective is to construct a framework/method which designs the successful procedure on the basis of wrapping knowledge: first of all, we must analyze the wrapping stages, dependent on transformed object shapes.    For this requirement, we enhance the existing Face Adjacency Graph (FAG) [8], which represents the connective relationships among faces in 3-dimensional space.    FAG is regarded as a graph structure for analyzing the feature of polyhedron: nodes represent faces of polyhedron and links indicate the corresponding edges.    It is possible to extract the features from the graph structure, if various attributes are assigned to the links in FAG.    We implement a stage analysis method so that our stage tree should correspond to the wrapping graph as an extended FAG.

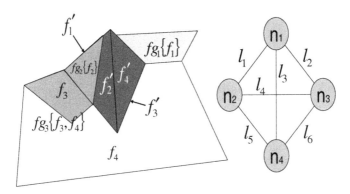

**Fig. 4.** Wrapping graph

In our wrapping model, each face is always allocated to the plane which contains the same face of target-object.    The nodes in the wrapping graph must keep the reference to both object plane and face group.    In addition, each link keeps the information about the plane to which 2 connective objects belong, and stores the check variable *Fold*, which indicates whether the wrapping operation is adaptable. All operations must be applied in the wrapping direction from nodes $n_i$ to $n_j$, even if the connected parts of paper sheet passed over the sheet size.

**Table 1.** Arguments in node

| Node# | $f_i$ | $fg_p$ |
|-------|-------|--------|
| $n_1$ | $f'_1$ | $fg_1$ |
| $n_2$ | $f'_2$ | $fg_2$ |
| $n_3$ | $f'_3$ | $fg_3$ |
| $n_4$ | $f'_4$ | null |

**Table 2.** Arguments in link

| Link# | $n_i$ | $n_j$ | Fold |
|-------|-------|-------|------|
| $l_1$ | $n_1$ | $n_2$ | 0 |
| $l_2$ | $n_1$ | $n_3$ | 0 |
| $l_3$ | $n_1$ | $n_4$ | 1 |
| $l_4$ | $n_2$ | $n_3$ | -1 |
| $l_5$ | $n_2$ | $n_4$ | 0 |
| $l_6$ | $n_3$ | $n_4$ | 1 |

Figure 4 shows an example of wrapping graph.    In this case, Table 1 arranges arguments attended to each node and Table 2 sets arguments associated with each link.    Each node holds the information about object faces, and contains the additional information about face groups of wrapping sheet.    While, individual links include the relationship between 2 connective nodes and store the integer variable *Fold*, which denotes the possibility that the operation is applicable between nodes. When *Fold=1* the operation is applicable in the direction from $n_i$ to $n_j$; when *Fold=-1* the operation does well from $n_j$ to $n_i$; and when *Fold=0* the corresponding operation is not effective between 2 nodes.    In this example, since *Fold=1* in $l_3$, the operation from $n_j$ to $n_i$ is possible: the operation which transforms the wrapping sheet of $fg_1$ into $f'_4$ is applicable.    Also, since *Fold=-1* in $l_4$, the operation from $n_3$ to $n_2$ (connected $fg_3$ to $f'_2$) is applicable.

## 4    Design of Wrapping Procedure

### 4.1    Construction of Stage Tree

The construction procedure of stage tree is shown in Figure 5.    First, the operation which is adaptable in each stage is determined.    When the adaptable operation was determined, it is judged whether the newly generated stage is added into the child node of stage tree.    If the newly generated stage is adjusted physically, the other nodes as the same stage have already existed and this newly stage is duplicated, then the newly generated stage is arranged by the pruning.

### 4.2    Design Based on Wrapping Knowledge

We compose the procedure with wrapping knowledge if the object shape is very clearly derived from our experience.    For example, we can apply the caramel wrapping or square wrapping to a cuboid, but all wrapping knowledge is not applicable in case that the object shape is a tetrahedron.    Our stage tree is expanded by using the best-first search based on the evaluation criterion, which represents how

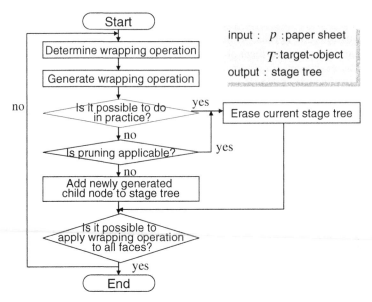

**Fig. 5.** Generation of stage tree

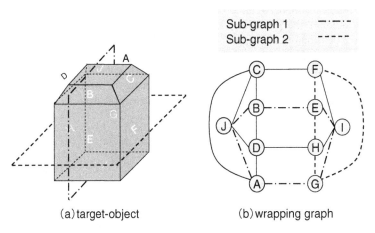

(a) target-object            (b) wrapping graph

**Fig. 6.** Shape feature graph in caramel wrapping

individual stages can make use of wrapping knowledge.    The evaluation criterion in each stage is dependent on the feature of object shape.    When the procedure composition step based on the best-first search aborts in its half way, the design process is controlled by all-search, after then.

## 4.3    Caramel Wrapping

The caramel wrapping is a procedure which covers directly every side of target-object. The shape feature of caramel wrapping is the topological symmetry for object sides as a sub-graph pattern and can divide the wrapping graph into 2 disjoint sub-graphs. As shown in Figure 6, we can observe that there are many shape features. In these cases, we can choose the graph whose unique link length is the longest in the shape feature graph.

Our wrapping procedure is designed by using the evaluation criterion.    In case that the shape feature graph **G** with wrapping nodes $n_l$, $n_{l+1}$, ..., $n_m$ is extracted, Expression (1) computes the evaluation value ***ecp***:

$$ecp = \Sigma_{i=l,m} \cdot |O_i, \text{list}| \qquad (1)$$

In Expression (1), $|O_i, \text{list}|$ is the total number of faces, which belong to $n_i$ in the shape feature graph.    The wrapping procedure can be designed so that the shape feature graph is selected at first under ***ecp***.    After all nodes in the shape feature graph were selected appropriately, ***ecp*** in all nodes is the same.

## 5    Experiment

Using our proposed method, we consider the caramel wrapping for pentagon-type object.    Figure 7 shows our designed wrapping procedure.    In the continuous stages from the initial stage to the stage level **d=7**, the wrapping operations attached closely to side-faces of object are selectively applied.    After the stage level **d=7**, the stage tree is constructed by all searches because all adaptable wrapping operations do not enforce to all face sides in the object.    Though the caramel wrapping is the best-selective in Figure 7, our system supports the interaction so that user can choose the

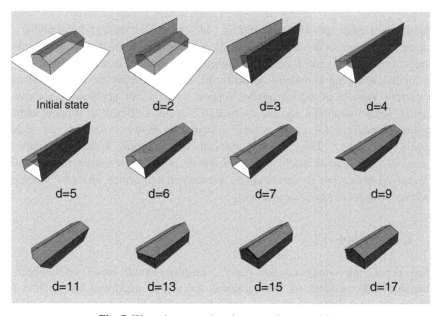

**Fig. 7.** Wrapping procedure in caramel target-object

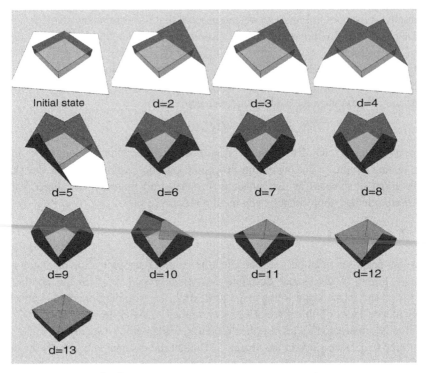

**Fig. 8.** Wrapping procedure in square target-object

wrapping knowledge apt to his preference.    In general, our strategy for applying the wrapping knowledge to the procedure design is better though the wrapping procedure for target-object in Figure 7 is well designed.    Of course, if the design ability is smart or the wrapping knowledge is powerful, these problems are not addressable. The current version of our wrapping support system can apply to the caramel wrapping, square wrapping and others, though it is not sufficient to support various wrapping procedures for many goods.    Figure 8 shows a sequence of square wrapping procedure.    This is partly because the wrapping knowledge must be prepared into the support mechanism.    However, our support system for designing the wrapping procedure is successful to accommodate various kinds of wrapping knowledge without any additional work.

## 6    Conclusion

In this paper, we composed the paper wrapping model based on connective relationships among faces in 3-dimensional space, and addressed the method for designing the wrapping procedure by using the predefined knowledge under such a model.    We proved that our method is effective to recognize the relationships between target-objects and wrapping sheets analytically.    In this article the wrapping knowledge was defined on the basis of our institutional features, derived from our analysis result and evaluation, but it may be not always an optimal definition for all wrapping activities.    With a view to supporting this successful process, it is desirable to extract automatically the wrapping knowledge to be transferred from experts.

# References

[1] Hull, T.: On the Mathematics of Flat Origami. Congress Numerantium 100, 215–224 (1994)

[2] Lang, L.: A Computational Algorithm for Origami design. In: Proc. of 12th ACM Symposium on Computational Geometry, pp. 98–105 (1996)

[3] Belcastro, S., Hull, T.C.: Modeling the Folding of Paper into Three Dimensions Using Affine Transformations. Linear Algebra and its Applications 348, 466–476 (1999)

[4] Shimanuki, H., Kato, J., Watanabe, T.: Analysis of Overlapping Faces for Constructing Paper-made Objects from Sketches. In: Proc. of 18th ICPR 2006, vol. 1, pp. 247–250 (2006)

[5] Miyazaki, S., Yasuda, T., Yokoi, S., Toriwaki, J.: An Origami Playing Simulator in the Virtual Space. The Journal of Visualization and Computer Animation 7, 25–42 (1996)

[6] Matsushima, K., Shimanuki, H., Watanabe, T.: Computer-Assisted Paper Wrapping with Visualization. In: Pan, Z., Zhang, X., El Rhalibi, A., Woo, W., Li, Y. (eds.) Edutainment 2008. LNCS, vol. 5093, pp. 114–125. Springer, Heidelberg (2008)

[7] Sugihara, K.: Robust Gift Wrapping for the Three-Dimensional Convex Hull. Computer and System Sciences 49(2), 391–407 (1994)

[8] Ansaldi, S., Floriani, L.D., Falcidleno, B.: Geometric Modeling of Solid Objects by Using a Face Adjacency Graph Representation. ACM SIGGRAPH Computer Graphics 19, 131–139 (1985)

# Personal Learning Environments and the Integration with Learning Management Systems[*]

Miguel Ángel Conde[1], Francisco José García-Peñalvo[1], María José Casany[2], and Marc Alier Forment[2]

[1] Computer Science Department. Science Education Research Institute (IUCE). GRIAL Research Group. University of Salamanca
{mconde,fgarcia}@usal.es
[2] Services & Information Systems Engineering Department, UPC - Campus Nord, building Omega, office 1116, 08034 Barcelona, Spain
mjcasany@lsi.upc.edu, marc.alier@upc.edu

**Abstract.** eLearning is continuously evolving and must be ready to integrate new paradigms and consider the student as the centre of the process. This shift will mean changing the tools currently used, giving way to other tools that take into account the customization. These changes are expensive and should not think only of replacing all previously existing but should seek to integrate new initiatives with those of success. This will ensure learning environments really powerful and effective. In this paper integration initiatives will be review and a new one will be proposed.

**Keywords:** Learning Management System, Personal Learning Environment, 2.0 web-based tools, Personalization.

## 1    Introduction

Learning will be one of the key processes in any society, because it facilitates the evolution of the individual and in many cases it could be a social or business improvement for her. Furthermore, learning could be understood as a living process, constantly evolving. Hence its evolution is influenced by changes of a different nature, such as sociological, educational or technological [1]. Let us consider one of those changes, in particular, the application of technology to learning, which is known as eLearning.

One of the most representative tools in the field of eLearning are learning platforms, also known as Learning Management Systems (LMS) or Virtual Learning Environments (VLE). Today, the LMSs are fully seated in educational settings [2, 3].

However, despite the acceptance they have, the LMS have not achieved the expected improvements [4]. Due mainly to the following reasons: 1) Learning should be focused on the user and not the institution or the course [5]. 2) It is necessary for

---

[*] This work was supported by Spanish Government projects TSI-020302-2009-35 and TIN2010-21695-C02-01 and by the Castile and Lion Regional Government through GR47 excellence project.

M.D. Lytras et al. (Eds.): WSKS 2011, CCIS 278, pp. 16–21, 2013.

learning environments give support to life long learning [6]. 3) It is essential to consider the informal learning and the support of 2.0 tools that promote this model of learning [7]. 4) Learning systems must be able to evolve with new technologies [8].

In order to solve these problems appear Personal Learning Environments (PLE). These new learning spaces are able to satisfy all new necessities but have to consider how to integrate formal, informal and non-formal tendencies. In this article we are going to study PLEs and different integration policies. In the first section the definition of Personal Learning Environment will be presented. The second will expose the different learning integration tendencies and finally some possible integration sceneries will be described.

## 2    Definition of PLE

PLE concept is something recent, but other concepts like personalization of learning in which they are based, not so. The concept emerge around 2001 [9] although does not take force until November 2004 when the title appears as part of the sessions of the JISC / CETIS Conference of that year.

From here there is a profuse contribution of different authors to what could become the definition of PLE. The definition of PLE is not easy and there is still debate about it, although they settled common ground. Among the possible definitions, could be a differentiation between those who stress the importance of the technological concept as central to the PLE and those that consider the pedagogical benefits of it.

From a technological point of view there are several definitions but here we are going to consider one of the most representative. "The PLE is not a piece of software. It is an environment where people where, people, tools, communities and resources interact in a flexible way "[10]. This author promotes an open environment to services and resources from multiple contexts, opened, bidirectional (not only consume services but are provided), customized to the user, that uses lightweight standards and interfaces, collaborative and open content-oriented the person but also the community in which they covered.

From a pedagogical point of view could be considered Atwell between others. This author believes that a PLE should not be seen as a software application: "Personalized Learning Environments are not an application but a new approach to the use of new technologies in learning. There are still many unresolved elements. But in the end the discussion about the use of PLE is not technical but philosophical, ethical and educational. The PLEs provide students their own space to develop and share their ideas, through learning environments that connect resources and contexts so far apart [5].

There are many definitions of PLE, but this section does not attempt to review them but to clarify the concept to facilitate understanding of existing integration trends.

## 3      Integration Tendencies and Proposal

The PLEs represent an opportunity for learning management seeking greater effectiveness in the process. But in any case they should be viewed as a substitute for the LMS [11]. The LMSs are tools fully established and should remain in the landscape of learning [12].

PLEs are going to open institutional walled-gardens [5] is therefore essential to establish solutions to integrate institutional and non institutional worlds, that is to say formal, non formal and informal learning.

But this will not be an easy task because, among other things, to: 1) the difficulties of the LMS to include interoperability standards [12]; 2) The integration of training activities in the PLE is not adequate because they are designed for representation, classification and tracking in other platforms [13]; 3) Problems of traceability of user activity in the PLE and, therefore, for consideration in the formal environment; [14] 4) single-sign-on implementation problems [15]; 5) Problems of information security [16].

In this situation, Wilson and others [10] proposed three possible scenarios for coexistence between LMS and PLE that would: 1) Existence of PLE and LMS in parallel, as formal and informal environments respectively. 2) The LMS open their structures to establish a means of interoperability with PLE. 3) Another possibility is that the LMS include elements of the PLE. This latter scenario limits the transformative power of PLEs.

The first of the proposed scenarios will not consider the integration but the coexistence, and hence will not be discussed further in this paper.

The second scenario refers to the opening of the LMS through the inclusion of Web services and interoperability initiatives. In this scenario may be included: iGoogle based initiatives [17], social networks connected with LMS [18], the LMS that offer support for implementations of interoperability specifications [19], PLEs with specific communication protocols [20] or integration based on service-oriented architecture [21]. Main difficulties of these initiatives are institutional barriers to the opening of formal environments that focus on the export of information and not the exchange interaction.

The third scenario considers the integration of external tools into the LMS. With possibility user could not decide which tools he is going to use and they will be limited to institutional decisions. Some initiatives in this scenario could be: LMS defined for the integration of external tools [22], Google Wave Gadgets integrated into Moodle [23], PLE introducing tools based on analysis of logs[24], initiatives based on the integration of tools based on learning design [25], integration architectures[26], etc.

Considering the initiatives discussed above we have proposed one that uses Moodle web services layer, the different existing connectors (to export information and interaction) and a new one based on IMS-LTI (IMS Learning Tools for Interoperability) specification in order to import the activities outcomes [27, 28].

# 4     Conclusions

As conclusions we have to take into account that PLEs provide us new possibilities in eLearning processes. 2.0 tools, social networks and so on are going to define the future of eLearning and must be included in our actual learning contexts.

That inclusion requires considering how PLE could be integrated with existing LMS and how interaction and information will be exchanged. In this sense there are several initiatives but none of them are providing efficient methods to guarantee full integration and interaction.

Considering this we have presented a possible solution that will not only facilitate integration but also promoted a model of PLE that is in between the institutional initiatives and the fully customized by the user.

# References

1. García Peñalvo, F.J.: Preface of Advances in E-Learning: Experiences and Methodologies. Information Science Reference, Hershey (2008)
2. Prendes, M.P.: Plataformas de campus virtuales de Software Libre: Análisis compartivo de la situación actual de las Universidades Españoles, pp. 228. Informe del proyecto EA-2008-0257 de la Secretaría de Estado de Universidades e Investigación (2009)
3. Wexler, S., Dublin, L., Grey, N., Jagannathan, S., Karrer, T., Martinez, M., Mosher, B., Oakes, K., van Barneveld, A.: Learning Management Systems. The good, the bad, the ugly, and the truth. The eLearning Guild (2008)
4. Brown, J.S., Adler, R.P.: Minds on Fire: Open Education, the Long Tail, and Learning 2.0. Educause Quarterly 42, 16–32 (2008)
5. Attwell, G.: The Personal Learning Environments - the future of eLearning? eLearning Papers 2 (2007)
6. Attwell, G.: e-Portfolios – the DNA of the Personal Learning Environment? Journal of e-Learning and Knowledge Society 3 (2007)
7. Ajjan, H., Hartshorne, R.: Investigating faculty decisions to adopt Web 2.0 technologies: Theory and Empirical Tests. The Internet and Higher Education 11, 71–80 (2008)
8. Mott, J., Wiley, D.: Open for Learning: The CMS and the Open Learning Network. In: Education - Exploring Our Connective Educational Landscape. University of Regina, Saskatchewan (2009)
9. Brown, S.: From VLEs to learning webs: the implications of Web 2.0 for learning and teaching. Routledge (2010)
10. Wilson, S., Liber, O., Johnson, M., Beauvoir, P., Sharples, P., Milligan, C.: Personal Learning Environments: Challenging the dominant design of educational systems. Journal of e-Learning and Knowledge Society 3, 27–38 (2007)
11. Adell, J., Castañeda, L.: Los Entornos Personales de Aprendizaje (PLEs): una nueva manera de entender el aprendizaje. In: Roig Vila, R., Fiorucci, M. (eds.) Claves para la investigación en innovación y calidad educativas. La integración de las Tecnologías de la Información y la Comunicación y la Interculturalidad en las aulas. Stumenti di Ricerca per l'innovaziones e la qualità in ámbito educativo. La Tecnologie dell'informazione e della Comunicaziones e l'interculturalità nella scuola. Marfil – Roma TRE Universita degli studi, Alcoy (2010)

12. Sclater, N.: Web 2.0, Personal Learning Environments, and the Future of Learning Management Systems. Research Bulletin (2008)
13. Palmér, M., Sire, S., Bogdanov, E., Gillet, D., Wild, F.: Mapping Web Personal Learning Environments. In: Wild, F., Kalz, M., Palmér, M., Müller, D. (eds.) Second International Workshop on Mashup Personal Learning Environments (MUPPLE 2009), vol. 506, pp. 31–46. CEUR-WS.org, Nize (2009)
14. Wilson, S., Sharples, P., Griffiths, D., Popat, K.: Moodle Wave: Reinventing the VLE using Widget technologies. In: Wild, F., Kalz, M., Palmér, M., Müller, D. (eds.) Mash-Up Personal Learning Environments - 2st Workshop MUPPLE 2009, vol. 506, pp. 47–58. CEUR Proceedings, Nize (2009)
15. Severance, C., Hardin, J., Whyte, A.: The coming functionality mash-up in Personal Learning Environments. Interactive Learning Environments 16, 47–62 (2008)
16. Casquero, O., Portillo, J., Ovelar, R., Benito, M., Romo, J.: PLE Network: an integrated eLearning 2.0 architecture from University's perspective. Interactive Learning Environments (in press)
17. Casquero, O., Portillo, J., Ovelar, R., Romo, J., Benito, M.: iGoogle and gadgets as a platform for integrating institutional and external services. In: Wild, F., Kalz, M., Palmér, M. (eds.) Mash-Up Personal Learning Environments - 1st Workshop MUPPLE 2008, vol. 388, pp. 37–42. CEUR-Workshop Proceedings, Maastricht (2008)
18. Torres, R., Edirisingha, P., Mobbs, R.: Building Web 2.0-Based Personal Learning Environments: A Conceptual Framework. In: EDEN Research Workshop 2008 (2008)
19. http://www.imsglobal.org/cc/statuschart.html
20. van Harmelen, M.: Personal Learning Environments. In: Proceedings of the Sixth IEEE International Conference on Advanced Learning Technologies, pp. 815–816. IEEE Computer Society (2006)
21. Peret, Y., Leroy, S., Leprêtre, E.: First steps in the integration of institutional and personal learning environments. In: Workshop Future Learning Landscape - EC-TEL 2010, Barcelona, Spain (2010)
22. Booth, A.G., Clark, B.P.: A service-oriented virtual learning environment. On the Horizon 17, 232–244 (2009)
23. Wilson, S., Sharples, P., Griffiths, D., Popat, K.: Moodle Wave: Reinventing the VLE using Widget technologies. In: Wild, F., Kalz, M., Palmér, M., Müller, D. (eds.) Mash-Up Personal Learning Environments - 2st Workshop MUPPLE 2009, vol. 506, pp. 47–58. CEUR Proceedings, Nize (2009)
24. Verpoorten, D., Glahn, C., Kravcik, M., Ternier, S., Specht, M.: Personalisation of Learning in Virtual Learning Environments. In: Cress, U., Dimitrova, V., Specht, M. (eds.) EC-TEL 2009. LNCS, vol. 5794, pp. 52–66. Springer, Heidelberg (2009)
25. de la Fuente-Valentín, L., Leony, D., Pardo, A., Kloos, C.D., M.I.L.D.: Mashups in Learning Design: pushing the flexibility envelope. In: Proceedings of the First International Workshop on Mashup Personal Learning Environments (MUPPLE 2008), Maastricht, The Netherlands, September 17 (2008)
26. Alario-Hoyos, C., Wilson, S.: Proceedings of the Comparison of the main Alternatives to the Integration of External Tools in different Platforms. In: International Conference of Education, Research and Innovation, ICERI 2010, Madrid, Spain (November 2010)

27. Alier, M., Casañ, M.J., Piguillem, J.: Moodle 2.0: Shifting from a Learning Toolkit to a Open Learning Platform. In: Lytras, M.D., Ordonez De Pablos, P., Avison, D., Sipior, J., Jin, Q., Leal, W., Uden, L., Thomas, M., Cervai, S., Horner, D. (eds.) TECH-EDUCATION 2010. CCIS, vol. 73, pp. 1–10. Springer, Heidelberg (2010)

28. Conde, M.Á., García-Peñalvo, F.J., Casany, M.J., Alier Forment, M.: Open Integrated Personal Learning Environment: Towards a New Conception of the ICT-Based Learning Processes. In: Lytras, M.D., Ordoñez De Pablos, P., Ziderman, A., Roulstone, A., Maurer, H., Imber, J.B. (eds.) WSKS 2010. CCIS, vol. 111, pp. 115–124. Springer, Heidelberg (2010)

# Applying Verbal Decision Analysis in the Selecting Practices of Framework SCRUM

Thais Cristina Sampaio Machado, Plácido Rogério Pinheiro,
and Henrique Farias Landim

University of Fortaleza (UNIFOR), Graduate Program in Applied Computer Sciences, Av.
Washington Soares, 1321 - Bl J Sl 30 - 60.811-905, Fortaleza, Brazil
Thais.Sampaio@edu.unifor.br, Placido@unifor.br,
Hflandim@gmail.com

**Abstract.** Considering that agile methodologies, in focus Framework SCRUM, are each time more popular for Development Software Companies, and noticing that the mentioned companies can't always apply every characteristics of the framework, this paper presents an application of the Verbal Decision Analysis (VDA) methodology ORCLASS to select some of the characteristics to be applied in the company, considering the preferences elicitation of a decision maker.

**Keywords:** VDA, ORCLASS, agile, SCRUM, preferences elicitation.

## 1 Introduction

Development Software Organizations used to focus on process definition for generating high quality products, but many plans and documentations became hard to maintain because of wrong estimative and projects deployed latter. So, companies which used to adopt maturity models, like Capability Maturity Model (CMMi), for defining and improving their processes, became interested in manager their projects applying agile methods [2].

The use of agile methodologies for management projects became more popular between Development Software Companies, objecting to create products of high quality in less time and spending less documentation.

The paper selected a specific agile methodology for studying: framework SCRUM. The framework is applicable for managing the development of software's, grouping the monitoring, feedback for the team and correction of impediments. SCRUM is composed by steps and practices to apply. The problem is that, usually, the organizations are not capable of implementing every characteristics of it. So, which would be the best practices of SCRUM to be implemented by the organization?

The SCRUM practices can be described qualitatively, based on a set of multiple criteria. Therefore, the paper studies an area called Multicriteria, what is an approach to support the process for decision making [6]. The characteristics were evaluated qualitatively, applying verbal decision analysis. The ORCLASS method, which

M.D. Lytras et al. (Eds.): WSKS 2011, CCIS 278, pp. 22–31, 2013.

belong to the Verbal Decision Analysis (VDA) framework, was used [4] for solving problems that has qualitative nature and difficult to be formalized, called unstructured [19]. The mentioned method has the objective to classify alternatives in different groups. The division in groups will be responsible to identify which SCRUM practices should be applied by the organization to implement a part of the project management framework studied, substituting the related practices of the process defined for the company, for project management in levels 2 and 3 of CMMi.

## 2     Framework SCRUM

Considered recent, the "agile" term for software development has created in 2001, as a response for the traditional models of software development.

The bigger concept for agile is "Agile Manifest" [3], which defines some important characterizations:

"We are uncovering better ways of developing software by doing it and helping others do it. Through this work we have come to value:

- Individuals and interactions over processes and tools
- Working software over comprehensive documentation
- Customer collaboration over contract negotiation
- Responding to change over following a plan

That is, while there is value in the items on the right, we value the items on the left more."

Framework SCRUM is an agile method different from the others for focusing in project management, not exactly development. It was developed by Ken Schwaber and Jeff Sutherland to help organizations to move on with complex projects [5].

SCRUM assumes that the software development is unpredictable to be planed completely initially, so it must guarantee visibility, inspection and fast adaptation, as can be seen in its pillars [5].

The framework is based on some practices, like: short iterations (from 1 to 4 weeks), close relation with the product owner, planning meetings, daily monitoring, visible charts of activities, and so on.

## 3     Verbal Decision Analysis

Decision making is a special kind of human activity aimed at the conclusion of an objective as for people, as for organizations. In the human world, emotions and reasons become hard to separate, and in personal decisions or when the consequences reach them, the emotions often influences the decision making process [1].

Generally, multi-criteria decision support methods are based on well structured mathematical models. Even if the description of the problems is initially defined in a qualitative way, later they become transformed into the required quantitative form, in accordance with the model established for the corresponding method [16].

According to [16] in the majority of multi-criteria problems, exists a set of alternatives, which can be evaluated against the same set of characteristics (called criteria or attributes). These multi-criteria (or multi-attribute) descriptions of alternatives will be used to define the necessary solution.

The Verbal Decision Analysis (VDA) framework is structured on the assurance that most decision making problems can be qualitatively described. The Verbal Decision Analysis supports the decision making process by the verbal representation of problems [7][8] [10][11][12][13][14][15][20][21][23][24].

The methodologies of decision making support allow evaluating the alternatives considering the multiple criteria and the decision maker's preferences, which become the responsible for the decisions. As a multi-criteria decision support approach, the process doesn't have the objective to show a solution for the decision maker, but it has the objective to help the decision making process [6].

The decision maker's ability to choose is very dependent on the occasion and the interest's stakeholders, although the methods of the decision making are universal.

According to [6], the methods of verbal decision analysis are: ZAPRO-III, ZAPROS-LM, PACOM and ORCLASS. The three firsts have the goal to establish a ranking of the alternatives from some order of preference. The last one is the only methodology for classification from the VDA framework.

# 4        Methodology ORCLASS

## 4.1        Overview

The ORCLASS methodology (Ordinal Classification) [6][17] differs from the other verbal decision analysis methods (ZAPROS, PACOM) because it doesn't consist of ordering alternatives in rank, but aims at classifying the multi-criteria alternatives of a given set: the decision maker only needs that these alternatives are categorized into a small number of decision classes or groups, generally two groups [1].

The method ORCLASS allows to elicit information in traditional form for human been: through verbal description of decision groups and criteria scales, about the verbal representation of problems. What is one of the main advantages of the method: dialog easily with the decision maker using verbal criteria values.

The method ORCLASS should compare a few quantity of criteria and criteria values, because the methodology works combining them. So, the combination may generate a high number of questions to the decision making.

The correct form to apply the methodology is presenting the combinations that generate new information, minimizing the number of combinations and simplifying the decision maker's comprehension. This is the property called Transitivity.

## 4.2        Structure

According to [17], Figure 1 presents the structure to apply the VDA method ORCLASS.

In accordance with the scheme described in Figure 1, the application of the method can be divided in three stages: Problem Formulation, Structuring of the Classification Rule and Analysis of the Information Obtained.

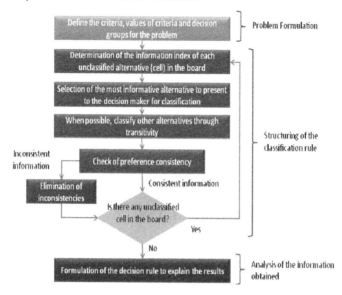

**Fig. 1.** Structure of process to apply the ORCLASS method

In the Problem's Formulation stage, the set of criteria and criteria values, and the groups to classify the alternatives are defined.

The Structuring of the Classification Rule stage will be done structured on the decision maker's preferences. For this stage, classification boards will be developed for filling. Each cell from the mentioned board is composed by a combination of determined values of criteria. During the decision making process, the elicitation of preferences is done and as long as the filling is accomplished, the classification board became filled.

The results of the decision rules are verbally formulated to be easily explained for the stakeholders.

## 4.3    Explaining the Application

Initially, an ORCLASS matrix may be created with the main decision rules.

The standard decision rule for any application of the method follows:

- An alternative composed by the best characteristics ([A1,B1,C1]), will always belong to Class I.
- An alternative composed by the worst characteristics ([A3,B3,C3]), will always belong to Class II.

Below is shown the classification board for illustration and better visualization of how many cells can be filled according to the decision maker elicitation of preferences.

| | B₁ | B₂ | B₃ |
|---|---|---|---|
| A₁ | I | 1+17 | 2+8 |
| A₂ | 1+17 | 3+11 | 5+5 |
| A₃ | 2+8 | 5+5 | 8+2 |

C₁

| | B₁ | B₂ | B₃ |
|---|---|---|---|
| A₁ | 1+17 | 3+11 | 5+5 |
| A₂ | 3+11 | 7+7 | 11+3 |
| A₃ | 5+5 | 11+3 | 17+1 |

C₂

| | B₁ | B₂ | B₃ |
|---|---|---|---|
| A₁ | 2+8 | 5+5 | 8+2 |
| A₂ | 5+5 | 11+3 | 17+1 |
| A₃ | 8+2 | 17+1 | II |

C₃

**Fig. 2.** Classification boards composed by the quantities of generated information

It was concluded that the most informative alternative is the cell [A2,B2,C2] [6] (which enables seven new classifications for either answer), so that is the better option to be presented to the decision maker for classification.

# 5    Application of Method ORCLASS

## 5.1    Criteria Definition

As the first step to apply ORCLASS, there were defined the criteria, which the alternatives are going to be evaluated against. For each criterion, there is a scale of values associated [8][9][18]:

**Table 1.** Criteria and associated values

| Criteria | Values of Criteria |
|---|---|
| A – Difficult degree for implementation | A1. Low: It's implementation doesn't require experience with the framework SCRUM.<br>A2. Medium: It's implementation requires a little bit of experience with the framework SCRUM or can be learned on the job.<br>A3. High: It's implementation requires experience (maturity) about framework SCRUM. |
| B – Time consumption | B1. Gain: The consumption of time in the project for executing the activity is less than the previous model.<br>B2. Not changed: There is no extra time in project for executing the activity than the previous model.<br>B3. Lose: There is extra time in project for executing the activity comparing to the previous model. |
| C – Cost for the project | C1. Gain: The new activities are able to provide to the project an economy of cost.<br>C2. Not changed: The new activities don't change the cost of the project.<br>C3. High cost: The new activities are able to increase to the project new costs. |

## 5.2    Alternatives

The alternatives for the application will be the practices of SCRUM. Notice that the characteristics of the framework selected to be alternatives are practices that can be assigned to any project (the organization may have a process defined in maturity model or not).

The practices selected by the decision maker were described in Table 2.

**Table 2.** Identification of Alternatives Board

| ID | Alternatives |
|---|---|
| Prac1 | Sprints (or iterations) with 1 to 4 weeks |
| Prac2 | A product backlog and a sprint backlog |
| Prac3 | Planning meeting 1 and Planning meeting 2 in the beginning of each iteration |
| Prac4 | Stand up meeting of 15 minutes |
| Prac5 | Burn down chart |
| Prac6 | Visible activities board |

## 5.3    Definition of Groups

A set of decision groups must be defined:

- The first group was chosen to support the practices of framework SCRUM which will be selected after the application of ORCLASS, to be utilized by the organizations;
- The second group will support the set of practices that shouldn't be utilized by the organization which want to implement part of SCRUM.

## 5.4    Characterizing the Alternatives

Analyzing each alternative and having the right support by the decision maker, an experienced ScrumMaster, it was possible to classify the alternatives in criterion values. Table 3 presents the characteristics of the alternatives about each criterion values identified in Table 1.

**Table 3.** Classification boards composed by the quantities of generated information.

| Criteria<br>Alternatives | Difficult degree for implementation | Time consumption | Cost for the project |
|---|---|---|---|
| Prac1 | A1 | B2 | C2 |
| Prac2 | A2 | B1 | C1 |
| Prac3 | A3 | B1 | C1 |
| Prac4 | A3 | B2 | C1 |
| Prac5 | A1 | B1 | C1 |
| Prac6 | A1 | B1 | C1 |

# 6        Computational Results of ORCLASS

After applying the entire ORCLASS method according to the decision maker choices, the final classification board became as follows:

|       | $B_1$ | $B_2$ | $B_3$ |
|-------|-------|-------|-------|
| $A_1$ | I     | I     | I     |
| $A_2$ | I     | I     | I     |
| $A_3$ | II    | II    | II    |

$C_1$

|       | $B_1$ | $B_2$ | $B_3$ |
|-------|-------|-------|-------|
| $A_1$ | I     | I     | I     |
| $A_2$ | I     | I     | II    |
| $A_3$ | II    | II    | II    |

$C_2$

|       | $B_1$ | $B_2$ | $B_3$ |
|-------|-------|-------|-------|
| $A_1$ | I     | II    | II    |
| $A_2$ | II    | II    | II    |
| $A_3$ | II    | II    | II    |

$C_3$

**Fig. 3.** Classification boards updated after first elicitation of preferences

For conclusion, it was possible to select the following alternatives for the first group:

- Prac1: Sprints (or iterations) with 1 to 4 weeks;
- Prac2: A product backlog and a sprint backlog;
- Prac5: Burn down chart;
- Prac6: Visible activities board;

The second group will be composed by the following practices:

- Prac3: Planning meeting 1 and Planning meeting 2 in the beginning of each iteration;
- Prac4: Stand up meeting of 15 minutes;

## 6.1        Decision Rules

The decision rule [6] is made in the end of the application of the method of verbal decision analysis and it is used to do an explanation of the results described in verbal way to the decision maker or stakeholders.

Analyzing the computational results obtained from the application of ORCLASS, it's possible to identify several options of decision rules. Bellow follows some examples:

- For SCRUM practices which requires extra time in project for executing the activity than the previous model (B3), only practices which implementation don't require experience with the framework SCRUM (A1) must be accepted by the organization to be implemented;
- For SCRUM practices which implementation requires experience (maturity) about framework SCRUM (A3), the practices must never be accepted by the organization to be implemented;

# 7    Conclusions

The framework SCRUM is an agile model for managing the development software process which is very discussed usually.

It is composed by practices that can be described qualitatively, based on a set of multiple criteria. Therefore, the paper studies an area called Multicriteria, what is an approach to support the process for decision making [6]. The characteristics were evaluated qualitatively, applying verbal decision analysis.

This paper presents SCRUM practices for deciding, verbally, which should be implanted in a Software Development Company that can't implement all the characteristics.

The ORCLASS method was applied and divided the SCRUM practices (alternatives) in different groups: in the first group it is going to be the alternatives that should be implanted by an organization and in the second one will be the others practices, which shouldn't be implanted in an organization.

The paper contribution is to prove that verbal decision analysis methodologies can be applied in real problems of elicitation of preferences process and decision making.

# 8    Future Works

As future works, more research can be done applying other methodologies for classification [22][26][27], or studying another SCRUM practices to increase the alternatives, or considering another criteria to evaluate the alternatives, or applying hybrid methodologies in the problem [1].

More research will be done when use the practices selected before applied the methodology in a real software development organization, to study the results of the SCRUM practices for projects.

**Acknowledgment.** The first author is thankful to the Organization FUNCAP and the second author is thankful to the National Counsel of Technological and Scientific Development (CNPq) for the support received on this project.

# References

1. Machado, T.C.S., Menezes, A.C., Tamanini, I., Pinheiro, P.R.: A Hybrid Model in the Selection of Prototypes for educational Tools: An Applicability In Verbal Decision Analysis. In: IEEE Symposium Series on Computational Intelligence SSCI (2011) (to appear)
2. Marcal, A.S.C., Freitas, B., Furtado, M.E.S., Soares, F.S.F., Belchior, A.D., Maciel, T.M.: Blending SCRUM Practices and CMMI Project Management Process Areas. Innovations in Systems and Software Engineering 4, 23–35 (2008) (print)
3. Beck, K., et al.: Manifesto for Agile Software Development. Disponível em (2001), http://agilemanifesto.org/

4. Larichev, O.: Ranking Multicriteria Alternatives: The Method ZAPROS III. European Journal of Operational Research 131 (2001)
5. Schwaber, K.: Agile Project Management With Scrum. Microsoft (2004)
6. Larichev, O.I., Moshkovich, H.M.: Verbal decision analysis for unstructured problems. Kluwer Academic Publishers, The Netherlands (1997)
7. Tamanini, I., Pinheiro, P.R.: Challenging the Incomparability Problem: An Approach Methodology Based on ZAPROS. In: Modeling, Computation and Optimization in Information Systems and Management Sciences, Communications in Computer and Information Science, vol. 14(1), pp. 344–353. Springer, Heidelberg (2008), doi:10.1007/978-3-540-87477-5 37
8. Tamanini, I., Machado, T.C.S., Mendes, M.S., Carvalho, A.L., Furtado, M.E.S., Pinheiro, P.R.: A Model for Mobile Television Applications Based on Verbal Decision Analysis. In: Sobh, T. (Org.) Advances in Computer Innovations in Informations Sciences and Engineering, vol. 1, pp. 399–404. Springer, Heidelberg (2008), doi:10.1007/978-1-4020-8741-7 72
9. Machado, T.C.S., Menezes, A.C., Pinheiro, L.F.R., Tamanini, I., Pinheiro, P.R.: Toward The Selection of Prototypes For Educational Tools: An Applicability In Verbal Decision Analysis. In: 2010 IEEE International Joint Conferences on Computer, Information, and Systems Sciences, and Engineering, CISSE (2010)
10. Tamanini, I., Carvalho, A.L., Castro, A.K.A., Pinheiro, P.R.: A Novel Multicriteria Model Applied to Cashew Chestnut Industrialization Process. Advances in Soft Computing 58(1), 243–252 (2009), doi:10.1007/978-3-540-89619-7 24
11. Tamanini, I., Castro, A.K.A., Pinheiro, P.R., Pinheiro, M.C.D.: Towards an Applied Multicriteria Model to the Diagnosis of Alzheimer's Disease: A Neuroimaging Study Case. In: 2009 IEEE International Conference on Intelligent Computing and Intelligent Systems (ICIS), Proceedings of 2009 IEEE International Conference on Intelligent Computing and Intelligent Systems, Shanghai, China, vol. 3, pp. 652–656. IEEE Press, Beijing (2009), doi:10.1109/ICICISYS.2009.5358087
12. Larichev, O., Brown, R.: Numerical and verbal decision analysis: comparison on pratical cases. Journal of Multicriteria Decision Analysis 9(6), 263–273 (2000)
13. Moshkovich, H., Larichev, O.: ZAPROS-LM– A method and system for ordering multiattribute alternatives. European Journal of Operational Research 82, 503–521 (1995)
14. Larichev, O.I.: Method ZAPROS for Multicriteria Alternatives Ranking and the Problem of Incomparability. Informatica 12, 89–100 (2001)
15. Tamanini, I., Pinheiro, P.R., Carvalho, A.L.: Aranau Software: A New Tool of the Verbal Decision Analysis, Technical Report, University of Fortaleza (2007)
16. Gomes, L.F.A., Moshkovich, H., Torres, A.: Marketing decisions in small businesses: how verbal decision analysis can help. Int. J. Management and Decision Making 11(1), 19–36 (2010)
17. Tamanini, I.: Improving the ZAPROS Method Considering the Incomparability Cases. Master Thesis I Graduate Program in Applied Computer Sciences, University of Fortaleza (2010)
18. Machado, T.C.S., Menezes, A.C., Pinheiro, L.F.R., Tamanini, I., Pinheiro, P.R.: Applying Verbal Decision Analysis in Selecting Prototypes for Educational Tools. In: 2010 IEEE International Conference on Intelligent Computing and Intelligent Systems (ICIS), Shanghai, China (2010)
19. Simon, H., Newell, A.: Heuristic Problem Solving: The Next Advance in Operations Research. Oper. Res. 6, 4–10 (1958)

20. Dimitriadi, G.G., Larichev, O.I.: Decision support system and the ZAPROS-III method for ranking the multiattribute alternatives with verbal quality estimates. European Journal of Operational Research (December 2002)
21. Tamanini, I., Pinheiro, P.R.: Applying a New Approach Methodology with ZAPROS. In: XL Simpósio Brasileiro de Pesquisa Operacional, João Pessoa, Brazil. XL Simpósio Brasileiro de Pesquisa Operacional, pp. 914–925 (2008)
22. Brasil Filho, A.T., Pinheiro, P.R., Coelho, A.L.V.: The Impact of Prototype Selection on a Multicriteria Decision Aid Classification Algorithm. In: Sobh, T. (Org.) Innovations and Advanced Techniques in Computing Sciences and Software Engineering, vol. 1, pp. 379–382. SpringerLink (2010)
23. Mendes, M.S., Carvalho, A.L., Furtado, E., Pinheiro, P.R.: Towards for Analyzing Alternatives of Interaction Design Based on Verbal Decision Analysis of User Experience. Internacional Journal of Interactive Mobile Technologies (iJIM) 4, 17–23 (2010)
24. Mendes, M., Carvalho, A.L., Furtado, E., Pinheiro, P.R.: A co-evolutionary interaction design of digital TV applications based on verbal decision analysis of user experiences. International Journal of Digital Culture and Electronic Tourism 1, 312–324 (2009)
25. Pinheiro, P.R., Furtado, M.E.S., Mendes, M.S., Carvalho, A.L.: Analysis of the interaction design for mobile TV applications based on multi-criteria. In: IFIP International Federation for Information Processing, pp. 389–394 (2007)
26. Brasil, A.T.: A Novel Approach Based on Multiple Criteria Decision Aiding Methods to Cope with Classification Problems. Master Thesis I Graduate Program in Applied Computer Sciences, University of Fortaleza (2009)
27. Brasil Filho, A.T., Pinheiro, P.R., Coelho, A.L.V.: Towards the Early Diagnosis of Alzheimer's Disease via a Multicriteria Classification Model. In: Ehrgott, M., Fonseca, C.M., Gandibleux, X., Hao, J.-K., Sevaux, M. (eds.) EMO 2009. LNCS, vol. 5467, pp. 393–406. Springer, Heidelberg (2009)

# Mixed Methods Research Design

Heli Aramo-Immonen

Tampere University of Technology, Department of Industrial Management
Pohjoisranta 11, 28100 Pori, Finland
heli.aramo-immonen@tut.fi

**Abstract.** Mixed methods research is an approach to inquiry that combines or associates both qualitative and quantitative forms. Mixed methods designs provide researchers, across research disciplines, with a rigorous approach to answering research questions. In the case of holistic analysis of complex systems, such as the mega-project, this is a relevant approach. Mixing the data, the specific types of research designs, the notation system, terminology, diagrams of procedures includes a risk of entering to chaos. Therefore research design has to be clearly articulated to readers. Triangulation is an important part of research design. Denzin [10] has identified four basic types of triangulation. In this exploratory paper are discussed mixed method research, theory triangulation, economic science, design science and systems development. Finally is introduced utilization of mixed methods in multiple-case study conducted in industry.

**Keywords:** mixed methods, triangulation, multiple-case study, economic science, design science, systems development.

## 1 Introduction

Science can be defined as a process of inquiry. This can be distinguished by three procedures: answering questions, solving problems, and/or developing more effective procedures for the first two. Science both informs and instructs [1], [2]. In order to answer questions, the researcher requires tools, techniques and methods considered to be scientific (Table 1). In this conceptual paper is explored the research question: How to utilize mixed methodology in research practice? Conducted research example represented applied sciences. The research questions posed in original research project were an immediate problem in the research domain, i.e. in the mega-project management environment. Mega-projects are large-scale, complex projects delivered through various partnerships, often affecting both public and private stakeholders [3]. Multiple methods were applicable to this research environment. To gain a holistic understanding of the complex object of research, here the mega-project management system, a multimethodological research strategy was relevant [4]. The research domain of industrial management is economic science. However, this study also had features of design science, systems development and social science.

M.D. Lytras et al. (Eds.): WSKS 2011, CCIS 278, pp. 32–43, 2013.
© Springer-Verlag Berlin Heidelberg 2013

**Table 1.** Scientific tools, techniques and methods [2], [5], [6], [7]

| Scientific tools; techniques and methods | |
| --- | --- |
| Tools | Instruments utilized in scientific inquiry. Mathematical symbols and formulas, computers and software, thermometers etc ; in social sciences concepts and taxonomies; in action research scholars themselves as actors. |
| Techniques | Scientific course of action. Means of utilizing scientific tools. Eg. conceptual techniques, classification techniques, sampling techniques. The researcher decides about selecting the technique. |
| Methods | Methods are the rules of choice. In case studies, field studies, and sample surveys selecting the set of tools is ruled by the |
| Methodology | The study of scientific methods. The logic of science. |

In the conceptual part of this paper will be discussed mixed method research and triangulation. The methods utilized in case research are introduced and finally the case study will be introduced in light of discussed methods.

## 2      Mixed Method Research

Recently mixed methods research has been accepted among research designs as the third main stream beside the purely qualitative and purely quantitative research methods. Mixed methods research is an approach to inquiry that combines or associates both qualitative and quantitative forms [8]. It involves both collecting and analyzing quantitative and qualitative data [9]. Mixed methods designs provide researchers, across research disciplines, with a rigorous approach to answering research questions. In the case of holistic analysis of complex systems, such as the mega-project, this is a relevant approach. To put both forms of data (qualitative and quantitative) together as a distinct research design or methodology is new. Thus the idea of mixing the data, the specific types of research designs, the notation system, terminology, diagrams of procedures, and challenges and issues in using different designs are features that have emerged within the past decades (see e.g. [10], [9]).

### 2.1      Triangulation

To gain a holistic view of the research domain it is necessary to use approaches that systematically explore the new avenues of research that methodological diversity affords. Methodological styles reflect not only differences in technique (such as qualitative versus quantitative procedures), but also different views of the epistemology of science and its ultimate goals and contributions to human thought and endeavor [11, p. 26]. Denzin [10] discusses triangulation as an important part of research design. He has identified four basic types of triangulation [12, p. 391]:

1. Data triangulation: the use of a variety of data sources in a study
2. Investigator triangulation: the use of several different researchers or evaluators
3. Theory triangulation: the use of multiple perspectives to interpret a single set of data
4. Methodological triangulation: the use of multiple methods to study a single problem

If we asses discussed multiple-case research through triangulation typology, we can conclude that all four types of triangulation are represented. First, the researcher compiled a database of 16,200 responses to qualitative research statements. Each individual evaluation is valuable qualitative information for the researcher, thus also statistical evaluation is possible by converting the linguistic scale to a numerical form as with the Likert scale [7], [13]. Second, the empirical study is based on a multiple-case study instead of one single case. Each case company can be studied both separately and as part of a network. Third, in this particular research project several researchers conducted partial projects (e.g. [14], [15], [16], [17]). Fourth, the mixture of methods used in the research process varied from self-assessment (multiple-choice questions), workshop observations (action research), and Friedman tests (statistical analysis, e.g. [18]). According to theory triangulation, the research domain was studied from the angle of economic science, design science and systems development. These areas will be introduced in the following sections.

# 3    Three Research Methods

## 3.1    Economic Science

The five common research approaches used in economic science (in the industrial management domain) are listed in Table 2: concept analytic, nomotetic, decision methodological, action research, and constructive research [14]. The research approach was normative, and the acquisition of knowledge was empirical in the research introduced. The method was partially constructive and action-oriented (case studies), hence a descriptive conceptual study of the qualitative features of project management disciplines was also presented. The construction, namely a qualitative analysis, was built in the decision model designed for mega-project management. The substance of the analysis is an artifact, a classification of the qualitative features affecting mega-project success. This classification can also be termed an ontology. This artifact is the product of the conceptual analysis of the researcher and of the hermeneutical interaction between the researcher and the actors in the mega-project environment.

**Table 2.** Business economics research approaches [19], [5], [6]

| Business economics research approaches | |
| --- | --- |
| Concept analytic | Both the positivistic and hermeneutic comprehension of science. Its objective is to create a concept system which assists in the description of different phenomena and creates instructions for present and future actions. In this research, the project knowledge taxonomy is mostly descriptive and empirical, but it also has normative characteristics. |
| Nomotetical | Consists mostly of the positivistic comprehension of science. The purpose of this research approach is to explain the causes of phenomena and occurrences subject to the constraints of laws. |
| Decision methodological | Consists of mostly positivistic comprehension of science. The objective of this research strategy is to create a solution method which is based upon mathematics and logic. |
| Action research | Consists primarily of the hermeneutic comprehension of science. Its purpose is to understand and describe problems or situations which are difficult to explain with a positivistic method. Problems in the situations where action research is utilized are usually holistic and it is difficult to separate them into specific sub-parts of the problem. This research approach is both descriptive, normative and empirical. One of the objectives is to produce critical knowledge from a system and to change the system after that. The objective of action research is to identify a hidden theory in the research target and see whether it is possible to support it with empirical research. The catalytic role of the researcher is vital for the process in action. |
| Constructive research | The objectives of this research strategy are normative and they create a method for problem solutions. It combines elements of decision methodological research and of the action research strategy and design science. The empirical study connects the research strategy to a practical situation. The research strategy is usually a case study. |

The project management ontology created in research is based upon a conceptual analysis. Concepts are abstract notations or symbols; they assist the solidification, structuring and illustration of both phenomena and their characteristics at the qualitative level [20].

The case study method [20], [21] was applied to collect data. According to Olkkonen [20], the results obtained through the case study method are often new hypotheses or theories, explanations of change or development processes, even normative instructions. The material and its processing are empirical, although often the material is formed from a small number of cases. However, it is worth emphasizing that for this particular study the data were collected from ten project organizations. The multiple-case method provides rich qualitative evidence supporting the research conclusions [21]. The linearity of the result graphs indicated broader generalizability than in a single case study. Hence, affecting features, such as organizational culture, management style or work atmosphere in a single case, can be eliminated from multiple-case results.

## 3.2    Design Science

The method of design science is developed within information technology research. While natural science explains how and why things are, design science is concerned with devising artifacts to attain goals. In other words, natural science attempts to understand reality whereas design science attempts to create artifacts that serve human purposes [22]. Instead of producing general theoretical knowledge, design science produces and applies solution-oriented knowledge. This is typical of operations research, systems development and management science. Theories are expected to explain how and why systems work within their operating domain [22]. Table 3 lists the research activities and outputs in design science.

The design science research activities used in this study were as follows: 1) the artifact designed in this research was a decision model with a built-in qualitative analysis; 2) evaluation of the artifact was conducted via case studies in a mega-project environment; 3) the theories discussed explicate the characteristics of the decision model. However, this solution-oriented research provided no direct generalization of theory. Hence the research is qualitative; the justification was made according to the natural science methodology (e.g. surveys, case experimentations and observation) [2]. The theoretical framework in this research was formed from organizational behavior theories: knowledge management, activity theory, systems dynamic and theories of organizational learning.

## 3.3    Systems Development

In the case of complex systems, such as mega-project organizations, the multi-methodological approach will generate holistic knowledge of the research area. The methods discussed and employed in this research were complementary in the multidimensional domain. These research approaches are required to investigate aspects of the research questions and to execute the objective of the design task of the focal research project (namely the project learning model, introduced in WSKS2009 conference).

**Table 3.** Design science research activities and outputs [22]

| Design science research activities | |
|---|---|
| **Build** | The objective is to build an artefact to perform a specific task. These artifacts then become the object of study. Artifacts are constructs, models, methods and instantiations. The research question is "does it work?". |
| **Evaluate** | The objective is to evaluate the artifact. Evaluation requires the development of the measurement of artifacts. The research question is "how well does it work?". |
| **Theorize** | Discussed theories explicate the characteristics of the artifact and its interaction with the environment that results in the observed performance. This requires an understanding of the natural laws governing the artifact and of those governing the environment in which it operates. The interaction of the artifact with its environment may lead to theorizing about the internal working of the artifact itself or about the environment. |
| **Justify** | If a generalization of theory is given, the explanation has to be justified. For artifacts based on mathematical formalism or whose interaction with the environment is presented mathematically, this can be done by utilizing mathematics and logic to prove posited theorems. Justification for non-mathematically represented IT artefacts follows the natural science methodologies governing data collection and analysis. |
| **Design science research outputs** | |
| **Constructs** | Concepts from the vocabulary of the domain. They constitute a conceptualization used to describe the problems in the domain. They form the specialized language and shared knowledge of a discipline. |
| **Model** | A set of propositions or statements expressing relationships among constructs. A solution component to an information requirement determination task and a problem definition component to an information system design task. An example of this is expert systems where knowledge is modeled as a set of production rules or frames. |
| **Method** | A set of steps (a guideline) utilized to perform a task. Methods are based upon a set of constructs (a language) and a representation (a model) of the solution space. |
| **Instantiation** | The realization of an artifact in its domain. Instantiations operationalize constructs, models and methods. It demonstrates the feasibility and effectiveness of the model or method it contains. It is an empirical discipline. Instantiations provide working artifacts. |

**Table 4.** Systems development research approach [23]

| Systems development - a multimethodological approach to research | |
|---|---|
| **Theory building** | Includes the development of new ideas and concepts and the construction of a conceptual framework, new methods or models. Theories are usually concerned with generic system behavior. Because of emphasis on generality, the outcome of theory building has limited practical relevancy to the target domain. Theories may be utilized to suggest research hypotheses, guide the design of experiments, and conduct systematic observations. |
| **Experimentation** | Research strategies such as laboratory and field experiments; computer and experimental simulations. Experimental designs are guided by theories and facilitated by systems development. Results may be utilized to refine theories or/and to improve |
| **Observation** | Research methodologies such as case studies, field studies and sample surveys. Observation assists the researcher to arrive at generalizations, which helps focus later investigations. Research settings are natural, therefore holistic insights may be gained and results are more relevant to the domain. Sufficient contextual and environmental conditions are to be reported to enable judgement of the limitations of conclusions. |
| **Systems development** | Consists of five stages: concept design, the construction of the system architecture, prototyping, product development and technology transfer. Multiple methodologies appear to be complementary, providing valuable feedback to one another. To gain a holistic understanding of a complex research area such as mega-project management systems, a multimethodological approach is effective. |

As regards systems development, this research was applied, developmental, and exploratory [2], [5], [23]; applied as a solution-oriented, problem-solving approach; developmental in order to search for a construction or model for a better course of action in the system; and exploratory (formulative) to identify problems for a more precise investigation. The systems development research approach is explained in Table 4.

In summary, the research approach matrix is mapped in Appendix 1. The connection between different stages of the research process and the original publications (indicated with Roman numbers I-IX) are also systematized in the appendix 1.

# 4     Utilizing Mixed Methods in Multiple-Case Study

The common underlying research topic in research project introduced was the management of learning in project organizations in order to gain successful project results. Interrelated topics are project managers' personal memory aids (IV in Appendix 1) and the idea generation capability of project members (II in Appendix 1). The process of planning the research, executing the empirical study, and documenting the results occurred in 2004-2009. The connection between the reported results, research methods and original publications is shown in Appendix 1.

The project organizations that participated in this research and their view of the qualitative features of a mega-project were evaluated. Each individual's assessment was collected through the evaluation of various statements which describe the project's features. The assessment consisted of 150 statements describing the ontology of 40 features that affect a project's success. The classification of the project management ontology is based upon the literature study and interviews carried out in project organizations. In the process, the project performer evaluated the current state of the project and its desired future state. The gap between the states describes the proactive vision, which is the potential for development in each project management feature. During the research, a database of 16,200 evaluation responses was compiled. This provides a comprehensive information resource for statistical calculations in this research and also for future review. [13], [14], [16], [17]

This study was limited to the qualitative research of the mega-project network organization. Quantitative methods were limited to a selection of relevant statistical calculations. An empirical study was conducted in two large case mega-projects. Limitations of a case study always lie in the generalizability of results [6], [21], [20], [24]. This research did not attempt to construct any new general project management theory based on the research results. However, the multiple-case study on the ten project-based companies participating in the two mega-projects provided interesting empirical results of qualitative mega-project management characteristics. These multiple-case results also have general value [21]. On the basis of these results, a learning model for a project-based organization is introduced. These empirical results may also be valuable to further discussion on general project management theories.

The research approach was qualitative. In the field of management science, project management has been acknowledged as an object of independent research only quite recently. There has been an army of consultants and plenty of fads available in this field, but fewer real professional approaches supported by the scientific community [25], [26], [27], [28]. Acquisition of a variety of qualitative methods in project management science is needed. Qualitative research consists of several aspects simultaneously. It is multiparadigmatic in its focus, and its value is its multimethodological approach. The interpretive understanding of human experience is crucial (e.g. [29], [30]). Qualitative implies an emphasis on qualities of entities and processes. Meanings are not examined in terms of quantity, amount, intensity or frequency. However, in the tradition of positivist economic science (the domain of industrial management and engineering), statistical measures and documents are utilized as a means of locating groups of subjects within a larger population [30].

Hence, qualitative research results and the reporting of the results in the "quantitative" form as graphs have to be distinguished carefully. The result remains qualitative. This research was qualitative in the domain of organizational behavior and management and it employs survey tools and classification methods derived from the social sciences [5], [7].

The research discussed was hermeneutical. The researcher can be seen as a research instrument in the process of gaining insight into and the significance of the concepts and the causality of the management features modeled in the study [2], [6], [23]. The researchers' preunderstanding of the fields studied (first-hand preunderstanding), as well as the capability to search and obtain new information via intermediaries (second-hand preunderstanding), is essential for research of this type [6]. The challenge is to gain a holistic view of the subject. The hermeneutic approach process uses open lateral thinking, whereas in the positivistic approach the researcher, thinking vertically, attempts to gain an exact result for a limited research objective [6]. The solution-orientated study of the qualitative features of the complicated, fragmented and networked construction of the mega-project organization's functions requires lateral thinking in order to gain a comprehensive view of the issue.

The design science method was utilized to design the project learning model. Models have inputs and outputs. Inputs can be described as the outline of possible choices of action, whereas the output variable represents the index (or the quantitative measure) of the value of alternative choices to the decision-maker. Focus in this research is on modeling a qualitative decision situation. In this domain, the choice available to the decision-maker cannot be presented with a quantitative variable. Hence the choice is between discrete qualitative alternatives [2].

The systems development method closely resembles design science; however, it focuses on the development of the system itself. In this research, strategies such as experimental simulations were guided by theories of organizational behavior and facilitated by systems development. The results may be employed to improve systems [23].

## 5    Discussion and Conclusions

Both the mixed methods approach and triangulation was discussed in this paper. Furthermore was introduced the economic science, design science and systems development research approaches. The tools and techniques considered were described shortly and the connection between the research process and methodology was discussed.

Applied research in the domain of mega-project organizations in the context of the offshore and marine industries requires the researcher's basic understanding of these fields. Asking relevant research questions and applying valid research methodologies to address research tasks in such broad systems requires both the researchers' holistic understanding and involvement [6], [23]. In the domain of industrial engineering, several researchers are involved in research. This is relevant in practice in order to be able to conduct empirical research in real settings. It is also possible source of triangulation in research process.

The decision to choose two case mega-projects was based upon the researcher's understanding and practical knowledge of the industry sector. The ten case organizations were selected from hundreds available, according to the theoretical sampling of the cases [20], [21], [24].

Validity of the research starts from a meaningful research question in the domain explored. This is a challenge. Researchers' understanding of the research domain and the practice are essential. After the relevance of the research problem is established, the research approach and chosen methods should support the validity of the research (Appendix 1). Subject variation [7], the subject's motivation, and the basis of volunteering and co-operating in an empirical study are essential for validity. The motivation of each respondent in the analysis was compared to his/her own median of answers. Therefore it was possible to evaluate the involvement of a single respondent. In the case study research, the knowledge searched for and gained is not context-free. Reliability of the research is provided by structuring the methodology (Appendix 1) and reporting the results accordingly. A multiple-case study (also called a collective case study) provides stronger evidence of the domain than a single case study.

To conclude, in order to gain holistic view over a complex problem scientists do need requisite variety of methods. Karl Popper [31] encouraged researchers to be innovative year 1959 in his famous book "The Logic of Scientific Discovery" with following words:

*"I do not care what methods a philosopher (or anybody else) may use so long as he has an interesting problem, and so long as he is sincerely trying to solve it."*
(In Karl Popper: Preface to the first English Edition, 1959 pp. xx)

# References

1. Ackoff, R.: From Data to Wisdom. Journal of Applied Systems Analysis 16, 3–9 (1989)
2. Ackoff, R.: Scientific method, optimizing applied research decisions. John Wiley & Sons, United States of America (1962)
3. van Marrewijk, A., Clegg, S.R., Pitsis, T.S., Veenwijk, M.: Managing public-private megaprojects: Paradoxes, complexity, and project design. International Journal of Project Management 26, 591–600 (2008)
4. Nunamaker Jr., J.F., Chen, M., Purdin, T.D.M.: Systems development in information systems research. Journal of Management Information Systems 7, 89–106 (1990)
5. Bailey, K.D.: Typologies and taxonomies an introduction to classification techniques. SAGE, Thousand Oaks (1994)
6. Gummesson, E.: Qualitative methods in management research. SAGE, Thousand Oaks (2000)
7. Blalock, A., Hubert, M.J.: Methodology in social research. McGraw-Hill, New York (1968)
8. Creswell, J.W.: Research design - qualitative, quantitative, and mixed methods approaches. SAGE, London (2009)

9. Creswell, J.W., Plano Clark, V.: Designing and conducting mixed methods research. SAGE, London (2007)
10. Denzin, N.K.: The research act: a theoretical introduction to sociological methods, 2nd edn. McGraw-Hill, New York (1978)
11. Brewer, J., Hunter, A.: Multimethod research a synthesis of styles. SAGE, Thousand Oaks (1989)
12. Denzin, N.K., Lincoln, Y.S.: Handbook of qualitative research. SAGE, Thousand Oaks (2000)
13. Aramo-Immonen, H., Porkka, P.L.: Shared knowledge in project-based companies' value chain. International Journal of Knowledge Management Studies 3, 364–378 (2009)
14. Aramo-Immonen, H., Kantola, J., Vanharanta, H., Karwowski, W.: Mastering qualitative factors of uncertainty in mega projects. In: Dussauge, P. (ed.) 5th Annual International Conference Proceedings of EURAM 2005 European Academy of Management (2005)
15. Suominen, A., Jussila, J.J., Koskinen, K.U., Aramo-Immonen, H.: Requisite variety of expertise in idea generation within a group. In: Huizingh, K.R.E., Torkkeli, M., Conn, S., Bitran, I. (eds.) Proceedings of the XIX ISPIM Conference, Tours, France (2008)
16. Aramo-Immonen, H., Porkka, P.L., Koskinen, K.U.: The role of formal training in project-based company. In: Kähkönen, K., Kazi, A.S., Rekola, M. (eds.) The Human Side of Projects in Modern Business, pp. 695–708. Project Management Association Finland (PMAF) in collaboration with, VTT Technical Research Centre of Finland, Helsinki (2009)
17. Aramo-Immonen, H., Vanharanta, H.: Project management – the task of holistic systems thinking. Human Factors and Ergonomics in Manufacturing 19, 582–600 (2008)
18. Conover, W.J.: Practical nonparametric statistics. John Wiley & Sons, New York (1999)
19. Neilimo, K., Näsi, J.: Nomoteettinen tutkimusote ja suomalaisen yrityksen taloustiede - Tutkimus positivismin soveltamisesta. (Nomothetic research approach and economics in Finland - a study of applications of positivism). University of Tampere, Tampere (1980)
20. Olkkonen, T.: Johdatus teollisuustalouden tutkimustyöhön. (An introduction to the research on industrial management). Helsinki University of Technology, Otaniemi (1993)
21. Eisenhardt, K.M., Graebner, M.E.: Theory building from cases: opportunities and challenges. Academy of Management Journal 50(1), 25–32 (2007)
22. March, S.T., Smith, G.F.: Design and natural science research on information technology. Decision Support Systems 15, 251–266 (1995)
23. Nunamaker Jr., J.F., Chen, M., Purdin, T.D.M.: Systems development in information systems research. Journal of Management Information Systems 7, 89–106 (1990)
24. Siggelkow, N.: Persuasion with case studies. Academy of Management Journal 50, 20–24 (2007)
25. Görög, M., Smith, N.: Project management for managers. PMI, Pensylvania (1999)
26. Turner, R.J.: Handbook of project-based management, improving processes for achieving strategic objectives. McGraw-Hill Companies, London (1999)
27. Kerzner, H.: Project management - A systems approach to planning, scheduling, and controlling. John Wiley & Sons, New Jersey (2003)
28. Levine, H.A.: Project portfolio management - A practical guide to selecting projects, managing portfolios, and maximizing benefit. Jossey-Bass A Wiley Imprint, San Francisco (2005)
29. Turner, R.J.: People in project management. Gower, Aldershot (2003)
30. Denzin, N.K., Lincoln, Y.S.: The landscape of qualitative research theories and issues. SAGE, Thousand Oaks (2003)
31. Popper, K.: The Logic of Scientific Discovery. Hutchinson & Co. (1959)

# Appendix 1

| Business economics research | | | | Design science research | | Systems development research | |
|---|---|---|---|---|---|---|---|
| **Constructive** | **Research process** | **Conceptual** | **Research process** | **Design science** | **Research process** | **Systems development** | **Research process** |
| Formulate the research problem (Kasanen et al., 1991; Olkkonen, 1994) | *Define the need for qualitative analysis in mega-project management. II, IV* | Define the research problem area (Kasanen et al., 1991; Olkkonen, 1994) | *Define the need for project management ontology: II, IV* | Build (March and Smith, 1995) | *Design the project organization learning model and use of the emulator metaphor. I, III, VI, VII* | Construct a conceptual framework (Nunamaker et al., 1990) | *Define the need for qualitative analysis and ontology in mega-project management. Execute the conceptual analysis of the ontology and discuss theoretical framework for learning model. II, IV, V* |
| Building the preunderstanding (Kasanen et al., 1991; Gummesson, 2000) | *Literature study, researchers experience, discussions in industrial domain.* | Classify (Kasanen et al., 1991; Olkkonen, 1994; Bailey, 1994) | *Conceptual analysis, Typological classification of project management features, creating project management ontology: V* | | | | |
| Innovate (Kasanen et al., 1991) | *Design Ontology and create the 150 statements to application.* | | | Evaluate (March and Smith, 1995) | *Multiple case study in 10 project organizations.* | Develop a system architecture (Nunamaker et al., 1990) | *Utilize Evolute architecture. Create 150 statements to application. I, V.* |
| Justify the construction (Kasanen et al., 1991) | *Laboratory testing of application at university and field testing at one company.* | Justify (Kasanen et al., 1991) Appendix 2 | *Comparison between other project knowledge area classifications. IPMA, APM, IPM, ISO, DMO* | Theorize (March and Smith, 1995) | *Interaction of the model with its environment understanding of systems dynamics laws.* | Analyze and design the system (Nunamaker et al., 1990) | *Project organization learning model and project management ontology in mega-project systems environment. I, VI, VII* |
| Justify the theoretical framework (Kasanen et al., 1991) | *Conceptual analysis and literature study. V* | | | Justify (March and Smith, 1995) | *study in case organizations.* | Build the (prototype) system (Nunamaker et al., 1990) | *Project organization learning model. I, VI* |
| Study the feasibility (Kasanen et al., 1991) | *Case study project 1 / Case study project 2* | Evidence (Kasanen et al., 1991; Olkkonen, 1994) | *Case study project 1 / Case study project 2* | | | Observe and evaluate the system (Nunamaker et al., 1990) | *Case study project 1 / Case study project 2 / Feasibility study in three case organizations* |

# Constructivist and Person-Centered Learning in Higher Education – Using Indicators and Case Examples for Comparing Good Practice

Renate Motschnig-Pitrik[1] and Lucie Rohlíková[2]

[1] University of Vienna, Computer Science Didactics and Learning Research Center
[2] University of West Bohemia in Pilsen, Lifelong Learning Centre
renate.motschnig@univie.ac.at, lrohlik@ucv.zcu.cz

**Abstract.** Constructivist and humanistic, person-centered education stand out as two well-known educational paradigms. Their commonalities and differences, however, have not yet been systematically investigated. Thus we compare principles and our experiences in facilitating constructivist and person-centered learning in order to derive implications for educational practice, research, and technology support. Results suggest that while the two paradigms overlap considerably, they exhibit subtle differences concerning the paths to reach their primary objectives. With numerous illustrations we aim at inspiring educators to move forward in their educational offerings and grow cognitively as well as (inter)personally with their students.

## 1    Introduction

Constructivist and person-centered education have been successfully applied in the context of technology-enhanced or blended learning (Jonassen, 2004; Motschnig-Pitrik, 2005; Motschnig-Pitrik & Derntl, 2005; Rohlíková, 2009). They appear to be highly overlapping and amenable to support/enhancement by technology, but equally exhibit different roots, terminology, practices, and emphases. Hence, we aim to identify the differences between the approaches and the ways they impact the design and realization of courses. Furthermore, we'll explore the option of integrating person-centered and constructivist learning in technology-enhanced environments.

After briefly introducing constructivist and person-centered learning, we compare basic "ingredients" of the two approaches. Thereby we borrow the concise constructivist overview of E. Murphy (1997) available online, and refer to Carl Rogers' original writing on the Person-Centered Approach. The main part of the paper provides illustrative examples from educational practice clustered along 5 themes: multiple perspectives, authenticity, function/role of "instructor", student-centeredness, and knowledge construction/acquisition. Theoretical considerations as well as examples will confirm our experience, namely that each of the approaches can well be enriched by the other one. This is because constructivism is primarily a paradigm of knowledge construction while the Person-Centered Approach contributes

M.D. Lytras et al. (Eds.): WSKS 2011, CCIS 278, pp. 44–57, 2013.

a psychological perspective on personality development in a constructive interpersonal atmosphere and hence focuses on qualities of relationships. Both aspects, certainly, are essential in our knowledge society.

## 2     Constructivist Learning in a Nutshell

In constructivism, learning is considered to be an active knowledge construction process that builds upon knowledge already possessed by the learner. Because knowledge is constructed by the individual through his or her interactions with their environment, learning methods cannot be prescribed (Von Glasersfeld, 1995). Principally, teachers cannot teach knowledge, rather they take on the role of coaches who help the learners to acquire knowledge themselves.

Woolfolk (1993, p. 485) states that the key idea is that students actively construct their own knowledge: the mind of the student mediates input from the outside world to determine what the student will learn. Learning is active mental work, not passive reception of teaching. In the context of eLearning, Gottlieb (2000) presents a few guiding principles of constructivist education:

1. Learning is an active process. E-learning designs need to engage the learner with sensory input. The learner needs to do something.
2. People learn to learn as they learn. Each meaning we construct makes us better able to give meaning to other scenarios that fit a similar pattern.
3. The crucial action of constructing meaning is mental. We need to model both the behavior and the thinking that generates the behavior.
4. Learning is contextual. People learn new things developmentally in relation to what they already know. So, interventions must be scaled to a particular group or be flexible to accommodate differing levels of expertise.
5. Learning is a social activity. Designs need to encourage interaction among the participants either synchronously or asynchronously.
6. Motivation is a key component of learning. Learners need to know why they have to learn, and how it will be applied.

The different interpretations of the theory have produced radical and moderate constructivists (Bertrand, 1995; Dalgarno, 2001). Radical constructivists hold the view that learners should work independently, with limited teacher support, while the moderates believe that learning can occur within a formal and structured environment. In our practice (Rohlíková, 2009, 2009b; Rohlíková &Vejvodová, 2010) we apply didactic constructivism (Koohang et al., 2008) in a way to focus on students' active engagement without aiming at methodological purity.

When characterizing constructivist learning, terms like: schemas, objects, concept maps, organization, construction, cooperation, knowledge creation, thought process, reflection, action, representation, tool are in the forefront. Thus, emphasis is on knowledge and cognition as a means for the organization of experience (Piaget, 1972). This is somewhat different to person-centered learning that more strongly integrates feeling and meaning, aiming at a holistic functioning based on the actualizing tendency that energizes and orients the assimilation of experience resulting from a person's interaction with their environment (Rogers, 1951).

# 3     Basics of Person-Centered Learning

The American psychologist Carl Rogers (USA: 1902 – 1987) was the founder of the Person-Centered Approach (Rogers, 1951, 1961). His work on "student-centered learning" illustrates how a teacher or, as Rogers preferred, a "facilitator of learning" could provide the trust, understanding and realness to free students to pursue significant, person-centered, whole-person learning. According to Rogers (1983, p. 20) "Significant learning combines the logical and the intuitive, the intellect and the feelings, the concept and the experience, the idea and the meaning. When we learn in that way, we are whole, utilizing all our masculine and feminine capacities." According to Rogers (1983, p. 20), the elements that are involved in significant learning are:

- There is a quality of personal involvement – the whole person in both feeling and cognitive aspects being in the learning event.
- Learning is self-initiated. Even when the impetus or stimulus comes from the outsides, the sense of discovery, the reaching out, of grasping and comprehending, comes from within.
- Learning is pervasive. It makes a difference in the behavior, the attitudes, perhaps even the personality of the learner.
- Progress is evaluated by the learner. She knows whether it is meeting her need, whether it leads toward what she wants to know, whether it illuminates the dark area of ignorance she is experiencing. The locus of evaluation resides definitely within the learner.
- Its essence is meaning. When such learning takes place, the element of meaning to the learner is built into the whole experience." (Rogers, 1983, p. 20)

Rogers emphasizes the importance of relationship qualities on learning. Significant learning requires the following personal attitudes on the side of the facilitator that must be perceived by the students at least to some degree:

- Realness, genuineness, congruence, openness to experience, authenticity or transparency in the facilitator. This means that he or she must be real in the relationship with their students, be the person he/she is and not hide behind any masks or facades when communicating with students.
- Acceptance, prizing, or respect towards student. This implies that the facilitator accepts and respects the whole personality of the student and feels basic trust in his or her constructive tendency, his/her striving for solutions in his/her own way.
- Deep understanding, often called empathic understanding. It is reflected in the attitude and practice of the facilitator to actively listen to the students with the ultimate goal to profoundly understand their questions, meanings, motivations, intentions, and also limitations.

A challenging task in teaching/learning scenarios, hence, is how such interpersonal qualities can be transformed into promotive actions in technology-enhanced environments. Tausch and Tausch (1963/1998) have identified and extensively researched a set of activities that tend to foster significant learning. Follow-up work investigated in which ways promotive activities can be supported in technology-enhanced environments (Bauer et al., 2006; Derntl, 2006; Motschnig-Pitrik, 2006).

# 4    On Comparing Constructivist and Person-Centered Learning

**Comparison Based on Characteristic Features and Examples.** The comparison is guided by 18 criteria of the constructivist checklist proposed by E. Murphy (1997) and available online. For easier comprehension, we have clustered the criteria along 5 major features or themes: 1) multiple perspectives, 2) authenticity, 3) function/role of "instructor", 4) student-centeredness, and 5) knowledge construction. In the following, each of the 5 major themes extracted from Murphy's list (1997) is devoted a Table. The entries describe the theme by quoting the indicators from Murphy's list (left upper field) and subsequently give examples from constructivist academic practice in the left columns, respectively. In analogy, respective themes and examples from the practice of person-centered learning are provided in the right columns.

**Table 1.** Multiple perspectives

| *Constructivist learning* | *Person-Centered learning* |
|---|---|
| Multiple perspectives and representations of concepts and content are presented and encouraged. (No. 1) Knowledge complexity is reflected in an emphasis on conceptual interrelatedness and interdisciplinary learning. (No. 15) Collaborative and cooperative learning are favoured in order to expose the learner to alternative viewpoints. (No. 16). | Rather than being presented, multiple views are encouraged to *emerge* from students' interest, experience, questions, engagement. Self-complexity is acknowledged, with meanings and feelings being increasingly more differentiated and gaining form and clarity in awareness. A kind of crystallization process is set free in the learners, influenced by their *interactions* with colleagues, material/electronic resources and the facilitator. |
| **Example** from "technology of production": *Discussions.* Discussion is offered primarily to approach hard and complex topics that need to be explained from multiple viewpoints. It is expected that the discussions help to reveal issues that generally are prone to misinterpretation at an early point in time. This shall prevent educators from bad surprises at exams where they find out that | **Example** from "communication": *Online reaction sheets.* A reaction sheet is an online reflection of a course participant written to encompass anything the participant has to say in response to a course unit. Reaction sheets are applicable whenever a constructive climate has been established in class and students feel safe to express their honest reactions. It is essential that the |

issues that seemed to be clear pose problems and turn out not to have been explained sufficiently.

**Example** from "marketing communication": *Team projects.*

In ethics, teams of students can choose their topics from a list /e.g. ethics of marketing). After some workshops, two weeks before the submission deadline, there is a brainstorming-workshop concerning the topics in which students can inspect the intermediate works of their colleagues and consult the instructor regarding their ideas and work procedures. At the end of the term, students are expected to discuss which marketing activities appear not to be ethical to them, their relatives and to others, and how they explain their judgments. The goal thereby is to become aware of the different valuing regarding ethics across people and the difficulties of an ethical marketing management.

**Example** from "systemic design of technical products": *Interdisciplinary projects.*

Teams of students from the faculty of construction who are expected to propose a new product always cooperate with one designer from the faculty of design and art. As a result, the proposed products are not only functional but also nice. Furthermore students learn to negotiate with a person who may hold different views. Furthermore, students from economics and production often join the teams such that real world situations are closely approximated.

**Example** from "personal management": *Decrease course content.*

It is important to consider the amount of content to be presented in order to leave space for discussion.

teacher/facilitator is genuinely interested in having students' reactions expressed and is willing to read them and to react on them. Practically, an online facility for submitting and displaying reaction sheets and some space in the curriculum in order to be able to react to students' expressed thoughts, questions, wishes, etc. Soliciting students' reactions has proved most effective in terms of having positive effects on the course process and on students' cooperation in intensive classes (Motschnig-Pitrik, 2005; Motschnig-Pitrik & Figl, 2008) and classes with up to 55 students

**Example** from "organizational development": *Student surveys.*

Online student surveys can be employed in the elaboration of topics. Typically, some discussion starts in a face-to-face session and in case it can't be finished, students can be asked to continue online. For example, in a course on organizational development (Motschnig-Pitrik et al., 2007) we started to discuss what it meant for an organization to move forward. The initial discussion was continued online in surveys, in which each student expressed what it meant to him or her for an organization to move forvard. Subsequently, a team used the survey to write an essay.

**Example** from "project management": *Peer evaluation.*

Project-based teamwork accompanied by peer reviewing supports students in developing skills of giving and receiving feedback, increasing their reflection ability, developing awareness of their own work's quality, and getting to know others' work and styles. The facilitator can use peer-reviews to inform the grading process thus enriching it to include not only his or her own evaluation but also that of others.

**Table 2.** Authenticity

| *Constructivist learning* | *Person-Centered learning* |
|---|---|
| Learning situations, environments, skills, content and tasks are relevant, realistic, authentic, and represent the natural complexities of the 'real world'. (No. 6) | Facilitators are authentic in their relationship to students and subject matter and communicate their "reality". "It is only by providing the genuine reality which is in me, that the other person can successfully seek for the reality in him." (Rogers, 1961, p. 33) |
| Primary sources of data are used in order to ensure authenticity and real-world complexity. (No. 7) | Facilitators provide learning resources from within themselves,, from books or materials, and encourage the learners to add resources. |
| Assessment is authentic and interwoven with teaching. (No. 18) | |
| **Example** from "systemic design of technical products": *Product design for a company.* | **Example** from "communication": *Being authentic and open.* |
| For their term-assignment student teams are expected to design technical products for external companies. At the end of the term there is a contest in which student teams present their products and the best team gets a financial reward. In the case of high quality results, further cooperation with the external firm is considered. | Two Asian students, who had shared that they needed to work to earn their living, missed 3 out of 6 workshops and came to the 5th workshop. I (Renate) felt upset: I understood their situation but couldn't excuse their long absence in a course in which presence was essential. I decided to share my thinking and feeling with the group. One of the Asian students responded: "I see and fully understand this. Still, we liked the course and wanted to ask whether it was okay to just sit in the course, without being graded." The strained situation immediately became relaxed and the group proceeded with more openness. |
| **Example** from "English": *Using real books and sources of literature.* | |
| Students can get acquainted with literature not only orally but also practically: Key books are brought to class and web-resources are presented on an interaction board. Students can suggest and try out exercises. | |
| **Example** from „personal management": *Multi-facetted evaluation.* | **Example** from "project management": *Changing the course mode.* |
| The complex achievement of each student is assessed: The quality of the presentation and report of the seminar thesis, the student's activities throughout the term, the exam, etc. Special effort is made to value students' contributions more highly and to appreciate their work rather than to devalue students' questions or comments. Feedback is encouraged. Furthermore, students are lead to more self-evaluation, for example they are asked to analyze the strengths and weaknesses of their seminar theses. | One of the authors taught a (4 ECTS) lecture in project management. This course type implied that there was one final exam and ruled out grading of intermediate achievements. The personally felt tension between this formal requirement and the experience that making assessment part of continuous learning was more effective caused her to apply for a change of the course mode. After some discussion, the the course mode was revised to become "mixed lab and lecture". There students solve real, small projects, give each other feedback, deliver and revise milestone documents and reflect online on the course units. While more time consuming due to intensive interaction, this course is "alive" and all concerned tend to enjoy learning from real situations. |

**Table 3.** Function/role of instructor

| Constructivist learning | Person-Centered learning |
|---|---|
| Teachers serve in the role of guides, monitors, coaches, tutors and facilitators. (No. 3) | Teachers are facilitators, meaning not just to carry a role but to be all one is in the particular relationship and experience. |
| **Example** from "management of sport": *Feedback.* <br> For their term-project, student teams always receive feedback on the parts that they elaborate in an incremental fashion. At the end of the term, the final version tends to have a higher quality because it already incorporates the comments. Students elaborate individual as well as team tasks. Such tasks always must be precisely specified and assigned such that subsequently they can be compared and evaluated. <br> **Example** from "mathematics": *Presentation of a problem from practice.* <br> Students' activity is encouraged by introducing each lecture with a problem, situation or example from practice. This raises first common questions for the theme of the lecture and motivates students to complement concepts and issues they do not know yet to solve problems and find responses. | **Example** from "soft skills in project management": *Facilitator as an experienced group member.* <br> Since soft skills can't be taught through lecturing, a good contact and relationship between facilitator and students is essential. This is brought about by a genuine interest of the facilitator in students' expectations, fears, past and recent experiences. After listening actively to students, the facilitator engages participants in small team work, encourages them to propose themes to be elaborated cooperatively and provides appropriate resources. He/she shares their perceptions and encourages open feedback while always respecting students and trying to thoroughly understand their meanings as well as feelings. The facilitator shares his or her power of grading including students' self- and peer-evaluations into the grading process. Facilitators flexibly react on the unfolding process. Typically, they lead less and less as the course proceeds, almost making themselves obsolete as leaders. |

**Table 4.** Student-centeredness

| Constructivist learning | Person-Centered learning |
|---|---|
| Goals and objectives are derived by the student or in negotiation with the teacher or system. (No. 2) <br> The student plays a central role in mediating and controlling learning. (No. 5) <br> The learner's previous knowledge constructions, beliefs and attitudes are considered in the knowledge construction process. (No. 10) | "The facilitative teacher shares with the others – students and community members – the responsibility for the learning process." (Rogers, 1978, p. 73) Goals and objectives are derived in dialogue between students and facilitator. "The discipline necessary to reach the student's goal is a self-discipline and is recognized by the learner as being his or her own responsibility." (Rogers, 1978, p. 73). |
| **Example** from "Hebrew language": *Students' choice of text.* | **Example** from "human computer interaction": *ePortfolios documenting learning process.* |

| | |
|---|---|
| In the beginning students choose a classical Hebrew text that interests him or her and that they want to understand. During the term, this text is used to exemplify the grammar that is taught, vocabulary, etc, such that students can devote their time also to literature that they themselves are interested in.<br>**Example** from "multimedia": *Free choice of project themes.*<br>Students are completely free to choose the themes of their projects. At the beginning they are just given the intended outcome, for example, to produce a poster for dissemination and some conditions, such as to use only open source software, and the control conditions, such as to present once every 2 weeks. Students can also cooperate with colleagues from other teams. Each month they present their progress and discuss their work with the other teams. | Throughout the course, several open questions and tasks arise, such as the evaluation of a web-site or comparing mobile phones for their usability. Students can follow up these and other self-chosen themes in their ePortfolios. Some tasks are discussed in class, others are just presented during a final interview used for grading by both the instructor and the student (self-evaluation).<br>**Example** from "communication": *The group co-determines the activities.*<br>Students' feedback, such as that shared in the reaction sheets, has an influence on the process and design of upcoming course units: Students and facilitator can cooperate to address expressed perceptions and change something, such as to revisit a difficult topic, to extend a break, to bring more//less theory, etc. In this way, the group can learn from their experience, diversity, creativity, "mistake", experiments. |

**Table 5.** Knowledge construction

| *Constructivist learning* | *Person-Centered learning* |
|---|---|
| Activities, opportunities, tools and environments are provided to encourage metacognition, self-analysis -regulation, -reflection & -awareness. (No. 4)<br>Knowledge construction and not reproduction is emphasized. (No. 8)<br>This construction takes place in individual contexts and through social negotiation, collaboration and experience. (No. 9)<br>Problem-solving, higher-order thinking skills and deep understanding are emphasized. (No.11)<br>Errors provide the opportunity for insight into students' previous knowledge constructions. (No. 12)<br>Exploration is a favored approach in order to encourage students to seek knowledge independently and to manage the pursuit of their goals. (No. 13) | First of all, an interpersonal relationship is lived that encourages students to participate ways they consider most constructive for themselves as well as the group. In a climate of realness and openness, respect, and understanding there arises genuine interest in students' meanings and feelings such that dialogue, discussion, and encounter tend to happen and unfold in the group, leading to personally and interpersonally discovered meanings, activities, and behavior.<br>Every symbolic expression is regarded without judgment and can be a source of learning and reorganization.<br>Students need to find out how they learn, hence their self-exploration and expression are favored in order to encourage them to seek understanding interdependently, in harmony with the group's goals. "It can be |

| | |
|---|---|
| Learners are provided with the opportunity for apprenticeship learning in which there is an increasing complexity of tasks, skills and knowledge. (No. 14)<br><br>Scaffolding is facilitated to help students perform just beyond the limits of their ability. (No. 17) | seen that the focus is primarily on fostering the process of learning." (Rogers, 1978, p. 73)<br><br>Learning is more self-directed and arising from the „here-and-now" rather than being strictly engineered. |
| **Example** from "computer networks": *Consecutive tasks with increased difficulty.*<br>The lab activities are partitioned into three categories according to students' stepwise control of the problem:<br>    1. First, students test the basic configuration of the equipment that is described in the tasks following a step by step approach.<br>    2. Subsequently students can approach a more advanced configuration that illustrates further extensions and additional properties that can be used.<br>    3. After successfully managing the first two steps, students are capable of finding and fixing errors in configurations in the third step.<br>In this way, students build insight on already acquired knowledge and extend their insights.<br>**Example** from "computer networks": *Teams and forum-discussions.*<br>Students work on various projects in teams having three members. In this way they not only acquire knowledge but also build their interpersonal, communicative, and analytical competences. Activities are arranged from simple ones to advanced ones such as searching for errors in solutions. This supports experiential learning. Throughout the teamwork, students can compare their knowledge with that of colleagues and can compensate deficiencies with the help of colleagues. However, this compensation shall only be temporary, students are motivated to spend more time for preparing the next unit. Each | **Example** from "project management": *Talking to teams individually.*<br>In class, small teams are formed to elaborate questions that emerge throughout the process, e.g. what is the nature of good feedback or how can cost be estimated. The facilitator visits each team to see how they are doing, what questions they have, how far they have come, etc. to establish interpersonal contact and to share some of his/her feelings and meanings in immediate situations.<br>**Example** from "communication" and "organizational development": *Encounter group sessions.*<br>While in their full form person-centered encounter groups typically last for at least 1,5 days to a few weeks, some of their qualities can be experienced in sessions lasting for a few hours. There is no structure and everybody is free to share his or her thoughts, feelings, meanings. Participants can experience how it feels to talk in front of a whole group, how they are received by others, what ore others' responses to their messages, how it feels to be silent or equally not able to get a turn in an excited group. Often students reflect that experiences they make in encounter groups are deep, lasting, and even unique. In some sense they understand that what seems most personal often turns out to be of deep general interest, such as difficulties in listening to partners or communicating divergent views to superiors. However, it happens that some students don't understand the processes in groups and wish to be taught more theory or participate in exercises. It is essential that encounter group |

exception to the ordinary configuration needs to be discussed. If the discussions proceed in the forum they can be accessed also by students who have not encountered the same problem.

**Example** from "mathematics": *Working with errors.*

Students are encouraged to be active during seminars. Also a wrong opinion is an opinion and it is not criticized but used as an incentive for another thought or further discussion. Thereby also self-reflection in the student can be achieved.

**Example** from "macro-economy": *Exploring and searching for information.*

Active searches for articles for every training session lead to the establishment of useful habits for the future. Students should get accustomed to retrieving recent information about economy from printed media or the internet such that even after passing the course or their studies they are capable of retrieving important information.

sessions are introduced thoughtfully and empathically, they must not be imposed on students. Reflecting the process usually helps to make it more transparent and raise curiosity for more by almost every student, as evident from feedback.

**Example** from "Soft skills in project management": *Student teams moderate a 3-hour session.*

An important soft skill is to work in teams and to present/elaborate ideas interactively. This is why the facilitator uses various moderation techniques such as small team work, collecting ideas on a flipchart, constellations, feedback rounds, etc. in the initial sessions. In this phase students get a chance to experience these moderation techniques through participating in them. A few weeks later, after having consulted the concept of the moderation sequence with the facilitator, each team moderates a 3 hour workshop and provides underlying materials on the web-site. This scenario has proved particularly powerful in learning how to present ideas, initiate dialogue and discussion, manage time, and give and receive feedback face-to face as well as online.

**Reflections and Insights.** We get the impression that constructivist and person-centered learning, while both valuing subjectivity and sharing highly related goals, follow complementary directions:

- In constructivist education the predominant insight is that knowledge serves the organization of the experiential world and thus the construction of knowledge is the primary activity to be supported. There is a clear focus on assimilating, accommodating, constructing *knowledge*.
- In person-centered education organismic (i.e. stemming from the body and senses) experience guides, better motivates (due to the actualizing tendency) the organization of the self-structure that can be thought to fluently organize knowledge (of very different kinds, partly tacit) that has some, how dim so ever, relevance to a person. Of course, the structure of the self (corresponding to what we conceive of as "I know") can influence organismic experience, but there will, in a psychologically mature person, always be a flow between organism and self,

perceiving/subceiving/sensing and knowing. Thus in the PCA there appears to be a clear focus on assimilating *experience*.

The high value and depth of experiential learning, as acknowledged and actively endeavored in constructivist and person-centered learning, can be understood in so far as this kind of learning possesses the complex experiential, organismic evidence, comparable to a kind of birth process to knowing that typically is void in purely receptive learning that addresses primarily the cognitive structures. Receptive learning produces structures that are well shaped, but tend to lack organismic searching and sourcing. They can be compared to items you can buy ready-made, off the shelf, fitting some preconceived purpose but useless in new, unexpected situations.

The above may support the understanding of the tendency of constructivist educators to act as coaches who hint students to relevant experiences for knowledge constructions while person-centered educators are more strongly non-directive and more likely to rely on the learners' actualizing tendencies for whole-person enhancement. This leaves us with the questions: What are the consequences of these differences for higher education? Can the two paradigms be integrated in a synergistic way that allows them to maintain their strengths and overcome weaknesses?

## 5      On Integrating Constructivist and Person-Centered Learning

In our view, constructivist and person-centered learning in practice are often integrated – in particular, if a constructivist coach is congruent, acceptant, and endeavors to deeply understand students. In this case, he or she will be particularly attuned to students' needs arising in the here and now. From the perspective of the person-centered facilitator, in an integrated approach he or she will suggest activities and exercises which he/she considers worthwhile while always being highly interpersonally present to students and letting them have the final choice of engaging in some activity or proposing self-initiated alternatives. Criteria relevant for deciding on some educational paradigm or scenario include:

- Personality and experience, skills, background of the educator
- Educational goals/mission of the institution offering education
- Degree of freedom versus following requirements and learning outcomes specified in the curriculum
- Class size, course type, subject matter, time available
- Previous knowledge, attitudes, diversity, maturity, and various competences of the student cohort

## 6      Conclusion

We feel that any educational offering can be positioned on a continuum whereby the multidimensional axes that span the space are individual educational paradigms. It is helpful, though, to know the – sometimes clear-cut, at other times subtle – differences in order to be more aware of their implications for the learner as well as for oneself. For example, one may ask the question: Am I prepared to let myself influence by students in how the course will be conducted? Can I trust them to be self-directing or should I better guide them to reach the learning outcomes? Can I establish sufficient contact with a large number of students in a given time such as to have them co-decide on learning outcomes? Overall, when comparing constructivist and person-centered "philosophies" we get the impression that their focus is complementary: Constructivism emphasizes knowledge construction and appropriate cognitive methods and tools. The Person-Centered Approach, however, concentrates on the (pre)conditions under which deep or significant learning is most likely to take place and consequently emphasizes the unfolding of a constructive learning climate, growing from facilitative interpersonal relationships (Cornelius-White & Harbaugh, 2010) and providing space for the assimilation of experience. The integration of the two paradigms is likely to add value to both. Still, further research is necessary to confirm this hypothesis and to explore specific conditions for the blend to be most effective.

Learning technology is likely to support either paradigm, since it facilitates personalized and cooperative activities, networking, and almost continuous communication and contact, even though through a restricted electronic "channel" only. Constructivist and person-centered learning put similar demands on technology support, using technology to make it easier to find, access and share information, to extend contact between participants beyond the class hours, to supply information and hence trade some time/space that otherwise would be used for lecturing for more communication in class.

Last but not least, we need to find out, how constructivist coaches and person-centered facilitators can best be "trained" or developed to fulfill the high demands posited on their professional coaching, "personhood", and interpersonal presence.

**Acknowledgement.** Sincere thanks are due to Ladislav Nykl, Elfriede Ederer, Oswald Comber, David Haselberger, Jana Vejvodová and Jana Nema for their encouragement and constructive comments to an earlier version of the manuscript. The authors also express their sincere thanks to their colleagues and students who have contributed to the examples given in the tables. Without their active cooperation this paper couldn't have been written.

# References

1. Bauer, C., Derntl, M., Motschnig-Pitrik, R., Tausch, R.: Promotive Activities in Face-to-Face and Technology-Enhanced Learning Environments. The Person-Centered Journal 13(1-2), 12–37 (2006)
2. Bertrand, Y.: Contemporary theories and practice in education. Magna Publications, Madison (1995)

3.  Cornelius-White, J.H.D., Harbaugh, A.P.: Learner-Centered Instruction: Building Relationships for Student Success. SAGE, Thousand Oaks (2010)
4.  Dalgarno, B.: Interpretations of Constructivism and Consequences for Computer Assisted Learning. British Journal of Educational Technology 32(2), 183–194 (2001)
5.  Derntl, M.: Patterns for Person-Centered e-Learning. Aka Verlag, Berlin (2006)
6.  Gottlieb, M.: Foundations of E-Learning. Online Communication Project Magazine, Vol. 3.1 (2000), http://www.comproj.com/Gottlieb.html
7.  Jonassen, D.H. (ed.): Handbook of research on educational communications and technology, 2nd edn. Lawrence Erlbaum Associates, Mahwah (2004)
8.  Koohang, L., Riley, L., Smith, T.: E-Learning and Constructivism: From Theory to Application. Interdisciplinary Journal of E-Learning and Learning Objects 5 (2008), http://ijklo.org/Volume5/IJELLOv5p091-109Koohang655.pdf
9.  Motschnig-Pitrik, R.: Person-Centered e-Learning in action: Can technology help to manifest person-centered values in academic environments? Journal of Humanistic Psychology 45(4), 503–530 (2005)
10. Motschnig-Pitrik, R., Derntl, M.: Can the Web Improve the Effectiveness of Person-Centered Learning? Case Study on Teaching and Living Web-Engineering. IADIS Int. Journal of WWW/Internet 2(1), 49–62 (2005)
11. Motschnig-Pitrik, R.: Two Technology-Enhanced Courses Aimed at Developing Interpersonal Attitudes and Soft Skills in Project Management. In: Nejdl, W., Tochtermann, K. (eds.) EC-TEL 2006. LNCS, vol. 4227, pp. 331–346. Springer, Heidelberg (2006)
12. Motschnig-Pitrik, R., Figl, K.: The Effects of Person Centered Education on Communication and Community Building. In: Proceedings of ED-MEDIA, World Conference on Educational Multimedia, Hypermedia and Telecommunications, pp. 3843–3852. AACE, Vienna (2008)
13. Motschnig-Pitrik, R., Kabicher, S., Figl, K., Santos, A.M.: Person Centered, Technology Enhanced Learning in Action: Action Research in a Course on Organizational Development. In: Proceedings of 37th ASEE/IEEE Frontiers in Education Conference, Milwaukee, WI (2007)
14. Murphy, E.: Constructivist Learning Theory (1997)
15. http://www.ucs.mun.ca/~emurphy/stemnet/cle2b.html
16. Piaget, J.: Psychology and Epistemology: Towards a Theory of Knowledge. Penguin, Harmondsworth (1972)
17. Rogers, C.R.: Client-centered therapy: Its current practice, implications, and theory. Houghton Mifflin, Boston (1951)
18. Rogers, C.R.: On Becoming a Person - A Psychotherapists View of Psychotherapy. Constable, London (1961)
19. Rogers, C.R.: On Personal Power. Constable (1978)
20. Rogers, C.R.: Freedom to Learn for the 80's. Charles E. Merrill Publishing Company, Columbus (1983)
21. Rohlíková, L.: The Importance of ICT for the Development of Constructivist Methods of Instruction at Universities. In: Šimonová, I., Poulová, P., Šabatová, M., Bílek, M., Maněnová, M. (eds.) On Contribution of Modern Technologies Towards Developing Key Competences. M. Vognar, Hradec Králové (2009)
22. Rohlíková, L.: E-learning and didactic constructivism in higher education. In: Proceedings of eLearning Conference 2009 Proceedings. Univerzita Hradec Králové, Hradec Králové (2009b)

23. Rohlíková, L., Vejvodová, J.: Blended learning in staff developement: Toward constructivism by constructivism. In: Proc. of Distance Education Conference DisCo 2010. University of West Bohemia in Pilsen, Pilsen (2010)
24. Tausch, R., Tausch, A.-M.: Erziehungs-Psychologie (Educational Psychology) Hogrefe. 11. Auflage 1998, Göttingen, Deutschland (1963/1998)
25. Von Glasersfeld, E.: A constructivist approach to teaching. In: Steffe, L., Gale, J. (eds.) Constructivism in Education, pp. 3–16. Lawrence Erlbaum Associates, Inc., New Jersey (1995)
26. Woolfolk, A.: Educational psychology, 5th edn., p. 643. Allyn & Bacon, Boston (1993)

# Key Factors in Managing IT Outsourcing Relationships

Hari Nugroho[1], Gamaludin Al Afghani[1], Georg Hodosi[2], and Lazar Rusu[2]

[1] School of Information and Communication Technology,
Royal Institute of Technology (KTH)
Isafjordsgatan 39, 164 40 Kista, Sweden
[2] Department of Computer and Systems Sciences, Stockholm University
Isafjordsgatan 39, 164 40 Kista, Sweden
{nugroho,gaaf}@kth.se, {hodosi,lrusu}@dsv.su.se

**Abstract.** Relationship management in IT Outsourcing (ITO) is today an important concern in many organizations. In the review of research literature regarding relationship management in IT outsourcing we have found a lot research on best practices but not on key factors. Therefore our research goal has looked to find the key factors in managing IT outsourcing relationships that are including the best practices in ITO relationships. The results of this research has due to a list of six key factors that includes the best practices that were elicited from the IT outsourcing relationships research and which were applied in the case of three organizations in Sweden. The analysis of the results has shown both deviations as well as compliances between the theory and practices, but also deviations between the views of these key factors in the studied organizations.

**Keywords:** Key Factors, IT Outsourcing, IT Outsourcing Relationships, Best Practices, Sweden.

## 1 Introduction

Since the "Kodak effect" in 1989 (that refers to an agreement through which IBM has developed and managed the data centre for Eastman Kodak with the purpose of decreasing the Kodak company's costs associated with IT operations) outsourcing has expanded as a company's strategic choice and as a key method to manage their IT portfolio [1][2]. According to Huber cited in [3] IT has a significant effect in organizational performance. Concerning Information Technology Outsourcing (ITO) this is defined as a decision conducted by an organization to delegate various IT functions and activities such as operations, supports, development, and maintenance, to outside suppliers, who in exchange provide those services for financial returns within an agreed period of time [4][5][2]. In this context IT outsourcing relationships is one of the important research areas in IT outsourcing because IT outsourcing performance has major effects to the whole organizational performance.

M.D. Lytras et al. (Eds.): WSKS 2011, CCIS 278, pp. 58–69, 2013.

## 1.1    Transaction Cost Economics (TCE)

In research in ITO, Transaction Cost Economics (TCT) is an important theory developed by [6]. According to [7] that are mentioning [8] as the one who has introduced transaction cost as the main determinant of firm boundary and in his opinion firms will grow until the operational cost for managing transactions is the same as the cost of making the same transactions in other firm. Hence, as [8] is mentioning transaction cost as the main reason of firm existence. Later on Williamson [6] has explained that the un-ability to predict the future due to bounded rationality causes incomplete contract which will trigger renegotiations when the power balance shifts to one party. Moreover according to [7] a firm will outsource its IT department if there are cheaper alternatives in the open market compare to operational cost for running IT department. On the other hand the IT outsourcing service providers exists to substitute the IT department and to reduce the IT operational cost. However, [9] argued that there is also a switching cost related to IT outsourcing decision.

## 1.2    Selection of Best Practices and Key Factors

For finding the best practices in IT outsourcing relationships we have reviewed the research literature and a summary with a brief explanation of the main findings from outsourcing relationship research is presented in Table 1. The findings of this literature review will serve as foundation to figure out the key factors in managing IT outsourcing relationships. In this direction we consider key factors as those few important factors that could guide ITO decision makers in having successfully ITO relationships.

**Table 1.** A Summary of Research done in IT Outsourcing Relationships

| No. | Researchers | Main Findings |
|-----|-------------|---------------|
| 1 | Williamson in [7] | • Transaction costs as the main determinant of the firm boundary.<br>• It is impossible to make contract which covers all possible future state because of bounded rationality.<br>• Incomplete contract causes renegotiations when the power balance moves to one party. |
| 2 | Kern and Willcocks [10] | Core interactions are IT outsourcing relationships focus, such as products, services, financial, and information exchanges. |
| 3 | Alborz et al. [11] | • Three phases in IT outsourcing relationships model: pre-contract, contract, and post-contract.<br>• Eight factors that influenced IT outsourcing relationships: outsourcing strategy, due dilligence, contract development, governance, performance management, contract management, working relationship management, and knowledge management. |

**Table 1.** (*continued*)

| 4 | Hodosi and Rusu [12] | Contract fulfillment measurement. |
|---|---|---|
| 5 | Lee, Miranda and Kim [13] | The contract is the main issue in outsourcing relationship. |
| 6 | Jiang-ping, Yong-hua and Qing-jing [14] | Six dimensions based on the Relational Exchange Theory: trust, flexibility, communication, collaboration, management, risk and benefit sharing. |
| 7 | Wilcocks [15] | The CIO should play a major role in IT outsourcing. |
| 8 | PriceWaterhouseCoopers [16] | Effective management in a long term is important in IT outsourcing relationships. |
| 9 | Clark, Zmud, and McGray in [17] | Vendor governance is a main critical success factors in outsourcing. |
| 10 | Mingay and Govekar in [18] | Service Level Agreements (SLAs) are often used as key for controlling parties' behavior and measuring outcome in IT outsourcing relationships. |
| 11 | Sargent Jr [19] | The CIO should ensure that the contract is well-managed and govern the IT architectural plan throughout IT outsourcing. |
| 12 | Barthélemy in [20] | IT management on soft side which refers to trust has more impact compare to IT management on hard side. |
| 13 | Lee et al.(2003) | Guidance to make productive partner relationship which consists of: Mutual business understanding, Define short and long term objectives, Specify clear and reasonable expectations, Risks and benefits sharing, Develop performance measurements, Anticipate revisions and changes, Prepare for unpredicted, Take care of the relationships. |
| 14 | Mehta and Mehta [22] | Improving client and outsourcing provider partnership requires relational investment from the client. |
| 15 | Perrin [23] | Five factors for successful outsourcing relationship: high level of communication, trust, conflict resolution, co-operation, proactive management. |
| 16 | Ahituv and Wilcocks in [24] | Good project management as a key for successful outsourcing project. |
| 17 | Oza et al.[24] | Trust-based relationships shows a better result for outsourcing project. |
| 18 | Kishore et al. [2] | • The FORT framework.<br>• The detail of IT outsourcing contract depends on the IT outsourcing relationships type. |
| 19 | Cullen and Willcocks [25] | • Eight building blocks of successful IT outsourcing.<br>• Eleven factors for successful IT outsourcing.<br>• Four factors that causes failure in IT outsourcing. |
| 20 | Chorafas [26] | Outsource only good processes. |

Based on findings in IT outsourcing relationships research described in Table 1, we have proposed six key factors in managing IT outsourcing relationships. The key factors are built based on the review of the research literature in IT outsourcing relationships as important factors for having a successfully IT outsourcing relationship. The six key factors we have identified are including the best practices in managing IT outsourcing relationships and are presented in Table 2.

**Table 2.** List of Key Factors with Associated Best Practices in Managing IT Outsourcing Relationships

| Key Factors | Best Practices |
|---|---|
| **IT Outsourcing Strategy** | • The executive management of client should have long-term objectives before deciding to outsource [11] [16].<br>• Due diligence. The company should conduct pre-planned activities before signing the outsourcing contract with an outsourcing service provider [11].<br>• Define short-term and long-term goals. Prioritize middle goal without forgetting long-term focus [21].<br>• Defines realistic expectations clearly. Both parties should define clear and reasonable expectations and prepare a learning curve [21].<br>• Cost and financial management. The client and supplier should have the cost and financial management integrated in the IT outsourcing strategy [25].<br>• Outsource only good process as outsourcing is not a solution for a problem [26]. |
| **The CIO role in IT Outsourcing** | • Senior management plays strategic roles and supports the successful IT outsourcing (Kern and Willcocks in [11], Clark, Zmud, and McGray in [17]).<br>• The CIO should ensure that the contract is well-managed and govern the IT architectural plan [15][19]. |
| **Contract Management** | • The outsourcing contract should have high level of detail to prevent opportunism in the future (Williamson in [7]).<br>• The contractual foundation guides the outsourcing relationship over its contractual term [10].<br>• The client should develop specific SLAs and flexibility into outsourcing contract which allow adjustments in the future (Fitzgerald and Willcocks in [2],[11]).<br>• The contract is not self-enforcing or self-adjusting, it needs different management style (Kern and Quinn in [11],[21] [25]).<br>• Flexibility. Both parties are able to adapt with the environmental changes by renegotiation [14][21][25] .<br>• The organization should control the contract and processes to ensure that it stays competitive [25]. |

**Table 2.** (*continued*)

| Interactions | <ul><li>Working relationship management. It is a combination of interactions and behaviors between outsourcing service provider and the client [11][25].</li><li>Knowledge management. It refers to the ongoing and knowledge and expertise exchange between outsourcing service provider and the client (Klepper and Jones in [11]).</li><li>The outsourcing service provider should provide professional training for effective IT outsourcing implementation [14] [25].</li><li>Trust. It means expecting others to fulfill their responsibility and have fair performance even though opportunism exists [14], Barthélemy in [20][23] [24], Ahituv and Willcocks in [24].</li><li>Communication. Both sides should share the significant formal/informal, and timely information [14][23][25].</li><li>Collaboration. It refers to conducting positive actions for achieving mutual benefits [14].</li><li>Understanding each other's business. Both parties should share important goals and policies [21][25].</li><li>Nurture the relationship. IT outsourcing relationships requires continual maintenance from both parties [21].</li><li>Relational investment from the client. The client should also contribute in IT outsourcing relationships [22].</li><li>Co-operation. Both sides should work together for achieving a mutual goal [23].</li><li>Proactive. The outsourcing service provider should provide the service in a proactive manner [23].</li></ul> |
|---|---|
| **Performance Management** | <ul><li>Measuring the performance of outsourcing service provider provides empirical data for measuring outsourcing relationships success (Gartner in [11][21]).</li><li>The performance of outsourcing service provider should be measured against SLAs [12].</li><li>SLAs act as key for managing parties' behavior and outcomes (Mingay and Govekar in [18],[25]).</li><li>The service should not only be delivered to meet expectations and specifications, but it needs to be improved continuously [25].</li><li>The outsourcing service provider should deliver services which meet client's needs [25].</li></ul> |
| **Risk Management** | <ul><li>Risk and benefit sharing. Both parties should not only consider their own interests [14][21].</li><li>Prepare for unexpected. Both sides should identify the potential problems [21].</li><li>Conflict resolution. Both parties should resolve the conflicts jointly and mutually agree to the solution [23].</li></ul> |

## 2      Research Methodology

This research aims is to analyze how to manage successfully IT outsourcing relationships using as case study three different Swedish organizations. The main research question of this study is looking to find the key factors in managing IT outsourcing relationships. The research process of selecting the key factors in managing IT outsourcing relationships has the following steps:

1. A review of research literature in IT outsourcing relationships for extracting the best practices in IT outsourcing relationship in any type of organization.
2. The identification of key factors coming from best practices in managing IT outsourcing relationships.
3. The application of the key factors previously mentioned in three case studies in organizations from Sweden which have outsourced part or whole of their IT operations.

According to [27] case study is able to achieve same scientific goals through different ways. Therefore this research is using case study as research methodology to test the key factors based on best practices in IT outsourcing relationship and elaborate the results from the observation data. The authors have started this research by conducting a review literature to elicit the best practices in IT outsourcing relationships. After that interview questions were developed based on several theoretical backgrounds in IT outsourcing that were presented in chapter 2. Further on the authors have conducted semi structured interviews in Spring 2010 with the CIO or Head of IT Sourcing or other decision persons who had responsibilities in IT Outsourcing. In final step we have analyzed the data from the interviews regarding the application of the key factors in IT outsourcing relationships in three different organizations (a small size, a medium size, and a large organization) in Sweden.

## 3      Data Analysis and Results

In finding how these key factors can be applied in managing IT outsourcing relationships we have used as case study three different categories of organizations (a small size, a medium size, and a large organization). A short description of the organizations and an analysis of the data collected from the interviews performed with IT decision makers in ITO are below presented.

### 3.1    Organization A: Service Company

Organization A is according to [28] a medium company because it has less than 250 employees. Organization A outsources several application developments and IT infrastructure, such as servers, hardware, workstations, and office applications to support business activities because they are not its core competencies. Organization A still develops in-house main application. Based on the interview with the CIO of organization A, we have found that the size difference between Organization A as a medium company and IT outsourcing provider as large company cause unbalance in IT outsourcing relationships. Due to that reason, the CIO prefers to choose other IT outsourcing provider for the next IT outsourcing contract. Organization A can terminate the contract anytime by paying exit fee. However this could be a bad situation because they don't mention the exit fee amount. The CIO argued that IT outsourcing relationships should be based on trust and they believe that the IT outsourcing provider will not cheat. Organization A uses SLAs (Service Level Agreements) to measure IT outsourcing provider performance. Upon failure in fulfilling those parameters, the IT outsourcing service provider should pay penalties. However, the CIO argued that the IT outsourcing relationships are similar like love and hate relationships which are difficult to satisfy both parties.

### 3.2    Organization B: Telecommunication Company

Organization B is according to [28] a large company because it has more than 250 employees. Organization B has well IT outsourcing relationships, as explained by the Head of IT Sourcing of this organization. Acquiring benefits from IT expertise is the reason of why organization B has decided to outsource basic support operation of mobile division which is not its core competencies. The combination of price, quotation and trustworthiness are the main determinants in supplier selection process. There were several renegotiations to adapt with the changing environment. Organization B can measure the service quality of IT outsourcing provider by using Service Level Agreements (SLAs) and Key Performance Indicators (KPIs).

### 3.3    Organization C: Non-profit Organization

Organization C is according to [28] a small company because it has less than 50 employees. To manage IT outsourcing, organization C hires an IT specialist because it doesn't have dedicated IT staff. In the interview we had with the IT specialist he has explained us that the main reason to outsource IT is there is lack of internal IT resources. Therefore references are very important in building the trust in IT outsourcing relationships. For selecting the best IT outsourcing provider there are specific criteria in which both parties signed an open-ended contract. In organization C the measuring of the service quality of IT outsourcing service provider performance is based on the contract.

### 3.4    Data Analysis

The six key factors in managing IT outsourcing relationships have been tested in the case of the three organizations A, B and C and the results of this analysis are presented below.

### 3.4.1  IT Outsourcing Strategy

All the three organizations have outsourced IT because IT is not their core competency and they want to focus on their core business. The CIO of organization A argued that trust-based relationship is important in IT outsourcing and a higher trust prevents IT outsourcing provider to misbehave its client. Meanwhile the Head of IT Sourcing of organization B explained that IT outsourcing provider fulfillment to contract and obligation without any deviation create trustworthiness which is the foundation in IT outsourcing relationships. The trust is also supported by the IT specialist of organization C, which mentioned that references are important in gaining trust in IT outsourcing relationships.

### 3.4.2  The CIO Role in IT Outsourcing

The whole IT portfolios, except in two branches are responsibility of the CIO of organization A which reports directly to the CEO. The Head of IT Sourcing of organization B is also responsible in IT Outsourcing and reports directly to the CIO. Hence, both companies can get IT outsourcing benefits because the CIO plays major role in IT outsourcing [15]. On the other side, there is no dedicated IT staff in organization C which results in poor IT management and as a consequences, it delays the IT outsourcing process.

### 3.4.3  Contract Management

Both organizations A and B managed to renegotiate the contract due to unhappiness and also to adapt with the changes. The CIO of organization A prefers to have a smaller IT outsourcing provider in order to avoid size difference. Organization A can terminate the contract anytime by paying penalty. Meanwhile organization C has an open-ended contract which allows renegotiations in the future. However advance notification is needed to terminate the contract.

### 3.4.4  Interactions

All three organizations have monthly regular meetings with their IT outsourcing provider to nurture the relationships. Initially employees of organization A could not adapt with the new working policy because they should share ideas and problems externally. This situation did not happen in organization B because most of the IT outsourcing staff are former employees of organization B. They still have the same job descriptions but are working for the IT outsourcing provider. Meanwhile organization C communicates regularly with the IT outsourcing provider by using the telephone or email depending on issues category.

### 3.4.5  Performance Management

Organizations A and B are using SLAs to evaluate the IT outsourcing provider performance, moreover organization B also applies KPIs. In case of failure in fulfilling the promising performance, the IT outsourcing provider should pay penalties. Meanwhile organization C measures the IT outsourcing provider performance using a contract in which is define the services and penalties upon failure of fulfilling the promises.

### 3.4.6  Risk Management

Organizations A, B and C are managing the risk by identifying the potential risk and composing the mitigation plans. When a problems occurs, organization A judge them based on complexity to find whose party is responsible. Further on organization A can launch their applications with minimum features when the system crashes. On the other hand organization B considers risk management as an ongoing task which changes over the time. While in organization C, the main factor to minimize IT outsourcing risk is concern of selecting the best IT outsourcing provider. In fact according to [29] a good risk management in IT outsourcing is required and as we have noticed this is presented in all these organizations.

## 3.5    Results

From the interviews we have had in three organizations in Sweden with ITO decision makers we have found that there are slight deviations between theory and observation data of these companies. In fact we have found that some best practices part of our key factors in IT outsourcing relationships  and which were presented in Table 2 are less important for a successful IT outsourcing. We also have observed that both organization A and organization C has less bargaining power with the IT outsourcing service provider due to size difference. The provider in the case of these organizations A and C is a large company while the clients are small and a medium company. The results of the analysis in these three organizations using the key factors in ITO relationship are shown in Table 3.

**Table 3.** Results of the analysis using the key factors in ITO relationship in three organizations

| Key Factors in ITO relationship | Organization A | Organization B | Organization C |
|---|---|---|---|
| IT Outsourcing Strategy | Selective outsourcing | Selective outsourcing | Minimal outsourcing |
| The CIO Role in IT outsourcing | High involvement | High involvement | Low involvement |
| Contract Management | Medium-term contract | Medium-term contract | Short-term duration |
| Interactions | Formal communication | Formal and informal communication | Formal communication |
| Performance Management | SLAs | SLAs + KPIs | Contractual-based |
| Risk Management | Risk & reward contractual, Fixed fee contractual | Fixed fee contractual | Fixed fee contractual |

## 4    Conclusions

In summary this research has looked to identify the best practices in IT outsourcing relationships through a review of the research literature and define some key factors for managing IT outsourcing relationships. In this direction our research has defined six key factors that were applied in three organizations from Sweden. In order to use effectively these key factors in having a successful IT outsourcing relationship guidelines of using them are presented below.

**1. IT Outsourcing Strategy**

Companies need long-term strategy for conducting IT outsourcing to avoid failure which can cause high transaction cost in the future.

**2. The CIO Role in IT outsourcing**

The CIO or even better the CEO should have a major role during IT outsourcing process because they have the strategic bargaining power.

**3. Contract Management**

Both parties should have flexible contract which allow renegotiations without any difficulty to adapt with changing business environment and requirements. However opportunistic behavior potential should also be considered when we make a contract.

**4. Interactions**

Communication is important to diminish conflict or disagreement between both parties as well as information sharing to build trust in IT outsourcing relationships.

**5. Performance Management**

The IT outsourcing providers should fulfill agreed performance indicators as promised in the contract. Furthermore the companies can measure their performance by using Service Level Agreements (SLA) and apply penalties upon failure in fulfilling the promises.

**6. Risk Management**

Companies should identify the potential risk and make plans for mitigation of this risk. Risk and reward contractual type is one of the solutions to prevent opportunistic behavior from IT outsourcing providers.

The importance of the key factors described before is an attempt to focus the relationship management in ITO on the important key areas in managing ITO relationships and support in this way the ITO decision makers in their efforts to have a successful IT outsourcing relationship in their organizations.

# References

1. Loh, L., Venkrataman, N.: Diffusion of Information Technology Outsourcing: Influence Sources and the Kodak Effect. Information System Research 3(4), 334–358 (1992)
2. Kishore, R., Rao, H.R., Nam, K., Srinivasan, R., Chaudhury, A.: A Relationship Perspective on IT Outsourcing: A longitudinal study at four companies provides valuable insights about the evolution of IT outsourcing relationships. Communication of the ACM 46(12), 87–92 (2003)
3. Dewett, T., Jones, G.R.: The Role of Information Technology in The Organization: a Review, Model and Assesment. Journal of Management 27(3), 313–346 (2001)
4. Lacity, M., Hirschheim, R.: Information System Outsourcing: Myths, Metaphors, and Realities. John Wiley & Sons, Chichester (1993)
5. Rao, H.R., Nam, K., Chaudhury, A.: Management of information systems outsourcing: A bidding persepective. J. MIS 12(2), 131–159 (1995)

6. Williamson, O.E.: The Economic Institutions of Capitalism. The Free Press, New York (1985)
7. Gottschalk, P., Solli-Sæther, H.: Managing Successfull IT Outsourcing Relationship. IRM Press, London (2006)
8. Coase, R.H.: The Nature of the Firm. Economica 4(16), 386–405 (1937)
9. Whitten, D., Wakefield, R.L.: Measuring Switching Costs in IT Outsourcing Services. Journal of Strategic Information Systems 15(3), 219–248 (2006)
10. Kern, T., Willcocks, L.: Exploring Information Technology Outsourcing Relationships: Theory and Practice. Journal of Strategic Information Systems 9, 321–350 (2000)
11. Alborz, S., Seddon, P.B., Scheepers, R.: A Model for Studying IT Outsourcing Relationships. In: Proceedings of 7th Pacific Asia Conference on Information Systems, Adelaide, Australia, July 10-11, pp. 1297–1313 (2003)
12. Hodosi, G., Rusu, L.: Information Technology Outsourcing: A Case Study of Best Practices In Two Swedish Global Companies. In: Proceedings of the Mediterranean Conference in Information Systems, Hammamet, Tunisia, October 23-26 (2008)
13. Lee, J.-N., Miranda, S.M., Kim, Y.-M.: IT Outsourcing Strategies: Universalistic, Contingency, and Configurational Explanations of Success. Information Systems Research 15(2), 110–131 (2004)
14. Jiang-ping, W., Yong-hua, Z., Qing-jing, L.: Empirical Study on IT Outsourcing Partnership with Relational Exchange Theory. In: Proceedings of 15th International Conference on Management Science & Engineering, Long Beach, USA, September 10-12, pp. 378–384 (2008)
15. Wilcocks, L.: The Next Step for the CIO: Moving IT-enabled Services Outsourcing to the Strategic Agenda. Strategic Outsourcing: An International Journal 3(1), 62–66 (2010)
16. PriceWaterhouseCoopers: The Partnership Bridge: Building Successful IT Outsourcing Relationship, PriceWaterhouseCoopers 2007, http://www.pwc.co.uk/pdf/building_successful_it_outsourcing_relationships.pdf (retrived from February 17, 2011)
17. Gellings, C.: Outsourcing Relationships: The Contract as IT Governance Tool. In: Proceedings of the 40th Annual Hawaii International Conference of System Sciences, Hawaii, USA, January 3-6 (2007)
18. Goo, J.: Structure of Service Level Agreements (SLA) in IT Outsourcing: The Construct and its Measurement. Information Systems Frontiers 12(2), 185–205 (2010)
19. Sargent Jr, A.: Outsourcing Relationship Literature: An Examination and Implications for Future Research, Claremont, USA, April 13-15, pp. 280–287. ACM (2006)
20. Lennerholt, C.: Achieving Trust in IT Outsourcing Relationships, Master Dissertation in Computer Science, School of Humanities and Informatics, Högskolan Skövde (2006)
21. Lee, J.-N., Huynh, M.Q., Kwok, R.C.-W., Pi, S.-M.: IT Outsourcing Evolution Past, Present and Future. Communications of the ACM 46(5), 84–89 (2003)
22. Mehta, N., Mehta, A.: It Takes Two to Tango: How Relational Investements Improve IT Outsourcing Partnerships. Communications of the ACM 53(2), 160–164 (2010)
23. Perrin, B.: IT Outsourcing Relationship Management and Performance Measurement System Effectiveness. In: Proceedings of 16th Australasian Conference on Information Systems, Sydney, Australia, November 29-December 2 (2005)
24. Oza, N.V., Hall, T., Rainer, A., Grey, S.: Trust in Software Outsourcing Relationships: An Empirical Investigation of Indian Software Companies. Information and Software Technology 48, 345–354 (2006)
25. Cullen, S., Willcocks, L.: Intelligent IT Outsourcing. Butterworth-Heinemann, Oxford (2003)

26. Chorafas, D.N.: Outsourcing, Insourcing and IT for Enterprise Management. Palgrave Macmillan, New York (2003)
27. Lee, A.S.: A Scientific Methodology for MIS Case Studies. MIS Quarterly, 33–50 (March 1989)
28. European Commission, The New SME Definition, User Guide and Model Declaration (2010), http://ec.europa.eu/enterprise/policies/sme/files/ sme_definition/sme_user_guide_en.pdf (accessed on February 22, 2010)
29. Earl, M.J.: The Risk of Outsourcing IT. In: Sloan Management Review, Spring 1996, pp. 26–32 (1996)

# An Approach to the Relationship between Efficiency and Process Management

Inés González, Enric Serradell, and David Castillo

Business and Sciences Department, University Polytechnic of Barcelona and Open University of Catalonia, Barcelona, Spain,
{igonzalezg,eserradell,dcastillo}@uoc.edu

**Abstract.** The economic situation we are living the Western company has led the urgent need for companies not only have focus their efforts on improving technology, but also, to be implementing new management techniques that are provide a competition between satisfaction customer and increased performance obtained. For this reason we relieve show the importance of good management processes such as one of the techniques better management to cut costs. This work conducts an empirical study based on statistical analysis of responses obtained through a questionnaire to companies in Spain, specifically in Catalonia, which seeks found empirical evidence about the positive effects for firms of the implementation of process management methods in terms of efficiency, and in particular, in productivity.

**Keywords:** process, quality, efficiency, productivity, flexibility.

## 1 Introduction

The biggest problem arises when required total quality in all that is done, as the functional head can not carry out a monitoring of all and each of the operations being implemented. However, this type of organization may be adequate in business where the required level of qualification is very low and tasks easy and repetitive; but does not hold in reality in which we find ourselves today, an emerging reality defined by globalization, liberation of the industry, technological innovation and a market where supply has gone into the background, as the customer satisfaction the ultimate objective of the company, always without forgetting, of course, the profitability of the organization.

In this context, the objective of our article is to examine whether the introduction of process management system in the company, as instruments to pursue and at the same time enhance the entrepreneurial approach to total quality, allows the achievement of an improvement of efficiency in the allocation and use of resources which it is in a

Impact Process Management in Business Efficiency. Empirical Case Catalonia-Spain main determinant of the increase in business productivity rates. To this end we have divided this article into six sections. Following the introduction, the second

M.D. Lytras et al. (Eds.): WSKS 2011, CCIS 278, pp. 70–77, 2013.

paragraph describes the theoretical framework underlying the relationships between process management, flexibility of labour, business productivity and cost efficiency. The third paragraph is intended to establish the research hypothesis and explain the database used in the empirical analysis. The fourth sets out the methodology used and the variables defined. The fifth, gathers the main results obtained. And, finally, the sixth paragraph sets out the findings of the investigation, as well as future lines open through this work.

## 2          Theoretical Framework

According to specifies the standard ISO 9000: 2000: "Process-based approach consists in the Systematic of the processes developed in the Organization and in particular identifying interactions between such processes". Therefore, process management is a systemic company vision, so that if a process is ineffective or inefficient system it will be.

We propose a simple example that clarifies the vision system exposed: the human body, consisting of a set of organs acting independently but are closely interrelated. If the heart does not work neither will the rest of the bodies, or what is, if one does not work, neither will the rest or, if they work, they will in poor conditions.

Having clarified this point, we list the principles of process management that can be summarized in four principles: the first is that any organization should be composed of processes, the latter argues that virtually any activity is located in a process, item third said that to produce the existence of a process is necessary a product or service and vice versa, and the fourth and final principle states that there has to be customer- product/service.

Therefore, by way of conclusion, process management involves the need to identify and classify them, producing a series of indicators that measure the effectiveness, efficiency and flexibility of these and, finally, a responsible allocation of each process or process owner.

Therefore, the key element of the process management system is, without a doubt, the management of the processes that make up. Although business literature we found a wide range of approaches to the concept of process, we in this article, we believe appropriate to mention the provided by experts in the field under study, which define the process as a "system that uses resources to transform inputs at outputs generating added value". Subsequently, the definition has been expanded considering that the process is "the sequence of activities that consume time and resources, aims to Inés González, Enric Serradell, David Castillo generate added value of an entry to get a result or output that meets the requirements of the customer" [4].

It is clear that the decisive process will be those that provide greater value to the client that the efficiency of the organizations will depend on these process. Anyway, there is a false perception that any company that has identified its most important processes - the so-called key - enjoys this type of management. However, it is vital that they are interrelated in the search for a common goal, the satisfaction of the client.

In addition, we agree with [11] when indicated, on the one hand, that the processes must be subjected to continuous revisions in order to adapt to changes in the market, customers, and new technologies and, on the other constantly seek ways to improve the process in terms of productivity of operations or the reduction of defects.

The flexibility of human resources can be defined as "the capacity of human resources management" to facilitate the ability of the Organization to adapt effectively and quickly to the changes or diversity of the demand in the interior of the company or in its surroundings. The flexibility of a company's human resources can be internal and external [7] And can distinguish between functional and numerical flexibility. Functional internal flexibility refers to the ease of adaptation to changes in demand. The related variables taken into account the degree of reorganization of the jobs through the valuation of work in flexible and adaptive equipment or versatility. Internal numerical flexibility, tries to adapt the pace and volume of work through flexible part-time or hourly contract.

In conclusion, effective management is the key to success in business management. This success is based on the innovation of the processes that make up the company, therefore can be considered one of the pillars in the Organization and in the development of a system of management indicators.

# 3    Hypothesis and Data

## 3.1    Hypothesis

According to the theoretical framework, we are willing to verify the following hypothesis:

*H: the process management entails an improvement in the efficiency cost of the company*

Through this study we found that an implementation of process management in the enterprise is reflected in its efficiency

## 3.2    Database

The population under study for this work is composed of companies surveyed in the PIC[1] project. From the data base SABI[2] proceeded to select 2038 companies... The data sheet of the sample is detailed in table 1

The methodology of personal interview with the directors of contact of each of the companies was used from the selection. The technical data of the survey are reflected in the following table.

---

[1] Research project conducted by researchers from the studies of Economics and business of the UOC: draft Internet Catalunya (http://www.uoc.edu/in3/pic/esp/).

[2] Iberian balance sheet analysis system, developed by Bureau Van Dijk Electronic Publishing, S.A. and the company advises, economic intelligence, S.A.

**Table 1.** Technical details of the questionnaire

| Universe | Companies in Catalonia |
|---|---|
| Dimension | 2038 personal interviews with entrepreneurs and senior managers |
| Margin of error | ± 2.22 for the aggregated data in the case of maximum uncertainty (p = q = 50) for a confidence level of 95.5% |
| Quota | By size in terms of workers and business sector |
| Margin of error | Between + 4.20 and 5.45 for the different dimensions in terms of number of workers and between 4.82 and +5.67 + for different business sectors, in the case of maximum indetermination (p = q = 50), to a confidence level of 95.5% |
| Shows resulting | Determined by weighting |
| Fieldwork period | From January to May 2003 |
| Selection of the sample | Through a process of marginal quotas and random selection |

# 4    Methodology

To test the hypothesis, we have used the following relations form:

$$GP = f \text{ (FLEX)}$$
$$EC = f \text{ (GP)}$$
$$A = f \text{ (PM)}$$

Where:

- PM is the variable process management. It's a binary variable which takes the value 1 if the company States have adopted a process Management system and 0 otherwise.
- FLEX is the flexibility of labour. In order to be able to adequately capture the flexibility used four indicators: one for each of the dimensions of internal flexibility: functional and numerical and two, external flexibility.

With regard to the external flexibility, mainly try to adapt to changes in demand through variations in the number of temporary jobs with workers not in template. Use of temporary or autonomous work or relationships with third parties in order to obtain valuable knowledge when it does not exist within the company, through cooperation agreements with third parties, such as for example companies of consultancy, or universities.

- EC is cost efficiency. Two indicators have been used: the first is the proportion of fixed costs on the total of costs; the second, is the ratio of the direct costs on the total costs of the company.
- Is the overall efficiency of the company. It has used the calculation carried out of the total factor productivity (TFP) from the financial data available for the

exhibition, through the implementation of the formulation of [6] accepted in international literature.

Defined variables and their indicators of measure are summarized in the following table:

**Table 2.** Variables used and measurement

| Variable Nome | Concept | Variable Type | Values / Range |
|---|---|---|---|
| External flexibility | Percentage of contracts freelance (% of total) | Scale | 0-100 |
| | Percentage of workers with temporary contract | Scale | 0-100 |
| Internal Flexibility | | | |
| Functional internal flexibility | Workers can share and exchange information | Binary | 0 -1 |
| Functional Internal Flexibility | Work teams are flexible and adaptable | Binary | 0 -1 |
| Internal Numerical Flexibility | Part-time contracts (% of total) | Binary | 0-100 |
| Costs | | | |
| | Fixed costs on total costs | Scale | 0-100 |
| | Fixed direct costs on total costs | Scale | 0-100 |
| Productivity | Total Factor Productivity | Scale | |
| Process management | Process management | Binary | 0 -1 |

## 5    Results and Discussion

At the beginning, our analysis has been to determine the relationship of the practices by process management with the strategy of competitiveness of enterprises. According to [3] companies should adopt an internal strategy that has to support innovation in the processes of production and the products themselves, as well as a continuous cost reduction. A question in which the Steering had to describe was included in the questionnaire in this line of research, which was the predominant strategy of competitiveness, based on a closed list of five options, which should be decided one and only one of the options raised. In the first place should be noted that most of the companies (40.7%) chose a 25.8% for the quality of the product or service as a strategy of priority competitiveness, differentiation of the product or service, and 11.8% flexibility or rapid response.

A total of 563 enterprises applied process management being the percentage a 27.6%. The rest of the companies, with 68.4 per cent with a total of 1393 companies do not perform organizational approaches where recourse to the process management.

It is important to note that given the multi-sectoral nature of the sample, the results are of a generic nature in order to describe in a more objective way what organizational practices on process management, and especially their impact and influence on the flexibility, efficiency in cost and productivity of enterprises. From the fixed variables has been to perform an Anova analysis in order to verify if there are significant differences between the population taking into account the existence or not of procedures of process management (table 3). The test has been to scale variables, allowing for binary variables will be after the test chi - square.

**Table 3.** Anova Analysis

|  | F | S |
| --- | --- | --- |
| Percentage of contracts related to total costs | 13,369 | 0 |
| Percentage of workers with temporary contracts | 8,521 | 0,004 |
| Workers can share and exchange information | 8,746 | 0,003 |
| Fixed costs on total costs | 8,044 | 0,005 |
| Percentage of direct costs of total costs | 8,127 | 0,004 |
| Total Factor Productivity | 25,999 | 0 |

The analysis has allowed us to obtain the following results:

External flexibility variables such as the number of contracts made with freelancers and number of contracts of character temporary show as significant. In addition, taking into account the carried out analysis of mean, business process-oriented tend to make temporary recruitments greater than those not aimed at the process; and at the same time, they made fewer hiring self-employed. From the point of view of external flexibility, businesses organized around processes tend to internalize the hiring of employees necessary for the development of productive activities. Tending to a greater extent own hiring, even if temporary. This result would show an orientation of enterprises internal control of the activities carried out.

With respect to the variables of internal flexibility, the functional internal flexibility "workers may exchange and share information", after the analysis Chi-square, the obtained probability ($p < 0,05$) allows us to assert that the data are incompatible with the null hypothesis of independence of the data and conclude that the variables are related. However, a more detailed analysis of the association between the two variables indicates that this Association is negative; the guidance to the process management is negatively related to the variable for the exchange of information. This result could suggest that business-oriented processes limit to some extent internal flexibility, not to allow relations between workers carried out outside the established processes.

With respect to the variable "Flexible and adaptable work teams", corresponding also to functional internal flexibility, not shown significant association with process management, perhaps suggesting an explanation on the line as seen in the previous paragraph. Internal numerical flexibility "Part-time contracts" is shown as significant in relation to the process management. In addition the analysis carried out, shows within the studied sample, 9,77% per cent of the contracts made is on time partial, against 9,41% from the rest of the companies. This difference according to the assessment is shown as significant. For what it is clear that companies aimed at the process and in the line as seen in the external flexibility, made more temporary contacts and more part-time contracts as the rest of the companies.

In the section on costs, business process-oriented present 39.1 per cent of costs fixed with respect to the total costs, while the rest of the companies obtained a 44%., and the statistically significant difference. Therefore, the companies managed  by processes have a structure which on average is lower than that of other companies. At this point one might ask what the composition of these fixed costs, in order to obtain results of higher quality. However, the global figure is indicative of flexibility.  With regard to the direct costs, business process-oriented feature 57.3 per cent of the total costs, compared to 51.7% of the other companies. With regard to the productivity of the factors, and as we anticipated in the formulation of the assumptions made the productivity of the process-oriented business is higher than that of other companies, and the significant difference statistically. For this reason, we confirmed the proposed hypothesis.

# 6     Conclusions

Indeed, the analysis allows us to confirm that there is a positive and significant relationship between the consciously of process management by the Catalan companies and an increase in their rates of productivity, key to the survival and long term business success. This result is consistent with the international empirical evidence, according to which the improvement of business efficiency in the current economic situation requires the adoption of new organizational methods focused on the management of business processes (for example, [8] - for the countries of the European Union or [1]- to United States).

On the one hand, the introduction of process management systems enables companies to obtain a more flexible cost structure, with a presence predominant of variable costs, and adaptable to the productive needs, fact that entails as it has been demonstrated in specific industries that the total volume of costs on resources is less. On the other hand, the achievement of greater flexibility of work, embodied in the greater capacity of enterprises which are oriented to the process management to better identify the activities likely to be outsourced  and carry out a more efficient adaptation of the staffing of the factor work to the production needs. Both factors have also been confirmed by [2] in the case of Italy and by [9] to United States. The results form a solid empirical evidence of the importance of the process management as key to business productivity, so it opens up a field of applied research of great importance that has allow, through the sectoral analysis more detailed and the incorporation of additional variabilities build a both pattern to serve companies as a reference in your design process of the organizational structure suitable for the development of its activity.

# References

1. Bresnahan, T.F., Brynjolfsson, E., Hitt, L.M.: Information Technology, Workplace Organization, and the Demand for Skilled Labor: Firm-level Evidence. Quarterly Journal of Economics 117(1), 339–376 (2002)
2. Cristini, A., Leoni, R., Gaj, A., Labory, S.: New workplace practices in Italy: adoption and performance effects. Università degli Studi di Bergamo, Mimeo (2001)
3. Fernández, A., Muñoz, C.: La actuación estratégica de la empresa y la contabilidad de gestión, vol. XXV(89), pp. 821–836 (1996)
4. González González, I.: Un modelo de valoración de la implantación de la gestión por procesos en la empresa. Análisis específico del sector automoción. Tesis doctoral, Universidad de Valladolid (2009)
5. González, J.M., Zamora, C., Escobar, B.: La reingeniería de procesos de negocio (BPR) aplicada a la gestión de tesoreria: su estudio en una compañía de electricidad española, vol. XXXVI(135), pp. 537-568 (2007)
6. Jorgenson, D.W., Ho, M.S., Stiroh, K.J.: Productivity. Information Technology and the American Growth Resurgence. MIT Press, Cambridge (2005)
7. Martínez Sánchez, A., Vela Jiménez, M.J., Pérez Pérez, M., Luis Carnicer, P.: Flexibilidad de recursos humanos e innovación: competitividad en la industria de automoción. Universia Business Review, Cuarto trimestre (2009)
8. Murphy, M.: Organizational Change and Firm Performance, OCDE Science, Technology and Industry Working Papers, No. 2002/14 (2002)
9. Osterman, P.: Work Reorganization in an Era of Restructuring: Trends in Diffusion and Effects on Employee Welfare. Industrial and Labor Relations Review 53(2), 179–196 (2007)
10. Such, M.J., Parte, L.: La financiación de la actividad productiva: una aproximación empírica a los determinantes del endeudamiento de las empresas hoteleras española, Revista española de financiación y contabilidad, vol. XXXVI(133), pp. 147–174
11. Zaratiegui, J.R. La gestión por procesos: su papel e importancia en la empresa, vol. 6(330), pp. 81–88 (1999)

# Support of Service Systems by Advanced SOA[*]

Jaroslav Král[1,2] and Michal Žemlička[1]

[1] Charles University, Faculty of Mathematics and Physics Malostranské nám. 25,
118 00 Praha 1, Czech Republic
{kral,zemlicka}@ksi.mff.cuni.cz
[2] Masaryk University, Faculty of Informatics,
Botanická 68a, 602 00 Brno, Czech Republic
kral@fi.muni.cz

**Abstract.** SOA is often considered to be the philosophy good for large projects and large enterprises. We propose a variant of SOA good for small enterprises meeting the requirements of service systems. The proposal uses specific organizational services increasing the dynamics of the resulting systems and enabling agile methods systems development and agile business processes. The structure of resulting SOA has common features with cloud systems. It semantically reflects more features of real life systems as the organizational services fulfill the tasks of infrastructure and business services in human society.

## 1 Introduction

Modern knowledge society is as a rule also the society of services (SoS) [1]. Knowledge must be therefore often used in environment of services, it must be supported by proper skills usable in such an environment. The skills must be trained.

It is natural to support, manage, and control SoS by the help of service-oriented information systems having the software-oriented architecture (SOA) [2,3]. There are, however, objections [4,5] stating that SOA as specified by many SOA standards like [6] and by many SOA textbooks like [3] is not dynamic enough. The rules of governing the collaboration of the services are unnecessarily rigid. SOA can be in principle dynamically modified. It is, however, rarely the case as the precondition of the on-line governance of SOA supporting SoS are coarse-grained user-friendly interfaces being usually not available.

The solution of the issues can be achieved by allowing the system users to modify the rules of the cooperation of the services. It is enabled by a variant of SOA formed by software services of two types: basic (kernel) services KS providing basic (business) capabilities, *architectural services* ArS providing no basic business capabilities. The resulting SOA has the properties preferable to support the activities of service society.

---

[*] This work has been supported by the grant of Czech Science Foundation No. 201/09/0983.

M.D. Lytras et al. (Eds.): WSKS 2011, CCIS 278, pp. 78–88, 2013.

# 2  Towards Atomic Services

The development of such SOA (denoted as ASOA) starts from a collection of "kernel" services being a properly wrapped software applications. The wrapping enables the applications to communicate asynchronously. The wrapping can use various tools, typically a variant of MQ (Fig. 1) enabling the applications to send messages asynchronously via a middleware. The kernel service is the pair (Application A, Wrapper W) often shortened to AW.

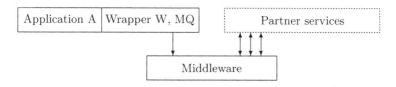

**Fig. 1.** Kernel service

The interfaces provided by the wrappers tend to be fine grained and developer-knowledge-domain oriented. Such interfaces are typically based on Remote Procedure Call (RPC) primitives. Why to use fine-grained services?

1. They are well understood and they can be easily used by system developers.
2. There are many tools supporting such a solution.
3. There is a great chance that all the capabilities of A will be accessible.
4. Various optimization techniques inside the pair AW can take place

There are cons:

A) The communication based on RPC is not user friendly. It in practice hinders, often even excludes, the involvement of users to manage and to control a SoS. Without easy human involvement the behavior of the service-oriented systems cannot be, however, dynamic enough.
B) The changes of the wrappers tend to be difficult.
C) Fine-grained interfaces overload communication lines and complicate the analysis of logging records, and reduce the power of supervision, logging, simulation, training, emergency control, and prototyping [7,8].
D) Fine-grained services break the rule of information hiding [9].
E) The changes of the wrappers require the accessibility of the source code of A or can require specific structure of A.

We conclude that there are therefore important reasons not to use fine-grained interfaces. There are, however, substantial reasons to have them. A good solution is based on services used as a service adapters. We call them front-end-gates (FEG) to stress that they in fact act as gates in front of the wrappers.

## 3   Towards User-Friendly Interfaces, Service Adapter as a Service

The FEG works as follows:

1. It transforms sequences of fine-grained input messages coming from A via W into sequences of coarse-grained output messages for partner services.
2. It transforms sequences of coarse-grained input messages from the partner services into sequences of fine-grained output messages for A.
3. Every message for A must be sent to the FEG, the message is, after the transformation described in point 2, sent to A.
4. Every message for any partner service must be sent by A to the FEG, it is after the transformation described in point 1 is sent to the partner service.
5. No other messages are sent to FEG and AW.
6. The messages communicated between FEG and partner services (external messages) are coarse-grained and user-domain oriented.

The pair (kernel service, front-end gate) is called atomic service. It, under the above condition, behaves like a service having coarse-grained user-oriented interfaces. The fine-grained interface of the wrapper W of A is not under the above rules directly accessible from the partner services.

The communication between AW and its FEG can use another middleware than the communication between FEG and the partner services. It is therefore possible to construct a SOA behaving for its users like a SOA using exclusively coarse-grained user-oriented messages. We can therefore use the atomic service as a black box.

It is easy to see that the proposed solution is a good mixture of the fine-grained and coarse-grained interfaces. All the capabilities of A are accessible. The optimization of the wrapped A is possible provided that the source codes of A and W are available. The FEG can be developed as a white box and therefore can be adapted to the needs of partner services and users. The formats of messages hide implementation details of AW. We show that our solution enables an easy implementation of the capabilities listed in point D) above and offers many powerful generalizations. In order to show it we simplify the notation from Fig. 1 into the one in Fig. 2. The kernel service has in its front-end gate(s) a special treatment – the service is in the FEG(s) distinguished. It is important to point out that FEG provides no basic business capabilities, it supports the exclusive collaboration of other services in SOA.

**Fig. 2.** Simplified notation of atomic service; W can be possibly omitted

The structure of an atomic service can be modified so that there are several kernel services instead of only one. It then implements the compositions of the kernel services. Let us now generalize FEG to enable the dynamics needed for the control of services networks. We need to have tools for the analysis and control of the processes in services networks.

The activities in real-life services networks are dynamic [4]. It implies that they must use permanent on-line user involvement. The users must then have information on: what are the capabilities of atomic services; it is enabled by the user oriented interfaces of atomic service, what happens just now, what has happened lately. The last point can be easily met if we equip FEG by logging memory storing typically all coming and leaving messages. The messages should be textual, typically in XML format. The snapshot look can be provided direct user (supervising) access into FEG. The FEG then have the structure shown in Fig. 3. It is simple in modern SOA to redirect the messages to other destinations.

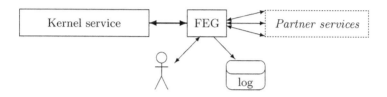

**Fig. 3.** Supervision and logging in FEG

The most useful capability is the cheap implementation of the tools, generalized prototyping inclusive. ASOA integrating atomic services only are confederations in the sense [8]. ASOA described below is a sophisticated enhancement of SOA.

## 4 Prototyping and Simulation

Suppose that the messages sent to Final service in Fig. 4 are in XML and that they are redirected to a user interface [10]. It is then possible to present them on the user screen. They can be answered as they would be answered by Final service provided that the manual simulation interface is properly programmed.

- The FEG (and therefore its kernel service) need not be aware that Final service does not exist. The Final service is in fact simulated.
- The simulation can be made more sophisticated using specific simulation service. It enables simulation of real-time systems [11].
- It can be used as a mock-up prototype on the site of the distinguished service of FEG.

Up to now we have discussed the front-end gates as service adapters. We can substantially enhance their capabilities if we allow them to transform sequences of external messages into the sequences of external messages. They are then no merely service adapters. We call them therefore *architecture services* (ArS).

Individual architectural services can be prototyped or simulated in the way shown in Fig. 4 provided that the kernel services there are also architecture services.

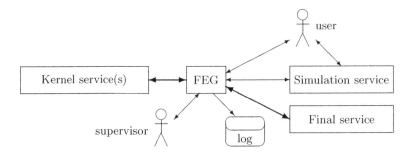

**Fig. 4.** Redirecting, prototyping, and simulation

# 5 Architectural Services

Any FEG can be viewed as an instance of an abstract architectural service (AAS), Fig. 5. It consists of:

- Head of architectural service (HAS). It accepts messages. Tuples of input messages are transformed into tuples of output messages.
- Interface of a supervisor used to modify message destinations and the transformation of messages, it provides an on-line supervision.
- Logging memory.
- Optional data store. There are two main cases:
  - Data store enabling integration of batch applications and the combination of bulk data transfer and message data transfer.
  - Message store enabling e.g. construction of user defined multipoint communication protocols, typically over point-to-point protocols.

There can be further rules providing additional capabilities. Examples are: the rules (disciplines) of communication, e.g. the requirements on the paths of the messages and on the grouping of messages and services. Another example is the design of atomic service described above.

The concept of the abstraction of architecture service (AAS) from Fig. 5 is multidimensional. It is therefore extremely flexible. Let us now show the instances of AAS for particular capabilities and needs.

## 5.1 Head of Composite Service

The general principles of service composition are clear from Fig. 6. FEG in Fig. 6 is with respect to Fig. 2 slightly generalized – it is not merely a service adapter, we call it *Head of Composite Service*. The difference is that the distinguished services need not be kernel services only. It is technically a negligible change. It, however, enables infinite composition of services as technically any (composite) service can be a part of a (higher level) composite service.

The communication must obey the rules described in the points 1 though 6 in paragraph 3. The difference is that A is replaced by a group of services. Note

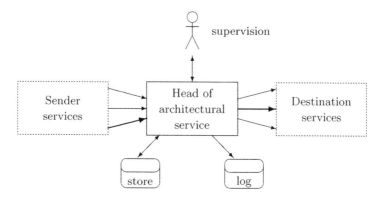

**Fig. 5.** Abstraction of architecture services (AAS). Thick arrows indicate "distinguished paths".

that no data store or message store is usually needed. The Head of Composite Service behaves (is used) as a common facade for all the distinguished services. They can be completely hidden.

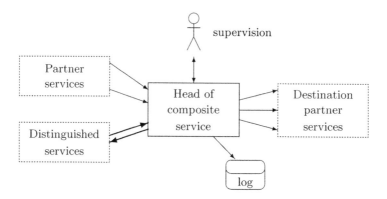

**Fig. 6.** Composition of services

## 5.2 Router

The sources or destinations of messages can be autonomous systems having SOA. It is especially the case when they have the structure we discuss here, i.e. they are ASOA. The router can transform point-to point communication protocols as provided e.g. by SOAP into various multipoint communication protocols. It can be the advantageous to equip the router by a message store. An example is implementation of a precedence queue.

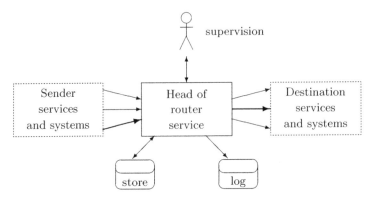

**Fig. 7.** Router

## 5.3    Integration of Batch Systems into SOA

The ability of (SOA) systems to integrate batch systems is important but largely underestimated. There are cases when it is not feasible not too use batch applications:

– They provide very complex computations (scheduling)
– They are available and are very stable
– Various security reasons
– Their computation is quite cheap.

The integration can sometimes use a common database. It can be easily overloaded, not accessible properly or not secure enough. A quite simple solution uses an architecture service with data store, Fig. 8.

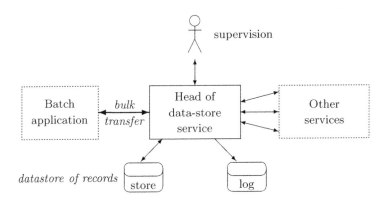

**Fig. 8.** Integration of batch subsystems

## 5.4  Business Process Manager

Manager of a business process (Fig. 9) uses process data generated during the process initialization from appropriate process model requested by Process owner. The models can be incomplete and in different languages. Process owner then can modify the process execution in an agile way (on-line). The system enables continuous adaptation of the system and training of its users. It enables the improvement of business intelligence. Note that especially in small and medium enterprises the business process models must be as a rule used in an agile way due to changing business conditions.

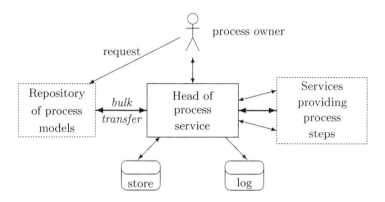

**Fig. 9.** Business process manager

# 6  Cloud-Like Structure of ASOA

Architectural services are able to implement the crucial features proposed by some SOA standards like the standards by OASIS [6]. The resulting systems can use coarse-grained interfaces. Architectural services simplify the use of integration-oriented standards like OSIMM [12].

We have experience that our proposals can be well used in small projects by small teams. Our analysis indicates that they could be applied in e-government. There are no technical obstacles here. A problem can be that it can be against the interests of powerful lobbies.

SOA using architectural services (ASOA) is technically network of services where nodes are of three types: kernel services, user interfaces, and architectural services – see Fig. 10:

Such a structure reminds the structure of cloud computing systems. Cloud systems are formed by a network of infrastructure services and by applications (jobs) to be executed. It is open whether the similarity is superfluous only. We believe it is not.

Note that the architectural services fulfill the roles similar to the roles of organizational institutions and trade companies in human society.

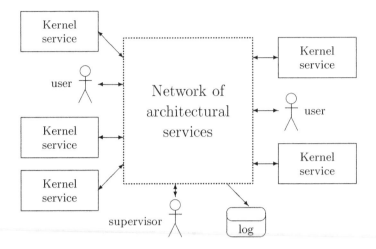

**Fig. 10.** The two tier structure of SOA using architecture services

# 7 Software Engineering Advantages of Architectural Services

We have seen that minimal technical changes of the structure of an architectural service changes substantially its semantics and even yet more the properties of the whole ASOA. The changes are often independent and can be combined.

The second main source of the dynamics of ASOA are the consequences of the fact that the effects of a given architecture service depend substantially on the rules how it is used (compare the heads of composite services and the rules of message routing).

The third source of the dynamics of ASOA is the possibility of agile involvement of users (supervisors) into the activities of architectural services. It enables ASOA to be changeable in an agile way. It also enables the agility of the business processes supported by ASOA.

Coarse-grained messages hide implementation details effectively. The implementation of an individual service is therefore an almost independent task. It moreover enables an easy integration very heterogeneous systems. The systems can be then either bought, developed, reused or outsourced. Then there is a good chance that the services as well as the entire systems can be executed in SaaS style in a cloud system.

The coarse-grained messages are something like commands of high level programming languages whereas the messages using RPC have some features of commands of assembly languages. The user orientation of the messages implies user involvement. It follows that atomic services must be coarse grained and that there must not be too many of them. It can be too limiting in large enterprises. It is however necessary in small to medium enterprises and also in e-government.

The concept of architectural services is technically (not politically) easily applicable in e-governments of some countries where the concept of electronic mail room (called data box) is used. The data box used as a electronic mail room can also provide a sophisticated variant of MQ.

## 8  Conclusions

We have shown, that architectural services can substantially increase the dynamics, agility and openness of SOA typical for small to medium enterprises (SME) and e-government. Their challenges and promises will be investigated yet. The most promising issues of further research are:

- Challenges and opportunities outside SME.
- What is the optimal combination of ASOA and the principles of cloud computing?
- Can architectural services cover further organizational roles in human societies?
- ASOA can be used as the models of agent systems studied in artificial intelligence. Is the concept of architectural (organizational) services supporting the collaboration of other agent meaningful?

Service orientation is according to Gartner Group a fully mature IT philosophy. It is often believed that there are almost no open important issues. We believe that we have shown that it is not the case yet.

## References

1. Maglio, P.P., Kieliszewski, C.A., Spohrer, J.C. (eds.): Handbook of Service Science. Service Science: Research and Innovations in the Service Economy. Springer, New York (2010)
2. Král, J., Žemlička, M.: Autonomous Components. In: Hlaváč, V., Jeffery, K.G., Wiedermann, J. (eds.) SOFSEM 2000. LNCS, vol. 1963, pp. 375–383. Springer, Heidelberg (2000)
3. Erl, T.: Service-Oriented Architecture: Concepts, Technology, and Design. Prentice Hall PTR (2005)
4. Galliers, R.D.: Strategizing for agility: Confronting information systems inflexibility in dynamic environments. In: Desouza, K.C. (ed.) Agile Information Systems: Conceptualization, Construction, and Management, pp. 1–15. Butterworth-Heinemann (2006)
5. Carroll, N., Whelan, E., Richardson, I.: Applying social network analysis to discover service innovation within agile service networks. Service Science 2(4), 225–244 (2010)
6. MacKenzie, C.M., Laskey, K., McCabe, F., Brown, P.F., Metz, R.: Reference model for service-oriented architecture 1.0, OASIS standard, October 12 (2006)
7. Král, J., Žemlička, M.: Implementation of business processes in service-oriented systems. International Journal of Business Process Integration and Management 3(3), 208–219 (2008)

8. Král, J., Žemlička, M.: Software architecture for evolving environment. In: Kontogiannis, K., Zou, Y., Penta, M.D. (eds.) Software Technology and Engineering Practice, pp. 49–58. IEEE Computer Society, Los Alamitos (2006)

9. Parnas, D.L.: Designing software for ease of extension and contraction. IEEE Transactions on Software Engineering 5(2), 128–138 (1979)

10. Král, J., Žemlička, M.: Implementation of business processes in service-oriented systems. In: 2005 IEEE International Conference on Services Computing (SCC 2005), vol. 2, pp. 115–122 (2005)

11. Král, J., Žemlička, M.: Service orientation and the quality indicators for software services. In: Trappl, R. (ed.) Cybernetics and Systems, vol. 2, pp. 434–439. Austrian Society for Cybernetic Studies, Vienna (2004)

12. The Open Group: The Open Group service integration maturity model, OSIMM (2009)

# A Characterization of Non-buyers in B2C E-Commerce and the Drivers to Turn Them into E-Shoppers

Ángel Hernández-García, Santiago Iglesias-Pradas, and Alberto Urueña-López

Universidad Politécnica de Madrid. Dpto. de Ingeniería de Organización,
Administración de Empresas y Estadística. Escuela Técnica Superior de Ingenieros de
Telecomunicación. Despacho A-126. Av. Complutense, 30. 28040 Madrid
{angel.hernandez,s.iglesias,alberto.uruena}@upm.es

**Abstract.** This exploratory study deals with the characterization of non-buyers groups in the context of business-to-consumer electronic commerce (B2C-EC), based on their motivations for not purchasing on the Internet and explores which factors would incline them to make a first purchase on a website. In order to do so, a household panel survey was taken to 1075 Spanish respondents and analyzed with a Latent Class Analysis (LCA) approach for grouping both consumers' motivations to reject online shopping and possible motivations to start buying online. After the definition of both sets of groups, a k-means clustering was performed in order to relate both groups in disjoint sets. The results from our study show that there are mainly three types of causes for not shopping through the electronic channel –namely, absence of physical presence of the goods or channel preference, security concerns and privacy risks, and lack of internet access and/or skills– and six different attitudes towards future use of Internet as a shopping channel, revealing a total of ten different sets of non-buyers. Implications for theory and practice are discussed in the final section.

## 1 Introduction

In the last decade, the generalization of Internet use has made it possible to increase sales through e-commerce websites. Nevertheless, this increase has not been exempt from difficulties, and thus the study of consumer attitudes and beliefs towards business-to-consumer electronic commerce (B2C-EC) has raised a high interest for researchers, marketers and company managers.

In a first stage, this interest focused on the barriers and drivers of Internet adoption. But during the last years the focus has been set in the study of the factors that affect purchase and repurchase behavior. Most of the research that deals with this topic is based on technology acceptance and marketing theories, using samples with previous experience with online shopping. Therefore, although they make a significant contribution to the understanding of the online purchase mechanisms, they fail to explain why there are people who do not shop on the Internet.

Yet, according to the reality, there are still a great number of people who have not made any purchase on the Internet, and the reasons behind this fact are

M.D. Lytras et al. (Eds.): WSKS 2011, CCIS 278, pp. 89–97, 2013.

under-researched to this date. Furthermore, even though the information that could be extracted from such analysis would be of great value for researchers and marketers, so that actions could be taken for the promotion of B2C-EC, the literature about what are the characteristics of these non-buyers is scarce.

Thus, the aim of this article is to study the specific nature of the attitudes of non-buyers −or consumers who have not purchased on the Internet yet. In order to do so, and due to the lack of recent research in this field, an empirical approach has been taken, expecting to confront the results from our analysis to those from B2C-EC acceptance related literature.

## 2     Theoretical Background

Segmentation of customers has always been a fundamental tool in marketing for a long time, allowing to focus on the appropriate target when launching a new product or target [19]. However, although the study of Internet consumer behavior is well advanced at the present time regarding attitudinal factors which have influence on online purchasing and repurchasing, the heterogeneity and diversity of Internet users has caused a strange scarcity of studies dealing with online consumer classification and segmentation even though this issue, when addressed, is considered a most beneficial tool in order to be able to address consumers' needs and increase sales [3].

Internet shopper segments have traditionally been studied from different approaches [2]: management-imposed, with fixed sets of customers, and consumer-revealed, from clustering after costumers' self-reports. Generally, both approaches include a later demographic segmentation.

Consumer-revealed segmentation, nonetheless, may be attitudinal/behavioral, such as the ones based on motivations to buy online [9][12][15][17] or shopping orientations [6][11], and also psychographical, such as lifestyle segmentation based on declared AIOs (activities, interests and opinions) [16].

In this sense, the greatest effort made during the last decade was the extensive research of Swinyard and Smith [20], which developed an instrument scale in order to perform the segmentation of online shoppers and non-shoppers based on lifestyle scales. Swinyard and Smith's research discovered eight types on online customers, four of them belonging to the Internet shopper segment (shopping lovers, adventuresome explorers, suspicious learners and business users) and the other four classified as non-shopper types. Non-shoppers were thus classified as:

- Fearful browsers: consumers with a relatively high level of computer literacy, usual Internet users who practice window-shopping, and with distrust towards online shopping.
- Shopping avoiders: consumers who prefer to see the products they purchase and tend to avoid mail delivery.
- Technology muddlers: consumers who have low computer literacy and are not excited about Internet shopping.
- Fun seekers: consumers who use the Internet for entertainment purposes but are afraid of online shopping.

The results from Swinyard and Smith's research have later been subject to cross-cultural validation in Belgium [5] and China [24], giving as result similar classifications with some variations, such as the division of technology muddlers into positive and negative technology muddlers.

These studies, however, present three drawbacks when considering the behavior of non-shoppers: (1) they rely on a closed scale instrument which –although in the case of [20] derived from the analysis of open-ended questionnaires– may not cover some of the aspects that may be gathered from self-reported open answers; (2) they are applied to *both* shoppers and non-shoppers, thus increasing the range of possible situations; (3) they explain the behavior of non-shoppers and their market appeal but do not question the customer beliefs about what would drive them to start shopping.

The first drawback may be overcome with a latent class analysis approach such as the one performed by Bhatnagar and Ghose [4], who apply it to e-shoppers, while the second requires limiting the research to non-shoppers and the third implies trying to go beyond the explanation of the behavior and including and inquire about non-shopper motivations.

# 3     Research Methodology

## 3.1     Sample Selection and Demographics

The sample was extracted from a Spanish household panel of 2137 people, who were contacted by telephone and were explained the purpose of the study during November of 2009. Of these, 1075 people (50.3 percent of the total) claimed to have no prior experience purchasing on the Internet

Then, the interviewees who claimed to be non-buyers were asked two open questions, allowing as many answers as the respondents considered appropriate:

1. What are the reasons why you do not buy any product or service on the Internet?
2. On what depends that you will shop on the Internet in the future?

Based on the different answers received, reasons for not buying on the Internet and motivations for future purchases were classified into twenty-seven categories each, which were marked as present or absent in the interviewee's answer.

## 3.2     Analysis Method

Once collected and classified, we proceeded to analyze the results, where each category had a value of 1 –in case the respondent had mentioned it– or 0 if it had not been mentioned. Since data were binary variables, the usual methods used for factoring –such as exploratory factor analysis– were not considered valid for our study because of the misleading parameter estimates that it may introduce when using categorical data [23], and instead a latent class analysis (LCA) approach was performed. Latent class analysis factor analysis of categorical data, where there is no assumption of linearity, normal distribution or homogeneity of variance from input data [8]. As a method for setting latent variables from the observed variables, it is also a subset of structural equation modeling.

When LCA is used on confirmatory analysis, the number of expected latent variables –or classes– is known by the researcher, but for exploratory purposes this number is unknown. LCA offers goodness of fit, such as the likelihood ratio chi-square ($G^2$), and parsimony statistics, such as the Bayesian information criterion, or BIC [18] and the Akaike information criterion, or AIC [1], which help determine the best underlying model to explain the manifest variables. Since conditional independence is assumed for the different responses, observations with the similar sets of answers tend to cluster into the same latent classes. LCA may also be extended by a latent class regression model to include covariates and predict latent class membership [10].

# 4    Data Analysis and Results

To perform the latent class analysis, the package poLCA for R software environment [13], version 2.10.1, was used. Since the number of latent variables was unknown, the analysis was repeated for a number of classes starting in 2, until the best values for AIC, BIC and $G^2$ were achieved. For each model, 10000 iterations were made, with 100 estimations for each model in order to find the global maximum of the log-likelihood function [14].

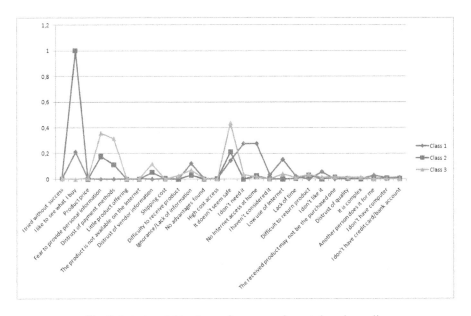

**Fig. 1.** Latent variable classes for reasons for not shopping online

The criterion for the selection of classes is given by the goodness of fit values from AIC, which lowest value reflects the best fitting model a better fit, taking into account model parameters and complexity. The models that best fit the two different sets of clusters were achieved for nclasses=3 in the first set –reasons for not shopping online– and nclasses=6 in the case of future motivations to buy online. In both cases, the value of $G^2$ was lower than the degrees of freedom for the model and lower than the critical value.

The latent class analysis results provide a share of each manifest variable belonging to the latent variable. The results from this analysis of both datasets are shown graphically in figures 1 and 2.

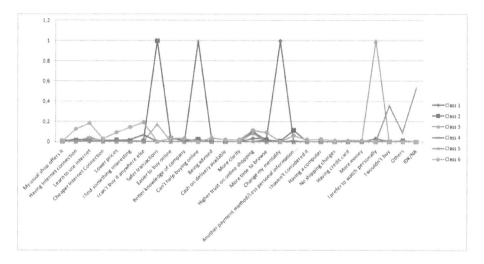

**Fig. 2.** Latent variable classes for drivers for future online purchases

From figure 1, three types of non buyers can be identified (in parentheses, predicted class memberships are shown):

1. *Physical-experiential (26.8 percent)*: they are those consumers who prefer the traditional retail channel. These people value the physical presence of the good or service above everything else, even though they may be regular Internet users. This group would include various types of purchasers, from the ones who like to try and evaluate physically the good they plan to buy to those who prefer to include social presence in their transactions. They also show some concerns about the safety of their transactions, payments and personal data on the Internet.

2. *Security concerned (31.6 percent)*: this type of consumers are fundamentally worried about security concerns and have a special awareness of the risks associated to making transactions on the Internet. The risks they find are both channel and vendor related.

3. *Technology avoiders (41.6 percent)*: they are mostly digital illiterates, who do not have Internet access, use it very occasionally or have not learnt to use it.

When evaluating motivations for future online purchases, six groups were identified; consumers stated the following reasons to buy products on the Internet in the future: (1) admitting they needed a change of mentality; (2) demanding improved security systems; (3) preferring to be able to *see* the product; (4) real need for the product and no other means to buy it; (5) do not know or are not willing to purchase online in any case; (6) miscellanea, or a mix of different reasons.

Once identified all three types of non-buyers and the six motivations or actions which would lead them to make their first purchase in the future, each respondent was assigned by the latent class analysis to one of the clusters from each class. These two new datasets were then analyzed with K-means cluster analysis with the help of the statistical software SPSS PASW Statistics 18, in order to make the correspondences between the two sets of clusters. The results revealed ten different final clusters. Table 6 shows the clusters and the number of predicted members for each one.

**Table 1.** K-means clustering analysis results for the combination of both LCA datasets

| CLUSTER | CLASS (STAGE 2) | CLASS (STAGE 3) | No. of members | Percentage |
|---------|-----------------|-----------------|----------------|------------|
| 1 | | Improved security | 201 | 18.7 |
| 2 | Technology avoiders | Will not buy/do not know | 50 | 4.7 |
| 3 | | Miscellanea | 37 | 3.4 |
| 4 | Physical-Experiential | Need to buy/no alternative | 55 | 5.1 |
| 5 | | Miscellanea | 285 | 26.5 |
| 6 | | Change of mentality | 116 | 10.8 |
| 7 | | Improved security | 158 | 14.7 |
| 8 | Security concerned | Personally be able to see | 3 | 0.3 |
| 9 | | Need to buy/no alternative | 159 | 14.8 |
| 10 | | Will not buy/do not know | 11 | 1.0 |

As it can be seen above in table 6, only ten different clusters are created. A quick look at the table shows that the percentage of consumers who are not willing to buy irrespective the actions taken is very small (a total of 5.7%), while an improvement of security –or, al least, perceived security– could drive a total of 33.4% of the customers make a first online purchase. Regarding the set of miscellaneous measures –tagged as *miscellanea*–, it could be used as a driver to online shopping, for near another third of the whole non-buyers population (29.9%). The third situation where more non-buyers could be turned into online shoppers would happen when the customers would want to buy some product they needed and this product was available only on the Internet.

## 5      Conclusions and Discussion of Results

### 5.1      Contributions of the Study

First of all, this research makes a significant contribution to theory by providing a new characterization of the different types of non-buyers in B2C-EC. This characterization differs largely from the ones made at the first steps of e-commerce because it takes into account that several of the previously studied groups have, in any given time from there, used Internet as a medium to make any kind of purchase. Therefore, our classification reflects the three kinds of people who have not made an online purchase yet, and what could drive them to become online consumers.

From the methodological point of view, our study presents a different approach for exploratory studies dealing with attitudes and beliefs. Although data gathering may require a great effort, we believe that it could also be applied to other consumer-behavior related research fields as a means to contrast established theories.

It also must be emphasized that perceived trust and perceived risk –mainly for the security concerned class– are still one of the greatest barriers for the growth of B2C-EC. This result is consistent with established and present consumer behavior and e-commerce-related technology acceptance theories (e.g. [7][21]). It could be highly interesting to evaluate technology acceptance models comparing the influence of the different factors for online buyers and these three groups.

Finally, we would like to point out that, although first time online purchasers tend to mention the relevance of price and convenience on online shopping [22], non-buyers rarely mentioned it in their answers. The reason behind this practice could be that Internet is already associated with those benefits, and even though non-buyers are aware of them, it is not a motivation as strong as those unveiled in this study.

## 5.2    Implications for Practice

The implications for marketers can be deduced straightforward from the results in table 1. First, it can be observed that the number of people who are not willing to buy products or services on the Internet is very small and that improved security mechanisms may raise considerably the online consumer base. There are some good practices that may help to achieve these improvements, such as the presence of quality seals or easier-to-understand messages, especially for technology avoiders. These actions would probable become more effective if they are encompassed with governmental support and monitoring.

Second, findings for the *miscellanea* group of motivations reveal that Internet access, use and cost is still far from the desirable levels, at least in the Spanish case, and that a great effort to extend the use of Internet must be made from local, national and international authorities, as well as ISPs.

Third, there is a significant amount of consumers that express a channel preference for traditional shopping; for this type of consumers, mechanisms should be provided so that social and product presence could be raised on the Internet. Social presence may be achieved by different methods, such as building communities around a company or product, with the help of social networking tools, or increasing the number of ways to contact the company's support center and improving its quality by solving promptly any enquiry from consumers; in the case of product presence, multimedia and interactive display of information may help the consumer to decide without the need to go and evaluate the product physically.

Fourth, our results show that there is a group of people who are aware of the benefits of using the web as a purchasing channel, but admit that they need to change their mentality in order to use it. These people belong to the security concerned group, so the aforementioned security improvements must be made along with institutional information campaigns, courses and workshops in order to help to achieve this goal.

Fifth, the "need it/no alternative" motivation (almost a 20% of the total) shows clearly how important is for online vendors to cover business niches, where traditional shops rarely offer competition, except in the case of capitals and big cities.

# References

[1] Akaike, H.: Information Theory and an Extension of the Maximum Likelihood Principle. In: Petrov, B.N., Csake, F. (eds.) Second International Symposium on Information Theory, pp. 267–281. Akademiai Kiado, Budapest (1973)

[2] Aldred, C.R., Smith, S.M., Swinyard, W.R.: E-shopping lovers and fearful conservatives: a market segmentation analysis. International Journal of Retail & Distribution Management 34(4/5), 308 (2006)

[3] Barnes, S.J., Bauer, H.H., Neumann, M.N., Huber, F.: Segmenting cyberspace: a customer typology for the internet. European Journal of Marketing 41(1/2), 71–93 (2007)

[4] Bhatnagar, A., Ghose, S.: A latent class segmentation analysis of e-shoppers. Journal of Business Research 57, 758–767 (2004)

[5] Brengman, M., Geuens, M., Weitjers, B., Smith, S.M., Swinyard, W.R.: Segmenting Internet shoppers based on their Web-usage-related lifestyle: a cross-cultural validation. Journal of Business Research 58, 79–88 (2005)

[6] Brown, M., Pope, N., Voges, K.: Buying or browsing? An exploration of shopping orientations and online purchase intention. European Journal of Marketing 37(11), 1666–1684 (2003)

[7] Chen, S., Li, J.: Factors Influencing the Consumers' Willingness to Buy in E-Commerce. In: International Conference on E-Business and Information System Security, EBISS 2009, May 23-24, pp. 1–8 (2009)

[8] Garson, G.D.: Latent class analysis, from Statnotes: Topics in Multivariate Analysis (2009),
http://faculty.chass.ncsu.edu/garson/pa765/statnote.html
(Date of retrieval: October 30, 2009)

[9] Ganesh, J., Reynolds, K.E., Luckett, M., Pomirleanu, N.: Online Shopper Motivations, and e-Store Attributes: An Examination of Online Patronage Behavior and Shopper Typologies. Journal of Retailing 86(1), 106–115 (2010)

[10] Hagenaars, J.A., McCutcheon, A.L.: Applied Latent Class Analysis. Cambridge University Press, Cambridge (2002)

[11] Jayawardhena, C., Wright, L.T., Dennis, C.: Consumers online: intentions, orientations and segmentation. International Journal of Retail & Distribution Management 35(6), 515–526 (2007)

[12] Kau, A.K., Tang, Y.E., Ghose, S.: Typology of online shoppers. The Journal of Consumer Marketing 20(2), 139 (2003)

[13] Linzer, D.A., Lewis, J.: poLCA: Polytomous Variable Latent Class Analysis. Version 1.1 (2009), http://userwww.service.emory.edu/~dlinzer/poLCA (Date of retrieval: November 05, 2009)

[14] McLachlan, G.J., Krishnan, T.: The EM Algorithm and Extensions. John Wiley & Sons, New York (1997)

[15] Ng, C.F.: Satisfying shoppers'psychological needs: From public market to cyber-mall. Journal of Environmental Psychology 23, 439–455 (2003)

[16] Plummer, J.T.: The Concept and Application of Life Style Segmentation. The Journal of Marketing 38(1), 33–37 (1974)

[17] Rohm, A.J., Swaminathan, V.: A typology of online shoppers based on shopping motivations. Journal of Business Research 57, 748–757 (2004)

[18] Schwartz, G.: Estimating the Dimension of a Model. The Annals of Statistics 6, 461–464 (1978)

[19] Smith, W.R.: Product Differentiation and Market Segmentation as Alternative Marketing Strategies. Journal of Marketing 21(1/4), 3 (1956)

[20] Swinyard, W.R., Smith, S.M.: Why people (don't) shop online: A lifestyle study of the internet consumer. Psychology & Marketing 20(7), 567 (2003)

[21] Udo, G.J.: Privacy and security concerns as major barriers for e-commerce: a survey study. Information Management & Computer Security 9(4), 165–174 (2001)

[22] Urueña, A.: e-commerce B2C 2009. National Spanish Observatory of Telecommunications and Information Society (Ministry of Industry, Trade and Commerce) (2009), http://www.ontsi.red.es/articles/detail.action?id=4001&requ est_locale=en (Date of retrieval: September 20, 2010)

[23] Vermunt, J.K., Magidson, J.: Latent class cluster analysis. In: Hagenaars, McCutcheon (eds.) Advances in Latent Class Models, ch. B1. Cambridge University Press, Cambridge (2000)

[24] Ye, Q., Li, G., Gu, B.: A cross-cultural validation of the web usage-related lifestyle scale: An empirical investigation in China. Electronic Commerce Research and Applications 10(3), 304–312 (2011)

# Extrinsic Benefits and Perceived Quality as Determinants of Perceived Satisfaction: An Application to a B2C Repurchase Model

Alberto Urueña-López, Santiago Iglesias-Pradas, and Ángel Hernández-García

Universidad Politécnica de Madrid. Dpto. de Ingeniería de Organización,
Administración de Empresas y Estadística. Escuela Técnica Superior de Ingenieros de
Telecomunicación. Despacho A-126. Av. Complutense, 30. 28040 Madrid
{alberto.uruena,s.iglesias,angel.hernandez}@upm.es

**Abstract.** This study presents a B2C electronic commerce repurchase model, introducing current purchasing habits and satisfaction as determinants, explained in terms of the extrinsic benefits and perceived quality. To carry out the study, a survey was carried out among 1307 Spanish users from a household panel; the results from the survey have confirmed the proposed predictive model, which gives an explanation of 61.4 percent of the repurchase intention. Data was analysed by the partial least squares (PLS) method for validation and predictive ability assessment. The results confirm all hypotheses, including a significant influence of extrinsic benefits and perceived quality on satisfaction. The most significant conclusion was that B2C electronic commerce managers need to achieve high levels of satisfaction from Internet purchasers by enhancing perceived quality and perceived benefits obtained. On the discussion of results, the authors offer some hints in order to achieve this goal.

## 1 Introduction

Despite the growth experienced in the recent years, the expenditure of individuals on the Internet channel only represents a small percentage of total sales –a bit over 1% of global purchases in Spain. However, companies have begun to realise that in the digital economy competitors are "just a click away". Attracting consumers to make their first purchase is only the first step in the creation and establishment of a competitive and sustainable advantage in the long term, with loyal and profitable customers. In order to characterise the behaviour of these loyal and profitable customers, models of repurchase intention for electronic commerce between businesses and consumers (EC-B2C) have traditionally been used. This article presents a study based on purchasing habits and customer satisfaction as fundamental factors in the process of repurchase. Perceived extrinsic benefits and perceived service and website quality have been used as satisfaction predictors. For this purpose, existing scientific literature on the phenomenon of satisfaction-based repurchase intention based was thoroughly reviewed.

M.D. Lytras et al. (Eds.): WSKS 2011, CCIS 278, pp. 98–106, 2013.

# 2 Literature Review

An important research line in EC-B2C repurchase theory started with models based on the Expectation Confirmation Theory (ECT) [3-4][26-27], which addresses repurchase intention –understood as the intention to continue using EC-B2C systems– based on user satisfaction. Satisfaction occurs when perceived benefits from using a product or service are deemed higher than the expectations held prior to its use. Thus, according to this theory, satisfaction is the result of an ex-post evaluation by consumers of their own service experience, which may be neutral, positive or negative [4], although other authors maintain that satisfaction is itself an emotional response associated with the purchasing experience [14]. On the other hand, some authors [13][17] argue that perceived value is only constituted by benefits –not benefits and sacrifices. In this study, we measure satisfaction in B2C-EC through quality and obtained benefits, as it has been made previously in other fields before (e.g. in the field of scenic arts) [14].

## 2.1 Extrinsic Benefits

Benefits can be classified as extrinsic and intrinsic [15]. Although there are a number of different motivations for purchasing, these two generic classes are usually considered; the first group, known as extrinsic, is instrumental, functional or utilitarian, whilst the second, called intrinsic, is hedonic, emotional or affective. Both dimensions underlie in the majority of consumer phenomena [2].

With intrinsic motivation, the person carries out the consumer activity as a goal in itself [15] and, therefore, a task is performed because it results in certain benefits (pleasure, aesthetics, new experiences, etc.). By contrast, when people are motivated in an extrinsic manner, they perform an action as a means to achieve other goals. Hence, for example, obtaining a discount voucher, or the time saved by using online purchasing does not generate immediate consumption benefits, but can be used to obtain benefits from future actions.

Of these two types of benefits, this study is only concerned about extrinsic benefits since the influence of intrinsic benefits has not yet been considered substantial [32] or has a degree of influence that is "between low and moderate" [10].

Thus, our research focuses on studying the importance of extrinsic benefits and quality –which will be explained below–, as factors that have a direct influence on satisfaction –and, indirectly, on repurchase intention. The literature review on these aspects enable identification of various types of extrinsic benefits [1][7][32]:

- Discounts/promotions on price: reduction of expenditure, presents or free gifts.
- Time savings: reduction in the time spent on a task or increased efficiency in the task.
- Convenience.
- Ease of purchase.

Prospecting theory postulates that price reductions can have an influence on prospecting other product alternatives [19]. This way, if the promotions and discounts through B2C electronic commerce are higher than those available in physical shops, this may provoke a desire to make a higher number of online purchases [23]. As a consequence of the above:

*H1. Perceived extrinsic benefits have a significant positive effect on satisfaction*

Bhattacherjee [4] proposed that satisfaction with a product or service is the main motivation for consumers to continue making purchases through EC-B2C. Therefore:

*H2. The relation between satisfaction with electronic commerce on the Internet and the intention to repeat the purchase in EC-B2C is significantly positive.*

## 2.2    Customer Loyalty

Customer loyalty is crucial for the success of any business and it is a fundamental pillar for success and growth of "customer–centric" companies, as it drives both revenue and profit growth [28-29]. If there is no customer ready to purchase again in a certain online shop, its business value will be zero, irrespective of the company's commercial and management skills [21]. Customer loyalty is vital because a shop's value is determined mainly by the number of loyal customers [21]. Customer loyalty is defined as "a deeply held commitment to repeat the purchase of a product or service consistently in the future, despite possible changes in circumstances or the marketing of other companies endeavouring to influence a change in behaviour" [28]. Empirical studies [33] confirm the relationship between customer satisfaction and loyalty, as well as the fact that these concepts mutually reinforce each other. This leads to the following hypothesis:

*H3. The relation between satisfaction with electronic commerce on the Internet and customer loyalty is significantly positive.*

## 2.3    Perceived Quality

Perceived quality can be defined as an assessment of a product's excellence or its superiority over other products or services on the market [34]. It is a different concept from objective quality, since it goes beyond the evaluation of the product attributes [30]. Various authors have demonstrated the relation between quality and satisfaction, including a description of existing works related to quality, value and satisfaction [9]. Furthermore, it has been demonstrated that an electronic commerce shop's web page design, purchasing experience and security are very important factors which affect the quality perceived by Internet purchasers [6][20]. According to this, the following hypotheses can be established:

*H4. The quality perceived by the customer has a positive effect on perceived satisfaction.*

*H5. Positive perception of the electronic commerce website has a positive effect on perceived quality.*

## 2.4    Purchasing Habits

A purchasing habit can be defined as the "automatic behavioral tendency shown historically by an individual" [22]. Therefore, it is a present behavioral preference that is often performed unconsciously, and which affects behaviour beyond social attitudes and norms and generally extends current behaviour into the future [5][31]. This automatic tendency drives the individual towards a preservation of their habits; and thus, an individual who is used to purchasing over the Internet will maintain this behaviour in the future. Therefore:

*H6. The relation between the current purchasing habits and EC-B2C repurchase intention is significantly positive.*

# 3    Research Model

Taking into account the proposed hypotheses, the following model is proposed:

**Fig. 1.** Proposed repurchase model

## 3.1    Data Collection and Survey

The proposed model in figure 1 was validated through a telephone survey to a sample of Spanish population, obtaining 1,307 valid responses from Internet purchasers. The sample used comes from a survey panel, which will enable longitudinal studies to be carried out in the future.

The items for the survey, measured with a Likert-7 scale, have been validated in previous studies. Specifically, the repurchase intention and satisfaction measures were adapted from [4]. Measurement of extrinsic benefits was adapted from [1] and perceived quality and website quality were taken from [20][35], and [6][20], respectively. Items measuring customer loyalty were adapted from [11][16][18]. Finally, measurement of current purchasing habits was adapted from [22].

## 3.2    Statistical Analysis

Data was analysed by the partial least squares method using PLS Graph software, version 3.00 build 1130, for its validation and predictive ability assessment [8]. Firstly, the validity of the measurement instrument was verified and subsequently, the structural model was validated. In order to check for discriminant validity, following the recommendations of [12], SPSS 16.0 was additionally used as a tool for calculating the bivariate correlations.

Individual item reliability offered values close to -or higher than -the recommended 0.80. However, the value of one indicator for purchasing habits was near the threshold, with a value of 0.6984. The relatively low value of this indicator ("I buy on the Internet every week") can be explained because the average number of purchases by product type oscillated between 2.07 and 8.73 per year [24], which implies that purchases are not made with a weekly frequency in general.

Convergent validity was studied by compound reliability and average variance extracted, with values of 0.878 and 0.709, respectively. Discriminant validity was tested and confirmed by comparing the average variance extracted (AVE) of each construct and the bivariate correlation with each other construct.

The evaluation of the structural model was analyzed through three different indicators: path coefficients ($\beta$), explained variance ($R^2$) and t-statisticals. The values of $R^2$ indicate a good explanation of the model based on the proposed constructs, given that the relations enable an explanation of at least 47.9 percent of the variance in all cases. For the dependent variable, the variance explained for repurchase intention is 61.47 percent. A blindfolding procedure [8] was also applied to measure the predictive relevance of the model constructs (parameter $Q^2$ from a Stone-Geisser test) obtaining results that assure the predictive validity of the model ($Q^2 > 0$ in all cases). Path coefficients easily exceed the limit value of 0.2 in all cases. The values of the t-statistics also exceeded the recommended minimums. Statistical significance ($p<0.001$) was obtained for the weights and loading of the model items by bootstrap resampling. The results for the structural model are represented graphically in Fig. 2.

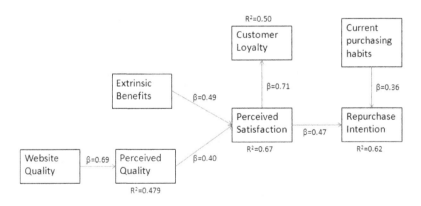

**Fig. 2.** Research results for the structural model

# 4     Conclusions and Discussion of Results

The results confirm the predictive ability of the proposed repurchase model and support all the hypotheses. It has predictive capacity for all the proposed relations (the explained variance was 61.47 percent) in EC-B2C, considering the purchasing habits and perceived satisfaction of an Internet purchaser as explanatory factors. The model also explains 66.75 percent of the Internet purchaser's satisfaction through extrinsic benefits obtained and perceived quality.

Perceived satisfaction stands out then as a more important factor than purchasing habits in the explanation of the repurchase process. The low average number of purchases made in Spain may explain these findings, and it implies that EC-B2C has still not been generalised as a habit among Spanish Internet purchasers.

In creating satisfaction, extrinsic benefits obtained have a greater weight for the Internet purchaser than perceived quality. Also, satisfaction has a significant influence on customer loyalty, explaining more than 50 percent of loyalty.

Additionally, electronic commerce website quality has a significantly positive effect on perceived quality. Therefore, providing users with purchasing experiences with a design that produces satisfaction, simple navigation and tools providing utility and security are revealed as important elements for increasing perceived quality.

## 4.1    Contribution to Existing Research

Even though perceived satisfaction has been a recurrent research field in consumer behavior theory, this is one of the first models for EC-B2C repurchase based on purchasing habits and perceived satisfaction, involving the concept of benefits obtained –referred to in previous studies as value [13][17]– and perceived quality. The results suggest that the modeling of perceived satisfaction from these constructs offers a better explanation than that which can be found in previous literature.

## 4.2    Implications for Decision Taking

The authors' first indication for decision takers in B2C electronic commerce is that, in the current state of B2C electronic commerce in Spain, they should seek customer satisfaction, offering proposals that focus on increasing perceived quality and benefits obtained.

In order to increase perceived quality, it is necessary to provide transaction security and a design that provides simple and useful navigation and purchasing experience. However, it is still more important that the customer perceives the electronic commerce site as "living up to what it offers", fundamentally in terms of delivery dates and obtaining the requested product in the condition expected by the customer. In order to achieve this, a first measure would be the use of quality seals, since their presence in considered positive and it is taken into account by two out of three purchasers [25].

With respect to promise fulfillment by the e-commerce website, one of the main problems stated by purchasers was that "they did not receive the product they requested". The authors think that more and better information for the consumer is a critical step to help improving the perception that an EC-B2C site delivers what it promises.

The element that most influences perceived satisfaction are the benefits obtained, which consist mainly of providing functionality and utility to the consumer (fundamentally saving time and money in online purchasing, ease in the purchasing process and delivery and convenience with respect to traditional purchasing). Time-saving in online purchasing compared to the physical purchasing process seems evident. Therefore, managers should constantly monitor their prices compared to traditional "off-line" sites and, taking advantage of their lower disintermediation costs, always offer a better price to the Internet purchaser than the off-line purchase option. These prices should be adapted in real time, informing at the time of payment of any possible price discounts in the product since the time it was selected. The use of tools that make it possible to record consumer preferences is also recommended, offering the best options in the final delivery process (in terms of delivery time and location).

These measures should lead to an increase in benefits perceived by the customers, and in turn reflect a natural increase in online purchasing habits, which as previously mentioned in this study is "an automatic behavioral tendency that is unconscious" and which is therefore difficult to stimulate directly.

# References

[1] Atchariyachanvanich, K., Okada, H., Sonehara, N.: Exploring Factors Effecting the Continuance of Purchasing Behavior in Internet Shopping: Extrinsic Benefits and Intrinsic Benefits. IPSJ Digital Courier 4, 91–102 (2008)

[2] Babin, B.J., Darben, W.R., Griffin, M.: Work and/or fun: Measuring hedonic and utilitarian shopping value. Journal of Consumer Research 20(1), 644–656 (1994)

[3] Bhattacherjee, A.: An Empirical Analysis of the Antecedents of Electronic Commerce Service Continuance. Decision Support Systems 32, 201–214 (2001)

[4] Bhattacherjee, A.: Understanding information systems continuance: An expectation-confirmation model. MIS Quarterly 25, 351–370 (2001)

[5] Campbell, J.Y., Cochrane, J.H.: By force of habit: A consumption-based explanation of aggregate stock market behaviour. Journal of Political Economy 107(2), 205–251 (1999)

[6] Chen, L., Gilleson, M.L., Sherrel, D.L.: Consumer Acceptance of Virtual Stores: A theoretical model and critical success factors for virtual stores. ACM SIGMIS Database 35(2), 8–31 (2004)

[7] Childers, T.L., Carr, C.L., Peck, J., Carson, S.: Hedonic and utilitarian motivations for online retail shopping behaviour. Journal of Retailing 77(4), 511–535 (2001)

[8] Chin, W.W.: The Partial Least Squares Approach to Structural Equation Modeling. In: Marcoulides, G.A. (ed.) Modern Methods for Business Research. Lawrence Erlbaum Associates, Mahwah (1998)

[9] Cronin Jr., J.J., Brady, M.K., Hult, G.T.: Assessing the effects of quality, value, and customer satisfaction on consumer behavioral intentions in service environment. Journal of Retailing 76(2), 193–218 (2000)

[10] Éthier, J., Hadaya, P., Talbot, J., Cadieux, J.: B2C Web site quality and emotions during online shopping episodes: an empirical study. Information and Management 43(5) (July 2006)

[11] Gefen, D.: Customer loyalty in E-commerce. Journal of the Association for Information Systems 3, 27–51 (2002)

[12] Gefen, D., Straub, D.W.: A Practical Guide to Factorial Validity Using PLS-Graph: Tutorial and Annotated Example. Communications of the Association for Information Systems 16, 91–109 (2005)

[13] Hamel, G., Prahalad, C.K.: Computing for the Future. Harvard Business School Press, Boston (1994)

[14] Herrero Crespo, Á., García de los Salmones Sánchez, M.M., Rodríguez del Bosque, I.: Calidad y valor percibido como condicionantes de la satisfacción: una aplicación en el sector de las Artes Escénicas. Revista de Economía y Empresa XXIII(54/55) (2005)

[15] Holbrook, M.B.: Consumer Value: A Framework for Analysis and Research. Routledge, New York (1999)

[16] Homburg, C., Giering, A.: Personal characteristics as moderators of the relationship between customer satisfaction and loyalty. Psychology and Marketing 18(1), 43–66 (2001)

[17] Hunt, S.D., Morgon, R.M.: The competitive advantage theory of competition. Journal of Marketing 59, 1–15 (1995)

[18] Jones, T.O., Sasser, W.E.: Why satisfied customers defect. Harvard Business Review 73(6), 88–99 (1995)

[19] Kahneman, D., Tversky, A.: Prospect theory: An analysis of decision under risk. Econometrica 47(2), 263–291 (1979)

[20] Lee, G., Lin, H.: Customer perceptions of e-service quality in online shopping. International Journal of Retail & Distribution Management 33(2), 161–176 (2005)

[21] Lee, J., Jinwoo, K., Yun Moon, J.: What makes Internet users visit cyber stores again? key design factors for customer loyalty. In: Proceedings of the SIGCHI Conference on Human Factors in Computing Systems, The Hague, The Netherlands, April 01-06, pp. 305–312 (2000)

[22] Liao, C., Palvia, P., Lin, H.-N.: The roles of habit and web site quality in e-commerce. International Journal of Information Management 26(6), 469–483 (2006)

[23] Nowak, G.J., Phelps, J.: Direct marketing and the use of individual-level consumer information: Determining how and when 'privacy' matters. J. Direct Market. 11(40), 94–108 (1997)

[24] Observatorio Red.es: "Comercio Electrónico B2C 2008". Observatorio de las Telecomunicaciones y Sociedad de la Información de Red.es (Ministerio de Industria, Turismo y Comercio) (2008), http://observatorio.red.es/hogares-ciudadanos/articles/id/3051/estudio-b2c-2008.html (Date of retrieval: February 20, 2009)

[25] Observatorio Red.es: "Comercio Electrónico B2C 2009". Observatorio de las Telecomunicaciones y Sociedad de la Información de Red.es (Ministerio de Industria, Turismo y Comercio) (2009), http://www.ontsi.red.es/hogares-ciudadanos/articles/id/3945/estudio-b2c-2009.html (Date of retrieval: October 24, 2009)

[26] Oliver, R.L.: Effect of Expectation and Disconfirmation on Postexposure Product Evaluations - an Alternative Interpretation. Journal of Applied Psychology 62(4), 480 (1977)

[27] Oliver, R.L.: A cognitive model for the antecedents and consequences of satisfaction. Journal of Marketing Research 17(4), 460–469 (1980)

[28] Oliver, R.L.: Satisfaction: a behavioral perspective on the consumer. Mc Graw Hill, New York (1996)

[29] Oliver, R.L.: Whence consumer loyalty? Journal of Marketing 63(5), 33–44 (1999)

[30] Olson, J.C., Reynolds, T.J.: Understanding consumers' cognitive structures: implications for advertising strategy. In: Percy, L., Woodside, A. (eds.) Advertising and Consumer Psychology. Lexington Books, Lexington (1983)

[31] Ouellette, J.A., Wood, W.: Habit and intention in everyday life: The multiple processes by which past behavior predicts future behaviour. Psychological Bulletin 124(1), 54–74 (1998)

[32] Shang, R.-A., Chen, Y.-C., Shen, L.: Extrinsic versus intrinsic motivations for consumers to shop on-line. Information and Management 42(3), 401–413 (2005)

[33] Shankar, V., Smith, A.K., Rangaswamy, A.: Customer satisfaction and loyalty in online and offline environments. International Journal of Research in Marketing 20(2), 153–175 (2003)

[34] Zeithaml, V.A.: Consumer perceptions of price, quality and value: a means-end model and synthesis of evidence. Journal of Marketing 52, 2–22 (1988)

[35] Wolfinbarger, M., Gilly, M.: e-TailQ: "Dimensionalizing, measuring and predicting retail quality". Journal of Retailing 27, 183–198 (2003)

# A Multi-criteria Decision Model for Planning Inter-organizational Global Agile Software Development Projects

Luis Henrique Almeida[1], Adriano Albuquerque[2],
and Plácido Rogério Pinheiro[2]

[1] CPQi IT Offshore Solutions,
R. Chico Lemos, 946, 60822-780, Fortaleza, Brazil
lhenrique@cpqi.com
[2] University of Fortaleza, Graduate Program in Applied Computer Science,
Av. Washington Soares, 1321, 60811-905, Fortaleza, Brazil
{adrianoba,placido}@unifor.br

**Abstract.** Inter-organizational Global Software Development (GSD) has become a common reality for many projects. It is well established that distance makes difficult to interact and to cooperate effectively. Scrum, a consolidated Agile methodology, emphasizes communication, reduces coordination and control overhead and has been increasingly used in a distributed fashion. Successfully planning and managing the combined use of GSD and Scrum is a complex task and requires carefully planning. Despite the importance and complexity of this type of problem, there seems to be a lack of reports, in the literature, of models that could support managers dealing with these decision contexts. This paper presents a multi-criteria decision model for planning and fine-tuning such project plans. This model was developed using cognitive mapping and MACBETH[1]. The application of the model is demonstrated, followed by conclusion and future work.

**Keywords:** Global Software Development; Project Management; Multi-Criteria Decision Analysis; Cognitive Mapping; MACBETH.

## 1 Introduction

Due to numerous business reasons Global Software Development (GSD) projects have become a common reality. Organizations look for ways to reach a larger pool of skilled professionals, to optimize costs and to reduce time of delivery. Software development projects involve numerous activities that require a well coordinated effort from multiple organizational actors or units in order to be successful.

In addition to the usual challenges faced by any project, the distance between team members directly affects the process of communications and coordination, and control activities in GSD[2]. In order to ensure success of the project, all members of the team have to work and cooperate efficiently. According to [3],

M.D. Lytras et al. (Eds.): WSKS 2011, CCIS 278, pp. 107–116, 2013.

actors who envision gaining collaborative advantage from aligning with others in an inter-organizational partnership face the often-daunting prospect of trying to integrate their diverse perspectives and frequently competing goals.

Agile Development is another software engineering paradigm that has been consolidated in the past decade, bringing methodologies like Scrum, XP, FDD, Lean. Scrum is an iterative framework for managing software projects according to agile principles. It enables teams to deliver the right features on time, on budget, and with great quality[6]. Scrum helps a software development organization adapt to changing business requirements and stakeholders needs while protecting the team from unproductive disruptions to their workflow[6]. Scrum has been used to develop complex products since the early 1990s and has been increasingly used for GSD as well. Scrum emphasizes communication, reduces coordination and control overhead; therefore it helps the management of distributed projects. The primary tools that agile processes use, to effectively solve complex problems, rely on frequent communication and quick feedback, special challenges are presented to the agile processes by GSD projects[4][2]. Successfully managing the combined use of GSD and Scrum is not an easy task and requires carefully planning. Despite the importance of this problem, there seems to be a lack of reports, in the literature, of models that could support project managers dealing with such decision contexts.

Multi-criteria Decision Analysis (MCDA) is a discipline that aims to support decision makers facing complex problems, that requires making numerous and sometimes conflicting evaluations. A well structured MCDA model highlights these conflicts and derives a way to come to a compromise in solid and clear process. The multi-criteria approach can be accomplished by structuring the model through exploring actors interests, evaluating alternatives under different perspectives, robustness analysis against uncertainties and analyzing inter and intra personal conflicts[11]. While MCDA has been employed for task allocation in GSD and portfolio management we believe it may also be useful for supporting planning global inter-organizational software engineering projects.

This paper presents a multi-criteria decision model for planning and fine-tuning inter-organizational global Scrum software development projects. The remainder of the paper is organized as follows. Section 2 describes the decision setting that inspired the development of the model and discusses the challenges faced when planning inter-organizational distributed Scrum projects. The development of the model is explained in Section 4. Section shows the results obtained of an example of use. Finally, Section 5 provides concluding remarks.

## 2    Decision Setting

This section presents the context that motivated the structuring of the model. A real world intervention scenario is briefly described. Challenges faced by project managers planning Inter-organizational GSD projects with Scrum are listed.

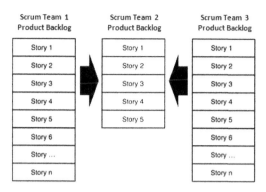

**Fig. 1.** Example of backlog strategy. Multiple teams feeding the backlog of another team [4]

## 2.1 Real World Scenario

The client company is a leading banking technology specialist in Brazil working for the international and domestic markets. It has deep and broad experience in investment banking and all major asset classes, from front to back for key international and domestic platforms. The company was born as global operation and has been growing organically with development offices in London UK, São Paulo Brazil, Fortaleza Brazil and Bangalore India. Its customers are global organizations from UK, US, Netherlands, Switzerland, Brazil and Chile to mention a few. The company is the unique partner in Latin America for two major investment banking technology providers and one of the two partners for another major technology provider. All of the projects require inter-organizational cooperation between at least three companies: the company in question, the major technology provider and the end customer company. The software development projects effort is distributed over sites, separated across time and space, operating in different time zones, with team members from different culture dealing with customers that also work in a similar distributed fashion.

One of the recent business cases involved planning and advising project planning decisions for an end customer organization that has competency centres in London, Ultrech and São Paulo. The end users were in São Paulo. Business and technical analysts could stay in London and São Paulo. Technology infrastructure personnel were in London, Ultrech and São Paulo. Software developers were in Fortaleza and London. The project management methodology of choice has been Scrum, due to its successful record of emphasizing communication, reducing coordination and control overhead. The product owner could stay in São Paulo or London and was responsible for prioritizing the backlog of solutions. The scrum master could stay in London or Fortaleza. In addition to the decision context characteristics typical to distributed software development projects, Scrum factors had also to be considered in the decision making process. Scrum factors, like backlog strategy in Figure 1 for instance, were important factors to be taken in consideration. The tools that were supposed to be used for communication, for managing the backlog and to perform daily scrums were also important factors on planning and fine-tuning the project plan alternatives. Sprint synchronicity had to be considered as well. The next section will get into more details on the challenges faced by decision makers on planning globally distributed scrum projects.

### 2.2    Planning Inter-organizational Global Scrum Projects

**Inter-organizational Factors:** Some factors could turn into a pitfall and significantly decrease chances of success for globally distributed scrum projects. [5] refer to as collaborative inertia by slowing or inhibiting the formation or continuation of collaborative relationships. Challenges identified were: a1) Limited vision of domain; b1) Perceived loss of control; c1) Perceived loss of constituent support; d1) Internal conflicts; e1) History of conflict and mistrust; f1) Power Differences.

**Challenges of distributed projects:** A large body of research suggests that time and spatial distance can have powerful and negative effects in business[2]. Challenges identified were: a2) Communicating with distributed team members; b2) Time zones and working hours; c2) Cultural differences; d2) Language differences; e2) Tools; f2) Software engineering practices; g2) Team dynamics; h2) IT Infrastructure for collaboration; i2) Different knowledge levels; j2) Asymmetry in Processes Policies and Standards; k2) Tracking and control; l2) Intellectual Property issues; m2) Creating team spirit.

**Challenges in Distributed Scrum Projects:** Scrum has three levels of planning: Release Planning, Sprint Planning, and Daily Scrums. Some of the challenges are: a3) How to organize Scrum teams; b3) Create and prioritize the backlog; c3) Estimating the stories as a team; d3) Create the release plan; e3) Sprint length; f3) Managing dependencies; g3) Product Owner effectiveness; h3) Continuous integration.

**Challenges in any Type of Project:** Obviously there are factors that are related to any software development project. Challenges identified were: a4) Cost management; b4) Risk management; c4) Skill fit; d4) Managing ROI; e4) Use of the right technologies; f4) Product delivery estimate; g4) Knowledge management; h4) Quality management; i4) Task allocation; j4) Scope and change management; k4) Project management tools.

## 3    Developing the Model

How MCDA treats a decision problem and what are the various phases that should be carried out to develop models have been properly documented in [1][7][9][8]. According to[1], the decision support process involves three phases:

structuring; evaluation; and recommendation. The problem structuring phase usually is the longest phase and it may take a while to even scope the decision context. This is consistent with the literature and research findings. The model was developed using cognitive mapping and MACBETH (Measuring Attractiveness by a Categorical Based Evaluation Technique).

Cognitive mapping, a solid tool for analyzing and structuring decision making problems, was used in order to carry out the identification of the criteria. This tool has been applied in diverse knowledge areas, more specifically in administration. The main advantage it presents for the decision makers is the possibility to increase the level of knowledge of the subject, during the construction of the map, leading him/her to reflect on more coherent and intelligent decision making, according to the problem to be structured[10]. The following steps where were used for the construction of the cognitive map:

## 3.1   Defining the Problem

Decision makers perceive and interpret the same situation in different ways and since the exclusive use of reason is highly debatable, one should not regard the stakeholders as completely rational. One of the MCDA premises is that a problem belongs to someone, as it is a construction that an individual makes about events. Therefore, each stakeholder has its own subjective view about the decision context. Another premise is that preferences and models are generated.

Cognitive mapping allows for the representation of the problem generated. The first step to build a cognitive map is to define, working with the decision makers/actors, a label that describes the problem that will need intervention. Below is the output of the first step performed.

**Label** : "To chose a globally distributed scrum project plan that has good chance of success."

## 3.2   Defining Primary Evaluation Elements

Following the definition of the problem, brainstorming sessions and interviews with project managers and Scrum Masters, experienced in DSD were performed. In initial interactions, with the goal to promote creativity, any criticism was avoided. Questions addressed were regarding what aspects the interviewee would consider when analyzing the problem; the characteristics that distinguish a good decision or action from a bad one; what were the main challenges in the decision setting prior to the intervention.

Additional discussions were about the consequences that would be considered to be good, bad and inacceptable; what goals, restrictions and general guidelines that should be adopted; what were the strategic goals for the decision context. The output of this step was: Risk; Cost; Distribution Level; Cultural Difference Level; Language Difference Level; Team Formation Age; Team Skills Fit; Communication Efficiency; Communication Frequency; Level of Coordination and Control Required; Product Backlog Strategy; User Stories Dependence; Sprint Length Synchronization.

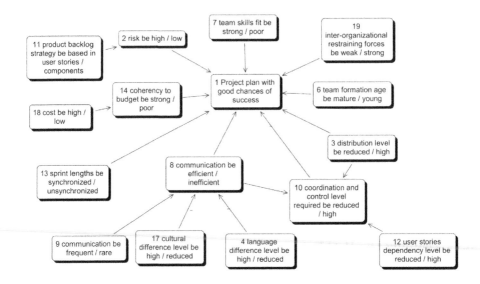

**Fig. 2.** Cognitive Map Generated in The First Iteration

## 3.3  Building Concepts

For every PEE there should be a concept. Initially the primary evaluation element is oriented to action, that way providing the first pole to the concept. The meaning for the concept is partially based in the actions that is suggests. This dynamic can be obtained placing the verb in the beginning.

The map developed was supposed to be action oriented. After having the first pole the opposite should be regarded as well. Both poles are separated by , which should be read as as opposed to. There a few pitfalls if one does not think on the opposite pole. Important and different interpretations can be missed. The concepts extracted from the PEEs are listed below.

### Concepts Extracted from (PEEs)

1:  cost be high ... cost be low
2:  risk be high ... risk be low
3:  distribution level be reduced ... distribution level be high
4:  cultural difference level be high ... cultural difference level be reduced
5:  language difference level be high ... language difference level be reduced
6:  team formation be mature ... team formation be young
7:  skill fit be strong  skill fit be poor
8:  communication be efficient  communication be inefficient
9:  communication be frequent  communication be rare
10:  coordination and control level required be reduced  coordination and control level required be high
11:  product backlog strategy be based in user stories  product backlog strategy be based in components

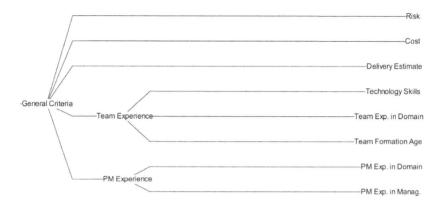

**Fig. 3.** General criteria concepts hierarchy for supporting planning distributed Scrum projects

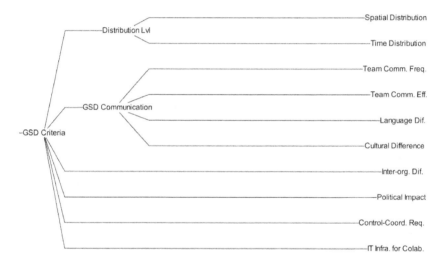

**Fig. 4.** GSD criteria concepts hierarchy for supporting planning distributed Scrum projects

12:  user stories dependency be reduced  user stories dependency be high
13:  sprint lengths be synchronized  sprint lengths be unsynchronized

After listing the concepts and taking each of the concepts, physically drawing of a map for the first iteration started.

### 3.4   The Concept Hierachy and MACBETH

The cognitive map resulted from the first iteration **??** is depicted in Figure 2. In order to obtain the end result, the feedback of several actors were obtained

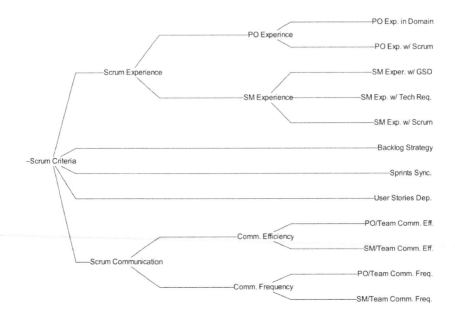

**Fig. 5.** Scrum criteria concepts hierarchy for supporting planning distributed Scrum projects

| Which Plan? | Weight | Plano A | Plano B | Plano C | Cumulative Weight |
|---|---|---|---|---|---|
| General Criteria | 5 | 17,6 | 18,3 | 22,7 | 35,7 |
| GSD Criteria | 6 | 22,2 | 24,6 | 22,9 | 42,9 |
| Scrum Criteria | 3 | 7,4 | 8,4 | 15,2 | 21,4 |
| TOTAL | 14 | 47 | 51 | 61 | 100,0 |

**Fig. 6.** Evaluation of the different plans

through interviews where interviewees answered questions like: which aspect would be the most important for the solution? Another step towards the construction of the model was performed, in order to construct the concept hierarchy that served as input to the MACBETH method. Figure ?? shows the end result for the concept hierarchy. As it has been previously said, this method provides for the evaluation of alternatives considering the multi-criteria.

The main fundamental difference between MACBETH and other multi-criteria methods is that it requires qualitative judgments about different attractiveness with the goal to generate about differences to help a decision maker or a decision-advising group quantify the relative attractiveness of alternatives available.

The qualitative judgments were performed using the seven semantic categories introduced by MACBETH for different levels of attractiveness: no, very weak, weak, moderate, strong, very strong and extreme. The comparisons were performed always in pairs of alternatives, evaluating qualitatively the difference in attractiveness and choosing one of the categories[9].

For a set of judgments to be considered consistent it must be possible to deduce, starting from the scores of the project plans alternative, in such a way that: 1) alternatives equally attractive obtain the same score; 2) an alternative more attractive than other obtain a higher score; 3) if the difference of attractiveness between two alternatives is greater than the difference of attractiveness between two other alternatives then the difference of score between the first pair of alternatives is greater than the difference of score between the other two alternatives. Figures 3, 4 and 5 show the segregated concept hierarchy.

# 4   Evaluation and Recommendation

In order to test the model that was developed, three different alternatives of plans where evaluated. For each criteria comparisons were performed in pairs as it has been mentioned in the previous section. Plan C was recommended as the best alternative of plan. Figure 6 shows the total values for the alternatives.

# 5   Conclusion

The development of the Multi-criteria Model for Planning Inter-organizational Global Agile Software Development Projects achieved the initial goal of supporting the decision making process for choosing which plan should be carried out or to fine-tuning project plans typical to the decision contexts of the offshore solutions client company and its partners organizations. The construction of the model allowed for the improvement of success rates of the projects. The proposed model was based in judgment of values of the decision makers, giving a subjective character to the model. This work allowed for a new approach sustained by the MCDA methodology replacing an old decision process that worked in the past without any multi-criteria method and mainly focused on cost reduction and task allocation. The MCDA methodology proved to be suitable for modeling the problem setting being handled. Future work can be done with regards to deepening the concept hierarchy, identifying other criteria related to inter-organizational factors.

**Acknowledgements.** The first author is thankful to the Foundation for Support of Scientific and Technological Research of Ceara  FUNCAP and the third author is thankful to the National Council of Technological and Scientific Development (CNPq) for the support received on this project.

# References

1. Bana e Costa, C.A., Sanchez-Lopez, R., Vansnick, J.C., De Corte, J.M.: Introduccin a MACBETH. In: Leyva Lpez, J.C. (ed.) Anlisis Multicriterio para la Toma de Decisiones: Mtodos y Aplicaciones, pp. 233–241. Plaza y Valds, Mxico (2011)
2. Jimenez, M., Piattini, M., Vizcano, A.: Challenges and improvements in distributed software development: a systematic review. Adv. Soft. Eng. Journal (2009)
3. Gray, B.: Intervening to Improve Inter-organizational Partnerships. In: Cropper, S., Ebers, M., Huxham, C., Ring, P.S. (eds.) The Oxford Handbook of Inter-Organizational Relations. Oxford University Press, Oxford (2008)
4. Woodward, E., et al.: A practical guide to distributed Scrum. IBM Press (2010)
5. Vangen, S., Huxham, C.: Nurturing Collaborative Relations: Building Trust in Inter-organizational Collaboration. Journal of Applied Behavioral Science (2003)
6. Sutherland, J., Viktorov, A., Blount, J., Puntikov, N.: Distributed scrum: Agile project management with outsourced development teams. In: 40th Annual Hawaii Int. Conference on Software Systems, System Sciences, p. 274a (2007)
7. Rodrigues, A., Pinheiro, P.R., Rodrigues, M.M., Carvalho, A., Gonalves, F.M.: Applying a multicriteria model for selection of test use cases: a use of experience. Int. Journal Social and Humanistic Computing 1, 246–260 (2010)
8. Nunes, L.C., Pinheiro, P.R., Pequeno, T.C., Pinheiro, M.C.D.: Toward an Applied to the Diagnosis of Psychological Disorders. Advances in Experimental Medicine and Biology 696, 23–31 (2011)
9. Pinheiro, P.R., de Souza, G.G.C., de Castro, A.K.A.: A Estruturao do Modelo Multicritrio para Produo de Jornal. Pesquisa Operacional 28, 203–216 (2008)
10. Gomes, L.F.A., Rangel, L.A.D., Jeronimo, R.: A study of professional mobility in a large corporation through cognitive mapping. Pesqui. Oper. 30(2), 331–344 (2010)
11. Takeuchi, H., Nonaka, I.: Hitotsubashi on Knowledge Management. In: Towards an Integrative Model of Organizational Culture and Knowledge Management. John Wiley & Sons (Asia), Singapore (2004)
12. Paasivaara, M., Durasiewicz, S., Lassenius, C.: Using scrum in distributed agile development: A multiple case study. In: Fourth IEEE International Conference on Global Software Engineering, ICGSE 2009, pp. 195–204 (2009)

# Social Networking and Teachers' Professional Development

Paula Antunes[1,3], Isabel Barbosa[2,3], and António Moreira[3]

[1] Research Center CIDTFF – Universidade de Aveiro
Sponsored by Foundation for Science and Technology's Portugal (SFRH/BD/70607/2010)
[2] Research Center CIDTFF – Universidade de Aveiro
Sponsored by Foundation for Science and Technology's Portugal (SFRH/BD/69151/2010)
[3] Universidade de Aveiro - Portugal
{paulucha.antunes,immbarbosa}@gmail.com, moreira@ua.pt

**Abstract.** Are teachers able to take advantage of technological tools to informally promote their professional development? On one hand, we acknowledge the utility of 2.0 tools for teaching and learning - connecting, communicating, sharing and collaborating, the pillars of knowledge development in the global society. On the other hand teachers face new challenges as educators and professionals in the global society of the 21th century. This is the underlying research question of two joint investigations – a survey and a case study – that aim to investigate to what extent professional networks, as informal learning environments, can contribute towards teachers' growth. The survey intends to investigate if teachers perceived digital skills are conditioning their participation in online professional networks, as well as the importance teachers give to these communities for their professional development, and the impacts they perceive. The case study will analyze an online teacher's network, investigating the reasons and motivations that drive teachers to belong to the community, as well as the interactions established. The data collected will contribute to a better understanding of the potential of professional networks in lifelong learning for teachers.

**Keywords:** ICT Skills; Informal Learning; Professional Development: Social Networking; Web 2.0.

## 1 Web 2.0 and Knowledge Building

Information and communication technology (ICT) has irreversibly changed the way people work, communicate, interact, invest, learn and spend their leisure time [1]. During the last decade evidence has revealed that a crucial shift occurred in the way knowledge is acquired, mainly related to the context in which knowledge is available, its characteristics and ways of dissemination [2]. The generation of learners of the digital age, the "New Millennium Learners" or the "digital natives" use computers on a daily basis and are excellent multitaskers, easily shifting between tasks [3]. They are

M.D. Lytras et al. (Eds.): WSKS 2011, CCIS 278, pp. 117–120, 2013.
© Springer-Verlag Berlin Heidelberg 2013

also autonomous and independent in their learning processes, but more outgoing and more involved in group work. The knowledge society expects individuals to be independent thinkers, collaborative, and "The critical community of learners ... encourages cognitive Interdependence simultaneously" [4] resulting from the fusion of two different worlds, an individual and a shared one.

Knowledge is built from the relationships and the interactions established between individuals [2]. Siemens described the basic principles of connectivism, a theory that aims to characterize learning in the digital era: learning and knowledge are drawn from a multiplicity of opinions, in a process of linking nodes or sources of knowledge. So, in order to increase and update knowledge throughout life, a concept inherent to New Millennium Learners (NML), it is mandatory to nurture and maintain links between individuals, particularly through the use of Web 2.0 tools, through a learning process that combines conversation/communication, interaction, sharing, creation and participation [5].

## 2     Informal Learning and Teachers' Continuous Professional Development

Learning is a lifelong, permanent process, built individually or in a community [2]. Alongside the formal learning in educational institutions in order to obtain a certification or a diploma, there is non-formal learning, parallel to the above, which is not validated by a formal certification and may be provided by work institutions or through activities sponsored by organizations or civil society groups. Furthermore, informal learning is a non-intentional form of learning and results from everyday experiences [6].

The contexts of informal learning are regarded as alternative learning models that are generally time-consuming, poorly organized, difficult to assess, but perhaps more effective in a process of changing practices and innovation [7]. Nonetheless, the formal context of teacher training can offer some gains, if supported by the use of social software and, at the same time, provide the required certification. This understanding can enhance formal training, creating informal learning approaches and environments that may increase a more reflective learning attitude.

As an alternative to a more formal training, informal training supported by Web 2.0 tools, well known by teachers who use them mainly for personal purposes, can facilitate their integration in online teachers' communities. Social networking is a potential informal learning context, because it promotes an inevitable exchange and sharing of knowledge and experience. Hi5, Facebook, Plaxo, Twitter, Ning and other 2.0 tools allow teachers to get in touch with the Web in an intuitive way and can lead to eliminate professional development in a collaborative environment, providing not only the development of ICT skills, but also the scientific and pedagogical teachers' skills necessary to increase innovation in education and establish a better "connection" with their students – "The net generation" [8].

The report "Implementing Web 2.0 in Secondary Schools: Impacts, Barriers and Issues" [9] gives further evidence that the use of Web 2.0 contributes to a greater autonomy and creativity, as it allows teachers to publish content on the Web, fosters collaborative learning activities and promotes the development of lifelong learning.

# 3     Ongoing Research

The two joint studies mentioned here aim to contribute to a better understanding about the potential role of social networking as an informal learning environment for teachers. The survey's objective is to describe the skills and uses of digital technologies by teachers of basic and secondary public schools from Aveiro, Portugal, (11 schools/groups of schools – about 1300 teachers), as well as the importance these teachers attribute to social professional networks for their professional development and the perceived impacts on: i) ICT skills; ii) pedagogical skills using technology; iii) subject knowledge. The skills and the uses of digital technologies refer to both basic ICT and social web skills. It is our intention to clarify if teachers consider the use of web 2.0 tools and services an important means of development of their skills. Concerning professional development, the study aims to identify the perceptions of teachers about the growing importance of lifelong learning and informal learning contexts as a recognized way of facing the challenges of the knowledge society. Another dimension present in this study is the impact teachers believe can occur from their participation in social professional networks in their practices.

The survey is designed in two phases. The first one refers to the processes required to prepare the questionnaire application, that is, contact the schools administrators to obtain data about the number of teachers and students, and the local ICT coordinator contact. Later on, ICT coordinators will be asked to give information related with the school ICT resources and services, as well as about the school context and policies on ICT use. The second phase concerns the application of the survey questionnaire. With the support of the schools administrators and ICT coordinators, the main questionnaire survey will be deployed to teachers (online survey), in order to get the data required to answer the research questions.

At this stage of the research we don't discard the possibility of conducting interviews with those teachers who declare belonging to Interactic 2.0[1] – the professional social network that is the object of the previously mentioned case study.

The case study aims to analyze and understand how social networks, as tools to create and develop online learning communities, can contribute towards teachers' professional development. In particular, we aim to explore the impact of teachers' participation in social networks on the collaborative work they develop within the online community and at school, as well as evaluate the impact of the use of a social network on the growth of a professional community of practice and verify the effects of these learning informal contexts on teachers' professional development. Thus, an online questionnaire is being applied to the members of an online teachers' community - Interactic 2.0 - , and the interactions of these teachers in forums and blogs of some specific groups (inside Interactic 2.0) will be analyzed. The case study design also contemplates interviewing Interactic 2.0 administrators to obtain data about their motivations to create this social network, as well as about their expectations and how they are being achieved.

---

[1] http://interactic.ning.com

Finally, and according to a perspective that is common to both studies, we aim to understand the teacher's needs to effectively consider their participation in a social professional network as a means of professional growth.

# 4    Expected Results

From this joint research we expect to obtain significant data about teachers' motivations, benefits and obstacles to the development of communities of practice supported by social networking, and find evidence of impacts of their participation in such communities on teachers' ICT skills and professional development. Simultaneously, we wish to contribute towards the promotion of consciousness about the potential growth of innovative pedagogical "spaces" as a result of more collaborative work within teachers.

The results of these studies are expected to raise the awareness for the need to prevent some flaws that condition the sustained development of teachers' social professional networking, so they can be minimized. By achieving this, we believe our findings may contribute towards supporting Interactic. 2.0.

# References

1. Kozma, R.B.: Comparative analysis of policies for ICT in Education. Consultado em 10 de Fevereiro de 2010 (2008),
   `http://robertkozma.com/images/`
   `kozma_comparative_ict_policies_chapter.pdf`
2. Siemens, G.: Knowing Knowledge. A Creative Commons Licensed version - disponível, obtido em 20 de Março de 2008 (2006), `http://www.knowingknowledge.com`
3. Redecker, C.: Review of Learning 2.0 Practices: Study on the Impact of Web 2.0 Innovations on Education and Training in Europe. Office for Official Publications of the European Communities, Luxembourg (2009)
4. Garrison, D., Anderson, T.: E-Learning in the 21st Century. Routledge, New York (2003)
5. Downes, S.: An Introduction to Connective Knowledge. Consultado em 23 de Maio de 2009 (2005), `http://www.downes.ca/cgi-bin/page.cgi?post=33034`
6. Longworth, N.: Lifelong learning in action: transforming education in the 21st century. Kogan Page, London (2003)
7. Moreira, A., Loureiro, M.J.: Enquadramento das TIC na Formação Contínua de Professores. In: Competências TIC. Estudo de Implementação, GEPE, vol. 2, pp. 118–160. Editorial do Ministério de Educação, Lisboa (2009)
8. Oblinger, D., Oblinger, J.: Educating the Net Generation. Consultado em 4 de Agosto de 2008 (2005), `http://www.educause.edu/~educatingthenetgen/`
9. BECTA: Implementing Web 2.0 in Secondary Schools: Impacts, Barriers and Issues. Consultado em 09 de Julho de 2009 (2008),
   `http://partners.becta.org.uk/upload-dir/downloads/`
   `page_documents/research/web2_benefits_barriers.pdf`

# Intellectual Capital Management in SMEs and the Management of Organizational Knowledge Capabilities: An Empirical Analysis

Darwin Romero-Artigas[1], Félix Pascual-Miguel[2],
and Ángel Francisco Agudo-Peregrina[2]

[1] Universidad Centroccidental Lisandro Alvarado (UCLA). Dpto. de Sistemas, Decanato de Ciencias y Tecnología. Av. Las Industrias, Redoma el Obelisco, 3001 Barquisimeto, Venezuela
[2] Universidad Politécnica de Madrid. Dpto. de Ingeniería de Organización, Administración de Empresas y Estadística. Escuela Técnica Superior de Ingenieros de Telecomunicación.
Despacho A-126. Av. Complutense, 30. 28040 Madrid, Spain
dromero@ucla.edu.ve, {felixjose.pascual,af.agudo}@upm.es

**Abstract.** Knowledge management is a complex concept of difficult implementation in the organizations and only possible to understand from a socio-technical point of view, where the human component establishes a relation of synergy with technological and cultural elements that allow him to extend their capabilities. The proposed model is based on a cause-effect relation, as the result of the influence of IT/IS presence, organizational culture and human capital in organizational knowledge management, within the framework of a maturity model. The investigation was developed on a group of Latin American SMEs from the industrial and manufacturing sector, using a Partial Least Squares (PLS) approach and k-means clustering for statistical analysis. Structural validity of the model was verified and reliability consistency, stability, and prediction ability were demonstrated. The analysis shows that Latin American SMEs have not found yet the balance that allows them to efficiently take advantage of the installed technology and the capacity of their human resources to operate its intellectual capital.

## 1 Introduction and Motivation

This research seeks to discover and to verify if small and medium enterprises (SMEs) have overcome the barriers of their nature and internal structure, in order to extend at operation levels which help to develop competitive advantage from their own knowledge.

Historically, the need to measure and manage intellectual capital has raised a high interest among researchers [1-3], especially in the case of SMEs –since they represent a very high percentage of many national economies– and their development has a direct impact at regional and national scale. Nevertheless, it is accepted that SMEs must learn to develop a balance between the accumulation of human capabilities, their technological potential and reliable processes for the handling of information and knowledge [4].

M.D. Lytras et al. (Eds.): WSKS 2011, CCIS 278, pp. 121–128, 2013.

Starting off from a constructivist approach, from an epistemological point of view this represents the creation of a knowledge repository as a source which contributes to supply information to all employees and helps to create a knowledge network. From the ontological point of view, specifically in the social aspect, this repository may be shared, together with experiences and shared points of view from everyone in the company. For such reason, we propose a theoretical model whose aim is to demonstrate that, from a socio-technical perspective, the influence of technologies and information systems, the organizational culture and the human capital in the sustained development of organizational knowledge management capabilities determine a level of maturity of such capabilities to manage the intellectual capital in SMEs.

Therefore, SMEs may progress and develop their capabilities to manage organizational knowledge and finally reach an acceptable level of maturity to manage intellectual capital if three conditions are met: (a) the presence of a technological platform supporting the processes of information and knowledge handling; (b) an organizational culture based on the free exchange of information, teamwork and continued improvement; and (c) human capital prepared to face the challenges of information and knowledge management, supporting and enriching it with their experience, and their general and technical education.

## 2    Theoretical Foundations

The framework for this study is based on the concept of Intellectual Capital, upon three basic dimensions (human, structural and relational capital) of intellectual capital [3, 5]; these are associated with a set of respective internal sub-dimensions: (1) employee capabilities, skills, satisfaction, education and training; (2) organizational culture, processes and technology; and (3) clients, suppliers, partners, stakeholders and community [7, 8].

Once established this general framework, a comparative structural analysis of the principal intellectual capital measurement methodologies –Skandia Navigator [6], Monitor of Intangible Assets [9], Balanced Scorecard [10] and the Technological Manager [7] – is needed in order to define the parameters for the model in a similar context to those from literature.

From a knowledge management point of view, the approach of "space of information" (i-space) proposed by Boisot [11] was adopted. This approach identifies knowledge management based on information processing [11-14]. Boisot defines the "space of information" as a three-dimensional area that is present, to a lesser or higher degree, within all the organizational elements and which consists basically of the processes of information encoding, information abstraction and information dissemination or diffusion. Information encoding groups the names and internal language used within the company as part of its operations and processes; information abstraction relates to the way the company stores all the information about its business; and distribution of information comprises the mechanisms for information retrieval and distribution in a clear common language for everyone in the company.

As part of a definition of capabilities' maturity patterns, a relatively new subject in the managerial area, essential foundations were found upon empirical research from knowledge management in SMEs [15-21] and theoretical studies based on CMMI [22-24].

Furthermore, there is empirical evidence of the relation between the dimensions of intellectual capital and organizational performance [25], between social capital (a mental dimension) and intellectual capital –based in information processing –[26], and between human capital, structural capital and relational capital [27]. Additionally, there is a notable interrelation of human resources, technology, context and performance in SMEs contexts [25].

Additionally, and in order to observe specific characteristics of measurement parameters, it is necessary to review aspects related to excellence in knowledge-based organizational culture -where teamwork, information exchange and continuous improvement flourishes [29-34]-, human capital characteristics in organizational contexts -especially personal and technological experience and education [5, 13, 35-36]-, as well as the impact of information and communication technologies (ICTs) in knowledge management processes in SMEs [15, 37-39]

## 3    Research Model

To reinforce the theoretical context of the research and to help to define the areas covered by this study, from a socio-technical perspective and derived from classic intellectual capital theory, the relevant aspects about collaboration between employees and with competitors were taken into account, integrating them as recommended by the European Foundation for Quality Management [40].

Each of the following areas was treated as independent variables –or exogenous latent constructs–: information technologies and systems (IT/IS), organizational culture and human capital capabilities, represented by the following indicators:

- IT and IS: Presence and use of technological infrastructure (hardware) and applications (software).
- Organizational culture: team work, information exchange and continuous improvement
- Human capital or personal factors: experience, general education and technological training.

The second part of the model includes a comparative guide with the different areas and characteristics of capabilities' maturity levels so as to perform an effective management of the company's intellectual capital, according to CMMI. This characterization is based on the type of relation between the research variables, giving as result a set of stages arranged in "maturity contexts", from the simplest to more complex contexts.

Therefore, the following general research hypothesis is formulated: the maturity level of the skills necessary to manage intellectual capital in SMEs has a direct positive relation to the development level achieved by organizational knowledge management capabilities, as a consequence of the influence of IT/IS, organizational culture and human capital capabilities.

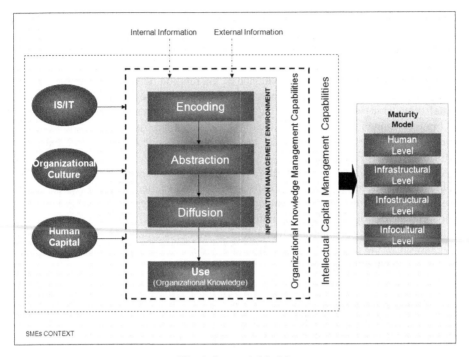

**Fig. 1.** Research Model

## 4      Empirical Study and Data Analysis

Data for the analysis was obtained from a survey instrument delivered by e-mail to 334 SMEs in the industrial and manufacturing sector in the Latin America and registered in the Alpymes database –created by the Community of SMEs of Latin America. A total of 83 answers to the questionnaires were received –24.8 percent of the total–, with the following distribution by country: Argentina (12), Brazil (14), Chile (5), Colombia (10), Ecuador (6), Mexico (12), Uruguay (7) and Venezuela (17). It seems an acceptable number considering the complexity and novelty of the subject. The statistical error was set at a 9 percent with a margin of confidence of 95%.

Data was analyzed using PLS Graph 3.0 (fig. 2), and then a k-means cluster analysis was performed using SPSS 15.0 to group the SMEs according to their maturity level of intellectual capital management.

Results from the cluster analysis show that approximately 82 percent of SMEs reported high maturity levels of intellectual capital management, with high level of capabilities to manage organizational knowledge, IT/IS infrastructure and human capital.

But it also must be noted that not all the relationships from the model were significant. For instance, IT/IS elements had no significant relation to the different processes involved in managing organizational knowledge, and neither had the other two factors in their relation with the diffusion process.

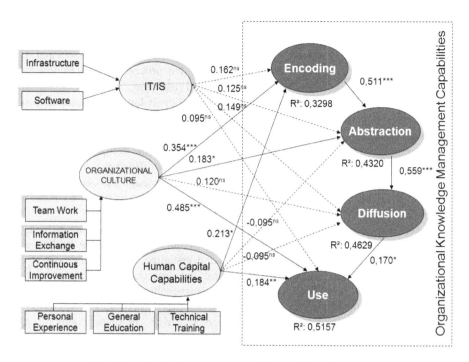

**Fig. 2.** Results for the structural model using PLS Graph v.3.0

In regard to the predictive ability of the model, all values for the Stone-Geisser's test were positive, assuring predictive ability.

## 5     Conclusions and Discussion of Results

From the analysis, the proposed model was sufficiently consistent, reliable and with predictive ability in the estimation of knowledge management in SMEs in a socio-technical context.

The general hypothesis, though, was not be completely validated in the context of this study, and while it was possible to demonstrate that Latin American SMEs reported high levels of maturity in their ability to manage intellectual capital, it was found that these maturity levels were not achieved through all the three proposed elements (IT/IS, organizational culture and human capital). The main reason behind this finding is that IT/IS infrastructure and applications might not play a significant role for any of the capabilities associated to organizational knowledge management. Contrary to the expected result, companies in this study do have an information processing environment based on IT/IS platforms, but not in terms of a goal-oriented knowledge management support. This phenomenon means they might tend to support their knowledge management processes on everyday tools for information management, diverting the focus from the strategic to the operational use. Furthermore, in the context of this study, IT/IS infrastructure is possibly not being incorporated actively as fundamental part of the social learning cycle, or maybe its influence is indirect and could not be observed by the model.

However, from the point of view of management capabilities associated to organizational knowledge, it is noteworthy the fact that processes of environmental information processing (encoding, abstracting and use and, to a lesser extent, dissemination), are well consolidated, and have a sufficient level of development in general terms. Regarding the specific relation of organizational culture with the capabilities associated to knowledge management, the main reason for this finding would be that even though knowledge is available within the company for anyone who needs it, there are neither clear policies nor culture of diffusion, probably due to the lack of mechanisms facilitating access for all. It could be concluded that organizational culture has predominance in the development of skills to manage organizational knowledge.

Moreover, the analysis highlights the fact that human capital only has influence over the encoding and use of organizational knowledge, mostly because it plays an important role in document capture, retrieval and encoding, whereas the way it is stored and disseminated is seen as more cultural and procedural than related to the human capital, which then takes part again in the use of this information; a common practice in SMEs, where only a small group manages information and knowledge.

Finally, we might conclude that Latin American SMEs, although having strong capabilities to manage their intellectual capital, are not able to empower them from the socio-technical point of view; that is to say, they do not take advantage of IT/IS and human resource skills to achieve a significant development of a knowledge management-oriented culture.

# References

[1]  Marr, B., Gray, D., Neely, A.: Why do firms measure their intellectual capital? Journal of Intellectual Capital 4(4), 441 (2003)

[2]  Martin, W.: Demonstrating knowledge value: a broader perspective on metrics. Journal of Intellectual Capital 5(1), 77 (2004)

[3]  Sveiby, K.: Measuring Intangibles and Intellectual Capital - An Emerging First Standard (1998),
     http://www.sveiby.com/articles/EmergingStandard.html
     (Date of retrieval: January 18, 2011)

[4]  Llisterry, J., Angelelli, P.: Guía Operativa para programas de Competitividad para la Pequeña y Mediana Empresa 2002. Banco Interamericano de Desarrollo. División de Micro, Pequeña y Mediana Empresa, Washington (2002)

[5]  Bontis, N.: Intellectual capital: an exploratory study that develops measures and models. Management Decision 36, 63 (1998)

[6]  Edvinsson, L., Malone, M.: El Capital Intelectual. Editorial Norma, Colombia (1998)

[7]  Brooking, A.: Intellectual Capital: Core Asset for the Third Millenium Enterprise. International Thompson Business Press, London (1996)

[8]  Kaplan, R., Norton, D.: Using the Balanced Scorecard as a Strategic Management System. Harvard Business Review, 75–85 (1996)

[9]  Sveiby, K.: The Intangible Assets Monitor (1997),
     http://www.sveiby.com/articles/CompanyMonitor.html
     (Date of retrieval: January 18, 2011)

[10] Kaplan, R., Norton, D.: The Balanced Scorecard: Translating Strategy into Action. Harvard Business School Press, Boston (1996)
[11] Boisot, M.: Knowledge Assets: Securing Competitive Advantage in de Information Economy, ed. K.A.S.C.A.i.d.I. Economy, Great Britain (1999)
[12] Alavi, M., Leidner, D.: Knowledge Management and knowledge Management Systems: Conceptual Foundations and Research Issues. MIS Quarterly 25(1), 109 (2001)
[13] Davenport, T.: Ecología de la Información: Por qué la tecnología no es suficiente para lograr el éxito en la era de la información. Oxford University Press (1999)
[14] Malhotra, Y.: Knowledge Management and New Organization Forms: A Framework for Business Model Innovation. Information Resources Management Journal 13(1), 5 (2000)
[15] Butler, T., Murphy, C.: An exploratory study on IS capabilities and assets in a small to medium software enterprise. Journal of Information Technology 23, 330–344 (2008)
[16] Egbu, C., Hari, S., Renukappa, S.: Knowledge management for sustaintable competitiveness in small and medium surveying practice. Structural Survey 23(1), 7 (2005)
[17] Hussain, I., Si, S., Ahmed, A.: Knowledge Management for SMEs in Developing Countries. Journal of Knowledge Management Practice 11(2) (2010)
[18] Rehman, M., et al.: Implemention of Knowledge Management in Small and Medium Enterprises. Journal of Knowledge Management Practice 11(1) (2010)
[19] Sparrow, J.: Knowledge Management in Small Firms. Knowledge and Process Management 8(1), 3 (2001)
[20] Supyuenyong, V., Islam, N., Kulkarni, U.: Influence of SME characteristics on Knowledge Management Processes. Journal of Entreprise Information Management 22(1/2), 63–80 (2009)
[21] Zevallos, E.: Micro, Pequeñas y Medianas empresas en América Latina. Revista de la CEPAL 79, 18 (2003)
[22] Dayan, R., Evans, S.: KM your way to CMMI. Journal of knowledge Management 10(1) (2006)
[23] Kruger, C., Snyman, M.: Formulation of strategig knowledge management maturity model. OpenUP, Departament of Informatión and Knowledge Management. University of Johannesburg (2007)
[24] Ramanujan, S., Kesh, S.: Comparison of Knowledge Management and CMM/CMMI Implementation. Journal of American Academy of Business 4 (2004)
[25] Chen, Z., Zhu, Z., Xie, H.: Measuring intellectual capital: a new model and empirical study. Journal of Intellectual Capital 5(1), 195 (2004)
[26] Vandaie, R.: Developing a Framework to describe the interaction of Social and Intellectual Capital in Organizations. Journal of Knowledge Management Practice 8(1) (2007)
[27] Moon, Y., Kim, H.: A Model for the Value of Intellectual Capital. Canadian Journal of Administrative Sciences 23(3), 253 (2006)
[28] Wong, K., Aspinwall, E.: An Empirical study of the important factors for knowledge-management adption in the SME sector. Journal of Knowledge Management 9(3) (2005)
[29] Al-Alawi, A., Al-Marzooqi, N., Mohammed, Y.: Organizational culture an knowledge sharing: critical success factors. Journal of Knowledge Management 11(2), 22–42 (2007)
[30] Bontis, N., Serenko, A.: A causal model of human capital antecedents and consequents in the financial services industry. Journal of Intellectual Capital 10(1), 16 (2009)
[31] Bratianu, C., Orzea, I.: Tacit Knowledge Sharing in Organizational Knowledge Dynamics. Journal of Knowledge Management Practice 11(2) (2010)

[32] Lai, M., Lee, G.: Relationships of organizational culture toward knowledge activities. Business Process Management Journal 13(2), 306–322 (2007)

[33] Staplehurst, J., Ragsdell, J.: Knowledge Sharing in SMEs: A Comparison of two case Study Organisations. Journal of Knowledge Management Practice 11(1) (2010)

[34] Water, N., Beruvides, M.: An empirical Study Analysing Tradicional Work Schemes versus Work Teams. Engineering Management Journal 21(4), 9 (2009)

[35] Bontis, N., Fitz-enz: Intellectual Capital ROI: a causal map of human capital antedents and consequents. Journal of Intellectual Capital 3(3) (2002)

[36] Chen, L.: What Individual-level Antecedents influence Knowledge Management Effectiveness. Journal of Knowledge Management Practice 10(2) (2009)

[37] Abdulgader, F.: Impact Assessment of I/S Technology utilization on Knowledge Management Creation and Conversión: An Empirical study in Jordania Universities. Journal of Knowledge Management Practice 9(1) (2008)

[38] Casalet, M., González, L.: Las Tecnologías de la Información en las Pequeñas y Medianas Empresas Mexicanas. Scripta Nova revista Electrónica de Geografía y Ciencias Sociales VIII(170) (2004)

[39] Sattar Chaudhry, A., Ainah Ali, N., Iman Abadi, D.: Exploiting the potencial of Intranet for Managing Knowledge ini Organisations. Journal of Knowledge Management Practice 9(2) (2008)

[40] Ehms, K., Langen, M.: Holistic Development of Knowledge Management with KMMM. Knowledge Management & Business Transformation 8 (2002)

# Multi-rep: An e-Learning Reputation System Aggregating Information from Heterogeneous Sources

Alessandro Grande[1], Andrea Sterbini[1], and Marco Temperini[2]

[1] Computer Science, Sapienza University of Rome,
Via Salaria. 113, 00198 Rome, Italy
[2] Computer and System Science, Sapienza University of Rome,
Via Ariosto. 25, 00185 Rome, Italy
`alessandro.grande@gmail.com,`
`sterbini@di.uniroma1.it, marte@dis.uniroma1.it`

**Abstract.** Reputation systems are used both as a motivational and an assessment tool in cooperative and classic e-Learning. They can prove useful in accompanying learners along the paths of their didactic activities, by fostering their involvement in the socio-cooperative didactic game. A problem arises, though, when learners (and teachers) participate in different web systems and possibly in different reputation systems, as it is the case when the learners are in proper e-learning systems, such as Moodle, and/or blogs, forums, or wikis. Then, the difficulties in computing reputation, across heterogeneous platforms, may overcome the teacher, and eventually force her towards the use of a single system. We present the initial work done and the design of Multi-Rep, a reputation aggregator, able to collect data from heterogeneous sources, by tracking the participation actions of learners across diverse e-learning tools, and compute the related reputation. Being able to deal with different reputation algorithms and to merge the results of students' interaction in several arenas, appears to be a key factor in allowing more freedom for teacher and students (who can use a wider array of socio-collaborative tools). Moreover, we want to easily define different roles for the students depending on their reputation, so that we can empower some of them (e.g. letting them be co-tutors or peer teachers), rewarding their involvement with higher capabilities/responsibilities, and thus recognizing their important role in the cooperative didactic game.

**Keywords:** Reputation systems in e-learning, multiple-source reputation systems, Student empowerment.

## 1 Introduction and Motivations

Reputation is used in a variety of applications, related to the support of web communities' interaction. It e-commerce and recommender systems it is used as a means to establish and maintain mutual trust [1]; moreover, both in e-learning and in social communities, reputation can help showing how much a user's participation is valuable to the community goals [2,3,4,5,6]. In these contexts, higher reputation levels give recognition to the good work done, and reputation functions as both a motivational tool to "content producers", and a recommendation tool to "content

M.D. Lytras et al. (Eds.): WSKS 2011, CCIS 278, pp. 129–134, 2013.

consumers": while the former may feel rewarded by their participation's prominence, the latter can be supported while selecting their best valued information in the system.

On the other hand, the structure and the management of reputation is usually quite tightly connected with the features and organization of the system at hand: computation and exploitation of reputation in a system, basing on data coming from another system, may reveal an hard tasks for systems developers, let alone systems managers and users. In the past we have introduced a reputation-based e-learning system (SOCIALX) to help students sharing their solutions to assignments, and to involve them in cooperative learning, by discussing their homeworks, reusing them and looking for better solutions and/or for mistakes [7]. The leaning activities in our system are not particularly specific to discipline or type of resources to be produced; this gives the system a wide applicability, yet it still lacks the extensibility that can be obtained by connecting it to other cooperative e-learning systems or to other Web 2.0 tools. Basically from this observation we were convinced of the usefulness of extracting the reputation module from SOCIALX and building a more comprehensive and modular reputation system, able to support merging and using of the various heterogeneous sources that are presently available. In this paper we present the design and first implementation of the mentioned modular system, which is called Multi-Rep. Multi-Rep is able to collects the learner's actions from a variety of e-learning and collaborative systems (which we call *the joining systems*), and to allow for 1) computing the user's reputation out of the wider picture provided collectively by those systems and 2) provide the joining systems with the possibility to adapt their behavior and services to such wider definition of reputation.

## 2    A Bouquet of Sources for Reputation

Different collaborative and e-learning systems use rather different models to compute the user's reputation: those systems may have different educational and collaborative strategies, and the very structure and organization of the user's contributions may vary widely (ranging, for instance, from notes and observations to well structured documents, from questions to answers, from informative essays to solutions to due homeworks). In the following a set of such systems is examined.

ⴰ    **DLDE** (Digital Library and Digital Education): the reputation in DLDE is user-driven, and it is designed to recognize and to encourage the participation of the students, seen both as consumers and producers of information. To this aim, DLDE rewards the production of good quality documents, blog posts, evaluations and interactions, by weighting the various activities in the system. The users' reputation is computed as the sum of a SystemScore (capturing her competency in doing the available activities) and of a CollaborationScore (capturing interactions with others through the exchange of documents, their evaluation and thus their perceived utility). See [6] for more details.

ⴰ    **Wikipedia**: the reputation in Wikipedia is content-driven, i.e. it depends only on the work done by the contributors by adding/editing content to the wiki. Users do not grade other users or documents, but obtain their reputation through their edits. The wiki is in general very resilient to disruption, first because the removal of information affects only the reputation of the disruptor, and second, because the ratio between people improving the wiki and disruptors is high.

Documents are ranked depending on their change history (i.e. the document quality increment depends on the quantity of text remaining after an edit and on the editor's reputation). See [8] for more details.

⋏     **CELS** (Collaborative E-Learning System): In CELS the user's contributions are ranked by using a modified PageRank® algorithm, designed to weight the documents more when they are highly referenced by others and when the people referencing the document has higher reputation. On the other side, the user's reputation depends on the rank of her documents. Moreover, an expiration mechanism is introduced to weight more a newer contribution [5].

The **SocialX** reputation system was designed to collect the student's interactions (forum posts, answers, submission of solutions, others' solutions marks, self judgment, reusing of solutions, and some more) in a series of learning indicators:

○     **involvement**: a qualification of the active participation in the system. It can be measured by the number of contributions submitted by the student (posted solutions, posed questions, given grades, propriety and extension of judgments);

○     **usefulness**: how the learner's work is beneficial to others in the system (such as the reuse of learner's solutions, and the appreciation of her/his questions);

○     **competence**: an appraisal of the skills shown by the learner (deriving from the grades and judgments coming from peer students and from the teacher;

○     **judgment**: how well the student has evaluated other's solutions, questions, answers and products (with respect to the teacher's grades and evaluations)

○     **self-judgment**: how well the student has evaluated her/his own answers and products (with respect to the teacher's grades and evaluations);

○     **active critical thinking**: a measure of the conceptual work issued to understand and critically appraise others' work, in order to modify, reuse, and start from such work (such as when a solution is the first produced for a problem, or is the correction of another).

A general multiple-source reputation system, able to manage the various interpretations of reputation shown in the above systems, and to integrate them so to provide a feedback to such systems, would 1) relieve the teacher from the constraints imposed by being forced to use only one e-learning tool, and 2) empower the learner according to her merits, entitling her to further roles in the system depending on the reputation gained through the learning activities performed. We designed the initial version of the Multi-Rep system to make the following characteristics available:

⋏     it is interfaced with the platforms' databases; it imports users ids and activities;

⋏     all the evaluations/marks expressed by the users (teacher included) for the activities and the documents submitted are collected

⋏     the evaluations can be filtered with various strategies

⋏     for each system, the indexes of the reputation schema are computed

⋏     the facets are aggregated as the student's reputation in one system

⋏     roles can be defined with conditions to be met to activate new capabilities for the student, see figure 1 (yet, the activation of roles is manual)

⋏     the different reputations for the different intervening systems are aggregated

⋏     in particular, the granularity of the reputation can be computed both at course, at single system and at overall (all systems) level.

## 3    Design of Multi-rep

As we have described earlier, diverse reputations reflect different social strategies that focus on different goals. A general unified reputation system, to emulate and/or merge other reputation schemas in a single reputation, is designed through a unified description of the different entities and actions available in the intervening systems:

- users         (students, teachers, tutors ...)
- documents  (posts, activities, solutions, questions, files ...)
  - o    documents have one or more authors
- actions       (grade, edit, delete, ask, answer, comment, best, offtopic ...)
  - o    actions are made by a user on a document
- roles         (guest, student, tutor, assistant, teacher, ...)
  - o    roles define the set of capabilities for a given reputation level and tag
- facets        (competence, participation, ...)
  - o    indicators capturing une aspect of the user's behavior
- tags          (math, physics, derivative, automa, ...)
  - o    keywords associated to documents, identify related sets of documents

**Actions' Weight Depending from Reputation:** The SocialX reputation definition was not recursive (i.e. the weights of the user's actions did not depend from her current reputation), while it is common to consider an action more or less important depending on the student's usefulness to the group, i.e. on her current reputation. We enhance the computation to allow dependency of action weights from the current reputation levels. To avoid recursion and to radically simplify the computation we update the user's reputation only once a day, thus making it dependent only onto the previous day's values and the last day activities.

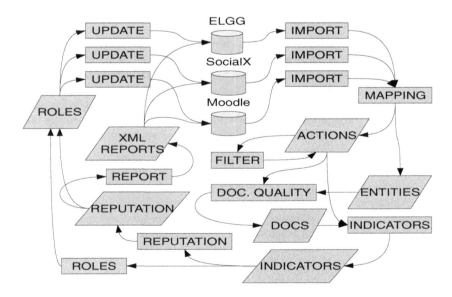

**Fig. 1.** Multi-Rep structure: modules and data flow

**Reputation granularity and roles:** The granularity of the reputation (in our current system being computed at course/system/overall levels) should be more detailed, allowing the teacher to use the reputation as an assessment index for the single topics of the course [9]. To this aim, e-learning activities should be tagged with appropriate keywords. Reputation stemming from the actions on such e-learning activities will, then, be indexed by tag.

**Students empowerment:** When a student has shown competence/participation on a given topic/tag, a prompt recognition for the good work done is imperative, e.g. by making her a tutor in the related learning activities (allowing for deeper involvement). To this aim a suitable set of XML reports is produced, to be processed by the joining systems and to enable more functionality when given reputation levels are reached.

Multi-Rep is built by the following modules (see Fig. 1):

- an **import** module, specific for each intervening system, to query the system's databases and to extract the base entity tables and the last day's actions,
- a **mapping** module, to map corresponding entities in different systems,
- a **filtering** module, to normalize the student's actions/grades if needed,
- a **document quality** module, updating the documents' importance in the system depending on the actions and on the current reputation of the actors,
- a **indicators** module, aggregating documents and actions to update the reputation indicators for each user,
- a **reputation** module, computing one or more of the available reputation schemes by merging indicators,
- a **roles** module, updating the enabled roles of the students depending on the reputation reached in each course topic (tag),
- a **report** module, producing the XML reputation reports, to be used both for display and to adapt the behavior of the intervening system,
- a **update** module, updating the user roles in the intervening systems.

Currently, we have ready the extraction modules for the systems Moodle, ELGG and SOCIALX. To comprise a further system into Multi-Rep one should:

- analyze the system's database and write a Java class for a new extraction module, defining the mappings from the DB internal representation to the various XML descriptions of entities and actions, used by the other modules,
- if needed, define the student's roles and the corresponding reputation levels to be reached to unlock more capabilities/responsibilities,
- define a mapping between e-learning activities and tags if not yet in the system)
- define the update module to automatically apply roles to the system.

## 4    Conclusions

We have presented the design of Multi-Rep, a unified reputation system to manage heterogeneous sources. Currently we are in the process of:

⅄  standardizing the description of the student's interaction (the actions), to make easier the construction of the extraction modules,
⅄  implementing the remaining parts of the above mentioned design,
⅄  designing the report module so that Multi-Rep can be used as a **web-service**, to be easily integrated into other systems.

   In a near future we would like to:

⅄  declaratively describe the mappings between events in the intervening systems and actions in the Multi-Rep action language.
⅄  Create a gui to make easier the definition of new reputation schemas.

# References

1. Vu, L., Papaioannou, T.G., Aberer, K.: Synergies of Different Reputation Systems: Challenges and Opportunities. In: Proc. World Congress on Privacy, Security, Trust and the Management of e-Business, pp. 218–226 (2009), doi:10.1109/CONGRESS.2009.8

2. Jin, F., Niu, Z., Zhang, Q., Lang, H., Qin, K.: A User Reputation Model for DLDE Learning 2.0 Community. In: Buchanan, G., Masoodian, M., Cunningham, S.J. (eds.) ICADL 2008. LNCS, vol. 5362, pp. 61–70. Springer, Heidelberg (2008)

3. Wei, W., Lee, J., King, I.: Measuring credibility of users in an e-learning environment. In: Proc. 16th Int. Conf. on World Wide Web, pp. 1279–1280. ACM, New York (2007)

4. Weller, M.: The distance from isolation: Why communities are the logical conclusion in e-learning. Computers & Education 49 (2007)

5. Yang, S., Zhao, J., Zhang, X., Zhao, L.: Application of PageRank Technique in Collaborative Learning. In: Leung, E.W.C., Wang, F.L., Miao, L., Zhao, J., Kleinberg, R.D. (eds.) WBL 2008. LNCS, vol. 5328, pp. 102–109. Springer, Heidelberg (2008)

6. Jin, F., Niu, Z., Zhang, Q., Lang, H., Qin, K.: A User Reputation Model for DLDE Learning 2.0 Community. In: Buchanan, G., Masoodian, M., Cunningham, S.J. (eds.) ICADL 2008. LNCS, vol. 5362, pp. 61–70. Springer, Heidelberg (2008), doi:10.1007/978-3-540-89533-6_7

7. Sterbini, A., Temperini, M.: SocialX: Reputation Based Support to Social Collaborative Learning Through Exercise Sharing and Project Teamwork. International Journal of Information Systems and Social Change (IJISSC) 2(1) (2011)

8. Adler, B.T., De Alfaro, L.: A Content-Driven Reputation System For Wikipedia. In: Proceedings of the 16th International Conference on World Wide Web (2007)

9. De Marsico, M., Sterbini, A., Temperini, M.: The Definition of a Tunneling Strategy between Adaptive Learning and Reputation-based Group Activities. In: IEEE International Conference on Advanced Learning Technologies, ICALT 2011 (2011) (to appear)

# Current Trends and Difficulties in Knowledge-Based e-Health Systems

Katarzyna Ewa Pasierb, Tomasz Kajdanowicz, and Przemysław Kazienko

Institute of Informatics, Wrocław University of Technology
Wyb.Wyspiańskiego 27, 50-370 Wrocław, Poland
{katarzyna.pasierb,tomasz.kajdanowicz,kazienko}@pwr.wroc.pl

**Abstract.** discussion on matters arising from encountered problems while designing and introducing e-health systems is presented in this paper. In particular, some difficulties in the adaption of ICT to e-health systems have been emphasised. Additionally, the future vision of healthcare evolution by means of information technology is analysed. Questions which arose as to the main challenges for healthcare systems were both technological and non-technological.

**Keywords:** e-health, e-healthcare system, medical information system, knowledge-based system, telemedicine, electronic medical record (EMR), electronic health record (EHR).

## 1    Introduction

E-Health is facilitating access to healthcare by utilising Information and Communication Technologies (ICT) tools and services for health. E-health refers to structured and managed services including: electronic health (medical) records (EHR / EMR), telemedicine (telehealth), Healthcare Information Systems, mHealth (mobile health), Connected Health. Also a new term emerged from e-health in terms of web 2.0 services: health 2.0.

Despite the economic downturn, the use of ICT services, such as mobile phones and the Internet, continues to increase worldwide (Fig. 1) [1]. High-speed mobile Internet access in an increasing number of countries will further raise the number of Internet users, especially in the developing world. It may break the barrier of high quality of data traffic medium and from an e-health viewpoint - medical services would be available for more and more people worldwide.

Medical information systems involve subsystems containing among others patient information, reporting tools, decision support systems and clinical scheduling. Due to the highly complex and enormous nature of collected medical data, medical information systems should comply with basic and well-proven trends of data management. It considers all available medical resources in context of data acquisition, storage, retrieval and further processing and utilisation. As acquisition, storage and retrieval of data are providing only the platform for operational activities, the major focus on knowledge-based e-health systems should deal with extended processing, analysis and reasoning. The basics of such operations include

M.D. Lytras et al. (Eds.): WSKS 2011, CCIS 278, pp. 135–140, 2013.

functionalities providing reporting and data mining analysis. As presented in Fig. 2, information systems overall should be extended with new abilities incrementally. Knowledge-based systems benefit mainly from advanced data mining tasks: statistical analysis, extraction and prediction.

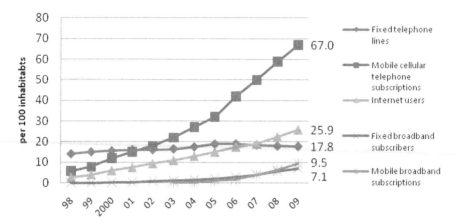

**Fig. 1.** The mobile miracle, based on ITU World Telecommunication/ICT Indicators database [1]

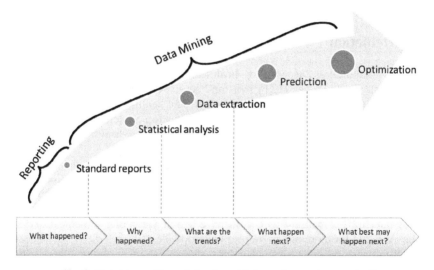

**Fig. 2.** The stages of knowledge-based information systems maturity

We can distinguish a range of services that combines contemporary ICT from traditional methods and delivers:

1) technologies supporting patient self-care and necessary education,
2) patient-provider and provider-provider communication,
3) electronic data storage and data sharing across providers,

4) systems that support decisions made every day by doctors and nurses, pharmacists,

5) technologies that combine all of the applications above [2].

Finally, there is growing awareness of the importance of evaluating the use and impact of information systems. Both barriers and facilitators exist regarding the successful implementation of e-health services.

## 2    Difficulties

Nowadays we can note a growing pressure to provide management information, control operating costs, facilitate quality management and improve patient safety. The Institute of Medicine estimates that about 98,000 deaths occur each year due to medical errors [3]. Lyytinen and Lyytinen and Hirschheim in 80' reported a 50% failure rate for information systems with a suggestion that technical problems were the underlying cause [2].

The success of implementation and utilisation of knowledge-based systems depends on integrating the computer system into a complex organisational setting. The assessment of organizational environment is based on a measure of technology compatibility which plays an important role in the adoption of ICT. Also any errors made in the transition to new technologies are less acceptable in sectors other than healthcare (severe and irreversible consequences). In spite of technical problems Lyytinen and Lyytinen and Hirschheim enumerated several causes of failure in information systems implementation. Mainly these are: problems with format and content of the data, user problems related to skills, competence and motivations [2, 4]. They also mention organisational difficulties. For example, in the United States the electronic medical record (EMR) which stores health information to assist health professionals with decision-making and treatment, was used by only 20-25% of physicians in the ambulatory care setting, and by only 5% of all hospitals for computerised treatment entry, while in the UK and New Zealand this rate was above 50% [5, 6].

Evaluating information systems requires not only an understanding of computer technology, but also an understanding of the social and behavioural processes that affect and are affected by usage of e-health applications that changes people's lifestyle, e.g. in attitude towards healthcare and in technology readiness [7].

## 3    Trends

Current visions of innovation in healthcare systems identify both an approach to join different technological sectors as well as the need for technological platforms. Main technological challenges include bioinformatics, DNA/protein sensors, self-powered micro and nanosystems, standards and interoperability [8], and furthermore, data protection, enhanced security, where more than one layer should be covered by the security mechanisms in order to achieve high quality protection of the e-healthcare system [9].

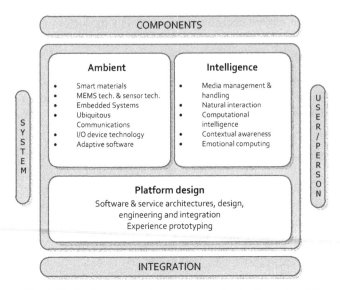

**Fig. 3.** Technology research requirements for AmI based on [8]

One of the topics that have so far received much attention is the creation and development of the/a patient personalised interface. It uses Medical/Patient/Health Records (EMR, EPR, EHR) which should be always available for processing and protected from unprivileged access. These will have to be accessible from mobile devices. It is for this reason that modelling medical records and simulation of complex systems need to be performed. This is crucial because EMRs can provide lifelong clinical information and can be used by professionals. They should be coordinated with the help of applications such as calendars for event-planning and communication services, and in fact all activities around patient management.

Another point to be discussed is knowledge management. An ongoing challenge is how to integrate standalone information repositories into a single logical repository.

Also non-technological challenges have to be solved. For example, the equal participation of users needs to be ensured [5]. A holistic approach to the non-technological aspects concerns aspects affecting society at large and healthcare systems in particular, e.g. political commitment, financial resources and liability of healthcare providers [10]. By way of illustration follow the case of Thailand [11].

One of the proposed ideas in Europe is that of Ambient Intelligence (AmI) designated for information society where the emphasis is on user-friendliness, efficient and distributed service support, and support for human interactions will allow healthcare to go beyond the simple provision of e-doctors [10]. The value of any ICT is fundamentally linked to the ability to share that information and connect with other users. These ideas are included in the European concept of AmI:

"The 'Ambient Care' environment is a responsive and proactive environment that enables easy participation of the individual in their own healthcare management, including communication with professional carriers, friends, family and the wider community. It will enable remote monitoring of activity and physical well-being and will include people with physical disabilities" [8].

There are a number of research domains for which significant progress is expected in order to develop further and realise the AmI vision (Fig. 3). For instance free software and open source endeavours in e-health should be encouraged by authorities. Besides, there is a need to share knowledge and find methods to evaluate the impact of investments [12].

Nowadays development of e-health services is also aimed at GRID-based applications and technologies around Geographic Information Systems working with location-based services [13]. In this context data mining and expert systems are used for knowledge extraction.

# 4     Conclusions

The healthcare sector is increasingly becoming a knowledge-based community that depends fundamentally on knowledge management activities to improve the quality services. As outlined in this report, a systemic approach to innovation in e-health needs to be connected with a holistic approach to the non-technological aspect. E-health will facilitate the provision of information at the right time, and support decision-making and knowledge management when making diagnoses. In parallel with these processes the development of a common open source base should take place. The objective of future endeavours is to integrate processes of normalisation by working on standards, paying attention to enabling ICT knowledge transfer by diminishing organisational and financial obstacles.

# References

1. Measuring the Information Society. Executive Summary, International Telecommunication Union (ITU-D) (2010) ISBN 92-61-13111-5
2. Anderson, J., Aydin, C.: Evaluating the Organizational Impact of Healthcare Information Systems. Introduction, Health Informatics. Springer, Heidelberg (2005)
3. Sartipi, K., Najafi, M., Kazemzadeh, R.S.: Data and Mined-Knowledge Interoperability in eHealth Systems. In: Giannopoulou, E.G. (ed.) Data Mining in Medical and Biological Research. InTech (2008) ISBN: 978-953-7619-30-5
4. Murray, et al.: Why is it difficult to implement e-health initiatives? A qualitative study. Implementation Science 6(6) (2011)
5. Jha, A.K., Ferris, T.G., Donelan, K., DesRoches, C., Shield, A., Rosenbaum, S., Blumenthal, D.: How Common Are Electronic Health Records in the United States? A Summary of the Evidence. Health Affairs, Web Exclusive, 496–507 (2006)
6. Anderson, J., Aydin, C. (eds.): Evaluating the Organizational Impact of Healthcare Information Systems. Research and Evaluation: Future Directions, Health Informatics. Springer, Heidelberg (2005)
7. del Hoyo-Barbolla, E., Carisio, E., Ortega-Portillo, M., Arredondo, M.T.: Results of a Tailored Communication Framework Through E-Health. In: Harris, D. (ed.) HCII 2007 and EPCE 2007. LNCS (LNAI), vol. 4562, pp. 269–278. Springer, Heidelberg (2007)
8. IST Advisory Group, From vision to reality, for participation – in society & business. In: Riva, G., Vatalaro, F., Davide, F., Alcañiz, M. (eds.) Ambient Intelligence, pp. 45–68. IOS Press (2005)

9. Marković, M.: On Secure e-Health Systems. In: Domingo-Ferrer, J., Franconi, L. (eds.) PSD 2006. LNCS, vol. 4302, pp. 360–374. Springer, Heidelberg (2006)
10. eHealth in 2010: Realising a Knowledge-based Approach to Healthcare in the EU – Challenges for the Ambient Care System. European Foresight publications, EUR 21486 EN
11. Tangcharoensathien, V., Wibulpholprasert, S., Nitayaramphong, S.: Knowledge-based changes to health systems: the Thai experience in policy development. Bull. World Health Organ. 82(10), 750–756 (2004)
12. Rahimi, B., Vimarlund, V.: Methods to Evaluate Health information Systems in Healthcare Settings: A Literature Review. Journal of Medical Systems 31(5), 397–432 (2007)
13. Varshney, U.: Pervasive healthcare. Computer 36(12), 138–140 (2003)

# Filtering Learning Objects Repositories by a Didactic Search Engine

Carla Limongelli[1] , Filippo Sciarrone[2,3], and Marco Temperini[2]

[1] Department of Information and Automation, University RomaTRE, Roma, Italy
limongel@dia.uniroma3.it
[2] OpenInformatica srl, E-learning Division – Pomezia, Italy
f.sciarrone@openinformatica.org
[3] Department of Computer and System Sciences, Sapienza University, Roma, Italy
marte@dis.uniroma1.it

**Abstract.** Nowadays, thanks to the Internet, the request for distance learning is increasing. Private companies and public institutions are very sensitive to the saving of costs that such type of education could implicate, i.e., with no limits in time and place. Besides, the results obtained by this kind of learning are comparable to those reached by the classic in-presence lessons. Consequently, instructional designers need didactic instruments to build courses in a rapid way, especially if they would build their courses starting from learning objects already posted into Learning Object Repositories by other peers. Our work proposes a system, at a very early stage of development, with the aim to help instructional designers to find and retrieve learning objects suitable for their courses, starting from the classic conceptual map of the course to be built. The system contains an OLAP module to let teachers to drill-down into concepts as well.

**Keywords:** E-learning, Learning Objects, Business Intelligence.

## 1 Introduction

Nowadays, the request for distance learning is surging thanks to the new internet-based technologies: open source Learning Management Systems (LMSs), such as Moodle[1] or ATutor[2], and Web-based Educational Systems (WES), either generic (such as LecompS [1]) or AI-based (such as BLITS [2] or HyperCase [3]) empower teacher and learner with convenient and augmented instructional opportunities, and support an increasing demand for them. At the same time, the development and application of standards for e-learning is originating wide availability of Learning Objects (Los) Repositories (LORs) on the internet, providing a growing portfolio of structured learning material. In this respect, one standing problem in the area of web-based e-learning is how to support teachers' capability to retrieve and select effectively and efficiently learning materials appropriate for their educational

---

[1] http://www.moodle.org
[2] http://atutor.ca

M.D. Lytras et al. (Eds.): WSKS 2011, CCIS 278, pp. 141–145, 2013.

purposes. Business Intelligence (BI) has been recently shown to be suitable to approach that problem [4]. Here we present a system to help instructional designers to configure courses, at its very early stage of development, which, starting from the conceptual map of a course, i.,e., Novak Maps [5], produced by the instructional designer, acts as a didactic search engine, retrieving just those LOs from standard LORs (see  the SLOOP project as an example of this kind of repositories [6]). The main goal of the system is to  help instructional designers to configure a course on a particular learning domain, through a sort of *Extract-Transform-Load* (ETL) process based on intelligent software agents bringing back new LOs retrieved from LORs. Besides, through a classic OLAP engine teachers can drill-down into concepts and LOs, using the open source OLAP engine PENTAHO[3], an approach already used in [4] where instructional designers could be helped to select LOs. In [4] teachers can drill down into some concept dimensions where facts table were composed by the number of LOs tagged with the IEEE-LOM tag matching the ones proposed by teachers in the conceptual map of the course. Here we propose to overcome the limitations of that system by means of a didactic searching engine, based on intelligent software agents that surf LORs bringing back useful didactic material. This system is currently at its very early stage of development. This paper is structured as follows. Section 2 shows the system design; Section 3 reports on an example of the use of the BI engine, while in Section 4 conclusions are drawn.

## 2    The System Design

In this section we show design issues of the system, basing on a description of the process that brings instructional designers to the production of a course. Then the architecture of the system is shown.

### 2.1    Building a Course

A course is usually made up as a sequence of LOs, selected from a wide repository in order to respond to learner's learning goals. Such a selection is performed by the instructional designer, as a direct application of the learning objectives and teaching strategies stated by the teacher. So the teacher is required to design a clear conceptual map, for instance using the open source tool *CMAP tools*[4]. Then the elements of that conceptual map are linked to learning goals, which are in turn mapped over the actual learning material. Novak maps [5] allow teachers to express their didactic needs in a very simple way, as shown in Figure 1. The whole process is shown in Figure 2, from where the efficacy of a BI approach to the selection f learning material can be appreciated: in particular the instructional designer can select LOs from the local LOR through the OLAP engine, using drill-down and roll-up functions performed into concepts linked to the appropriate didactic material. One advantage of this organization would be that the instructional designers can focus their work rather exclusively on didactic aspects, than on technical aspects, such as learning objects authoring.

---

[3]  Pentaho BI Suite: http://www.pentaho.com

[4]  http://cmap.ihmc.us/

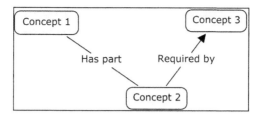

**Fig. 1.** An example of Novak Map

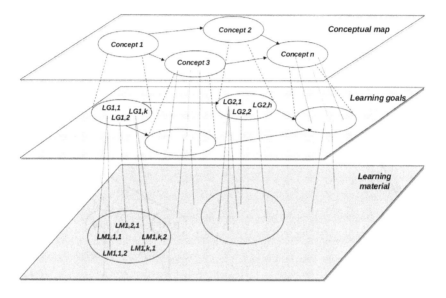

**Fig. 2.** Building a course

## 2.2    Functional Architecture

The general architecture of the system is shown in Figure 3. The instructional designer interacts with the system for building her own course monitoring or participating into the activation of several modules.

- The CMAP TOOLS module provides teachers with an environment supporting the definition of the conceptual map of the aimed course. The output of the module is the actual semantic net of the course, as intended by the teacher: it is represented as a direct graph where the nodes are the concepts to learn and the arcs are the relationships among them.
- The *Didactic Expander* module produces the $n$ learning goals $LG_1$, $LG_2$, …$LG_n$ corresponding to the $m$ concepts $c_1$, $c_2$, … $c_m$, as shown in Fig. 2.
- The *Didactic Query Expander* expands the learning goals in order to obtain $p$ query terms: $q_1$, $q_2$, …, $q_p$, that will play as the input for the next module.
- The *Didactic Search Engine* launches $q$ *Didactic Search Agents,* whose goal is to retrieve LOs from the visited LORs. In particular, the specific work

protocol of the Didactic Search Engine is to launch various software agents with the task of retrieving, analyzing and bringing back (links to) LOs relevant for the course, i.e., adhering to the conceptual requirements specified by the teacher.

-    The retrieved LOs are stored in a local LOR (labeled LOCAL DIDACTIC REPOSITORY in Fig. 3).

-    Finally, the OLAP engine provides users with the capability of analyzing the LOs stored in the local LOR. In particular, through *multidimensional analysis*, instructional designers can perform a deep analysis of retrieved learning material.

In the presented framework, the modules work through software Intelligent Agents that go through the LOs stored in the internet and allow to match them against the concepts specified by the teacher by the concept map. In that, the software agents do actually behave as real users, that filter learning material in search of LOs suitable for their own use.

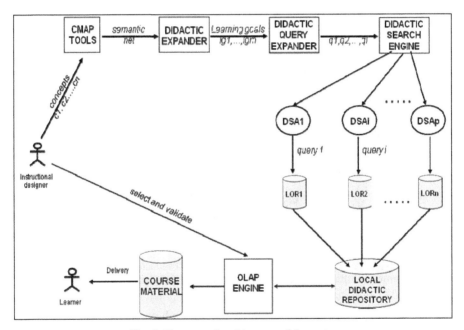

**Fig. 3.** The general architecture of the system

## 3    Conclusion

We have shown the design a novel system, enabling the support to teachers and instructional designers in the process of development of courses. The courses are made up of learning objects possibly selected from repositories throughout the internet, and such selection is driven by the conceptual specification given by the teacher about the learning and teaching strategies and aims of the course. The system is based on a didactic search engine capable of matching the specified concepts with the contents of the approached LORs. Then, by means of an OLAP engine, the instructional designer can configure the actual course content, by exploiting classic functions to analyzing data, such as drill down and roll-up. We are in an early stage of development, planning to implement all the system in the very next future.

# References

[1] Limongelli, C., Sciarrone, F., Temperini, M., Vaste, G.: The Lecomps5 Framework for Personalized Web-Based Learning: a Teacher's Satisfaction Perspective. Computers in Human Behaviour (2011) (to appear)

[2] Micarelli, A., Gasparetti, F., Sciarrone, F.: A Web-based Training System for Business Letter Writing. Knowledge-Based Systems 22, 287–291 (2009)

[3] Micarelli, A., Sciarrone, F., Gasparetti, F.: A Case-Based Approach to Adaptive Hypermedia Navigation. Int. J. of Web-based Learning and Teaching Technologies. Special Issue on Adaptive and Intelligent Web-based Educational Systems 4(1), 35–53 (2009)

[4] Limongelli, C., Sciarrone, F., Starace, P., Temperini, M.: An Ontology-Driven OLAP System to Help Teachers in the Analysis of Web Learning Object Repositories. Information Systems Management 27(3), 198–206 (2010)

[5] Novak, J.D.: Concept Mapping: A Useful Tool for Science Education. Journal of Research in Science Teaching 27(10), 937–949 (1990)

[6] Gentile, M., Taibi, D., Allegra, M., Fulantelli, G.: A collaborative 'open Learning Objects' management system. In: Proceedings of WSEAS - Engineering Education 2006 (EE 2006), Vouliagmeni Beach, Athens, Greece, July 11-13 (2006); Special Session: Methods and Tools for Managing Learning Objects

# Literature Review in Game-Based Learning

Miroslav Minović, Miloš Milovanović, and Dusan Starcevic

Faculty of Organizational Sciences, Laboratory for Multimedia Communications,
University of Belgrade
{mminovic,milovanovicm,starcev}@fon.rs

**Abstract.** In this paper we will give literature review related to game-based education, in first place at university, as well as analysis of existing solutions which should enable this type of eLearning. Main topic of this research will be capacity for applying modern information technologies for developing game-based learning platform. When we choose this topic, we started form the fact that there are no applied game-based eLearning systems at universities. During analysis phase, we found that more research is needed in order to improve application of games in education. At first place, these researches should cover listed problems: how to design educative games in order to achieve better learning effects; how to develop software tools to automate educative game development process; establish methods and techniques for knowledge and skills assessment utilizing educative games.

**Keywords:** Game-Based Learning, eLearning, Games, Motivation for learning.

## 1    Introduction

The first computer games appeared in the fifties of the 20th century - since then, their development has proceeded at a vertiginous speed. It was almost impossible to assume that they will become one of the dominant social phenomena, and that, in the last decade of the 20th century, the industry of computer games generate more revenue from the film industry.

The popularity of computer games led to thinking about their application in education. Games became an integral part of modern society. They are the ideal platform for presenting new content and new technology - a lot of people play computer games and accept them as a normal form of entertainment. Research shows that not only youth who play games - big part of the playing population are adults [1]. According to the report of the American Association for entertainment software (ESA - Entertainment Software Association) in 2006. The 69 percent of the U.S. population plays video or computer games. The average age of players is 33, and 25 percent are older than 50. Men make up 62% of the population [2].

Electronic games are a new mass medium, with its characteristics, as compared to the now traditional media such as books, television, film or music. In contrast to all existing media, games have the opportunity to interact, allowing the user to actively participate, not just passivly receive information. That is why the last few years we

M.D. Lytras et al. (Eds.): WSKS 2011, CCIS 278, pp. 146–154, 2013.
© Springer-Verlag Berlin Heidelberg 2013

can see more and more use of computer games for education. Educational games are social, card, or computer games that are specifically designed to teach people about a certain subject, expand concepts, reinforce development, understand an historical event or culture, or assist in the development of certain skills.

## 2    Educational Games

The paper focuses on educational computer games [3]. They combine education and entertainment in a concept known as edutainment. This concept usually assumes that users provide lessons in a fun environment recognizable: television, computer games, movies, music, websites, multimedia software and so on.

It is known that computer simulation has long been used to train civilian and military pilots. Modern flight simulation games are so highly developed that greatly surpassed the commercial software, especially in the quality of sound, graphics, and the degree of realism in general. In Germany is already working on a program very similar to computer games that simulate driving a car in the city and on the open roads. The advantage of these flights and car-simulation is that the represent a cheap way to simulate incidents and enhance response by participants. Disadvantage is that in comparison to modern computer games they reminiscent to clumsy attempts at 3D animation of the twentieth century.

There are indications that even a shooting game in first person in some areas can be used as an educational tool. Some armies take them to be cost-effective way to supplement tactical knowledge of military and anti-terrorist unit, as well as orientation and coordination skills. Many social and computer games that are not intended to be strictly educational in themselves carry a significant educational aspect. Monopoly teaches us basic principles of market economy, Microsoft's Age of Empires series, Total War games, and Civilization teach political economy, history, military theory, and even sociology and ecology. There are also many games that teach management: Transport Tycoon (management of urban and intercity transport), Railroad Tycoon (managing railway), Rollercoaster Tycoon (managing amusement park), Sim City I-IV (management of the modern city), Football Manager (managing a football club) and many others.

It is significant to mention the educational games for kids. Sales of classic toys shown a downward trend from year to year, and the kids all spend more time next to the screen. Thus, this genre of computer games is becoming extremely important. Children's educational games are educational in the true sense of the word. There are games for all ages, from those that resemble picture books in electronic format, to games like The Sims to help teenagers to cope with and resolve problems in the real world.

We decided to name the classification given by Chris Crawford, in his book 'The art of computer games' [4], published for the first time back in the 1970th year. It is a classification by type of game, and essentially cover the actual games today.

1. Games of skill and action (a. Combat game; b. Maze; c. Sports Games; d. Games blow; e. Racing Games; f. Various other games)

2. Strategy Games  (a. Adventures; b. D & D (Dungen & Dragons) game; c. War Games; d. Games of Chance; e. Educational and children's games ; f. Interpersonal games)

# 3    Development Trends

Although the use of games in education recently become a hot topic, games have always been one of the available techniques for education. Education is often the first field to test new technologies [5], and video games can be considered as a type of technology for education [6]. After several years of intensive research, during which the main focus was to attract attention to the possibility of using games in education, the situation has changed and led to wider interest in this area. Most people still believe that games can attract the attention, they can be effective and to have a place in the field of education [7].

## 3.1    Edutainment

Most of the works that attempt to link the play and education are among the edutainment category. Although the word is formed by merging the two words, education and entertainment (education and entertainment), the term is often used for each game that puts the focus on educational content. Basically it comes to placement of official educational content (mostly elementary school programs) in an environment that resembles the game. From the point of designing games, these works goes from educational content, which is later added to the logic of the game. Many authors believe that this is not good approach, and that it has negative consequences for the reputation of educational games [8,9,10,11]. This is because if the game is not well designed, it has no positive effect on motivation and engagement of players, so the effect on learning is not a positive at all [12].

## 3.2    Use of Existing Commercial Games for Training

On the other hand there are initiatives to use existing commercial games for educational purposes. Although in these games educational aspect is not taken into account during design, some of them have a rich enough model and content that can be used for education, if properly used. The two most famous examples of such games are SimCity and Civilization:

In the SimCity game, player has a mayor role, and manage the development of the city. The work presented in [13] describes the experiences of the use of this game, how it can be used for discussion on topics such as social dynamics and development. After the success of SimCity titles, appeared much more similar, with the prefix 'Sim', with a focus on economic and practical problems of management in different environments. Such games are SimFarm and SimHealth used as a tool for education, as described in [14].

Civilization is a series of games, realized as simulation games, where players manage the development of entire worlds, and infrastructure, military, research and scientific progress, which starts with an empty ground and ends with the developed world civilization [15].

Work of Barab and Squire [16] gives an overview of experience with students who were in history class used the game, and then analyze and discuss the subject. These example suggest that successful integration of commercial games in the process of education is possible. The basic advantage of this approach is low cost: the development of entirely new educational games that will be at par with commercial games is too high to be profitable, which makes access to the use of existing games very appealing [17]. On the other hand, there are limitations that may impact negatively on educational potential. One of the main disadvantages is that these games are still designed for fun, without taking a pedagogical and educational factors into account. Although realism and historical accuracy may contribute to the success of the game, every decision in which the party was threatened to be made in favor of fun at the expense of education. Some of the concepts in these games are too simplistic and can lead to erroneous conclusions, as indicated by the papers presented in this section. Therefore, this approach should always be combined with the supervision of instructors, and frequent discussions.

## 3.3    Educational Games

After a short analysis of the previous two extreme approaches, we can conclude that none of them is optimal. The main factor for success is to achieve a balance between fun and learning in the model of game design [18]. Unfortunately, this is not an easy task. Design of the game is not an exact science, primarily because of the sophisticated nature of fun [12]. However, there are plenty of successful games that have managed to achieve a given goal, and that are given to players who are not interested in themes, make them to be motivated to play the game to the end, and learn without being aware of it, playing the game. Examples of these games belong to the wide range of games, from action shooter games to strategic and logic games. Here are some interesting examples: Monkey Wrench Conspiracy – first-person shooter intended to be learning tools for the design. In the game, the player must construct their own weapons in the console that operates much like a software tool for that task. View given in [18] provides additional analysis of that game and the incredible results they achieved in terms of training as well as advertisements for a given software tool.

Virtual Leader [19] - game with a focus on learning advanced management. The game consists of a number of scenarios, representing different meetings at different levels and different subjects. The player can follow the participants at the meeting, their mood, and the ideas proposed and being discussed. The aim of the player is to present their ideas on how to be accepted and that the morale of other participants is not compromised.

Virtual UTM [20] - the player takes the role of the rector of the university, with a mission to lead the entire university, including budget management, staff, quality of teaching, research and other activities.

On the other hand, despite the existence of such successful titles, many other initiatives have not led to successful implementation of educational games. A major problem is that the high costs of developing games, and the problem of finding a balance between fun and learning, so the game is fun, interesting and educational in the same time.

Another possible approach would be modifications of existing commercial games to improve their educational value [21]. Although this approach would drastically reduce development costs, still remains the problem of finding a suitable game design for education. If the original game is engine specific, then it is a limiting factor for educational upgrading. On the other hand, when we utilize a generic engine (basically provides only low-level operations) technical requirements for development are high. Although the reduction of costs and technical requirements of educational games is desirable, however, recommendation is to use engine made specifically for the creation of educational games, which increases their pedagogical value, allowing educators to develop educational games. Such engines should be able to support creation of certain genre of games, which were described using domain-specific language developed for a particular genre. Given that these languages are specific for the domain, they would be easy to use and would allow educators to create and maintain their own educational games.

Hence, we promote using known approaches to the development of software engineering for developing software that will allow easy creation and maintenance of educational games. The first step is to determine the pedagogical features essential for the development of engine and educational games [22].

### 3.4    Games and Human Brain

Some authors argue that if the children spend a lot of time playing games while growing up, it changes the structure of their brain. According to Carsten and Beck [23]: "Time spent with the games while growing up led to the fact that their brains are differently connected than brains of people who did not play the games well enough." Similarly, [18] argues that: "the vast changes in the development of technologies in the last thirty years, of which video games are an important part, led to a dramatic and discontinuous changes the way people think, learn and process information ... The change is so great that young people today have, according to the intellectual style and preferences, a different brain than their parents and older generation".

### 3.5    Games and Types of Intelligence

It is known that different people learn in different ways and at different pace. Research shows that learning style is inheriting. Some people visualize things when they think about them, others are more oriented to the description of words. While one group of people mostly use logic, others are more likely to rely on intuition. It is known that IQ is distributed according to a bell-shaped distribution, as is also well known that IQ tests do not measure all forms of intelligence. [24] says that in fact there are seven forms of intelligence, as follows: 1. Linguistic; 2. Logical-mathematical; 3. Bodily-kinetic; 4. Spatial; 5. Musical; 6. Interpersonal; 7. Intrapersonal (directed inward, self-motivation). Different people will be interested in different types of games because of differences in their natural talents. We should not forget that people will not solve puzzles that they percieve as noise and are not given clear and known. Greater probability is that they will choose the issues they think that are likely to be solved. People with bodily-kinetic intelligence will gravitate toward sports, while those with linguistic will end up solving a crossword or Scrabble.

## 3.6    The Balance Between Motivation and Learning

Aim of game-based learning is to provide an environment that is both fun and enables the achievement of learning goals. [25,26] have identified four motivational factors in games:

1. Challenge: the structure of the game must be neither too simple nor too complicated
2. Control: A player must have a sense of manageability, that may affect the outcome of the game
3. Curiosity: for example, opportunities to explore the world in the game can lead to unexpected outcomes
4. Fantasy: the perception of participation in the imagined world.

The main challenge when designing educational games is the realization of a balance between factors that stimulate the motivation to play in a way that does not harm the learning process. Games or simulations can easily distract players in a way that is counterproductive to learning. For example, games that have a fast logic does not leave time for reflection. Games or simulations that have a very detailed and realistic visualization and audio effects can lead to memory overload of players. Also, games or simulations with rich worlds, can lead to significant activities of players, but with very little learning. The solution lies in the careful selection of motivational elements in the game in the way that they support and not interfere with the basic psychological mechanism of learning. Nicole Lazzaro has conducted research looking at people when they play games, based on which has found four groups of emotions that the players show in their facial expression: hard to have fun, easy entertaining, altered state, and human factors [27].

When we successfully resolve the issue given to us, we stimulate the brain with a dose of satisfaction [12]. If the inflow of new problems slow down, pleasure will disappear and can induce boredom. If the inflow of new problems increase through our capacity, we will not feel the satisfaction, as we will be unable to make progress.

## 3.7    State of Flow (Flow)

The time that most of the players referred to as 'being in the zone'. One of mostly cited academic definitions is one given as Csikszentmihalyi's concept of 'flow' (flow)

- is a condition in which the player enters when experiencing an absolute concentration on the task (physical, mental or both), so he lose sense of time and the outside world [28].

Lazzaro [27] calls this phenomenon 'hard fun' (hard fun).

This condition is not achieved very often, but when it happens it is a great experience. The problem is precisely match the challenges and the capabilities of the player, which is a very difficult task.

If they were in this situation, the players usually ascertained "This was really fun." If it was not the case, they can say: "... it was fun" but with less enthusiasm. Does not mean that there is no fun if there was no entry in this condition. So the fun is not a state of flow, also the state of flow can be experienced in many situations that are not fun.

### 3.8    Evaluation and Verification of Knowledge

Thibault also talks about the need for constructing a framework to test the learning through play, based on cognitive psychology, design, games, machine learning, neurobiology and theories of education. Until a unique methodology come which will be widely accepted, we will require the presence of people in the process of testing knowledge. Full automation of the test can not be expected before that [29].

Currently the knowldege verification is reduced to the traditional ways of testing and self-checking which is given to the player before and after playing the game. On the other hand, video games have the potential to change the way of how we perform tests [30]. Utilizing the games as a tool for testing knowledge, need to use conventional tests will be reduced, since knowledge verification will be integrated in the course of the game. Lecturer, or the software itself, will be able to determine whether student understood some of the material or not, based on the behavior of the players. This is the direction we should go in the future.

## 4    Conclusion

There are many open questions on the application of games in education. Van Eck [7] pointed out that research should explain why educational games are effective, and to provide practical guidance on how educational games should be successfully implemented with the aim of maximizing the educational potential. In addition to research in the filed of educational games, he pointed out the problem of how to operate different types of games and how that affect learning. For example, simple card games can be good for pattern recognition and connecting concepts, and adventure games, on the other hand, promote access to test hypotheses and solve problems.

There is still no unimpeachable evidence of the efficiency of games in the classroom, as well as educational games compared with traditional methods. Eric Klopfer, a professor at MIT says that the question: "Are games educational?" is set too wide. It is clear that some games are educational, while some are not.

Investigations are still at an early stage, but some studies are promising and demonstrate the potential benefits of applying games in education.

From the foregoing, our proposal is to develop a unified framework for development of educational games, which will define the methods, techniques and tools for production of educational games. Developing such a framework requires a multidisciplinary approach and cooperation between scientific disciplines, such as psychology, computer science, human-computer interaction. Single framework for development should resolve most of these problems, and to identify systemic approach to educational games, which would reconcile the different roles of the participants in this process. Method development should define the process of development that will include the creation of educational content, design and logic games, as well as the development of software systems, using the experience gained in each of these areas independently, in such a way as to allow the creation of effective educational games.

**Acknowledgments.** This work is part of a project "Corporate portal for employee long life learning", funded by the Ministry of science and technology Republic of Serbia, grant no: 32028.

# References

1. De Aguilera, M., Mendiz, A.: Video games and Education. Computers in Entertainment 1(1) (2003)
2. Clark, R., Mayer, R.: E-learning and the science of instruction. John Wiley & Sons, Inc. (2008)
3. Rouse, R.: Game design: theory and practice. Wordware Publishing, Plano (2001)
4. Crawford, C.: The art of computer game design (1982)
5. Cantoni, L., Di Blas, N.: Comunicazione. Teoria e pratiche. Apogeo (2006)
6. Miller, C.T.: Games: Purpose and Potential in Education. Springer Science (2008)
7. Van Eck, R.: Digital Game- Based Learning: It's Not Just the Digital Natives Who Are Restless. EDUCAUSE, 17–30 (March/April 2006)
8. Kirriemur, J., McFarlane, A.: Literature review in games and learning. NESTA Futurelab. NESTA Futurelab, Bristol (2004)
9. MacFarlane, S., Read, J.: Evaluating interactive products for and with children (2004)
10. Sim, MacFarlane: All work and no play: Measuring fun, usability, and learning in software for children. Computers and Education 46(3), 235–248 (2006)
11. Egenfeldt-nielsen, S.: Beyond Edutainment: Educational Potential of Computer Games. Continuum International Publishing Group Ltd. (2007)
12. Koster, R.: A theory of fun for game design. Paraglyph Press, Scottsdale (2005)
13. Kolson: The politics of SimCity. Political Science and Politics 29(1), 43–46 (1996)
14. Starr: Seductions of Sim. The American Prospect 2(17) (1994)
15. Bittanti, M.: Civilization: Virtual history, real fantasies. Ludilogica Press, Milan (2005)
16. Squire, Barab: Replaying history: Engaging urban underserved students in learning world history through computer simulation games. Lawrence Erlbaum Associates, Santa Monica (2004)
17. Burgos, Tattersall: Re-purposing existing generic games and simulations for e-learning. Computers in Human Behaviour 23(6), 2656–2667 (2007)

18. Prensky, M.: Digital Game-Based Learning (2001)
19. Aldrich: Simulations and the future of learning: An innovative (and perhaps revolutionary) approach to e-learning. Pfeiffer, San Francisco (2004)
20. Virtual U: Virtual U. Preuzeto sa Virtual U (2008), http://www.virtual-u.org/
21. Purushotma: Commentary: You're not studying, you're just? Language Learning & Technology 9(1), 80–96 (2005)
22. Moreno-Ger, P., Burgos, D., Martínez-Ortiz, I., Sierra, J.L., Fernández-Manjón, B.: Educational game design for online education. Computers in Human Behavior 24(6), 2530–2540 (2008)
23. Carstens, A., Beck, J.: Get Ready for the Gamer Generation. TechTrends 49(3), 22–25 (2005)
24. Howard, G.: Intelligence reframed: Multiple Intelligences for the 21st century. Basic Books (2000)
25. Malone, T.W.: Towards a theory of intrinsically motivating instruction. Cognitive Science 4, 333–369 (1981)
26. Malone, T.W., Lepper, M.R.: Learning Fun: A Taxonomy of Intrinsic Motivations for Learning. In: Snow, R., Farr, M.J., Urednici (eds.) Aptitute, Learning and Instruction: III. Conative and Affective Process Analyses, pp. 223–253 (1987)
27. Lazzaro, N.: Why We Play Games: Four Keys to More Emotion Without Story. XEODesign,® Inc. (2004)
28. Csíkszentmihályi, M.: Creativity: Flow and the Psychology of Discovery and Invention. Harper Perennial, New York (1996)
29. Thibault, A.: Assesment and The Future of Fluid Learning Environments. Presentation at Serious Game Summit, Washington, D.C (2004)
30. Smith, G., Ferguson, D.: Student attrition in mathematics e-learning. Australasian Journal of Educational Technology 21(3), 323–334 (2005)

# PRIOR-W&K: A Collaborative Tool for Decision Making in the Knowledge Society

Alberto Turón[1,2,*], Juan Aguarón[2], Jesús Cardeñosa[2], María Teresa Escobar[2], José María Moreno-Jiménez[2], José Ruiz[2], and Adrián Toncovich[2]

[1] Alberto Turón, Facultad de Economía y Empresa, Gran Vía n° 2, 50005 Zaragoza, Spain
turon@unizar.es.
[2] Grupo Decisión Multicriterio Zaragoza, Facultad de Economía y Empresa,
Universidad de Zaragoza, Gran Vía n° 2,
50005 Zaragoza, Spain
http://gdmz.unizar.es

**Abstract.** This paper presents a new module devoted to knowledge extraction and diffusion, based on a previously developed decision making tool concerning the Internet and related with the multicriteria selection of a discrete number of alternatives. Quantitative and Qualitative procedures using data and text mining methods have been employed in the extraction of knowledge. The resulting collaborative tool may be considered as the methodological support for the cognitive democracy known as e-cognocracy.

**Keywords:** Decision Making, Knowledge Society, e-Cognocracy, Knowledge Extraction, Knowledge Diffusion.

## 1 Introduction

This paper extends the software PRIOR, used as the methodological support of the democracy model known as e-cognocracy [1-4]), in order to meet the challenges and needs of the Knowledge Society. PRIOR [5, 6], developed by the Zaragoza Multicriteria Decision Making Group (http://gdmz.unizar.es) and employed in the multicriteria selection of a discrete set of alternatives, has been extended by adding two modules associated with the Internet (the Web) and the democratization of knowledge (Knowledge), two of the most important aspects of public decision making in the Knowledge Society.

Decision making is one of the essential characteristics of the human being and is the key factor of the Knowledge Society. In this context, the scientific resolution of public decision making problems should be oriented towards the education of the actors who are implicated in the resolution process, and in the decision making in general.

In order to facilitate the educational process of the individuals and, at the same time, of the society itself (social or collective intelligence), it is recommended that decision making includes the specification of the arguments that support the decisions that are taken.

---

* Corresponding author.

M.D. Lytras et al. (Eds.): WSKS 2011, CCIS 278, pp. 155–161, 2013.

The identification of these arguments is based on the analysis of the opinions provided in the e-discussion stage of the e-cognocracy's methodology by the actors involved in the decision making process (qualitative approach), and by the exploitation of the mathematical model employed in the decision making (quantitative approach).

The consideration of the e-discussion stage has led to the extension of the social software known as PRIOR-Web [7], through the incorporation of a new module aimed at the extraction and diffusion of the relevant knowledge in the problem resolution, that is to say, the identification and democratization of the arguments that support the decisions. The resulting collaborative tool, denominated as PRIOR-W&K, is outlined in this paper, the structure of which is as follows: Section 2 describes PRIOR-Web tool. Section 3 presents both the quantitative approach based on data mining techniques and used to identify the relevant messages, and the qualitative approach based on text mining techniques and used to identify the arguments that support decisions. Section 4 briefly includes some comments about the security issues associated with the use of the Web in the valuation and discussion processes followed in the PRIOR-W&K platform. Finally, Section 5 summarises the most important points discussed in the paper.

## 2     PRIOR-Web

The software PRIOR-Web [7], based in the discrete multicriteria prioritization tool PRIOR [5, 6], has been developed with the aim of providing the spatially distributed actors implicated in the resolution process of a problem with a tool for the secure incorporation of their judgments using the Internet.

PRIOR-Web was conceived to be used by means of open standards technologies, based on the World Wide Web. In this way, the decision makers need only a browser to participate in the whole process. Together with the consistency stability intervals for judgments, alternatives and criteria [8] and the secure elicitation process [9], a multiactor decision making module is provided [10], it includes the consistency consensus matrix [11, 12], the aggregation of individual preference structures [13] and graphical visualization tools [14], as well as web functionalities for the elicitation of judgments when the actors are spatially distributed.

## 3     Knowledge Extraction in PRIOR

The new module incorporated to PRIOR includes functionalities oriented to knowledge extraction and diffusion. The extraction is made by means of data and text mining tools, and the diffusion by means of graphical visualisation ones.

### 3.1     Quantitative Knowledge Extraction

We have designed a procedure [15, 16] that identifies the comments and messages included in the discussion stage of e-cognocracy [3] that support the different patterns of behaviour and changes in preferences that appear in the problem resolution stage.

By exclusively taking into account the quantitative information existing in the resolution process (the priorities of the alternatives in the two rounds and the information on comment importance), the quantitative approach identifies the arguments which support each alternative.

From the priorities of the alternatives and the quantitative information (importance, valuations and direction) associated with the message or comments under consideration, the approach determines the importance that each alternative has in the thread, following a procedure [15, 16] which synthesizes the existing information.

The procedure calculates the valuation assigned to each alternative in each discussion thread by summing up the valuation given to each alternative for each message of the thread made by a given decision maker. This valuation is obtained by multiplying the weight assigned to the message made by the decision maker and the priority given to the alternative by this same decision maker using the multicriteria decision making technique (AHP). The weight assigned to a message made by a given decision maker is calculated taking into account the importance given to the message by its author, the number of assessments received by the message, the mean assessment of the message and the mean direction of the assessments of the message.

Finally, the quantitative procedure assigns to each discussion thread the alternative with the greatest valuation. This process allows the identification of the comments and messages that support each alternative and the different patterns of behavior.

## 3.2    Qualitative Knowledge Extraction

A qualitative approach, based on text mining tools, has been used to identify the arguments embedded in these messages that support the different positions of the actors [17]. The methodology followed in the qualitative approach is based on the analysis of the different patterns that an expert defines in order to classify a message. These patterns are implemented in a text mining system that aims to emulate the lines of reasoning of the expert. The text mining system is backed by the linguistic knowledge codified in a tailor-made grammar and a specific lexical resource. Its main purpose is to ascribe each comment to the different positions identified in the resolution of the problem.

The qualitative approach follows a knowledge-based methodology. Firstly, an expert performs a manual classification of the messages, taking into account the presence of specific assertions that allow the expert to reasonably infer the participant's position underlying in the message. Next, the set of identified assertions are analyzed and codified into linguistic patterns that are implemented in a text mining system. The design and implementation of the whole process consists of the following steps:

1. *The Role of the Expert*: The expert reads the messages, classifies each according to the postulated categories, and marks up the expressions that support the proposed classification.

2. *Extraction of Patterns*: Once the expert has classified the messages and identified the supporting expressions, common features and regularities have to be identified. The key aspect for identifying patterns is the presence of expressions with

either positive or negative connotation. This work therefore requires lexical units (in particular, adjectives, nouns and verbs) to be classified as positive, negative, or neutral. The system of automatic classification mainly seeks noun and verb phrases and then assigns a global connotation to the message according to the nature of the identified expressions.

3. *Creation of the Lexical Resource*: The unique information registered in the dictionary is the grammatical category of the word. The postulated categories for the work are for open categories: verb, noun, adjective, and adverb; for functional categories: determinant, conjunction, preposition, and pronoun; and, finally, two ad-hoc categories for the domain: hedge, and quantifier. This classification is a simplification of the categories present in natural languages, but it is sufficient for the work where linguistic accuracy is not a priority. Words belonging to open categories are marked with either positive or negative connotation. This is the only semantic feature allowed in the dictionary.

4. *Pattern Codification and Generation*: Once the first version of the lexical resource is obtained, it is necessary to define a grammar that can identify simple phrases and assigns a positive/negative connotation to the phrase as a whole. The grammar is restricted to the identification of noun, verb, and adjective phrases.

5. *Assignment of Category Labels*: Category labels are ascribed to each message according to rules which constitute the core of the automatic classification.

## 4     Knowledge Diffusion and Security in PRIOR

In order to favour knowledge extraction, the discussion through collaborative web tools, the negotiation processes between the actors involved in the problem resolution and, in general, the learning process either individual or collective, we resort to the use of graphical visualization tools, following the approach taken in [14].

The *ternary diagram* (Figure 1) represents the individual priorities and the consensus priorities of each group of actors that can be identified when dealing with group decision making problems with a large number of individuals. Moreover, when an intermediate discussion is carried out, they demonstrate how the decision makers and the decision making groups vary their preferences with respect to each alternative after the debate.

The *Euclidean bi-plots* (Figure 2) use the Euclidean distance in order to measure the magnitude of the distance between any pair of points representing the preference structures of each voter in a problem with several rounds and intermediate discussion.

To carry out the e-voting and e-discussion stages of e-cognocracy, the technological properties usually demanded for this kind of electronic participation need to be guaranteed. A new voting protocol [9, 18] ensures the technological security of the e-voting process in e-cognocracy. A number of rounds are allowed (usually two) and this forces the linking of the ballots as both the options preferences and the distribution of intensities among them are incorporated.

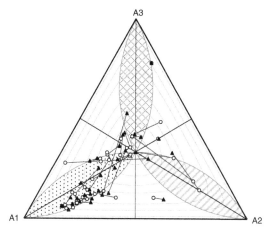

**Fig. 1.** Ternary diagram

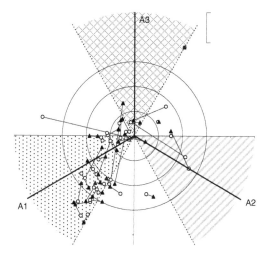

**Fig. 2.** Euclidean bi-plot

The technological security of the other key stage in e-cognocracy (the e-discussion carried out by means of a collaborative tool: e-forums, wiki, etc.) is also guaranteed by this security protocol. The protocol is based on the use of short linkable ring signatures, a cryptographic primitive that allows one person to sign as a member of a group without giving any information about his own identity. All the signatures from the same signer can be linked together whilst maintaining anonymity [19-21].

## 5    Conclusions

The participation of citizens in the public decision making relative to the government of the society is one of the most important social and institutional requisites at the beginning of the 21st century. In response, a number of e-participation (e-democracy) models have been suggested.

In accordance with the needs and challenges of the Knowledge Society, and based on the evolutionism of living systems, a new model of cognitive democracy named e-cognocracy was proposed in [1].

This citizen's representation model allows, by use of the Internet, a co-decision between the representatives and the represented. In addition to achieving greater transparency, participation and control of the citizens in the government of the society, e-cognocracy will improve the quality of life of the citizenry by means of its continuous education and training in a key aspect of the human being: decision making.

In order to generate the participation in the public decisions of spatially distributed citizens (Internet) and to favour the democratisation of the knowledge, it is necessary to use decision support systems. The collaborative tool PRIOR-W&K provides the methodological and cognitive support required in the e-cognocracy, through the incorporation of two new modules (Web and Knowledge) to the software PRIOR, developed in mid 90s by the Zaragoza Multicriteria Decision Making Group (GDMZ) for the multicriteria selection of a discrete set of alternatives.

The Web module allows decisions to be made with spatially distributed multiple actors in a technological secure environment. The module Knowledge, in which data and text mining tools are combined, facilitates the extraction the relevant knowledge in the decisional process, that is to say, the arguments that support the decisions made. Finally, the diffusion of the behaviour patterns of the citizens, as well as that of the critical points and opportunities of the decisional process, will encourage continuous education and training, one of the main objectives of the Knowledge Society.

The new collaborative tool has been trialled in a case study carried out with a group of students. The application is currently being used in a real case in the municipality of Cadrete (Zaragoza, Spain); the citizens will participate in the public politics by selecting cultural and sporting activities and events.

**Acknowledgments.** This research was partially funded under Research Projects "e-Government, Citizen Participation and Knowledge Democratization" (Ref. PI 127/2009) and "Collaborative Decision Making in e-Cognocracy" (Ref. TIN2008-06796-C04-04/TSI).

# References

1. Moreno-Jiménez, J.M.: Las Nuevas Tecnologías y la Representación Democrática del Inmigrante. IV Jornadas Jurídicas de Albarracín. Consejo General del Poder Judicial (2003)
2. Moreno-Jiménez, J.M.: E-cognocracia: Nueva Sociedad, Nueva Democracia. Estudios de Economía Aplicada 24(1-2), 559–581 (2006)
3. Moreno-Jiménez, J.M., Polasek, W.: E-democracy and Knowledge. A Multicriteria Framework for the New Democratic Era. Journal Multicriteria Decision Analysis 12, 163–176 (2003)
4. Moreno-Jiménez, J.M., Polasek, W.: E-cognocracy and the participation of immigrants in e-governance. In: Böhlen, et al. (eds.) TED Conference on e-Government 2005. Electronic Democracy: The Challenge Ahead. Schriftenreihe Informatik, vol. 13, pp. 18–26. University Rudolf Trauner-Verlag (2005)

5.  Aguarón, J., Escobar, M.T., Moreno-Jiménez, J.M., Turón, A.: A Module for Discrete Multicriteria Selection in Environmental Decisional Systems. In: Mendes, I. (ed.) Decision Support Systems: Viewpoints and Applications, pp. 9–20. European Commission. Joint Research Center, CL-NA-EUR 17295 EN-C, Ispra, Italia (1996)

6.  Aguarón, J., Escobar, M.T., Moreno-Jiménez, J.M., Turón, A.: PRIOR: Priorización Multicriterio Discreta con el Proceso Analítico Jerárquico, private property (1996)

7.  Aguarón, J., Escobar, M.T., Moreno-Jiménez, J.M., Turón, A.: PRIOR-WEB: A discrete multicriteria prioritization tool for the global economy context. In: Respicio, A., et al. (eds.) Bridging the Socio-Technical Gap in Decision Support Systems. IOS Press, Lisbon (2010)

8.  Aguarón, J., Escobar, M.T., Moreno-Jiménez, J.M.: Consistency Stability Intervals for a Judgement in AHP-Decision Support Systems. European Journal of Operational Research 145(2), 382–393 (2003)

9.  Salazar, J.L., Piles, J., Ruiz, J., Moreno-Jiménez, J.M.: E-cognocracy and its voting process. Computer Standards and Interfaces 30(3), 124–131 (2008)

10. Escobar, M.T., Aguarón, J., Moreno-Jiménez, J.M.: A Note on AHP Group Consistency for the Row Geometric Mean Priorization Procedure. European Journal of Operational Research 153(2), 318–322 (2004)

11. Moreno-Jiménez, J.M., Aguarón, J., Raluy, A., Turón, A.: A Spreadsheet Module for Consistent AHP-Consensus Building. Group Decision and Negotiation 14(2), 89–108 (2005)

12. Moreno-Jiménez, J.M., Aguarón, J., Escobar, M.T.: The Core of Consistency in AHP-Group Decision Making. Group Decision and Negotiation 17, 249–265 (2008)

13. Escobar, M.T., Moreno-Jiménez, J.M.: Aggregation of Individual Preference Structures. Group Decision and Negotiation 16(4), 287–301 (2007)

14. Turón, A., Moreno-Jiménez, J.M., Toncovich, A.: Group Decision Making and Graphical Visualization in e-Cognocracy. Computación y Sistemas 12(2), 183–191 (2008)

15. Moreno-Jiménez, J.M., Escobar, M.T., Toncovich, A., Turón, A.: Arguments that support decisions in e-cognocracy: A quantitative approach based on priorities intensity. In: Lytras, M.D., Carroll, J.M., Damiani, E., Tennyson, R.D., Avison, D., Vossen, G., Ordonez De Paldos, P. (eds.) WSKS 2008. CCIS, vol. 19, pp. 649–658. Springer, Heidelberg (2008)

16. Toncovich, A., Turón, A., Escobar, M.T., Moreno-Jiménez, J.M.: A quantitative approach to identify the arguments that support decisions in e-cognocracy. Submitted to International Journal of Knowledge Society Research

17. Moreno-Jiménez, J.M., Cardeñosa, J., Gallardo, C.: Arguments That Support Decisions in e-Cognocracy: A Qualitative Approach Based on Text Mining Techniques. In: Lytras, M.D., Damiani, E., Carroll, J.M., Tennyson, R.D., Avison, D., Naeve, A., Dale, A., Lefrere, P., Tan, F., Sipior, J., Vossen, G. (eds.) WSKS 2009. LNCS(LNAI), vol. 5736, pp. 417–426. Springer, Heidelberg (2009)

18. Moreno-Jiménez, J.M., Piles, J., Ruiz, J., Salazar, J.L.: E-cognising: the e-voting tool for e-cognocracy. Rio's Int. Jour. on Sciences of Industrial and Systems Engineering and Management 2(2), 25–40 (2008)

19. Salazar, J.L., Piles, J., Ruiz, J., Moreno-Jiménez, J.M.: Security approaches in E-cognocracy. Computer Standards and Interfaces 32(5-6), 256–265 (2010)

20. Moreno-Jiménez, J.M., Piles, J.J., Ruiz, J., Salazar, J.L., Turón, A.: Securization of policy making social computing. An application to e-cognocracy. Computers in Human Behavior 27(4), 1382–1388 (2011)

21. Turón, A., Moreno-Jiménez, J.M., Piles, J., Ruiz, J., Salazar, J.L.: Securization of the discussion stage in e-cognocracy. Int. J. Social and Humanistic Computing 1(3), 219–231 (2010)

# IM-TAG: Informal Mentoring Improved by Means of Social Web Contents Tagging

Ricardo Colomo-Palacios[1], Cristina Casado-Lumbreras[2],
Ángel García-Crespo[1], and Pedro Soto-Acosta[3]

[1] Universidad Carlos III de Madrid, Computer Science Department
Av. Universidad 30, Leganés, 28911, Madrid, Spain
{ricardo.colomo,angel.garcia}@uc3m.es
[2] Universidad Complutense de Madrid, Department of Development Psychology
and Education, Faculty of Education
Rector Royo Villanova s/n, 28040, Madrid, Spain
cristinacasadolumbreras@pdi.ucm.es
[3] University of Murcia, Department of Management & Finance,
Campus de Espinardo, 30100 Murcia, Spain
psoto@um.es

**Abstract.** Corporations are facing an era in which human capital is crucial for their sustainability. In such scenario, personnel development is decisive for both personnel and organizations. On the other hand the importance of social web for business is unquestionable in terms of knowledge management and information sharing. This paper presents IM-TAG, a tool to use web 2.0 contents in informal mentoring processes. This tool is based on the processing of semantic tagging of blog contents as well as opinion tagging made by users. The results of the process are recommendations of mentoring contents built upon personal characteristics of the mentee combined with content and opinion tagging.

**Keywords:** Informal Mentoring, Social Web, Tagging, Recommender System, Semantic technologies.

## 1 Introduction

People are crucial for the knowledge society. The development of workers represents one of the most significant challenges for today's managers, and one of the most fertile fields for business innovation, human resource management and education research [1]. Mentoring has received much attention recently as a tool for personnel development [2].

On the other hand, the advent of various ICTs, and moreover the amazing capacities of emerging technologies (with Web 2.0 and Semantic Web among others), certainly provide a fruitful basis for a new era in human development [3]. Web 2.0 is about participation and reuse [4]. In the last few years, there has been an increasing focus on social software applications and services as a result of the rapid development of Web 2.0 concepts [5]. Web 2.0 opens a whole new world of social

M.D. Lytras et al. (Eds.): WSKS 2011, CCIS 278, pp. 162–168, 2013.

interconnectivity in which academics, experienced professionals and students alike can now much more easily network with each other for life-like collaborative knowledge construction [6]. According to these authors, the advent of Web 2.0 has caused a significant change in the way the technology is used in all the fields of human development as it is characterized by social learning, active participation and easy to use tools.

In latest years, the number of Social Web Sites has increased very quickly; these webs allow the knowledge to be generated just by using the contributions of the users via blogs, wikis, forums, online social networks… [7]. The Web 2.0 phenomenon made the Web social, initiating an explosion in the number of users of the Web, thus empowering them with a huge autonomy in adding content to WebPages, labeling the content, creating folksonomies of tags, and finally, leading to millions of users constructing their own WebPages [8]. Moreover, the advantages of "Web 2.0" have increased the interest of companies as a way to obtain benefits from this technology [9].

The aim of this paper is to present IM-TAG, an initiative in which social content published by informal mentors is tagged using an evolution of SOLAR [10] tool, in this case applied to an Intranet environment. The main benefit of this approach is the recommender system that SOLAR provides which has been adapted to informal mentoring scenarios. This feature gives informal mentees the possibility to obtain good quality mentoring pieces from Blog posts. The recommender system advices social web contents based on users tagging of posts and intelligent profile matching.

The remainder of the paper is organized as follows. Section 2 outlines relevant literature in the area about mentoring both formal and informal. In Section 3, the tool is presented along with the main effects of its implementation. Conclusions and future work are discussed in Section 4.

## 2    Mentoring: Formal and Informal

The concept of mentoring dates back to the earliest stages of human civilization [11]. More specifically, it dates back to Homer's Odyssey where Odysseus, before leaving to fight in the Trojan War (traditionally dated 1193 BC-1183 BC), entrusted his older friend Mentor to teach and educate his son, Telemachus [12].

There are many definitions of mentoring in the literature, for instance, [13] identified approximately 40 different definitions used in empirical literature since 1980. For the purpose of this paper, Mentoring is defined as the matching of a novice with a more experienced person in the same role [14]. Furthermore, mentors use their experience to provide not only skills but also personal support and guidance. Mentoring activities are organized around knowledge, skills and process to deploy competency-based competences [15].

Literature reports benefits to both mentor and mentee. On the one hand, by means of mentoring, the protégé achieves success in his or her career (e.g. [16]; [17]; [18]), higher salaries [19], more satisfaction and social acceptance in the working environment [11] and higher job performance [20]. In sum, research shows that individuals who have been mentored have greater opportunities to advance in their professional career, get higher salaries and achieve better satisfaction [21].

Nevertheless, according to [22], although mentoring matters for career success, it represents only a part of a constellation of career resources embedded within the relationships. Moreover, in [23] authors stated that the distance between the theoretical program and its implementation decreases the efficiency of mentoring in software development companies.

In contrast to spontaneously-derived informal mentoring relationships, formal mentoring programs, which are sanctioned by the organization, are usually in the form of voluntary assignment or matching of mentee and mentor [24]. Ragins and Cotton [25] discussed the differences between formal along three dimensions: initiation of the relationship, structure of the relationship and processes in the relationship. The initiation of formal mentoring relationships is externally directed while informal mentoring relationships are initiated when two people are attracted to one another based on the foundation of perceived similarity. With respect of the structure and the processes of the relationship, informal mentoring relationships last from three to six years; meetings and activities occur when desired as opposed to a set schedule; and, the goals of informal mentoring relationships evolve over time [24].

# 3    IM-TAG: Annotating Contents for Mentoring Recommendations

Mentoring programs are expensive [26]. Informal mentoring can be also expensive taking into account that the global costs include personnel costs that in many cases are high. Technology has been changed the way mentoring is applied (e.g. [27]), but E-mentoring processes must be performed in a one on one basis.

Social web can provide a solution to this problem. More precisely, blog posts can act as informal mentoring instruments. Thus, a single post can influence thousands of informal mentees from all over the world.

Taking this novel scenario into account, IM-TAG proposes the collaborative tagging of internal blog-posts to produce content recommendations in an intranet environment. The purpose of this limited scope is to give exact recommendations based on consistent profiles and reliable recommendations in an scenario in which corporate culture is uniform.

## 3.1    IM-TAG: The Tool

As mentioned above, IM-TAG is based on a previous tool, SOLAR [10]. As a consequence of this, IM-TAG presents similar technical characteristics of its predecessor namely semantic technologies and open-source widely accepted platforms, as depicted in what follows:

- Semantic technologies. Several consolidated tools were combined to provide a consistent architecture. The first is the Web Ontology Language (OWL) as the cornerstone conceptual and underlying language, particularly its OWL DL flavor, since it builds on the formal foundations of Description Logics (DL). OWL DL supports the use of subsumption as the selected reasoning. The second is the Java based Renamed ABox and Concept Expression

Reasoner (RACER) reasoning engine and the Jena framework as the backbone technology for the Application Logic Manager layer, the former for the reasoning and the latter for the RDF Management and SPARQL Querying.

- Open-source widely accepted platforms. The graphic user interface of the tool was designed to be a set of PHP based extensions of the plug-ins for annotation in Wordpress (PHP based blog platform which has gained momentum over the last years becoming the most used according to the blogging community). The graphic user interface was developed using Asynchronous JavaScript and XML (AJAX, for short). It provided a set of loosely-coupled features to optimize the application efficiency and ease of use from the user standpoint.

## 3.2    IM-TAG: The Case Study

To explain the realization of IM-TAG in a functional environment, as referred to in the previous section, a use case is included in this paper. MINT-INC (fiction name) is an IT consulting company focused on software development on demand. During the last years the company developed projects for different clients including other consulting companies and public and private end-clients. The company has its headquarters in Madrid, Spain but has branches in four more cities in Spain including Barcelona, Valencia, Sevilla and Bilbao and three delegations in Latin-America: Buenos Aires, Argentina, Mexico DF and Bogotá, Colombia. The total workforce stood at 2,500 employees in 2010.

MINT-INC has designed and implemented formal mentoring programmes in order to facilitate the transfer of tacit knowledge among employees. Informal mentoring occurs among employees in a natural way during work time. However, there are two mentoring sources that employees use to know about the company: CEO and CIO blogs. These blogs present posts related to the company and its environment and it is a good source of information about the values present in the culture of MINT-INC. The company has detected the full potential of social media in knowledge management and values spread and has promoted the use of blogs among both managers and IT workers alike.

Taking this into account the company wants to use this information for informal mentoring and boost the potential of social web contents to provide good information to newcomers and veteran workforce. To do so, IM-TAG is installed on Wordpress to provide bloggers with a tool to tag content. Before the tool was installed the ontology of the domain was adapted to cover all issues relative to MINT-INC knowledge and culture. This ontology presents concepts that cover company competences and culture issues. Once a given content (a post) is written IM-TAG permits the blogger to tag the post using the ontology.

The second phase of the process comes when a user that is recognized as an employee of MINT-INC reads the content and wants to express his or her opinion about that. This can be done using the classic comment tool that almost every blog presents, but it can be enriched using IM-TAG also. In this case the user expresses his or her emotions about the content and usefulness for other employees.

IM-TAG gathers all this information and matches employees' profiles with blog content tagging and personnel opinions. The result of this process is a recommendation that IM-TAG provides to users in forms of contents published in the intranet or spreads using RSS.

## 4     Conclusions and Future Work

This paper presents IM-TAG, a recommender system based on a knowledge based architecture. IM-TAG offers a new solution to a well-known objective in the personnel development domain: offering wise advice to less senior individuals. IM-TAG enables collaborative tagging of blog contents and provides content recommendations to users based on their profiles and tags to support informal mentoring. Counting on a tool that enables personnel development that will influence employee performance in a positive way could be a competitive advantage for the firm.

Taking into account the possibilities initiated in IM-TAG, three separate lines of future research may be considered. In the first place, the expansion of IM-TAG to include more Web 2.0 contents, Wiki contents to be more precise. Wikis are knowledge oriented Social Web tools that can improve the efficiency of IM-TAG taking into account that their contents are oriented to the transmission and formalization of knowledge. In the second place, include Natural Language Processing tools to provide automatic assessment of the comments given by users of the posts under consideration in IM-TAG. This evaluation can be integrated with human intellectual capital management tools to provide richer personnel performance assessment. Lastly, it is aimed to increase the scope of IM-TAG to a multi-corporation environment. This swell must be performed carefully, since culture spread is one of the main outputs of mentoring and culture is different among organizations.

## References

1. Casado-Lumbreras, C., García-Crespo, Á., Colomo-Palacios, R., Gómez-Berbís, J.M.: Emotions and Interpersonal Skills for IT Professionals: an Exploratory Study. International Journal of Technology Enhanced Learning 2(3), 215–226 (2010)
2. Casado-Lumbreras, C., Colomo-Palacios, R., Soto-Acosta, P., Misra, S.: Culture dimensions in software development industry: the effects of mentoring. Scientific Resarch Essays (2011) (in press)
3. Lytras, M.D.: Teaching in the knowledge society: an art of passion. International Journal of Teaching and Case Studies 1(1-2), 1–9 (2007)
4. Lux, M., Dösinger, G.: From folksonomies to ontologies: employing wisdom of the crowds to serve learning purposes. International Journal of Knowledge and Learning 3(4/5), 515–528 (2007)

5. Chatti, M.A., Jarke, M., Frosch-Wilke, D.: The future of e-learning: a shift to knowledge networking and social software. International Journal of Knowledge and Learning 3(4/5), 404–420 (2007)
6. Perifanou, M.A., Mikros, G.K.: Italswebquest': a wiki as a platform of collaborative blended language learning and a course management system'. International Journal of Knowledge and Learning 5(3/4), 273–288 (2009)
7. Kinsela, S., Passant, A., Breslin, J.G., Decker, S., Jaokar, A.: The Future of Social Web Sites: Sharing Data and Trusted Applications with Semantics. Advances in Computers 76(4), 121–175 (2009)
8. Breslin, J.G., Decker, S.: The Future of Social Networks on the Internet: The Need for Semantics. IEEE Internet Computing 11(6), 86–90 (2007)
9. Ferreira, N.: Social Networks and Young People: A Case Study. Int. J. Human Capital and Information Technology Professionals 1(4), 31–54 (2010)
10. García-Crespo, A., Colomo-Palacios, R., Gómez-Berbís, J.M., García-Sánchez, F.: SOLAR: Social Link Advanced Recommendation System. Future Generation Computer Systems 26(3), 374–380 (2010)
11. Kammeyer-Mueller, J.D., Judge, T.A.: A quantitative review of mentoring research: Test of a model. Journal of Vocational Behavior 72(3), 269–283 (2008)
12. Gentry, W.A., Wever, T.J., Sadri, G.: Examining career-related mentoring and managerial performance across cultures: A multilevel analysis. Journal of Vocational Behavior 72(2), 241–253 (2008)
13. Haggard, D.L., Dougherty, T.W., Turban, D.B., Wilbanks, J.E.: Who Is a Mentor? A Review of Evolving Definitions and Implications for Research. Journal of Management 37(1), 280–304 (2011)
14. Reiss, K.: Leadership and coaching for educators. Corwin Press, Thousand Oaks (2007)
15. Curtis, B., Hefley, W.E., Miller, S.A.: People Capability Maturity Model (P-CMM®) Version 2.0, 2nd edn. CMU/SEI-2009-TR-003 (2009)
16. Blicke, G., Witzki, A.H., Schneider, P.B.: Mentoring support and power: A three year predictive field study on protégé networking and career success. Journal of Vocational Behavior 74(2), 181–189 (2009)
17. Ng, T.W.H., Eby, L.T., Sorensen, K.L., Feldman, D.C.: Predictors of objective and subjective career success. A meta-analysis. Personnel Psychology 52(2), 367–408 (2005)
18. O'Brien, K.E., Biga, A., Kessler, S.R., Allen, T.A.: A meta-analytic investigation of gender differences in mentoring. Journal of Management 36(2), 537–554 (2008)
19. Blicke, G., Witzki, A.H., Schneider, P.B.: Self-initiated mentoring and career success: A predictive field study. Journal of Vocational Behavior 74(1), 94–101 (2009)
20. Scandura, T.A., Williams, E.A.: Mentoring and transformational leadership: The role of supervisory career mentoring. Journal of Vocational Behavior 65(3), 448–468 (2004)
21. Knouse, S.B.: Virtual mentors: Mentoring on the Internet. Journal of Employment Counselling 38(4), 162–169 (2001)
22. Singh, R., Ragins, B.R., Tharenou, P.: What matters most? The relative role of mentoring and career capital in career success. Journal of Vocational Behavior 75(1), 56–67 (2009)
23. Casado-Lumbreras, C., Colomo-Palacios, R., Gómez-Berbís, J.M., García-Crespo, Á.: Mentoring programmes: a study of the Spanish software industry. International Journal of Learning and Intellectual Capital 6(3), 293–302 (2009)
24. Blake-Beard, S.D.: Taking a hard look at formal mentoring programs. A consideration of potential challenges facing women. Journal of Management Development 20(4), 331–345 (2001)

25. Ragins, B.R., Cotton, J.L.: Easier said than done: gender differences in perceived barriers to gaining a mentor. Academy of Management Journal 34(4), 939–951 (1991)
26. Grybek, D.D.: Mentoring the gifted and talented. Preventing School Failure 41(3), 115–119 (1997)
27. Soto-Acosta, P., Casado-Lumbreras, C., Cabezas-Isla, F.: Shaping human capital in software development teams: the case of mentoring enabled by semantics. IET Software 4(6), 445–452 (2010)

# Blogs as User Based Social Networks for Learning: An Exploratory Study

Aline M. Marques[1], Rafael Krejci[1], Sean W.M. Siqueira[1], Mariano Pimentel[1], and Maria Helena L.B. Braz[2]

[1] Department of Applied Informatics (DIA/CCET), Federal University of the State of Rio de Janeiro (UNIRIO): Av. Pasteur, 458, Urca, Rio de Janeiro, Brazil, 22290-240
[2] ICIST, IST, Technical University of Lisbon: Av. Rovisco Pais, Lisbon, Portugal, 1049-001
{aline.marques,rafael.krejci,pimentel,sean}@uniriotec.br,
mhb@civil.ist.utl.pt

**Abstract.** Nowadays social networks have a prominent place in human communication. Blogs are as user based social networks and its use in the context of formal learning can contribute to increase student's motivation and to get better learning outcomes. This paper discusses message structuring on social networks and presents an exploratory study on the use of three different collaborative learning dynamics supported by blogs with groups of undergraduate and graduate students. Then, it also explores message structuring aspects in blogs in a collaborative learning dynamic.

**Keywords:** Online Social Networks, Blog, Collaborative Learning, Communication, Message Structuring.

## 1    Introduction

Online social networks have attracted thousands of users, which have integrated the networks into their lives and in their daily activities. There are different strategies guiding the development and maintenance of such networks, which vary as they incorporate new information and communication tools, such as mobile connectivity, blogging and multimedia content sharing.

Boyd and Ellison [1] provided an overview of the literature related to online social networks, which were defined as: "web-based services that allow individuals to (1) construct a public or semi-public profile within a bounded system, (2) articulate a list of other users with whom they share a connection, and (3) view and traverse their list of connections and those made by others within the system."

Therefore, besides providing information about the users through their profiles, there is the articulation of the users throughout their connections. The main contribution of online social networks it to enable users to articulate while making visible their social networks. The display of connections is important in the online social networks as it allows users to navigate through the connections, exploring the contacts' profiles.

M.D. Lytras et al. (Eds.): WSKS 2011, CCIS 278, pp. 169–178, 2013.

In order to provide such interactions among users, online social networks offer mechanisms for users to communicate with their contacts. It can be through private messaging (similar to webmail), instant messaging, discussion forum or blogging. The communication tools and the structuring of messages are important as they result on more (or less) interactions among the users and they also influence the type and value of such interactions.

The structuring of messages in communication tools represents the possibility of relationships among messages. As illustrated in Fig. 1, the best known ways to structure messages are [2]: Linear Organization of messages (List structure), Hierarchical Organization (Tree structure) and Net Organization (Graph structure).

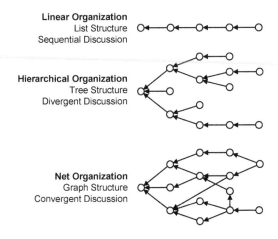

**Fig. 1.** Message Structuring in Communication Tools [2]

The List structure is a particular case of Tree structure, which in turn is a particular case of the Graph - each of these structures is used depending on the communication activity one wishes to establish through the system. The List-structured leads a Linear Organization of messages: a discussion is established in a sequence in which messages are listed according to some perspective such as posting date, author's name or message title. There is no explicit relationship among the messages. The linear organization is typically used in e-mail and discussion list tools. The Tree-structured leads to a Hierarchical Organization: each message is associated with a single father-message (the sender chooses a message to reply to), and thus each message contains ramifications that result in a divergent discussion. The hierarchical organization is typically used in discussion forum tools. The Graph-structured leads a Net Organization: multiple relationships may be established for each message. This structure has the potential for convergence of the discussion [3].

In order to better understand the influence of using online social networks and different message structures on learning, an exploratory study was conducted covering three collaborative learning dynamics and diverse groups of students in a formal learning context. As blogs were chosen to communicate in the exploratory study, next section discusses blogs as user based social networks. On section 3 the collaborative learning dynamics used on the study are presented and discussed considering the use of blogs for their deployment. Section 4 presents the main results regarding students' participation in the experiment and section 5 discusses some issues that arise from the study. Section 6 discusses ongoing work based on connection based social networks and section 7 concludes presenting some final remarks.

## 2     User Based Social Networks and Blogs

In this paper, user based social networks are characterized as online social networks whose focus is on the user, his/her profile and messages. Therefore, user interactions are published as a notice board, just like traditional blogs. The user is the center of the news production and therefore his/her publications are on his/her profile or mural.

A blog is a Web page to which the owner sends messages called "posts". The posts are usually listed in chronological order, with the most recent messages displayed first. Posts are sent to the blog by one or more authors, and readers are able to leave comments for each post. As the Internet becomes more social, it is necessary to consider how people communicate through the web, how they exchange ideas and knowledge.

The blog is one of the most promising communication tools. Several studies highlight the blog as an important means of communication, where participants can express their opinions, share their knowledge, disseminate information, make their work visible and discuss and exchange ideas. Some researchers have investigated the potential of the blog for the democratization of information in a journalistic context: the blog has been considered a relevant medium for the production and dissemination of content, and for the participation and expression of opinion and criticism from readers [4] [5].

Through blogs, participants communicate and form virtual communities based on similar interests which strongly influence the way they relate, act and make decisions [6] [7]. Participants communicate by reading posts and commenting on each other's blogs. Bloggers are encouraged to post new content when they realize that readers read and comment on their posts [8]. Comments made by visitors, besides being considered a form of communication and information exchange, also promote social ties and form bonds among participants [9]. The use of blogs has also been investigated as a means to favor the internal communication among employees in a company to promote collaboration, knowledge exchange and socialization [10] [11].

**Centralized Organization**
Star-Graph Structure
Focused Discussion

**Fig. 2.** Message Structuring in Blogs

In a Blog, messages are structured through the Star Graph, represented in Fig. 2, where the central vertex of the graph represents the post provided by the blog's author, and the leaves represent the comments issued by its readers. This structure leads a centralized organization of messages: all comment-messages are associated with a single post-message, resulting in a focused discussion.

In typical blogs, two common relationships are available: One-to-All (posting) and All-to-One (comments-to-post). These are the kinds of messages considered in the Exploratory Study.

A possible All-to-All relationship in Blogs is through the Inter-Blogs Link Mechanism, which allows authors to add to their blogs a list of references to other blogs (Blogroll): generally, those publishing related issues or having similar interests, or to friends' blogs. The All-to-All relationship is set by reading and commenting on each other's blogs. The links among blogs characterize a communication distributed among multiple blogs, which can follow several different paths, and involve and connect several scattered participants [12]. Some authors emphasize that the essence of blog communication is the establishment of links among blogs [9] [12]. That leads to a characterization of blogs as a user based online social network.

## 3     Blogs as a Collaborative Platform for Learning

Some studies highlight blogs as a relevant system in the context of education, as they promote dialogue and the exchange of ideas, enable debate situations, promote collaboration and motivate student participation through interactions among teacher-and-students, among students-and-students of the same class, and among students of different classes, grades and schools [13] [14].

**Table 1.** Collaborative Educational Dynamics in Blogs Compared in the Exploratory Study

|  | Collaborative <u>Problem-Based</u> Learning with the use of Blogs | Collaborative <u>Project-Based</u> Learning with the use of Blogs | Collaborative <u>Discussion-Based</u> Learning with the use of Blogs |
|---|---|---|---|
| Blog's Owner | The teacher | Learners keep their own blogs (alone or in groups) | Teacher and Learners keep the class blog |
| Teacher's actions | To define tasks or exercises to be solved by the students (post); and to coordinate the answers (comments) | To define and coordinate the development of the stages of the students projects (not in the blog) | To propose topics to be discussed (post); and to coordinate the students discussion (comments) |
| Student's actions | To contribute to the solution of the problem or exercise (comments) | To present part of his project (post); to make critics to the other projects (comments) | To propose topics to be discussed (post); and to discuss the posted topics (comments) |

In order to investigate the potential of using blogs in the process of teaching-learning, an exploratory case study was developed according to the methodology presented in [15], in which three collaborative education dynamics were conducted with classes of different levels (information systems graduate and undergraduate) and institutions (private and public education) during the first semester of 2009. The dynamics are briefly compared as presented in Table 1.

Blogs can be used as a support for Problem-Based Collaborative Learning [16]. In the exploratory study, the teacher is the blog owner, defines a problem and follows the students' answers through the blog. Each student makes a contribution to the solution of the problem through comments. Although the process is still centered in the teacher and with predetermined content (similar to the traditional teaching), the dynamics provides an interaction and collaborative environment among the students that contributes with each other in the search for the solution of the problem.

Blogs can be used as a support for Project-Based Collaborative Learning [17]. In the exploratory study, the teacher's action is to define and coordinate the projects' stages. The students, alone or in groups, create and maintain the blogs for posting the parts of the underdevelopment project. Students are motivated to send comments with critics and evaluations about each part of the posted project. This dynamics establishes a collaboration environment among the students, incentives the critics about the works of the colleagues and the thinking about the own work [18].

Blogs can be used as a support for Discussion-Based Collaborative Learning [19]. In the exploratory study, the blog is created by the teacher (or by the students). Then, the subject is posted, the students send their comments about the subject (or topic) and the teacher coordinates the discussion among the students, while also sending comments. The dynamics promotes collaboration and learning through group discussion.

## 4    Exploratory Study: Participation in the Educational Dynamics

Considering the collaborative educational dynamics described in section 3, four classes were prepared and executed according to that proposal in order to allow analyzing messages exchanged among the students and their engagement in the classes. Table 2 presents a brief comparative analysis of the educational dynamics. Some data was also obtained from the answers to questionnaires applied to the students after the dynamics (pseudonyms are used to preserve students' identity).

**Table 2.** Comparative frame of data from the educational dynamics

| Educational Dynamics | Collaborative Problem-Based Learning with the use of Blogs | Collaborative Project-Based Learning with the use of Blogs | | Collaborative Discussion-Based Learning with the use of Blogs |
|---|---|---|---|---|
| Class | Class 1 | Class 2 | Class 3 | Class 4 |
| Educational level | Undergraduating | Undergraduating | Graduate | Graduate |
| # of Students | 10 | 22 | 16 | 8 |

Table 2. *(continued)*

| Posting and Discussion | Teacher-centered | Distributed, students | Distributed, groups | Distributed, students and teachers |
|---|---|---|---|---|
| Stages (usually one week each) | 10 | 11 | 8 | 2 |
| Messages average by student (post + comments) | 4,1 | 21,9 | 50,0 | 4,2 |
| # Messages sent by student each stage | 0,4 | 2,0 | 6,2 | 2,1 |
| Expected # of messages by student each stage | 1 | 6 | 7,5 | 3 |
| Engagement rate (#sent msg / #expected msg) | 42% | 33% | 83% | 70% |

Summarizing the main results, some characteristics can be emphasized.

**Educational Level Affects the Participation and Engagement in the Dynamics.** The engagement rate in the dynamics conducted with the graduate classes was much higher than those in the undergraduate level (averages of 77% and 38%, respectively).

**Expected Number of Messages Affects the Amount of Messages.** In all cases, the student participation was below the expected, although they were warned about the expected amount. However, as bigger is the expectation, bigger the amount of messages sent by students (85% of correlation).

**Blog Promotes Interaction and Collaboration Among the Students.** Through postings, students showed their works and sent comments with contributions to their colleagues, which promoted interaction and collaboration in the classes. Jussara emphasized the importance of the contributions: "receiving and making constructive critics so that my colleagues could help me and to help others was what I liked most in blogs". For Tatiana, other important aspect was the interaction among the students: "everybody could see my work and make opinions about it and that helped joining the students."

Other interesting results can be obtained at [20].

## 5    Reply and Quotation in Blogs

The exploratory study also showed an important issue related to message structuring:

**It is Difficult to Follow the Comments and Identifying the Senders.** In some reports, there were references to the difficulty of following the comments and visualizing the answers to the tasks and on identifying the comments' authors. Maria said: "the comments were muddled" and Mario said: "it is kind of tiring to visualize the tasks in the comments." Marcelo reported: "Sometimes, there were a lot of comments and they were long, making it hard to see." According to Luis "some anonymous comments or pokes made hard to identify the participant." This problem was also reported by Daniel: "I think it was confusing, I had some problems regarding the identification of comments' sender."

However, the exploratory study considered only posting and comments to posts (One-to-All and All-to-One relationships). Nevertheless, some blogs have established mechanisms that allow the All-to-All relationship: through comments on another comment (replies to a comment) and through quotes to other comments (quotation).

Blogs allow readers to comment a post, but usually readers start communicating among themselves through comments. If that occurs, according to the Linear Organization, then the result is going to be confusing (as related at the exploratory study). Some blog tools enable authors and readers to discuss among themselves through the mechanism to Reply to Comments. Participants, including readers and authors, can discuss with each other. Each participant can choose a message to reply and thus send a response-comment. This type of communication (with the reply mechanism explicitly implemented or not) characterizes the All-to-All relationship in the blog, as anyone can respond to any message. The ability to respond to comments (explicitly implemented) allows the structuring of related comments and leads to the Hierarchical Organization of comments. However, the problem with the use of this mechanism is that it modifies the typical blog conversation centered on the author/posts and enables the occurrence of divergent discussions such as those typically established in discussion forum tools.

Another possible common All-to-All relationship in blogs is the quotation, in which a reader can quote the comment of other readers, creating a Net Organization. This mechanism enables the occurrence of a convergent discussion.

Therefore, it was decided to conduct a study with the objective of investigating the influence of quote and reply (to comment) functionalities through blogging. This study was executed in a class of the same characteristics of Class 2. Blog's records, questionnaires and interviews were used to understand the use of these functionalities in the study. Table 3 summarizes some results.

In the total, 290 common comments were sent, 38 reply-to-comment and 5 quotations. The quote functionality was available in stages 1, 2, 7 and 8, but it was used only in the first two stages. The functionality reply-to-comment was available in stages 3, 4, 7 and 8, but no reader used it (only the authors used it). The educational dynamics was designed to promote the use of the interaction functionalities by the project authors in order to comment the messages received from the colleagues (readers). As opposed to the expectative, the quote functionality was hardly used and the reply-to-comment was fairly used. These results indicate the need for additional strategies for improving the use of the right structures for the messages, such as user training, for instance.

**Table 3.** The Use of Quote and Reply-to-Comment *versus* Comment

| Stages | Available Functionality | | | Use Frequency | | | | | |
|---|---|---|---|---|---|---|---|---|---|
| | Common comment | Reply to comment | Quote | Common comment | | Reply to comment | | Quote | |
| | | | | Readers | Authors | Readers | Authors | Readers | Authors |
| 1 | ✓ | ✗ | ✓ | 48 | 4 | 0 | 5* | 1 | 3 |
| 2 | ✓ | ✗ | ✓ | 36 | 11 | 0 | 3* | 0 | 1 |
| 3 | ✓ | ✓ | ✗ | 25 | 4 | 0 | 11 | 0 | 0 |
| 4 | ✓ | ✓ | ✗ | 27 | 8 | 0 | 7 | 0 | 0 |
| 5 | ✓ | ✗ | ✗ | 27 | 8 | 0 | 1* | 0 | 0 |
| 6 | ✓ | ✗ | ✗ | 24 | 9 | 0 | 0 | 0 | 0 |
| 7 | ✓ | ✓ | ✓ | 23 | 5 | 0 | 6 | 0 | 0 |
| 8 | ✓ | ✓ | ✓ | 26 | 5 | 0 | 5 | 0 | 0 |
| **Total:** | | | | 236 | 54 | 0 | 38 | 1 | 4 |

* The functionality "reply-to-comment" was not available in stages 1, 2 and 5, but, after the customization of the blogs with this functionality, some authors-students went to the previous stages and rewrote the comments using this functionality

# 6    Ongoing Work

The work presented in this paper allowed understanding message structuring in communication tools of online social networks. In particular, the studied blogs had the same focus of user based social networks, in which it is necessary to go to the information, in the place it is. In the study, it was necessary to go to the blog to see the posts and the comments. However, a new kind of communication tools regarding the next generation of social networks (the connection based social networks) is under study. In these networks, the user receives information regarding to their connections in his page, thus having up to date information in his own place. The ongoing work investigates message structuring in such connection based social networks and how educational dynamics are affected by the message structuring.

Some implementations of these connection based social networks are the microblogs. The term microblog has appeared with the advent of the web 2.0 or social web. A microblog is an asynchronous communication tool in which it is possible to send messages, in general smaller than those of blogs (usually 140 characters).

Besides the different functionalities that such tools can have, the way that messages are presented and structured can influence its use or misuse in specific domains or situations [21]. Therefore, the ongoing work intends to investigate the different ways for message structuring in microblogs and their use in collaborative educational dynamics.

## 7    Final Remarks

This work described the characteristics of user based social networks and how blogs can be considered such kind of online social networks. Then, messages structuring in blogs were discussed as well as how it provides communication capacities and interactions among the contacts of this network. In addition, blogs were also presented in the context of a collaborative learning platform. This platform based on blogs was used with three different educational dynamics that were also described.

An exploratory study was conducted in order to understand student interactions and motivation through the use of blogs in the mentioned setting. From this study, it was possible to notice that there were difficulties on dealing with the structure of the messages and on identifying the senders, which is related both to authentication and to message structuring. Another study was conducted with the use of reply-to and quote functionalities, but they were not used by the students as expected.

The use of connection based social networks and microblogs in the context of formal learning is now under research and similar studies are going to be conducted to better understand the advantages and disadvantages brought by these platforms to collaborative learning.

**Acknowledgments.** The authors would like to thank the students that participated in the case studies. This work was partially supported by FAPERJ (through grants E-26/170028/2008 INC&T Program - Project: Brazilian Institute of Research on Web Science, and E-26/ 101.509/2010 - BBP/Bursary Representation and contextualized retrieval of learning content), CNPQ (project: 557.128/2009-9, INCT on Web Science) and by FCT Portugal, through funds of ICIST.

## References

1. Boyd, D.M., Ellison, N.B.: Social Network Sites: Definition, History, and Scholarship. Journal of Computer-Mediated Communication 13, 210–230 (2008)
2. Gerosa, M.A., Pimentel, M., Fuks, H., Lucena, C.J.P.: No Need to Read Messages Right Now: Helping Mediators to Steer Educational Forums Using Statistical and Visual Information. In: The 2005 Conference on Computer Support for Collaborative Learning, pp. 160–169. Lawrence Erlbaum Associates, Taiwan (2005)
3. Pimentel, M., Fuks, H., Lucena, C.J.P.: Linking to Several Messages for Convergence: A Case Study in the AulaNet Forum. In: Briggs, R.O., Antunes, P., de Vreede, G.-J., Read, A.S. (eds.) CRIWG 2008. LNCS, vol. 5411, pp. 196–203. Springer, Heidelberg (2008)
4. Schiano, D.J., Nardi, B.A., Gumbrecht, M., Swartz, L.: Blogging by the Rest of Us. In: Conference on Human Factors in Computing Systems, CHI 2004, pp. 1143–1146. ACM Press, New York (2004)
5. Higgins, C.J., Reeves, L., Byrd, E.: Interactive online journaling: a campus-wide implementation of blogging software. In: 32nd Annual ACM SIGUCCS Conference on User Service, pp. 139–142. ACM Press, New York (2004)
6. Agarwal, N., Liu, H., Tang, L., Yu, P.S.: Identifying the Influential Bloggers in a Community. In: International Conference on Web Search and Web Data Mining, pp. 207–218. ACM Press, New York (2008)

7. Herring, S.C., Kouper, I., Paolillo, J.C., Scheidt, L.A., Tyworth, M., Welsch, P., Wright, E., Yu, N.: Conversations in the Blogosphere: An Analysis "From the Bottom Up". In: IEEE 38th Hawaii International Conference on System Sciences, p. 107b. IEEE Computer Society, Washington (2005)
8. Nardi, B.A., Schiano, D.J., Gumbrecht, M.: Blogging as Social Activity, or, Would You Let 900 Million People Read Your Diary? In: 2004 ACM Conference on Computer Supported Cooperative Work, pp. 222–231. ACM Press, New York (2004)
9. Recuero, R.C.: Information flows and social capital in weblogs: a case study in the Brazilian Blogosphere. In: The 19th ACM Conference on Hypertext and Hypermedia, pp. 97–106. ACM Press, New York (2008)
10. Yardi, S., Golder, S.A., Brzozowski, M.J.: Blogging at Work and the Corporate Attention Economy. In: CHI 2009 Social Software in Office, pp. 2071–2080. ACM Press, New York (2009)
11. Efimova, L., Grudin, J.: Crossing Boundaries: A Case Study of Employee Blogging. In: The 40th Annual Hawaii International Conference on System Sciences, p. 86. IEEE Computer Society, Washington (2007)
12. Efimova, L., Moor, A.: Beyond personal web publishing: An exploratory study of conversational blogging practices. In: IEEE 38th International Conference on System Sciences, p. 107a. IEEE Computer Society, Washington (2005)
13. Xu, B.: Research of Collaborative Learning Platform Based on Blog Group. In: The 2008 International Conference on Computer Science and Software Engineering, vol. 05, pp. 27–30. IEEE Computer Society, Washington (2008)
14. Shaohui, W., Lihua, M.: The Application of Blog in Modern Education. In: International Conference on Computer Science and Software Engineering, pp. 1083–1085. IEEE Computer Society, Washington (2008)
15. Yin, R.K.: Case Study Research: Design and Methods, 4th edn. Sage Publications, Inc., Thousand Oaks (2009)
16. Stahl, G., Koschmann, T., Suthers, D.: Computer-supported collaborative learning: An historical perspective. In: Sawyer, R.K. (ed.) Cambridge Handbook of the Learning Sciences. Cambridge University Press, Cambridge (2006)
17. Dillenbourg, P., Baker, M., Blaye, A., O'Malley, C.: The Evolution of Research on Collaborative Learning. In: Spada, E., Reiman, P. (eds.) Learning in Humans and Machine: Towards an Interdisciplinary Learning Science, pp. 189–211. Elsevier, Oxford (1996)
18. Ugulino, W., Nunes, R.R., Pimentel, M.: Em Busca de Diferentes MODUS de Realizar Dinâmicas Educacionais. In: WIE 2009 - XV Workshop sobre Informática na Escola. SBC, Porto Alegre (2009) (In Portuguese); Free Translation of the title: In the Search of different MODUS of Executing Educational Dynamics
19. Dillenbourg, P. (ed.): Collaborative learning: Cognitive and computational approaches. Pergamon, Elsevier Science, Amsterdam (1999)
20. Marques, A.M., Pimentel, M.G., Siqueira, S.W.M.: Dinâmicas Educacionais com o Uso de Blogs: Requisitos a partir de Experiências. In: XVI Workshop sobre Informática na Escola (WIE 2010), pp. 1177–1186. SBC, Porto Alegre (2010) (In Portuguese); Title: Educational Dynamics with the use of blogs: Requirements from Experiences
21. Theartguy: Academic Aesthetic 165: Twitter vs Plurk, http://academicaesthetic.com/2008/08/06/academic-aesthetic-165-twitter-vs-plurk/ (last accessed on: May 10, 2011)

# Advanced Personalized Feedback in e-Assessment Systems with Recommender Engine

Constanta-Nicoleta Bodea[1], Maria-Iuliana Dascalu[1], and Miltiadis D. Lytras[2]

[1] Economic Informatics Department, The Bucharest Academy of Economic Studies, Calea Dorobanţi, no.15-17, Sector 1,010552 Bucharest, Romania
[2] University of Patras Argolidos 40-42, 153-44 Gerakas Attikis, Greece

**Abstract.** The paper presents an recommender engine, embedded in the feedback module of an e-assessment platform for project management. The objective of this engine is to provide links to the web pages connected with the identified knowledge gaps of the students making the assessments. An ontology-based clustering algorithm is used to generate these recommendations. The authors argue that using a recommender engine the formative value of the e-assessment will increase, the students having the opportunity to take control of their own learning and actively participate in the learning process. The evaluation of the utility of the recommendations is also provided.

**Keywords:** educational recommender systems, personalized feedback, e-learning, e-assessment, project management.

## 1    Introduction

There is a wide range of activities, instruments and materials in e-learning [1]. Using e-learning services is no longer a real challenge, but choosing the most efficient ones for a specific purpose still is. One of the most important concern of the developers and suppliers of e-learning services is to efficiently guide students during the learning process. Considering the information overload, one solution is to give the possibility to students to get personalized recommendations for their knowledge enhancement [2].

The current paper describes the design of a recommender engine within the feedback module of an e-learning system. The e-assessment domain is project management and the knowledge assessment is made during the preparation course for certification. This course is included in the curricula of the project management master degree program, delivered by the Bucharest Academy of Economic Studies (AES). The certification preparation course is based on the cooperation between AES and Project Management Romania, the national association, delivering IPMA project management certification in Romania. Using a recommender engine during e-assessment could increase the formative values of the e-assessment, which not only evaluates knowledge, but also creates knowledge. A set of personalized recommendations, consisting in web bibliography is given at the end of the e-assessment session, when wrong answers are detected, providing future learning directions. Students receive recommendations, but are not forced to use them, thus gaining the opportunity to take control of their own learning. The interaction between

M.D. Lytras et al. (Eds.): WSKS 2011, CCIS 278, pp. 179–184, 2013.
© Springer-Verlag Berlin Heidelberg 2013

students and the e-assessment system is taken at an upper level, the final purpose being the quality increase of the learning process.

## 2     The Relevance of the Recommender Systems in E-learning

In the last years, numerous repositories of educational digital resources have been created [5], [6], [7]. These repositories are added to the unclassified resources provided by Internet itself. In this overcrowded space of online educational resources, the e-learning users feel the need of services which can help them identify the proper learning objects. RS serve this purpose [3].

A RS guides the user to interesting objects (concepts) in a large space of possible options [8]. Usually RS must choose which of the items should be shown to the user or when and how the recommendations must be shown [9]. In educational area, RS started to spread more and more [10], [11]: some assist students to plan their semester schedule, by checking courses that comply with constraint regulation and with students' preferences [12], others are used at course ranking [13] or to give proper knowledge to proper members in collaborative team contexts, by respecting role, tasks, members' level of knowledge [14]. Interesting researches have been made for comparing existing educational RS, such as QSIA (Questions Sharing and Interactive Assignments), CoFind, ISIS, ReMashed, RACOFI (Rule-Applying Collaborative Filtering) [3] or eInkPlusPlus [2].

## 3     The Recommender Engine Design

The current section describes an innovative e-assessment system for project management domain, having a recommender engine. The system has a service-oriented and components-based architecture which ensures its flexibility. The architecture is further described.

### 3.1     The Architecture of the Adaptive Formative E-assessment System

The system has the following main components: the *admin* module, the *trainer* module and the *student* module. The *admin* module offers the possibility to accomplish operations on levels, competences, trainers, users or questions. The *trainer* module allows the creation of rules-based tests, visualization of previously created tests and visualization of students. The *student* module contains the web application used by the students to run the online tests.

The tests offered to the students have multiple-choice questions (see Fig. 1). Each question has five possible answers, which can be true or false. The score sheet has incorporated an automated feedback mechanism. The user can return to the incorrectly answered questions (which are marked in red in Fig. 1) or to the correctly answered questions (which are marked in green). The user can also ask for an exam report, which will give him a "pdf" document (see Fig. 1) with the correct answers. The formative dimension of the test can be increased by pressing the "Search on WEB" button from Fig. 1. A recommender engine is called and the users obtain a set of links to web documents related to the knowledge assessed by the questions which were incorrectly answered. The algorithm standing behind this recommender-based feedback is an ontology-based clustering algorithm.

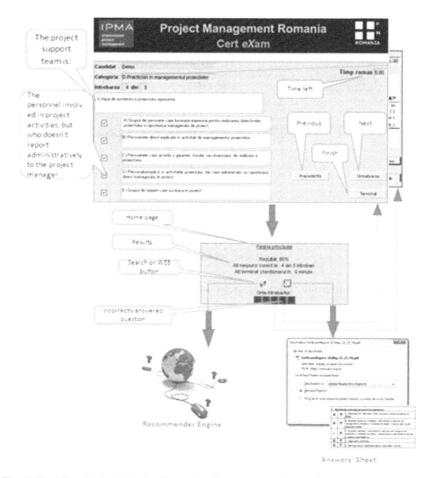

**Fig. 1.** Workflow in the Adaptive Formative E-assessment System for Project Management

## 3.2    The Mechanism of the Recommender Engine

Each question of an e-assessment session checks a certain number of concepts from the knowledge domain in project management. This knowledge domain is represented by an educational ontology [14], which is correlated with the relational database used to stock the educational content. The recommender engine should search for web documents related to the concept of the incorrectly answered question, but also for web documents related to the parent node of the concept in the domain ontology and other child nodes of that parent. The lexical instances of these concepts are the entry points for a clustering algorithm. Thus, the web pages are grouped into relevant clusters, offering the users a friendlier list of results. The concepts are converted to their lexical instances, using the educational ontology. The recommender engine is a C# web-service. The mechanism of the recommender engine is presented in Fig. 2.

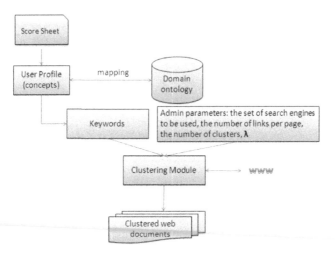

**Fig. 2.** The RS Mechanism

According to Fig. 2, the following steps are available in the recommender engine mechanism:

| | |
|---|---|
| 1. | The user takes the test. |
| 2. | The user finishes the test and the 'user profile' is built: a set of concepts related to the incorrectly answered questions. |
| 3. | The user profile is mapped in the domain ontology, taking account a $\lambda$ parameter used as an entry data: according to that parameter, child nodes from the initial set of concepts might be chosen. For all chosen concepts, lexical instances are extracted and further used for web-search. |
| 4. | The web search is processed for the lexical instances from Step 3 and for the following admin parameters: the set of search engines to be used (the administrator of the e-assessment application can choose the available engines from a combo-box), the number of links per page, the number of clusters. |
| 5. | The clustering algorithm is applied. Clustering will be realized after a predefined number of iterations. This number will be determined experimentally in order to find a compromise between computing time and quality of clusters obtained. By default, we make 6 clusters, the 7th cluster representing unclassified documents and we use a threshold value of 0.3 for classification of instances in clusters. After each clustering, we recalculate the centroids and we reset the clusters' components. The new centroids are calculated using the average weigh of words reached in that cluster. |

### 3.3    The Evaluation of the Recommender Engine

Taking into account the directives of the directives of the Australian Flexible Learning Framework, which drew the attention to the the tendency of developers and suppliers of e-assessment applications to be concerned only with the technical aspects of the success and usefulness of products in the learning process per se (Australian Flexible Learning Framework), we focused on the evaluation of the utility of the recommendations to the users. We calculate the utility of the recommended web documents using formula (1).

$$\text{Utility}_u = \frac{\sum\limits_{i=0}^{n} P(u, i)}{n}, \text{ where } P(u, i) \in \{0,1\} \tag{1}$$

Where:

u = an user;

P(u,i) = the utility of the document $i$ to the user $u$;

P(u,i)=0, if document $i$ is considered useless by the user;

P(u,i)=1, if document $i$ is considered useful by the user;

n = the total number of recommended documents;

The formula was successfully used by other researchers, too [9]. In order to apply the formula (1), we made a short experiment, at which 39 users of the e-assessment application participated. All the users were students in the second year of a project management master and were preparing themselves for taking the same type of certification in project management. The results of the experiment are the following: 21 users considered that the recommendations were very valuable (their utility was higher than 75%), 13 users considered that the utility was valuable enough (between 50% and 75%) and the rest of the users classified the recommendations to be not very useful (the utility was under 50%).

## 4     Conclusions

The article presents a recommender engine which is activated each time the e-assessment system is used. The recommender engine offers the users a list links to the web documents related to the mistakes made by the students during the e-assessment session. The documents are clustered, taking into account their content and the relevance of the content to the users' knowledge gaps. By using the recommender engine, the feedback mechanism of the e-assessment system is highly improved. It gives proper knowledge (through reading recommendations) to proper users (users receive these recommendations, depending on their mistakes). The feedback mechanism is generally considered to be very important for the formative dimension of an e-test. The article states that, if it uses a recommender engine, it efficiently adjusts learning.

In order to increase the usability of the solution, we should migrate the clustering process on the web and go for a distributed architecture: the ontology can stay on a machine, the clustering process on other machine and so on. For the moment, the recommender engine works only for Romanian language. In the future, it should be extended to other languages, too.

# References

1. Súilleabháin, G.Ó.: Principles, Structure and Framework of e-Learning. Learning Services, Ericsson (2003),
   `http://learning.ericsson.net/socrates/doc/cork.docTallent-Runnels`
2. Crespo, R.G., Martinez, O.S., Cueva Lovelle, J.M., Pelayo García-Bustelo, B.C., Labra Gayo, J.E., Ordoñez de Pablos, P.: Recommendation System based on user interaction data applied to intelligent electronic books. Computers in Human Behavior 27, 1445–1449 (2011)
3. Manouselis, N., Drachsler, H., Vuorikari, R., Hummel, H., Koper, R.: Recommender Systems in Technology Enhanced Learning. In: Ricci, F., Rokach, L., Shapira, B., Kantor, P.B. (eds.) Recommender Systems Handbook, pp. 387–420. Springer, Heidelberg (2010)
4. Project Management Romania, `http://www.pm.org.ro`
5. Multimedia Educational Resource for Learning and Online Teaching, `http://www.merlot.org`
6. Open Educational Resources, `http://www.oercommons.org/`
7. Learning Resource Exchange for Schools, `http://lreforschools.eun.org/`
8. Burke, R.: Hybrid Web Recommender Systems. In: Brusilovsky, P., Kobsa, A., Nejdl, W. (eds.) Adaptive Web 2007. LNCS, vol. 4321, pp. 377–408. Springer, Heidelberg (2007)
9. Hernandez del Olmo, F., Gaudioso, E.: Evaluation of recommender systems: A new approach. Expert Systems with Applications 35, 790–804 (2008)
10. Yang, S.-Y.: Developing an ontology-supported information integration and recommendation system for scholars. Expert Systems with Applications 37, 7065–7079 (2010)
11. Kardan, A.A., Abbaspour, S., Hendijanifard, F.: A Hybrid Recommender System for E-learning Environments Based on Concept Maps and Collaborative Tagging. In: The 4th International Conference on Virtual Learning, Iasi, pp. 200–207 (2009)
12. Hsu, I.-C.: SXRS: An XLink-based Recommender System using Semantic Web technologies. Expert Systems with Applications 36, 3795–3804 (2009)
13. Farzan, R., Brusilovsky, P.: Encouraging user participation in a course recommender system: An impact on user behavior. Computers in Human Behavior 27, 276–284 (2011)
14. Bodea, C.-N.: Project Management Competences Development Using an Ontology-Based e-Learning Platform. In: Lytras, M.D., Damiani, E., Carroll, J.M., Tennyson, R.D., Avison, D., Naeve, A., Dale, A., Lefrere, P., Tan, F., Sipior, J., Vossen, G. (eds.) WSKS 2009. LNCS(LNAI), vol. 5736, pp. 31–39. Springer, Heidelberg (2009)

# An Introduction to Community Detection in Multi-layered Social Network

Piotr Bródka[1], Tomasz Filipowski[1,2], and Przemysław Kazienko[1,2]

[1] Wrocław University of Technology, Wyb. Wyspiańskiego 27, 50-370 Wrocław, Poland
[2] Research Engineering Center Sp. z o.o., ul. Strzegomska 46B, 53-611 Wrocław, Poland
{piotr.brodka,tomasz.filipowski}@pwr.wroc.pl,
kazienko@pwr.wroc.pl

**Abstract.** Social communities extraction and their dynamics are one of the most important problems in today's social network analysis. During last few years, many researchers have proposed their own methods for group discovery in social networks. However, almost none of them have noticed that modern social networks are much more complex than few years ago. Due to vast amount of different data about various user activities available in IT systems, it is possible to distinguish the new class of social networks called multi-layered social network. For that reason, the new approach to community detection in the multi-layered social network, which utilizes multi-layered edge clustering coefficient is proposed in the paper.

**Keywords:** social network, multi-layered social network, communities in social networks, community extraction, social network analysis, multi-layered edge clustering coefficient.

## 1   Introduction

Area of science which in recent years is rapidly growing is social network analysis. One of the main reasons for this is growing number of different social networking systems and simple way to obtain data from which we can extract those social networks. Depending on the type of social network we want to build, data can be found in various places, e.g.: blogs [1], telecommunication data [2], bibliographic data [3], social services like Facebook [9], e-mail systems [10] and more.

Group extraction is among those topics which arouse the greatest interest in the domain of social network analysis. Finding groups among the system users opens the new possibilities and can be utilize in such disciplines as human resource management, advertisement, information propagation and lots of others.

Many methods and algorithms have been proposed[3], [8].They are becoming faster [2] and better reflect the real groups in social network [6]. These upgrades have to be significant since social networks are growing very fast those days. However few years ago social networks stopped to grow only in "width", and also began to grow "up". While information technologies became more and more popular, people have expanded their everyday communication on many new channels. They start to build

M.D. Lytras et al. (Eds.): WSKS 2011, CCIS 278, pp. 185–190, 2013.

their social environments basing on various web activities. Social networks have become multi-layered (*MSN*).

*MSN* is a kind of social network where people are connected by many different relationships. Some examples may be complex social networking sites (e.g. Facebook), where people are linked as friends, via common games, "like it", etc. or regular companies where people are at the same time: department colleagues, best friends, colleagues from the company football team, etc. The existing community extraction methods do not concern this multidimensionality of human relations and allow only to group each layer separately. They do not allow to look at the social network as a whole and extract multi-layered groups based on all network layers. For that reason, the new approach to community detection in multi-layered social networks is proposed in the paper.

## 2    Multi-layered Social Network

**Definition 1:** A multi-layered social network (*MSN*) is defined as a tuple $<V,E,L>$, where: $V$ – is a not-empty set of nodes (social entities: humans, organizations, departments etc.); $E$ – is a set of tuples $<x,y,l>$, $x,y \in V$, $l \in L$, $x \neq y$ and for any two tuples $<x,y,l>$, $<x',y',l'> \in E$ if $x=x'$ and $y=y'$ then $l \neq l'$; $L$ – is a set of distinct layers.

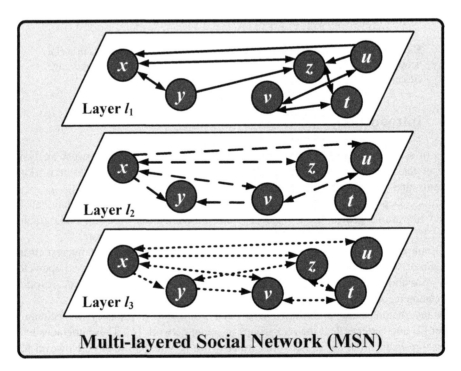

**Fig. 1.** An example of the multi-layered social network MSN

Each tuple $<x,y,l>$ is an edge from $x$ to $y$ in layer $l$ in the multi-layered social network (MSN). The condition $x{\neq}y$ preserves from loops, i.e. reflexive relations from $x$ to $x$. Moreover, there may exist only one edge $<x,y,l>$ from $x$ to $y$ in a given layer $l$. That means any two nodes $x$ and $y$ may be connected with up to $|L|$ (cardinality of a set $L$) edges coming from different layers. Edges in *MSN* are directed and for that reason, $<x,y,l>{\neq}<y,x,l>$. Each layer corresponds to one type of relationship between users [4]. Examples of different relationship types can be real world friendship, Facebook friendship, family bonds or work ties. A separate relationship can also be defined based on distinct user activities towards some 'meeting objects', for example publishing photos, commenting photos, adding photos to favourites, etc. See [4], for details. Depending on variety of user activities types, the *MSN* will have more or less layers.

Nodes $V$ and edges $E$ from only one layer $l{\in}L$ (such edges form set $E_l$) correspond to a simple, one-layered social network $SN <V, E_l, \{l\}>$.

A multi-layered social network $MSN=<V,E,L>$ may be represented by a directed multi-graph. In Figure 1, the example of three-layered social network is presented. The set of nodes consists of $\{x, y, u, v, z, t\}$ so there are five users in the network that can be connected with each other within three layers: $l_1$, $l_2$ and $l_3$. In layer $l_1$, eight relationships between users: $<x,y,l_1>$, $<y,x,l_1>$, $<x,z,l_1>$, $<z,x,l_1>$, $<y,z,l_1>$, $<u,z,l_1>$, $<u,v,l_1>$, $<v,u,l_1>$ can be distinguished.

# 3   Social Community

A group, often also called a social community, in the biological terminology is a number of cooperating organisms, sharing a common environment. In sociology, in turn, it is usually defined as a group of people living and cooperating on a particular area. However, due to the rapid growth of the Internet, telecommunication and transportation, the concept of community has lost its geographical limitations. Overall, a general idea of the social community has become a set of people in a social network, whose members more frequently collaborate with each other rather than with members of this social network who do not belong to the group.

This concept of social community can be easily transposed to the graph theory, in which the social network is represented by a graph. Group is a set of vertices with high density of edges between them, and low edge density between those vertices which do not belong to this set.

However, the problem appears in the quantitative definition of community. There is no general definition of the group (social community) in social networks [8]. There are several of them, which are used depending on the authors' needs.

Most definitions are built based on the idea presented above. Nevertheless, none of them has been commonly accepted. Additionally, groups can also be algorithmically determined, as the output of the specific clustering algorithm, i.e. without a precise a priori definition [5]. In such case, group definition is determined by the algorithm and its parameters. In this paper, we will use such definition.

In this article, we assume that the group $G$ in the social network $SN=<V,E>$ is a subset of vertices from $V$ ($G\subseteq V$), extracted using any community extraction method (clustering algorithm) and the multi-layered group $MG$ in multi-layered social network $MSN=<V,E,L>$. is a subset of vertices from $V$ ($MG\subseteq V$) extracted using community extraction method which takes into account all layers of $MSN$.

# 4     Multi-layered Edge Clustering Coefficient

Before the new measure can be introduced the concept of multi-layered neighbourhood has to be presented. The neighbourhood $N(x)$ of a given node $x$ for regular one-layered social network $SN=<V,E>$ is defined as:

$$N(x,l) = \left\{ y :< y,x,l >\in E \vee < x,y,l >\in E \right\} \tag{1}$$

In other words, all nodes connected with the particular node by any edge in the given layer belong to this node neighbourhood in this layer.

Multi-layered neighbourhood, $MN(x,\alpha)$, of a given node $x\in V$ is a set of nodes, which are neighbours of node $x$ on at least $\alpha$ layers in the $MSN$:

$$MN(x,\alpha) = \left\{ y : \left| \{ l :< x,y,l >\in E \vee < y,x,l >\in E \} \right| \geq \alpha \right\} \tag{2}$$

So a node is a muli-layered neighbour of the given node if they are connected by any edges in at least $\alpha$ layers.

For MSN from Figure 1, we have $MN(x,1)=\{u,v,y,z\}$, $MN(x,2)=\{u,v,y,z\}$ $MN(x,3)=\{u,y,z\}$

The cross-layer edge clustering coefficient ($CLECC$) is an edge measure which was developed based on idea of edge clustering coefficient measure introduced by Radicchi et. al [7].

Edge clustering coefficient for an edge $<x,y>$ expresses how much the neighbours of the user $x$, and neighbours of the user $y$ are interconnected. The edge clustering coefficient is defined as:

$$ECC(x,y) = \frac{z_{x,y}+1}{s_{x,y}} \tag{3}$$

where $x$ and $y$ are the users connected by the edge $<x,y>$, $z_{x,y}$ is the number of triangles built upon the edge $<x,y>$ and all edges between x, y and their neighbours, $s_{x,y}$ is the possible number of triangles that one could build based on edge$<x,y>$ and all possible edges (even those that do not exist) between $x$, $y$ and their neighbours.

$CLECC$ measure is slightly modified and express the similar neighbours interconnectivity but for the multi-layered social network.

$$CLECC(x,y,\alpha) = \frac{\left| MN(x,\alpha) \cap MN(y,\alpha) \right|}{\left| (MN(x,\alpha) \cup MN(y,\alpha))/\{x,y\} \right|} \tag{4}$$

Thus, it can be described as a proportion between the common multi-layered neighbours and all multi-layered neighbours of $x$ and $y$

*CLECC*, by utilizing multi-layered neighborhood, considers all layers at the same time. The α parameter allows to adjust the measure strictness depending on differences in the density of each layer. This latter feature is particularly important when there are very large differences in the density of each layer.

For instance, imagine that we have four layers and 1000 users. Two of them are very dense (50,000 edges), while the two other quite sparse (5,000 edges). Now, thanks to the α parameter the measure can be adjust. It can be very restrictive and require the connection to exist on all layers (α=4), or it can be gentle and require connections only in few of them (α=2). We can also choose a middle ground and assume that the connection exists on two existed dense layers and one of the sparse (α=3).

## 5     Community Detection in Multi-layered Social Network

After introducing the *CLECC* measure the method for community detection in multi-layered social network can be presented:

---

**Input:**   The multi-layered social network
**Output**: The list of groups within the *MSN*

1. Calculate the *CLECC(x,y,α)* for each pair *(x,y)* where *x∈ MN(y)* and selected α
2. Remove all edges between par *(x,y)* for which the CLECC was the lowest. In case there are two pairs with the lowest CLECC select randomly one of them.
3. Recalculate the *CLECC(x,y,α)* for all *z:z∈ MN(x)∪MN(y)* and selected α
4. If the deletion of edges will lead to the separation of network into the subgraphs, validate them against selected condition for the group existence (in the original *MSN*). If the subgraph is a multi-layered group do not remove any more edges.
5. Repeat from step 2 until there are only groups or single nodes.

---

This approach looks similar to approaches presented by Girvan and Newman [3], and Radicchi [7] but by using the new *CLECC measure* it allow us to extract multi-layered communities in multi-layered social networks.

## 6     Conclusions and Future Work

In this paper, the general concept of the new measure called multi-layered edge clustering coefficient was presented. This measure can be used to detect how strongly are connected the neighbourhoods of two nodes linked by an edge. In consequence, this measure can be utilized to detect communities in the multi-layered social network.

Future work will focus on complex examination of the proposed measure and method. Additionally, the new version of *CLECC*, which will also take into account the weights and directions of the *MSN* edges, will be developed.

**Acknowledgments.** The work was supported by: Fellowship co-Financed by the European Union within the European Social Fund, The Polish Ministry of Science and Higher Education, the development project, 2009-2011 and the research project, 2010-13, and the training in the "Green Transfer" project co-financed by the European Union from the European Social Fund

# References

1. Agarwal, N., Galan, M., Liu, H., Subramanya, S.: WisColl: Collective Wisdom based Blog Clustering. Information Sciences 180(1), 39–61 (2010)
2. Blondel, V.D., Guillaume, J.-L., Lambiotte, R., Lefebvre, E.: Fast unfolding of communities in large networks. J. Stat. Mech., 10008 (2008)
3. Girvan, M., Newman, M.E.J.: Community structure in social and biological networks. Proc. the National Academy of Sciences 99(12), 7821–7826 (2002)
4. Kazienko, P., Bródka, P., Musial, K., Gaworecki, J.: Multi-layered Social Network Creation Based on Bibliographic Data. In: The Second IEEE International Conference on Social Computing (SocialCom 2010), Minneapolis, August 20-22, pp. 407–412. IEEE Computer Society Press, USA (2010)
5. Moody, J., White, D.R.: Structural Cohesion and Embeddedness: A Hierarchical Concept of Social Groups. American Sociological Review 68(1), 103–127 (2003)
6. Palla, G., Barabási, A.L., Vicsek, T.: Quantifying social group evolution. Nature 446, 664–667 (2007)
7. Radicchi, F., Castellano, C., Cecconi, F., Loreto, V., Parisi, D.: Defining and identifying communities in networks. PNAS 101, 2658–2663 (2004)
8. Fortunato, S.: Community detection in graphs. Physics Reports 486(3-5), 75–174 (2010)
9. Traud, A.L., Kelsic, E.D., Mucha, P.J., Porter, M.A.: Community structure in online collegiate social networks, eprint arXiv:0809.0690 (2009)
10. Tyler, J.R., Wilkinson, D.M., Huberman, B.A.: Email as spectroscopy: Automated discovery of community structure within organizations. In: Communities and Technologies, pp. 81–96. Kluwer, B.V., Deventer (2003)

# Communication and Cooperation Pragmatism: An Analysis of a Community of Practice by Non-deaf and Deaf to Study Sign Language

Daniela de F. Guilhermino Trindade[1,3], Cayley Guimarães[1], Diego Roberto Antunes[1], Rafaella A. Lopes da Silva[1], Laura Sánchez García[1], and Sueli Fernandes[2]

[1] Informatics Department, Federal University of Paraná, Curitiba, Brazil
`{danielaf,cayleyg,diegor,rafaellaa,laura}@inf.ufpr.br`
[2] Linguistic Department, Federal University of Paraná, Curitiba, Brazil
`suelif@globo.com`
[3] Center of Technological Sciences, State University of Paraná, Bandeirantes, Brazil
`danielaf@uenp.edu.br`

**Abstract.** The Deaf community lives in a historical period of affirmation of social rights they have been denied for over at least a century. It is important that Computer Science research be based on the needs and specificities of people, to develop systems that respect and take into account their differences, in order to inform design and to deliver tools to mitigate the communication barriers and to promote knowledge access and social inclusion: for the Deaf, this means more systems in Sign Language. This article studies the knowledge creation process of a Community of Practice of non-deaf and Deaf members around the domain of Libras (Brazilian Sign Language). The main goal is to investigate whether traditional theories of collaboration (acts of speech, pragmatism, cooperation principles) hold in an environment where the language of choice is not spoken, but, rather, a Sign Language. Results show strong evidence in favor of such premise, and suggest further studies to enrich CP, collaboration and Sign Language studies.

**Keywords:** Acts of Speech, Pragmatism, Collaboration, Sign Language.

## 1 Introduction

The Deaf community lives in a historical period of affirmation of social rights they have been denied for over at least a hundred years. According to Fernandes [5], we find that "*among their most important claims is the right to be allowed to use Sign Language in the different contexts of social interaction, and access to knowledge*". There are still many challenges surrounding the issue of social integration of the Deaf, along with the full acceptance of their rights and duties to effectively participate in society, and to fully exercise citizenship, the lack of knowledge about Sign Languages (relegated to special schools, some churches, a few associations – all mostly in big metropolis) being one of those challenges.

M.D. Lytras et al. (Eds.): WSKS 2011, CCIS 278, pp. 191–205, 2013.

Mindful of the differences existing in the Brazilian population, particularly the issues surrounding special needs individuals, the Sociedade Brasileira de Computação (SBC) – Brazilian Computing Society – has elected as one of its priorities for the next 10 years the *"participative and universal access of the Brazilian citizen to knowledge"*. This challenge addresses the importance of computer research based on the needs and specificities of people, that respect and take into account their differences, in order to inform design and to deliver tools to mitigate the communication barriers and to promote knowledge access: for the Deaf, this means more systems in Sign Language (SL) – considering that most Brazilian Deaf don't know Portuguese.

Human-Computer Interaction (HCI) has long established the responsibility to dig deeper into more complex features of users (e.g. culture). Technology should serve the needs of humans, not the other way around. The surveyed studies fail to deliver on that premise by a plethora of factors: lack of information on how the Deaf real needs are understood or taken into account; on how the participation of the Deaf occurs; on how the SL is correctly treated and so on.

But there is a lack of research on how these considerations should inform design [1]. *"The need is pressing [...]"* especially when our work extends into differing communities and constituencies that are not our own. Thus, this work is justified. Good will alone will not do, since the best-intended researcher who may "feel" the plight of the deaf still work under the conceptual frame that hearing is a far more viable, natural and normal feature than deafness [33].

Communities of Practice (CP) (i.e. group of people who share an interest in a domain of human endeavor and engage in a process of collective learning that creates bonds between them) may represent an adequate space to cultivate collaboration; a space in which non-deaf and Deaf may act to promote access and share information, in order to create knowledge.

In this context, this article presents the results of an ethnographic analysis of a CP (brought together to study SL phonological theories), composed by non-deaf and Deaf students of an undergraduate linguistic course in Brazilian Sign Language (Libras). The CP was cultivated by the knowledge creation of the phonetics of Libras, mediated by a Phonetic Structure of Libras (PSL), and by a computer system that described the signs as per the model, with respective Knowledge Management (KM) tools (to collect, organize, store, retrieve and use) for the knowledge created. The system served as a catalyzer specially designed for the CP in question. The analysis used the 3C model [4] and the mapping between acts of speech and principles of the model in order to analyze how communication, coordination and cooperation occurred within the CP. The study also allowed for very strong evidence that the classical principles of speech act from spoken language do apply to SL.

## 2    Deaf Culture

The Deaf identity is intimately connected to the visual manner in which they experience the world [8]. But that has not always been the case: the Deaf have been deprived of freedom to express themselves in SL [9]. Fernandes [5] asserts that the use of SL by a deaf person presupposes a specific relationship with her world, a different way of being and also a different way of learning. The author states that the deaf communities suffered at least 100 years of exclusion of their language, thus rendering their communication tool as disqualified, and, therefore, SL was never the object of serious research, with direct implications as seen by the exclusion of the deaf from the oral society.

The 60´s, the seminal work of Stokoe [10] showed that SL have all the linguistic aspects of a natural language, and brought forth a series of linguistic studies of SL, and the beginning of a cultural, political and scientific awakening that allowed for a new regard of SL used by deaf people everywhere.

SL are complete, legitimate linguistic systems of gestural, visual-spatial modality, with communication occurring by means of signalized movements and non-manual expressions perceived by vision. They are not universal (different from country to country) with dialects and regionalisms between different deaf communities.

SL are not mere spelling, and definitely are not mimes, and their lexicon is vast and rich; SL should be studied encompassing all linguistic aspects in order for its correct use to be able to promote access to information, create knowledge and serve as means to social inclusion [5], [11]. In order to better develop, the Deaf should be educated in the bilingualism theory, with Libras as the maternal language, and the other language being that of her country (e.g. Portuguese) [12]

Deaf communities have SL as a tool for communication and social integration; SL are a major part of their culture, of which they are very proud, and the tools to aid them in their integration process should include SL and respect such culture.

Collaborative interactions may be of great importance to social, historical, political and human formation and may contribute to the Deaf identity. In such activities involving the Deaf, the non-deaf participants must act as interlocutors, aiding in the sharing of social languages. For the Deaf, such practices, with CP, enhance knowledge sharing and creation [3].

## 3     Communities of Practice: A Space for Collaboration

Wenger [14] says that a *"[...] community of practice is a group of people who share an interest in a domain of human endeavor and engage in a process of collective learning that creates bonds between them: a tribe, a garage band, a group of engineers working on similar problems"*.

A CP is structured in three elements [14]: i) the domain (common interest of the group); ii) the community (interaction and bonding dictated by the common interest); iii) the practice (process by which members of the CP learn about their subject of interest).

CP favor collaborative work scaffolded by communication, allowing the joint action and coordination of individuals. CP create collaboration opportunities that promote cooperation and knowledge creation and sharing through interaction, based on trust, among other things [32]

**Table 1.** Seven principles for implementing Communities of Practice (Wenger, 2002)

| |
|---|
| To find out ways to excite a community by the identifying factors that would absorb potential members (weekly meetings, web site construction); |
| Collect community member experiences to discover her internal perspective that allows for appreciation and understanding of the issues that are part of her domain about the knowledge, and to understand the community's potential for knowledge creation and administration (sustain a dialogue about what the community may gain from external information); |
| Invite members of the community to participate in the three levels: in the core group as a coordinator; in the active group, as a regular participant in the meetings, and as occasional participant in the forums; in the peripheral participation group (i.e. those comprised of members who rarely participate, but watch the interactions, and, thus, also grow through more private conversations); |
| Develop public and private spaces within the CP through meetings, in order to share suggestions, solve problems, and explore new ideas, in physical or virtual presence; |
| Create a systematic body of knowledge that is easily accessible and to conduct discussions so that other stakeholders may understand the impact of the value of the community (that may, otherwise, take long to emerge); |
| Combine familiarization and excitement; |
| Create a rhythm for the community. |

A CP may be implemented according to seven principles Wenger [15] presents in Table 1.

In this sense, an approach that deserves consideration due to its concern about the aspects of collaboration within groups is the Computer Supported Collaborative Work (CSCS). CSCW stands out by taking into account the necessary tools to allow collaboration. According to Nielsen [16], CSCW may be defined as the study of techniques, methodologies and technologies to support group work. Most works in CSCW try to minimize the barriers encountered during group collaboration, thus maximizing the output of the collaboration.

A CSCW model that is widely used for above *groupware*[1] development is the collaboration 3C model [4], based on the idea that, in order to collaborate, group members need communication, coordination and cooperation. The 3C model is equivalent to the Clover model [17].

According to the 3C Model, to collaborate, people need to communicate; during the communication, compromises are generated and negotiated. The compromises are tasks that are needed for the execution of the job, and are managed by coordination, that organizes the group and makes sure the tasks are performed in the correct order, time and within the restrictions and goals. During cooperation, group members act together in a shared space, the tasks are performed, and renegotiate status and make decisions [7].

---

[1] Groupware designates the technology developed by CSCW work.

CP promote communication, coordination and cooperation among members, revolving around an specific common domain of interest. In a CP involving non-deaf and Deaf it is necessary to address specific issues, specially those related to communication (e.g. a SL interpreter, or a computer mediated translator).

# 4    Communication and Cooperation Theories

The gamut of diversity among members of the CP, with distinct culture, characteristics and needs, it is important to investigate techniques and methodologies to support communication, coordination and cooperation that may occur in such environments.

Considering the communication situations that are paramount to cultivate CP, and the fact that SL are natural, complete linguistic systems, this research applies classical theories such as pragmatism, acts of speech, cooperation and problem solving principles: the main goal of such theoretical choice was to determine whether these classical theories do apply, and whether they could be used in order to scaffold the various practices that cultivate CP.

## 4.1    Acts of Speech Theory and Principles of Cooperation

Pragmatism is a particular perspective from the philosophy that relates the meaning of signs to the effects they have on other signs, thus making them relevant for the users to understand intellectual activities. Pragmatism (i.e. theory of the acts of speech) has been used in HCI for CSCW [18], [19], [20].

The theory of the acts of speech claims that language is used not only to represent states of reality, but, also, to affect such given reality, to do things. Austin [18], presents acts of speech that are not used to describe the world, but rather, are alternative ways people use to perform actions: locutionary, illocutionary and perlocutionary.

Locutionary act is present at utterance and recognition that the sentence has a structure related to the norms and grammar of a language. Illocutionary act happens at utterance time, and represents the user intention; among the verbs that characterize illocutionary actions described by [18], we may find: informing, ordering, warning, undertaking, among others. Perlocutionary act also occurs at utterance, but it is related to the effect that results from the sentence utterance; some of the verbs in this act are: *convincing, persuading, deterring, surprising or misleading* [18].

For example, consider the analysis of the utterance: "Do not plagiate". The utterance is an locutionary act, with syntax, semantics, phonetics and other elements of grammar that represent a warning so that you do not plagiate a work (illocutionary act), and, if you respect the warning, then there was success in guiding you not to plagiate (perlocutionary act).

Searle expanded Austin's studies and described five basic classes for the illocutionary act [19]:

1. Assertives (instructions, affirmations): truth.
2. Directives (requests, orders): attempts of several degrees from the speaker to persuade the listener to perform something;
3. Declaratives (alter the world): must be in accord with reality;
4. Comissives (promises): commit the speaker to some action in the future; and
5. Expressives (reprimands, condolences): aim at attracting attention to some psychological state or attitude, with sincerity.

Such classical concepts summarized above are present and complement Grice's principles of Cooperation's [19], [20], [23], [24]:

1. Quantity: a proposition should achieve the informative level required, without being excessive.
2. Quality: a proposition should be articulated with enough information to make sense.
3. Relation: a proposition should contain only relevant information to the cooperation goal.
4. Manner: refers to the form (rather than the content): a proposition should be uttered clearly, without ambiguity, brief and ordered.

These principles are important in conversations to coordinate rational behavior related to a goal; they have a powerful descriptive force when they help explain and/or understand some rules. In HCI work, for example, the rules of consistency (related to the manner) [21]; visibility of the system's status (related to quality) and minimalist design (quantity, quality, relation and manner) [22].

## 4.2    Problem Solving Principles

Still in line with interpersonal relations, Leech [24] formulated a series of principles to solve problems, and that may be used in conjunction with the theories of acts of speech [19].

1. Tact maxim (applicable to Directive and Comissive): when using language to give orders or make promessis, it is polite to minimize the cost for the interlocutors, or maximize the benefits;
2. Generosity (Directive and Comissive): when using language to give orders or make promessis, it is polite to minimize the benefit to the emissor or maximize the cost to the emissor;
3. Approbation (Expressive and Assertive): when expressing a state, or indicating something that affects the interlocutor, it is polite to minimize the desprise or maximize the praises;
4. Modesty (Assertive): when expressing a state or indicating something that affects the interlocutor, it is polite to minimize praise to self;
5. Agreement (Expressive and Assertive): when using language to make a statement, it is polite to minimize disagreement or maximize agreement;
6. Sympathy (Expressive and Assertive): when making a statement, it is polite to minimize antipathy or maximize sympathy.

The elements chosen in a communication influence in its result and continuation; choice does not necessarily mean a conscious process by the speaker. A functional analysis aims at finding out the reasons the speaker uttered one thing instead of any other, in a given context [25].

For Macedo [26:40] *"meanings are attained by means of choices the speaker makes in face of the possible choices available"*. Thus, a choice is tied with the intention of the speaker, and carries a meaning that interferes in the problem-solving task.

These principles must be understood under the light of culture: modesty may be interpreted as fake; pragmatism is based in principles, rather than rules; productive conversation results from decision-making more than from linguistic competence or domain knowledge. Therefore, HCI must mediate user decisions, in an adequate manner (i.e. in the case of this study, with the use of SL interfaces) about how to interact. Knowledge is usually formatted in positive terms (explanations); decisions are presented in comparative terms (cost/advantage, problem-solving instructions, etc.).

# 5    A Collaborative Environment to Support Interaction among Non-deaf and Deaf

A computer mediated environment was developed to support meetings and create and cultivate a CP centered on the study of SL phonological aspects with non-deaf and Deaf members. The domain was the knowledge creation of Libras parameters that describe the phonology of Libras signs, its characteristics, structure, variation and limitations, in order to validate the Phonetic Structure of Libras (PSL) model.

The PSL model is a computational representation model based on a compilation and adaptation of phonological models that aggregates a high degree of details for sign description. Such finesse in describing the signs render the model presented as adequate for computational treatment of SL. Validated elsewhere [34], and during the collaborative meetings of the CP, the model helps in the development of tools to support the deaf community. The PSL model was presented in details in [27] e [28].

The CP was composed by researchers, co-authors of this article, interpreter and Deaf students of an undergraduate course in Linguistic/Libras. The knowledge management system was used to mediate the meetings; a role also played by the interpreter.

The co-authors were mediators of the collaboration that took place, in order to organize and coordinate the tasks. Care was taken to make the environment adequate for the Deaf needs (e.g. the knowledge management system, in Libras), in order to allow each and every participant to have equal say and responsibility during the meetings. The Deaf students acted as the main stakeholders, knowledgeable of SL, and capable of validating the PSL. The Deaf were the main contributors for the knowledge creation within the domain of the CP, sharing information, experiences and skills to improve the model.

The PSL model was presented to the CP as a model to describe and standardize the signs in Libras. The CP had the common goal of validating, improving, and adopting it. One of the main goals of the meetings that cultivated such CP was that of identify a set of Libras signs for each of the parameters from the model. The chosen signs were described as per the model, in all its aspects, to form a set with the minimum number of signs that covered the maximum number of parameters. This set is necessary for Computer Vision recognition of signs, 3-D representations of the signs, and gestural-based interface design, among other future works. The Fig. 1 presents a snapshot of one of such meetings.

**Fig. 1.** The snapshot of a environment of the collaborative meetings

Seen in Fig. 1 is a part of the members of the CP, discussing and analyzing a given sign. The system was used to describe the results. Consensus was achieved through many forms, as seen later in the article. The meetings were recorded, for analysis of the chosen methodology to cultivate the CP. At the end of each meeting, the chosen signs were recorded for future reference

## 6    Methodology

The research presented here is exploratory in character, developed with the general aim to determine whether the use of classical theories (i.e. Acts of Speech, Communication and Cooperation and Problem Solving, among others) were admissible in analyzing and cultivating CP between non-Deaf and Deaf members. This type of research is used when it is hard to state precise and operational hypothesis on the chosen theme, and it serves as basis to develop, clarify and change concepts and ideas in order to better define the object of study and to formulate robust working hypothesis [2].

The research was conducted under the general premise that the classical theories would apply in a CP where all the elements of group work would take place, with the additional issue of the language being SL: not know to all members, and, mainly, of a different manner (i.e. gestural, visual, special) than that of spoken language. It was understood that, since SL is a complete linguistic system, that the classical theories would hold. Thus, the study would give deeper insight on how to use them to cultivate the CP with the fewer disturbances, and the most profit to the CP as possible. It is in order to raise awareness to such issues, in an orderly, profound, scientific discussion about the lack of such knowledge, and the consequences of the lack thereof. These are not the only issues at stake, but the point here is to give food for thought: start with simple things the user can relate to, and then, for future research, build on that, towards an ambitious goal to raise the bar on SL understanding and use.

The methodology used was to select and analyze cases where the classical variables occurred during the performance of the tasks by the members of the CP in their goal to enhance knowledge of the phonetic aspects of Libras signs as per the proposed PSL model. The results presented here serve to inform on the relations between the theories variables and the occurrence in real usage situation; and (when possible) to show lack of usage of such variables and the instances when they were (or not) most effective. The results will serve for grounds for further research on the subject, specifically on how they should be used in virtual environments in SL.

The research was based on ethnographic studies on special meetings of the CP. The meetings were designed to allow the improvement of the PSL model by means of knowledge, information and experience sharing. The communication between non-deaf and Deaf is here analyzed in order to determine the appropriateness of using the classical theory of acts of speech, the decision-making principles, the collaboration, the computer mediation among others.

A special information system was implemented, with all the parameters from the PSL model. The system allowed for KM of the knowledge created during the CP process. The information provided by the system, and its adequate interface, in SL, allowed for a concrete illustration of the knowledge creation process. Additionally, the system was crucial in the interactions, mostly aiding the members in some of the acts and principles being used.

The system presents the user with a graphical interface with the parameters compiled in the PSL model. The user, then, is able to visually choose the adequate parameters to describe the desired sign, and, most importantly, it helped the users to standardize their knowledge, store and share experience, and create knowledge about the signs that were closest to the model as possible (i.e. clarifying any doubts that occurred). In this sense, considering the particular way the research is using the classical theories (act of speech, cooperation principles, etc.), the system showed to be available addition to the process (as will be discussed later in the paper).

The authors [34] describe the meetings and the results on validating the PSL model. In total, 15 meetings, each lasting approximately 2 to 3 hours was conducted. An average number of 10 participants were present. Of those, approximately 5 were Deaf. The interpreter (non-Deaf) was present in all meetings. The ages varied from 22 to 45, of both sexes, and all had at least undergraduate education

The variables used to analyze the meetings can be thus summarized:

- Mapping of the acts of speech theory: the main goal was to verify whether the use of this classical theory would be useful in a SL environment. They were studied in regards to the communication, coordination and collaboration needed to cultivate such CP.
- Principles of Cooperation: the main goal was to determine the barriers and facilitators that occurred, and how they must be addressed to improve collaboration within the CP. Quantity of information, its relevance, quality and dissemination manner were studied to determine their relevance and pertinence.

The analyses were done based on the tasks the CP had to perform during the meetings, such as: disclaimers; goal explanation; task instructions; comprehension and execution of the tasks; consensus achievement among others

## 6.1    Mapping of the Acts of Speech

As mentioned before, the basic assumption is that the underlying background of the CP was to be mediate linguistically, although the language of choice was not spoken, but signed. It was, then, a very important research question to determine whether the classic theories would apply. This study, as seen in the following sections, strongly suggests that they might be of importance to inform design and be employed to cultivate CP using SL.

According to de Souza [29] the intention of the language user and the resulting effects of the language have a considerable degree of relevance to communication. Therefore, this study aimed at map the actions of language in the aid on the coordination of the collaborative meetings, during the tasks performed:

- Disclaimers: During the disclaimers, the co-authors used approximately 80%[2] of Directive and maxim of Tact, in order to excite the participants to fully cooperate, pointing out the benefits of the end result for the Deaf and the community. Expressive with the maxim of approbation was also used (albeit less frequently), to express thankfulness and respect and appraise.
- Presentation of the CP goals: 55% of the utterances were Assertives. It was used with the maxim of Consensus to strength the cooperation among the participants; and with the maxim of Modesty to emphasize the lack of knowledge by the researchers in relation to Libras and the Deaf community issues. In 20% of the cases the Commissive was used with the maxim of Generosity to point out the benefits for the Deaf community, to demonstrate the engagement of the researchers and to guarantee the privacy of the participants. Another 25% of occurrences were of Directives, with the maxim of Tact, to promote cooperation and execution of the tasks.
- Task information: more than 80% of the utterances were Directives to motivate collaboration. It was some times used with the maxim of Tact to reassure the benefits to the Deaf community. Expressives were also used, with the maxim of Consensus to strengthen collaboration. In some points, Declaratives were used to help participants in some stalled decision situation.
- Translation of the information: this task was mainly performed by the translator, respecting the modulators of the interlocutors, with, however, a high usage of Expressives. This degree of Expressiviness is due to the nature of Libras, where non-manual expressions are essential to demonstrate the intentions of the speaker.
- Transmission of tasks results: Assertives were the modulator of choice. In case of doubt by the participants, intense use of Expressive was made, together with Assertives.

---

[2] Frequency of utterances during the execution of the task.

The analysis of the interactions of these initial tasks indicated a high frequency of use of the modulators of the acts of speech, to aid communication and coordination in the collaboration environment. It was also observed that the modulators included some of the maxims to support problem solving and to allow the achievement of the desired goals.These indications are important to the extent that they provide grounds for additional research of classical concepts in the realm of SL.

**Table 2.** Cooperation Principles of Quantity and Manner

| Task/Occurrence | Quantity | Manner |
|---|---|---|
| Presentation of Disclaimers and Research goals Responsible: co-author | The information was considered sufficient (due to comprehension and agreement for collaboration). In some occasions, there was excessive information with the (wrong) assumption to convey the importance of the CP. | The conveyed information promoted an attitude of approval and commitment (expressed clearly and objectively). |
| Task information Responsible: co-author | Initially, the information wasn't sufficient. The feedback from the members prompted a greater detailment. There were information losses when the mediators tried to simplify or minimize content. | In some situations there were communication difficulties due to the complexity of the subject, and due to the fact that they were not part of the member's context. It is, thus, important, to consider the need to use scaffolding materials that are of interest of all participants. |
| Task results Responsible: Deaf participants | Because the choice of signs were random and out of context, some members had difficulties to produce the required signs. Even though a scenario was used, it is clear that the scenario should be extended to incorporate situations of use, context, in order to facilitate sign selection. | Results were reported clearly and objectively. There were, however, some divergences about the signs, due to the dynamic nature of the language (neologisms, regionalisms, etc.) as different constituents of a natural language. |
| Feedback to tasks results Responsible: co-authors | The amount of information was sufficient (as per acceptance or doubts about the results and the description of the signs using the PSL model) both by all members of the CP. | Feedback was used in order to obtain consensus. |
| Information Translation Responsible: interpreter | The mediation was necessary and sufficient, although some information loss was observed due to simplification by the interpreter. | Translation was clear and objective. The lack of knowledge about the phonetic elements of the SL, though, caused some doubts to the interpreter. This shows the importance of the PSL model: that of standardize and universalize SL knowledge. |

## 6.2     Cooperation Principles

During cooperation, people need to perform tasks in group, in a shared space. The principles of cooperation proposed by Grice [23] may provide important guidance for the members in a CP in order to achieve their collaboration goals through communication, coordination and cooperation. As pointed out before, this article aims at studying how these classical theories may inform the cultivation of CP where the language of choice is SL. This way, the tasks executed by the members of the CP were analyzed for quality, relevance, quantity and manner. Table 2 presents a summary of such analyzes of the occurrences of quantity and manner. These two principles presented a greater variation during the process when compared to quality and relevance, which were used constantly and consistently during the process.

The Quality principle seems to be fairly applied by the members of the CP during the execution of the tasks, and the participants were really involved, showing a high degree of commitment and responsibility during the execution of the tasks. When in doubt, the members were at easy to freely present their reservations, and to amply discuss all the aspects deemed relevant. Once a consensus was reached, the information was conveyed and inputted into the system in a firm and precise manner.

The interpreter had been somewhat distant from the domain (i.e. the phonetic structure of Libras) and of the community, which presented her with some signification problems (neologisms, regionalisms etc.). The mediators (mostly the co-authors) also had difficulties to identify the directions and nuances the communication process was undergoing. In collaborative environments, the mediators should guide the speech in an strategic way in order for all the group to perceive. It was found (by try & error), that positioning that encompassed both the interpreter and the Deaf was to be optimized, considering that the Deaf must be visually aware of all aspects of communication. As for relevance, the information transmitted, during most part of the process were within the scope of the domain of the CP.

## 7     Conclusions and Future Works

Discussions are presented here grouped by the variables used:

1. Mapping of Act of Speech: The main goal of this article was to verify whether classical principles, such as acts of speech (mainly for spoken language) would fit an environment based in SL. It was observed that, although Libras has its specificities, due to its gestural, visual, spatial manner, it is a complete linguistic system, thus allowing for all the linguistic potentialities and resources of a natural language. Therefore, the analysis of the modulators of the theory indicates strong evidence that they could be used in order to aid coordination in collaborative meetings.
2. Principles of Cooperation. As far as the cooperation principles related to information (i.e. Quality, Quantity, Relevance and Manner), it was observed, mainly, that members participation were both informative and necessary. The careful attention to the needs of the participants in the form of clear, objective and unambiguous information transmission proved to be essential. The mediators, responsible for the coordination, attempted to convey information that was contextualized within the CP.

Additionally, the use of an information system that implemented all the parameters of the PSL model, in a graphical interface, adequate for the Deaf, proved to be crucial in the process of knowledge creation by the CP. The use of the system was determinant to the successful end result of the tasks performed to the extent that they were incorporated in the process of the CP meetings (e.g. the system, unorthodoxly, was used to simulate, exemplify, illustrate the concepts, tasks, results, acts of speech among other uses). Given the particular use that this research makes of the classical theories, enough evidence was found that the use of such a system may be incorporated and proves suitable for HCI research and cultivation of CP.

These indications (that the classical theories may be relevant to cultivate CP based on SL) could be used as a basis from which to investigate further into the subject. Some research issues:

– Are the traditional theories really applicable for SL environments?
– What aspects of those theories should be altered and/or improved for such environment?
– How the findings of such theories should be used to advantage when cultivating CP that involves SL?
– Among others.

Despite our best efforts, however, some additional problems aroused, and are very much worth mentioning and discussing for future practices:

– Difficulties, by the Deaf, to understand complex tasks: due to lack of adequate context, and inability from the mediators to communicate specific contents;
– Loss of information: occurred when mediators and interpreter tried to simplify or minimize information;
– Difficulties, by the mediators, to identify the communication dynamics: its is important, in a collaborative environment, for the mediators to convey the information strategically to all members.
– Difficulties in minimize noise during communication: careful consideration must be taken into account about the gestural manner of SL, specially during times of informal interactions in order to avoid misunderstandings.

Additional considerations were of issue during the cultivation of the CP involving non-deaf and Deaf members:

– Locomotion: the Deaf need proper, precise directions as how to get to the meeting venue.
– Localization: once at the venue, the Deaf also need precise directions. The lack of adequate information (visual, textual etc.) for the Deaf in public and private venues are a constant source of problems, and are included under the accessibility concern.
– Lack of context, proximity and factual knowledge of the interpreter. This is true for many situations: an interpreter for a medical seminar, for instance, is not expected to know all the terms: this presents a challenge and an opportunity to develop tools (such as thesaurus, controlled vocabulary, dictionaries, specialization, etc.) to aid the interpreter in her job.

Groupware tools may support interaction and promote collaborative environments for knowledge creation and dissemination among CP [30]. Information Technologies may reduce temporal, spatial and organizational barriers among members of an organization; they provide a standard medium and define some rules of communication; and the CP allow a better physical and virtual balance for collaboration environments: virtual users are dispersed, without the benefit of unification provided by the physical world, and, additionally, there is no information conservation rule; this way, the virtual world must address several issues, such as that of identity, communication, interaction etc [31:5-12].

Such needs are premises for future works, which aim at expanding on the knowledge acquired during physical meetings of the members of the CP, as hypothesis for the development of collaborative tools and applications that are efficient and effective for the target public (the members of the Deaf communities). Thus informed, the collaborative environments stand a better chance to increasilly promote social inclusion.

# References

1. Tedre, M., Sutinen, E., Kahkkonen, E., Kommers, P.: Ethnocomputing: ICT in cultural and social context. Communications of the ACM 49(1), 126–130 (2006)
2. Ariboni, S., Perito, R.: Guia prático para um projeto de pesquisa – exploratória, experimental, descritiva. UNIMARCO, São Paulo (2003)
3. Arcoverde, R.D.L.: Digital technologies: a new interative space of social in the written production of the deaf. Cad. CEDES 26(69) (May/August 2006)
4. Ellis, C., Gibbs, S., Rein, G.: Groupware: Some issues and experiences. Comunications of the ACM 34(1), 39–58 (1991)
5. Fernandes, S.: Avaliação em Língua Portuguesa para Alunos Surdos: Algumas considerações. SEED/SUED/DEE, Curitiba (2006)
6. Fuks, H., Raposo, A.B., Gerosa, M.A.: Engenharia de Groupware: Desenvolvimento de Aplicações Colaborativas. In: XXI Jornada de Atualização em Informática, Anais do XXII Congresso da Sociedade Brasileira de Computação, vol. 2, Cap.3 (2002) ISBN 85-88442-24-8
7. Gerosa, M.A., Raposo, A.B., Fuks, H., Lucena, C.J.P.: Combinando Comunicação e Coordenação em Groupware. In: $3^a$ Jornada Ibero-Americana de Engenharia de Software e Engenharia de Conhecimento – JIISIC 2003, Anais Eletrônicos, Valdivia, Chile, November 26-28 (2003)
8. Quadros, R.M., Perlin, G. (odg.): Estudos surdos II. Arara Azul, Petrópolis (2007)
9. Barros, M.E.: ELiS – Escrita das Línguas de Sinais: proposta teórica e verificação prática (Tese de Doutorado). UFSC, Florianópolis (2008)
10. Stokoe, W.C.: Sign Language Structure. Linstok Press, Silver Spring (1960)
11. Skliar, C.: Atualidade da educação bilíngüe para surdo. Mediação, Porto Alegre (1999)
12. Goldfeld, M.A.: Criança Surda. Linguagem e cognição numa perspectiva Sóciointeracionista. Plexus Editora, São Paulo (2002)
13. Wenger, E.: Communities of practice and social learning systems: the career of a concept. In: Blackmore, C. (ed.) Social Learning Systems and Communities of Practice, ch. 11, p. 179. Springer, Dordrecht (2010)

14. Wenger, E.C.: Supporting communities of practice - survey of community oriented technologies. Technical Report 1.3, Etienne Wenger Research and Consulting (2001)
15. Wenger, E., McDermott, R., Snyder, W.M.: Cultivating Communities of Practice. Harvard Business School Press, Massachusetts (2002)
16. Nielsen, J.: Multimedia and Hypermedia: The Internet and Beyond. Academic Press (1996)
17. Laurillau, Y., Nigay, L.: Clover architecture for groupware. In: Proceedings of the Conference on Computer-Supported Cooperative Work (CSCW 2002), pp. 236–245 (2002)
18. Austin, J.L.: How to Do Things with Words. Harvard University Press, Cambridge (1962)
19. Searle, J.R.: Expression and Meaning. Studies in the Theory of Speech Acts. Cambridge University Press, Cambridge (1979)
20. Searle, J.R.: Speech Acts: an essay in the philosophy of language. University Press, Cambridge (1969)
21. Shneiderman, B.: Direct Manipulation: a step beyond programming languages. IEEE Computer 16(8), 57–69 (1983)
22. Nielsen, J.: Heuristic Evaluation. In: Nielsen, J., Mack, R.L. (eds.) Usability Inspection Methods, pp. 25–62. John Wiley & Sons, New York (1994)
23. Grice, H.P.: Logic and Conversation. In: Cole, P., Morgan, J.L. (eds.) Syntax and Semantics, Speech Acts, vol. 3, pp. 41–58. Academic Press, New York (1975)
24. Leech, G.: The Principles of Pragmatics. Longman, London (1983)
25. Thompson, G.: Introducing functional grammar. Arnold, London (1996)
26. Macêdo, C.M.M.: A reclamação e o pedido de desculpas: uma análise Semântico – Pragmática de cartas no contexto Empresarial. Tese de Doutorado. PUC, São Paulo (1999)
27. Guimarães, C., Antunes, D.R., Trindade, D.F.G., da Silva, R.A.L., Garcia, L.S.: Structure of the Brazilian Sign Language (Libras) for Computational Tools: Citizenship and Social Inclusion. In: Lytras, M.D., Ordonez de Pablos, P., Ziderman, A., Roulstone, A., Maurer, H., Imber, J.B. (eds.) WSKS 2010, Part II. CCIS, vol. 112, pp. 365–370. Springer, Heidelberg (2010a)
28. Guimarães, C., Antunes, D.R., Trindade, D.F.G., da Silva, R.A.L., Fernandes, S., Miranda Jr., A., Garcia, L.S.: Techonological artifacts for social inclusion: Structure of the Brazilian sign language (LIBRAS), gestures for citizenship. In: IADIS Internacion Conference WWW/INTERNET 2010, Timisoara, Romenia, pp. 267–271 (2010b)
29. De Souza, C.S.: The Semiotic Engineering of Human-Computer Interaction. The MIT Press, Cambridge (2005)
30. Wenger, E., Snyder, W.: Learning in Communities. Disponível em, http://www.linezine.com/7.2/articles/ewwslc.html (access in February 01, 2011)
31. Kimble, C., Li, F., Barlow, A.: Effective Virtual Teams through Communities of Practice. Management Science – Theory, method & Practice. Strathclyde Business School Management Science Working Paper No. (2000)
32. Tremblay, G.: Communities of Practice: Are the conditions for implementation the same for a virtual multiorganization community – EnANPAD (2004)
33. Winchester, W.W.: III REALizing Our Messy Futures: Toward Culturally Responsive Design Tools in Engaging Our Deeper Dives. ACM's Interactions 18(6), 14–19 (2010)
34. Antunes, D.R., Guimaraes, C., Trindade, D., Silva, R.A.L., Garcia, L.S., Fernandes, S.: Evaluation of a Computational Description Model of Libras (Brazilian Sign Language): Bridging the Gap Towards Information Access. In: Proceedings of the Fifth IEEE International Conference on Research Challenges in Information Science, IEEE RCIS 2011, Guadeloupe, France, May 19-21 (2011) (in press)

# Simulation-Based IT Process Governance

Vladimir Stantchev[1,2], Gerrit Tamm[3,4], and Konstantin Petruch[5]

[1] Berlin Institute of Technology, Berlin, Germany
stantchev@computer.org
[2] Hochschule für Oekonomie und Management (FOM), Berlin, Germany
[3] SRH University of Applied Sciences, Berlin, Germany
[4] Humboldt-University at Berlin, Germany
[5] Deutsche Telekom AG, Germany

**Abstract.** IT departments within enterprises often utilize incident management and ticketing systems. While performance data from such systems is often stored in logfiles it is rarely evaluated extensively. In this work we assess the applicability of an approach for extended evaluation of logged data from such systems. Our evaluation is focused on Key Performance Indicators (KPIs) and aims to discover more in-depth insights as compared to typical data visualization and dashboard techniques.

We also present a practical case study where we demonstrate the feasibility of the approach using real-life logfiles from an international telecommunication provider. Our modeling methodology is based on the approach of System Dynamics.

**Keywords:** simulation, IT processes, IT governance, incident management.

## 1 Introduction

Modern enterprises and organizations conduct a wide range of operative processes electronically. Data gathered by such operative systems often hides nontrivial insights. Visualization is often a first step towards a more detailed data analysis. This is the application domain of the business dashboards. One specific example is the usage of Google analytics[1] to visualize web server logfiles. More complex application scenarios involve the aggregation of multiple data sources and the subsequent analytical processing of data within a data warehouse.

Operative data can provide insights about two distinct types of measurements – key goal indicators (KGIs) which provide insights about the results of an operative task, and key performance indicators (KPIs) which define the way these results were achieved (e.g., speed, transaction rate). When we define such indicators with respect to specific business processes we can apply an approach known as process mining [1].

In this work we extend this approach with more complex simulation techniques. Our focus lies on KPIs and we address the question whether an extended

---

[1] www.google.com/analytics/

M.D. Lytras et al. (Eds.): WSKS 2011, CCIS 278, pp. 206–215, 2013.
© Springer-Verlag Berlin Heidelberg 2013

data analysis using simulation methodologies can provide an additional value as compared to standard data visualization.

The rest of this work is structured as follows: Section 2 presents the state of the art in the measurement of process indicators and the terminology we use. In Section 3 we give an overview of our assessment framework for such indicators in the area of IT operations. In Section 4 we describe a specific data transformation and simulation process that we have assessed within an industry case study with an international telecommunications provider. Section 5 contains a summary of our results and outlook on our future research activities.

## 2 Preliminaries

In this section we introduce the motivation for performance and output metrics. We also discuss the possible insights from existing datasets.

### 2.1 Concepts of Indicators

As stated above, indicators can be generally divided into two groups – key performance indicators (KPIs) and key goal indicators (KGIs). KPIs measure how well a process is performing and are expressed in precisely measurable terms. KGIs represent a description of the outcome of the process, often have a customer and financial focus and can be typically measured after the fact has occurred [2]. While KGIs specify what should be achieved KPIs specify how it should be achieved.

### 2.2 Objectives of Data and Log File Analysis

Various algorithms [3,4] have been propose to discover different types of models based on a log file. A special issue of Computers in Industry on process mining [5] offers more insights. In the context of process model verification there are several notions for equivalence of process specifications such as behavioral equivalence [6,7], trace equivalence, and bisimulation [8] that have been developed. Traditional equivalence notions like bisimulation or trace equivalence are defined as a verification property which yields a yes-or-no boolean value, but no insights on the degree of equivalence. When comparing a reference model with a process model, it is not realistic to assume that their granularities are the same. Therefore, the equivalence analysis with classical equivalence notions will most likely not be conclusive. In the context of process mining we should apply notions searching for behavioral similarity. Examples include causal footprint [6] and fitness function [7]. In [6], the authors introduce an approach for determining the similarity between process models by comparing the footprint of such models. Thereby the footprint describes two relationships between activities – the soc. look-back and look-ahead links and returns the degree of the process similarity expressed in [0, 1]. This value is not conclusive and requires further explanation. It is not possible to trace the missing or differing activities.

Since traceability is an important requirement of the organization, the approach is not suitable in general. In [7], the authors introduce the behavioral and the structural precision and recall. The behavioral equivalence of the process models compares a process model with respect to some typical behavior recorded in log files. The structural precision and recall equate the term "'structure"' with all firing sequences of a Petri net that may occur in a process model. Other related works exist in the areas of pattern matching or semantic matching. Existing approaches [9] assume that the correspondence of activities can be established automatically. Since they suppose that the same label implies same function, they try to identify the content of an activity by using an automated semantic matching algorithm based on the label of activities. One specific approach for quality improvement in compliance is IT supported compliance evaluation [10]. The notion of compliance has also been discussed in the context of business alignment [11].

# 3    Assessment Framework for IT Governance

## 3.1    IT Governance Frameworks

IT governance frameworks aim to define standardized processes and control metrics for IT provision. Commonly applied frameworks in this area include the IT Infrastructure Library (ITIL) [12] and the Control Objectives for Information and Related Technology (CObIT) [13]. They typically provide best practices for measurement and control of IT-specific indicators.

## 3.2    IT-Specific Indicators

IT indicators should demonstrate the added value of IT to the business side. A well accepted view of business objectives is Porter's distinction between operational effectiveness (efficiency and effectiveness) and strategic positioning (reach and structure) [14]. This view can be translated directly into corresponding goals and indicators for IT [15].

Organizations require well designed business processes to achieve excellence in a competitive environment: Here, not one-time optimized business processes play the essential role, but rather the ability to quickly react to new developments and to flexibly adapt respective business processes are decisive[16]. It is important that these processes are effectively supported through IT. These requirements have consequently been catalyzing increased interest in reference modeling for IT process management. Reference models such as ITIL and CObIT represent proven best practices and provide key indicators for the design and control of IT services [12]. On the one hand, utilization of reference models promises to enhance quality and facilitates better compliance according to statutes and contractual agreements. On the other hand, IT processes have to correspond to corporate strategy and its respective goals. Therefore, the question arises how best practices can be implemented in a particular corporate environment. Another challenge lurks in the checking of reference process execution as well as in assuring compliance to IT procedure in respect to new or altered business processes [17].

### 3.3   Aligning IT and Business Indicators

One way towards IT and business alignment can be the application of approaches such as CObIT and ITIL for the optimization of IT organizations. We recently introduced an approach for the continuous quality improvement of IT processes based on such models [1] and process mining. An organization can also try to assure the continuous provision of service levels as demonstrated in our previous work with such reference models and our work in the area of service level assurance in SOA [18,19,20]. Furthermore, in order to coordinate and govern IT production, we can assess operative data and try to analyze it more deeply with the help of simulation models.

### 3.4   Cloud Governance Aspects

Governance of cloud computing should regard different deployment models. Abstracting services at the level of infrastructure (IaaS) allows comparatively easy virtualization – the user organization can configure and customize the platform and the services within the virtual image that is then being deployed and operated. This includes the definition of performance parameters for specific services (e.g., parameters of a Web Service Container), the security aspects of service access, and the integration of services within the platform.

When using a standardized platform (the PaaS approach) the user organization deploys the services in a virtualized operating environment. This operating environment is typically provided as a service – the virtualization technology and the operating environment are managed by the provider. Integration capabilities are always provider-specific and there are currently no commonly accepted industry standards for integration between services operated in different PaaS environments.[2] The usage of software services itself (the SaaS approach) precludes fine-grained control and enforcement of non-functional aspects (e.g., QoS, response time) and security parameters of the infrastructure and the platform by the user organization.

These different levels of virtualization require different levels of security and abstraction. The grade of control and responsibility for security aspects declines with higher levels of abstraction – in IaaS the configuration is generally in the hand of the user organization, while in SaaS it is primarily a responsibility of the Cloud provider.

There are several emerging patterns for cloud usage. The first one is a natural consequence of the trend to outsource IT-Operations (aka. IT-RUN functions) to external providers and results in demand for IaaS. IaaS is typically used for the implementation of test projects and as a way to overcome underprovisioning in on-premise infrastructures. The second one is coming from the SaaS area and focuses on the provision of Web 2.0 applications. Some well-known sites

---

[2] Two current standardization activities at the IEEE Standards Association are IEEE P2301, Draft Guide for Cloud Portability and Interoperability Profiles, and IEEE P2302, Draft Standard for Intercloud Interoperability and Federation, see http://standards.ieee.org/news/2011/cloud.html

offer the user the chance to develop simple applications (a la PaaS) and offer them in a SaaS-like manner later on. This usage pattern could also be called extension facilities. PaaS is an optimal environment for users seeking testing and development capabilities, these are two new emerging use patterns which are gaining popularity. Probably, gaming will be one of the most remarkable usage patterns for Cloud technologies, due to an inherent scalability, endowing such applications with virtually unlimited graphical power and players. Also the rise of netbooks in the computer hardware industry triggered the development of Clouds. These slim devices depend on services being deployed in remote Cloud sites since their own capacity is limited. Behind this stand the idea of getting access to everything, from anywhere, at any time.

A set of general Corporate Governance rules has to be specifically refined and targeted for every operational area in an enterprise. The idea of manageability in Cloud Computing is closely related to the operationalization of Corporate Governance in the different phases of the use of a Cloud Computing offering.

A specific manifestation of such operationalization can be the introduction of SLA-based Governance. This would mean that the organization has to incorporate specific governance requirements as part of a service level agreement for a Cloud Computing offering. Suitable examples include the so called "four-eyes-principle" that can be part of the SLA for a SaaS offering, or data availability requirements that can also be part of the SLA for a SaaS offering.

In order to introduce such transparent Cloud Governance mechanisms an organization has to consider all phases of the usage of a Cloud Computing offering. During the first phase of requirements identification and elicitation (often called the Plan-Phase) these requirements need to be specified and formalized. This allows addressing them already within a first assessment of the Cloud Computing market for the specific offering. Potential Cloud Computing providers can then be specifically evaluated with respect to the requirements and specific SLAs can be negotiated with them during the second phase. The third phase can focus on the transparent communication of values and benefits of the SLA during start of production for the specific business unit. The fourth phase would deal with performance monitoring and assessment of SLA fulfillment and associated bonuses or penalties.

These phases and their associated activities can be introduced as specific Cloud Computing extensions to more traditional IT-Governance approaches such as CObIT and ITIL. This introduction is typically non-trivial, as there are significant differences between the abstraction levels and the semantics of Cloud Computing and IT-Governance.

In the specific area of SaaS a more straightforward approach can focus on the introduction of a more specific approach from the area of SOA Governance – the SOA LifeCycle [21]. It describes a governance approach for software functionality as provided by web services which makes its paradigms and concepts more applicable to the aspects of SaaS Governance. On the other side, the SOA LifeCycle can be incorporated as part of a general IT-Governance strategy based on CObIT and ITIL.

# 4   Case Study: Transforming and Simulating Log Data

In this case study we describe our approach for extended log data evaluation using System Dynamics [22].

## 4.1   Operative Log Data

The operative log data is generated by software applications that provide service support as a set standardized IT functions. It describes request processing for three different IT services of an international telecommunications provider. The IT services are an e-mail service, an IP-based video-on-demand service, and a web-hosting service. Data is generated in a comma separated values (CSV) format and includes an incident number, as well as the following fields:

- priority,
- short description,
- affected service,
- start of incident,
- end of incident,
- range of impact,
- number of process steps needed.

## 4.2   The Concept of System Dynamics

System Dynamics allows to represent and analyze complex causality structures. It can often provide insights that are not easily derived from the original data and are sometimes even counterintuitive. Sometimes such analyzes can lead to the revision of already made decisions. Figure 1 shows an example for such model.

## 4.3   Selection of a Simulation Tool

There exist several tools for the definition and conduction of System Dynamics models. Our next objective was the selection of a suitable tool for the enterprise application scenario. Our assessment was based on cost benefit analysis and the analytical hierarchy process (AHP) and included the following categories of requirements with their weightings.

- Technical (15%)
- Functional (50%)
- Environment (25%)
- Supplier / Support (10%)

Figure 2 shows exemplary an excerpt from the assessment of the technical requirements of the four alternatives.

The final decision was to use the simulation software Consideo Modeller.[3]

---

[3] http://www.consideo.de

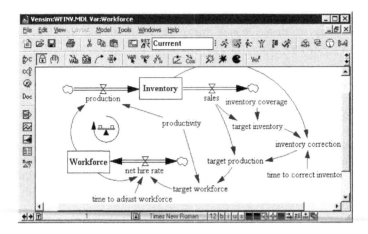

**Fig. 1.** A Sample System Dynamics Model

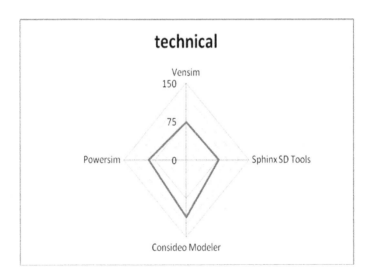

**Fig. 2.** An Excerpt from the Technical Assessment

## 4.4   Data Transformation

The use of the log data as input for the System Dynamics simulation required
further transformation. Examples for two specific transformations that we had
to conduct are:

- The original log data includes timestamps (start and end of an incident)
  UNIX-type datetime data. It had to be transformed to the supported
  DD.MM.YYYY HH:MM:SS format.

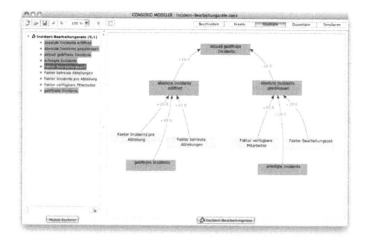

**Fig. 3.** An Excerpt from the Quantitative Model

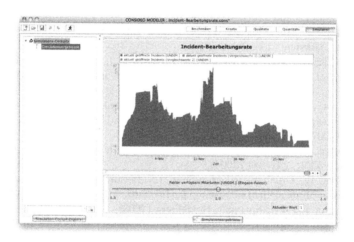

**Fig. 4.** Simulation of the Incident Processing Rate

- We had to include an incident increment that we then facilitated to model coordinates between a time value and the number of incidents that are processed.
- We used only an excerpt of the available log data that covered several years. Using data blocks per month allowed us to keep the execution time of the simulation short.

### 4.5   Sample Simulation Models and Results

Figure 3 shows an excerpt from our quantitative modeling approach.

Specific KPIs and KGIs that we can simulate from the log data include the incident processing rate (see Figure 4) and further indicators such as timing and responses dependencies.

## 5  Conclusion and Outlook

Objective of this work was to better evaluate enterprise indicators through facilitation of an extended analysis of operative log data. We used a System Dynamics model in order to map log data to established indicators from ITIL. The case study demonstrated the feasibility of our approach. Furthermore, it can be a suitable environment for the evaluation of knowledge and learning objects, processes, strategies, systems, and performance as defined in [23].

## References

1. Gerke, K., Tamm, G.: Continuous Quality Improvement of IT Processes based on Reference Models and Process Mining. In: AMCIS 2009 Proceedings, p. 786 (2009)
2. Van Grembergen, W. (ed.): Strategies for Information Technology Governance. IGI Publishing, Hershey (2003)
3. van der Aalst, W.M.P., van Dongen, B.F., Herbst, J., Maruster, L., Schimm, G., Weijters, A.J.M.M.: Workflow mining: a survey of issues and approaches. Data Knowl. Eng. 47, 237–267 (2003)
4. de Medeiros, A.K.A., Weijters, A.J.M.M., van der Aalst, W.M.P.: Genetic process mining: an experimental evaluation. Data Mining and Knowledge Discovery 14(2), 245–304 (2007)
5. van der Aalst, W.M.P., Weijters, A.: Process mining: a research agenda. Computers in Industry 53(3), 231–244 (2004)
6. van Dongen, B., Dijkman, R., Mendling, J.: Measuring Similarity between Business Process Models. In: Bellahsène, Z., Léonard, M. (eds.) CAiSE 2008. LNCS, vol. 5074, pp. 450–464. Springer, Heidelberg (2008)
7. van der Aalst, W.M.P., de Medeiros, A.K.A., Weijters, A.J.M.M.: Process Equivalence: Comparing Two Process Models Based on Observed Behavior. In: Dustdar, S., Fiadeiro, J.L., Sheth, A.P. (eds.) BPM 2006. LNCS, vol. 4102, pp. 129–144. Springer, Heidelberg (2006)
8. Van Glabbeek, R.J., Weijland, W.P.: Branching time and abstraction in bisimulation semantics. Journal of the ACM (JACM) 43(3), 555–600 (1996)
9. Ehrig, M., Koschmider, A., Oberweis, A.: Measuring similarity between semantic business process models. In: Proceedings of the Fourth Asia-Pacific Conference on Comceptual Modelling, vol. 67, pp. 71–80. Australian Computer Society, Inc. (2007)
10. Sackmann, S., Kähmer, M.: Expdt: A layer-based approach for automating compliance. Wirtschaftsinformatik 50(5), 366–374 (2008)
11. van der Aalst, W.M.P.: Business alignment: using process mining as a tool for delta analysis and conformance testing. Requir. Eng. 10, 198–211 (2005)
12. Van Bon, J.: Foundations of IT service management based on ITIL V3. Van Haren (2008)

13. Lainhart IV, J.W.: COBIT: A Methodology for Managing and Controlling Information and Information Technology Risks and Vulnerabilities. Journal of Information Systems 14, 21 (2000)
14. Porter, M.E.: What is strategy? Harvard Business Review 74(4134), 61–78 (1996)
15. Tallon, P.P., Kraemer, K.L., Gurbaxani, V.: Executives' perceptions of the business value of information technology: a process-oriented approach. J. Manage. Inf. Syst. 16, 145–173 (2000)
16. Borzo, J.: Business 2010 - Embracing the Challenge of Change. Technical report (2005)
17. Stantchev, V., Tamm, G.: Addressing non-functional properties of services in it service management. In: Non-Functional Properties in Service Oriented Architecture: Requirements, Models and Methods, pp. 324–334. IGI Global, Hershey (2011)
18. Stantchev, V., Schröpfer, C.: Service level enforcement in web-services based systems. International Journal on Web and Grid Services 5(2), 130–154 (2009)
19. Stantchev, V., Malek, M.: Translucent replication for service level assurance. In: High Assurance Services Computing, pp. 1–18. Springer, Berlin (2009)
20. Stantchev, V., Schröpfer, C.: Negotiating and Enforcing QoS and SLAs in Grid and Cloud Computing. In: Abdennadher, N., Petcu, D. (eds.) GPC 2009. LNCS, vol. 5529, pp. 25–35. Springer, Heidelberg (2009)
21. Stantchev, V., Malek, M.: Addressing dependability throughout the soa life cycle. IEEE Transactions on Services Computing 99(PrePrints) (2010)
22. Richardson, G.P., Pugh, A.L.: Introduction to System Dynamics Modeling with Dynamo. MIT Press, Cambridge (1981)
23. Lytras, M.D., Sicilia, M.A.: The Knowledge Society: a manifesto for knowledge and learning. International Journal of Knowledge and Learning 1(1/2), 1–11 (2005)

# A Social Network for Sharing Learning Segments and Compositions

Edmar Welington Oliveira[1,2], Sean W.M. Siqueira[3], and Maria Helena L.B. Braz[4]

[1] Computer Science Department (DCC), Federal University of Juiz de Fora (UFJF):
R. José Kelmer, s/n Campus Universitário, São Pedro, Juiz de Fora, Brazil, 36036-330
[2] Computer Science Department, Pontifical Catholic University of Rio de Janeiro (PUC-Rio):
R. Marques de Sao Vicente, 225, Gavea, Rio de Janeiro, Brazil, 22453-900
[3] Department of Applied Informatics (DIA/CCET), Federal University of the State of Rio de Janeiro (UNIRIO): Av. Pasteur, 458, Urca, Rio de Janeiro, Brazil, 22290-240
[4] ICIST, IST, Technical University of Lisbon: Av. Rovisco Pais,
Lisbon, Portugal, 1049-001
edmar.oliveira@ufjf.edu.br, sean@uniriotec.br,
mhb@civil.ist.utl.pt

**Abstract.** The development of learning content using information technologies is an expensive, time-consuming and complex process. Therefore, it is important to consider reusing already developed instructional artifacts. This reuse approach is particularly interesting as it is observed that both teachers and learners perform searches for learning content, according to their needs and interests in order to create units – or compositions – of instructional content, aiming to accomplish a particular learning objective. Previous works discussed how the learners can learn from sharing instructional segments, but the composition of these segments is also important in the learning process. Therefore, in this paper different strategies for composition of learning segments are discussed and an educational social network oriented to instructional segments, is presented. A prototype was developed and a case study was performed in order to evaluate the proposed strategy.

**Keywords:** Learning Objects, Segments, Content Objects, Composition, Segmentation, Reasoning.

## 1 Introduction

The development of instructional content using information technologies is an expensive, time-consuming and complex process [1]. So, in order to reduce costs and improve development speed it is important to consider the reuse of existing instructional materials and other available documents. In this context the term Learning Object (LO) was coined and it is possible to find in literature many different approaches based on this concept aiming at increasing reusability of learning materials. The most cited definition of LO is provided by IEEE LTSC [2]: "a LO is any entity, digital or non-digital, that can be used for learning, education and training". Usually LOs are considered reusable digital content units.

M.D. Lytras et al. (Eds.): WSKS 2011, CCIS 278, pp. 216–225, 2013.
© Springer-Verlag Berlin Heidelberg 2013

When considering the reuse of LOs, it is observed that both teachers and learners perform searches for LOs, according to their needs and interests, and create units of instructional content, aiming to accomplish a particular learning objective. In general, teachers are interested in the preparation of courses, lessons or classes. Learners, on the other hand, are interested in gaining support during the study of some subject. In fact, both teachers and learners are interested in compositions of learning content, able to support them in some educational process. Basically, this composition can be understood as a set of learning materials, which together, consist in a new and more complex content. The approach of creating content compositions is intrinsically associated to the activities of searching and sequencing LOs. The search comprises in selecting appropriate materials to a particular need and the sequencing comprises ordering the selected materials in a suitable way. However, these new learning materials are still manually assembled, possibly because there is a great difficulty in finding suitable LOs and, especially, making its subsequent sequencing. In this scenario, teachers and learners spend considerable time and efforts in (i) searching for learning content that promotes a gain in knowledge and (ii) trying to understand how to sequence those that were selected. Thus, from this point of view, the reusability of LOs is not as high as desirable.

An important aspect associated with lack of reuse of LOs is the LOs' granularity. In fact, as stated by [3] and discussed by [4], there is an inverse relationship between LO size and reusability. Nowadays, LOs are still complex units, usually corresponding to multimedia files. Therefore, although the access and reuse of only parts of a specific LO could be desirable, in general, it is only possible to obtain the entire LO, which limits its reuse. In this context, it is essential to provide strategies to promote reuse of parts of LOs' content, instead of the whole content. In [5] it was presented a strategy to segment LOs in small portions - called "segments" -, making it possible to use them in different learning contexts. With the segmentation approach, it would be possible to teachers and learners to use specific parts of the content embedded in LOs, appropriated to a particular need. However, although the use of segments can be considered as a strategy to improve reusability, segmentation itself is not sufficient to solve problems regarding searching and sequencing. When considering composition - even using segments - , it is necessary define approaches able to support users.

This paper presents some strategies for composing content segments. It also describes the use of relationships between the segments and logic reasoning for providing a semi-automatic approach for sequencing. A social network that provides a collaborative environment for sharing instructional content was created. This network allows exploring segments of instructional content and their compositions. In order to verify the applicability of this environment, in special related to the composition strategy, a case study was performed. It showed the importance of using relationships between the segments and their practicability for supporting content composition. The collaborative environment also motivated students in their learning process.

The remaining of this paper is organized as follows: Section 2 discusses composition strategies. In section 3 the proposed approach for content segmentation and composition is presented while in Section 4 the case study performed in order to evaluate the reasoning strategy is described. Section 5 presents some final remarks, also discussing some ongoing and future works.

## 2      Composition Strategies of Instructional Segments

This section presents different learning content composition approaches. In [6], the focus was in pedagogical approaches and learning theories. Basically, it considered a metamodel for representing learning content and practice. The definition of this metamodel was based on previous experiences and proposals on information processing, learning content structuring and the classification of learning content and practice. Particularly, to accomplish LOs composition, it was considered the use of pedagogical approaches (an organized set of principles that explain how individuals acquire, retain and recall knowledge) for extracting and sequencing the instructional content and practice. The teacher's model is associated with learning theories and approaches which they often adopt in their classes. This strategy for searching, extracting, and sequencing instructional content and practice, supports a teacher to better control the implementation of complex LO (a lesson or a course) reducing errors in the authoring process and  reusing existing instructional material stored in a repository and modeled according to the conceptual metamodel. Although interesting, this approach has focus on the teacher and his didactical-pedagogical influences when composing a LO. In addition, it does not provide any information about getting those concepts into a real media, which implements the LO.

Searching for LOs through navigating in repositories is also described in [7], which proposed the navigation through a curricular specification. This is a limited way for composing learning content.

Aroyo et al. [8] suggest using topic maps as a way for implementing the interoperability and possible reuse of LOs, providing means for getting a suggestion for looking for LOs in a manual way in repositories. Although topic maps provide a conceptual structuring of concepts, the relationships allow navigating through the concepts. However, making a composition from these topic maps is harder because of the semantics of the relationships.

There are some relationships already defined in LOM[1] for connecting LOs. The use of these relationships from LOM categories for providing learning paths from these relationships is proposed by Farrel et al. [9]. In their proposal, learning paths consider the time for learning and a topic graph, which is built from the LOM information. The composition combines xml documents according to a structure defined by the user or using an automatic approach. However, the composition is restricted to categories such as introduction, concepts, procedures and conclusion, and the system deals only with textual information.

## 3      Proposed Approach for Learning Content Composition

The proposed approach for learning content composition is related to LOs and their possible segments - obtained through a segmentation process. Basically, given a LO,

---

[1] Learning Objects Metadata, a standard proposed by IEEE LTSC for describing LOs: http://ltsc.ieee.org/wg12/files/LOM_1484_12_1_v1_Final_Draft.pdf

the segmentation process comprises segmenting it in small portions, according to a user's need or interest. The segmentation architecture was proposed in [5] and an evaluation of segmentation process was discussed in [10]. A strategy for allowing students to segment and share segments was discussed in [11].

Once created and properly described, the segments could be reused in other learning contexts. Then, when necessary, instead of reusing a whole LO, it would be possible to reuse specific parts of the content embedded on it. This reuse should comprise creating compositions – a set of related segments disposed in a specific sequence. The learner could select - from a repository - a set of segments, according to his/her needs and interests, and create a new and more complex learning material, appropriated to his/her current instructional process.

In order to create compositions, it is necessary to search for appropriated segments – in general, a time-consuming task, mainly considering large repositories. Therefore, aiming to support a semi-automatic composition development, the proposed approach comprises specifying relationships among segments and performing logic inferences over these relationships.

The relationship strategy is based on the definition of relationships among different segments, making it possible to a search engine, during a search processing, not only to return segments according to the search's parameters, but also to return other segments that are related to these ones. Let's consider a repository with segments S1 and S2, for instance. Suppose that S1 and S2 are related to each other: S1 complements S2. In this case, if S1 is returned by the search engine as result of a user' search, then S2 could be returned as well, since it is related to S1. This is interesting to learners, mainly when considering the composition process. In fact, learners would be able to analyze possible relationships of the segment of interest with other ones, possibly considering these related segments as part of a composition. The idea is to support learners during composition process, assisting them to choose and sequence segments. However, for the success of the discussed strategy it is important to specify, whenever possible, relationships among learning segments. Figure 1 presents an example of relationships among segments.

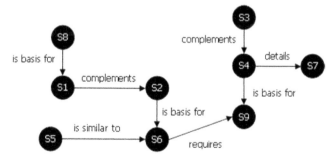

**Fig. 1.** Example of relationships between segments

Although it is necessary to define relationships among segments, there is a problem regarding this process. In fact, the larger a segment repository, the more complex is specifying all possible relations among segments. Actually, for larger repositories this is an impracticable task. It would be a very time consuming task whenever storing a new segment in a repository to analyze all segments already stored in order to verify possible relationships with the new one. In this sense, a feasible proposal to deal with the difficulties associated with defining relationships between segments, mainly when considering large repositories would be an automatic specification of relationships, performed during searches processing. This approach comprises the performing of logical inferences over the relationships defined between segments. These inferences would be executed every time a search is performed. It would allow identifying relationships among segments which where not defined during segments' storage. As example, a learner, interested in a specific subject, could perform searches for segments. Let's consider the relationships defined in Figure 1, and that a learner's search has returned the segment S2. In a traditional search process, only the segment S2 would be returned by learners' search. However, adopting the relationships strategy, it would be also returned S1 and S6, since they are related to S2. But, using the reasoning strategy and considering the use of pre-defined inference rules, it would be possible to return, for instance, S4. In this case, the relationship between S2 and S4 was inferred, using the inference rule and a reasoner engine. Figure 2(a) and Figure 2(b) illustrate, respectively, the scenarios of relationship and reasoning strategies. In the last one, it was considered the following logic rule: "If SX is basis for SY and SW is basis for SZ and SY requires SZ → SX requires SW" – which was applied over the components described in Figure 1. The correspondences with Figure 1 are: SX/S2, SY/S6, SW/S4 and SZ/S9. In this case, the logic rule could be translated to: "S2 is basis for S6 and S4 is basis for S9 and S6 requires S9 → S2 requires S4".

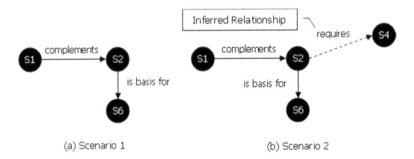

(a) Scenario 1                    (b) Scenario 2

**Fig. 2.** Scenarios of relationships and reasoning strategies

The relationship "requires", illustrated through the dotted arrow in Figure 2(b) represents the result of the logic inference, using the logic rule already discussed over the relationships presented in Figure 1. In other words, the expression "SX requires SW" is valid if the assumptions "SX is basis for SY", "SW is basis for SZ" and "SY requires SZ" are true. Therefore, in this context, a reasoner engine could infer that "S2 requires S4" (a relationship not explicitly defined during the storage of these segments). The main objective of using the reasoning strategy is to (i) avoid, whenever possible, the time-consuming task of finding all possible relationships among segments every time a new segment is stored in the repository and (ii) to improve results of segments' search by presenting to users the larger semantic network of related segments.

Obviously, it would be possible to configure the system in order to return all the segments directly or indirectly related to S2. Moreover, it would be possible to specify levels of depth of relationships that should be considered by the reasoner. In this context, if S2 was returned according to learner's search parameters, the segments illustrated in Figure 3 would be returned – considering a depth of level 2. Considering level 1, the segments returned would be those illustrated in Figure 2(b). The authors argue that the composition development becomes easier to the users as relationships among segments can be visualized. Considering Figure 1, for instance, a learner could create a composition with the segments S1, S2 and S4. Moreover, based on the semantic of the relations, the sequence could be: S4, S2 and S1 since S4 it is necessary to S2 and S1 complements S2.

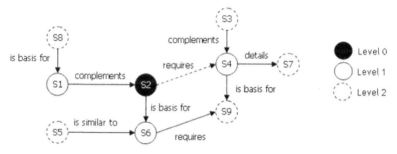

**Fig. 3.** Levels of search depth

## 4    Case Studies and Their Evaluation

In order to understand how users (in the case, learners) would react to the composition of segments of educational content, it was used a prototype based on the architecture proposed at [5]. The experiment was developed in a class of the "Introduction to Information Systems" Course in the Federal University of the State of Rio de Janeiro. Twenty-four learners participated of the study and were distributed into eight groups, each one with three members. The number of groups and members were defined based on the infrastructure available to carry out the study. Particularly, the prototype was configured to work with videos. So, twenty-three videos were selected from the Web: 12 related to "Strategic Planning" topic and 11 related to "Object-Oriented Programming". These topics were chosen since both of them were subjects of the course and were of possible interest to the learners. The number of videos was bounded by time restrictions for the considered tasks as well as content evaluation by the instructors.

The study was configured to be performed in stages. In each one, learners should execute specific tasks and, after the completion of each one, evaluation questionnaires were applied in order to collect data. The learning content composition activities were evaluated focusing on the segments, including a segmentation process, the searching for segments, and the composition of segments. For the proposal of this paper, it was essential to analyze learners' interest on using segments of learning content in order to create new learning materials - according to their needs and interest. In other words, the authors were interested in evaluating how learners would react to the possibility of creating new composed objects, performing a knowledge aggregation. This motivation is important to consider in an online social network, in special, working as a learning collaborative environment. It was analyzed, for instance, learners' interest on creating and using segments (motivation), how they understood an learning content in order to segment it (conceptualization or abstraction for representing concepts), how they looked for learning segments (classification and summarization for searching) [4] and how they reacted to acquired segments (critical thinking) [11]. Figure 4 shows a summary of the study, particularly regarding to the segmentation and composition processes.

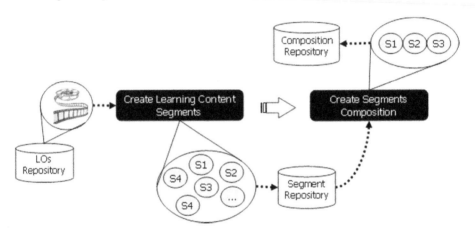

**Fig. 4.** Segmentation and composition processes

Initially, the groups should access the available videos (previously stored in the LOs Repository) and choose – according to their interest – the ones that would be segmented. Once selected, the videos were segmented and the resulting segments were stored in the Segment Repository. Then, the groups should access it and perform searches for segments, selecting those according to their needs and interests in order to create compositions (in other words, new and more complex learning materials). During the search process, logic inferences were performed by the prototype aiming to support the composition task. Once created, each composition was appropriately stored in the Composition Repository. It is important to emphasize that, during the composition process, the groups were allowed to use segments created by other groups. Therefore, it was some kind of social network for sharing learning segments and compositions.

Analyzing the answers of the questionnaires, the possibility of visualizing related segments during the composition process were useful according to 87.5% of the learners. They argued that it is easier to create segments compositions analyzing how segments are related to each other - in other words, analyzing the semantic of the relationships. Moreover, 100% of the learners would like to use related segments during a new composition process. The questionnaires also showed that 91.66% of the learners agreed that the relationships between segments are important in the learning process. In fact, according to them, defining relationships between segments can support user's learning process by presenting segments - results of segments search - in a meaningful sequence that enables an exploratory navigation approach between different segments. In addition, for 91.66% of the learners, the segments which were related to those returned as query results were useful in order to create their compositions. Finally, 100% of learners argued they would recommend to other learners their related segments - created through the segmentation process – as a way to support as well as promote learning. This motivation for collaboration is essential in a collaborative learning environment, building social networks.

# 5     Conclusions

The development of instructional content using information technologies is an expensive, time-consuming and complex process. Therefore, there is a great interest in reusability – that's why the Learning Objects (LOs) approach is considered. When reusing LOs, usually teachers and learners perform searches for LOs, according to their needs and interests, and create units of educational content, aiming to accomplish a particular learning objective. The approach of creating content compositions is intrinsically associated to the activities of searching and sequencing LOs – which makes the composition itself a time-consuming task.

In the work presented in this paper, the emphasis was in collaboratively building sequences (compositions) of educational segments. Users (usually learners) search for specific parts of learning materials (segments) in order to create compositions that could support them at accomplishing learning objectives. It was showed the importance of specifying relationships among different segments, which should also be provided through a reasoning strategy. A scenario of relationships among segments was presented, as well as the use of logic inferences over it. A case study was performed and its results were presented. The learner's motivation on dealing with educational segments and their compositions showed it is a good approach for a collaborative learning environment.

Therefore, it is useful to perform segmentation of learning content. However, the search, composition and sequencing of the resulting learning segments are high cognitive load tasks which demand time and effort. The approaches of relationships and logic reasoning could be used in order to facilitate these tasks. Other alternatives are under investigation as ongoing works focus on dealing with the composition according to two layers: the conceptual and the physical. Based on semiotics, it considers the former from a domain ontology, trying to find a path from the necessary concepts to learn a subject. Then, in the physical layer it consider aspects as solving media execution, defining which content can be executed in parallel or in a sequence according to cognitive aspects. This approach seems to provide a solution for dealing with different media, as opposed to the solution proposed in this paper that only deals with sequencing the same media.

Future works could consider more automatic approaches such as the use of HTN networks for planning the compositions. Recently, planning techniques in Artificial Intelligence have been successfully used for determining the sequence of instructional actions. In this sense, it would be possible use or adapt these techniques in order to promote learning content composition, mainly considering segments of instructional materials.

**Acknowledgments.** The authors would like to thank the participants of the case study. This work was partially supported by FAPERJ (through grants E-26/170028/2008 INC&T Program - Project: Brazilian Institute of Research on Web Science, and E-26/ 101.509/2010 - BBP/Bursary Representation and contextualized retrieval of learning content), CNPQ (project: 557.128/2009-9, INCT on Web Science), CAPES (RH-TVD project #133/2008) and by FCT Portugal, through funds of ICIST.

# References

1. Christiansen, J., Anderson, T.: Feasibility of course development based on learning objects: Research analysis of three case studies. International Journal of Instructional Technology and Distance Education 1(2), 21–38 (2004)
   IEEE LTSC. IEEE P1484.12.3, Draft 8: Draft Standard for Learning Technology - Extensible Markup Language (XML) Schema Definition Language Binding for Learning Object Metadata Draft P1484.12.3/D8 (2005), http://ltsc.ieee.org/wg12/files/IEEE_1484_12_03_d8_submitted.pdf
2. Wiley, D.A.: Learning object design and sequencing theory. Dissertation submitted to the faculty of Brigham Young University, Department of Instructional Psychology, USA (2000)
3. Oliveira, E.W., Siqueira, S.W.M., Braz, M.H.L.B.: Approaches to Use Segments of Learning Objects. Revista Brasileira de Informática na Educação 18(1), 76–90 (2010)
4. Oliveira, E.W., Siqueira, S.W.M., Braz, M.H.L.B.: Structuring Segments of e-Learning Multimedia Objects with LOM and MPEG-7. In: Proceedings of IASTED International Conference on Computers and Advanced Technology in Education, pp. 353–358. Acta Press, Calgary (2008)
5. Braz, M.H.L.B., Siqueira, S.W.M., Silva, D.S., Melo, R.N.: A semi-automatic strategy for achieving learning content and practice repurposing. Computer in Human Behavior 27(4), 1344–1351 (2011)
6. Janssen, J., Berlanga, A., Vogten, H., Koper, R.: Towards a learning path specification. International Journal of Continuing Engineering Education and Life Long Learning 18(1), 77–97 (2008)
7. Aroyo, L., Dicheva, D.: The new challenges for e-learning: The educational semantic web. Educational Technology & Society 7(4), 59–69 (2004)
8. Farrell, R.G., Liburd, S.D., Thomas, J.C.: Dynamic assembly of learning objects. In: Proceedings of the 13th International World Wide Web Conference, pp. 162–169. ACM, New York (2004)

9. Oliveira, E.W., Braz, M.H.L.B., Siqueira, S.W.M.: Evaluating the Reuse of Learning Content through a Segmentation Approach. In: Proceedings of the IEEE International Conference on Advanced Learning Technologies, pp. 319–321. IEEE Computer Society, Washington (2009)
10. Oliveira, E.W., Siqueira, S.W.M., Braz, M.H.L.B., Melo, R.N.: Learning by Sharing Instructional Segments. In: Lytras, M.D., Damiani, E., Carroll, J.M., Tennyson, R.D., Avison, D., Naeve, A., Dale, A., Lefrere, P., Tan, F., Sipior, J., Vossen, G. (eds.) WSKS 2009. LNCS, vol. 5736, pp. 346–355. Springer, Heidelberg (2009)

# Improving the Efficiency of Web Searches
# in Collaborative Learning Platforms

João Carlos Prates[1], Eduardo Fritzen[1], Sean W.M. Siqueira[1],
Leila C.V. de Andrade[1], and Maria Helena L.B. Braz[2]

[1] Department of Applied Informatics (DIA/CCET), Federal University of the State of Rio de
Janeiro (UNIRIO): Av. Pasteur, 458, Urca, Rio de Janeiro, Brazil, 22290-240
[2] ICIST, IST, Technical University of Lisbon: Av. Rovisco Pais, Lisbon, Portugal, 1049-001
{joao.santos,eduardo.fritzen,sean,leila}@uniriotec.br,
mhb@civil.ist.utl.pt

**Abstract.** The web is nowadays one of the main information sources and
information searching is one important issue where many advances have been
reported. However, in learning environments, web searches do not consider the
learning context in order to provide more adequate learning content. As
collaborative learning platforms are usually web-based systems, it would be
important to add a contextual web query tool to provide additional learning
material from the web. This paper describes a strategy for incorporating such
functionality in online social networks, as they can be used as collaborative
learning platforms. In this study, the learning environment was a learning
community in an online social network, in which a course was implemented.
Contextual search was provided through a prototype that implements the
proposed query expansion, which was evaluated using learning documents.
Some results are summarized and presented.

**Keywords:** Social Networks, Web Search, Information retrieval, Context,
Personalization.

# 1    Introduction

The Web is still growing on importance as people incorporate its tools and
functionalities in their daily activities. The existence of so many documents available
online and the need to be able to find information in such a rich repository have led to
the development of search engines. A lot of research effort has been directed to obtain
more efficient solutions on getting the right information from the web and search
engines receive several hundred million queries each day through its various
services[1]. On the other hand, the disseminated use of the web has provided a whole
category of online social networks.

Online social networks are another important tool that allows users to share ideas,
activities, events, and interests within their individual networks. Boyd and Ellison [1]

---

[1] http://en.wikipedia.org/wiki/Google_Search

M.D. Lytras et al. (Eds.): WSKS 2011, CCIS 278, pp. 226–234, 2013.
© Springer-Verlag Berlin Heidelberg 2013

provided an overview of the literature related to online social networks, which were defined as: "web-based services that allow individuals to (1) build a public or semi-public profile within a bounded system, (2) articulate a list of other users with whom they share a connection, and (3) view and traverse their list of connections and those made by others within the system."

The potential brought by these tools for human development is enormous and it is clear that the area of education can not remain indifferent to the existence of such opportunities. There are now many Web-based collaborative platforms where students and teachers interact and communicate and because many students are already using social networking sites, teachers have begun to familiarize themselves with this trend and are exploring new possibilities for increasing learning outcomes. There are now many examples of social networks and other web tools being used by teachers and students as communication tools [2], [3].

Nevertheless, when analyzing the search tools included in these environments it is possible to realize that searching for information on these platforms does not take advantage of the corresponding context in order to provide more adequate content from the web. It becomes more critical when the social networks are used as learning environment and the web searches do not consider the learning context.

This is an open issue and the work described in this paper addresses the possibility of building a contextual web query tool to be able to offer better search results. The work presented in this paper builds a strategy based on getting contextual information from shared content used in the learning platform and using a query expansion approach to get more suitable documents for the learning activities.

To be able to evaluate the value of these ideas, a prototype, based on the proposed strategy, was built and a case study was conducted in a real learning scenario at a Brazilian public university, with the aim of helping students to find educational resources in the Internet that complement their learning processes.

The remaining of this paper is organized as follows: Section 2 describes how context can be used to drive the information retrieval process. On Section 3, the architecture of the contextual query tool is presented and discussed. Section 4 presents the case study and the experiments done to evaluate the query expansion strategy and section 5 concludes presenting some final remarks.

## 2    Contextual Information Retrieval

In general, context is modeled through some knowledge representation. The information considered in the context can be the knowledge domain, the user profile, the business process or the user activity, the search history or even information obtained from sensors. The context model is used to make information retrieval more adequate to the user's need, thus it alters the normal process of documents retrieval. This process implies on providing new terms for expanding the original query, or removing other terms. Other possibilities for the alteration on the retrieval process are related to using the context as a basis for reclassification of the relevance order of an initial set of retrieved documents.

The context model can be created manually or automatically. In the first possibility there is direct interference of experts or users, for example through the creation of ontologies, filling out preferences forms or marking relevant documents [4], [5]. The latter provides the automatic capacity through inferences based on user behavior (analysis of clickthrough, navigation and queries history) or information from the environment [6], [7].

Although performing well in making the search tool adaptive to the context, and therefore providing more useful results, the manual context creation presents as main drawbacks the time and effort spent by users (experts or end users) in building the context model. On the other hand, the automatic creation of contexts may cause incorrect results if the inferred context does not reflect the current information needs of the user.

Another form of automatically creating the context model is through text mining, using techniques such as stemming, clustering and co-occurrence of terms. Some works that use query expansion with clustering (like the solution strategy used in this work) are presented in [5].

In advanced learning technologies, some works address the use of context in information retrieval. Zhuhadar and Nasraoui [8] capture the context with the use of domain taxonomies and user profile, and reclassify the search results according to the similarity between the terms contained in the search results and in taxonomies. Khribi et al [9] recommend educational resources based on web mining techniques. From the log files (records of visited addresses), user sessions are grouped according to similarity, and association rules are created between these sessions and visited elements. Ambrosio et al [10] use text mining techniques in selected presentations to recommend documents stored in a repository and suggest query expansion to be executed on the web.

## 3     The Proposed Architecture

In order to make web searching context sensitive, the tool for query expansion proposed in this work supposes that the most frequent terms in documents (links or messages) that are representative of a domain have higher probability to be in other documents that are available on the Internet and are relevant and related to this domain. Therefore, these terms are good candidates to be used to expand the queries entered by the users aiming at getting more useful results on web search engines.

As online social networks become more and more incorporated to everybody's daily tasks, they are also investigated as possible environments for other business situations. They usually provide content (media) sharing sometimes through the use of communication tools. These functionalities allow using online social networks as a collaborative learning platform. In some networks it is possible to create groups of users who share the same interest (for instance, students in a class or a course). Content sharing allows providing the necessary content material for a course, the communication tool enables exchanging ideas and therefore collaborative tasks. According to the proposal presented in this paper, through the available content it is possible to get the domain context and, then, use this context to expand user web queries in order to obtain additional learning resources related to the subject to be learned.

For the implementation of the proposed approach, it was considered the social network facebook[2]. The first step on creating the learning environment is to create a group, illustrated as Context Group in Fig. 1. The Learning context is acquired through published text and links.

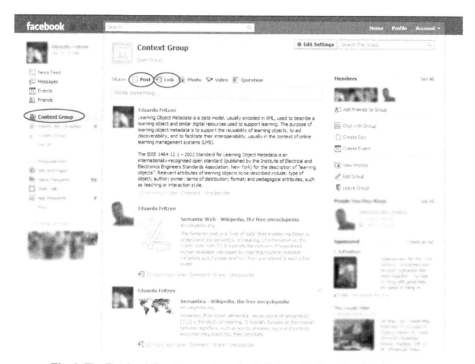

**Fig. 1.** The Facebook Implementation of a Collaborative Learning Environment

For retrieving data from facebook, it is necessary to use a communication SDK/API (Open Graph API or Facebook Graph API), which is officially supported for PHP, Javascript, C#, Android and iOS. All the communication between partner app and the facebook is through the use of a JSON (JavaScript Object Notation) specification.

Some activities for preparing the text of the documents before extraction are necessary: (i) Tokenization, the process of decomposing textual content into terms; (ii) stop words removal, a list of common terms that occurs with high frequency in texts but have almost no value at all, such as prepositions, pronouns and articles; and (iii) stemming, the process of reducing a term to its root form, removing endings, affixes and thematic vowels [11].

---

[2] www.facebook.com

Considering that each document (text or link) that is representative of a context can contain different subjects, although all of them related to the context, just extracting terms based on occurrences can combine terms from different subjects in a query, thus reducing the probability of getting useful results in the web query.

Therefore it was decided to make two term extractions: one calculating the weights of the terms based only on the frequency of these terms in the whole collection of documents (in the group) in order to get the "general terms of the context"; and other in which the calculus considers the terms' frequency in the documents of each subject that was identified in the context, the "specific terms by subject". Each extraction of terms provides different query expansions.

In order to extract specific terms by subject it is necessary to process contextual information with information extraction activities. In order to avoid terms from different subjects being added to a query, the content of each piece of contextual information is segmented in topics, making each segment to treat a different subject and being considered an independent document in the collection.

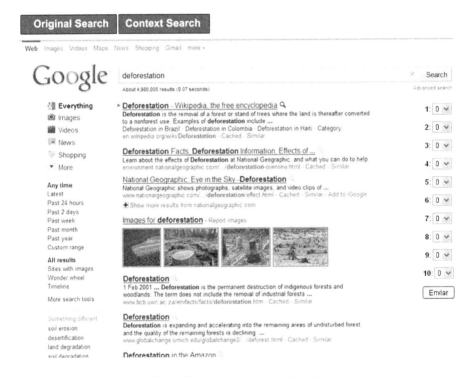

**Fig. 2.** The Query App's user interface

After segmenting all the pieces of information, the segments are grouped according to their similarity, making subsets of segments. These subsets represent the different subjects that were identified in the context. For each subset, the most frequent terms are extracted.

A domain specialist must identify, for a group of selected documents, the amount of different subjects that are considered. This number defines how many groups of segments are going to be created and therefore the quantity of query expansions that will be created in the search module.

The search module gets three pieces of information from the users: the domain context, the query expression and the search engine. With these pieces of information, this module searches for the terms in the information extraction module, makes the query expansion and runs the expanded queries on the query engine.

Therefore, the students have to access the Query Application in order to make a contextualized query (Fig. 2).

## 4    A Case Study

To test the feasibility of these ideas a prototype was developed considering at this time only the core of the proposal and not being used in the facebook environment yet. Nevertheless it was valuable to demonstrate the applicability of the proposed approach for query expansion. The case study was conducted in a real learning scenario at a Brazilian public university, with students attending the undergraduate course "Information Systems". Context was defined as a lesson about Knowledge Management and Expert Systems. The main objective of this case study was to use the prototype to help students finding educational resources in the Internet that complement the learning process in this lesson.

The participants should express their information needs by specifying queries that represented these needs, and then the prototype with the automatic expansion facility was used to make the search. Afterwards the students evaluated the results obtained from the searches according to their relevance. In addition, after using the tool, the participants answered a questionnaire to collect data on qualitative aspects of the tool assessment.

Eighteen evaluations were collected as the class had twenty-six students, but some were allowed to work in groups. Each student or group should formulate a search expression and select the number of terms that the tool would include in the original query. They were allowed to execute the query as many times as necessary, testing a different number of terms until they felt comfortable to start the evaluation of the search results.

The results were evaluated according to three metrics proposed by different researchers and consolidated by Tang and Sun [12] for the evaluation of web search engines: first 10 full precision, search length and rank correlation.

Precision is a metric widely used in information retrieval, representing the fraction of relevant documents among all retrieved documents [11]. However, the binary judgment of relevance adopted in traditional evaluations does not take into account the different amounts of relevant information found in each document. The full precision metric tries to consider the total amount of relevant information found in the first 10 results, through the use of a five positions scale for the relevance judgments. The value "0" indicates that the result has no relevance and value "4" indicates high relevance. Therefore, the students had to judge the relevance of the first 10 results displayed on all tabs of the search results, using a 5-point scale (as shown in the right side at Fig. 2).

The second metric was the search length, which reflects the number of not relevant documents that the user must evaluate until finding a certain number of consecutive documents considered relevant. Therefore, the lower the value, lower the effort for the user to find relevant results. As in [12], in this study the search length was defined as the number of documents evaluated until two consecutive results were found with the value of relevance greater than or equal to three. Therefore, it was possible to use data from the same evaluation tool (the 5-point scale of relevance of the first 10 results).

The last metric, called rank correlation, aims to compare the correlation between the priority that was obtained in the search with an ideal priority, where the results are sorted in descending order of relevance. The higher the correlation between the relevance of search results and the ideal prioritization, more effective is the search tool. Since the first ten results were evaluated, and the evaluation scale is five positions, the prioritization has to be considered ideal if in the first two positions it has documents with evaluation four, next two with value of evaluation equals to three, and so on until the last two results with evaluation value equals to zero.

The results are presented in percentages, representing the amount of times the result obtained in each tab was better than the others tabs.

In all metrics, the expansion with general terms of the context and the expansion with specific terms of the subjects showed better results than those obtained with the original query (Table 1).

**Table 1.** Results of the Metrics

| Expansions / Metrics | Full Precision | Search Length | Rank Correlation |
|---|---|---|---|
| Original query | 25% | 16.67% | 33.33% |
| Context expansion | 66.67% | 33.33% | 16.67% |
| Subject expansion | 41.67% | 25% | 58.33% |
| Any expansion | 75% | 41.67% | 58.33% |

In the full precision metric, an improvement in 75% of the cases in at least one of the expansions was observed, while the original query result only showed better results in 25% of cases. The percentage improvement was observed in the comparison of the results from the original query with the results of the expanded query with general, terms of the context (66.67%), and comparing results from the original query with the results of expanded queries with specific terms of subjects (41.67%).

Improvements in results were also observed in the search length metric and in the correlation rank metric, but in smaller proportions than the full precision.

## 5     Final Remarks

The work presented in this paper proposes a strategy for contextual query based on shared content of a learning community implemented in an online social network. The collaborative learning was provided through content sharing and communication tools while a web query engine was used for retrieving web documents with the learning context of the community. In order to make the query results more useful, it was considered information extraction and query expansion techniques, which were tested through a case study. The results of the experiment were presented and showed better results for the queries.

The strategy for query expansion and contextualized search presented in this paper has as main differences from related works: (i) the use of topic segmentation before clustering processes, with the objective of grouping all the different subjects found in the shared content, (ii) the use of terms of all clusters, not only the terms of the cluster most related to the query terms and (iii) quality assurance in the selection of content, consisting of educational shared resources published by the community according to its interests.

The use of activities of information extraction and query expansion can be considered to make search results more contextualized and therefore more useful to students, helping them to search for educational resources on the web, complementing the published content. The contextualization is done through the expansion of queries entered by students, adding in these queries the terms extracted from existing educational shared resources published by the community members.

A case study showed that the query expansion could be used in an educational environment to improve the educational process. Ongoing works are integrating the query module with the online social network and a case study is being conducted to evaluate the whole solution.

Some future works are: (i) analysis of the terms of the queries done by the users as a criterion for the terms expansion, for example, using as a criterion for calculating the weights of the terms the distance of each term with the terms informed in the query, in addition to frequency in the context information; (ii) improvements in the display of search results, which is tiring in cases where many expansions are showed; (iii) further analysis with bigger communities and student interactions on different communities; and (iv) providing mechanisms for reputation and rules for weighting the terms in the query expansion.

**Acknowledgments.** The authors would like to thank the participants of the case study. This work was partially supported by FAPERJ (through grants E-26/170028/2008 INC&T Program - Project: Brazilian Institute of Research on Web Science, and E-26/ 101.509/2010 - BBP/Bursary Representation and contextualized retrieval of learning content), CNPQ (project: 557.128/2009-9, INCT on Web Science) and by FCT Portugal, through funds of ICIST.

# References

1. Boyd, D.M., Ellison, N.B.: Social Network Sites: Definition, History, and Scholarship. Journal of Computer-Mediated Communication 13, 210–230 (2008)
2. Richardson, W.: Blogs, Wikis, Podcasts and Other Powerful Web Tools for the Classroom, 2nd edn. Corwin Press, Thousand Oaks (2009)

3. Mora-Soto, A.: Collaborative Learning Experiences Using Social Networks. In: International Conference on Education and New Learning Technologies (EDULEARN 2009), Academia.edu (2009),
   `http://uc3m.academia.edu/ArturoMoraSoto/Papers/114887/Collab`
   `orative_Learning_Experiences_Using_Social_Networks`
   (last access: May 1, 2011)
4. Chanana, V., Ginige, A., Murugesan, S.: Improving information retrieval effectiveness by assigning context to documents. In: International Symposium on Information and Communication Technologies (ISICT 2004), pp. 2239–2244. IEEE Press, New York (2004)
5. Bhogal, J., Macfarlane, A., Smith, P.: A review of ontology based query expansion. Information Processing and Management: an International Journal 43(4), 866–886 (2007)
6. Chien, B.C., Hu, C.H., Ju, M.Y.: Intelligent Information Retrieval Applying Automatic Constructed Fuzzy Ontology. In: Proc. Conference on Machine Learning and Cybernetics, pp. 2239–2244. IEEE Press, New York (2007)
7. Wang, C., Chang, G., Wang, X., Ma, Y., Ma, H.: A User Motivation Model for Web Search Engine. In: Proc. Conf. Hybrid Intelligent Systems (HIS 2009), pp. 327–331. IEEE Press, New York (1999)
8. Zhuhadar, L., Nasraoui, O.: Semantic Information Retrieval for Personalized E-Learning. In: Proc. IEEE Conf. on Tools with Artificial Intelligence (ICTAI 2008), pp. 364–368. IEEE Press, New York (2008)
9. Khribi, M.K., Jemni, M., Nasraoui, O.: Automatic Recommendations for E-Learning Personalization Based on Web Usage Mining Techniques and Information Retrieval. In: IEEE International Conference on Advanced Learning Technologies (ICALT 2008), pp. 241–245 (2008)
10. Ambrósio, A.P., Silva, L.O., Neto, V.G.: Automatic Retrieval of Complementary Learning Material for Slide Presentations. In: International Conference on Interactive Computer Aided Blended Learning, ICBL 2009 (2009),
    `http://www.valdemarneto.com/pdfs/artigoICBL.pdf`
    (last access: May 1, 2011)
11. Manning, C.D., Raghavan, P., Schütze, H.: Introduction to Information Retrieval. Cambridge University Press, Cambridge (2008)
12. Tang, M.C., Sun, Y.: Evaluation of Web-Based Search Engines Using User-Effort Measures. LIBRES Research Electronic Journal 13(2) (2003),
    `http://libres.curtin.edu.au/libres13n2/tang.html`
    (last access: May 1, 2011)

# Children's Performance with Digital Mind Games and Evidence for Learning Behaviour

Rosa Maria Bottino, Michela Ott, and Mauro Tavella

Istituto Tecnologie Didattiche – CNR
Via De Marini, 6, Genoa Italy
{bottino,ott,tavella}@itd.cnr.it

**Abstract.** This paper investigates the relationship between the possession of some of the reasoning abilities required to play digital mind games and the school performance of primary school pupils. It draws on an in-field experiment involving 60 Italian primary school children; the experiment was based on the use of the standardized test LOGIVALI which foresees ten one-hour gaming sessions with five mind games. The pupils were divided in three groups according their school achievement (high, medium and low achievers) and their performance at the test was studied; a substantial consistency was found between school achievement and ability to solve the adopted digital games. A closer insight was also given into the specific reasoning abilities actually possessed by the three different categories of pupils, thanks to the fact that the LOGIVALI test also allows a finer distinction among the different types/levels of reasoning abilities required to perform the proposed gaming tasks.

**Keywords:** Game-based learning, reasoning abilities, mind games, primary education, students' performance.

## 1    Introduction

Computer games are broadly regarded as emerging technologies offering a high potential to foster and support learning [1]. One of the key issues to be investigated to nourish this general claim is the relationship between academic performance and the use of computer games in relation to different disciplines, educational settings and underpinning cognitive tasks. At present few studies have been carried out with this objective, even if its importance is increasingly acknowledged [2], [3].

A number of significant research studies have been carried out that look, from different perspectives, at the actual relationships among types of games, learning objectives to be met and learning population to be addressed (i.e. which kind of games better serve the scope of fulfilling specific learning objectives and how this can be done in specific learning contexts and with a specific target population [4], [5].

M.D. Lytras et al. (Eds.): WSKS 2011, CCIS 278, pp. 235–243, 2013.
© Springer-Verlag Berlin Heidelberg 2013

This paper focuses on mainstream [6] mind games[1] when used in formal educational settings with the aim of fostering primary school pupils' reasoning abilities, those "transversal" abilities that are recognized as underpinning the majority of learning tasks and sensibly contributing to enhance global academic achievement [9], [10].

With the ultimate aim of understanding whether early interventions in the area of reasoning skills conducted by means of mind games can contribute to noticeably enhancing school performance [11], this paper investigates the possible relationships between the possession of some of the reasoning abilities required to solve mind games and the school performance of primary school pupils. It draws on an in-field experiment involving 60 Italian primary school children and it is based on the use of the LOGIVALI Test, a game-based standardized test assessing primary school pupils reasoning abilities [12]. In the following, after introducing the LOGIVALI Test, the paper presents the methodology adopted to carry out the in-field experiment and discusses some of the obtained results, with a view on future trends and possible new research objectives.

## 2     The LOGIVALI Test

The LOGIVALI Test is a norm-referenced test that follows a custom set-up, specific methodology with the aim to investigate and assess the possession of some specific logical and reasoning abilities by the target population; to this end, the test employs five digital mind games selected on the basis of previous in-field research experiments [13]. In the following the types of games adopted and the considered abilities are briefly illustrated, and the administration methodology adopted to standardize the test is summarized.

### 2.1     LOGIVALI Test: The Games Adopted

The test is grounded on the use of five mind games that fall into the category of "mini-games", that is "games that take less than an hour to complete [7]; they do not require specific prerequisites in curricular school subjects, beyond vey basic literacy and, most importantly, do not imply the possession of specific mathematical skills; some of the games are the computerized versions of well known board games (e.g. battleship, master mind).

Figure 1 shows screenshots of the games adopted in the LOGIVALI Test; reference are provided on their availability, since all of them are Open Source or free (two as limited demo-trials).

---

[1] The term mind games is used in this paper to define games that are elsewhere called brain teasers or puzzles [7], [8]; they differ from brain training games in that they require at an higher extent to devise and enact problem solving strategies to reach the game solution.

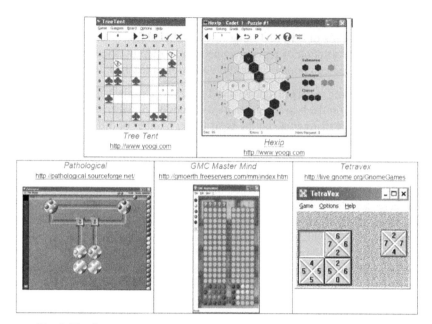

**Fig. 1.** The five games adopted in the LOGIVALI Test and related reference

## 2.2    LOGIVALI Test: The Considered Reasoning Abilities

The experience acquired during previous projects [14] and the detailed analysis of the mind games at hand allowed us to identify a set of reasoning abilities that we considered as essential for effectively playing with the adopted games. For the purpose of our work, it was decided to consider a restricted number (six) of specific reasoning abilities identified as crucial although they are, obviously, only a subset of the abilities required to deal with the games at hand.

The following six abilities (which we have identified as common to the five games even if in each of them they may assume a specific connotation) are those investigated through the LOGIVALI Test:

*Ability 1*    "knowing the rules of the game": to know the rules underlying a given game and to be able to apply them in concrete game situations.

*Ability 2*    "first level reasoning": to be able to make an inference taking into consideration a single given datum.

*Ability 3*    "second level reasoning": to be able to make an inference taking into consideration two given information or game constraints.

*Ability 4*    "third level reasoning": to be able to make an inference taking into consideration more than two given information and game constraints.

*Ability 5*    "managing uncertainty": to be able to establish whether the data available at a given moment of the game are sufficient to decide whether a certain guess is correct or not. This requires flexibility in reasoning and meta-cognitive awareness.

*Ability 6*    "operatively applying reasoning abilities": to be able to implement into
the game the results of own reasoning (actions should follow thoughts); this entails
approaching the solution of a given game step by step by showing the capacity to
be able to proceed autonomously until the solution is reached.

An important finding emerged during the LOGIVALI project is that the ability of
making inferences on the basis of given data cannot be considered as a unique ability
but it is necessary to distinguish on the basis of the number of different data, information and constraints to be dealt with. The standardization procedure of the LOGIVALI
test evidenced that a reasonable way to do this is to differentiate the abilities to make
inferences taking into account one, two, and three or more data (abilities 2, 3 and 4).
As to their relative difficulty, it emerged that the number of correct answers progressively decreased: Ability 2 (80%); Ability 3 (63%); Ability 4 (46%). This confirms
that the three abilities can be considered as increasingly complex abilities for the target population. This finding is consistent with the empirical observations we have
often made during the experimental work with students: pupils usually are able to
process one information, but they often show difficulties when it is necessary to take
into account two or more information and the passage from one to two (or more) data
is crucial. The standardization procedure of the LOGIVALI test showed that all the
abilities considered are different and that, at a more general level, all the entailed
abilities, even if distinct, are related to a common cognitive area, that of logical reasoning.

## 2.3    LOGIVALI Test: Structure and Administration Methodology

The LOGIVALI test encompasses five different sub-tests, one for each of the games
employed. Each sub-test is composed of eight exercises, each containing multiple
items in the form of multiple choice questions [15] or, when possible, practical drills
(e.g. "fill in the schema with the needed moves"). Each of the test items (question or
drill) was conceived so that it could be considered directly related to the enactment of
one of the considered abilities. The standardization procedure of the LOGIVALI test
involved 26 primary school classes (4th and 5th grades) of a sample of schools in two
Italian regions. The LOGIVALI project involved around 540 students and 52
teachers.

The administration methodology of the LOGIVALI Test implies that:

a. Teachers explain the games to the students.
b. Students play individually with five digital mind games; each game is used twice,
   in two different one-hour playing sessions.
c. Teachers monitor students at work during the playing sessions, but abstain from
   intervening with suggestions and help.
d. After completing the two playing sessions with each game, each student individually takes a specific test on that game (sub-test); tests are administered by the
   teachers who also are in charge of making students aware of the fact that no curricular evaluation is foreseen for the tests but that they are contributing to a research
   project.

In detail: each sub-test is administered immediately after the two playing sessions where the children have the opportunity to play one of the games; the order in which games are presented to the students is fixed: it was established a priori following a number of criteria including perceived difficulty of the games, similitude/difference among tasks, interface attractiveness, etc. For each sub-test, students have at their disposal one hour during normal school time; teachers are in charge of administering the test and monitoring the process.

To avoid, as far as possible, non-homogeneity in the way teachers carry out the overall process, specific guidelines and detailed sheets (one for each game at hand) were produced aimed at supporting the three tasks of: explanation of the game, monitoring of the work and administration of the test.

## 2.4 LOGIVALI Test: Validation and Standardization

The test validation procedure was aimed at verifying both the test reliability and validity, namely if the test is self consistent and can be considered able to measure what required: in the case at hand, if it is able to account for the individual differences existing among children as to the considered reasoning abilities. To this end, first of all, the suitability of the sample population (size and composition) has been verified, subsequently the test internal consistency has been analyzed and, finally, its ability to measure what it was claimed to assess was investigated. On the basis of the results obtained with the involved sample population the test was standardized and the reference norms were defined on the percentile ranking basis. In [12] the whole test validation and standardization procedure is presented.

## 3    The In-field Experiment Based on the LOGIVALI Test

The experiment, aimed at assessing primary school students' reasoning abilities and grounded on the game-based LOGIVALI Test, was carried out in twenty Italian primary schools classes ($4^{th}$ and $5^{th}$ grades) of the Lombardia region; it was held during school hours within the school computer laboratory.

The students involved in the experiment were globally around 500; for the purpose of this study 60 pupils were selected and monitored while individually playing with digital mind games. The students were classified in three groups according to their school achievement (school actual results plus teachers' judgments): group A (high achievers); group B (medium achievers); group C (low achievers). The target group of 60 students comprised three students per class (out of 20 classes), one student for each group A, B and C.

The LOGIVALI test was administered and the performance of each student at the test was computed according to the percentile ranks determined by the test, namely:

- from 0 to 25: *poor* performance
- from 26 to 50: moderately low performance *(fair)*
- from 51 to 75: moderately high performance *(good)*
- from 76 to 99: *very good* performance

Data on pupils' performance at the test were analyzed and compared with the level of school achievement; further on, since the LOGIVALI test also allows a finer distinction among the different types/levels of reasoning abilities required to perform the various gaming tasks, a closer insight was given into the six specific reasoning abilities considered to investigate to what extent they were actually possessed by the three different categories of pupils.

## 4    Results

*A substantial consistency exists between school achievement and the students' performance at the test.*

As a matter of fact, Figure 2, where dark parts stand for low performances (actually 2 levels of low performances: poor and fair) and light parts for high performances (actually 2 levels of high performances: very good and good) shows that:

- Only students in Group A show prevailing high performances at the LOGIVALI test (light parts in the figure) with respect to the other two categories where dark parts are prevailing; more than half of the students of this group perform at the two highest levels.
- The very majority of the students in group C perform at low levels (fair and poor); most performances of these students are at the lowest level.
- Students in group B performances are comparable to those of students in group C if we consider dark and light parts but performances at the fair level prevail on performance at poor level.

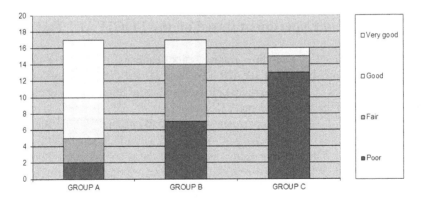

**Fig. 2.** Performances of the three groups of students at the LOGIVALI Test

*High achievers show better performances in each of the abilities.*

The structure of the data doesn't allow us to directly compare the performances of the three groups of students in the different abilities: our data are, in fact, based on the calculation of the percentiles which varies in the different abilities (treated as independent) as a consequence of the different number of correct answers given by the sample population. Notwithstanding this, if we look singularly at the six considered reasoning abilities, we see that high achievers always perform better than the other two groups; this is true for all the abilities in play, despite reasonable differences linked to the intrinsic level of difficulty of each reasoning skill considered. A closer insight (Fig. 3) in the three abilities of the test related to the capacity to make inferences on the basis of given data (namely Ability 2, 3 and 4), we see that performances of high, medium and low achievers are always scaled (with the prevalence of good performances for high achievers and of poor performances for low achievers).

**Fig. 3.** Performances of the three groups at the three "core" abilities considered

Students in group C appear to have difficulties also in Abilities 5 and 6, while students in group B and those in group A have higher performances. As to Ability 1, which actually deals with a simplest cognitive task, namely the recalling of the game rules, the difference among the performance of the students in the three groups is narrower, probably due to the lower amount of cognitive load required.

**Fig. 4.** Performances of the three groups at the three "other" abilities considered

Differences in performances can also be compared to the level of attention and autonomy students showed during the use of the games. For this reason, during the project, considered pupils have been singularly monitored by the teachers while playing and observations sheets were filled in. The analysis of such sheets will allow to have a closer look at the relationship between attention and level of autonomy showed by pupils and their school performance.

## 5    Conclusive Remarks

The first results of the experiment showed that a substantial consistency can be found between school achievement and ability to play and solve games. Not surprisingly, high achievers' performance on the test was far better with respect to that of the other pupils; conversely, low achievers performance was quite poor.

These former findings, on the one hand, seem to support the idea that at primary school level there is a relationship between school achievement and ability at mind games, and, on the other hand, they also seem to suggest that early intervention aimed to develop and exercise pupils reasoning abilities through games and motivating activities can have an impact on their learning behavior.

This suggests as a possible future line of intervention aimed at improving reasoning abilities by employing mind games that allow a fine graduation of reasoning tasks and that are able to conveniently scaffold the pupils' identification and processing of relevant data.

## References

1. Prensky, M.: Digital game-based learning. McGraw-Hill, New York (2001)
2. Kebritchi, M., Hirumi, A., Bai, H.: The effects of modern mathematics computer games on mathematics achievement and class motivation. Computers & Education 55(2), 427–443 (2010)
3. Milovanović, M., Minović, M., Kovačević, I., Minović, J., Starčević, D.: Effectiveness of Game-Based Learning: Influence of Cognitive Style. In: Lytras, M.D., Ordonez de Pablos, P., Damiani, E., Avison, D., Naeve, A., Horner, D.G. (eds.) WSKS 2009. CCIS, vol. 49, pp. 87–96. Springer, Heidelberg (2009)
4. Mc Farlane, A., Sparrowhawk, A., Heald, Y.: Report on the educational use of games: an exploration by TEEM of the contribution which games can make to the education process. Teem, Cambridge (2002)
5. Mitchell, A., Savill-Smith, C.: The use of computer and video games for learning. A review of the literature. Learning and Skills Development Agency, Ultralab, M-learning (2004)
6. Kirriemuir, J., McFarlane, A.: Literature Review in Games and Learning. Report 8: Futurelab (2004),
   http://archive.futurelab.org.uk/resources/documents/
   lit_reviews/Games_Review.pdf
7. Prensky, M.: Educational Games Complexity Matters: Mini-games are Trivial - but "Complex" Games Are Not. An important Way for Teachers, Parents and Others to Look At Educational Computer and Video Games. Educational Technology 45(4), 1–15 (2005)
8. Schiffler, A.: A heuristic taxonomy of computer games (2006),
   http://www.ferzkopp.net/joomla/content/view/77/15/
9. Rohde, T.E., Thompson, L.A.: Predicting academic achievement with cognitive ability. Intelligence 35(1), 83–92 (2007)
10. Robertson, D., Miller, D.: Learning gains from using games consoles in primary classrooms: a randomized controlled study. Procedia Social and Behavioral Sciences 1(1), 1641–1644 (2009)

11. Franco, C., Mañas, I., Cangas, A.J., Gallego, J.: Exploring the Effects of a Mindfulness Program for Students of Secondary School. International Journal of Knowledge Society Research (IJKSR) 2(1), 14–28 (2011)
12. Bottino, R.M., Ott, M., Tavella, M., Benigno, V.: Can digital Mind Games be Used to Investigate Children's Reasoning Abilities? In: Meyer, B. (ed.) Proceedings of the 4th ECGBL Conference on Games Based Learning Copenhagen. Academic Conferences, pp. 31–39 (2010)
13. Bottino, R.M., Ott, M.: Mind games, reasoning skills, and the primary school curriculum: hints from a field experiment. Learning Media & Technology 31(4), 359–375 (2006)
14. Bottino, R.M., Ferlino, L., Ott, M., Tavella, M.: Developing strategic and reasoning abilities with computer games at primary school level. Computers & Education 49(4), 1272–1286 (2007)
15. Serradell-Lopez, E., Lara, P., Castillo, D., Gonzales, I.: Developing Professional knowledge and Confidence in Higher Education. International Journal of Knowledge Society Research, IJKSR 1(4), 32–41 (2010)

# Mobile Learning as an Asset for Development: Challenges and Oportunities

María José Casany[1], Marc Alier[1], Enric Mayol[1], Miguel Angel Conde[2],
and Francisco José García Peñalvo[2]

[1] Universitat Politècnica de Catalunya, C/Jordi Girona Salgado 1-3,
Office Omega 116 08034 Barcelona, Spain
[2] Universidad de Salamanca, Plaza de los caidos S/N. 37008, Salamanca
{mjcasany,malier,mayol}@essi.upc.edu,
{mconde,fgarcia}@usal.edu

**Abstract.** Education is a key objective and asset for development. While elearning has proven to be a key element for difusion and improvement of education, an analisys of trends shows that mobile devices – not desktop computers or laptops – are going to become the ubiquitous universal computing and networking device. Thus the mission of elearning will have to be complemented by mobile learning. This paper analyzes the challenges and oportunities for the unfolding of mobile learning in developing countries.

**Keywords:** Mobile Learning, Net neutrality, Sustainable Development.

## 1   Introduction

Universal Education is a human right as well as one of the Millennium Goals proposed by the United Nations for human development. Nowadays, individuals need to learn new abilities to face life challenges, instead of learning perishable or encyclopedic knowledge. Among these new abilities, digital competences are necessary to develop in the Information Society. In the Information Society, digital competences are key aspects to change the current educational models to include Sustainable Development.

The *Human Development Report* 2001 [1], postulates a direct relation between the Digital Divide and the opportunities for development of a region or country. The Digital Divide concept refers to the differences between groups or countries to access ICT technologies. Addressing the Digital Divide problem, means working in different dimensions: infrastructures, access to ICT equipment as well as teaching the basic skills to interact with ICT. This last dimension, presents a new challenge for education: teaching digital competencies.

The digital divide separates countries and social groups in two groups: the ones that have access to ICT technologies and the ones that do not have. But among ICT technologies, there is one technology that has the potential to break the digital divide, because it is widely used in developing countries: mobile phones.

M.D. Lytras et al. (Eds.): WSKS 2011, CCIS 278, pp. 244–250, 2013.

According to the *International Telecommunication Union* (ITU) [2], there are 370 million mobile users only in Africa. Wireless coverage and mobile phones is a technology that is spreading really fast in Africa (mobile cellular penetration in Africa in 2010 is about 68%), and is being adopted for multiple purposes by its inhabitants. In the Information Society Report published by the *International Telecommunication Union*, the developing countries are experiencing an important increase on the use of mobile phones. The ITU states that: *"It is a technology that has permeated more widely than any other into new areas, and we must examine how we can utilise this technology going forward, to help narrow the digital divide"*.

Since mobile phones are widely used both in developed and developing countries, we propose to use this technology to implement e-learning in developing countries (this is called mobile learning or m-learning). Authors believe that m-learning will not replace e-learning but complement it.

The organization of this paper is the next: Section 2 describes some of the major problems that face ICT infrastructures in developing countries. One of the only technologies that remain in most developing countries is mobile technology. So, section 3 reviews some of existing the m-learning initiatives for development. Section 4 summarizes some of the challenges that face m-learning and finally section 5 presents some conclusions.

## 2     ICT Infrastructure in Developing Countries

IT infrastructures face many problems in developing countries. Problems such as intermittent electric supply, overheating of networking components, lack of adequate infrastructures and IT systems personnel, problems generated by climatic conditions (sand and dust), and even theft of hardware. Because of these handicaps, it is very hard and expensive, to build and maintain information systems applications; because servers cannot last. Only government and huge companies, usually owned by foreign capital, are able to build and maintain data centres. Despite the hostile environment there are two IT technologies that remain functional in most developing countries: Internet access and mobile phones.

Internet or DSL connections are still very expensive and can be accessed only by companies and small part of the population. Meanwhile Internet access is still provided to a high percentage of the population by Internet cafe businesses. Internet cafes are widespread, relatively cheap and allow individuals and small businesses access to the Internet without the need to own and maintain a computer.

Mobile phones are spreading really fast in developing countries. The proliferation of mobile phones in developing countries is due to several factors. One of the most important ones is the relatively low cost of the mobile terminal. In most of the world countries, it is possible to find a mobile phone for about 40$. Besides, there is a second hand market that allows people from developing countries to buy a mobile phone for a low price. These second hand market starts in the developed countries, where people tend to change their mobile phone regularly. These terminals that are no longer used in the developed countries, are sold in the developed countries for a lower price.

Mobile phones are personal devices that serve many purposes for its owner: communications (voice, sms - Internet access is not widespread yet), photo and video camera or music. Sometimes mobile phones are used as lanterns, since public illumination coverage is very low and many homes do not have electric power supply. For many people in developing countries [3]:

- Mobile phones are their only computing device.
- They are portable networked computers.

In developing countries there are high demand of information related to health, agriculture and education. SMS-based applications have covered this gap in the last years, creating a huge market for SMS. So SMS-based applications and in general mobile technologies are providing information services to a large percentage of population. Mobile phones are being used intensively throughout Africa for a lot of purposes such as heath, agriculture, education or banking services [3]. Mobile phones allow:

- Communication with family and friends.
- Access to information by subscription to various short code services such as news updates. These updated may be coffee or other agricultural price updates. The user types a short code and then receives and update of information.
- Emerge of innovative mobile services such as mobile payment (for example, this service is called m-pesa in Kenya).
- Innovative individuals are building solutions based on mobile phones to different types of problems.
- Job creation.

The successful stories around mobile technologies in developing countries share one element in common: the solutions are envisioned, applied and adopted bottom up, instead of top down. When mobile technologies offer open and general-purpose systems, the people have figured out ways to use the technologies to satisfy the needs they need the most. Meanwhile top down designed services are usually destined for failure, because they usually miss the real needs of the population and become very expensive due to communication campaigns to foster adoption.

## 3     Mobile Learning for Development

The rapid growth of mobile technologies and services in developing countries make academics and other professionals think that mobile technology has a great potential to help improving education in developing countries and achieving universal primary education (one of the Millennium Goals proposed by the United Nations). Mobile technology may also be used to fight against the digital divide and for sustainable development.

This section presents a review of some m-learning projects for development in developing countries.

From the learner point of view, [4] proposes a model for m-learning in Africa. He states that m-learning may help learners from third world rural or remote areas who have access to a mobile phone. The University of Pretoria (South Africa) started a m-learning pilot project at 2002. Three existing programmes of the Faculty of Education adopted the m-learning pilot project. This pilot project was launch based on the fact that 99% of the students had mobile phones and that most of them lived in rural areas with no fixed ICT infrastructure. The pilot project used bulk SMS to provide students with basic administrative support. The SMS focussed on reminders of important dates for activities like contact classes or examination registration as well as notification of study material distribution.

The project was successful because learners responded in mass and almost immediately on information provided in SMS-messages. Instead of using SMS bulks, using print and postal service to distribute the necessary information to students, would have been more than 20 times the cost of the bulk SMS. While SMSs provided just-in-time information, the posted information would have taken between 3 and 18 days to reach the learners. Some conclusions of the project were that:

- m-learning is a supportive mode of education.
- m-learning provides flexibilities for various learning and lifestyles.
- the most appropriate mobile device for learners in Africa is the mobile phone.

[5] and [6] described a master in mobile computing developed at the Makerere University (Uganda) that will help develop more advanced mobile services adapted to the socio-economic situation of developing countries. This master programmes provide students with knowledge to develop software applications and services for mobile devices as well as to promote sustainable development because:

- Students that finish the programme go back to their home village with a mobile service to be tested by the people of the village.
- Students learn important knowledge to develop mobile services.

From the teacher point of view [7] developed two initiatives to bring universal primary education to developing countries. The *Digital Education Enhancement Project* (DEEP - www.open.ac.uk/deep) carried out an initial study into the potential of ICT for teacher education in developing nations, working with teachers and institutions in Egypt and South Africa.

The over-arching research questions for DEEP were:

1. How does ICT transform the pedagogic knowledge and practice of teachers and the communities in which they live and work?
2. What is the impact of ICT- enhanced strategies on pupil achievement and motivation?

The SEMA project was started in Kenya in 2003 to support school based teacher development. The project used SMS messages broadcasting for several purposes such as: delivering study guide material, content such as hints, tips or summaries, reminders or urgent messages about errata or cancellations.

Both projects analyse the impact of mobile technologies in the pedagogy of teachers. Both projects use different hardware: the DEEP project uses PDAS and laptops while the SEMA project uses GSM mobile phones. The number of teachers involved is also very different. While the DEEP project involved about 50 teachers, the SEMA project involved about 100000 teachers. Both projects conclude that the long temp sustainability of the project is one of the challenges of m-learning in Africa.

[8] and [9] suggest that it important to find strategies to implement low-cost m-learning projects. [9] propose some work directions in order to use m-learning to fight against the digital divide. They consider that some of the initial expectations of m-learning in developing countries have not been archieved because the projects are not yet consolidated. There may be needed a larger period of time to analyse the results of these projects.

# 4    Challenges of Mobile Learning in Developing Countries

Although mobile phones have rapidly spread in developing countries, the availability and accessibility of this technology does not assure that it will succeed in fighting against the digital divide.

There is another dimension of the digital divide that affects the attitude of people towards technology. Depending on the attitude of people towards technology, we can find consumers and producers of information and knowledge. Consumers are those people that only use ICT to find information and applications. Creators are people that do not only look for information or applications but also create or produce information and knowledge.

To break the digital divide, it is important to break the divide between consumers and producers. It is not enough to learn how to use technology to find information. It is necessary to learn how to contribute in the creation of information and knowledge [9].

The previous point is very important in developing countries because if they only use information provided by developed countries, they may risk from cultural colonization. For example, like the cultural colonization suffered in Europe from the EEUU TV series in the 1970s.

This tendency towards the creation of knowledge and contents is already developing in many places. From 2000, new elements that influence the learning process started to appear. Technologies such as the Web 2.0 are elements that are influencing the way we learn as well as the way teachers teach. Tools such as blogs, wikis, podcasts or social networks are changing the learning process. For example, students may be able to discuss a variety of topics with people of different countries around the world. They use the acquired knowledge to do their assignments. With the introduction of Web 2.0, e-learning is changing because students participate in the creation of contents. Students became producers of contents [10].

Net neutrality, the guaranty that the quality and cost of Internet access is independent from the kind of service that is used and intended for, is a key quality that needs to be preserved if mobile Internet has to become an asset for education, innovation and development. Last year Google and Verizon signed an agreement stating that net neutrality should be preserved in landlines, but could be overseen on the mobile space to foster its development and economical viability. But this development and economical viability is only on behalf of the operator, who by the way is already earning a lot of money. In Europe we have already seen with WAP phones, how a crippled Internet access only delays the adoption of the use and kills innovation. Europe had the lead in mobile technologies because its adoption of the GSM standard for digital mobile communications, and lost it to American companies (Apple, RIM and Google) because of a true open Internet access and experience. If developing countries get a crippled Internet access it will only slow down or prevent its adoption and the benefits presented in this paper.

## 5    Conclusions

In the Information Society, information and knowledge have a central role in development. A country can grow and develop in the Information Society without large infrastructures because information and knowledge is the key to social-economic growth. This is one of the reasons why mobile technology has succeeded in developing countries, while other ICT technologies have not. Mobile phones do not need large communication infrastructures and the cost of the device as well as the cost of mobile services is relatively inexpensive.

Mobile technology may encourage young entrepreneurs from developing countries who create new mobile services or applications. This socio-economic activity may provide new job creation among other benefits. If the Information Society must succeed in developing countries, it is necessary to incorporate basic ICT skills in education. It is also important to improve Internet access, maximize the use of open source software and adapt it to the local socio-economic situation.

## References

1. Human Development Report (2001),
   http://hdr.undp.org/en/reports/global/hdr2001/
2. International Telecommunication Union,
   http://www.itu.int/en/pages/default.aspx
3. Colaço, J.: Mobile Technology and Social Change (2009),
   http://ictlogy.net/20091019-uoc-tech-talks-jessica-colaco-mobile-technology-and-social-change/ (January 20, 2011)
4. Brown, T.H.: The role of m-learning in the future of e-learning in Africa. Distance Education and Technology: Issues and Practice, 197–216 (2004)
5. Mekuria, F.: Using Mobile Technology and Services for Sustainable Development in Africa. Special Topics in Computer ICT Research. Strengthening the Role of ICT in Development (2008)
6. Mekuria, F., Rai, I.: Issues in Next Generation Wireless Network Technologies and Services for Developing Regions. In: Proceedings WiNS-DR 2008 (2008)

7. Traxler, J., Leach, J.: Innovative and Sustainable Mobile Learning in Africa. In: Fourth IEEE International Workshop on Wireless, Mobile and Ubiquitous Technology in Education (2006)
8. Litchfield, A., et al.: Directions for m-learning research to enhance active learning. In: Proceedings Ascilite, Singapore (2007)
9. Laouris, Y., Laouri, R.: Can Information and Mobile Technologies Serve to Close the Economic, Educational, Digital, and Social gaps and Accelerate Development? World Features 64(4), 254–275 (2008)
10. Downes, S.: Models for Sustainable Open Educational Resources. Interdisciplinary Journal of Knowledge and Learning Objects 3 (2007)

# Using a Crowdsourcing Knowledge Base to Support the Sustainability and Social Compromise Skill in Computer Science Engineering Studies

Marc Alier Forment[1], David López[2], Fermin Sánchez Carracedo[2],
Jordi Garcia Almiñana[2], Jordi Piguillem Poch[1], and Martha Velasco[2]

[1] Universitat Politècnica de Catalunya, C/Jordi Girona Salgado 1-3,
Office Omega 116 08034 Barcelona, Spain
{ludo,jpiguillem}@essi.upc.edu
[2] Universitat Politècnica de Catalunya, C/Jordi Girona Salgado 1-3,
Building D6 08034 Barcelona, Spain
{david,jordig}@ac.upc.edu, fermin@ac.edu

**Abstract.** The Skill "Sustainability and Socia Commitment" is commonly accepted as essential in today's world. However it proves tricky to introduce into the curriculum, mainly because of lack of knowledgeable teachers. To address this issue we present a knowledge base that brings together scientific articles, books, videos, compilations of data, experiences, etc., related to sustainability and knowledge areas associated with computer science engineering. This is a valuable tool that should provide to the teacher accurate and useful information in the research task of finding links between her course and the "Sustainability and Social Commitment" skill.

**Keywords:** Education, Skills, Sustainability, Educational resources, knowledge society.

## 1 Introduction

The adaptation to the European Higher Education Area (EHEA) has brought us the inclusion of professional skills in the curricula of universities. There are many studies on the need to incorporate these skills [1, 4, 9, 10]. The need of most of these skills is not discussed while others have fewer consensuses. There are also skills with which the teachers feel more comfortable, because they have an idea of how to teach and evaluate them.

The professional skill "Sustainability and Social Commitment" (from now on SSC) is generally accepted as essential in the modern world (despite some detractors), but raises concerns between teachers due to the lack of knowledge about it. It is very common, when discussing the skill, to hear questions such as: What is sustainability? What is its relationship with my subject? What should my students learn? How to evaluate the skill?

M.D. Lytras et al. (Eds.): WSKS 2011, CCIS 278, pp. 251–260, 2013.
© Springer-Verlag Berlin Heidelberg 2013

There exist several studies on the overall relationship between computers and SSC [6, 7], how to include this skill in some subjects [3, 5, 8, 10], in a whole curriculum [11] or how to evaluate it [2, 5, 7, 8]. However, these studies do not solve a complex problem: that every teacher knows how it relates SSC competition with his subject.

In most schools, it is not a hard work to find a group of teachers who are interested in SSC. But once you have the group of teachers, they cannot be left alone, without supporting them, telling them to look for themselves the relationship between their area of knowledge and SSC, and asking them to develop new activities from scratch. If there is not some support, the initiative will fail.

Therefore, our University (UPC – Barcelona Tech) has developed the project STEP (*Sustainability, Technology and Excellence Program*). This project provided financial support to groups of teachers of every school at the University, to develop the tools, activities and ideas needed to introduce the SSC skill in the new degrees adapted to EHEA. The authors of this paper are the responsible of the STEP project at the Barcelona School of Informatics, and we must help to introduce the SSC skill in the new Degree in Computer Science. Among other activities, described in [9] we have developed a tool to support teachers interested in working in the skill: SSC Knowledge Base.

This tool brings together a selected group of articles in scientific and popular journals, databases related to SSC, pages of corporate social responsibility from software and hardware companies, a compendium of laws, directives, recommendations, good practice examples and activities to do in class, etc. All these inputs are oriented to relate SSC concepts with the typical knowledge areas of Computer Science.

All entries have a small comment made by the person who entered the data and a series of tags, the keywords associated with each entry that allow us to perform very specific searches.

The advantages of this tool versus a generic search engine such as Google, are:

- The information is bounded. With certain keywords, Google can go from hundreds to millions of responses, most of which are not relevant to the person searching. In our case, all entries have been shortlisted, so that the number of results will be much smaller, and the probability of finding the information you are searching for is greater.
- The information has been introduced with some comments. These comments can be from a couple of lines with a basic review, to a summary of the article or more elaborate information. These comments can offer a first look of the contents of the entry without access to it.
- The information is tagged, so the person who entered the data have read (albeit briefly) the content of the entry, and decided that the entry should be indexed under certain tags, which allows you to search quite efficient and accurate. The user can also search for words outside the list of tags, just on the title and comment from every input of the Knowledge Base.

With this tool, teachers can find items that relate his subject with the SSC skill, so they can search for activities, finding specific examples or just real information to design their own activities and exercises, all quickly and easily.

The rest of the paper is organized as follows: Section 2 presents the process of discussion that led to the organization of the Knowledge Base and tagging system. Section 3 presents the technical specifications of the tool. Section 4 presents an example of use. Finally, Section 5 presents some final thoughts and conclusions.

## 2     The Process of Definition of the Knowledge Base

To create the knowledge base was necessary to design initially its structure and functionality. We looked for a knowledge base which locates entries based on keywords, but in a very open way (almost any word you could imagine). Moreover, we wanted the association of keywords to entries was easy and comfortable to carry and update entries. We needed, therefore, a small set of keywords associated as labels to the entries, but we also wanted the search could be made by using a much higher keyword set. To allow for complex searches, a certain structure on keywords was required. After analyzing different possibilities, we decided to provide the knowledge base of a three-dimensional structure.

On the one hand, we have a two-dimensional structure of keywords: a main level and secondary level. We defined a minimal yet complete set of keywords on the main level to cover all aspect. These words have a very high level of abstraction. The secondary level consists of a short but comprehensive set of labels covering more specific concepts. A direct relationship exists between keywords on the main and secondary level. The same word at the secondary level can be related to one or more keywords in the main level. This multiple assignment allows the possibility of complex searches. For example, searching for entries related to the secondary keyword X you can find all entries labeled directly with X or, in addition, those associated with the main keywords related also to the mark X (all the word with an X in the column in Figure 1).

Keywords defined on the main level are the following:

1.   Education
2.   Technoscience
3.   Environment
4.   Models
5.   Case studies
6.   Life-Cycle Products
7.   Services
8.   Values
9.   Social issues
10.  Economic issues
11.  Strategies
12.  Tactics

Figure 1 shows the relationship between keywords from main and secondary level. The first column shows the list of keywords from the secondary level. Remaining columns indicate, with an X, when a word from the secondary level is directly related to one from the main level. As can be seen, the main level consists of words with a level of abstraction higher than the words from secondary level.

| SECONDARY TAGS | 1 | 2 | 3 | 4 | 5 | 6 | 7 | 8 | 9 | 10 | 11 | 12 |
|---|---|---|---|---|---|---|---|---|---|---|---|---|
| Technological advances | X | X | X |  | X | X |  |  | X | X |  |  |
| Training | X | X |  | X | X |  |  | X | X |  |  |  |
| Subjects | X | X | X | X | X |  |  |  | X |  |  |  |
| Innovation | X | X |  |  | X |  | X |  | X | X |  | X |
| Method | X | X |  | X | X |  |  |  |  |  |  | X |
| Institutions | X | X |  |  | X |  | X | X | X | X | X |  |
| Cultural change | X |  |  | X | X |  |  |  | X | X | X | X |
| Atmosphere |  |  | X |  | X | X |  |  | X |  | X | X |
| Water |  |  | X |  | X | X |  |  | X | X | X | X |
| Air |  |  | X |  | X | X |  |  | X | X | X | X |
| Biodiversity |  |  | X |  | X | X |  |  | X | X | X | X |
| Fuels |  | X | X |  | X | X |  |  | X | X | X | X |
| Energy | X | X | X | X | X | X |  |  | X | X | X | X |
| Earth |  |  | X |  | X | X |  |  | X | X |  |  |
| Minerals |  | X | X |  | X | X |  |  | X | X | X |  |
| Closing cycles |  | X | X |  | X | X | X |  | X | X | X | X |
| Reuse | X |  | X |  | X | X | X |  | X | X |  | X |
| Consumption | X |  | X | X | X | X | X | X | X | X |  | X |
| Distribution |  | X | X |  | X | X | X |  | X | X |  | X |
| Industrial production |  | X | X |  | X | X | X |  | X | X |  | X |
| Waste | X | X | X | X | X | X |  |  | X | X | X | X |
| Climate Change |  | X | X |  | X |  |  | X | X | X | X |  |
| Natural disasters |  |  | X |  | X |  |  |  | X |  |  | X |
| Acidification |  |  | X |  | X |  |  |  | X |  |  | X |
| Landscape |  |  | X |  | X |  |  |  | X | X |  | X |
| Greenhouse effect |  | X | X |  | X |  |  |  | X | X |  | X |
| Chemicals |  | X | X |  | X | X |  |  | X |  | X | X |
| Pollution |  |  | X | X | X | X |  |  | X | X | X |  |
| Globalization |  | X | X | X | X |  |  |  | X | X | X | X |
| Quality of life |  | X |  |  | X |  |  |  | X | X | X | X |
| Resources |  |  | X |  | X | X |  |  | X | X | X |  |
| Consumer | X |  | X |  | X |  |  | X | X | X | X | X |
| Marketing | X |  |  |  | X |  | X | X | X | X | X | X |
| Company |  |  | X | X | X |  | X | X | X | X | X | X |
| Sustainable development | X | X | X | X | X | X | X | X | X | X | X | X |
| ROI |  |  |  |  | X | X | X |  |  | X |  | X |
| Digital divide | X | X |  |  | X |  |  | X | X | X | X | X |
| Justice | X |  |  |  | X |  |  | X | X | X | X |  |
| Employment |  |  |  |  | X |  | X |  | X | X | X | X |
| Ergonomics | X | X |  |  | X |  | X |  | X |  |  | X |
| Demography |  |  |  | X | X |  |  |  | X | X | X |  |
| Health | X | X | X | X | X |  |  | X | X | X | X | X |
| Town planning | X | X | X |  | X |  | X |  | X | X | X | X |
| Society | X |  |  |  | X |  |  | X | X | X |  | X |
| Peace | X |  |  |  | X |  |  | X | X | X |  |  |
| Solidarity | X |  |  |  | X |  |  | X | X | X |  |  |
| Imbalance | X |  | X |  | X |  |  | X | X | X |  |  |
| Policy |  |  |  |  | X |  |  | X | X | X | X |  |
| Tourism | X |  | X |  | X |  | X | X | X | X |  |  |
| Human Rights | X |  | X |  | X |  |  | X | X | X | X |  |

**Fig. 1.** Relationship between keywords from the main and secondary levels

We spent four months in selecting keywords, both the main level and secondary level, meeting us weekly during this time. In the meantime between meetings we classified sites, papers and other entries by using the keywords we had selected, and provisionally we included new keywords when necessary. The definitive addition to the knowledge base was made in our weekly meeting, and always in agreement of all of us. Once all keywords were selected, we established the relationship between main and secondary level. To this end, each of us made his own assignment, which after was reviewed by all together. For those assignments we didn't agree, we performed a new individual assignment, after discussing each keyword, and we established those assignments that had majority agreement.

On the other hand, in parallel with the process above described, we define the third dimension of the table. To enable searching for entries from a large number of different keywords, we define for each keyword at the secondary level a set of synonyms or related words. Entries in the knowledge base can also be found by using this "synonymous", despite being labeled only by keywords from secondary level. For example, for the keyword "biodiversity" we defined as synonymous the following words: "Fauna, Flora, Species, Biosphere, Nature, Extinction, Animals, Plants, Forest, Trees, Hunting and Fishing." Thus, an entry could be labeled as biodiversity but also appeared when searching for any of these related words.

The existence of "related words" allows us to easily update the knowledge base and adding new keywords without having to review all entries, just adding the new keywords as related words. This third dimension has helped further the multilingual capabilities of the knowledge base, because related words can also be translations to other languages of all the words from the list. By orthogonal, we defined a list of related words also for each keyword on the main level.

The entire process of creating the structure of keywords, starting from the first discussions on its structure until the final definition of the words in each level and their related words, lasted over six months. This process, in addition to the undersigned authors, involved two fellows who are primarily responsible for maintaining the list and structure of keywords and catalog entries from pre-defined keywords. One of the fellows had extensive training on issues related to SSC (we select her right after she read her PhD thesis, concerning this topic), while the other was a non-graduate student of computer engineering. In the implementation of the knowledge base a postgraduate student was also been involved.

## 3    Specifications and Technical Details of the Implementation of the Knowledge Base

Prior to the implementation phase, there was a gathering of requirements for the Knowledge based that can be summarized as the following:

- It needed to be an online system, based on the web to maximize the ease of access, usability and for it to be cross platform.
- It needed to implement a documental database able to refer to different kinds of contents.

- It needed to implement a tagging engine, so the taxonomy described in section 2 could be implemented, and support search.
- It needed to allow access control with several different levels of granularity.
- It needed to keep access logs, so statistics and data-mining practices on its use could be performed
- It needed to be a really simple environment, with a fair learning curve; and if possible already familiar for the collective of professors and lecturers.

To use a relational database or a custom development where discarded in the first round of analysis, due to cost and time constrains, and also because the risk it would imply such project. It was seriously considered to use a Wiki engine, like the software Mediawiki (mediawiki.org) in which is based the Wikipedia (Wikipedia.org) Wikis are very powerful documental databases, collaboratively created, that allow virtually any kind of structure and navigation scheme. But as a drawback, wiki projects require a continuous attention and content curation; otherwise there is a good chance that the structure and information quality will degrade with the use. The complexity of the Mediawiki source code and other wiki engines that where considered for the project caused, at last the wiki option to be discarded.

A strong alternative was to use a service of Social Bookmarking, based on *freemium software as a service* online tools like http://Delicius.com and http://Diigo.com. These services allow the creation of collections of references to URIs (Universal Location Identifiers) tagged according to flexible taxonomies (defined organically) as the groups of users work on the knowledge base. Social Bookmarking services added a nice to have feature: each user can create and maintain its own list of references and re-tag it according to her own criteria. References could be shared among a group of users, adding a –so to speak- 2.0 flavor to the Knowledga base.

As a critical drawback to use Social Bookmarking services implies to give away the control of the Knowledge Base to an external company, located in another country, that provides a free service with a service agreement that do not gives guaranties of any kind that the Knowledge Base and service might prevail over time, nor gives any kind of guaranty in case of loss on information. While there is the option of getting a backup of one user Bookmarks, is not possible to get the whole Knowledge Base baceuse it would *belong* to several users. Thus a decision was taken to look for a software that would implement the features of a Social Bookmarkin that we could set up on the servers in our center.

On 2008 Jordi Piguillem Poch, PhD student of the ESSI department of the UPC and core developer of Moodle (http://moodle.org), developed a Moodle contrib module that implements a course activity that implements a social Bookmarking within the course. Moodle is the same LMS that implements the UPC and the vast majority of the spanish universities. For the academic personal Moodle a well known system, it also allows a very granular access control and keeps a detailed access log.

In a couple of weeks of work, Piguillem adapted the initial design of his module to support the specific requirements defined by the taxonomy described in section 2. The final implementation of the Knowledge base is based on Moodle 1.9.11 with a modified version of the Open Sourced Module that can be found at http://code.google.com/p/moodle-social-bookmarking/

## 4    Example of Use

The Knowledge Database described in this work is publicly accessible to any user through the web address http://sycs.fib.upc.edu/ and its use is very simple. After an initial presentation screen of the knowledge database, the user is routed directly to the search screen.

Figure 2 shows a screenshot of the screen, the search one. As you can see this screen contains, in the center, the text box to start a search, and a cloud box with information to the list of predefined tags.

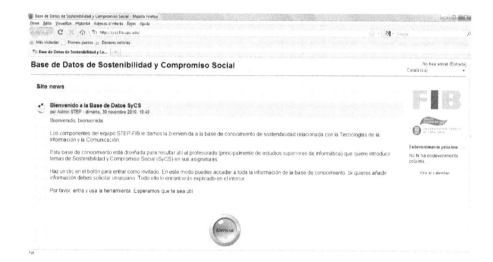

**Fig. 2.** Main screen

A search can be done in two ways:

- Using a predefined label with which all entries have been classified, or
- Using free text to be searched among the title and the description of the entry.

In order to search through a predefined label, the label can directly be selected from the right cloud box, or it can be written in the text box preceded by the mark "tag". For example, to search for entries tagged as *solidarity*, you can write directly: "tag: solidarity".

If you want to search using free text, you can type the text directly into the box. For example, typing *United Nations* all entries containing these words in the title or description fields will be displayed.

In Figure 3 you can see a screenshot example of the search results by "tag: operating systems". You can see a list of selected entries that contains the title, description, and the list of labels that classify that input. The title, in turn, is a link to the resource, either a web page, an article (usually in PDF format), a video, etc.

**Fig. 3.** Example of search results

A more restrictive search can be done as well by combining labels and / or free text, so that the search will be among the entries that meet all requirements. To make this type of search each parameter must be separated with a comma. For example, the search: "tag: solidarity, UN" (or "UN, tag: solidarity") will show the entries tagged with *solidarity* and that contain the word *UN* in the title or description texts. Another example: the search "tag: solidarity, tag: innovation" will show the entries tagged with *solidarity* and *innovation* simultaneously. In this way, any searches can be refined as desired.

Usually, the tool is accessed as a guest user profile. This profile is assigned by default, it does not require any identification and allows the user to perform any type of search. However, there is also an editor user profile, which requires identification, but can also add new entries or modify the existing ones. In order to have an editor profile, it has to be requested, and it is only required to be an academic in the area of ICT or to have an interest and professional background related to the project. The authorization is currently managed by the project team.

Of course, after the initial release of the tool, it is in constant evolution. Current efforts are focusing on:

- Improving the search capabilities, allowing the realization of specific searches made by algebraic combinations of labels and free text (for example, list the entries with a label or another, but in any case, with some free text),
- Providing a more graphical, less text-oriented, user interface.
- Improving the graphic design.

## 5    Final Thoughts and Conclusions

Introducing professional skills in University studies is not an easy task. We can find teachers who deny its importance, teachers who do not know how to start, or teachers with some knowledge of the skills, but inadequately trained in it.

In all these cases, the most important thing to succeed in introducing these skills in the new degrees is information. It is important for teachers to have articles, books, websites and other sources of information to explain the importance of each competency. Knowing good practices and examples is essential to incorporate correctly the development and evaluation of this skill in the curricula.

The professional skill "Sustainability and Social Commitment" (SSC) is particularly complex, since many teachers have experience in other skills such as "teamwork" or "communication", but there is great ignorance in regard to SSC. In this paper we have presented a Knowledge Base aimed at helping teachers relate their Engineering course with SSC concepts.

A tool of this style is very important for success in incorporating this skill to a specific subject. The tool presented is universal, so that all interested teachers can consult it. In addition, teachers may request access particularly interested as editors to help expand its content (write access is not universal to prevent degradation of the information).

Finally, we want to add that some colleagues who have seen the tool and the process of generating labels have asked us to use (and modify) the tool to implement this skill in other areas of knowledge (such as Urban Planning, for example). Similarly, the concepts used and the tool itself can be used for work other professional skills.

**Acknowledgements.** This project has been partially funded by the UPC –STEP project, the Learning Apps project funded by Spanish Ministry of Science and Innovation in the program INNPACTO, and the project miPLE Spanish Ministry of Science and Innovation within fundamental research TIN program.

## References

1. Cobb, C.L., Agogino, A.M., Beckman, S.L., Speer, L.: Enabling and Characterizing Twenty-First Century Skills in New Product Development Teams. International Journal of Engineering Education 24(2), 420–433 (2008)
2. Colby, A., Sullivan, W.M.: Ethics Teaching in Undergraduate Engineering Education. Journal of Engineering Education 97(3), 327–338 (2008)
3. Coyle, E.J., Jamieson, L.H., Oakes, W.C.: EPICS: Engineering Projects in Community Service. Int'l. J. of Engin. Educ. 21(1), 139–150 (2005)
4. Felder, R.M.: Sermons for grumpy campers. Chemical Engineering Education 41(3), 183–184 (2007)
5. Gößling-Reisemann, S., Von Gleich, A.: Training Engineers for Sustainability at the University of Bremen. Int'l. J. of Engin. Educ. 23(2), 301–308 (2007)

6. Huntzinger, D.N., Hutchins, M.J., Gierke, J.S., Sutherland, J.W.: Enabling sustainable thinking in undergraduate engineering education. Int'l. J. of Engin. Educ. 23(2), 218–230 (2007)
7. López, D., Sánchez, F., Cruz, J.-L., Fernández, A.: Developing Non-technical Skills in a Technical Course. In: Proceedings of the 37th Frontiers in Education Conference, Milwaukee, WI, USA, pp. F3B5–F3B10 (October 2007)
8. McLaughlan, R.G.: Instructional Strategies to Educate for Sustainability in Technology Assessment. Int'l. J. of Engin. Educ. 23(2), 201–208 (2007)
9. National Academy of Engineering, The Engineer of 2020. Visions of Engineering in the New Century. National Academy Press (2004)
10. Shuman, L.J., Besterfield-Sacre, M., McGourty, J.: The ABET Professional Skills—Can They Be Taught? Can They Be Assessed? Journal of Engineering Education 94(1), 41–55 (2005)
11. Siller, T.J.: Sustainability and critical thinking in civil engineering curriculum. Journal of Professional Issues in Engineering Education and Practice 127(3), 104–108 (2001)
12. Tam, E.: Developing a Sustainability Course for Graduate Engineering Students and Professionals. Int'l. J. of Engin. Educ. 23(6), 1133–1140 (2007)
13. Alier, et at.: Interoperability for LMS: the missing piece to become the common place for e-learning innovation. International Journal of Knowledge and Learning 6(2/3), 130–141 (2010)

# Is the Software Worker Competent? A View from Spain

Ricardo Colomo-Palacios[1], Cristina Casado-Lumbreras[2],
Edmundo Tovar-Caro[3], Pedro Soto-Acosta[4], and Ángel García-Crespo[1]

[1] Universidad Carlos III de Madrid, Computer Science Department
Av. Universidad 30, Leganés, 28911, Madrid, Spain
{ricardo.colomo,angel.garcia}@uc3m.es
[2] Universidad Complutense de Madrid, Department of Development Psychology
and Education, Faculty of Education
Rector Royo Villanova s/n, 28040, Madrid, Spain
cristinacasadolumbreras@pdi.ucm.es
[3] Universidad Politécnica de Madrid, Faculty of Computer Science
Campus de Montegancedo, 28660 Boadilla del Monte, Madrid, Spain
etovar@fi.upm.es
[4] University of Murcia, Department of Management & Finance,
Campus de Espinardo, 30100 Murcia, Spain
psoto@um.es

**Abstract.** This paper aims to identify competency gaps of software practitioners in Spanish software industry. Based on previous works, where a the description of a professional career and the competency levels for each role in the ladder are depicted, authors perform a study comparing an assessment performed using a 360 degree approach with such competency levels. Results show that certain roles present negative competency gaps and that, in general, technical competences present higher negative competency gaps than generic competences.

**Keywords:** Competences, Competency Levels, Software Engineering, Career.

## 1 Introduction

Human Factors represent one of the most important areas of improvement in Software Engineering [1]. But people are crucial for all business areas. Not in vain, the development of workers represents one of the most significant challenges for today's managers, and one of the most fertile fields for business innovation, human resource management and education research [2]. Competences and competence structures for IT professionals can be seen as enablers for the Knowledge Society, needed also of intellectual capital and competent IT workers [3]. Within Information Technology, software development is an intense human capital activity, more based in intellectual capital [4]. Moreover, according to Erdogmus [5], software development is an intellectual endeavour, and serious software development is a team activity. In words

M.D. Lytras et al. (Eds.): WSKS 2011, CCIS 278, pp. 261–270, 2013.

of Casado-Lumbreras et al. [6], Software development is a human centric and sociotechnical activity. Like any other industry, software industry needs to know the performance of their resources, in this case human resources. The scientific literature is full of evidences concerning the importance of personnel in the area. Thus, "Personnel attributes and Human Resource activities provide by far the largest source of opportunity for improving software development productivity" [7]. Moreover, qualified software engineers pertaining to software development teams are key factors in the software development process and their shortcomings and caveats [8]. Finally, Hazzan and Hadar [9] stated that there is abundant empirical evidence which proves that human aspects are the source of the main problems associated with software development projects

Since inadequate competence verification of software engineers is one of the principal problems when it comes to carrying out any software development project [10], this paper, based on previous works [1], [11] presents a study on the level of competence of software workers in Spain. This level of competence is calculated using 360 degree feedback and compared with competence levels defined for both technical [1] and general competences [11]. Thus, the aim of this paper is to show if there are differences between competence standards and real competence levels.

The remainder of the paper is organized as follows. Section 2 outlines relevant literature in the area about competence. In Section 3, the study conducted is presented along with the description of the sample and the methods used. Finally, conclusions are discussed in Section 4.

## 2     The Question of Competence: Origins, Taxonomies and Career Ladder

Competences are defined as behaviour models [12], as hidden characteristics of personality with an effect on the performance at work [13], as traits or features of human being [14] and as features related to an effective working performance [15]. That could be the reason why, competence is often used in the sense of performance, however, this is not entirely accurate [16].

Early 20th century scientific management used the concept of competence [17]. The concept is well established in the field of human resources management since the middle of the seventies, due to the works by McClelland [18]. Due to the popularity of the approach, competence frameworks, models, instruments and thinking have long been ingrained and utilized in management and organizational life [19]. McClelland [18] defines competence as the relation between humans and work tasks, that is, the concern is not about knowledge and skills in itself, but what knowledge and skills are required to perform a specific job or task in an efficient way. McClelland [20] suggested that competence ought to become the basis for a more effective method to predict individual performance in organizations.

In [21] a taxonomy of competences is presented. In this taxonomy, particular or technical competences are established as those that are necessary to carry out a very specific task of a particular job position and include knowledge, abilities, and skills. On the other hand, universal or generic competences are those that, though not linked to a specific activity or function, do make possible the competent performance of the tasks related to the work position, in as much as they refer to characteristics or abilities of the individual's general behaviour. These competences permit individuals to adapt to changes in a more efficient and rapid way [21]. Generic competences and may be crucial for IT project success [22] but also for a wider range of organizational contexts, including all knowledge workers [23].

Previous works [1],[11] presented a career ladder for software professionals. The professional ladder is based on an analysis aimed to extract similarities between definitions for each professional profile among all of the research sources, which includes industry practices, employment reports and technical literature. Figure 1 shows the seven steps of the career and the mappings to People-CMM [24] sample software engineering technical career:

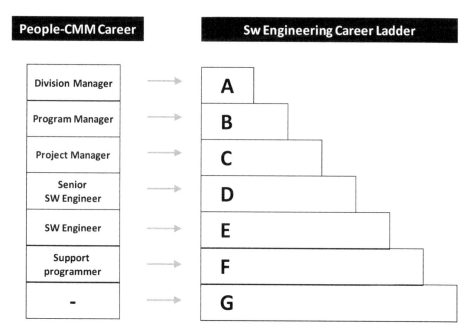

**Fig. 1.** Career ladder

Software engineering career ladder described in [1] consists in 7 consecutive steps from G (lower & entry level) to A (higher level). The second issue is to define a set of competences but technical and general and a competence level for all identified roles. Table 1 presents generic competence level per role, as suggested in [11]:

**Table 1.** Generic competence level per role

| Competence | A | B | C | D | E | F | G |
|---|---|---|---|---|---|---|---|
| Capacity for analysis and synthesis | 4 | 4 | 4 | 4 | 3 | 2 | 2 |
| Organization and planning | 4 | 4 | 4 | 3 | 3 | 2 | 2 |
| Oral and written communication in mother tongue | 4 | 4 | 4 | 3 | 3 | 2 | 2 |
| Problem solving | 4 | 4 | 4 | 4 | 3 | 3 | 2 |
| Decision-making | 4 | 4 | 4 | 3 | 2 | 2 | 1 |
| Critical thinking | 4 | 4 | 4 | 4 | 3 | 3 | 2 |
| Team work | 4 | 4 | 4 | 4 | 4 | 3 | 3 |
| Interpersonal skills | 4 | 4 | 4 | 3 | 2 | 2 | 2 |
| Ability to work on an interdisciplinary team | 4 | 4 | 4 | 3 | 3 | 3 | 2 |
| Information management | 4 | 4 | 4 | 4 | 3 | 2 | 2 |
| Ability to work in an international context | 4 | 4 | 3 | 3 | 2 | 2 | 1 |
| Ethical commitment | 4 | 4 | 4 | 3 | 3 | 3 | 3 |
| Environmental sensibility | 4 | 3 | 2 | 2 | 2 | 2 | 2 |
| Adaptation/flexibility | 4 | 4 | 4 | 4 | 3 | 3 | 2 |
| Creativity | 4 | 4 | 3 | 4 | 3 | 3 | 2 |
| Leadership | 4 | 4 | 4 | 3 | 2 | 2 | 1 |
| Understanding of other cultures and customs | 4 | 4 | 3 | 2 | 2 | 2 | 1 |
| Ability to work in an autonomous way | 3 | 3 | 3 | 3 | 3 | 3 | 3 |
| Initiative and enterprise | 4 | 4 | 3 | 3 | 3 | 2 | 2 |
| Quality concern | 4 | 4 | 4 | 4 | 4 | 3 | 3 |

On the other hand, Table 2 presents technical competence level as presented in [1].

**Table 2.** Generic competence level per role

| Competence | A | B | C | D | E | F | G |
|---|---|---|---|---|---|---|---|
| Software Requirements | 1 | 2 | 3 | 4 | 3 | 2 | 1 |
| Software Design | 1 | 2 | 3 | 4 | 4 | 3 | 2 |
| Software Construction | 1 | 1 | 2 | 3 | 4 | 4 | 3 |
| Software Testing | 1 | 2 | 3 | 4 | 4 | 3 | 2 |
| Software Maintenance | 1 | 2 | 3 | 4 | 4 | 3 | 2 |
| Software Configuration Management | 1 | 2 | 3 | 4 | 3 | 2 | 2 |
| Software Quality | 1 | 3 | 4 | 4 | 3 | 2 | 2 |
| Software Engineering Management | 3 | 4 | 4 | 3 | 3 | 2 | 1 |
| Software Engineering Tools and Methods | 1 | 2 | 4 | 4 | 3 | 2 | 2 |
| Software Engineering Process | 2 | 3 | 4 | 4 | 3 | 2 | 1 |

In what follows, the study that compares these levels with actual competency values of software workers is presented.

# 3    A Study on the Competence Level of Software Workers

## 3.1    Method

In order to analyze the competence level within software industry from a Spaniard point of view, a study was conducted. Authors applied the competency evaluation system for professionals figures C, D, E and F. The experimental groups should have average work experience of at least 1 year. This restriction is to set to allow that 360-degree assessments were carried out with sufficient data. The composition of the groups, as figures are concerned, presents a minimal structure of empirical validation of seven professionals who obey the hierarchical structure shown in Figure 2:

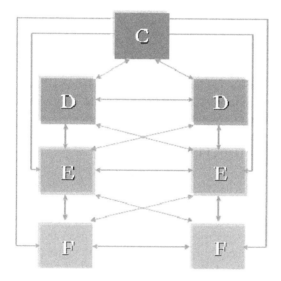

**Fig. 2.** Minimum composition of teams

Among the different evaluation methodologies that have been addressed in the relevant section of the state of the art, the two most used are the interview and the 360-degree assessment. We opted for the 360-degree assessment because of its good results [25] and its use in the assessment of IT personnel [26].

In the study, the results of an individual are composed by the assessment of the following stakeholders:

- His or her supervisor
- One or more subjects of the same level, ie, that shares the same professional figure.
- One or more subordinates

The scale used in the assessment presents a number of values from 1 to 4 points. The description of the scale will be generic to all competences, giving the following values:

1 = Low Level
2 = Medium Level
3 = High level
4 = Very High level

In order to provide a consensus in a single indicator the value is provided according the formula:

C. Level = ((Avg. supervisor rate) + (Avg. peers rate) + (Avg.subordinates rate)) /3

Prior to the completion by the subjects of the experimental task, the experiment was tested by two professionals with similar characteristics to the sample. The objective of this test was to improve procedures and ensuring the proper design and procedural implementation of the test.

## 3.2     Sample

The sample consisted on 22 subjects (5 women, 23% and 17 men, 77%) from three different corporations from Spain (a multinational IT consultancy corporation, a national IT consultancy corporation and a bank). The average age is 32.3. In average, subjects have 7.6 years of working experience. Subjects were classified on roles pertaining roles C (3), D (6), E(6) and F(7).

## 3.3     Results

Table 3 presents the results of 360 feedback including all competences. Table shows the number of responses per role (N), average rating (Av) and standard deviation (Sd).

With regard of technical competence, the role with highest technical competence is "D" averages, 27.9 points, followed by "E" with 25.2, "C" with 24.7, and finally, "F" with 20.7 points. Software Construction, Software Requirements and Software Design are the most valued technical competences. Software process closes this list. There is only a case of Standard Deviation over 1 point "D" and "Software Design" with 1.02 points.

Regarding generic competence, the role that leads the list of levels of competence, is the "C" with 68.5 points, followed by "D" with 64.8, the "E" with 62.5, and finally, the "F" with 61.1 points. The general competence ranking is led by "Capacity Analysis and Synthesis" with 13.2 points, followed by "Organization and Capacity Planning ". At the bottom are "Environmental sensibility" with 8.8 points and "Leadership " with 8.9 points. Similar to what has occurred in the case of technical skills, only presents a case of deviation above the unit, with a score of 1.02 for, like the previous case, the professional figure "D" and competition "Working in an international context".

In order to find out if there are differences between the evaluation and the competence levels defined in [1], [11] table.

**Table 3.** Assessment results

| | C | | | D | | | E | | | F | | |
|---|---|---|---|---|---|---|---|---|---|---|---|---|
| | N | Av | Sd | N | Av | Sd | N | Av | Sd | N | Av | Sd |
| Software Requirements | 6 | 3.5 | 0.8 | 24 | 3.2 | 0.6 | 38 | 2.8 | 0.6 | 31 | 2.2 | 0.9 |
| Software Design | 6 | 2.8 | 0.8 | 24 | 3.2 | 1 | 38 | 3.2 | 0.6 | 31 | 2.5 | 0.5 |
| Software Construction | 6 | 2.7 | 0.5 | 24 | 3.6 | 0.7 | 38 | 3.2 | 0.6 | 31 | 3 | 0.5 |
| Software Testing | 6 | 2.3 | 0.8 | 24 | 3.2 | 0.7 | 38 | 2.7 | 0.6 | 31 | 2.3 | 0.6 |
| Software Maintenance | 6 | 2.7 | 0.5 | 24 | 3 | 0.8 | 38 | 2.7 | 0.5 | 31 | 2.4 | 0.7 |
| Software Configuration Management | 6 | 2 | 0.9 | 24 | 2.4 | 0.8 | 38 | 2.2 | 0.7 | 31 | 1.8 | 0.5 |
| Software Quality | 6 | 2.2 | 0.8 | 24 | 2.8 | 0.6 | 38 | 2.5 | 0.7 | 31 | 2 | 0.8 |
| Software Engineering Management | 6 | 3.2 | 0.8 | 24 | 2.6 | 0.8 | 38 | 2.3 | 0.7 | 31 | 1.6 | 0.7 |
| Software Engineering Tools and Methods | 6 | 2 | 0.6 | 24 | 2.4 | 0.9 | 38 | 2.2 | 0.7 | 31 | 1.7 | 0.7 |
| Software Engineering Process | 6 | 1.3 | 0.5 | 24 | 1.5 | 0.5 | 38 | 1.4 | 0.5 | 31 | 1.2 | 0.5 |
| Capacity for analysis and synthesis | 6 | 3.7 | 0.5 | 24 | 3.4 | 0.8 | 38 | 3.2 | 0.7 | 31 | 2.9 | 0.6 |
| Organization and planning | 6 | 3.7 | 0.8 | 24 | 3.2 | 0.6 | 38 | 2.8 | 0.8 | 31 | 2.7 | 0.6 |
| Oral and written communication in mother tongue | 6 | 3.2 | 0.8 | 24 | 2.8 | 0.5 | 38 | 2.8 | 0.8 | 31 | 2.8 | 0.6 |
| Information management | 6 | 3.3 | 0.5 | 24 | 2.9 | 0.5 | 38 | 2.9 | 0.5 | 31 | 2.7 | 0.6 |
| Problem solving | 6 | 3.3 | 0.8 | 24 | 3 | 0.8 | 38 | 2.8 | 0.8 | 31 | 2.8 | 0.7 |
| Decision-making | 6 | 3.2 | 1 | 24 | 2.8 | 0.9 | 38 | 2.6 | 0.8 | 31 | 2.3 | 0.6 |
| Team work | 6 | 3.5 | 0.6 | 24 | 2.9 | 0.7 | 38 | 2.8 | 0.7 | 31 | 2.9 | 0.6 |
| Ability to work on an interdisciplinary team | 6 | 3.3 | 0.8 | 24 | 2.8 | 0.7 | 38 | 2.6 | 0.6 | 31 | 2.6 | 0.6 |
| Ability to work in an international context | 6 | 2.7 | 0.8 | 24 | 2.4 | 1 | 38 | 2.3 | 0.7 | 31 | 2.2 | 0.8 |
| Interpersonal skills | 6 | 2.7 | 0.8 | 24 | 2.9 | 0.8 | 38 | 2.7 | 0.7 | 31 | 3.2 | 0.6 |
| Critical thinking | 6 | 3.2 | 0.8 | 24 | 2.8 | 0.6 | 38 | 2.9 | 0.7 | 31 | 2.6 | 0.6 |
| Ethical commitment | 6 | 3.2 | 0.8 | 24 | 3.1 | 0.4 | 38 | 2.9 | 0.4 | 31 | 2.8 | 0.4 |
| Ability to work in an autonomous way | 6 | 2.8 | 0.8 | 24 | 3.1 | 0.7 | 38 | 3.2 | 0.5 | 31 | 3 | 0.6 |
| Adaptation/flexibility | 6 | 3.3 | 0.5 | 24 | 3 | 0.7 | 38 | 2.9 | 0.7 | 31 | 2.9 | 0.7 |
| Creativity | 6 | 3 | 0.9 | 24 | 3 | 0.8 | 38 | 2.7 | 0.5 | 31 | 2.9 | 0.7 |
| Leadership | 6 | 2.3 | 0.5 | 24 | 2.2 | 0.7 | 38 | 2.3 | 0.9 | 31 | 2.1 | 0.6 |
| Understanding of other cultures and customs | 6 | 2.7 | 0.8 | 24 | 2.6 | 0.5 | 38 | 2.5 | 0.6 | 31 | 2.5 | 0.6 |
| Initiative and enterprise | 6 | 2.5 | 0.6 | 24 | 2.5 | 0.6 | 38 | 2.6 | 0.8 | 31 | 2.5 | 0.5 |
| Quality concern | 6 | 2.7 | 0.8 | 24 | 3 | 0.4 | 38 | 2.7 | 0.7 | 31 | 2.5 | 0.6 |
| Environmental sensibility | 6 | 2 | 0.9 | 24 | 2.4 | 0.7 | 38 | 2.2 | 0.7 | 31 | 2.2 | 0.7 |

**Table 4.** Differences between assessment and competence levels

| | C | D | E | F |
|---|---|---|---|---|
| Software Requirements | 0,5 | -0,8 | -0,2 | 0,2 |
| Software Design | -0,2 | -0,8 | -0,8 | -0,5 |
| Software Construction | 0,7 | 0,6 | -0,8 | -1 |
| Software Testing | -0,7 | -0,8 | -1,3 | -0,7 |
| Software Maintenance | -0,3 | -1 | -1,3 | -0,6 |
| Software Configuration Management | -1 | -1,6 | -0,8 | -0,2 |
| Software Quality | -1,8 | -1,2 | -0,5 | 0 |
| Software Engineering Management | -0,8 | -0,4 | -0,7 | -0,4 |
| Software Engineering Tools and Methods | -2 | -1,6 | -0,8 | -0,3 |
| Software Engineering Process | -2,7 | -2,5 | -1,6 | -0,8 |
| Capacity for analysis and synthesis | -0,3 | -0,6 | 0,2 | 0,9 |
| Organization and planning | -0,3 | 0,2 | -0,2 | 0,7 |
| Oral and written communication in mother tongue | -0,8 | -0,2 | -0,2 | 0,8 |
| Information management | -0,7 | -1,1 | -0,1 | 0,7 |
| Problem solving | -0,7 | -1 | -0,2 | -0,2 |
| Decision-making | -0,8 | -0,2 | 0,6 | 0,3 |
| Team work | -0,5 | -1,1 | -1,2 | -0,1 |
| Ability to work on an interdisciplinary team | -0,7 | -0,2 | -0,4 | -0,4 |
| Ability to work in an international context | -0,3 | -0,6 | 0,3 | 0,2 |
| Interpersonal skills | -1,3 | -0,1 | 0,7 | 1,2 |
| Critical thinking | -0,8 | -1,2 | -0,1 | -0,4 |
| Ethical commitment | -0,8 | 0,1 | -0,1 | -0,2 |
| Ability to work in an autonomous way | -0,2 | 0,1 | 0,2 | 0 |
| Adaptation/flexibility | -0,7 | -1 | -0,1 | -0,1 |
| Creativity | 0 | -1 | -0,3 | -0,1 |
| Leadership | -1,7 | -0,8 | 0,3 | 0,1 |
| Understanding of other cultures and customs | -0,3 | 0,6 | 0,5 | 0,5 |
| Initiative and enterprise | -0,5 | -0,5 | -0,4 | 0,5 |
| Quality concern | -1,3 | -1 | -1,3 | -0,5 |
| Environmental sensibility | 0 | 0,4 | 0,2 | 0,2 |

Taking into account figures in Table 4, "C" role present a significant negative competence gap with and overall gap of 21 points, followed by "D" with 19.3, "E" with 10.4 and "F" with 0.2. These gaps are rooted on the higher exigency present in higher levels. With respect of the competences, the gap list is headed by two technical competences Software Engineering Process (7.6) and Software Engineering Tools and Methods (4.7) and a generic competence and Quality concern (4.1). In general there are higher gaps in technical competences. On the contrary positive gaps appear in Understanding of other cultures and customs, Environmental sensibility and Interpersonal skills. None of the technical competences present positive gaps.

# 4    Conclusions

This paper aims at the identification of competency gaps of software practitioners basing its study on two previous works. On the one hand, the pyramidal model for software engineering professional careers, identifying one single professional track going from Junior Programmer to IT Director, identified in [1]. On the other hand, competency levels provided in [1], [11]. Results show that, in general, there are negative gaps in technical competences and among them, Software Process is the one that presents higher gap. On the other hand, with respect to professional roles, figures "C", "D" and "E" present higher negative gaps than "F" role.

# References

1. Colomo-Palacios, R., Tovar-Caro, E., García-Crespo, A., Gómez-Berbis, M.J.: Identifying Technical Competences of IT Professionals. The case of software engineers. International Journal of Human Capital and Information Technology Professionals 1(1), 31–43 (2010)
2. Casado-Lumbreras, C., García-Crespo, Á., Colomo-Palacios, R., Gómez-Berbís, J.M.: Emotions and Interpersonal Skills for IT Professionals: an Exploratory Study. International Journal of Technology Enhanced Learning 2(3), 215–226 (2010)
3. Hernández-López, A., Colomo-Palacios, R., García-Crespo, A., Soto-Acosta, P.: Trust Building Process for Global Software Development Teams. A review from the Literature. International Journal of Knowledge Society Research 1(1), 66–83 (2010)
4. Sommerville, I., Rodden, T.: Human social and organizational influences on the software process. In: Fuggetta, A., Wolf, A. (eds.) Software Process (Trends in Software, 4), pp. 89–110. John Wiley & Sons, New York (1996)
5. Erdogmus, H.: Essentials of Software Process. IEEE Software 25(4), 4–7 (2008)
6. Casado-Lumbreras, C., Colomo-Palacios, R., Soto-Acosta, P., Misra, S.: Culture dimensions in software development industry: the effects of mentoring. Scientific Research and Essays (in press)
7. Boehm, B., Horowitz, E., Madachy, R., Reifer, D., Clark, B.K., Steece, B., Brown, A.W., Chulani, S., Abts, C.: Software Cost Estimation with COCOMO II. Prentice Hall, Upper Saddle River (2000)
8. Pressman, R.S.: Software Engineering: A practitioner Approach. Tata McGraw Hill Pub. Co. Ltd. (2005)
9. Hazzan, O., Hadar, I.: Why and how can human-related measures support software development processes. The Journal of Systems and Software 81(7), 1248–1252 (2008)

10. McConnell, S.: Professional Software Development. Addison-Wesley, Reading (2003)
11. Colomo-Palacios, R., Cabezas-Isla, F., García-Crespo, Á., Soto-Acosta, P.: Generic Competences for the IT Knowledge Workers: A Study from the Field. In: Lytras, M.D., Ordonez De Pablos, P., Ziderman, A., Roulstone, A., Maurer, H., Imber, J.B. (eds.) WSKS 2010. CCIS, vol. 111, pp. 1–7. Springer, Heidelberg (2010)
12. Roberts, G.: Recruitment and selection; a competency approach. Chartered Institute of Personnel and Development, London (1997)
13. Spencer, L.M., Spencer, S.M.: Competence at work: models for superior performance. John Wiley & Sons, Inc., New York (1993)
14. Zwell, M.: Creating a Culture of competence. John Wiley & Sons, Inc., New York (2000)
15. Boyatzis, R.E.: The Competent Manager. A model for effective performance. John Wiley & Sons Ltd., New York (1982)
16. Bassellier, G., Reich, B.H., Benbasat, I.: IT Competence of Business Managers: A Definition and Research Model. Journal of Management Information Systems 17(4), 159–182 (2001)
17. Taylor, F.W.: The Principles of Scientific Management. Harper & Brothers, New York (1911)
18. McClelland, D.C.: Testing for competence rather than for 'intelligence'. American Psychologist 28, 1–14 (1973)
19. Carroll, B., Levy, L., Richmond, D.: Leadership as Practice: Challenging the Competency Paradigm. Leadership 4(4), 363–379 (2008)
20. McClelland, D.C.: Human Motivation. Cambridge University Press, Cambridge (1987)
21. Levy-Leboyer, C.: La gestion des compétences (Competence management). Les Editions d'Organisation, Paris (1996)
22. Sukhoo, A., Barnard, A., Eloff, M.M., Van der Poll, J.A., Motah, M.: Accommodating Soft Skills in Software Project Management. Issues in Informing Science and Information Technology 2, 691–704 (2005)
23. Rimbau-Gilabert, E., Miyar-Cruz, D., López-de Pedro, J.M.: Breaking the boundary between personal- and work-life skills: parenting as a valuable experience for knowledge workers. International Journal of Knowledge and Learning 5(1), 1–13 (2009)
24. Curtis, B., Hefley, W.E., Miller, S.A.: People Capability Maturity Model (P-CMM®) Version 2.0, 2nd edn. CMU/SEI-2009-TR-003 (2009)
25. Wood, R., Payne, T.: Competency-based Recruitment and Selection. Wiley & Sons (1998)
26. Jiang, J.J., Klein, G., Roan, J., Lin, J.: IS service performance: self perceptions and user perceptions. Information & Management 38(8), 500–506 (2001)

# Establishing a Learning Culture: The Importance of Relationships within an Organization

Francesco Sofo[1] and Salvatore Ammirato[2]

[1] Faculty of Education, University of Canberra
ACT 2601, Australia
Francesco.Sofo@canberra.edu.au
[2] Department of Electronics, Computer Science and Systems, University of Calabria
via P. Bucci, 42\C, 87036 Rende (CS), Italy
ammirato@deis.unical.it

**Abstract.** Organizational learning is a relational concept and a social construct, intrinsically bound to the environment, involving interaction among individuals or between individuals and organizations. A learning culture can be represented as a range of complex relationships such as person-to-person relationships. Learning, to be productive within organizations, needs to be captured, realized, transformed and re-used. This requires relationships within an organization that support all types of learning at across the organization. This paper argues that a learning culture is a set of relationships and behaviors within an organization that transform tacit into explicit knowledge.

**Keywords:** organizational culture, learning culture, relationship.

## 1    Introduction

The concepts of knowledge and learning within organizational contexts have permeated the workplace and become popular over the past thirty years [15]. There have been numerous academic journals and books in the area beginning with Argyris and Schon [1], on organizational learning, arriving to Senge's work on the learning organization [21]. The importance of learning has also begun to be expressed simultaneously through other popular terms such as action learning [17, 11], knowledge management, team learning and reflective tools [7], talent retention, intellectual capital, emotional and social intelligence [6] and e-learning [14].

A learning culture therefore refers to sets of relationships that encourage a focus on balancing organizational interests with individual interests through transforming tacit knowledge to explicit knowledge [4]. Learning relationships need to be nurtured among organizational members where senior staff can act as coaches and mentors to more junior staff. Mentoring and leveraging leadership capability are ideal points of action for transforming the tacit to the explicit [8].

This paper analyzes the learning organization concept and argues that it makes sense within the context of a learning culture where relationships are nurtured that encourage learning at all levels. The paper reviews the concepts of organizational culture and examines the notion of learning culture as a set of relationships.

M.D. Lytras et al. (Eds.): WSKS 2011, CCIS 278, pp. 271–277, 2013.

## 2 Organizational Culture

The impact of culture on organizations is pervasive because it determines how work is done, the way organizations are led and how learning is undertaken and applied. Although there have been debates about the impact of culture on organizations there is general agreement that it is the key to influencing the operation and success of the organization [18, 5, 13].

There are multitudinous definitions of the term culture; all these scholars agreed that the essence of culture is values, beliefs, symbols and rituals and that these components are vitally important in both defining what an organization is and in acting as a glue to holding the organization together [10, 19, 9, 3]. Other researchers have created powerful metaphors in their analysis of workplace culture that are worth examining and noting the common elements among them as well as their distinctive differences [5, 16, 9, 23].

Deal and Kennedy use metaphors of a stable but hidden system of influences [5]. These metaphors include a stable collection of values, symbols, heroes, rituals and stories that operate beneath the surface as supports for behavior in the workplace. The metaphors are extended into vivid images through the use of four terms that describe four basic workplace cultures: 'the tough-guy, macho' culture characterized by individualists who are willing to take risks; the 'work hard-play hard' culture which encourages employees to maintain a high level of relatively low-risk activity but at the same time see work as a fun activity which is dependent on quick feedback; the 'bet your company' culture that operates in high risk, slow feedback environments and the 'process culture' in which there is little or no feedback, where employees, finding it hard to measure what they do, simply concentrate on how to do things, that is, doing things right rather than doing the right things.

The Competing Values Framework also classifies organizational culture along four dimensions [16]. Burchell and Saele use vivid metaphors to describe the four dimensions described by Quinn and Rohrburgh [3]. The first is the 'Clan Culture' which describes organizations that focus on flexibility, friendliness, concern for people and sensitivity to customers. The clan culture is like an extended family where the leaders, or the heads or the organization are considered to be mentors and perhaps even parent figures and the organization is held together by loyalty and tradition The organization places a great emphasis on teamwork, participation and consensus. The second dimension, the 'Adhocracy Culture' is entrepreneurial and creative where individual initiative and freedom are encouraged. The adhocracy type culture is characterized by risk-taking within the organization and is held together through the commitment of its members to experimentation and innovation. The third dimension, the 'Hierarchy Culture' is characterized by formality, structure and procedures to guide people in their work. The organization is held together by formal rules and policies since a smooth running organization is seen as critical. The organizational style is one where employees place a great deal of importance on secure employment and predictability. The fourth dimension, the 'Market Culture' emphasizes winning which is the glue that holds the organization together. The focus of this culture is on external positioning where the major concern is to get the job done. The people are competitive and goal-oriented with leaders who are tough and demanding. The organizational style is hard-driving competitiveness.

Handy's descriptions of four basic types of organizational culture are based on vivid metaphors of gods of ancient Greece [9]. His justification for the use of the Greek gods is based on the fact that the Greek gods possessed certain characteristics. The "Zeus" or club culture is dependent on an omnipotent head. He uses the metaphor of the spider's web to symbolize this type of culture as people in this type of culture can usually communicate directly with the omnipotent head as well as with others in the organization. In this type of organization, decisions are made quickly and there is quick feedback. This type of culture relies very much on empathy which itself is dependent on affinity and trust and is characteristic of small entrepreneurial organizations.

The second type of culture is the "Apollo" or role culture. Apollo was the god of order. This type of culture typically describes bureaucracies where the definition of the job not personalities is important. Handy uses the Greek temple as a metaphor for this type of culture where the pillars represent the different functions of the organization which are joined managerially at the top by the pediment. Handy describe s the third type as the "Athena" or task culture. In this type of organization, management is basically concerned with the allocation or drawing together of resources in order to achieve the successful solution of problems. He uses the metaphor of the net as it draws resources from various parts of the organization to focus on the solution of problems. This is the culture of teams in which expertise is the basis of power and influence. The fourth type of culture is represented by Dionysus and is the existential culture. In this type of culture, the organization exists solely to assist individuals achieve their purpose.

Trompenaars identifies four distinct workplace cultures whose names are derived from the attitude to people and authority figures and the ways of changing [23]. The first culture he describes is the 'family' where authority is ascribed to parent figures who are close and powerful. In this culture it is the father who changes course (equivalent to 'Zeus', 'clan', 'work hard-play hard). The second culture is what Trompenaars calls the 'Eiffel Tower' where status is ascribed to superior roles who are usually distant yet powerful and change is governed by rules and procedures (equivalent to 'Apollo', 'hierarchy', 'process'). The third he calls the 'guided missile' culture in which status is achieved by project group members who contribute to targeted goals. In this culture change is achieved by shifting aim as the target moves (equivalent to 'Athena', 'market', 'bet your company'). The fourth type is the 'incubator' culture in which status is achieved by individuals exemplifying creativity and growth. Change is achieved through improvisation and attuning (equivalent to ' Dionysus', 'adhocracy', tough-guy macho')..

The four types of workplace culture described by Deal and Kennedy [5], Quinn and Rohrburgh [16], Handy [9] and Trompenaars [23] can be aligned even though there is not an exact one to one correspondence among the various types. It is useful to gain a summary view of the power of metaphors in describing four distinctive types of culture which have some relationship to each other. There are different levels of congruence in the way these various authors have described organizational culture. First, it is interesting that all the authors who created their metaphors were able to distinguish four types, the same number of distinctive organizational cultures. Second, there appears to be a high level of congruence among the four types described as indicated above. Third, the authors suggest that subcultures exist and in fact one culture might be the dominant organizational culture while the others may exist in corners of the organization or as layers, as sub-cultures. All culture metaphors use basic concepts related to the nature of relationships especially how power and control are exercised.

For learning to take place and more importantly to be effective, there must be a supportive culture within the organization. This support can take many different forms and can include a reward system such as bonuses and promotion, financial support in order to undertake learning activities, coaching and mentoring from senior and/or experienced staff and most importantly there must be a direct relationship between the nature of the learning being undertaken and the duties of the job.

## 3    Learning Culture

Schein's more recent work defines culture as a pattern of shared basic assumptions learned by a group to solve its problems of external adaptation and internal integration, and that is taught to new members as the correct way to perceive, think, and feel in relation to those problems [20].

There is widespread support for the proposition that organizational culture is the critical element in developing a learning organization [2, 12, 22]. These authors have emphasised the need for developing a learning culture and identified different organizational imperatives for creating such a learning culture where ethical leadership is critical.

Some broad approaches taken in understanding learning in organizations promote a learning culture and therefore certain ways of behaving within organizations. First there is the mental models approach taken by Argyris and Schon [1] where they argue that sharing mental models leads to organizational learning especially when the models shared are made explicit and challenged through critical reflection. Where mental models are not taken beyond the tacit knowledge level then learning at productive and deep levels does not occur [4]. The second (systems) approach [21] also focuses on learning breakdowns that occur when mental models are ineffective due to their incompleteness and internal contradictions as well as to people's poor capacity to draw correct conclusions. The third approach focuses on organizational culture and the conditions necessary to sustain and nurture learning [18]. One reason that learning conditions do not exist in most organizations is that their cultures or typical behaviors do not support long-term learning [18]. Senge advocates the creation of cultures within organizations that cultivate an environment that both value the importance of learning and the supporting of learning as an important component of an organization's work [21].

Marquardt maintains that most organizational cultures are often anti-learning and anti-risk taking, which means that new approaches and information sharing are discouraged and rewards are offered for being compliant [12]. Marquardt provides us with a picture of groups of variables labeled 'organization, people, technology, knowledge management and learning' that have close relationships and how they intersect with each other. The indication is that all the relationships are important but learning is central and has the greatest impact and relationship with all the other factors. The central variable of 'learning' is the hub of the model and appears primary influencer for a learning culture. For learning to occur there needs to be a perception that the organization is permeated by relationships that support and encourage learning. Critical to the proposition that relationships are important is the notion that leadership is necessary for developing and implementing vision and culture,

Ortenblad maintains there are two perspectives within the literature on organizational learning stating that a functionalist perspective is more dominant than the interpretive perspective which now stands as a significant challenge to the functionalist view [15]. This contradicts the espousal theory of Argyris and Schon [1] which clearly places power at the individual level, as well as the works of most authors that Ortenblad classifies are functionalist in their perspective of organizational learning. The difference between a functionalist and interpretive perspective of a learning organization is that in the former, reality is regarded as persistent whilst in the latter reality is seen as requiring extensive use of the imagination.

A learning culture is based on a theory of action, of how one likes to do things. According to Argyris and Schon individuals have two such theories; the first is titled theory in use and refers to the behaviors actually used in a situation while the second one is titled espoused theory and refers to the behaviors that individuals espouse to use which may not be the same as the first [1]. The theory in use is similar across all cultures and that is where embarrassment or threat are sensed that may lead to losing face, honor or being uncivil. In this case, the behavior to avoid embarrassment (theory in use) is to avoid the potential loss of honor and pretend you are not escaping it. Different cultures have their own term for this behavior such as telling lies, telling white lies, being diplomatic or just using tactics. This maintains unilateral control, leads to winning and maintains rationality at all costs and the learning is limited, inhibited and leads to the persistence of the status quo. Argyris and Schon call this single loop learning and it describes a learning culture that fuels error processes and misunderstandings, is limited, uncreative, unchanging and reinforces existing routines [1]. It is a type of culture that insists on doing things right, persisting with the status quo, maintaining the same rules and doing little differently. This type of learning which can incorporate quite sophisticated defensive routines is inadequate for learning that leads to improvement and change. So it would seem that a culture of an organization that does not allow the organization to reduce its defensive organizational routines, be adaptable, flexible, organize situations where its staff can be original and learn new things and ways to protect each other overtly is not a learning culture.

## 4    Conclusion

This paper has argued that the concept of culture represents a set of relationships that need to be nurtured within organizations that empower both individuals and the collective organization. In theory there will exist a number of possible cultures that are capable of nurturing learning within organizations and the intention in this paper is to affirm frameworks that show possible cultures that are learning cultures.

In essence the work of Argyris and Schon points to some critical relationships required for a learning culture to exist [1]. Such a culture is based on relationships of honesty that can be actioned by individuals. This requires individuals who do not fear stating their complete views and organizations that value and seek to integrate those views and individual contributions into a creative endeavor. Part of this requirement is an unequivocal learning transfer process where the learning of individuals is valued and retained by the system processes. Revans emphasizes this notion of honest relationships in his theory of action learning as a key underpinning process for learning within organizations [17]. He describes action learning as the process of discovering what it means to be honest and then striving to be that. In some respects this notion of honesty epitomizes respect, openness and dispositional characteristics that capture the essence of learning culture. It seems, that instituting sets of relationships within organizations that are characterized by action learning, goes a good distance to building a learning culture.

## References

1. Argyris, C., Schon, D.: Organizational Learning; A Theory of Action Perspective. Addison-Wesley, Massachusetts (1978)
2. Armstrong, A., Foley, P.: Foundations for a learning organization: organization learning mechanisms. The Learning Organization 10(2), 74–82 (2003)
3. Burchell, R., Saele, C.: Organizational cultural diagnosis: Merits of employing the Competing Values Framework (CVF) in conjunction with shared values profiling. Paper presented at the Australian and New Zealand Academy of Management Conference, Sydney (2007)
4. Collis, B., Winnips, K.: Two scenarios for productive learning environments in the workplace. British Journal of Educational Technology 33(2), 133–148 (2002)
5. Deal, T., Kennedy, A.: Corporate Cultures. Penguin, Sydney (1982)
6. Goleman, D.: Emotional Intelligence. Bloomsbury, London (1996)
7. Gray, D.: Facilitating management learning: developing critical reflection through reflective tools. Management Learning 38(5), 495–517 (2007)
8. Hall, P.: Values development and learning organizations. Journal of Knowledge Management 5(1), 19–32 (2001)
9. Handy, C.: Gods of Management, 3rd edn. Random House, London (1991)
10. Harrison, R.: How to describe your organization. Harvard Business Review 50(3), 119–128 (1972)
11. Hind, M., Koenigsberger, J.: Culture and commitment: the key to the creation of an action learning organization. Action Learning: Research and Practice 4(1), 87–94 (2007)
12. Marquardt, M.: Building the learning organization: mastering the 5 elements for corporate learning. Davies-Black, California (2002)
13. Martin, J.: Culture in Organizations. Oxford University Press, New York (1992)
14. Newton, D., Ellis, A.: Development of an e-learning culture in the Australian Army. International Journal on E-Learning 6(4), 543–563 (2007)
15. Ortenblad, A.: Organizational learning: a radical perspective. International Journal of Management Reviews 4(1), 87–100 (2002)
16. Quinn, R., Rohrbaugh, J.: A spatial model of effectiveness criteria: towards a competing values approach to organizational analysis. Management Science 29(3), 363–377 (1983)

17. Revans, R.: ABC of action learning. Lemos & Crane, London (1998)
18. Schein, E.H.: Organizational Culture. American Psychologist 45(2), 109–119 (1990)
19. Schein, E.H.: Organizational Culture and Leadership. Jossey-Bass, San Francisco (1992)
20. Schein, E.H.: Organizational Culture and Leadership, New edition. Jossey-Bass, San Francisco (2004)
21. Senge, P.: The fifth discipline: the art and practice of the learning organization, 2nd edn. Random House, Sydney (2006)
22. Teare, R., Dealtry, R.: Building and sustaining a learning organization. The Learning Organization 5(1), 47–60 (1998)
23. Trompenaars, F.: Riding the waves of culture: understanding cultural diversity in business. Nicholas Brealey Publishing, London (1993)

# Collaborative Consensus and Knowledge Creation: Computer-Mediated Methodology for Sign Language Studies

Cayley Guimarães, Diego Roberto Antunes, Laura Sánchez García,
and Sueli Fernandes

UFPR, Computer Science Department, Curitiba, Brazil
profcayley@yahoo.com.br, drantunes@gmail.com, laura@inf.ufpr.br,
suelif@globo.com

**Abstract.** Historically, the Brazilian Sign Language (Libras) in particular, and most Sign Languages (SL) around the world in general, have suffered consequences of prejudice and lack of adequate scientific study. An evaluation of a computational representation of the phonology of Libras showed strong evidences of serious issues (e.g. prejudice, late acquisition, lack of knowledge, lack of standards among others). A Collaborative Consensus and Knowledge Creation (CCKC) Methodology was designed and tested in a Community of Practice centered at Libras Studies. Results showed a high degree of efficiency at addressing the issues. An extension is proposed to disseminate and enrich Libras.

**Keywords:** Sign Language, Knowledge Creation, Social Inclusion, Communities of Practice.

## 1 Introduction

Natural Language and its acquisition has long been the subject of researches, which have proven its crucial role in intellectual development, social integration and full citizenship exercise [6] [25]. As for the Deaf, they were once clinically defined by deafness (a "deficiency" that had to be removed to bring them back to "normality"), and thus, disregarded as subject, and deprived of their natural language [20].

The natural language of the Deaf (namely, Sign Language (SL) – Libras – Brazilian Sign Language) is their tool for communication, knowledge creation and other aspects that are language-dependent. SL are a major part of the Deaf culture. Deaf culture is a term applied to the social movement that holds deafness to be a difference in human experience (which includes the right to use SL) rather than a disability.

However, SL has been relegated (by society in general, and science in particular) for at least 100 years. SL only returned to the scientific agenda since the late 60's [21], thus lagging behind in its development, with consequences for the Deaf educational, social, political and citizenship dimensions [8] [20].

M.D. Lytras et al. (Eds.): WSKS 2011, CCIS 278, pp. 278–292, 2013.

The plight of the Deaf has been long and hard, with scarce progress related to their issues. Recently, There has been a shift in perception about the Deaf condition: they are now considered part of a minority, with identity, culture, belonging to a community that may be aided by medical advances, but, mostly, should have their social, political and educational dimensions considered. [20].

Guimarães et al. [10] compiled a series of phonological models into a computational model of the phonology of Libras (Brazilian Sign Language). In order to validate such model, a Community of Practice was formed with non-deaf members and Deaf students of an undergraduate course of Linguistics/Libras [11]. Community of Practice is defined by Wenger [26] as a group of people who share an interest or passion about a subject. Members of such a group try to interact regularly in order to augment their knowledge on the subject.

During validation of such model, with members of the Deaf society within the CP, the authors encountered several problems regarding the formational aspects of signs, its comprehension, correctness and the use of Libras: prejudices; late acquisition; lack of skills; lack of Libras standard; lack of adequate knowledge about the phonetics; dated scientific work about SL in general and Libras in particular among many others. Such problems are a dire consequence of the lack of enough advances in SL and Deaf issues, with implications for Deaf development.

In order to mitigate such problems, a methodology of Collaborative Consensus and Knowledge Creation (CCKC), to be used for educational purposes, knowledge creation and vector for standardization of Libras. The CCKC methodology is composed of two frameworks: (1) a process of CP cultivation evolving around Libras (2) a computer-mediated system, based on collaborative principles, to scaffold Libras learning.

The remainder of this article briefly summarizes SL and its relation to the Deaf issues; present the findings that prompted the development of the CCKC Methodology and present the results of its use in an educational CP (the main goal of this article). Results include: a) increase in consensus for knowledge creation in Sign Language; b) cultivation of a Community of Practice. Additionally, two extensions of the use of the Methodology are presented, along with their initial results.

## 2    Sign Language and Deaf Issues

Sign languages are considered a legitimate linguistic system. They are fully conventionalized (i.e. with rules and structure – phonetic and phonological (Brentari, 1995) [3] – morphology, syntax, semantics and pragmatics), of spatial-gestural-visual manner, capable of providing the deaf with an adequate means to realize all of their linguistic potentialities. Additionally, sign languages are suitable for computational representation, which allows for broader and richer tools [10].

Fernandes (2006:3) [8] tells us that humans use signs, codes and language, and socialization amplifies social-cultural aspects, and the use of sign language by the Deaf is a specific relationship between her and her surrounding world; a different way of being and learning. The traditional oppression of the oral tradition negatively affects the development of Deaf children, who are treated as inferior *"[...] because, after all, they lacked the essential property for society, that is, the oral and hearing language"*.

Oralism (the imposition, by society, of the spoken language) colonized the Deaf by disallowing them to speak their natural language of signs. Hearing aids were the tool to separate them from Deaf culture. This systematic behavior has left in its wake dire consequences (e.g. prejudice, social exclusion, lack of development, etc.) [8].

Boaventura de Souza Santos [19] states that science should not only "describe" the world, but, rather, that science should understand the world intimately, in order to unveil the human possibilities, turning the knowledge into practical, thus leading to inclusion. In this sense, the Deaf community's particular form of communication and understanding of the world must be a part in exercising citizenship.

The responsibilities to explore deeper into more complex features of users (e.g. culture) is a dear notion to Human-Computer Interaction (HCI) researchers in supporting design within people's lives. But there is a lack of research on how these considerations should inform design [23] and, mostly, there is a lack of studies of SL, and how they should be performed and incorporated, both in tools and SL advancements in general. *"The need is pressing [...]"* especially when our work extends into differing communities and constituencies that are not our own [27].

# 3    Computational Model of the Phonemes of the Libras (PSL)

Guimarães et al. [10] present a computational representation model based on a compilation and adaptation of phonological models that aggregates a high degree of details for sign description. The phonology of a SL is related to the study of sub-units that form a sign (e.g. hand configuration, location, movement among others) [21]. Such finesse in describing the signs render the model as adequate for computational treatment of SL. Figure 1 shows an adaptation of the basic structure of the model with some of its main parameters. The proposed structure (its use and the degree of computational details of signs) is important to solve a series of problems thus far encountered in the use of Libras.

The Phonetic Structure of Libras (PSL) model, one of the motivations that cultivated the CP, is defined as an Intellectual Artifact. Intellectual Artifact is a product created by an intellectual activity, based on the interpretation of a problem, and the conception of the solution, presented in a linguistic code [7].

When compared to existing models, the proposed model aggregates a high degree of details that allows for addition of new parameters, sequentiality of signs, dynamics of signs, among others. This completeness is important for the processing (use of the knowledge as described by the model for image recognition, translation etc.) and for the execution (e.g. to generate 3D avatars). Additionally, the proposed model includes the Non-Manual Expressions, which may be used in the intensity, sentence formation, and semantics and in the singular characterization of a sign. This singular characterization often occurs in disguised signs.

The model was internally validated by linguistic and members of the Deaf community. The evaluation, during the meetings, required a great deal of dedication and involvement by members of the deaf community and researchers, working together in the design and creation of knowledge around the subject. This involvement occurred within the collaborative meetings that cultivated the CP. The model was validated [10] [11] as helpful in teaching Libras, evaluating knowledge of Libras, standardizing it, to help designers to build computational tools.

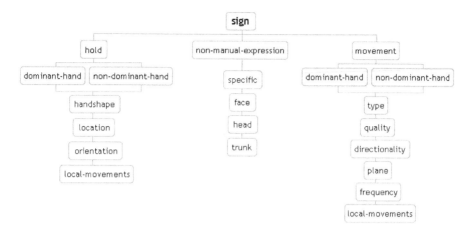

**Fig. 1.** Computational Description Model of the Phonetic Structure of the Libras (PSL)

# 4    Communities of Practice

Community of Practice is defined by Wenger [26] as a group of people who share an interest or passion about a subject. Members of such a group try to interact regularly in order to augment their knowledge on the subject.

According to Wenger [26:179]:

> *"The concept of community of practice was not born in the systems theory tradition. It has its roots in attempts to develop accounts of the social nature of human learning inspired by anthropology and social theory (Lave, 1988; Bourdieu, 1977; Giddens, 1984; Foucault, 1980; Vygostsky, 1978)".*

CPs are special environments that favor learning through the interaction of their members as individuals with similar interests, projects, motivations and challenges [24]. People bring different sets of skills, experiences and knowledge to the group, with each individual contributing in his particular manner to generate ideas, solve problems or make decisions. These opportunities to exchange knowledge and experience make learning and problem solving faster than the correspondent time period in which an isolated individual would achieve them [24].

A CP is structured in three elements [24]: (1) the domain (common interest of the group); (2) the community (interaction and bonding dictated by the common interest); (3) the practice (process by which members of the CP learn about their subject of interest). CPs and collaborative environments are very similar, as both bring people together for a common subject, and collaborate to achieve a common goal, through interactive activities that contribute for knowledge creation in a specific domain.

Knowledge creation in CP [5] [12] [26] is a continuous social process of goal clarification that requires commitment, constant encouraging of mutual learning and the increasing development of skills [5]. According to Picchiai et al. [16], CPs are an important tool for learning that favors the development of intellectual capital and consequent individual competences. KC has been recognized as strategically important for knowledge and innovation; several works about KC are centered in the organization of learning, with the goal to facilitate conversion and transfer of knowledge between its forms tacit and explicit [14].

Knowledge Creation in CPs occurs in various situations during collaboration, through information and experience exchanges, through observation and assimilation of specific intrinsic skills from each participant, by the exchange of ideas for decision-making and problem solving. In the CP, information exchange may occur tacitly or explicitly.

Additionally, knowledge refers to beliefs and commitments; it is related to action and, as such, it is a function of attitude, perspective or specific intention [14]. The authors also consider that "*knowledge is a dynamic human process of justifying the personal belief in regards to the truth*". These concepts emphasize knowledge as essential to human action.

Carroll et al. (2003) [5] describe the three characteristics a KC system must have in a CP: (1) it must be attractive and accessible in order to stimulate the users to make effective use of it and thus gain critical mass; (2) it must include interaction tools rich in authoring and material re-use; and (3) it must help the users is identifying the specialists and mediate the interaction with them.

# 5    Scaffolding

Scaffolds have been described as software features and its use to aid KC processes, to support learning, to aid in the overcoming of barriers (cognitive and others) in order to provide a better engagement in productive activities. The domain of Libras (and SL in general) calls for a greater participation from the HCI community to address such issues, and to design interactions that is effective. One of such challenges is to design scaffolds [18].

In order to be able to offer members of a KC environment with the proper tool, some of the requirements should include the requirements pointed by [5] above, in general; and, for Libras, in particular: a sound Model of Libras (in its chosen aspect, namely, its phonological elements); Sharing; Storage; Retrieval; Participation encouragement; Error Recovery; Problem-Solving mechanisms among others. Those challenges were incorporated in the information system developed in this research (and will be presented in section 7.2).

# 6    Validation and Evaluation: Methodological Steps

Qualitative research answers very particular types of questions. It is concerned with a level of reality that is hard to be quantified: it works with an universe of meanings, motivations, aspirations, values and attitudes, which incorporate a deeper space into relations, process and phenomena that are hard to be reduced to variables [2].

The research presented here is also exploratory in character, developed in two distinct phases: first, a validation and evaluation of a computer model allowed to compile evidence of issues that should be addressed. Then, a research in action (that acted upon the object with the general aim to change it) took place. This type of research is used when it is hard to state precise and operational hypothesis on the chosen theme, and it serves as basis to develop, clarify and change concepts and ideas in order to better define the object of study and to formulate robust working hypothesis [2].

In order to validate the model, a series of collaborative meetings were conducted involving members of the Deaf community, represented by undergraduate students of a linguistics course of Libras and an interpreter. The deaf had studied the main parameters used in the model. These meetings were designed to identify a minimum set of representative signs in Libras for each parameter (and the respective description using the Model) [11].

The approach of building such set yielded a corpus of culturally validated signs that are to be used by members of the research group and the Deaf community. This set, named minimum-maximum is a set with the minimal number of signs that cover the maximum numbers of parameters. The identified signs were described as per the model's parameters, considering all the possible variations of the signs. This procedure helped in verifying whether the model would be able to completely describe the chosen signs [11].

The meetings were schedule in advance according to the availability of the participants, and each session lasted for no more than 2 (two) hours, over a period of two months. For each meeting, a minimal of an interpreter and four members of the deaf community was required, along with the members of the HCI architecture research group. Previous instructions about the model, the meetings set up and objectives were sent via e-mail, and discussed with all participants prior to the beginning of the experiments [11].

Aspects of collaboration were carefully designed in order to cultivate an adequate environment permissive of productivity. For example, the consensus aspect was deemed highly important, and, thus, the meetings provided a democratic process that allowed each participant to have an active voice in determining the right sign and its description. Each participant was instructed as for her role and responsibilities in the meeting, and had the opportunity to reflect on her actions prior to acting. The consensus environment allowed for a decision-making process where all information was gathered and debated upon, to be universally absorbed and to be used in the concentration of efforts towards completion of the task at hand (that of selecting a sign and describing it) [11].

The meetings were divided into two phases: i) selection and recording of the signs and ii) description of the signs according to the model to be validated. For the first phase of the meetings, the following actions were taken: a) presentation of disclaimers; goals of the research and tasks to be performed; b) filling of disclaimers and compromise forms; c) discussion of the desired types of signs, and types to be avoided, such as composed signs (e.g. Church = house + Cross); d) presentation of each parameter of the model. The sign selection process can begin by the segment hold and hand shapes. For each of the 61 hand shapes, for instance, the following steps should be performed [11]:

1) Ask the participants for one or more sign that uses the given hand configuration;
2) Discuss the suggested sign (for correctness, form etc.);
3) Reach a consensus as for the sign that should compose the selection set;
4) Describe the sign in its elements as per the model; make sure that the most number of values is used;
5) Verify if that hand configuration also represents a number or a letter, or some unique sign;
6) Include the sign and its description into the selection set;
7) Repeat steps for the remainder of the hand configurations until the end.

## 6.1    Inadequacies about Knowledge of Libras

The experiments far surpassed expectations, and allowed the research group to incorporate new values for parameters (e.g. sadness, surprise, doubt as values for the set of pre-defined non-manual expressions). The original hand configuration set used, from Ferreira-Brito (1995) [9], was found to be incomplete, and the set from [17] was then added. As for location, the model detailed the space, but was lacking a neutral point during the articulation of a sign. Some signs, in the movement parameter, have local movement during suspension, and others have local movement during movement itself. Also, the orientation of the palm of the hand is better described by the orientation, also, of the base of the hand, combined with a parameter for the arm (horizontal or vertical).

Additionally, the validation and evaluation of the PSL model allowed for the compilation of evidence about the consequences brought about by the lack of use and studies of Libras. They came in form of problems, lack of knowledge, wrongful linguistics concepts, and prejudices. This section presents such issues. The following section presents a Collaborative Consensus and Knowledge Creation (CCKC) methodology created to mitigate the problems.

### A) Prejudices against SL and late acquisition of Libras

The Deaf members of the CP were children born into non-deaf families that imposed the oral culture. Most were tossed from school to school, and had no education in SL until their late teens (at the age of 14, in average). The following is a transcription of one of the statements (out of several others, similar in content) made by the Deaf interviewed:

> "[...] My mother didn't know I was deaf. Only when I was 2 did she suspect. She demanded a lot of me, there was no pity, she demanded. She forced me to oralize, and I oralized a lot. When I started school for the deaf, they beat me in the mouth. "You must learn how to talk. You can't Sign". I endured many difficulties. I had to go to the phono-audiologist. In school, I felt like a fool, I didn't understand anything. My mother didn't help in anything. She wasn't bad. She wanted me to learn how to read. I got beaten, she pulled my ears, and I was there, helpless [...]"

These types of statements show the problems faced by the child, mostly left to her own devices, suffering prejudices, and not properly developing social, affective and intellectual skills, and not being exposed to an environment permissive of language acquisition, and information access.

## B) Poor Libras Skills
The skills demonstrated by the Deaf were not consistent across the members, requiring several discussions about the utterances of signs. Evidence suggests that a general dissemination.

For example, in Brazil, the Portuguese language has a dissemination vector in the culture and national television network (films, soap opera, music, theater among others). This vector crosses the Brazilian borders, and allow for Portuguese speakers from other countries to understand it rather easily. The opposite is not so true: Brazilians have some difficulties to understand Portuguese spoken by non-Brazilians.

## C) Lack of Standards and Dissemination
There were several instances of inadequate skills due to the lack of dissemination of Libras.

- Errors: a student signed BANK - CHEQUE wrongly, with the strong conviction that she was correct, Figure 2-ab. It may be an evidence of pragmatics. But the sign is iconic [22], with little margin for misunderstanding as would be the correct combination of Figure 2-ac. Another student spelled her name with a completely wrong hand configuration for the letter "B". These, and other mistakes caused several instances of communicational barriers even among the Deaf speakers of Libras themselves.

**Fig. 2.** Bank Cheque. Wrong a-b. Correct: a-c.

- Lack of Knowledge about the phonetics of Libras (minimal elements that form a sign), which lead to several misunderstandings about meanings, uses, individualisms among others;

- Lack of use of necessary parameters: there was an indiscriminate use of the parameters (that may be sufficient for the Deaf but should not be considered acceptable). In this regard, the use of the PSL model proved crucial, by providing a detailed abstraction of the existing parameters;

- Non-parity between the phonological parameters described in the literature and the dynamicity of the language: There were Different sets: no agreement was reached as to the form; Unknown sets: for which no sign was produced; sets that were considered definitely wrong or non-existent: not accepted by the members of the CP; Differing nomenclature and numbers of parameters; sets whose formal aspects were non-Recognizable (but are very crucial when it comes to a computational formalism (e.g. the sign for "AMARELO" (YELLOW) had no definitive start-end points for the location parameter). Figure 3 shows the precise start location (a), but a rather pragmatic end location (necessary for formal computation)

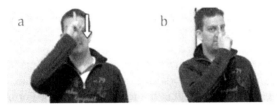

**Fig. 3.** Sign for AMARELO (YELLOW)

- Strong evidence that some of the formal parameters do not have to be known and specified, since they are incorporated and easily interpreted by the Deaf (such as a contraction or shortening of the sign). This was most preeminent especially when it comes to the natural gestural-visual perception of the Deaf. To illustrate, this would be the equivalent to the difference between "doing" and "doin'".

### D) Existing tools

Tools in Libras (be them educational or of another nature, such as sites, dictionaries etc.) are rare, and proved to be detrimental (rather than helpful) to the development of Libras [4] [28] [29]. Most of them perpetuate a view that contemplates what hearing developers consider to be sufficient, without taking into consideration the real needs of the Deaf. For instance, the dictionaries are mere compilation of several signs, presented as variations (some even go as far as calling them "regionalisms". This approach tends to create the impression that any sign is correct and acceptable (refer to the aforementioned of a name spelling using a completely wrong B hand configuration). Several signs are presented for the same meaning (without their being synonymous). Conversely, one sign is used for several meanings (without it being a polysemy). There are no classical elements to present the SL (such as phonology, etymology, neologism, context, explanation among others): signs are listed without any context, definition, and explanation [4] [28] [29].

- There is a lack of knowledge in Libras for a series of concepts: for example, there is no sign for some of the values of the parameters, such as "tip of the thumb".
- There is a very limited use of the parameters: most are a very limited set of such phonetic elements of the sign (one of them considers only the hand configuration), described in Portuguese. At most, they serve a Portuguese speaker to find out a possible sign in Libras. Consider the scenario where the Deaf sees a sign for which she doesn't know the meaning: she won't be able to find it, because the entry is in Portuguese. Even if she finds it (by shear luck), she may not understand its meaning.
- There is a lack of visual support (semiotic/iconic) to aid the definition of terms. One entry in the dictionary for Brother-in-Law had a picture of a

Queen, a King, and a prince (which had all members of the CP wondering about the possible relations).

- In that regard, there is a general lack of knowledge created in Libras: some concepts have no representation (as of yet): when using the Software Engineering concept "Waterfall", from Computer Science, (a software design model where each step of the process succeeds the next), the general translation left the Deaf considering whether the water wouldn't cause damage to the computer. This is a serious evidence and call for action that knowledge must be created in Libras (even though there is a case to be made for the other language of the country in which the Deaf lives, and for English being a "lingua-franca").

It may be the case that some exacerbation of errors may have occurred because the evaluation was lexically driven (i.e. out of a discourse or context). A scenario was used to help the members to produce the signs and its description, but it may have lacked additional elements (e.g. phrases, situations to help solve ambiguities of the signs). Discourse analysis is needed in order to establish the impact of such situation as related to meaning creation.

## 7    Collaborative Consensus and Knowledge Creation Methodology

Collaborative interactions are relevant for human, social, historical and political formation of the individual, and may aid in the creation of the Deaf's identity and KC within a CP. A good practice is that such activities be mediated (by computer systems or other members of the community of practice) as interactive interlocutors scaffolding the sharing of social languages, so that the Deaf may create and share knowledge with the non-deaf [1]. According to Arcoverde (2006) [1] "the ties established form the dialogic and ideological ties needed for the multi-lingual encounter of utterances, voices, intonations, themes and points-of-view, thus creating a new space for social interaction for the Deaf".

In that sense, in order to mitigate some of the problems presented in the above section, a Collaborative Consensus and Knowledge Creation (CCKC) Methodology was developed and tested. The CCKS methodology is composed of a framework for the study, fixation and KC of the phonetic parameters, and a computational framework to scaffold the process.

### 7.1    Collaborative Framework

The steps used in the evaluation process of the PSL model proved very efficient in identifying evidence of potential problems, and provided a privileged forum on which to debate and establish consensus on how to overcome the shortcomings and create knowledge. A deeper understanding of Libras, its parameters, nature, structure among other elements was achieved; the correct use of such elements was achieved, in the form of appropriation, acquisition and use of knowledge, as reported by all members of the CP.

## 7.2    Computational Framework

A KC tool, an intellectual artifact [7], was developed, with Libras as its primary language of interaction, based on the PSL model, to be used as mediator during the collaborative cultivation of the CP. Figure 4 is a screen shot of a search, in Libras, by signs using a given hand configuration. The result is a list of possible candidates selected from the database containing signs with the required handshape.

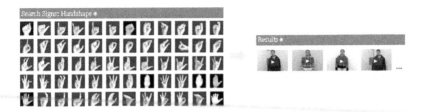

**Fig. 4.** Search Engine: Example of search for a sign in the database by a given hand shape

As seen in Figure 4, the search for a sign by its constituent parameter, in Libras, known to the Deaf signer, allows for a direct, more intuitive interaction. Once the sign is selected by the user, the system describes it in its parameters, as per the model. The output of possible candidates also generates a computational representation (XML) that can be used as input for several other systems, such as translators, 3D generator, SignWriting, Computer Vision, among others. Figure 5 represents a possible output of the system, with the description of a given sign in XML ("PATO", "DUCK").

**Fig. 5.** An output, in XML, of the description in PSL model of the sign for "PATO", "DUCK"

The system allowed for:
- Collaboration: show the standard parameters; present definitions etc.
- Discussion: each selected sign was discussed, studied, analyzed.
- Storage: complete, description of the signs, as per the consensus reached.
- Some standard: as per the theoretical background and KC process. The selected sign, stored for future use and further discussion, tends to aid in dissemination.

- Completeness: Detailed description of the signs in its basic phonetics elements. The systems served as a scaffold tool to aid the members to consider several aspects.
- In Libras: a more natural interface for the Deaf (in their own language). This paradigm, seldom seen in other information systems, presented a high usability evaluation (as per routine discount usability test [13] performed during the CP meetings with the Deaf).

### 7.3    Results of the Use of the CCKC Methodology

The CCKC methodology used allowed the CP to address most of the pressing issues found on the preliminary meetings for the creation of a set of signs correctly discussed, validated and described in enough detail to be of use in daily lives and as basis for the development of several intellectual artifacts (computational or other). It is important to remind that, although based on the phonology of Libras, the PSL model is, mostly, a computational representation of such phonology, with direct implications on its limitation.

The PSL model proved to be a potential dissemination and KC vector to inform design, and to enrich the Deaf's knowledge of Libras. Both linguistics and computational fields, such as virtual environments, Computer Vision recognition of signs, Natural Language Process, Written representation of the sign, 3-D avatars among others now have a patter from which to develop Libras.

The CCKC allowed for a co-local collaborative computer mediated environment around an intellectual artifact that provided support for discussion, KC, concept validation, sharing of experiences, fixation of learning, consensus. It proved to be a process for a greater understanding of Libras, its characteristics (dynamicity, rules, structure, uses, minimal components among others). The environment cultivated the CP in a deeper manner, with ample debate of Libras enrichment possibilities, as well as personal growth through mental processes that require language.

The system provided, among others, tools for: storage, sharing, consultation, retrieval, and correction among others, mainly for history, re-use, KC. The system also provided a structured computational description (that can be in XML or other formal aspect) to be used to inform intellectual artifacts development. The information system in Libras was crucial in managing the KC process, and was evaluated as necessary that further design should be thus informed, and present an adequate user interface.

# 8    Next Steps: Extension of Use

As seen, the SSKC methodology was designed to address issues found during evaluation of a small set of the many components of Libras: that of its phonetic parameters. This evaluation raised several evidences of the consequences Libras bears from enduring decades of neglect and proper development, studies, dissemination, standardization, knowledge creation among others.

The evidence calls for a more pro-active action towards those issues: there is a lack of studies of SL, and how they should be performed and incorporated, both in tools and SL advancements in general. "The need is pressing [...]" especially when our work extends into differing communities and constituencies that are not our own [27]. History has shown us that language is, also, a matter of cultural concern: society in general should partake in its development. Thus, the research CCKC methodology was adapted, extended and it is now being tested in two environments: undergraduate courses in Linguistics/Libras, with several objectives (e.g. acquisition, fixation of learning etc.) and CPs in general (involving deaf communities and its associations).

**A) Classroom Use**
The methodology is interactive and allows for evolution of the KC, and is composed of the following steps:

1. The use of a given, pre-determined, institutionalized set of signs, contexts, descriptions, uses etc. This set would be either internal (provided by the educational institution, the teacher) or external (provided by the Deaf community organizations that would aid in the development of the Libras).
2. This set would be incorporated into the pedagogical environment of the classroom settings, considering Production Conditions, Discourse Analysis [15], genres, real-use situation, scenarios, neologisms, regionalisms, pragmatism among many other possibilities.
3. The class would be divided into work groups for the assignment (the task being that of discussing the signs in particular and the language in general).
4. The signs selected during the discussion would be described and represented in the system.
5. Each group would present, discuss, validate, and correct its studies.
6. A consensus would be reached (the method for which would also be a matter of pedagogical choice).
7. Once the consensus is reached, it should be reflected on the system.
8. This set of evaluated signs would be the output for the institution.

**B) CP Use**
The institution, namely an organization of the Deaf community and society in general (called a CP for the sake of this article, but not limited), would receive the discussed set generated (reflecting the dynamic character of KC).

1. The discussed set would be analyzed and institutionally discussed.
2. Task groups, each specialized in a linguistic area, would be formed to perform the tasks.
3. The groups would receive feedback and study them.
4. The results would be jointly discussed, to reach a consensus.
5. The consensus would be represented in the system, for further use.
6. The final consensus would be thus made available for future evolution and iteration of the process.

Additionally, an ongoing research is being conducted in order to formally define the model. Such Computer Science formalization implies, among other things, the automatic description of signs in case the phonological structure description would be altered or modified in any of its main axis of expression.

# References

1. Arcoverde, R.D.L.: Digital technologies: a new interative space of social in the written production of the deaf. Cad. CEDES. Campinas 26(69) (May/August 2006)
2. Ariboni, S., Perito, R.: Guia prático para um projeto de pesquisa – exploratória, experimental, descritiva. UNIMARCO, São Paulo (2003)
3. Brentari, D.: Sign Language Phonology: ASL. In: Goldsmith, J. (ed.) The Handbook of Phonological Theory. The MIT Press, Cambridge (1998)
4. Capovilla, F.C., Raphael, W.D., Maurício, A.C.L.: Novo Deit-Libras: Dicionário Enciclopédico Ilustrato Trilíngue. Edusp, São Paulo (2009)
5. Carroll, J.M., Choo, C.W., Dunlap, D.R., Isenhour, P.L., Kerr, S.T., MacLean, A., Rosson, M.B.: Knowledge management support for teachers. Educational Technology Research and Development 51(4), 42–64 (2003)
6. Chomsky, N.: Language and Problems of Knowledge. The Managua Lectures. The MIT Press, Cambridge (1988)
7. De Souza, C.S.: The Semiotic Engineering of Human-Computer Interaction. The MIT Press, Cambridge (2005)
8. Fernandes, S.: Avaliação em Língua Portuguesa para Alunos Surdos: Algumas considerações. SEED/SUED/DEE, Curitiba (2006)
9. Ferreira-Brito, L.: Por uma gramática de Língua de Sinais. Tempo Brasileiro, Rio de Janeiro (1995)
10. Guimarães, C., Antunes, D.R., Trindade, D.F.G., da Silva, R.A.L., Garcia, L.S.: Structure of the Brazilian Sign Language (Libras) for Computational Tools: Citizenship and Social Inclusion. In: Lytras, M.D., Ordonez de Pablos, P., Ziderman, A., Roulstone, A., Maurer, H., Imber, J.B. (eds.) WSKS 2010, Part II. CCIS, vol. 112, pp. 365–370. Springer, Heidelberg (2010)
11. Guimarães, C., Antunes, D.R., Trindade, D., Silva, R.A.L., Garcia, L.S., Fernandes, S.: Evaluation of a Computational Description Model of Libras (Brazilian Sign Language): Bridging the Gap Towards Information Access. In: Proceedings of the Fifth IEEE International Conference on Research Challenges in Information Science, RCIS 2011, May 19-21, pp. 485–494. Guadeloupe (2011)
12. Lave, J., Wenger, E.: Situated learning: Legitimate peripheral participation. Cambridge University Press, Cambridge (1991)
13. Nielsen, J.: Multimedia and Hypermedia – The Internet and Beyond. Academic Press Inc. (1996)
14. Nonaka, I., Takeuchi, H.: A dynamic theory of organization knowledge creation. Organisational Science 5, 14–37 (1994)
15. Pêcheux, M.: Semântica e Discurso. Editora Unicamp, São Paulo (2009)
16. Picchiai, D., Lopes, M.S., Oliveira, P.S.G.: Knowledge Management and Communities of Practice. Gestão & Regionalidade – IBICT Review 23(68) (September/December 2007)
17. Quadros, R.M., Perlin, G. (org): Estudos surdos II. Arara Azul, Petrópolis (2007)

18. Quintana, C., Carra, A., Krajcik, J., Soloway, E.: Learner-Centered Design: Reflections and New Directions. In: Carroll, J.M. (ed.) Human Computer Interaction in the New Millennium, pp. 605–626. ACM Press (2001)
19. de Santos, B.S.: Um discurso sobre as ciências. Apontamentos, Porto (2002)
20. Skliar, C.: A Surdez: Um Olhar Sobre a Diferença. Mediação, Porto Alegre (1999)
21. Stokoe, W.C.: Sign Language Structure. Linstok Press, Silver Spring (1960)
22. Taub, S.F.: Language from the Body: Iconicity and conceptual metaphor in ASL. Cambridge University Press, Cambridge (2001)
23. Tedre, M., Sutinen, E., Kahkkonen, E., Kommers, P.: Ethnocomputing: ICT in cultural and social context. Communications of the ACM 49(1), 126–130 (2006)
24. Terra, J.C.C., Gordon, C.: Portais corporativos: a revolução na gestão do conhecimento. Ed. Negócio, São Paulo (2002)
25. Vygotsky, L.S.: Thougth and language. In: Hanfmann, E., Vakar, G. (eds.). MIT Press, Cambridge (1962)
26. Wenger, E.: Communities of practice and social learning systems: the career of a concept. In: Blackmore, C. (ed.) Social Learning Systems and Communities of Practice, ch.11, p. 179. Springer, Dordrecht (2010)
27. Winchester, W.W.: III REALizing our messy future: Towards culturally responsive design tools in engaging our depeer dives. ACM Interactions 18(6), 12–19 (2010)
28. de Sinais, D.B.: http://acessobrasil.org.br/libras
29. Rybená: http://www.rybena.com.br

# Alternative Agrifood Networks as Learning Communities: Some Issues for a Classification Model

Salvatore Ammirato, Marco Della Gala, and Antonio P. Volpentesta

Department of Electronics, Computer Science and Systems, University of Calabria
via P. Bucci, 42\C, 87036 Rende (CS), Italy
{ammirato,mdellagala,volpentesta}@deis.unical.it

**Abstract.** Recently, Alternative Agrifood Networks (AAFNs) are emerged in many countries in order to overcome limits of mainstream capital-intensive agribusiness system. Producers and consumers are brought together in different organizational forms depending on socio-economic characteristics of the reference territories. In this paper we introduce an original model to classify current worldwide AAFNs under a knowledge and learning perspective. Different organizational forms are mapped along two main dimensions: relationship types among networked groups of actors and their level of interaction/collaboration.

**Keywords:** Alternative Agrifood Network, Learning Communities, Classification model.

## 1    Introduction

Over recent years, the agribusiness sector has been facing new challenges due to deregulation and globalization of the markets. Food systems have become increasingly industrialized and globally extensive thus causing a standardized production which have led to uniformity in agricultural production, and significant ecological impact [5], [6], [9]. Industrialization of mainstream agrifood systems, results in concentrated control of product markets, with a small number of dominant organizations. Big organizations, monitor every transaction among millions of disconnected producers and consumers leading both to the loss of decisional power for farmers and producers and to the crisis of confidence in mass-production 'placeless and faceless', and the 'crisis of trust' among consumers [22], [15].

From the rural SMEs point of view, they are subjected to a continuous imbalance of their bargaining power; SMEs suffer to cost-price squeeze and unfair contractual agreement, rising production costs and declining commodity prices thus reducing their profitability [4], [15], [16], [22]. The general trend of liberalization and globalization of food markets, accompanied by an increasing disconnection between farming/food and producers/consumers, led to a widening consensus that conventional agriculture is no more sustainable and radical changes are needed [2]. The increasing consumer demands for quality and ethically correct food as well as

M.D. Lytras et al. (Eds.): WSKS 2011, CCIS 278, pp. 293–300, 2013.

societal pressure on issues such as sustainable development have been recognized as new opportunities for many farm households and a trigger for a process of synergic collaboration between SMEs searching for new ways of doing business [4], [7], [13].

Scholars are helping farmers to develop new and alternative business models able to guarantee competitive advantages, to improve farm revenue streams, to return in taking an active role in the agrifood system, and to develop new consumer market niches [4], [7], [13], [16], [21]. With this aim, different forms of collaborative networks have been introduced[1]: 'Alternative Food Initiatives' - AFI [1], 'alternative agro-food networks' AAFNs [7], 'alternative food networks' AFNs [22], Alternative Strategies – AS [10]. All these models refer to collaborative networks in the agrifood sector as characterized by a re-connection or close communication among producers and consumers, allowing for the development of new forms of relationship and governance of the actors' network and also enhancing a re-distribution of value for primary producers [15], [22].

In this paper, we refer to the "alternative agrifood network", briefly AAFN, to indicate these new forms of collaborative development, and focalize our attention on the different forms of AAFNs present in literature and on how these forms can be analyzed and classified. The paper is organized as follows. In section 2 theoretical background about AAFNs is proposed followed, in section 3, by a review of the different forms of AAFN in order to propose an original classification model for AAFN' forms in section 4. Finally, section 5 reports conclusion.

## 2     Theoretical Background

Since the mid-nineties, AAFNs were usually compared to the conventional food system using a set of contrasting terms like "traditional " compared to "rationalized", "standardized" to "localized", "quality" to "quantity", "extensive" to "intensive", "biodiversity" to "monoculture ", etc. [2].

Scholars from different disciplines have addressed the issue of AAFNs from different perspectives. Geographers focalize their attention to production, highlighting different ways of producing regional and local organic food as well as various ways of distribution networks such as box schemes, farm shops and farmers markets. Sociologists, agricultural economists, and anthropologists have faced up AAFNs from a more sociological and psychological view, focusing on community food cooperatives, the impact of such projects in low income territories, rural development and consumer's wellbeing and health [20].

From a geographical perspective, important differences can be found in the way in which North American and European researchers deal with the topic; different approaches are notable also in studies carried out in northern rather than southern Europe, [18]. North American studies consider AAFNs as something opposite to the

---

[1] A collaborative network (CN) is a network consisting of a variety of entities (e.g. organizations and people) that are largely autonomous, geographically distributed, and heterogeneous in terms of their operating environment, culture, social capital and goals, but that collaborate to better achieve common or compatible goals, (Camarinha-Matos & Asarmanesh, 2006).

dominant food system and refers to both a wider sense of protest, and an attempts to establish different modes of food transaction among producers and consumers. North American literature pays particular attention to social, ethical, environmental security and social equity that are substantiated by the cultural and political motivations of the consumer, [7], [10]. European studies discuss AAFNs in terms of their potential contribution to the survival of small rural enterprises and, more generally, for their contribution to the new paradigm of "territorially based rural development" [19]. The focus is on the processes of re-localization of agrifood networks and their attempts to embed agrifood products with a sense of geographical origin, and quality products. European scholars state that the term "food quality" assumes different meaning in southern and northern Europe countries. In Mediterranean countries the link between food and local context (culture, tradition, production processes, soil, climate, knowledge system, etc.) is particularly emphasized. In countries from northern European, quality is related to environmental sustainability, animals' welfare, health, hygiene and new marketing forms [18].

The concurrent analysis of all abovementioned contributes, leads towards a shared understanding of AAFNs as alternatives to the logic and organizational arrangements of the dominant agro-food system in the direction of shortening the distance (physical, social, cultural, and economic) between world production and world consumption, [8], [9], [15].

### 2.1    Knowledge and Learning Perspective

An important group of scholars propose the "knowledge perspective" looking at the importance of combinations of different knowledge forms for the economic and social success of the AAFN. Local, traditional tacit knowledge in products and production processes need to be integrated with scientific, technical and explicit knowledge and to be supported by organizational, managerial and marketing competences. In this perspective, intermediaries assume a strategic role in organizing and manage the AAFN, supporting members of the network, supplying technological platform and devices, managing information and knowledge flows among partners. AAFNs are described as learning systems based on a continuous experience-based learning process. Innovation is based on social interactions more than in technical new solutions and is linked with the other cultural, economic and touristic activities of the territory. According to Sofo et al. [17], the continuous knowledge and business exchanges, characterizing relationships among actors of the AAFNs, "enables people at every level to continually learning so that the initiative becomes, with time, a proactive learning community. The power of learning communities is that they form iterative relationship in partnership with their surrounding social, political, technological and economic structures by creating widespread social learning space for deeper trusting and open dialogue".

## 3    Forms of AAFNs

AAFNs have been developed in many countries shaping different organizational forms in relation to the socio-economic context of the reference territories and to the peculiarities of the many grassroots initiatives promoted both by producers and consumers. Most common and successful experiences of AAFNs can be summarized as below:

*Direct (on farm) sale - DoFS:* customers travels to the rural countryside to purchase food in its original cultural, geographical and economic context [15]

*Pick your own or U-pick - PYO:* it is a form of direct selling where consumers gather products by their own directly from the field. PYO is addressed to consumers looking for fresh and quality products at a reduced price; consumers enjoy the gathering as a recreational and dining experience. [12]

*Box schemes - BSs:* cooperatives and local consumption groups ensure a regular procurement of seasonal food grown up in a sustainable way and harvested in the local community or its close surroundings. [15]. Producers generally promote this kind of direct selling and regularly deliver fruit, vegetables, meat or cheese to a network of consumers. BSs are usually run on a subscription basis where customers, generally, sign up in advance to get what the scheme has available [4].

*Farmers' markets - FMs:* These are markets, generally placed in urban areas and with periodic frequency, where farmers direct sell their own food production to customers. Two main features characterize a FM: first, sold products are "local" (usually produced within 50 km from the market place); second, manufacturers are directly involved in sales [14], [15]. FMs enable a better consumers' awareness based on sharing a wider range of information, higher social interaction potential, learning opportunities for consumers, about the vendors and their food production practices, as well as for producers, about consumers' demand [5].

*Collective farmer shops - CFSs:* farmers act together to set up and jointly manage a shop in a market town or a suburban or urban where selling their local products. Operatively, products are sold (usually every day) by a qualified and trusted third organizations or by some of the farmers themselves. By agreeing to a CFS, producers reduce time spent in direct sales and face up an increased demand offering wide range of products. These results can be achieved only by applying management logics typical of a distribution structure that encompasses and exceeds that of the individual producer. It requires a shared agreement to regulate the behavior of individual producers, the store management and the joining of new participants [14].

*Community-supported agriculture - CSA.* It is a sort of alliance of concerned consumers and local farmers: the formers agree to buy seasonal food from the latters, who are responsible to delivery periodically at the consumers' home [15]. CSA, is a mechanism in which consumers become shareholders purchasing farm's products prior to be produced. The distinctive feature of these initiatives lies in the sharing of responsibilities among the farmer and all consumers involved. Community members purchase a share of agricultural production by paying in advance the equivalent, determined on the base of overall estimated production costs: in this way community members share risks with the manufacturer for a possible crop failure.

*Collective buying groups - CBGs:* organized consumers that choose to commonly buy directly from selected producers. Acting in a CBG, consumer is not only a purchaser of goods, but becomes an active participant of the AAFN. Group members are nodes of a network aimed to acquire and share information, as well as to define quality criteria for products to purchase. The interaction among producers and group members is mediated by a group leader. Consumers decide to share their "shopping lists" to create a unique cumulative order submitted, by the leader, to each producer who is charged to deliver ordered products to a unique pick up site [11].

# 4     AAFNs Classification Model

Two important evidences emerge from the analysis of literature on AAFN' forms:

1. main actors acting within the networks are producers and consumers
2. governance and business models depend on types of relationships established among main actors.

On this basis, we propose a classification models for AAFN' forms based on types of relationships among networked groups of actors.

Three main dimensions/perspectives are considered for the model: *1. Relationships among Producers; 2. Relationships among Consumers; 3. Relationships between producers and Consumers.*

For each dimension/perspective, 4 coalition's types can be recognized within a collaborative network, each of them represents a different level of integration among considered groups of actors: *networking, coordination, cooperation, collaboration.* According to Camarinha-Matos & Asarmanesh [3], "As we move along the continuum from networking to collaboration, we increase the amounts of common goal-oriented risk taking, commitment, and resources that participants must invest into the joint endeavor".

*Level 1 - Networking.* It involves communication and information exchange for mutual benefit. Each actor involved in the relationship can benefit from the information shared but there is not necessarily a common goal influencing individual contributions as well as there is no common generation of value.

*Level 2 - Coordination.* In addition to communication and information exchange, it involves aligning/altering activities so that more efficient results are achieved Nevertheless each entity might have a different goal and use its own resources. Values are mostly created at individual level.

*Level 3 - Cooperation.* In addition to level 2, it involves knowledge and resources' sharing for achieving compatible goals. In this case the aggregated value is the result of the addition of individual "components" of value generated by the various participants in a quasi-independent manner. There exists, a common plan, which in most cases is not defined jointly but rather designed by a single entity. Participants' goals are compatible in the sense that their results can be added or composed in a value chain leading to the end-product or service.

*Level 4 - Collaboration.* At this level entities share information, knowledge, resources and responsibilities to jointly plan, implement, and evaluate a program of activities to achieve a common goal. It implies sharing risks, resources, responsibilities, and rewards. Collaboration involves mutual engagement of participants to solve a problem together, which implies mutual trust and thus takes time, effort, and dedication.

In table 1 surveyed forms of AAFN are classified according to the model

**Table 1.** Forms of AAFN are classified according to the model

| Dimension \ Level | Level 1 Networking | Level 2 Coordination | Level 3 Cooperation | Level 4 Collaboration |
|---|---|---|---|---|
| *Relationships among Producers* | DoFS; PYO; CBG | FM; CBG | BS; CSA | BS, CFS; |
| *Relationships among Consumers* | DoFS; PYO; FM; CFS | | BS | CSA CBG |
| *Relationships between Producer and Consumers* | DoFS; FM; CFSs | DoFS; CBG; FM; CFSs | PYO; | BS; CSA |

Some important evidences emerge in all considered dimension/perspective when analysing classification results.

*Relationships among Producers.* CSA, BSs and CFSs require strong relationships among producers, meaning a more common goal-oriented risk taking, commitment, and resources that producers must invest into the joint endeavor. Goals of networked producers are at least compatible in the sense that their results can be added or composed in a value chain leading to the end-product or service. In some cases, when collaboration happens, mutual engagement of participants is necessary to solve a problem together which enables people at every level to continually learning so that these forms of AAFN become a proactive learning community. Other AAFN' forms like DoFs, PYO, CBGs, FMs and CBGs, need neither resource sharing resource nor common planning among producers.

*Relationships among Consumers.* Similar to the previous dimension/perspective, CSA and BSs, together with CBGs, are the AAFN' forms which require more complexity in managing relationships due to investments in resources, commitment, and risk sharing taken by groups of consumers. These forms of AAFN can be considered learning systems based on a continuous experience-based learning process Opposite to those, DoFs, PYO, CBGs, FMs and CFSs limit their activities to communication and information sharing together with activities adjustments; nevertheless each entity might have a different goal and use its own resources and methods of impact creation. Values are mostly created at individual level.

*"Relationships between Producer and Consumers".* Some forms of AAFN like BSs, CSA, and PYO require producers and consumers to invest in common goal-oriented risk taking, commitment, and resources into the joint endeavor. There exists a common plan that requires some level of co-working to achieve compatible or joint goals which implies mutual trust and thus takes time, effort, and dedication. The

power of these kind of learning communities is that they form iterative relationship in partnership with their surrounding social, political, technological and economic structures by creating widespread social learning space for deeper trusting and open dialogue. DoFSs, FMs, CFSs and CBGs show a low complexity in the management of relationships among groups.

# 5    Conclusion

In this paper we analyzed meaning and forms of Alternative Agrifood Network, under the different point-of-views present in the scientific literature. Moreover, we proposed an original classification model for AAFN' forms aimed to highlight levels of relationships integration among and within producers and consumers groups. Main forms of AAFN present in literature have been analyzed and classified according to the model.

Results of the study points to identify some forms of AAFN, particularly the Box Schemes and Community-Supported Agriculture which requires producers and consumers a high level of integration of knowledge exchange, planning and operations. These kinds of AAFNs manifest the characteristics of real learning systems based on a continuous experience-based learning process [17]. In Box Schemes and Community-Supported Agriculture, actually very similar in their deployment forms, innovation is based on social interactions more than in technical new solutions and is linked with the other cultural, economic and touristic activities of the territory. Other forms of AAFN can be considered kind of learning communities even restricted within one group of participants; in particular CFS forms for producers groups and CBGs for consumers' groups.

**Acknowledgement.** This research work was supported by AGROMATER LAB, a project funded by the EU and the Italian Government, and aimed to support both marketing of typical agrifood products and valorization of production territories in Calabria (Italy).

# References

1. Allen, P., Simmons, M.F., Goodman, M., Warner, K.: Shifting plates in the agrifood landscape: the tectonics of alternative agrifood initiatives in California. Journal of Rural Studies, 61–75 (2003)
2. Brunori, G., Rand, S., Proost, J., Barjolle, D., Granberg, L., Dockes, A.: Towards a conceptual framework for agricultural and rural innovation policies. IN-SIGHT-Project (2008)
3. Camarinha-Matos, L., Asarmanesh, H.: Collaborative Network. value creation in a knowledge society. In: Wang, K., Kovacs, G., Wozny, M., Fang, M. (eds.) Knowledge Enterprise: Intelligent Strategies in Product Design, Manufacturing and Management, pp. 26–40. Springer, Boston (2006)
4. Chiffoleau, Y.: From Politics to Co-operation: The Dynamics of Embeddedness in Alternative Food Supply Chains. Sociologia Ruralis 49(3), 218–235 (2009)

5. Covino, D., Mariani, A., Vastola, A., Viganò, E.: Which rules and criteria for a fairer market: a conceptual framework and some evidences about the Italian food supply chain. In: 119th EAAE Seminar 'Sustainability in the Food Sector: Rethinking the Relationship Between the Agro-Food System and the Natural, Social, Economic and Institutional Environments', Capri, Italy (2010)
6. Feagan, R., Morris, D.: Consumer quest for embeddedness: a case study of the Brantford Farmers' Market. International Journal of Consumer Studies 33, 235–243 (2009)
7. Goodman, D.: Editorial the quality "turn" and alternative food practices: reflections and agenda. Journal of Rural Studies, 1–7 (2003)
8. Higgins, V., Dibden, J., Cocklin, C.: Building alternative agri-food networks: Certification, embeddedness and agri-environmental governance. Journal of Rural Studies 24(1), 15–27 (2008)
9. Jarosz, L.: The city in the country: Growing alternative foodnetworks in Metropolitan areas. Journal of Rural Studies (24), 231–244 (2008)
10. Kirwan, J.: Alternative Strategies in the UK Agro-Food System: Interrogating the Alterity of Farmers' Markets. Sociologia Ruralis 44(4), 395–415 (2004)
11. Little, R., Maye, D., Ilbery, B.: Collective purchase: moving local and organic foods beyond the niche market. Enviroment Planning A 42(8), 1797–1813 (2010)
12. Lloyd, R., Tilley, D., Nelson, J.: Pick-Your-Own Markets. In: Direct Farm Marketing and Tourism, vol. 62. Russell Tronstad and Julie Leones, Tuscon, AZ (1995)
13. Renting, H., Marsden, T., Banks, J.: Understanding alternative food network: exploring the role of short food supply chains in rural development. Enviroment and Planning A 35, 393–411 (2003)
14. Rossi, A., Brunori, G., Guidi, F.: I mercati contadini: un'esperienza di innovazione di fronte ai dilemmi della crescita. Rivista di Diritto Alimentare (3), 1–11 (2008)
15. Sánchez Hernández, J.: Alternative Food Networks: concept, typology and adaptation to the spanish context. Boletín de la A.G.E. - Asociación de Geógrafos Españoles (49), 375–380 (2009)
16. Slee, B., Kirwan, J.: Exploring hybridity in food supply chains. In: 105th EAAE Seminar 'International Marketing and International Trade of Quality Food Products. Bologna (2007)
17. Sofo, F., Volpentesta, A., Ammirato, S.: Establishing a Framework for Collaborative Innovation Processes in a Technological District in Italy. The International Journal of Technology, Knowledge and Society 4(1), 169–176 (2008)
18. Sonnino, R., Marsden, T.: Beyond the divide: rethinking relationships between alternative and conventional food networks in Europe. Journal of Economic Geography 6, 181–199 (2006a)
19. van der Ploeg, J., Renting, H., Brunori, G., Knickel, K., Mannion, J., Marsden, T., et al.: Rural development: from practices and policies towards theories. Sociologia Ruralis 40(4), 391–408 (2000)
20. Venn, L., Kneafsey, M., Holloway, L., Cox, R., Dowler, E., Tuomainen, H.: Researching European 'alternative' food networks: some methodological considerations. Area (38), 248–258 (2006)
21. Volpentesta, A.P., Ammirato, S.: A Collaborative Network Model for Agrifood Transactions on Regional Base. In: Lytras, M.D., Ordonez De Pablos, P., Ziderman, A., Roulstone, A., Maurer, H., Imber, J.B. (eds.) WSKS 2010, Part II. CCIS, vol. 112, pp. 319–325. Springer, Heidelberg (2010)
22. Watts, D., Ilbery, B., Maye, D.: Making reconnections in agro-food geography: alternative systems of food provision. Progress in Human Geography 29(1), 22–40 (2005)

# Support for Collaborative Building of a Railway Technical Solution during Tendering

Diana Penciuc, Marie-Hélène Abel, and Didier Van Den Abeele

Alstom Transport,
93482 SAINT-OUEN Cedex , France
{diana.penciuc,didier.van-den-abeele}@transport.alstom.com
Heudiasyc CNRS UMR 6599
University of technology of Compiègne
BP 20529 , 60 205, Compiègne, France
{marie-helene.abel}@utc.fr

**Abstract.** As systems become more and more complex, more complex processes, organization and division of work are needed to achieve their conception and realization. The growing difficulty consists in the number and distribution of collaborators in disparate regions on the globe, the multifaceted communities that need to be coordinated in order to assure integration and coherence of their work. It is also the case of building railway technical solutions.The heterogeneity of customer market adds a supplementary challenge: adapt the solution to the customer background, context and real needs. In this context we propose a workspace to support collaboration when building customer technical solutions. We think that adequate collaboration support needs to be provided for each community and that a common backbone is needed between these communities to assure integration and coherence of their work. This paper gives a model and implementation of a dedicated workspace that can handle collaboration during complex processes like the construction of a railway technical solution.

**Keywords:** collaborative engineering, communities of knowledge, knowledge management, railway system engineering, product-line development.

## 1 Introduction

It is a fact that in the current economical context, building a system each time from the scratch, as demands come from the customers, is impossible to accomplish without a considerable cost and time loss. It is even more critical when it comes about complex system (or system of systems).

This is the reason why more and more companies adopt product-line engineering. Product-line engineering is an engineering method which consists in the use of a unique reference platform/ reference solution to create a set of distinct products. The role of the reference platform is dual: 1) it generalizes and extracts common functions and configurations; and 2) it provides a base for instantiating target systems that use that common base more reliably and cost effectively

M.D. Lytras et al. (Eds.): WSKS 2011, CCIS 278, pp. 301–310, 2013.

[8]. Re-use of the reference solution brings important benefits: improved quality, time-to-market and cost reduction [4].

Nevertheless, in railway context, only applying this method is not enough. The heterogeneity of railway market (customer background, culture, environment etc.) demands a further adaptation of the reference solution to each customer. In this paper we address one aspect of the adaptation of the reference platform: building the customers technical solution during Tendering, in the context of the company A (Alstom Transport).

The success of the adaptation process relies on two important factors which are the individual tacit knowledge [12] and a tight collaboration between the members of the Tendering communities. Tacit knowledge of key experts holding knowledge on specific technical and commercial professions are not enough, a constant collaboration between all the Tendering communities is a must in order to integrate the work of each community and to create a coherence and synergy between them.

By collaboration, tacit knowledge is externalized and exchanged, contributing thus to the increasing of the overall knowledge and innovation [9]. Our goal is therefore to answer to this complexity by providing means to support collaboration and tacit knowledge externalization by encouraging exchanges inside and outside communities.

When building the customer technical solution it is by collaboration that the teams try to respond to two challenges: 1) understand the user demand and his real needs and 2) find the way to adapt the reference solution to the customer demand in order to build the customer technical solution. In this paper we will discuss these challenges and we propose a collaborative model and a first implementation of the model that can answer to the collaboration needs of the Tender technical communities.

The paper is organized as follows. First, we explain the collaborative situations that appear when developing a customer technical solution in railway transport during Tendering. Next, we propose a collaborative model and we discuss several implementation solutions that we considered in our study. We justify our modeling and implementation choices with observations extracted from interviews and the actual context of the company. Then, we present the current implementation of a workspace based on the collaborative model proposed to support collaboration. We conclude with future directions.

## 2   Collaborative Situations When Building the Technical Solution

The purpose of the Tendering process is to propose a formal offer to the customer in order to answer to his request for proposal (RFP). The RFP consists of several resources (mainly text documents, but can also contain attached images, videos etc.) expressing the specification of the customer demand.

In order to propose an offer, multiple interdisciplinary teams are formed: technical, taxes, legal, etc. Division of work is necessary because of several reasons:

the complexity of the work is considerable, expertise from a heterogeneity of professions is needed, time is very short etc. Ad-hoc official teams are created, but beyond this strict organization there are other informal exchanges mechanisms that make the Tendering process work and nevertheless, they are not known. Extracting rules to make collaboration more efficient is necessary [13]. This can be done by supporting and analyzing the informal routines to improve the standard process.

Given the complexity of the whole Tendering process, we focus our research on one aspect of this process which is the conception of the technical solution, which we will further call as Build technical solution activity. In the following sections we provide more details about the collaborative situations that can appear during this activity.

*Needs elicitation:* The purpose of the needs elicitation is to assure that customer real need is correctly understood. This can be sometimes challenging because of several reasons: the need is not well expressed in the RFP, the need cannot be totally explicited. Drawbacks of needs elicitation are not few: the difference in language used, culture, customer environment, exploitation habits, limitation of the specification representation mainly throughout natural language, the complexity of the demand etc. Thus, the understanding of the customers needs cannot be limited to the reading of the RFP. For this purpose, several collaborative actions are possible: each of the members of the tendering team have to individually understand, anticipate or deduce important elements (from the RFP or external resources) and communicate them to the team; on-field observations to identify particularities of the customers environment where the system will be installed; internal meetings to share information and make decisions; etc.

*The technical analysis:* A technical analysis is performed during Tendering in order to propose to the customer a technical solution based on needs elicitation. This is done by the technical communities gathering system engineers experts in specific areas of railway system engineering, who need to collaborate in order to provide the overall technical solution. The main tasks during the technical analysis are: analyze demand, identify the gaps between the demand and the reference solution, choose reference solution elements to be considered, evaluate and solve the gaps, build the technical solution to be proposed to the customer, check the technical solution. Collaborative actions are: share of design choices, gaps and risks identified etc. at each sub-system level and overall system; arrive to a common agreement on the final solution.

## 3    Model to Support Collaboration

For the purpose of this paper we present a part of the collaborative model (Figure 1) that shows how knowledge is capitalized around pre-defined, well-known concepts of interest. Knowledge considered includes: explicit knowledge coming from diverse resources: annotations, RFP resource parts etc. as well as

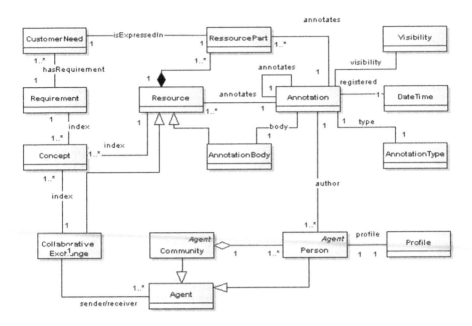

**Fig. 1.** The collaborative model

tacit knowledge made explicit and resulting from collaborative exchanges. The choice of this approach was motivated by the following reasons: both formal and informal knowledge need to be capitalized; once organized around given concepts, knowledge is easier to share, retrieve and reuse; a common backbone (provided by the concepts) is needed in order to assure work integration of communities focusing on specific areas of system engineering. The model was constructed as a result of a previous study realized in the company [10], [11].

In the following we discuss three aspects of our model: the modeling of the resources that can be exchanged, the management of persons and communities, and the common backbone that insures integration and coherence of the collaborative work.

*The modeling of the resources that can be exchanged:* The model of the annotation was created on the basis of the annotation model existing in DAML [3] and previous work on annotations realized by [5] and [7]. These models were then adapted to the needs of our workbench. According to [7], the base of the annotation may be one or several documents, a part of a document, another annotation or any other object (e.g. a post-it).

Adapting these previous models to our case, we consider that each Person can write annotations to the resources contained in the RFP (annotation of a document), to parts of an RFP resource (e.g. to statements of a document contained in the RFP) or to another annotation.

Annotations have a visibility which means that an author can decide to share his annotations with other members and thus the visibility of the annotations will change. Characteristics of an annotation related to its traceability are: the "author" of the annotation, the "registered" property which can be specialized in "created/updated" and which registers the date and time when the annotation was created/ updated.

Thus, annotations can be written individually or collectively (by several members of the same community or members of distinct communities). As shown in the model, an Agent (Community or Person) can exchange (send/receive) a Collaborative exchange which may be:

- any type of non-RFP resource: (e.g. a document, an image, a report etc.)
- annotations
- resources that can capture and support exchanges between the members (discussions, news publishing, questions/answers, collaborative editing etc.)

The collaborative exchanges may concern a resource (e.g. documents of the RFP), a part of a resource (e.g. a statement in a RFP resource), or annotations created on the RFP or on parts of the RFP. As the Resources, the Collaborative exchanges are indexed with one or more concepts which define points of interest.

*Persons and communities management:* Each Person has a Profile which allows him to be located by the others according to different search criteria: the geographical location, his expertise etc. The Profile describes in key-words expertise knowledge which are also mapped to one or more Concepts. This allows a uniform representation of expertise and facilitates expertise location and knowledge transfer when needed. Persons can be grouped in Communities, according to the necessity. Communities are usually created around a specific area of expertise or interest, thus members of one community will be interested in the same set of concepts, remark that should be taken in account when implementing the workspace.

*Common backbone to support collaborative work integration and coherence:* As explained before, in order to assure coherence and integration of work divided between different teams, a common structure is needed. This common structure is an ontology containing the concepts on which individual as well as resources resulting from collaboration are capitalized. As stated in [14], the role of the ontologies is to: assist communication between people and organizations (provide a common vocabulary), achieve interoperability between systems (once created, the ontology can be re-used in other applications), improve system engineering (allow consistency checking, improved search and information retrieval, speed, reliability).

In the context of the Tendering process, the ontology should provide integration and coherence of work by offering a shared understanding of multiple elements mandatory to successfully accomplish this process: the customer, the reference solution (knowledge about the system and the way to adapt it), the process itself, the organization.

## 4  Related Work

In order to implement a workspace dedicated to the activity of building the customer technical solution, we first looked for existing solutions that correspond to the collaborative model. Accordingly, we considered CSCW ([6], [15]). We discuss in the following subsections our findings and we explain the positive aspects and the inconvenient of each of the solutions found.

*Microsoft Word 2010 and OneNote 2010:* This solution consists in using Word, OneNote and a Word complement enabling link between the two (Linked notes). Once activated in Word, the complement is available under the Review tab. The user may use Word to visualize a document and when selecting a portion of the document, by clicking on the Linked notes button, OneNote will open enabling creation of annotations in the section/page selected by the user.

These annotations are all grouped in a notebook and the user can visualize anytime the base of the annotation (the statements selected in the Word document) when needed. Each notebook organizes notes in sections, pages, subpages etc. A page contains annotations related to the title of the page. Word and OneNote page where annotations were taken can be visualized simultaneously. User can share his notebook on the web or on the network or he may send pages by email. When used with a SharePoint server, OneNote allows users to work together and edit a shared notebook simultaneously. Modifications made by users are accompanied by the initials of their names and the time the change was made.

The main advantages of this solution are: 1) the availability of the tool (OneNote is available even on mobile devices supporting Windows operating system), 2) the flexibility of the formats in which notes can be captured: audio, video, etc., integration with other Microsoft tools allowing collaboration. The notebook hierarchy can be defined as to have at each level one concept and thus to group annotations under the corresponding concepts. Nevertheless, this solution cannot provide support for a more complex ontology, which is an inconvenient, provided that, more than subsumption links are needed to express the common knowledge we envisaged.

*E-MEMORAe2.0:* The aim, within the MEMORAe [2] approach, is to put into practice organizational learning by proposing to associate:

- knowledge management to support capitalization
- semantic Web to support sharing and interoperability
- Web 2.0 to support the social process

This approach was implemented in the E-MEMORAe2.0 platform [1] which is presented in the following paragraphs. Users of this platform can organize their work at individual or community level. Individuals and members of communities can organize (index) their resources around topics from a given ontology. The history of added resources is registered and can be visualized.

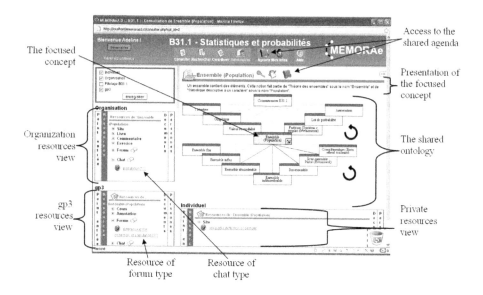

The focused concept

Organization resources view

gp3 resources view

Access to the shared agenda

Presentation of the focused concept

The shared ontology

Private resources view

Resource of forum type

Resource of chat type

**Fig. 2.** E-MEMORAe2.0 navigation interface (interface in French)

According to their rights, users have partial access to the resources indexed by the topics. In other words, it allows to have different points of view on the same ontology. The environment also provides two different views on the resources produced by users: the classical view (resources are displayed as they are produced) and the distributed view (from the visualization of concepts, accede to the corresponding resources: as seen in figure 2,when focusing a concept, all the resources indexed with the concept are shown in the resource panel). Annotation of both a concept and a resource are possible. Annotations are considered to be resources, so annotation of annotations is allowed.

Collaborative features are: forum, chat, semantic wiki and agenda which are considered as exchange resources. These can be added as resources and indexed with concepts from the ontology. The semantic wiki allows users to activate a term recognition function, which will underline the terms in the text that correspond to concepts in the ontology. The user may then decide if he wants to create links between the terms in the text and the recommended concepts.

Navigation in the ontology is realized by selecting concepts in the tree representation available in the center of the screen (see Figure 2). Entry points can be defined at individual, group and organization level by using the set of available concepts in the ontology. Entry points facilitate the access to the most frequently-used concepts. Entry points can be visualized in a dedicated panel.

The advantage of this solution is that it combines several groupware and knowledge management facilities which allow all resources and exchanges between collaborators to be structured around concepts of the ontology. The environment does not provide means to create annotations to part of resources.

## 5    Workspace Implementation

We decided to implement our workspace by customizing the E-MEMORAe2.0 platform and developing the supplementary features that are necessary. Our choice is justified by the capability of this platform to integrate knowledge capitalization around an ontology and collaborative features in the same environment.

For the purpose of this paper we present how collaboration is supported in the workspace we created from the point of view of: the exchange of resources and knowledge, the management of persons and communities and the ontology (which is the common backbone that handles knowledge capitalization).

Any type of resource (documents, images, videos) can be capitalized by the members of the Tendering team. As mentioned before, the platform allows capitalization in three spaces: the individual space, the group space and the organization space.

Resources can be easily exchanged with drag-and-drop from the individual space to the group space. The platform allows annotation of concepts and resources, authoring, registration of the date/time when the annotation was created, annotation of annotations.

In order to allow annotation of parts of a resource we are developing a dedicated module (see figure 3) in which the user can visualize and annotate the text of a selected RFP resource.

In the same way as for any other resource, the visibility of the annotations is implicitly determined by the space in which the user decides to place them. Thus, an expert can create his own annotations and share them with the rest of the community which is interested in his findings.

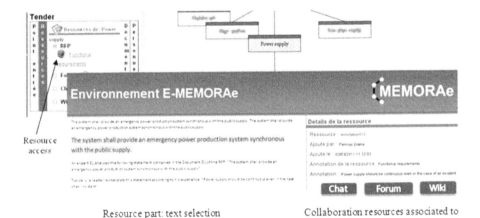

Resource part: text selection              Collaboration resources associated to
                                           the resource part: chat, wiki, forum

**Fig. 3.** Annotation on a part of a document and collaboration resources associated: forum, chat, wiki (interface in French)

Another type of resources available to the users are the Collaboration exchanges which are: the chat, the forum and the wiki. These can be used in different ways: to exchange knowledge about a given concept (e.g. the interlocking system), about a resource (e.g. a file provided by the customer), or a specific part of a document (e.g. a statement in a RFP document, see figure 3).

Thus, when needed, a user can create, for example, a forum as an annotation to a statement in the RFP. He may then write a question in the forum and wait for the other members of his team to answer to his question.

In the same way, users can create a chat to start a discussion on a statement which indicates for example, a possible risk. Moreover, wikis could be used to collaborate in order to edit any text resource that has to be produced by the team during the technical analysis.

Communities can be created as groups from the administration interface. Each user can decide on the groups that he wants to visualize in his working space, by a simple selection in a dedicated window. There is no support yet for user profiles but this feature will be developed in the future. For each community (group), entry points to concepts that are interesting for this community can be created, in order to facilitate access of the members to privileged areas of interest.

An ontology was developed that covers the areas mentioned before: the system (and the reference solutions), the organization, the customer and the process.

# 6 Conclusion

In this paper we presented a model to support collaboration during the Build technical solution activity in Tendering phase as well as an implementation of this model. We think that collaboration in complex system engineering need to be supported not only throughout the adequate collaboration tools, but also throughout coordination and integration of the work divided between multi-faceted communities. Our approach was to make available the collaboration tools in the context and at the granularity needed (in order to correspond to the specific needs of each community) and to propose an ontology as a backbone for a common understanding, integration and coherence of work produced by the different communities.

As a future work we want to further improve the usage of the process component of the ontology. In a second stage, we want to generalize our method for the whole Tendering process as well as for the other subsequent phases of a product lifecycle: project execution, installation etc.

# References

1. Abel, M.-H., Leblanc, A.: Knowledge Sharing via the E-MEMORAe2.0 Platform. In: Proceedings of 6th International Conference on Intellectual Capital, Knowledge Management & Organizational Learning, Montreal, Canada, pp. 10–19 (2009)

2. Abel, M.-H., Leblanc, A.: An Operationnalization of the Connections between e-Learning and Knowledge Management: the MEMORAe Approach. In: Proceedings of the 6th IEEE International Conferences on Human System Learning, Toulouse, France, pp. 93–99 (2008)

3. Annotation ontology. DAML Ontology Library,
   `http://www.w3.org/2000/10/annotation-ns#`

4. Birk, A., Heller, G., John, I., Schmid, K., von der Maen, T., Müller, K.: Product Line Engineering: The State of the Practice. IEEE Software, 52–60 (November/December 2003)

5. Bringay, S., Barry, C., Charlet, J.: A specific tool of Annotations for the Electronic Health Record. In: Proceedings of the International Workshop on Annotation for Collaboration - Methods, Tools and Practices, La Sorbonne, Paris, France, pp. 21–30 (2005)

6. Carstensen, P.H., Schmidt, K.: Computer supported cooperative work: New challenges to systems design. In: Handbook in Human Factors/Ergonomics, pp. 619–636. Asakura Publishing (2003)

7. Fogli, D., Fresta, G., Mussio, P., Marcante, A., Padula, M.: Annotation in cooperative work: from paper-based to the web one. In: International Workshop Annotation for Collaboration, Paris, France, November 24-25, pp. 1–10 (2005)

8. Nakagawa, E., Maldonado, J.C.: Reference architecture knowledge representation: an experience. In: Proceedings of the 3rd International Workshop on Sharing and Reusing Architectural Knowledge, Leipzig, Germany, May 13, pp. 51–54. ACM, New York (2008)

9. Nonaka, I., Takeuchi, H.: The knowledge-creating company: How Japanese companies create the dynamics of innovation. Oxford University Press, New York (1995)

10. Penciuc, D., Abel, M.-H., Van Den Abeele, D.: Requirements and modelling of a workspace for tacit knowledge management in railway product development. In: Proceedings of the International Conference on Knowledge Management and Information Sharing, KMIS 2010, Valence Espagne, pp. 61–70 (2010)

11. Penciuc, D., Abel, M.-H., Van Den Abeele, D.: From intangibles identification to Requirements for Intangibles Management. In: Proceedings of the 7th International Conference on Intellectual Capital, Knowledge Management and Organizational Learning, Hong Kong, Chine, pp. 628–634 (2010)

12. Polanyi, M.: The Tacit Dimension. Routledge (1966)

13. Suh, N.P.: Designing and engineering through collaboration and negotiation. Int. J. Collaborative Engineering 1(1/2), 1937 (2009)

14. Uschold, M., Gruninger, M.: Ontologies: principles, methods and applications. Knowledge Engineering Review 11(2) (June 1996)

15. Wilson, P.: Computer supported cooperative work: an introduction. Kluwer Academic Publishers, Norwell (1991) ISBN: 0-7923-1446-8

# Computer Science Teachers' In-service Training Needs and Their Technological Pedagogical Content Knowledge

Spyros Doukakis[1], Christos Koilias[2], Nikos Adamopoulos[3],
and Panagiota Giannopoulou[4]

[1] Dept. of Primary Education, University of the Aegean, Rhodes, Greece
[2] Dept. of Informatics, Technological Educational Institution (TEI) of Athens, Greece
[3] ICT Center of Primary and Secondary Education of Ileia, Greece
[4] Leonteio Lyceum, Greece
sdoukakis@rhodes.aegean.gr, ckoilias@teiath.gr, adamopou@sch.gr,
gianagia@gmail.com

**Abstract.** This study examines a national sample of 1127 computer science teachers who teach algorithms and programming in upper secondary education; it measures their knowledge with respect to three key domains as described by the TPACK framework: technology, pedagogy, content, and the combination of these areas. According to the results in the TPACK subscales, teachers state that their knowledge is between the values 4.38 (Content Knowledge) and 3.51 (Pedagogical Content Knowledge). Furthermore, according to the same study, teachers feel that they need further training in how to incorporate technology in their teaching as well as how to teach algorithms, two areas that relate to Pedagogical Content Knowledge and TPACK.

**Keywords:** Algorithms, TPACK, Training needs, in-service teachers, Computer Science.

## 1    Introduction

For many years, in different countries, computing has been included in the curriculum as a distinct discipline in secondary education. Computing focuses on how computers work (hardware) and on how they are programmed (programming and software development), whereas ICT (Information and Communication Technologies) focus on how to use computers. Teachers of Computer Science (CS) in secondary education belong to a special category that has a broad knowledge of both computing and ICT based on their academic studies. However, the ACM K-12 Education Task Force Report [1] draws attention to the need for appropriate Computer Science teacher training programs and notes "teachers must acquire both a mastery of the subject matter and the pedagogical skills that will allow them to present the material to students at appropriate levels" (p. 18). Moreover, according to Graham et al. [2], educators have realized that the knowledge of how to use technological tools is not enough; what they really need is the ability to use these tools effectively in order to facilitate the learning processes of their students. Thus, research interest has focused on ways to incorporate and integrate technological tools in teaching.

M.D. Lytras et al. (Eds.): WSKS 2011, CCIS 278, pp. 311–316, 2013.

Recently, Mishra and Koehler [3] have built upon Shulman's work [4] describing Pedagogical Content Knowledge (PCK) and have proposed a framework combining three important aspects of teacher knowledge: Pedagogical Knowledge, Content Knowledge and Technological Knowledge called the Technological Pedagogical Content Knowledge (TPACK) framework. So, according to the TPACK framework, it is important for teachers of CS to be able to integrate technological tools in their teaching practice, in such a way that these tools will not only form the subject matter but also a means to facilitate the learning process.

In this study, using quantitative analysis a) we measure the level of integration of technological tools according to the TPACK framework, and b) we explore how teachers' training needs are related to their TPACK.

## 2    Overview

In Greece, the teaching of Computing and ICT in secondary education is conducted by teachers holding an undergraduate degree in Computer Science, Computer Engineering or Applied Informatics. Secondary Education in Greece is divided into two cycles: compulsory lower secondary and non-compulsory Upper Secondary Education. Compulsory lower secondary education is provided in Gymnasium, while non-compulsory upper secondary education is provided in one of two types of schools: the General Lyceum (GL) and Vocational Lyceum (EPAL). In General Lyceum, both day and evening, ICT has been taught as an elective or direction course since 1999. In the last two classes of General Lyceum, students select one of three directions, (technological, scientific or theoretical). If students in the last grade select the technological direction, they attend a course in algorithms and programming, entitled "Application Development in a Programming Environment", for which they are assessed through national exams. The grade acquired in this examination is part of the consideration used in selecting students for admission in higher education programmes [5].

The overall aim of the course is to develop analytical and synthetic thinking, acquire methodological skills and be able to solve simple problems within a programming environment. Many basic algorithmic and programming concepts, such as conditions, expressions and logical reasoning, are fundamentals of general knowledge and skills to be acquired in general education; most of these concepts are not presented in other disciplines [6]. The curriculum states that this subject must be taught (at least partially) in a computer lab. The Greek Pedagogical Institute (Ministry of Education) has certified specific Educational Software to support the lab work. During the lab hour, teachers can use the technological tools to facilitate the learning process.

In this complex framework of ADPE, where examination pressure and requirements coexist with the use of technological tools for teaching algorithmic concepts, it was considered essential to investigate the TPACK of Computer Science secondary teachers who teach the subject, as well as to relate their TPACK with their training needs.

# 3    Research Context and Participants

We conducted a quantitative survey using a questionnaire with closed-ended questions. The questionnaire was available only through Internet browsers and participants answered electronically on-line.

The survey used a sample of 1127 teachers who had taught ADPE. The questionnaire consisted of 29 questions about TPACK and was based on the survey instrument developed by Schmidt et al. [7]. All questions were related to the three key domains as described by the TPACK framework (technology, pedagogy, content and the combination of these areas). The 29 questions in the questionnaire were divided into questions about Content Knowledge (CK) (4 questions), Technological Knowledge (TK) (4 questions), Pedagogical Knowledge (PK) (4 questions), Pedagogical Content Knowledge (PCK) (2 questions), Technological Content Knowledge (TCK) (5 questions), Technological Pedagogical Knowledge (TPK) (7 questions) and Technological Pedagogical Content Knowledge (TPACK) (3 questions). The response to each question was scored using a Likert-like scale where 1 stands 'strongly disagree', and 5 stands 'strongly agree' [8]. For each subscale the participant's responses were averaged. In addition to the survey instrument, participants filled out a questionnaire with 196 questions, all concerning the specific subject (ADPE). Moreover, the questionnaire included 10 questions which provided demographic data. Some of these answers were evaluated and used for this study. Participants completed the questionnaire between November 2009 and January 2010; in January, teachers are half way through the curriculum, having covered the appropriate material for all basic algorithmic components (sequential structure, conditional structure and loops).

There are 1712 CS teachers in upper secondary education in Greece [9]. The respondents came from the 13 regions of the country. The sample was representative of the population of educators of Computer Science by region.

# 4    Results

## 4.1    Sampling

The majority of teachers (66.4%) who completed the survey were male. 96% of the participants were under 50 years old, while 75% were under 40 years old. Teachers who were over 60 did not take part in the research study. The majority of teachers (61%) had, an undergraduate degree, while 35% had, a postgraduate degree and the remainder had PhDs.

## 4.2    Measuring Teachers' TPACK

The average mean for all items was 4.05. The range of response was 4, with a minimum response of 1, a maximum response of 5 and a standard deviation of .805. The respondents answered all of the questions; the mean and standard deviation are reported for each subscale in Table 1.

**Table 1.** Summary of descriptive statistics for subscales of TPACK components

| Subscale | Number of Items | Mean | Std. Deviation |
|---|---|---|---|
| CK | 4 | 4.38 | .488 |
| PK | 4 | 4.12 | .533 |
| TK | 4 | 4.16 | .552 |
| PCK | 2 | 3.51 | .692 |
| TCK | 5 | 3.68 | .802 |
| TPK | 7 | 4.18 | .511 |
| TPACK | 3 | 4.03 | .657 |

In addition to descriptive statistics measuring Computer Science Teachers' TPACK, the correlations among each of the subscales, using Pearson product-moment, were examined. With respect to correlations between subscales, coefficients varied from .235 (TCK and PCK) to .746 (PK and TK).

### 4.3    Training Needs

54% of the teachers who took part in the research claimed that they need training in ADPE while 46% of them claimed that they do not.

According to this research, teacher preference with regard to the sectors in which a training need is felt, 70% of the participant teachers wishes to be trained in how to incorporate the course educational software in their teaching. 43% wish to be trained in how to teach algorithms, while 37% agrees that they need training in using the educational software of their lesson.

## 5    Discussion

The results suggest that more than half of the teachers wish to be trained in ADPE and more particularly in the sectors of pedagogy, technology and the integration of technology in their teaching practice. On the other hand, there is quite a large number of teachers who does not wish to be further trained.

As far as teacher TPACK is concerned, it seems that those who participated in this survey rated their knowledge of content (4.38) higher than that of the other cognitive subscales. This suggests that teachers have very high CK, such as knowledge of algorithmic concepts presented in the subject, the general framework of the discipline and practical approaches used in order for students to acquire knowledge [4].

Technological Knowledge (TK) (4.16) is also very high. According to Koehler and Mishra [3], TK is associated with the ability to use technological tools but also the knowledge behind this technology. This is also reflected in questions concerning the type of training they consider as necessary. A small percentage of 37% of the respondents needs training in educational software to support the lab work.

The Pedagogical Knowledge rating (4.12) is very close to that of the Technological Knowledge. The high average implies that CS teachers have deep knowledge of the educative process and methodology of teaching and learning and thus can achieve the aim of the subject.

According to their responses, teachers seem to have very high Technological Pedagogical Knowledge (TPK, 4.18). This shows that educators have realized that teaching and learning are altered when using specific technological tools. This knowledge includes awareness of their tools' restrictions and affordances in designing pedagogical strategies.

The average scores for TCK and PCK are lower (3.68 and 3.51 respectively). For TCK, it seems that teachers rate themselves at a lower level in the understanding of how technology and subject matter both aid and limit each other. Therefore, teachers seem to need assistance in order to comprehend how the use of technology affects subject matter. This is also reflected in questions concerning the type of training they consider necessary, where a percentage of 70% of the respondents needs training in methods to integrate educational software in their teaching practice.

The last dyadic component (PCK) shows that, even if teachers of CS have both pedagogical knowledge and deep knowledge of their subject matter, they seem to be less confident in transforming and applying effectively their Content Knowledge to their teaching practice [4].

Finally, the high score in TPACK (4.03) shows that teachers are aware of the intersection between content, pedagogy and technology. Thus, it appears that teachers enhance teaching with a unique combination, a dynamic equilibrium, between the three teaching components (pedagogy, content and technology).

Despite the fact that CS teachers who teach this subject claim to possess the above qualities, it seems that only 62% use technological tools and the computer laboratory, while 38% teach the subject exclusively in the classroom. Out of the 62% of teachers who use technological tools and the laboratory, 65% consider that conducting sessions in the laboratory reduces the time needed to cover the curriculum. However, they use technological tools mostly to present algorithmic issues (41%) and less for students to practice with the available tools and relevant training scenarios (31%).

## 6    Conclusion

According to the results in the seven subscales, teachers state that their knowledge is between the values 4.38 (CK) and 3.51 (PCK). Moreover, it seems that the teachers who teach the course wish to be trained in how to incorporate educational software in their teaching practice so as to improve their TCK as well as their overall TPACK. This leads us to conclude that teachers wish to be able to determine when technology contributes and when it obstructs the teaching of ADPE. It seems, therefore, that teachers need that support which will help them judge/evaluate how technology affects their lesson. Teachers' high degree of independence in TPK indicates that they are capable of evaluating the consequences technology has on teaching and learning, but they are not ready to determine the way technology affects teaching and learning. As a result, it is important for teachers to acquire the experience that will allow them to distinguish those technological tools that are more appropriate to support specific cognitive goals during the development of algorithms and will also allow them to know how the content of their course can determine or modify the technology in use.

Finally, teacher preference for training in matters of teaching algorithms indicates that even though teachers have a) pedagogical knowledge and b) very good knowledge of their subject, they claim that they are less capable of transforming and applying effectively their knowledge on their teaching. Thus, we may claim that there is a need to train teachers in order for them to be able to identify the most common student misconceptions as well as to be able to find ways to overcome them.

The above results may prove very useful in the design of future training programmes for CS teachers of ADPE. According to these results, teachers are in search of a teaching framework that is far removed from the conventional classroom and which will incorporate more use of the laboratory, something that is in compliance with the nature of the course, too. Despite the fact that CS teachers are the ones with the greatest experience in and knowledge of computer use, it seems that they wish to be trained in the incorporation of technological tools in their teaching. On the other hand, special attention must be given to the development of appropriate educational scenarios and examples that will contribute to the improvement of student learning but also of teacher work.

# References

1. Tucker, A.: A Model Curriculum for K-12 Computer Science. Final Report of the ACM K–12 Task Force Curriculum Committee (2003)
2. Graham, C.R., Burgoyne, N., Cantrell, P., Smith, L., St. Clair, L., Harris, R.: TPACK Development in Science Teaching: Measuring the TPACK Confidence of Inservice Science Teachers. TechTrends 53(5), 70–79 (2009)
3. Mishra, P., Koehler, M.J.: Technological Pedagogical Content Knowledge: A new framework for teacher knowledge. Teachers College Record 108(6), 1017–1054 (2006)
4. Shulman, L.S.: Knowledge and teaching: foundations of the new reform. Harvard Educational Review 57(1), 1–22 (1987)
5. Eyrydice: Organisation of the education system in Greece (2008/2009), http://eacea.ec.europa.eu/education/eurydice
6. Vakali, A., Giannopoulos, E., Ioannidis, N., Koilias, C., Malamas, K., Manolopoulos, Y., Politis, P.: Applications Development in a Programming Environment. Pedagogical Institute, Athens (1999) (in Greek)
7. Schmidt, D., Baran, E., Thompson, A., Koehler, M.J., Shin, T., Mishra, P.: Technological Pedagogical Content Knowledge (TPACK): The Development and Validation of an Assessment Instrument for Preservice Teachers. Journal of Research on Technology in Education 42, 123–149 (2009)
8. Doukakis, S., Psaltidou, A., Stavraki, A., Adamopoulos, N., Tsiotakis, P., Stergou, S.: Measuring the technological pedagogical content knowledge (TPACK) of in-service teachers of computer science who teach algorithms and programming in upper secondary education. In: Fernstrom, K. (ed.) Readings in Technology and Education: Proceedings of ICICTE 2010, Corfu, Greece, pp. 442–452 (2010)
9. Hellenic Statistical Authority: Statistical data for Secondary Education (2009)

# Analysis of Educational Digital Storytelling Environments: The Use of the "Dimension Star" Model

Panagiotis Psomos and Maria Kordaki

Department of Cultural Technology and Communication, University of the Aegean,
Mytilene, Greece
{panagiotis.psomos,m.kordaki}@aegean.gr

**Abstract.** The focus of this paper is on the analysis of Educational Digital Storytelling Environments (EDSE) using the reference model «Dimension Star» [7]. More specifically, two EDSE were analyzed with the use of this model: (a) Toontastic [6] and (b) Kodu [9] which have been widely used in the educational process. The analysis of these environments showed that the diagrammatic analysis using the above model provides opportunities for easy and quick comparison of essential dimensions of the digital storytelling environments, which is particularly useful for researchers and educators. Finally, the completeness of the model «Dimension Star», as a tool for evaluating digital storytelling software in education, is investigated and possible extensions are suggested.

**Keywords:** digital storytelling, evaluation, education, "Dimension Star".

## 1    Introduction

Education through storytelling has been tested successfully in almost all the history of mankind unlike formal education at universities and schools which is a relatively recent institution. It seems that knowledge in any form (religion, technology, agriculture, hygiene etc.), is stored better in our brain if it takes the form of narration. According to narrative psychology, there are two modes of thinking: paradigmatic thinking (logico-deductive and classificatory discourse) and narrative thinking. Neurological findings seem to support this distinction, since narrative thinking (also called episodic memory) seems to lie in the hippocampus, while paradigmatic thinking lies in the cortex [4]. According to Papadimitriou (2003) narrative is an important epistemic modality. Epistemic modality refers to the way a speaker / writer communicates his doubts, certainties and predictions.

In recent years, however, multimedia and digital technology gave a new dimension to storytelling, the digital storytelling. Digital storytelling is therefore a modern expression of the ancient art of storytelling and derives its strength from the harmony between image, music, narration and voice, thereby giving bright color to characters, situations, experiences and ideas [2]. The advent of digital storytelling in educational environments is based on theories by which learning is a result of knowledge building and not just a knowledge transfer. Building on theories of constructivism, [5] digital storytelling is a great channel to apply these theories in

M.D. Lytras et al. (Eds.): WSKS 2011, CCIS 278, pp. 317–322, 2013.

practice. According to Ohler (2006) digital storytelling allows students to have active participation and not just be passive consumers in a society steeped in digital products. Creating digital stories is an educational process which strengthens the bonds between children in class, and at the same time between students and their teacher [1].

A number of requirements have been reported which may serve as criteria for digital story software evaluation [3] [8]. In this paper, we will study and evaluate with the "Dimension Star" model two representatives of EDSE: (a) Toontastic [6] and (b) Kodu [9]. This is the contribution of this work. In the next section the evaluation model mentioned above is described which is then used to analyze the aforementioned digital storytelling environments. Finally, the results of the analysis are discussed and appropriate conclusions are drawn.

## 2    "Dimension Star": An Evaluation Model for Digital Storytelling

All applications of digital storytelling have certain common characteristics. More specifically, the content of a digital story is either *default* or it is allowed to the user to *create his own (Concreteness).* Digital stories typically follow a conceptual *structure*. The structure shows whether the resulting narratives relate to the literary definitions of a story. The degree of conceptual structure has consequences in the *cohesion* and *continuity* of the story which show us the causal and temporal relationship between the elements of the story. It also affects the *cognitive effort* required to create a story. The presentation of a digital history varies depending on the degree of virtuality and spatiality. S*patiality* indicates whether the objects in space and space itself play a role in the evolution of the story. *Virtuality* refers to the extent to which the activity of storytelling takes place in a virtual world. Moreover, there is an interest in the degree of *collaboration* between users, the degree of *control* that users have in the evolution of events and the degree of *interactivity* that is allowed by the software. Finally, *immersion* shows the extent to which the user is drawn into the story.

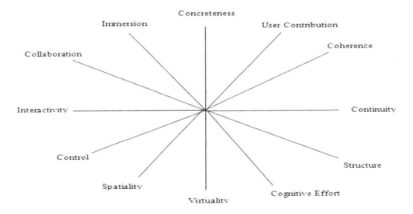

**Fig. 1.** A diagrammatic representation of the "Dimension Star" model

The «Dimension Star» [7], includes all the aforementioned features that may or may not have a DSE (Fig. 1). The length of each peak is proportional to the features of each digital story. In fact, each feature is evaluated using a 4-grade scale (low, medium, high, very high) and the result is reflected on the length of the appropriate peak of the «Dimension Star». The "Dimension Star" is therefore a reference model for the analysis of DSE.

# 3    Evaluation of Digital Storytelling Environments Using the "Dimension Star" Model

With the help of the evaluation model of digital stories "Dimension Star" an attempt has been made to evaluate two DSE, namely: (a) ToonTastic [7] that provides opportunities to create various stories on a variety of subjects and (b) Kodu [9] which supports the creation of various stories about a particular subject. Based on this evaluation analysis, the strengths and weaknesses of each DSE is highlighted (Fig. 2) while the completeness of the "Dimension Star" in the context of EDSE is also investigated.

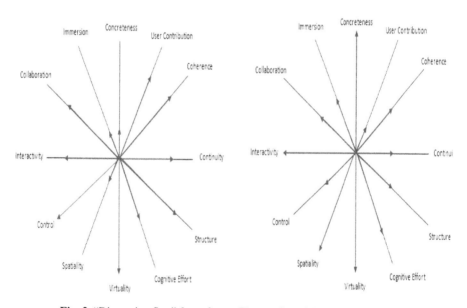

**Fig. 2.** "Dimension Star" for software Toontastic and Kodu respectively

## 3.1    ToonTastic

ToonTastic [7] (Fig. 3), is a collaborative digital animation creator that bridges the gap between game and more formal methods of storytelling. It is a constructive tool designed to help children capture and share their stories with other children around the world. It is designed to appeal to a broad group of users. As a drawing tool it is simple enough for six years old children and very interesting to entertain adults. However, ages that it is primarily addressed are between eight and twelve. The aim of this software -that underlines its theoretical background- is to provide children with opportunities to outline their internal representations and convert them to external, with visual and physical representation, so that children are able to debug and rebuild their mental models.

**Fig. 3.** Software ToonTastic

The analysis of digital storytelling software ToonTastic with the "Dimension Star" model is described as follows: As far as *User Contribution* is concerned, ToonTastic receives a high value. This is because the user can choose the types of scenes that will form the storyline. For the dimension *Concreteness* ToonTastic receives a low value because although there is supporting material (libraries backgrounds, designs, sounds), the user can create all the material needed from scratch. The dimensions of *Cohesion* and *Continuity* receive a high value, because the elements of the story have a logical and temporal flow since the software helps the user build the story with questions in each step. As far as the dimension *Structure* is concerned, ToonTastic receives a high value, due to the fact that the software helps the user with appropriate questions to create a well structured story. The dimension *Cognitive Effort* receives a medium value because considerable effort is needed to understand the functionality of the software. As far as the dimension Virtuality is concerned, ToonTastic receives a very high value since the story takes place entirely in a virtual environment, while on the dimension of *Spatiality* ToonTastic receives a low value because the motion of objects in the two dimensional space of the software does not play any special role in the evolution of each story. The dimension *Control* receives a very high value, because the user can build step by step, every piece of the story. Furthermore, the dimension *Interactivity* receives a medium value because the user can interact with the heroes of the story in the story construction, however there is no interaction during the narration. As far as the dimension *Collaboration* is concerned, ToonTastic receives a high value since five children can paint at the same time with the five digital pens that are available. Finally, the dimension *Immersion* receives a low value because even though the software is interesting, it doesn't create conditions of virtual reality.

## 3.2   Kodu

Kodu [9] (Fig. 4), is a visual programming language which is used for the creation of digital games. It is easy to use and includes tools for creating three-dimensional worlds. Kodu is a multi-dimensional tool for digital storytelling with a variety of possibilities for creating digital stories. It is designed to be user friendly and accessible for children aged between 8-18 years. The creation of digital stories is made through the selection of appropriate characters and objects (e.g. character Kodu, trees, clouds, rocks etc.) that can be used in specific situations. Kodu helps children build a sound programming literacy without complicated programming concepts.

**Fig. 4.** Software Kodu

The analysis of DSE Kodu with the "Dimension Star" model is described as follows: The objects and characters used in Kodu are pre-defined, so the dimension *Concreteness* receives a high value. The user can change the plot of the story by using strictly the default graphics library of the software. Therefore, the dimension *User Contribution* receives a medium value. In Kodu the user can create numerous well structured scenarios which can have temporal and logical consistency, however the software has no special function to help the user in this direction. Consequently, the dimensions of *Cohesion, Continuity* and *Structure* receive a medium value. The dimension Cognitive Effort receives high value because users need considerable effort to familiarize themselves with the environment and create complex stories. The dimension *Virtuality* receives a very high value because the story takes place entirely in a virtual environment, while the dimension of Spatiality receives a high value because the motion of objects in the three dimensional space of Kodu plays an important role in the evolution of each story. As far as the dimension *Control* is concerned, Kodu receives a medium value, because although the user can construct the story in detail, the default characters and objects provided by the environment should be used. Furthermore, the dimension *Interactivity* receives a high value because the user can interact with the characters and the objects of story during the creation and the presentation of the digital story. Moreover, the creation of digital stories can be done in groups but the software doesn't have any special utility that promotes cooperation, so the dimension *Collaboration* receives a medium value. Finally, the dimension *Immersion* receives a medium value, because the story space becomes to a certain extent real space for the user.

# 4     Conclusions

The diagrammatic analysis of digital storytelling environments (DSE) with the "Dimension Star" model allows the user to identify, at first glance, the strengths and weaknesses of the DSE at hand and make comparisons based on the dimensions of the edges of the star. Moreover, the "Dimension Star" can become a useful tool for software developers of digital stories especially in the early stages of conception and design of DSE. More specifically, by categorizing DSE using the dimensions described by the "Dimension Star", digital storytelling software designers have the opportunity to choose from successful examples. In addition, teachers can use the results of the analysis with the "Dimension Star" so as to choose appropriate DSE which are in line with the goals they want to achieve. As far as the completeness of the Shafer model is concerned, there should be noted that although the proposed dimensions for analysis of DSE are fundamental, there is room for the introduction of extra dimensions. More specifically, new dimensions can be added with an emphasis on constructivist learning, as for example, the software's ability to use "multiple representations" during the learning process. Extending the model "Dimension Star" is an imminent goal of this research effort.

# References

1. Di Blas, N., Boretti, B.: Interactive storytelling in pre-school: a case-study. In: Proceedings of IDC 2009, pp. 44–51. ACM, New York (2009)
2. Lowenthal, P.R.: Online faculty development and storytelling: An unlikely solution to improving teacher quality. Journal of Online Learning and Teaching 9(3), 349–356 (2008)
3. Mateas, M.: A Neo-Aristotelian Theory of Interactive Drama. In: Artificial Intelligence an Interactive Entertainment, pp. 56–61. AAAI Press, Menlo Park (2000)
4. Papadimitriou, C.H.: Mythematics: Storytelling in the Teaching of Computer Science and Mathematics. SIGCSE Bulletin 35(3), 1–1 (2003)
5. Papert, S.: Mindstorms: Children, Computers and Powerful Ideas. Basic Books, New York (1980)
6. Russell, A.: ToonTastic: A Global Storytelling Network for Kids, by Kids. In: TEI 2010, Cambridge, MA, USA, January 25-27, pp. 271–274 (2010)
7. Schafer, L.: Models for Digital Storytelling and Interactive Narratives. In: 4 th International Conference on Computational Semiotics for Games and New Media, Split, pp. 148–155 (2004)
8. Spierling, U.: Setting the scene: playing digital director in interactive storytelling and creation. Computers & Graphics 26(1), 31–44 (2002)
9. http://research.microsoft.com/en-us/projects/kodu/

# Towards a Social-Emotional e-Learning System

Michalis Feidakis and Thanasis Daradoumis

Department of Cultural Technology and Communication (D.C.T.C), School of Social Sciences,
University of Aegean, Mytilini, Greece
mfeidakis@sch.gr, daradoumis@aegean.gr

**Abstract.** In the current paper, we first review Emotion-Learning Theories and Emotion Assessment in Human-Computer Interaction (HCI) and then we lay the foundations of a Social-Emotional Computer Supported Learning System that is based on social-emotional competencies and can support emotion assessment.

**Keywords:** Emotion, Social-Emotional learning, Emotion assessment, Affect recognition, Affective Computing, Emotion Oriented Computing.

## 1    Introduction

Computer-Based Training/Learning was dynamically put forward in the 80's. After the WWW revolution, somewhere in the 90's, it has shifted to Web Based Learning/e-Learning, giving a social tone in the learning system's design. During that period, Artificial Intelligence in Education (AIED) was established, releasing its first Intelligent Tutoring Systems (ITS) and Intelligent Learning Environments (ILE). In our days, WEB is slowly turning to WEB 2.0, e-learning to e-learning 2.0 and social networks have become first topic in the agenda.

All these new technologies were aspired from the work of leading educators, like Bloom's Taxonomy, Gagne's Instructionism, Piaget and Papert's Constructionism, Vygotsky's Social Development, Bandura's Social Learning, Lave's Situated Learning, et al. The new systems were designed to be *Adaptive, Personalized, Cooperative, Collaborative, Constructive*.

Despite of the progress that has been achieved, the e-learning community is still talking about the promise of this technology whereas is questioning its realistic classroom use [1, 4, 15, 21]. Perhaps the innovative Human Computer Interactions (HCI) models have the tendency to focus exclusively on cognitive factors, and are often unable to adapt to real-world situations in which affective factors play a significant role [15]. Nevertheless, there is "rarely any learning process without emotion" [12].

A main pitfall identified in Computer Supported Collaborative Learning (CSCL) environments is the tendency to restrict social interaction to educational interventions aimed at cognitive processes, while social (psychological) interventions aimed at socio-emotional processes are ignored, neglected or forgotten [16]. Just because an environment makes it technologically possible, it does not mean that social interaction will take place. Students need to trust each other, feel a sense of warmth and

M.D. Lytras et al. (Eds.): WSKS 2011, CCIS 278, pp. 323–329, 2013.

belonging, and feel close to each other before they will engage willfully in collaboration and recognize the collaboration as a valuable experience [22]. Learners worry, hope, become bored, embarrassed, envy, get anxious, feel proud, and become frustrated, and so on. Expert teachers are very adept at recognizing and addressing the emotional states of students and, based upon impressions, taking some action that positively impacts learning [15]. Shouldn't expert tutoring systems do the same?

The consideration of student's emotions can offer a more interactive and challenging learning environment, enabling learners' demand of empowerment, social identity, and authentic learning experience. There are more than three decades of *Social & Emotional Learning (SEL)* Theory and Practice, and several models and theories that embody the dynamics of a learner's emotional state, have been put forth. Added feedback from recent neurological and psychological studies can shed light into our student's feelings and deep thoughts. Additionally, the advancements of AIED are already providing us with emotion recognition and assessment techniques that successfully classify students' emotions.

Research on emotions in e-learning is still quite limited, despite theoretical advances and calls for more empirical studies. An e-learning system that is fed by SEL paradigms and practices and provides its users (students, teachers, educators) with real-time emotion assessment, constitutes a challenging call for experimentation.

## 2     Emotion and Learning

Emotion, together with cognition and motivation are the key components of learning [4]. Newer research in the fields of neurobiology and psychology reveals the essential role of human's emotional centers (Limbic system-Hypothalamus, Amygdala, and Hippocampus) not only in perception and learning, but also in decision making [5, 18]. Although, much of our thinking takes place in the cortex, our memory involves the limbic system. The limbic system interprets all sensory information, external and visceral and sets the emotional tone of the information before its reaches the cortex.

The last decades, learning theories and models explore the links between emotions and learning [11]. For example, in circular models [15, 17], a typical learning experience involves a range of emotions, cycling the student around a cognitive-emotive space as they learn. Keeping them in the positive half is not the objective, but the fact that the cyclic nature is natural in learning, and "when learners land in the negative half, this is an inevitable part of the cycle. "Our aim is to help students to keep orbiting the loop, teaching them to propel themselves, especially after a setback [14]".

However, Emotion and Learning have been mainly ascribed by the term *Emotion Intelligence* (EQ) in many cases. In his homonymous book [10], Goleman presents convincing evidence that the emotional intelligence quotient (EQ) is just as important in academic success as cognitive intelligence, as measured by IQ or SAT scores. The early Emotional Intelligence theory was originally developed during the 1970s and 80s by the work and writings of psychologists Howard Gardner, Peter Salovey and John Mayer.

Since 1980, there have been hundreds of school-based programs that have been developed to assist people in gaining control of their emotions. These programs are better classified under the more general label *Social and Emotional Learning-SEL* (e.g. PATHs, Transaction Analysis, Social Development Curriculum, Resolving Conflict Creatively, Self Science, 6Seconds) and comprise basic lessons of emotional intelligence in the form of school-based programs.

In USA, CASEL (Collaborative for Academic, Social, and Emotional Learning) [2], researchers have directed the meta-analyses of more than 700 positive youth development, SEL, character education, and prevention interventions. They have identified five groups of inter-related core social and emotional competencies that SEL programs should address: Self-awareness, Self-management, Social awareness, Relationship skills, Responsible decision making.

The reviews include school, family, and community interventions designed to promote personal and social skills in children and adolescents between the ages of 5 and 18. The reviews indicate that SEL programs:

- Are effective in both school and after-school settings and for students with and without behavioural and emotional problems.
- Are effective for racially and ethnically diverse students from urban, rural, and suburban settings across the K-12 grade range.
- Improve students' social-emotional skills, attitudes about self and others, connection to school, and positive social behaviour; and reduce conduct problems and emotional distress.
- Improve students' achievement test scores by 11 to 17 percentile points.

A similar approach has been adopted in UK with the establishment of the Social and Emotional Aspects of Learning (SEAL) program, conducted by the DfES (Department of Education and Skills). In Australia, the Framework of Values for schools has also initiated an interest in social and emotional well-being and learning [13].

## 3    Emotion Assessment

Emotion research is susceptible to the risk to be focused on subjective emotional experience. Furthermore, there is still a debate between scientists, about the degree of consciousness when experiencing emotions [6]: if cognitive appraisal is a necessary pre-condition for affective arousal, or not [20]. As a result, there is a hesitance if we can assess emotions by asking "How do you feel" or "What do you prefer". More scientists prefer not ask at all. They "plug" the human subject into sensors, and start measuring its physiological responses. But how subjective is a subject, when he/she knows that he/she is taking part in an experiment [21]?

Affective Computing [20] or Emotion Oriented Computing [3] has focused on automated detection of affective states in a variety of learning contexts and it has shown promising results [1, 3, 4, 19, 20, 21]. By exploiting Computer Intelligence techniques, researchers are aiming at eliciting accurate automatic classifications of affective states and patterns that comply with three main categorizations [23]:

- Basic emotions: Emotions that are recognised universally, i.e. fear, anger, sadness and enjoyment [8].
- Emotion dimensions, i.e. arousal, valence, control, intensity, duration, frequency of occurrence, time dimension, point of reference, context [12].
- Eclectic approach that uses verbal labels that seem more appropriate.

Affect measurement can be grouped into three areas [19, 20]:

- Psychological-Profiling tools (verbal/non verbal self-reports, conductive chat, rating scales, standardized checklists, questionnaires, semantic and graphical differentials projective methods).
- Physiological signals-use of sensors (skin conductance-SC, electrodermal activity-EDA, electrocardiogram-ECG, blood volume pulse-BVP, electromyogram-EMG, respiration, pupillary dilation)
- Behavioral (facial expressions-face reader, voice modulation/intonation, hand tracking, body posture, motor behaviour-mouse-keyboard movements from log files, corrugator's activity)

Multimodal integration seems the likeliest key to real improvement.

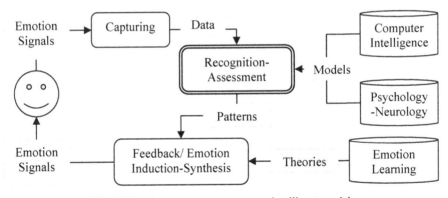

**Fig. 1.** Emotion-assessment computer intelligent model

## 4     Applying Social-Emotional e-learning in School

A 10% to 15% of elementary and high school students fall victim to various forms of "bullying" in school [7], while the drop out rate from school in the EU remains very high and in 2008 touched a total of 14.9% (14.8% in Greece) [14]. How effective can education systems be if we are indifferent to "what's on the students and teachers' deep minds"?

It is important to help students know how and when their "emotional intelligence" works to help or hinder their success. Salovey & Mayer [26] combined the work of several researchers to define the following measures of effective use of emotion. They used five attitudes to determine Emotional Intelligence:

1. Knowing one's emotions: Self-awareness
2. Managing emotions: Handling feelings
3. Motivating Oneself: Self-motivation
4. Recognizing emotions in others: Empathy
5. Handling Relationships: The art of relationships

There have been quite few isolated research projects on emotions in learning in Greek Language, which, however, lack of a systematic research. Moreover, emotion assessment is still out of schedule.

In a pre-pilot phase, we investigated the impact of a minimum number of lessons aiming at the Neuroscience of Learning and Emotion basic understanding, in two separate groups of students: 12-14 years (Lower Secondary School), and 15-17 years old (Technical Vocational Educational School). With the help of Multimedia (video-photos-animation), students became aware of the Emotional Brain and how it works in analogy with the Computer Architecture. They were also asked to define *emotions, affects, feelings* in groups, to describe cause and effects, to spot similarities and differences and to complete small case studies. The first results show a remarkable change in engagement, especially in the second group (age 15-17).

Our intention is to build a Social-emotional learning (SEL) program in Greek language that can be applied as an extracurricular activity, in a secondary education class. The proposed system purported to effectively involve learners in an educational, cultural and informative learning environment by assisting them in gaining control of their emotions. The suggested Learning Environment will consist of Learning Objects (Advanced-Content) that can complement Emotional Learning with Metaphors, Simulations, Educational Games, Storytelling, et al.

Assessment can be applied in two layers, academic and emotional:

- Students can be assessed both before and after the program in order to evaluate impact of Emotional Intelligence on their behaviour or academic performance.
- By combining signals from different modalities and different techniques (psychological, physiological, and behavioural) we can mine patterns of emotions that classify sequences of affective events.

Finally, we intend to formulate small groups according to students' talents based on Gartner's theory of Multiple Intelligence in order to mine successful collaborations. The latter has been already tested in a preliminary phase with promising outcomes. A more systematic and scientific approach will lead us to more safe results.

# 5     Conclusion

The role of emotion/affect in learning is at best in its infancy and there is still much to be discovered. We have described an educational scenario in which Social-Emotional Learning Theory can be applied into a Computer-Supported Learning Environment. We have considered not only academic assessment, but also (and mainly) emotion assessment.

**Acknowledgments.** This work has been partially supported by the European Commission under the Collaborative Project ALICE "Adaptive Learning via Intuitive/Interactive, Collaborative and Emotional Systems", VII Framework Programme, Theme ICT-2009.4.2 (Technology-Enhanced Learning), Grant Agreement n.257639.

## References

1. Calvo, R.: Incorporating Affect into Educational Design Patterns and Frameworks. In: 9th IEEE International Conference on Advanced Learning Technologies, Riga, Latvia, July 14-18 (2009)
2. Collaborative for Academic, Social, and Emotional Learning, http://www.casel.org/
3. Cowie, R.: Emotion-oriented computing: State of the art and key challenges (2010), http://emotion-research.net/
4. D'Mello, S., Craig, S., Gholson, B., Franklin, S., Picard, R., Graesser, A.: Integrating affect sensors in an intelligent tutoring system. In: International Conference on Intelligent User Interfaces, pp. 7–13. AMC Press, New York (2005)
5. Damasio, A.: Descartes's Error: Emotion, Reason, and the Human Brain. Papermac, London (1996)
6. Davou, B.: Interaction of Emotion and Cognition in the Processing of Textual Material. Meta: Journal des Traducteurs/Meta: Translators' Journal 52(1), 37–47 (2007)
7. Diamanti, I.: Bullying and violence in schools. Kathimerini (2009), http://www.kathimerini.gr/4dcgi/ _w_articles_ell_1_06/11/2009_336215
8. Ekman, P., Friesen, W.V.: Facial Action Coding System: A technique for the measurement of facial movement. Consulting Psychologists Press, Palo Alto (1978)
9. Gardner, H.: Frames of Mind. Basic Books, New York (1983)
10. Goleman, D.: Emotional Intelligence. Bantam Books, New York (1995)
11. Gratch, J. (n.d.): Emotion Research (2011), http://people.ict.usc.edu/~gratch/links.html (retrieved March 10, 2011)
12. Hascher, T.: Learning and Emotion: perspectives for theory and research. European Educational Research Journal 9, 13–28 (2010)
13. Hromek, R., Roffey, S.: Promoting social and emotional learning with games: "it's fun and we learn thinks". Simulation & Gaming 40, 626–644 (2009)
14. In12.gr Early school dropout in Greece and the EU (2010), http://www.in12.gr/article.php?a_id=1126&a_category=3
15. Kort, B., Reilly, R.: Analytical Models of Emotions, Learning and Relationships: Towards an Affect-sensitive Cognitive Machine. M.I.T. Media Laboratory (2002)
16. Kreijns, K., Kirschner, P.A., Jochems, W.: Identifying the pitfalls for social interaction in computer-supported collaborative learning environments: A review of the research. Computers in Human Behavior 19(3), 335–353 (2003)
17. Larsen, R.J., Diener, E.: Promises and problems with the Circurnplex model of emotion (1992), http://www.csun.edu/~gk45683/ Larsen%20and%20Diener%20%281992%29.pdf
18. LeDoux, J.E.: The Emotional Brain: The Mysterious Underpinnings of Emotional Life. Phoenix, London (1999)

19. Leon, S., Nikov, A.: Intelligent Emotion-Oriented eCommerce Systems. In: Proc. 9th WSEAS International Conference on Artificial Intelligence, Knowledge Engineering and Data Bases, pp. 202–207 (2010)
20. Picard, R.: Affective Computing. MIT Press, Cambridge (1997)
21. Picard, R.: Emotion research by the people, for the people. MIT Media Laboratory (2010)
22. Rourke, L.: Operationalizing social interaction in computer conferencing. In: Proceedings of the 16th Annual Conference of the Canadian Association for Distance Education, Quebec City (2000),
    `http://www.ulaval.ca/aced2000cade/english/proceedings.html`
23. Scherer, K.R.: Which emotions can be induced by music? What are the underlying mechanisms? And how can we measure them? Journal of New Music Research 33 (2005)
24. Salovey, P., Mayer, J.D.: Emotional intelligence. Imagination, Cognition, and Personality 9, 185–211 (1990)

# ICT and Universal Access to Education: Towards a Culture of Accessibility

Stefania Bocconi and Michela Ott

Istituto Tecnologie Didattiche – CNR
Via De Marini, 6, Genoa Italy
{ott,bocconi}@itd.cnr.it

**Abstract.** This paper deals with the issue of evaluating, documenting and spreading information about the accessibility of ICT-based educational products and also provides an example of how this can be done. This mainly goes in the direction of concretely supporting e-inclusion and Universal Access to education. As a matter of fact, provided that the accessibility of digital educational resources is carefully assessed and documented, teachers and educators have the possibility to choose and adopt those products that are fully "accessible" by "all" their students. From a wider perspective, this approach also goes in the direction of spreading the "culture of accessibility" and represents a further step onwards to guarantee the inclusion of students with disabilities.

**Keywords:** E-inclusion, Accessibility, Educational software, Digital resources.

## 1    Context and Challenges Addressed

There is a growing awareness that all students, including those with disabilities, have the right to expect the same standard of education [1]; this entails that all of them have the right to "access" and use the same educational tools, including those that are ICT based [2].

As a matter of fact, the use of educational software is often challenging for some students with disabilities: they are often prevented from using the same tools as their peers and this limits their educational opportunities.

The availability of Assistive Technologies (such as special keyboards, screen readers, speech synthesizers, etc.) *per se* doesn't completely solve the different accessibility problems posed by educational software products [3] and [4]. It is therefore very important that educational software databases and catalogues provide suitable information about the accessibility features of the products they list. Only when users of these information services (teachers, parents, students, etc.) have access to specific documentation they can gain understanding about the accessibility level of each product, thus also being able to make an informed decision about the product to be used [5].

The problem of providing and disseminating information about the accessibility features of educational software products has been recognized as significant by the Italian Ministry of Education which in 2006, in the framework of the national

M.D. Lytras et al. (Eds.): WSKS 2011, CCIS 278, pp. 330–337, 2013.

programme entitled "New Technology and disability" commissioned the Institute for Educational Technology of the National Research Council (ITD-CNR), to start a pilot research project to define models and methods for the evaluation of the accessibility of educational digital resources and for the spreading of related information.

In the framework of this project, ITD-CNR had the opportunity to define a method to evaluate the accessibility of educational digital products and to set up a dedicated documentation and information system, which is fully described in the following.

## 2    Evaluating and Documenting the Accessibility of Educational Digital Resources: The Approach Adopted

Since 1999, ITD-CNR under the auspices of Italy's Ministry of Education, University and Research, has been running Essediquadro [6], an online service providing comprehensive, up-to-date information on over 4,000 educational software products from both Italy and abroad.

At the heart of Essediquadro is a searchable catalogue listing educational software for all school levels and disciplines, with particular attention to special education needs. The system also offers support and guidance for integrating software and multimedia into the teaching / learning process: subject area software surveys, classroom reports, and more. Each software product is described in a sheet that comprises a number of pages with different contents: general information about the product (author, cost, availability etc.), educational information (subject area, topic, target users, educational strategy, pre-requisites etc.), summary of contents. The product system requirements are also listed and a few screenshots are available so that user may get an idea of the software interface. A further page called "Insights" offers information about software including teaching multiuse, subject area avails, classroom reports and study topics

Since 2006, in the framework of the above mentioned ministerial program on "New Technologies and Disability" an "Accessibility" sheet has been added to the description of each educational product in order to provide users with the possibility of being aware of software accessibility features.

The actual "Accessibility" sheet of Essediquadro comprises four main sections:

1.    *Suppliers/author's self-declaration*
2.    *Evaluation of compliance with legal requirements*[1]
3.    *Evaluation of the level of accessibility with respect to the different types of disability*
4.    *Results of field-testing.*

Figure 1 shows the accessibility page of the Essediquadro system, where the black arrows underline the above mentioned four different "fields" (which of course can be further exploited to access the full documentation).

---

[1] Italian Law 4/2004 Provisions to support the access to Information Technologies for the disabled http://www.pubbliaccesso.gov.it/normative/law_20040109_n4.htm

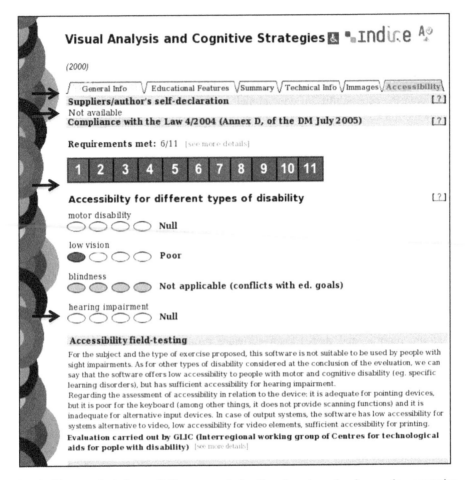

**Fig. 1.** The standard "accessibility page of the Essediquadro ed-software documentation system

## 1. Suppliers/author's Self-Declaration

In this specific section, Essediquadro recalls directly what the authors/ publishers officially say about the accessibility of their products. According to the Riga Ministerial Declaration on Inclusion [7], in fact, software authors and/or suppliers are entrusted to clearly state whether or not (and to what extent) each software product responds to the accessibility standards. Unfortunately, nowadays only very few multimedia educational developers provide such documentation.

## 2. Evaluation of Compliance with Legal Requirements

This section outlines the main results of the research efforts conducted at ITD for the design and application of an ICT-based grid (developed for this purpose by ITD-CNR) aimed at evaluating the accessibility of educational software [8]. The grid is shaped along the Italian law in force: Law no. 4/2004 (also known as "The Stanca

Act") which was followed by the Ministerial Decree (DM) 8 July 2005. Eleven requirements for both commercial/non commercial "on the shelf" software are indicated in the DM, following the main requirements outlined in Section 508 of the Rehabilitation Act of the US Federal Government [9].

Under this section, Essediquadro presents the data resulting from testing the compliance of each educational software product with the eleven accessibility requirements of the Italian Law. This analysis is carried out by expert evaluators using methodologies and tools designed and implemented, in the framework of the research project by ITD-CNR (namely the above mentioned specific evaluation grid). It is worth remembering that while the methodology adopted in Italy to carry out this type of evaluation (compliance with the national law in force) can easily be transferred to other national contexts the actual contents of the evaluation (fields of the grid) may vary according the differences of the national laws in force and related requirements.

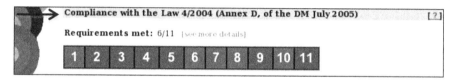

**Fig. 2.** Compliance with the law in force: number of matching requisites

As shown above in Figure 2 the results of the evaluation process are expressed in terms of numbers of requirements actually met (out of the eleven indicated in the DM): for instance, the result of 6/11 represented in the figure means that the product respects only 6 requirements of the regulation in force.

For a better understanding, details of which specific requirements are/are not met are also provided as shown in Figure 3.

| Details of compliance with the Law No 4/2004 | | | | | |
|---|---|---|---|---|---|
| Evaluation carried out on Windows operating systems (XP) and/or Linux (So_Di_Linux DVD) and assistive technology Jaws (vs 7.1). Evaluation completed on 27.7.2009 | **Law Compliance** | **Disability** | | | |
| | | Motor Dis. | Hearing Dis. | Low vision Dis. | Blindness |
| **Law Requirement No 1** [see more details] | ✗ | ● | | ● | ● CO |
| Terms: The functions provided by the user interface must be able to be activated by means of keyboard commands in cases where a description of the function or the result of executing it can be provided. | | | | | |
| **Law Requirement No 2** [see more details] | ✓ | ● | ● | ● | ● |
| Terms: Commands and functionalities of the user interface must not limit or disable the accessibility characteristics and functionalities of the operating system, made available by the manufacturer of the operating system. | | | | | |
| **Law Requirement No 3** [see more details] | ✓ | | | ● | ● |
| Terms: The application must provide sufficient information, such as identification information, operations possible and status, on objects contained in the user interface so that the assistive technology can identify them and interpret their functionalities. [More Requirements] | | | | | |

**Fig. 3.** Details of compliance with the law in force

## 3     Evaluation of the Level of Accessibility with Respect to the Different Types of Disability

Assessing and documenting the compliance of each product with the regulation in force is, of course, important but it is not enough to give an effective answer to all Essediquadro potential users. Typically educators ask for an answer to the question: "Is this product accessible for deaf (or blind, or dyslexic, etc.) students?" To answer this question, the methodology set up in Essediquadro draws on the correspondence between the law's requirements and each specific type of disability: if a product is not fully compliant with all of the eleven accessibility requirements, further information is supplied about the specific target for whom that product is not accessible (and, conversely, the eventual full or partial accessibility for other categories of disabled students is underlined). As an example, the product considered in Figure 4 appears to be fully accessible (compliant to all the DM requisites = all green circles) by motor and hearing disabled students while results scarcely accessible by sight impaired and partially by low vision students.

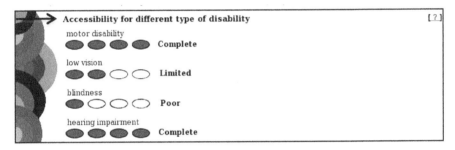

**Fig. 4.** Sheet showing the level of accessibility with respect to the different types of disability

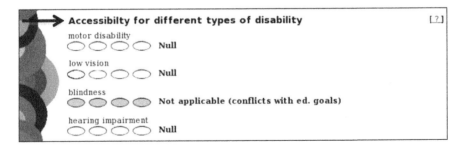

**Fig. 5.** Sheet showing the level of accessibility by type of disability- Conflict with educational goals suitable for blind students

To be more precise, Essediquadro also highlights whether there is a potential conflict between the educational goals of the application and a specific type of disability: this happens when using a product can be considered nonsense for a specific category of disabled students (i.e. most products aiming at teaching/supporting/practicing colour recognition skills are *per se* useless for blind students and investigating their accessibility for this category of disabled students can only be a waste of time).

Within the Essediquadro Accessibility Schema, the grey-coloured circles (Figure 5) alert users that the evaluation of such a product's accessibility features is not meaningful for that type of disability because of the mentioned conflict between legal requirements and the intended educational goals.

Another type of conflict is taken into account by the system, which entails a different approach to the accessibility evaluation: it happens when the lack of accessibility is due to a conflict between legal requirements and software educational goals [10].

As an example, one of the basic accessibility requirements foreseen by the Italian law entails the labelling of all software audio elements. However, educational products aimed at teaching foreign languages that present unlabelled dialogues should not be rejected out of hand as they serve a precise and very specific, educational objective (listening comprehension) and, furthermore, can be used by all disabled students other than the hearing impaired. Listening comprehension exercises are, of course, fundamentally based on audio presentations but they also require that such audio presentations are not backed with written labels, which may change the activity focus. Summarizing: Essediquadro, in case of lack of perfect compliance of a product with all the accessibility requirements indicates 'for whom' (type of disability) each product is not fully accessible and also indicates if there is a conflict between legal requirements and software educational goals and/or between legal requirements and educational activities cannot be performed by (are nonsense for) different types of disabled students.

## 4     Results of Field Testing

Thanks to the support of the Italian network of clinical centres specialised in the field of technological aids (GLIC) the data on accessibility provided in Essediquadro also include information about the actual usability of software products and about their

| Accessibility related to the types of device | | |
|---|---|---|
| keyboard: | OO | 0,33 |
| pointing devices: | OOO | 0,46 |
| alternative input dev.: | O | 0,00 |
| video: | OOOO | 0,79 |
| syst. alternative to video: | O | 0,00 |
| audio: | OOOO | 0,63 |
| print devices: | O | 0,00 |

**Fig. 6.** Accessibility field-testing results with reference to input /output devices

compatibility with the main assistive devices. In order to perform the evaluations, GLIC researchers constantly monitor the performances of some end-users while using specific educational software applications (often in conjunction with assistive devices); during the working sessions, they constantly take notes about software compatibility with specific assistive devices, record the obstacles encountered and the possible solutions, if any. A specific sheet in Essediquadro shows the results of such an in-field evaluation and Figure 6 shows one of the accessibility aspects taken into account by in-field testing namely those related to the accessibility with respect to different input/output devices.

## 5     Conclusions

In this paper the issue of the evaluation of the accessibility of educational software products has been tackled and the structured accessibility schema adopted in Essediquadro, (the Italian online documentation system for Educational Software) has been described in detail in order to put forward a concrete example shedding light on the complexity of the matter and on the variety of the aspects to be considered/taken into account. The proposed "Accessibility sheet" of Essediquadro can be regarded as an example of how to provide full and effective information about the accessibility features of educational software. As a matter of fact, the four sections of the Essediquadro accessibility sheet give different responses to different user questions: 1) Is the product labelled as accessible by the author/supplier, thus showing that it has been designed and implemented bearing in mind Universal Access criteria and requirements? 2) Is the product compliant with the requirements of the regulation in force? 3) For which types of disability can the product be considered accessible and to what extent? 4) Is the product tailored to specific needs and what kind of specific input and output devices are allowed?

We are convinced that, in order to foster school e-inclusion, providing information about the actual accessibility of educational software products is a key aspect. Dedicated documentation systems should, then, provide users with advanced search features allowing them to choose (and actually use in their educational activity) accessible tools able to facilitate inclusive practices. This approach can also have the side effect of allowing teachers/educators to gain a better global understanding of accessibility issues and challenges and can also stimulate software developers to design and produce more authentically accessible educational products.

The main critical factor that can hinder the actual transferability of the Italian experience carried out within Essediquadro to other EU countries is that different countries have different accessibility laws and that some of them have no accessibility laws at all. Policy makers, of course, play a major role at this end [11] and [12]; they should contribute to provide a common European framework for evaluating the accessibility of educational e- products and by defining the "rules" and the methods to spread the related information.

## References

1. UNESCO, Guidelines for inclusion: Ensuring access to education for all, http://unesdoc.unesco.org/images/0014/001402/140224e.pdf

2. Ott, M.: School of the Future: E-Tools and New Pedagogies to Build Up an Inclusive Learning Community. In: Ordóñez de Pablos, P., Zhao, J., Tennyson, R. (eds.) Technology Enhanced Learning for People with Disabilities: Approaches and Applications, pp. 105–120. IGI-Global (2011)

3. Croasdaile, S., Jones, S., Ligon, K., Oggel, L., Pruett, M.: Supports for and Barriers to Implementing Assistive Technology in Schools. In: Ordóñez de Pablos, P., Zhao, J., Tennyson, R. (eds.) Technology Enhanced Learning for People with Disabilities: Approaches and Applications, pp. 154–166. IGI-Global (2011)

4. Hitchcock, C., Stahl, S.: Assistive Technology, Universal Design, Universal Design for Learning: Improved Learning Opportunities. Journal of Special Education Technology 18(4) (2003)

5. Ribeiro, J., Moreira, A., Almeida, A.M.: ICT in the Education of Students with SEN: Perceptions of Stakeholders. In: Lytras, M.D., Ordonez De Pablos, P., Avison, D., Sipior, J., Jin, Q., Leal, W., Uden, L., Thomas, M., Cervai, S., Horner, D. (eds.) TECH-EDUCATION 2010. CCIS, vol. 73, pp. 331–337. Springer, Heidelberg (2010)

6. Essediquadro, http://www.sd2.itd.cnr.it

7. EU Ministerial Declaration, "ICT for an Inclusive Society" Conference, Riga, Latvia (June 11, 2006)
http://ec.europa.eu/information_society/activities/einclusion/events/riga_2006/index_en.html

8. Bocconi, S., Dini, S., Ferlino, L., Ott, M.: Accessibility of educational multimedia: in search of specific standards. iJET 1(3), 1–5 (2006)

9. Section 508 of the US Rehabilitation Act, http://www.section508.gov/

10. Bocconi, S., Dini, S., Ferlino, L., Martinoli, C., Ott, M.: ICT Educational Tools and Visually Impaired Students: Different Answers to Different Accessibility Needs. In: Stephanidis, C. (ed.) HCI 2007, Part III. LNCS, vol. 4556, pp. 491–500. Springer, Heidelberg (2007)

11. Sharma, R.S., Ng, E.W.J., Dharmawirya, M., Samuel, E.M.: A Policy Framework for Developing Knowledge Societies. International Journal of Knowledge Society Research 1(1), 22–45 (2010)

12. Meyer, I., Müller, S., Kubitschke, L.: eInclusion – Towards a Coherent European Policy Response to Social Inequalities in the Information Society. Paper presented at eChallenges Conference (2006)

# Exploring the Learning Profile of Information System Workers to Provide Effective Professional Development

Kordaki Maria[1], Thanasis Daradoumis[1,2], and Fragidakis Dimitrios[1]

[1] Department of Cultural Technology and Communication, University of the Aegean
81100 Mytilene, Greece
[2] Department of Computer Science, Multimedia and Telecommunications,
Open University of Catalonia, Barcelona, Spain
{m.kordaki,daradoumis}@aegean.gr, D.Fragidakis@nsk.gr

**Abstract.** This paper presents a research work that explores a variety of issues which, on the one hand, are related to the way the employees of a computerized workplace behave, work and learn and, on the other hand, try to identify the employees' knowledge, competencies, preferences, interests, deficiencies in knowledge, skills and abilities, training needs as well as socialization and health aspects. All these concerns lead to the construction of a rich learning profile of Information System employees which is a key issue for determining an adequate and timely training for the different types of employees and their needs. The methodology followed integrates a variety of profile assessment techniques, such as observation, questionnaires, interviews, focus groups, and documentation. This paper focuses more on the questionnaire technique where the main employee profile indicators are determined, analyzed and basic conclusions are drawn.

**Keywords:** learning profile, work-integrated learning, assessment techniques.

## 1 Introduction

This research aims at building a robust learning profile of employees who work with an Information System (IS) in a public organization. This learning profile will constitute then the base for developing a methodology and model that will allow the implementation of an adaptive and intuitive learning system which will be based on collaborative learning strategies and which will be used to provide training to the IS learners-employees, addressing both their particular goals, needs, preferences and interests and the increasing demands of the organization itself.

Literature research [1,2,3] shows that the development of a flexible and complete user learning profile is necessary so that to be able to provide him/her effective personalized training, monitoring, scaffolding and evaluation. Learners may also learn better and more effectively through an exploratory learning methodology and through collaboration in small groups, exchanging their personal experiences, helping each other, and learning/obtaining new knowledge together through experimentation, exploration, discovery, problem solving and critical thinking.

M.D. Lytras et al. (Eds.): WSKS 2011, CCIS 278, pp. 338–343, 2013.

As such, we initially need to extract knowledge about seven main indicators that concern the learner-employee profile. First, the learner-employee learning style; second, the aspects of the Information System (IS) that he/she would prefer to experience and learn about; third, aspects that include the workers' technical knowledge about the IS; fourth, the IS functionalities that the worker is using or would like to use; fifth, the workers' social past and current habits and how these habits have been changed due to the evolution of the IS in their work place; sixth, health issues associated with the use of the IS; and finally, information about the tasks that IS workers carry out in their work place. The first two indicators have been extensively explored and analyzed in the work of [4]. This paper focuses on the analysis of the last five indicators. The ultimate aim of the current study is to explore and build a solid and complete workers' learning profile in an IS-based working environment and then use it to provide them a better professional development, thus aiming at developing a live and more effective learning organization.

To explore and build the worker learning profile, we conducted a survey which took place in the central department of the Legal Council of the Hellenic State (hereafter, LCHS). Employees belong to several departmental sections and are all users of the IS. To identify the afore-mentioned aspects of the employees' learning profile regarding IS issues, we designed seven specific questionnaires, both with open and closed-type questions, the later following a five-point Likert scale. All questionnaires were given to the employees and those that were answered back were then evaluated and commented subsequently. The following sections describe the methodology (Section 2) and results obtained (Section 3). These results constitute the input data to build a complete learner profile module, which forms an important component of our adaptive, collaborative learning/training model. The final Section outlines the work done and makes reference to on-going and future work.

## 2    Research Objectives and Methodology

The research objectives that are set by this work coincide with the five specific analysis indicators and are explored and evaluated taking into consideration qualitative and quantitative characteristics. They are the following:

R1    Determine the user knowledge and skills with regard to the IS she/he is using.

R2    Identify specific functionalities/applications that a user would prefer the IS to have as well as the user behavior as regards e-environments and e-services.

R3    Find out the user socialization habits and how these have been evolved through his/her familiarization and use of the IS.

R4    Determine the main healthy issues that concern the user who works in a computerized environment.

R5    Identify and analyze the main tasks that an IS user is carrying out in his/her workplace.

# 3     Presentation-Annotation of the Aggregate Results of the Survey

In each questionnaire we have followed a five-point Likert scale. The five specific indicators regarding the users' profile are represented by the letters A to E. An indicator may be sub-divided into more specific variables or sub-factors (such as A1 and A2). Each indicator is measured by specific criteria/questions A.1.1., B.1.1.,…,E.1.1., where the first letter is the indicator, the first number is a sub-factor and the second number is a question associated with this subfactor.

## 3.1     Indicator A: The Workers' Knowledge and Technical Skills about the IS

This indicator is divided into two sub-factors (A1 and A2) which examine two important aspects of the IS workers: their basic background knowledge and skills about computers, as well as their knowledge and skills about some specific issues of an IS. These aspects are useful to identify for each individual user his/her area of interest which is more familiar with or not.

**A1: User's Basic Background Knowledge about Computers:** Interpreting the results which were obtained for the sub-factor A1 (8 questions were defined for this sub-factor) we came up to the following conclusions: The users of the IS know how to use the following applications quite well: (a) Microsoft office, (85%) (b) Workflow Management Systems (WMS), (74%),(c) E-mail Systems, (68%), (d) Real Time Web Meetings (Skype & Windows Messanger), (50%), (e) Social Networks (Facebook), (50%). They are not familiar (under 30%) with aspects like: DBase Management Systems, (b) Creation of web pages, and (c) Using Blogs. Here, it is significant to note that most users (75%) had enough previous experience in GUI environments and Web applications, but 80% of them had not any experience in WMS.

**A2: User's Knowledge about Some Specific Issues of the IS:** In this sub-factor, we examine whether the user knows about some specific issues that concern an IS, such as the development phases of an IS, its specification, the user ability about the languages and the Data Bases which are used, their capability to encounter errors, the use of manuals and help Desk. It is important to note that the most of the participants (more than 74%) answered 'NO' to the questions A2.1 – A2.11 that means that they have not any knowledge about these issues. It is also important to note that the rest of the users (26%) have more experience in these issues, but analyzing their answers to the open questions that accompanied each of the 14 initial questions indicated that they also need to learn more about aspects such as antivirus, Java, Oracle, and how to correct system errors. It is also detected that most of them (80%) expressed that they have not been involved or they did not know the development phases of an IS.

## 3.2     Indicator B: The IS Functionalities That Workers Are Using or Would Like to Use

This indicator examines two important aspects (sub-factors) that an IS worker prefers the IS to provide: the first one concerns the technical environment of the IS where the worker is carrying out his/her tasks, whereby the second one explores the networking environment of the IS, in particular those internet applications that facilitate the connection between employees, their training needs as well as the interconnection between branch offices.

**B1: The Technical Environment of the IS Where the Employee Is Working:** This sub-factor examines the functionalities of the IS and the user needs in accordance to the requirements of the LCHS. The results of the questionnaire showed that the employees have strong enough preferences toward specific functionalities that the IS should provide, namely: (a) a functional, user-friendly GUI, (95%), (b) a multiuser-multitasking environment, (90%), (c) a video file as guidance to understand the environment, (79%), (d) a voice file as guidance to understand the environment, (77%) and (e) a presentation with pictures to understand the environment, (63%).

As a result, the IS should have functionalities that provide information, assistance and services to the users of the system.

**B2: The Networking Environment of the IS:** This sub-factor shows interesting results. In particular, as it is shown from the participants answers, not all users have e-mail facilities (B.2.1) and not all users have access via Mini-Syzefxis network (B.2.7). The answers to the rest questions show that users do not have any access to facilities, such as: (a) Synchronous Learning Environment, (B.2.2), (b) Asynchronous Learning Environment, (B.2.3), (c) Web-conference, (B.2.4), (d) Application Sharing System, (B.2.5), and (e) Collaborative Learning System, (B.2.6). According the above, we detect that these users like GUI applications, as well as video, voice or presentation files in a multiuser-multitasking environment. However, despite the fact that, they do not have any access at all the aforementioned services, their answers indicated that they are willing to have all the above possibilities so that they be able to connect with other employees and collaborate with them.

### 3.3    Indicator C: The Workers' Social Past and Current Habits and How These Habits Have Been Changed due to the Evolution of the IS in Their Work Place

This indicator examines the workers' socialization habits, and how they have been changed due to the evolution of the specific IS in their work place. Thus, it is divided into two categories (C1 and C2). The results obtained according to the questionnaire (using the values "Agree" & "Strongly Agree") are as follows:

**C1: Past Habits of the IS Users of the LCHS**
C1.1: I used to be informed through the mass media (84%)
C1.2: I used to communicate by post and telegraph (26%)
C1.3: I used to be informed about my personal interests from the mass media (58%)
C1.4: I used to express my thoughts and concerns by phone63%
C1.5: I used to perform my financial transactions through the relevant organizations (74%)

**C2: Present Habits of the IS Users of the LCHS**
C.2.1: I read news from the Internet (news, technology development, etc.) (79%)
C.2.2: I use e-mail services (58%)
C.2.3: I buy consumer goods from the internet (11%)

C.2.4: I find information about my personal interests by using the Internet (63%)
C.2.5: I search information for consumer products via Internet (68%)
C.2.6: I express my thoughts and concerns in blogs, forums, etc. (11%)
C.2.7: I pay my financial transactions (banking, etc.) via Internet (16%)
C.2.8: I keep up with technological developments through appropriate sites (32%)

Based on the above, we can say, that the current e-socialization of the users is high enough. We can also see the evolution of their habits by comparing the above results.

### 3.4    Indicator D: Health Issues Associated with the Use of the IS

This indicator examines how Healthy the Work Environment (HWE) is, how the users' health is being affected by their working environment. The analysis of the data shows the percentages of the negative answers that concern the following aspects:

D1.1: How does the IS affect the health of the user (68%)
D1.2: What is the impact that the IS has on your health (63%)
D1.3: I am informed by my work about the notion of HWE (100%)
D1.4: I am informed about the necessary exercises to do to avoid "RSI" (89%)
D1.5: I am informed about the specific exercises that are necessary to do for the spinal column (89%)
D1.6: I recycle the printed paper that I do not need (58%)

Based on the above, it should be suggested to the LCHS to inform their users about HWE issues, so that they feel more confident and productive in their environment.

### 3.5    Indicator E: Main Tasks that IS Workers Carry out in Their Work Place

This indicator examines the main tasks that the IS workers of LCHS have to carry out in a daily basis. We have identified 8 main tasks and we asked how often the users execute these tasks, using a 4 Likert scale. Then we associated a number of close-type questions with each task, using a 5 Likert scale, in order to extract more specific information regarding each task. Below, we present the results obtained for each task and their associated questions; here the codes in parentheses represent the tasks and their associated questions, whereas the percentages concern the positive answers.

1. I carry out data entry and data processing (E.A: 95%): (a) The data entry requires many clicks (E.A1: 89%), (b) The data process is functional, effective and reliable (E.A2: 90%), (c) The access in the system is fast (E.A3: 94%), (d) There are unnecessary clicks at the registration process (E.A4: 73%), and (e) The system's response is immediate (E.A5: 94%)
2. I use the capabilities of IS to search for folders / documents files (E.B: 100%): (a) These capabilities cover completely the needs of my office (E.B1: 84%), (b) The data results in forms/reports are presented structured and clearly (E.B2: 90%).
3. I use office applications (E.C: 90%): (a) The computing resources of my PC (CPU) are sufficient for the applications of my office (E.C1: 79%), and (b) There is a direct or indirect notice in case of system failure (E.C2: 68%).

4. I use the IS WEB application (Document Management System) in LCHS (E.D: 58%): (a) There are procedures which control the functioning of the infrastructure and services offered by the IS (E.D1: 63%).
5. I exchange messages between users (E.E: 21%): (a) The exchange of e-mails helps the resolution of problems in my office (E.E1: 53%), and (b) The process of a case becomes easier through exchanging e-mails (E.E2: 68%).
6. I send electronic requests (Tickets) to the IS administrator (E.ST: 10%): (a) I use the phone to report a system error in my office (E.ST1: 79%), (b) I send e-mails (Tickets) to Administrators in order to declare a system fault (E.ST2: 16%).
7. I use the Calendar for due tasks – Reminders (E.Z: 10%): (a) I use the electronic way of the IS to keep future reminders or due tasks. (E.Z1: 10%), and (b) I use the traditional way (handwritten) to keep future reminders or due tasks (E.Z2: 68%).
8. I use other applications/services offered by the IS of LCHS (E.H: 10%).

Based on the above, we can say that, in general, the users carry out their tasks with the IS smoothly.

## 4    Summary and Future Work

In this paper we presented a methodology that analyses a variety of issues that concern the Information System (IS) workers' learning profile. The analysis of these issues shows interesting results and draws important conclusions that can be used to determine the behavior, performance and training needs of IS workers. The ultimate aim of this work is to build a complete analysis plan for determining the learning profile of IS workers. This in turn will be used to identify who needs training as well as to determine employees' readiness for training. It is very important for any organization to focus equal attention on the strengths and weaknesses of its workers' performances, give employees positive reinforcement when they perform well, make its employees aware that their work performance is being monitored continuously, increase management's support, involvement and resource allocation; all in all, take care that employees can receive adequate and timely help and training.

## References

1. Dolog, P., Schäfer, M.: A Framework for Browsing, Manipulating and Maintaining Interoperable Learner Profiles. In: Ardissono, L., Brna, P., Mitrović, A. (eds.) UM 2005. LNCS (LNAI), vol. 3538, pp. 397–401. Springer, Heidelberg (2005)
2. Eraut, M., Hirsh, W.: The Significance of Workplace Learning for Individuals, Groups and Organisations. SKOPE, Oxford & Cardiff Universities (2007)
3. Ley, T., Ulbrich, A., Scheir, P., Lindstaedt, S.N., Kump, B., Albert, D.: Modelling Competencies for supporting Work-integrated Learning in Knowledge Work. Journal of Knowledge Management 12(6), 31–47 (2008)
4. Kordaki, M., Daradoumis, T., Fragidakis, D., Grigoriadou, M.: Collaborative and Adaptive Design Pattern for the 'Students Team Achievement Divisions' Method: An initial implementation within Information Technology Work Place. In: Intelligent Adaptation and Personalization Techniques in Computer-Supported Collaborative Learning. Series "Studies in Computational Intelligence", Springer, Heidelberg (to appear)

# Towards Collaborative Complex Learning Objects by the Virtualization of Collaborative Sessions

Santi Caballé[1], Ian Dunwell[2], Anna Pierri[3], Francesco Zurolo[3], David Gañán[1],
Thanasis Daradoumis[1], and Néstor Mora[1]

[1] Open University of Catalonia, eLearn Center
Roc Boronat, 117, 08018 Barcelona, Spain
{scaballe,dganan,adaradoumis,nemonu}@uoc.edu
[2] Coventry University, Serious Games Institute
Cheetah Road, Coventry, West Midlands, CV1 2TL United Kingdom
IDunwell@cad.coventry.ac.uk
[3] Modelli Matematici e Applicazioni (MoMA, SpA)
via Aldo Moro, 1/P, 84081 Baronissi (SA), Italy
{pierri,zurolo}@momanet.it

**Abstract.** On-line collaborative learning has demonstrated the benefits of using collaborative activities to increase the learning efficacy. However, collaborative learning approaches cannot be applied in every e-learning experience because they require people's presence and collaboration, which is frequently difficult to achieve. In addition, collaborative learning resources lack of authentic interactivity, user empowerment and challenge, thus having a negative effect in learner motivation and engagement. To overcome these limitations, we propose a new paradigm named Collaborative Complex Learning Objects (CC-LO) defined as a special type of learning objects within Virtualized Collaborative Sessions (VCS) with the aim to leverage the knowledge elicited during live sessions of collaborative learning, which are augmented with author-generated information, in order to produce interactive and attractive resources to be played by learners. During the CC-LO execution, a VCS is animated so that learners can observe how avatars discuss and collaborate, how discussion threads grow and how knowledge is constructed, refined and consolidated. Furthermore, learners can interact with the CC-LO in order to modify some parameters observing the consequences and assessing their understanding. The research reported in this paper is currently undertaken within a FP7 European project called ALICE.

**Keywords:** Collaborative Learning, Collaborative Complex Learning Objects, Virtualized Collaborative Sessions.

## 1    Introduction

On-line collaborative learning is a mature research field in the educational domain dedicated to improve teaching and learning with the help of modern ICT [1]. Collaborative learning is represented by a set of educational approaches involving joint

M.D. Lytras et al. (Eds.): WSKS 2011, CCIS 278, pp. 344–350, 2013.
© Springer-Verlag Berlin Heidelberg 2013

intellectual effort by learners, or learners and teachers together [2]. Collaborative learning activities vary widely, but most of them are centered in students' exploration or application of the course material, not simply the teacher's presentation or explication of it. However, many researchers [1], [2], [3] argue that students must be meaningfully engaged in the learning resources for effective learning to occur. This lack of engagement is especially evident in collaborative learning content and can be attributed to the lack of (i) real interactivity (in many cases the only interaction available is to click on the "next" button to obtain the next message in a discussion forum); (ii) challenging collaborative tools, which fail to stimulate learners, making the collaborative experience unattractive and discouraging progression; (iii) empowerment, as learner expects to be in control of their own collaborative learning experiences.

To overcome these quoted limitations of current collaborative learning systems, we focus on defining a new type of Learning Object (LO) called Collaborative Complex Learning Object (CC-LO) embedded into a Virtualized Collaborative Session (VCS). A VCS is a registered collaboration session augmented by alternative flows, additional content, etc., during an authoring phase (subsequent to the registration phase). The VCS can be interactive and animated (by movies or comic strips) and learners can observe how knowledge is constructed, refined and consolidated. CC-LOs include also assessment, collaboration and communication features to enrich the learning experience provided by the VCS. The VCS containing the CC-LOs is eventually packed and stored as learning objects for further reuse so that individual learners can leverage the benefits from live sessions of collaborative learning enriched with high quotes of interaction, challenge and empowerment.

Focusing specifically on the objectives of a FP7 European project called ALICE[1] currently undertaken, in this paper we discuss on the notion and nature of a Collaborative Complex Learning Object embedded into the concept of Virtualized Collaborative Sessions. To this end, firstly in Section 2, the concept of a Learning Object is defined and extended to define a CC-LO. In Section 3, a methodological approach is provided that addresses how CC-LOs are created, managed, and executed. In Section 4 a definition and prototypes components of a VCS are provided in order to create and execute a VCS system containing CC-LOs. For evaluation purposes, these prototype components are technically tested by a proof of concept in Section 5. Section 6 concludes the paper by highlighting the key concepts covered and outlining ongoing and future work.

## 2    From LO to CC-LO: Definitions and Purpose

While the definition of a CC-LO may be new, the concept is reflected in a wide range of existing systems and studies which have looked at the challenges of repurposing LOs. An initial definition of LO was given by [4] as self-contained and reusable elements of learning. Furthermore, a number of other definitions have been put forward by researchers, such as [5] who defines a LO as "any digital resource that can be reused to support learning", while [6] emphasizes the need for LO to have learning goals and be reusable.

---

[1] ALICE project web site: http://www.aliceproject.eu

Following these principles, the notion of the CC-LO can be described as an extension of the LO paradigm by asking two fundamental questions: (i) what makes a learning object complex? (ii) what enables a learning object to be collaborative? As for the first question, there are two principle ways in which collaboration occurs [7]:

- Collaboration in creation (several platforms exist for the collaborative creation of LOs by educators).
- Collaboration in use, where a collaborative learning object is capable of responding to and facilitating interaction by multiple simultaneous learners.

As for the second question, LO complexity is considered at four levels:

- Applicability: A trait common to pedagogic as well as technical consideration is how widely an LO can be repurposed across technical domains.
- Evaluability: From the need for content rating and assessment, CC-LOs must support evaluability in pedagogic and technical terms.
- Internal dynamicism: The concept of creating 'intelligent' learning objects which are themselves able to adapt to context, removing the need for repurposing work.
- Composability: Need to have learning objects more easily composable so that they disassociate learning objectives from implementation issues.

In practice, there are common attributes specific to CC-LOs:

- Self-assessment by Q&A, alternative flows (non-linear paths through CC-LOs), relevant assessment of each path, and well-defined dependencies to other CC-LO.
- Animated and evolution over time allowing learners to observe how avatars discuss and collaborate and how knowledge is constructed, refined and consolidated.
- Instantiable and interactive by modifying some parameters and observing the effects and assessing the understanding.

## 3    Methodologies to Create, Manage and Execute CC-LO

Technologists have made many attempts to provide better tools for content creation, management, and execution of LOs to educators, but the transition from the role of content creator to moderator, generates inherent resistance in the educator [8]. The LO are usually customized and adapted for learners needs while the educators adaptation needs are not considered.

Commonly, methods for creating LO include mining existing information to construct learning objects autonomously and participatory techniques [9], which build upon the use of the creation process itself as a means for learning, instilling learners with increased engagement as a result of deeper engagement within the educational process [10]. However, learners are not often the best LO creators and the resulting LOs require careful validation to ensure quality.

Recently, the management of learning objects has benefited from semantic technology, which supports both bottom-up processes such as support registration, management, and sharing methods. Also, creates high-level elements such as courseware and e-learning tools autonomously, with remarkable benefits of ubiquity and interoperability, in-line with tutors needs.

The execution of learning objects has previously been achieved through methods such as the SCORM Run-Time Environment [11], allowing for user customization, adaptivity, high degree of dynamicism and evolution of learning objects over time across a range of formats. Overall, creating learning objects in an executable form represents a step-change in the context and autonomy in which they can be deployed, and reflects the transition of LOs from pedagogic material to semantic data constructs.

Considering all these approaches, widespread usage of CC-LOs implies conformance to core SCORM standards and representation formats, with CC elements added as independent extensions. Incorporation into more sophisticated systems would require the CC-LO to be enabled with the information required to generate the high-level tools required for collaboration, and support for complexity. As initial approach, existing methodologies for CC-LO can be grouped under three headings:

- Educator-centric: the educator assumes the role of author, moderator, and deployer of the CC-LO.
- Technology-centric: creation, management, and execution are handled by technology.
- Learner-centric: these methods advocate techniques such as participatory design to allow learners to be involved in the creation and management of CC-LOs.

# 4    Definition and Purpose of Virtualized Collaborative Sessions

Perhaps the best definition of a VCS can be achieved through analogy to a computer program, where CC-LOs exist as objects within the code, and the VCS is the overall execution of the program. As it runs, CC-LOs are created, evolve over time, and are subsequently disposed of. At termination, the VCS becomes ready to 'run' with new instances of CC-LOs, repeating the learning cycle to a new group of learners. This is illustrated in Fig. 1.

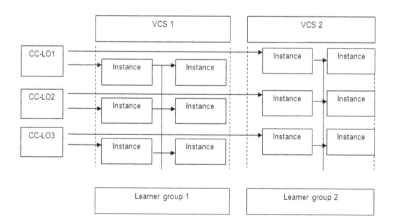

**Fig. 1.** Execution of CC-LO instances within VCS programs

A first approach to a VCS system is depicted in Fig. 2. The VCS is intended to be compatible with collaborative sessions in general, such as chats and forums, in order to create CC-LO as general as possible. For this purpose, the input of VCS system is a file with collaborative session data in a common format called Collaborative Session Markup Language (CSML) based on XML. For each source of collaborative session the data is converted into CSML by a specific plug-in and then processed to create a Virtual Collaborative Session Complex Learning Object (VCSCLO), containing information about scenes, characters, and other artifacts used during the visualization of this CC-LO (VCS Viewer). A VCSCLO can also be edited with a VCS Editor allowing for changing scenes order, adding assessment scenes, defining workflow, etc.

A VCS is a registered collaboration session augmented by alternative flows, additional content, etc. during an authoring phase. The VCS is animated and learners can observe how people discuss and collaborate, how discussion threads grow and how knowledge is constructed, refined and consolidated. Overall, a VCS produces an event in which CC-LOs are applied and consumed by learners, sessions evolve ("animate") over time, and the ultimate end-user interactions with CC-LOs are handled.

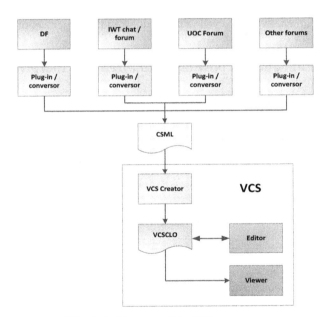

**Fig. 2.** Architecture of the VCS system

## 5     Prototyping a CC-LO Embedded into a VCS System

A VCS prototype with an embedded CC-LO was built as a proof of concept (Fig. 3). The VCS transforms a live discussion forum into an animated storyboard and shows[2] how people discuss and how the collaborative session evolves ("animates") over time.

---

[2] The demo can be watched at http://www.youtube.com/watch?v=-cOWewPjkF8

The resulting CC-LO is ready to be played and consumed by learners. To this end, the VCS containing the CC-LO is packed and stored for further reuse as any LO so that individual learners can be benefitted from live sessions of collaborative learning of others and in turn leverage the knowledge constructed collaboratively. Eventually, the CC-LO becomes an attractive learning resource so that learners become more motivated and engaged in the collaborative activities.

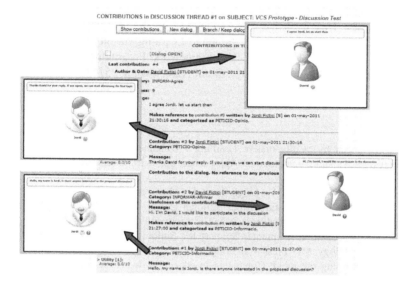

**Fig. 3.** Virtualization of a live collaborative session. Each text contribution of the discussion thread is converted into multimedia forming an animated storyboard.

## 6    Conclusions and Ongoing Work

This paper shows the current research work undertaken within a FP7 European project named ALICE devoted to provide on-line collaborative learning with authentic interactivity, challenging tools and user empowerment with the ultimate aim to influence learner motivation and engagement. To this end, a new type of LO called CC-LO is introduced embedded into a VCS prototype that registers live collaborative sessions and produces an animated CC-LO so that learners can observe how people collaborate and how knowledge is constructed.

Ongoing work is the evaluation of the VCS prototype in the real context of learning of the Open University of Catalonia[3]. Experimentation and validation will be conducted in on-line courses of UOC in order to provide attractive and challenging CC-LOs to support the collaborative learning activities, in particular in-class discussions. Moreover, current work within the ALICE project is the development of an editor tool

---

[3] The Open University of Catalonia (UOC) is found at: http://www.uoc.edu

to augment the VCS with author-generated information. Thus, e-assessment scenes are added to the VCS, such as tests (with optional jumps to storyboard scenes) as well as supporting videos to be connected with scene parts according to the dialogue time-line. In addition, tutors will be able to edit the storyboard by cutting scenes, modifying involved characters, and selecting correct emotional states, dialogues and connected concepts. The aim is to provide learners with CC-LOs with high quotes of interactivity, challenge and empowerment.

**Acknowledgements.** This work has been supported by the European Commission under the Collaborative Project ALICE "Adaptive Learning via Intuitive/Interactive, Collaborative and Emotional System", VII Framework Programme, Theme ICT-2009.4.2 (Technology-Enhanced Learning), Grant Agreement n. 257639.

# References

1. What do you mean by "Collaborative Learning"? Dillenbourg, P. (ed.) Collaborative Learning. Cognitive and Computational Approaches, pp. 1–19. Elsevier Science, Oxford (1999)
2. Goodsell, A., Maher, M., Tinto, V., Leigh Snith, B., MacGregor, J.: Collaborative Learning: A Sourcebook for Higher Education. National Center on Postsecondary Teaching, Learning, and Assessment, Pennsylvania State University (1992)
3. Stahl, G.: Group Cognition: Computer Support for Building Collaborative Knowledge. Acting with Technology. MIT Press, Cambridge (2006)
4. Gerard, R.W.: Shaping the mind: Computers in education. In: N. A. Sciences, Applied Science and Technological Progress (1967)
5. Wiley, A.D.: Connecting learning objects to instructional design theory: A definition, a metaphor and a taxonomy. In: Wiley, D.A. (ed.) The Instructional Use of Learning Objects. Association for Educational Communications and technology, Bloomington (2001)
6. Polsani, R.P.: Use and abuse of reusable learning objects. Journal of Digital Information 164 (1997)
7. Fuentes, L.M., Arteaga, J.M., Álvarez Rodriguez, F.: A Methodology for Design Collaborative Learning Objects. In: 8th IEEE International Conference on Advanced Learning Technologies (2008)
8. Mosley, P.: A taxonomy for learning object technology. J. Comput. Small Coll. 20(3), 204–216 (2005)
9. Singh, R.G., Bernard, M., Gardler, R.: Creating sharable learning objects from existing digital course content. In: 31st International Symposium on Computer Architecture, p. 8. ACM, Munich (2004)
10. Abad, C.L.: Learning through creating learning objects: experiences with a class project in a distributed systems course. In: 13th Annual Conference on Innovation and Technology in Computer Science Education, pp. 255–259. ACM, Madrid (2008)
11. Costagliola, G., Ferrucci, F., Fuccella, V.: Scorm run-time environment as a service. In: 6th International Conference on Web Engineering, pp. 103–110. ACM, Palo Alto (2006)

# Towards an Ontology to Model and Represent Collaborative Learning Data

Jordi Conesa, Santi Caballé, David Gañán, and Josep Prieto

Open University of Catalonia, Dept. of Computer Science
Roc Boronat, 117, 08018 Barcelona, Spain
{jconesac,scaballe,dganan,jprieto}@uoc.edu

**Abstract.** In this paper we propose a methodology for modeling and representing the collaborative learning data coming from collaborative sessions. To this end, we first provide a newly created ontology called Collaborative Session Conceptual Schema for modeling knowledge from online collaborative sessions within Web forums. We describe the knowledge this ontology needs to know and its relation with other well known ontologies. The data collected in our ontology is to be transformed later on into useful knowledge about what is happening during the collaboration. To make this step possible, the methodology is enriched with a dialogue-based model to represent specific collaborative interaction data from our ontology. This model is based on primitive exchange moves found in any forum posts, which are then categorized at different description levels with the aim to effectively collect and classify the type and intention of forum posts. The research reported in this paper is currently undertaken within a FP7 European project called ALICE.

**Keywords:** Collaborative Learning, Ontologies, Collaborative Session Conceptual Schema, Collaborative Session Markup Language, Knowledge Modeling and Representation.

## 1 Introduction

There has been a great effort in the semantic web community in order to provide specifications, standards and ontologies in order to facilitate semantic processes in the web [1]. In the particular field of eLearning, quite a few ontologies [1,2] and related standards [3] concerning the representation of CSCL have been defined so far. Representative approaches [4] propose to use the actions performed in the collaborative learning system to build a high-level representation of the process of collection and analysis of the interaction data. In [5] a theory-oriented interaction analysis approach based on theories of collaborative learning is provided. However, the social processes happening behind real collaborative learning practices are very complex and subjective and thus they fall far from a holistic view proposed by standards and ontologies. As [2] states, with a well-defined ontology structure, collaborative learning can accumulate the knowledge representation of learning objects and their use, including participant background, instruction designs, learning activities and outcomes, etc.

M.D. Lytras et al. (Eds.): WSKS 2011, CCIS 278, pp. 351–356, 2013.
© Springer-Verlag Berlin Heidelberg 2013

In order to support the specification of the collaboration activities that occur during the learning experience we can use some of the actual specifications and standards. Some of the most relevant specifications for collaborative learning are:

- Learning Object Metadata (LOM)[1] is a standard that allows for describing learning resources by a set of metadata. The main objective of this standard is to improve discovery, management, sharing and reusability of learning resources within and between different repositories. LOM is compatible with Dublin Core[2], which is another of the relevant metadata specifications.
- Friend Of A Friend (FOAF)[3] specification describes a language devoted to represent the linking information of people and information using the Web. FOAF describes the world using simple ideas inspired by the Web. FOAF allows describing people, groups and documents.
- Semantically-Interlinked Online Communities (SIOC)[4] provides a Semantic Web ontology for representing rich data from the Social Web in RDF: the SIOC Core Ontology. It can be used to express information contained within community sites (weblogs, message boards, wikis, etc) in a simple and extensible way. SIOC is commonly used in conjunction with the FOAF vocabulary for expressing personal profile and social networking information.

Our aim is to take advantage of these standards as much as possible for the purpose of modeling and representing information and knowledge of collaborative learning in the context of online forums. We then collect and classify the interaction occurred and registered in the context of online forums according to the classes and relationships of our ontology. This fact can significantly improve the way a collaborative system used for learning and instruction can collect all the necessary information produced from the user-user and user-system interaction in an efficient manner [6]. To this end, second section of this paper presents an ontology that represents the collaboration activities that have been realized using online forums. Third section shows how the information generated in collaborative learning forums can be captured and classified at several description levels. Section four concludes the paper by summarizing the main ideas and outlining ongoing and future work.

The ultimate aim of this approach is to provide an efficient and robust computational methodology that enables the effective collection and classification of data as part of the research undertaken in a FP7 European project called ALICE[5].

## 2    An Ontology for Representation of Collaborative Learning Sessions within Forums

The created ontology is named Collaborative Session Conceptual Schema (CS[2]) and will allow for representing the collaborative sessions several actors have enjoyed in

---

[1]  http://ltsc.ieee.org/wg12/

[2]  http://dublincore.org/

[3]  http://www.foaf-project.org/

[4]  http://sioc-project.org/

[5]  ALICE project web site: http://www.aliceproject.eu

learning experiences. The specification of such ontology is performed by means of a RDF language, which we call Collaborative Session Markup Language (CSML).

Our first approach is to use an existing specification as starting point, and add or change elements as needed. Since SIOC specification fits quite well our needs for describing collaborative sessions, we will reuse its RDF ontologies as a basis for the $CS^2$ ontology. Fig. 1 shows the main class structure of the SIOC core ontology.

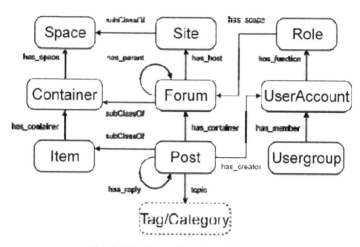

**Fig. 1.** SIOC Core Ontology Classes

## 2.1   $CS^2$ Origins

As said before, $CS^2$ is based on SIOC specification so it contains some of the elements defined on this and other related specifications, such as FOAF (Friend of a friend) or Dublin Core. However, some classes and properties of SIOC specification are not potentially useful to our domain. In this subsection we enumerate the elements from SIOC that are applicable to our ontology.

**SIOC Ontologies.** SIOC Core ontology includes classes relevant to our purpose of modeling data coming from collaborative learning sessions (e.g. discussion forums), such as *Forum, Item, Post, Thread*, and so on. In addition, SIOC types ontology defines classes that represent different kinds of Containers, Forums, Items and Posts. Some examples of these classes are: *Address Book, Image Gallery, Wiki, Chat Channel, Message Board*, etc. For the sake of simplicity, we will work at the level of forums and posts at this stage, but will consider using their subclasses in further versions. The SIOC types ontology also includes two classes used to define post topics: *Category* and *Tag. Category* is defined as a subclass of a SKOS Concept. For simplicity, literal topics will be used in CSML, but having the possibility to extend the language in the future with these two classes.

**Other Ontologies.** SIOC specification contemplates using some elements from other ontologies. Moreover, some of the SIOC elements are defined as subclasses or sub properties of that ontologies like FOAF or Dublin Core. For the sake of simplicity, $CS^2$ will adjust to the subset of SIOC defined in the previous section. Therefore, we need to include in our schema concepts from other ontologies that will take into account these new mechanisms, such as the class *Person* from FOAF that can help describe elements of *UserAccount* type with properties such as *firstName* and *lastName*, and also some elements from Dublin Core Terms that must be considered to include (e.g. *date*, *title*, *description* or *subject*).

## 2.2    $CS^2$ Schema

Previous section described the knowledge the $CS^2$ needs to know and the ontologies used in order to represent such knowledge. We have identified the building blocks from a schema structure of our ontology that allow for storing and working with collaborative session data. We can see in Fig. 2 the class hierarchy of the ontology.

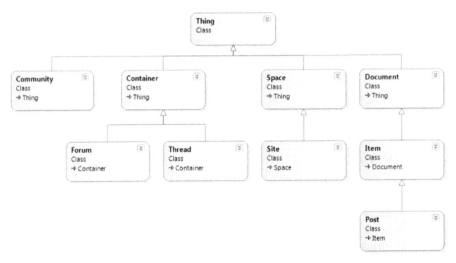

**Fig. 2.** Excerpt of the $CS^2$ Class hierarchy

# 3    Towards the Use of the $CS^2$ ontology

We now proceed with filling the ontology instances with the appropriate data collected and classified during the collaboration. This data will be afterwards transformed into useful knowledge about what is happening during the collaboration by means of analysis techniques (see [6] for a complete description).

To this end, we base the data collection and classification into our ontology on the interaction occurred and registered in the context of online forums. The focus is on student interaction among peers driven by posts in online forums, which is the cornerstone of this approach. Participants need indeed to interact with each other to plan an activity, distribute tasks, explain, clarify, give information and opinions, elicit information, evaluate and contribute to the resolution of problematic issues, and so on.

Next subsection deals with this issue by briefly presenting a methodological approach of a process of modeling interaction data from collaborative learning activity.

### 3.1    A Methodology to Model and Represent Collaborative Learning Interaction Data

The interaction model proposed here is based on the integration of several models and methods: the Negotiation Linguistic Exchange Model [8] a model of Discourse Contributions [9] and the types of learning actions underlying a participant turn [10]. The structure of a long interaction is constructed cooperatively by using the exchange as the basic unit for communicating knowledge. Following [8], three general exchange structure categories are considered: *give-information exchange, elicit-information exchange* and *raise-an-issue exchange*, which consist of different types of moves [11] and describe a generic discourse goal (see the complete model in [7]).

These three general types of exchanges represent standard discourse structures for handling information and suggest a certain type of knowledge building, as a result of giving and eliciting information or working out a solution on an issue set up. These discursive structures enable the participants to take turns, share information, exchange views, monitor the work done and plan ahead. Most importantly, they provide a means to represent and operationalize the cognitive product at individual level, that is, the way the reasoning process is distributed over the participants as it is shared in a collaborative discourse.

In overall, our model annotates and examines a variety of elements that contribute to the understanding of the nature of the collaborative interactions, such as the students' passivity, proactivity, reactivity as well as the effectiveness and impact of their contributions to the overall goal of the discussion. The aim is to provide both a deeper understanding of the actual discussion process and a more objective assessment of individual and group activity.

## 4    Conclusions and Ongoing Work

This paper shows the current research work undertaken within a FP7 European project ALICE devoted to provide on-line collaborative learning with authentic interactivity, challenging tools and user empowerment with the ultimate aim to influence learner motivation and engagement. To this end, a new ontology called $CS^2$ based on SIOC and FOAF has been created for modeling knowledge from online collaborative sessions within Web forums. The data collected in our ontology is to be afterwards transformed later on into useful knowledge about what is happening during the collaboration. In order to do so, a methodology based on a dialogue model is proposed to modeling and representing specific collaborative interaction data from our ontology.

Currently, we are exploiting our $CS^2$ ontology and CSML language within the ALICE project so as to model and represent in common format collaborative learning data coming from different data sources (i.e., discussion forums). Then, we will process the CSML format as an input to transform text-based forums into virtualized collaborative sessions with animated and interactive storyboards where learners can observe how avatars discuss and collaborate and how knowledge is constructed. The aim is to leverage the benefits of collaborative learning in on-line settings where collaboration is difficult to achieve, and eventually provide advanced collaborative learning resources with authentic interactivity, user empowerment and challenge, thus positively influencing learner motivation and engagement into the learning process

Furthermore, ongoing work is to expand the ontology to represent collaboration information from other sources. Thereafter, we plan to integrate the ontology within a virtual campus and apply the presented methodology in order to automatically infer the collaboration information generated during the virtual learning processes. Then, a set of services that use the collaboration information will be created in order to improve the learning experience of learners.

**Acknowledgements.** This work has been supported by the European Commission under the Collaborative Project ALICE "Adaptive Learning via Intuitive/Interactive, Collaborative and Emotional System", VII Framework Programme, Theme ICT-2009.4.2 (Technology-Enhanced Learning), Grant Agreement n. 257639 and by the IN3 institute.

# References

1. Wilson, R.: The role of ontologies in teaching and learning. TechWatch Reports (2004)
2. Babič, F., Wagner, J., Paralič, J.: The role of ontologies in collaborative systems. In: 6th International Symposium on Applied Machine Intelligence and Informatics, pp. 119–123. IEEE (2008)
3. Berlanga, A., Garcia, F.J.: Learning technology specifications: semantic objects for adaptive learning environments. International Journal of Learning Technology 1, 458–472 (2005)
4. Barros, B., Verdejo, M.F., Read, T., Mizoguchi, R.: Applications of a Collaborative Learning Ontology. In: Coello Coello, C.A., de Albornoz, Á., Sucar, L.E., Battistutti, O.C. (eds.) MICAI 2002. LNCS (LNAI), vol. 2313, pp. 301–310. Springer, Heidelberg (2002)
5. Inaba, A., Supnithi, T., Ikeda, M., Mizoguchi, R., Toyoda, J.: An overview of learning goal ontology. In: Workshop Analysis and Modelling of Collaborative Learning Interactions at the European Conference on Artificial Intelligence, ECAI 2000 (2000)
6. Caballé, S., Daradoumis, T., Xhafa, F., Conesa, J.: Enhancing Knowledge Management in Online Collaborative Learning. International Journal of Software Engineering and Knowledge Engineering 20(4), 485–497 (2010)
7. Caballé, S., Daradoumis, T., Xhafa, X., Juan, A.: Providing Effective Feedback, Monitoring and Evaluation to On-line Collaborative Learning Discussions. Computers in Human Behavior 27(4), 1372–1381 (2011)
8. Martin, J.R.: English text: System and structure. John Benjamins, Philadelphia (1992)
9. Clark, H.H., Schaefer, E.F.: Contributing to discourse. Cognitive Science 13, 259–294 (1989)
10. Self, J.A.: Dormobile: A vehicle for metacognition. In: Chan, T.W., Self, J.A. (eds.) Emerging Computer Technologies in Education, AACE, Charlottesville (1995)
11. Schwartz, D.L.: The productive agency that drives collaborative learning. In: Collaborative Learning: Cognitive and Computational Approaches, pp. 197–218 (1999)

# ICTs in Special Education:
# A Review

Athanasios S. Drigas and Rodi-Eleni Ioannidou

NCSR DEMOKRITOS,
Institute of Informatics and Telecommunications
Net Media Lab,
Ag. Paraskevi, 15310, Athens, Greece
dr@iit.demokritos.gr,
elena.ioan@hotmail.com

**Abstract.** The use of information communication technologies (ICTs) in a special educational needs (SEN) environment has gathered accumulative evidence around it during the last decade (2001-2010). In many settings ICT has become an important element of the learning and teaching process. ICT assessment tools can better recognize and integrate learning difficulties across students, while computer-based intervention tools can play a significant role in a child's life. In this report we provide a brief overview of the most representative articles for applications used for assessment and intervention purpose after classifying them according to the areas of needs they serve.

**Keywords:** ICT, special education, sensory and physical impairments, learning difficulties, assessment, intervention.

## 1    Introduction

Over the last decades the tremendous development of ICTs are changing the world and the way education is conducted. It is probably fair to say that the use of ICTs affects every aspect of our daily life. The impact of ICT in education has its roots back in the 1970s, where the governments in several countries started to realize the need of using technology in order to improve the relevance and quality of education [1]. ICT is considered a mean to bridge the gap between different groups of people such as the group of people with special educational needs. Recently, there has been a growing number of researches that supports the fact that, ICTs and assistive technologies more generally, enable people with special educational needs to lead more fulfilled lives [1], [2].

The term 'special educational needs' covers a range of problems which can cause difficulties in learning. Even though there have been many definitions over the years, comparative studies show that the term 'special educational needs' can mean different things to different countries [3]. One of the most dominant categorizations that recommends a graduated approach to educating learners in need of special provision is the one introduced below. 'The areas of needs' as defined in the 2001 SEN Code of

M.D. Lytras et al. (Eds.): WSKS 2011, CCIS 278, pp. 357–364, 2013.
© Springer-Verlag Berlin Heidelberg 2013

Practice are: Communication and Interaction, Sensory and/or Physical, Cognition and Learning, Behaviour, Emotional and Social Development [4]. Defining the area of 'Special Needs' has been a widely discussed issue. Titles as Learning Disabilities or Learning Disorders are also used to describe a group of the population that have problems in their school performance and maybe later in their lifetimes.

Even though the use of ICTs has been acknowledged for at least three decades, the first important program studies to support students with SEN start to appear amongst the latest years [1]. During the last decade there is a significant number of studies that address how ICTs are being used in practice and what impact they have on the life of children and adults with special educational needs. Dominant issues in the ICT literature report the benefits of alternative communication, assistive or enabling technology, internet applications, virtual environments, teacher education and technology integration [2]. In this report we will focus on the use the most popular applications that are used for assessment and intervention purposes of specific difficulties. They provide school staff, specialists and parents with the possibility to employ different ICT strategies which might lead to an easier understanding of children's learning differences. Moreover, several benefits are limited cost, greater precision, savings in time and labour [5]. For the past decade there has been conducted great progress in the design and the development of ICT software programs to provide students with special educational needs equal access to education [6]. In order for these applications to be presented we created a framework which consists of two main categories. The first one includes diagnostic and intervention tools regarding people with sensory and physical impairments, while the next one includes the major domains of learning difficulties.

## 2     Sensory and Physical Impairments

Students with sensory and physical impairments have different capabilities and needs. For this group of learners it is often necessary the use of assistive devices such as touch screens, trackerballs, joysticks, keyboards and mouse alternatives [2]. In order for an ICT intervention tool to be effective it is always best to discuss before implementing any adaptations to practice.

Fujiyoshi et al. (2010) introduced a testing system with a digital audio player and document structure diagrams for newly blind users who have difficulties in Braille or print. The system gives them the chance to take the National Center Test for university admission. This study showed that the audio tests results were almost similar to normal-print-format and braille-format tests in score [7].

Choi and Walker (2010) developed the Digitizer Auditory Graph, a sonification software tool which allows visually impaired users to take an image of a line graph with an optical input device (e.g. webcam) and then hear an auditory graph of the digitized graph image. This tool helps both teachers and students, since teachers have difficulties in explaining graphs and visually impaired students' access to graphs is limited.   Experimental results suggest that the users are able to understand the auditory output while using the optical input helps them create graphs easier and faster [8].

Drigas et al., in 2005 presented a Learning System designed for deaf and hard of hearing people. This prototype system offers Greek Sign Language videos in correspondence to all texts in the learning environment. The students for the first time have the opportunity to learn in their own language, the Greek sign language. The system includes also the involvement of the teacher and the administrator. Through appropriate training the users evaluate the knowledge they gained and they continue in further study [9].

In 2008 Drigas et al., presented 'Dedalos' project which deals with the teaching of the English language as a second language to deaf people. In developing this system, the researchers created a platform which includes methods such as distant linguistic training and an educational e-content designed specifically for the needs of this group of people. The project promotes a complete support system for the education of the deaf and hearing impaired individuals while at the same time opens the way for the inclusion of the deal and hearing impaired Greek students in Greece [10].

In 2008 Chin et al., introduced an integrated electromyogram and eye-gaze tracking cursor control system for individuals with motor disabilities. This system was designed for users who are unable to use their hands due to spinal dysfunction or other afflictions. The basic components of the system are the electromyogram (EMG) signals from muscles in the face and point-of-gaze coordinates produced by an eye-gaze tracking system (EGT). Additionally EMG-EGT system enables users to modify cursor position pixel by pixel and it provides a reliable left-click operation. However, the results of the EMG-EGT system was evaluated inside a laboratory environment, further experiments need to be conducted with learners with motor difficulties [11].

# 3    Learning Difficulties

## 3.1    Learners with Autistic Spectrum Disorders

One category within the group of 'Developmental Disorders' is known as Autistic Spectrum Disorders (ASD). ASD is a set of developmental problems that affect the social and communication skills. The latest years, important attempts have been made in the field of ICT assessment. Moreover, intervention is considered to increase the quality of life and functional independence of a child with ASD.

Ozonoff et al., (2004) developed the Cambridge Neuropsychological Test Automated Battery (CANTAB), a computer-administered set of neuropsychological tests designed to examine specific components of cognition. These tests examine the integrity of frontal functions since several studies support involvement of frontal cortex in autism. This method was tested to 79 participants with autism and 70 typical controls and the results indicated that the autism group had difficulties in planning efficiency and extradimensional shifting relative to controls comparing to the control group. Based on the results of this study, they argued that there is frontal lobe involvement in autism [12].

Vera et al., (2007) presented the use of 'Real Time' graphic applications as intervention tools in the educational process for people with learning difficulties.

Their main features are the use of 3D graphics, the user only needs a computer (with screen, keyboard, mouse and joystic) and he/she can interact with the tool easily. They can be used from people who have specific problems in attention, perception, memory, people with down syndrome and autism. These 'Real Time' applications give the users the chance to understand and control abstract concepts, very difficult to represent in real world [13].

## 3.2    Learners with Reading-Writing Difficulties and Difficulties in Mathematics

Proficient reading and writing is one of the major tasks a young learner will achieve in his or her lifetime. It is a process that depends upon a wide range of component skills and needs several years to master fully. Difficulties in mathematics affect also children with or without special needs. An early identification of these difficulties is of major importance in order to use later the appropriate intervention methods that will help the child overcome his or her difficulties.

One of the most widely used software tools is the Cognitive Profiling System (CoPS), a computerized psychometric assessment system which identifies the cognitive strengths and difficulties for ages 4-8. CoPS consists of eight tests in the form of games and a total assessment time of no longer than twenty minutes. The students are tested in sequential and associative memory, auditory and color discrimination and phonological awareness. CoPS is used across the UK, Scotland and British schools around the world [5], [14].

Lange et al., (2009) presented the effects of using an assistive software homophone tool on students with reading difficulties who were at least one year behind in reading. The homophone tool is used to point errors in learners' own writing. The pupils who participate in the research used Microsoft Word on a Windows-based laptop PC as the platform for accessing proofreading passages. Three groups were used to evaluate the effect of homophone tool by reading the passages under three conditions; with the homophone tool, with homophones highlighted only, or with no help. The different results amongst the three groups indicated that highlighting improve students' performance (14.6% improvement from no help) and offering homophonic choices could lead to additional benefits [15].

Starcic et al., in 2010 present the findings of the use of SEVERI, an e-learning environment for students who have difficulties with reading, writing and perceiving. It includes tools such as guidance messages, a learning diary, calendar, library, tasks, materials and group-specific discussions. The SEVERI project was adapted to the education context of five countries. This research supports the fact that SEVERI provides students guidance in their learning when at the same time helps teachers to improve the planning and organization of their teaching. In addition it supports networking and co-operation between specialists and parents [16].

In 2006 Wilson et al., developed an adaptive computer game for intervention of dyscalculia, 'The Number Race'. This software aims at training children on an entertaining numeral comparison task by introducing problems adapted to the performance level of every individual. According to the authors' study this method was tested by using mathematical simulation and by a group of students with difficulties in mathematics. The results indicated that this software application could be effective in the remediation of dyscalculia, at least for children aged 7–8 and under [17].

### 3.3    Dyslexic Learners

One of the most common and most studied types of Developmental Disorders is the difficulty in reading as well as in spelling and writing, known as dyslexia. The Code of Practice highlights the importance of an evidence-based diagnosis and provides also the framework for all the professionals to examine and identify students' needs through the use of assessment tools [4]. Recently, the use of technology provides school staff the opportunity to engage in identification and intervention tools.

Lucid Adult Development Screening (Lads) was introduced by Singleton et al., in 2002. Lads is developed to screen for dyslexia from age sixteen and older in different settings (e.g. schools, colleges). Areas such as speeded lexical access, memory, phonological coding are examined in an approximately twenty minutes short test. It is a self-administered test and it is currently used in over one thousand establishments [18], [19].

Gregor et al., (2003) developed 'Seeword', a word processing environment which assist dyslexic computer users when producing and reading text. The initial prototype was designed in Microsoft Wordtm version 7 in 'word basic', the built in macro language. The program has been tested on dyslexic school students aged 14-16 years and the experimental results have indicated that they were able to read standard texts from a screen more accurately by using 'Seeword' [20].

### 3.4    Learners with Difficulties in Memory

Memory skills of children with special needs have been a domain of great research for professionals over the latest years. There is evidence that shows that poor memory skills characterize children failing to progress normally in different areas of needs [21], [22].

Alloway in 2007 presented the 'Automated Working Memory Assessment' (AWMA), a standarised computerized tool. This tool enables teachers and psychologists to assess working memory skills with a user-friendly interface. AWMA includes three levels of assessment.  AWMA Screener is designed for students with suspected working memory difficulties, AWMA: Short Form (AWMA-S) is used for screening learners who are suspected to have memory deficits, but the specific area of their difficulties is not known and AWMA: Long Form (AWMA-L) is suitable for confirmation of working memory problems for learners identified as having working memory problems in the classroom. The results of AWMA's use suggest that working memory skills in individuals with memory deficits are relatively stable over the course of the school year. There was also a high degree of concurrence in performance between the AWMA and the WISC-IV Working Memory Index [23].

Van der Molen et al., (2010) created the 'Odd Yellow' training, a computer-based working memory tool to train adolescents with mild to borderline intellectual disabilities. In the 'Odd Yellow' method a sequence of three similar looking images is shown on the computer screen. One of the three figures is slightly different called the 'odd-one-out' while the other two are identical. They are all drawn in black apart from one of the two identical shapes, which is yellow. The user has to recreate the location of the odd-one-out and the location of the yellow figure shape. Experimental results showed improvement of students' working memory on several outcome measures [24].

## 4    Conclusions

This scoping study drew upon some of the most representative studies over the last decade which exploiting ICT, could facilitate the life of learners - students with special educational needs and the people around them as teachers, educators parents etc. ICT is increasingly seen as a tool in terms of creating independent learning environments, ensuring access to the curriculum and enhancing the social inclusion of all individuals. Given the multitude of manifestations of special educational needs, we attempted to examine various articles-studies for software applications regarding both assessment and intervention processes. Computer-based assessment appears to help teachers, the professionals involved as well as parents to understand deeper and to point the needs of every child. In addition, computerized intervention tools could be of great benefit since they can be used in school and home settings in a way that they promote the quality of offered education as well as self-advocacy. However, further research needs to be conducted in order to make sure that every learner has access to technology. Adaptations have to be made in relation to equity, ethnicity, culture and language for an effective delivery of technology services. Understanding the rights and needs of every child and providing a good quality of teaching, assessment and intervention via ICTs, are the most important factors to help individuals ensure access to appropriate learning and life skills programs.

## References

1. Stevens, C.: Information and communication technology, special educational needs and schools: a historical perspective of UK government initiatives. In: Florian, L., Hegarty, J. (eds.) ICT and Special Educational Needs: a Tool for Inclusion, pp. 21–34. Open University Press, Buckingham (2004)
2. Williams, P., Jamali, H.R., Nicholas, D.: Using ICT with people with special education needs: what the literature tell us. Aslib Proceedings 58(4), 330–345 (2006)
3. Meijer, C., Soriano, V., Watkins, A.: Inclusive Education across Europe: Reflections upon 10 Years of Work from the European Agency for Development in Special Needs Education. Childhood Education 83(6), 361 (2007)
4. Department for Education and Skills, Special Educational Needs Code of Practice. DfES, London (2001)

5. Singleton, C.: Using computer-based assessment to identify learning problems. In: Florian, L., Hegarty, J. (eds.) ICT and Special Educational Needs: a Tool for Inclusion, pp. 46–63. Open University Press, Buckingham (2004)
6. Adam, T., Tatnall, A.: Using ICT to Improve the Education of Students with Learning Disabilities. In: Kendall, M., Samways, B. (eds.) Learning to Live in the Knowledge Society, pp. 63–70. Springer, New York (2008)
7. Fujiyoshi, M., Fujiyoshi, A., Aomatsu, T.: New Testing Method for the Dyslexic and the Newly Blind with a Digital Audio Player and Document Structure Diagrams. In: Miesenberger, K., Klaus, J., Zagler, W., Karshmer, A. (eds.) ICCHP 2010. LNCS, vol. 6179, pp. 116–123. Springer, Heidelberg (2010)
8. Choi, S.H., Walker, B.N.: Digitizer Auditory Graph: Making Graphs Accessible to the Visually Impaired. In: Proceedings of the 28th of the International Conference Extended Abstracts on Human Factors in Computing Systems, pp. 3445–3450 (2010)
9. Drigas, A.S., Kouremenos, D., Kouremenos, S., Vrettaros, J.: An e-Learning System for the deaf people. In: ITHET 6th Annual International Conference on Information Technology Based Higher Education and Training (2005)
10. Drigas, A.S., Kouremenos, D., Vrettaros, J.: Teaching of English to Hearing Impaired Individuals Whose Mother Language Is the Sign Language. In: Lytras, M.D., Damiani, E., Tennyson, R.D. (eds.) WSKS 2008. LNCS (LNAI), vol. 5288, pp. 263–270. Springer, Heidelberg (2008)
11. Chin, C.A., Barreto, A., Cremades, J.D., Adjouadi, M.: Integrated electromyogram and eye-gaze tracking cursor control system for computer users with motor disabilities. Journal of Rehabilitation & Development 45(1), 161–174 (2008)
12. Ozonoff, S., Cook, I., Coon, H., Dawson, G., Joseph, R.M., Klin, A., McMahon, W.M., Minshew, N., Munson, J.A., Pennington, B.F., Rogers, S.J., Spence, M.A., Tager-Flusberg, H., Volkmar, F.R., Wrathall, D.: Performance on Cambridge Neuropsychological Test Automated Battery Subtests Sensitive to Frontal Lobe Function in People with Autistic Disorder: Evidence from the Collaborative Programs of Excellence. Journal of Autism and Developmental Disorders 34(2), 139–150 (2004)
13. Vera, L., Campos, R., Herrera, G., Romero, C.: Computer graphics applications in the education process of people with learning difficulties. Computer and Graphics 31, 649–658 (2007)
14. Singleton, C.H., Thomas, K.V., Leedale, R.C.: CoPS 1 cognitive profiling system manual, 2nd edn. Lucid Research Ltd., Beverley (2001)
15. Lange, A.A., Mulhern, J., Wylie, J.: Proofreading Using an Assistive Software Homophone Tool: Compensatory and Remedial Effects on the Literacy Skills of Students With Reading Difficulties. Journal of Learning Disabilities 24(4), 322–335 (2009)
16. Starcic, A.I., Niskala, Colloquium, M.: Vocational students with severe learning difficulties learning on the Internet. British Journal of Educational Technology 41(6), 155–159 (2010)
17. Wilson, A.J., Dehaene, S., Pinel, P., Revkin, S.K., Cohenand, L., Cohen, D.: Principles underlying the design of "The Number Race", an adaptive computer game for remediation of dyscalculia. Behavioral and Brain Functions 2(19) (2006)
18. Singleton, C.H., Horne, J., Thomas, K.V., Leedale, R.C.: LADS version 1.0 administrator's manual. Lucid Innovations Ltd., Beverley (2002)
19. Singleton, C., Horne, J.: Computerised screening for dyslexia in adults. Journal of Research in Reading 32(1), 137–152 (2009)

20. Gregor, P., Dickinson, A., Macaffer, A., Andreasen, P.: SeeWord - a personal word processing environment for dyslexic computer users. British Journal of Educational Technology 34(3), 341–355 (2003)
21. Gathercole, S.E., Pickering, S.J., Knight, C., Stegmann, Z.: Working memory skills and educational attainment: Evidence from national curriculum assessments at 7 and 14 years of age. Applied Cognitive Psychology 18, 1–16 (2004)
22. Bull, R., Scerif, G.: Executive functioning as a predictor of children's mathematics ability: Inhibition, task switching, and working memory. Developmental Neuropsychology 19, 273–293 (2001)
23. Alloway, T.P., Gathercole, S.E., Kirkwood, H., Elliot, J.: The working memory rating scale: A classroom-based behavioral assessment of working memory. Learning and Individual Difference 19(2), 242–245 (2009)
24. Van der Molen, M.J., Van Lult, J.E.H., Van der Molen, M.W., Klugkist, I., Jongmans, M.J.: Effectiveness of a computerized working memory training in adolescents with mild to borderline intellectual disabilities. Journal of Intellectual Disability Research 54(5), 433–447 (2010)

# Reflections on Educational Technology, Research and School Innovation

Rosa Maria Bottino

Istituto Tecnologie Didattiche – CNR
Via De Marini, 6, Genoa Italy
bottino@itd.cnr.it

**Abstract.** In this paper four main perspectives are sketched as a framework to consider accomplishments in the educational technology research field and, in particular, in the school education sector: (a) the computational perspective which is focused on what technology makes possible; (b) the cognitive perspective which is focused on what the individual can learn under certain conditions; (c) the pedagogical perspective which considers how the design of ICT mediated situations can provide an answer to concrete educational problems; (d) the social and cultural perspective which is focused on the opportunities and needs brought about by different contexts. In the paper, these perspectives are exemplified making reference to research studies carried out at the Institute of Educational Technology of the Italian National Research Council (ITD-CNR) in the specific field of school education.

**Keywords:** educational technology, school innovation, research perspectives.

## 1    Introduction

Educational systems are based on learning models that are traditionally oriented towards knowledge transmission. Nowadays, in a society increasingly challenged by many transforming factors, there is the need to provide students with methods, tools and skills allowing them to fruitfully live in an accelerated and complex world [1].

Schools have a responsibility to prepare individuals to deal with a body of knowledge that is rapidly changing, ever increasing in size, strongly dynamic in nature, and distributed over many places and peoples. Moreover, schools have to find new answers to problems that, even if traditionally present in our educational systems, increasingly need to be faced according to new approaches and methodologies. One can think, for example, of the results of international comparative studies, such as the Programme for International Student Assessment (PISA), the Trends in Mathematics and Science Study (TIMSS) or the Progress in Reading Literacy Study (PIRLS), quantitatively showing that school systems are facing serious problems in crucial sectors like language, science and mathematics.

The objective of educational technology research is to study the role that information and communications technologies can have in teaching and learning processes. Under this main umbrella a variety of topics and themes are addressed and studied. In any case,

M.D. Lytras et al. (Eds.): WSKS 2011, CCIS 278, pp. 365–373, 2013.
© Springer-Verlag Berlin Heidelberg 2013

it is important to note that an effective impact on school could be obtained if and only if technological innovation is developed together with pedagogical innovation [2]. On one hand the use of new tools results in little pedagogical gain if novel educational strategies and the activities in which teachers and students are involved are not carefully reconsidered and planned. On the other hand, pedagogical innovation should be based on the opportunities offered by technological advances and on a critical examination of how such advances change substantially, in direct or indirect ways, the needs, the modalities and the content of teaching and learning activities.

Currently educational technology comprises research studies from a variety of research traditions, and consequently produces different results that need appropriate frameworks to be interpreted and contextualized. In this paper a framework is sketched and exemplified through making reference to some of the research studies carried out at the Institute of Educational Technology of the Italian National Research Council (ITD-CNR).

## 2     Educational Technology as a Research Sector

Educational Technology is a non-traditional and relatively new research field that was born in the past century around the mid-sixties. Even if it was at times regarded as belonging either to pedagogy, information and communication technologies, cognitive science or to the specific disciplinary fields where new technologies are applied, in recent decades it has progressively established itself as an autonomous interdisciplinary research sector with its own journals, university and research centres and proper funding programmes.

An important role for the consolidation of the educational technology research field in Europe has had funding from the European Commission of networks of research organizations in this field, the so-called Networks of Excellence[1]. Currently educational technology is considered as one of the Europe's key priorities for ICT research and innovation as evidenced by the results of a wide open consultation promoted by the European Commission [3].

Due to its interdisciplinary nature, educational technology is characterized by approaches, models and methodologies that derive from a number of different disciplines. Consequently, to understand at a non superficial level how the different approaches have been concretely applied to the design, practical implementation and analysis of learning environments that incorporate technology it is necessary to refer to some overarching notions through which it is possible to link theoretical reflections and the pedagogical and technical considerations that one has to face when designing or analysing learning environments integrating technology.

This paper sketches a framework to support the understanding of research studies in the field of educational technology at the school level which is based on the notion of perspectives.

Such framework can provide, on one hand, a tool to analyse research projects according to their main distinctive features and, on the other hand, a reference to look at

---

[1]   See, http://cordis.europa.eu/fp7/home_en.html

the outcomes of specific projects according to different reading keys exemplified through key research questions. The idea is not to provide an overall categorization of developments in educational technology and success indicators, since this is a goal too broad and ambitious for the scope of this paper, but to propose some possible entry points when examining specific examples educational technology projects.

## 3    Perspectives for Framing Educational Technology Research

As observed in the "legacy" book of the Kaleidoscope network of excellence [4], educational technology has grown out of different areas of research that together can be used to describe evidence of changing conditions and effects of technology in education and that can be also used to individuate new directions for research and development. Building on some of the areas mentioned in such introduction, in this paper a frame is briefly outlined as a mean to situate research questions and to interpret the results obtained.

As a matter of fact, different approaches may be assumed when considering the field of educational technology. Consequently, research questions which derive from different traditions and angles of investigation can be formulated. For this reason, it is useful to structure research approaches according to a set of perspectives which can be used as lens through which changes and results may be described. For the purpose of this paper four complementary perspectives are considered and then briefly exemplified:

− The computational perspective
− The cognitive perspective
− The pedagogical perspective
− The social and cultural perspective

In Figure 1 such perspectives are sketched by means of some related crucial questions.

The computational perspective establishes a link between educational technology and the computer science sector. The analysis of learning environments integrating ICT-based tools, in such a perspective, pays attention to what technology makes possible (e.g. platforms, simulations, microworlds, mobile and tangible devices, etc.). Consequently, it focuses on how the characteristics of the tools can change the way knowledge is accessed (e.g. how tangible interfaces can support the introduction of scientific concepts) and on how the presence of technology can change the content itself to be learnt.

The cognitive perspective considers how computational tools can change cognitive performance. According to this perspective, the analysis of learning environments integrating technology focuses on what the individual can learn under certain conditions and on the cognitive abilities that new technologies require, foster or hinder.

The pedagogical perspective, considers how the design and co-evolution of new learning activities and new technologies can provide solutions to concrete teaching and learning problems. It considers new pedagogical needs as well as how technology can provide new answers and approaches to traditional ones.

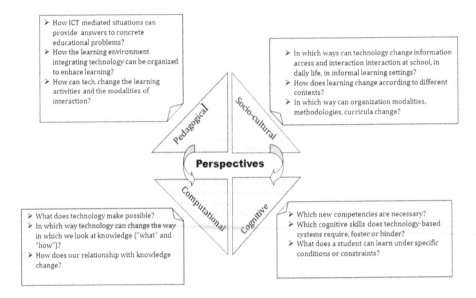

**Fig. 1.** Some TEL crucial questions according to different perspectives

The social perspective stresses the social and cultural factors that influence learning and the way in which knowledge is accessed and shared. Specific attention is paid to issues such as accessibility, equal opportunities, digital divide, etc. Moreover, in this perspective, technologies are considered in relation to the changes they can bring to activities in institutional education as well as in workplaces and informal settings.

The distinction between the above mentioned perspectives is, of course, not rigid and often there is a close interaction between them when looking at the same research study. As a matter of fact, the elaboration of new pedagogical practices is often interwoven with the design and implementation of systems and with their evaluation. Cognitive issues can emerge from the analysis of the interactions in different settings and among different actors and specific social needs (e.g. e-inclusion, cultural differences) are often to be considered when technology is integrated in real learning environments. Moreover, cognitive and pedagogical assumptions can guide the development of specific software features, and this can have an impact on how technologies are perceived and used.

The outlined perspectives can be a useful conceptual framework to situate and to understand educational technology approaches, to specify research objectives and to analyse the results obtained.

In the following, the above outlined framework is exemplified making reference to some projects and research studies carried out at the Institute of Educational Technology of the Italian National Research Council (ITD-CNR) in the specific field of school education.

# 4      Some Examples

## 4.1      ICT-Based Systems for Mathematics Education

How ICT mediated situations can provide an answer to concrete pedagogical problems? How the learning environment can be organized to enhance learning? How can technologies change the activities and the modalities of interaction?...

Mathematics teaching and learning is usually considered a difficult task by the different actors involved (teachers, students, parents and researchers), as confirmed by the results of international tests (e.g. PISA OECD surveys or the TIMSS study) that pointed out the necessity to tackle it according to new approaches and methodologies. In ITD-CNR multi-environments systems have been designed to allow students to approach maths concepts through the direct manipulation of concrete representations seen as the link between formal and abstract mathematics knowledge and the actual student experience. A long-term project concerned, for example, the design of a multi-environment system (the ARI-LAB system) that was aimed at developing arithmetic problem solving skills in primary and lower secondary school students.

As is commonly experienced, most students that have to solve an arithmetic problem tend to guess the correct operation and lose sight of the relation between the problematic situation to be examined and the sense of symbols to be used for its quantitative interpretation. Hence, students' learning difficulties often derive from their difficulty in associating the right meaning to arithmetic symbols. In the design of the ARI-LAB system, a social constructive approach is adopted to help overcoming such difficulties. Thus, a crucial role is ascribed not only to individual actions but also to the social context where actions are performed [5]. The teacher uses the ARI-LAB system in order to plan and manage the educational activity (editing problem texts; building examples of solved problems; sending problem and solutions to the students, etc.). The student has at his/her disposal environments (Microworlds) to solve problems, and a specific environment (the Solution Sheet) to externalize the solution process. Moreover, a Communication environment is available to exchange messages and problem solutions. Eight microworlds have been designed to model common situations in every-day life such as "purchase and sales" or "time measure" problems or to tackle arithmetic problem solving tools (abacus, number-line, graphs, spreadsheets, etc.). For instance, to solve a problem involving a money transaction, the student enters the "Euro" microworld where s/he can generate Euros, move them on the screen to represent a given amount, change them with other Euro of an equivalent value, etc. To learn how to calculate the value of money, the student can represent a numerical value on the Abacus or on the Number-Line microworlds, comparing the different representations in order to conceptualize them better. While solving a problem, the student can send messages or solutions to schoolmates and/or to the teacher. Figure 1 shows the interface of the Solution Sheet environment with an example of a problem solution obtained pasting the representations built in the microworlds (icons at the top right-hand side) and adding comments through the "post-it" function.

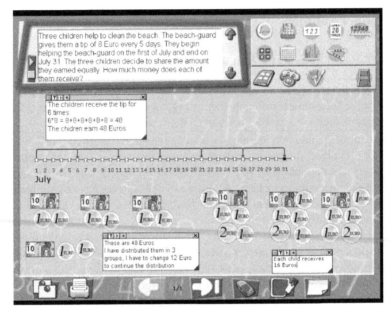

**Fig. 2.** Interface of the Solution Sheet environment with an example of a problem solution

ARI-LAB was tested for several years in long-term, real-class experiments. Outputs showed that the direct manipulation and coordination of different concrete representations has a crucial role in linking mathematics knowledge to the actual experience of the students. Moreover, it has been also evidenced that the development of problem solving abilities is the result of all the interactions established within the learning environment, not only of the interaction of the student with the software.

## 4.2    Playing with Robots

What does technology makes possible? How technology can change the relationship with knowledge? …

Activities of robot construction and programming by young children that have been carried out in ITD draw on the opportunities offered to scientific education by tangible devices. Such tools can be used to support the establishment of a correspondence between mental operations on conceptual entities and concrete operations performed in an iconic and motor-perceptive space [6]. Which educational goals can have a learning environment based on robot programming? Let's imagine a group of primary school children involved in the construction of cybernetic objects – assembling wheels, sensors, engines etc., and programming them via a specific iconic language. Through a discussion on robot behaviour (movements, reaction to obstacles and to stimuli like brightness and temperature) the group carries out a real activity of elaboration of theories by comparing different hypotheses and verifying them thanks to the robot reactivity.

In a computational perspective, the characteristics of the robot and of the programming language through which the robot is governed make the cause-effect relationships concrete and give the pupil a linguistic tool to communicate and reason on the robot behaviour ("if the temperature increases, the robot switches on the fan"). The immediacy of interpretation allows pupils to face problem solving in an innovative way ("let's add this action to teach the robot to switch on the fan when it is hot..."). The physicality of the robot is a key element since it makes ideas real and operative and becomes the motor of the conceptual construction process [7]. Learning is the outcome of the active engagement of the individual and of his/her relation with the group. ITD activity in this field has concerned the construction of cybernetic objects to develop scientific concepts (e.g. basic physics concepts, case, probability) and related educational activities tested in primary and lower secondary schools.

## 4.3    Digital Games and the Development of Reasoning Skills

What cognitive skills does technology-based systems require, foster or hinder? What does a student can learn under specific conditions or constraints? ...

It is generally recognized that the learning performance of students closely depends on basic skills that can be considered as transversal to curricular disciplines. Among them reasoning skills, connected with strategic thinking and problem solving, play a crucial role [8].

Assuming a cognitive perspective, the LOGIVALI project was carried out in ITD with the aim of investigating and assessing primary school students' logical and reasoning abilities by means of digital mind games (also called puzzles or brainteasers). To this end the main cognitive abilities involved in playing with a selection of mind games were investigated and their technical characteristics analyzed. The main final output of the project was the LOGIVALI test that, following a set-up on purpose, specific methodology, employs digital mind games to evaluate primary school students' specific reasoning abilities. On the basis of the results obtained with the sample population (around 540 primary school pupils), the test was standardized and the reference norms were defined [9].

The project outcomes go beyond the possibility of using the test at school for diagnostic purposes; in fact they are the grounding for a better understanding of how logic reasoning skills can be supported in actual terms and stimulated using exactly those means that today pupils, the "digital natives", widely use and appreciate – digital games. Games, however, are not merely used as a motivating tool, but are studied to understand the cognitive significance of the "added value" supplied by technology to the development of cognitive skills. The possibility of graduating the level of difficulty for each student, the availability of features such as feedback and backtracking, as well as the support offered to memorization and anticipation activities, are examples of such value.

### 4.4    Information Problem Solving

In which way can technology change information access and interaction at school, in daily life, in informal learning settings? In which way learning organization, methods and content can change? …

The Internet is becoming the main source of information and the way to build autonomous learning paths. Network information integrates communication codes different from traditional ones – it is immediately accessible, interactive and manipulable and yet, its quality is difficult to evaluate. Knowledge is represented through different conceptual networks having uncertain borders and continuously moving connections. This representation is scarcely compatible with subject matter and encyclopaedic classifications we have been used to for centuries. Hence, there is the problem of how to fruitfully exploit new opportunities offered by ICT developments to change pedagogy and to promote new activities in different learning settings. The field of information problem solving is of particular importance in this regard. Learning environments can be settled with the aim of promoting abilities such as, for example, question asking, hunting for clues, making hypotheses, recognizing appropriateness and reliability signals, using search tools and strategies in an informed and flexible way. This research theme was investigated at ITD-CNR starting from a critical analysis of current pedagogical practices on web use. Then a proposal for teacher training on the pedagogical use of the web was formulated and validated in various courses [10]. The main idea behind such work is the consideration of the double role played by technology: on the one hand it is the context where exploring factors and skills that influence the effectiveness of the information problem solving process and, on the other, it is the learning environment itself which stimulates and develops such competencies.

## References

1. Collins, A., Halverson, R.: The second educational revolution: rethinking education in the age of technology. Journal of Computer Assisted Learning 26(1), 18–27 (2010)
2. Guzman, A., Nussbaum, M.: Teaching competencies for technology integration in the classroom. Journal of Computer Assisted Learning 25(5), 453–469 (2009)
3. European Commission: Shaping the ICT research and innovation agenda for the next decade (2009),
   http://ec.europa.eu/enterprise/~newsroom/cf/
   itemlongdetail.cfm?item_id=2521
4. Balacheff, N., Ludvingsten, S., de Jong, T., Lazonder, A., Barnes, S.: Technology Enhanced Learning: a Kaleidoscope view. In: Technology-Enhanced Learning – Principles and Products, pp. V–XVI. Springer, Heidelberg (2009)
5. Bottino, R.M., Chiappini, G.: Using activity theory to study the relationship between technology and the learning environment in the arithmetic domain. In: English, L. (ed.) Handbook of International Research in Mathematics Education, pp. 838–861. Routledge, New York (2008)

6. Chioccariello, A., Manca, S., Sarti, L.: Children's playful learning with a robotic construction kit. In: Siraj-Blatchford, J. (ed.) Developing New Technologies for Young Children, pp. 93–112. Trentham Books Limited, Stoke on Trent (2004)
7. Cerulli, M., Chioccariello, A., Lemut, E.: Randomness and Lego Robots. In: Proceedings of the Fourth Congress of the European Society for Research in Mathematics Education, pp. 591–600. Universitat Ramon Llull (2006)
8. Rohde, T.E., Thompson, L.A.: Predicting academic achievement with cognitive ability. Intelligence 35(1), 83–92 (2007)
9. Bottino, R.M., Ott, M., Tavella, M., Benigno, V.: Can digital Mind Games be Used to Investigate Children's Reasoning Abilities? In: Meyer, B. (ed.) Proceedings of the 4th ECGBL Conference on Games Based Learning, Academic Conferences, Copenhagen, pp. 31–39 (2010)
10. Ferraris, M., Caviglia, F.: Web searching for learning: observing web users working out an information problem. In: Proceedings of International Conference on Cognition and Exploratory Learning in Digital Age, pp. 440–442. IADIS (2006)

# Guideline to Select Knowledge Elicitation Techniques

Diana-Marcela Vásquez-Bravo, Maria-Isabel Sánchez-Segura,
Fuensanta Medina-Domínguez, and Antonio Amescua

Computer Science Department, Carlos III University of Madrid,
Avda. De la Universidad, 30 28911 Leganés (Madrid), Spain
{dvasquez,misanche,fmedina,amescua}@inf.uc3m.es

**Abstract.** Knowledge elicitation process allows acquiring and transferring the knowledge. Actually, this process presents difficulties to select the appropriate elicitation technique. This paper presents a classification of the elicitation techniques used in software engineering and the relationship between the elicitation techniques and some elements of knowledge management as assets knowledge, epistemological dimension of knowledge and the knowledge creation phases. This classification provides a guideline to select a technique or a set of techniques for knowledge elicitation based on phases of Nonaka's model.

**Keywords:** Knowledge Elicitation, Knowledge Acquisition, Knowledge Elicitation Techniques, Knowledge Assets, Knowledge Management.

## 1    Introduction

For several years it has stressed on the importance of knowledge for organizations seeking to survive in today's competitive market, and it has demonstrated a clear relationship between knowledge and organizational success [3][14] [20] [16].

Knowledge management is presented as a discipline which focuses on the development of knowledge. The phases of knowledge management are identification, capture, organization, distribution, preservation, use and measurement [17][11].

Within knowledge management process, many authors have argued that one of the major bottlenecks in the process of building a knowledge-based system is the process of acquiring knowledge that corresponds with the phases of identifying and capturing the knowledge life cycle [9] [6][5] [13] [11][12].

Knowledge acquisition refers to the process of extract and makes accessible the knowledge of an organization. However, this activity is currently in experimental period due to the difficulty that represents to elicit the knowledge of the people, represent it adequately this knowledge and make it accessible to all members of an organization (see Fig. 1).

Knowledge elicitation involves acquiring and transferring the knowledge of human beings (as such it exists in the minds of experts in a specific domain) to an abstract and effective representation, to organize it, to model it and finally to express this knowledge in an understandable and reusable format through a formal representation.

M.D. Lytras et al. (Eds.): WSKS 2011, CCIS 278, pp. 374–384, 2013.
© Springer-Verlag Berlin Heidelberg 2013

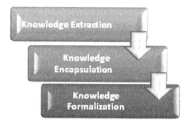

**Fig. 1.** Knowledge Elicitation Process

Knowledge elicitation process presents difficulties as in the elicitation techniques used, because of they are not complete enough to capture all the relevant knowledge for a specific domain, as in the same process of elicitation because a lot of the information that people knows is less than information verbalized. "We can always know more than we can tell, and we will always tell more than we can write down" [18]. Within Software Engineering field, one of the first phases in software product development is the requirement elicitation that allows characterizing the product type to be developed as well as the needs and features of the environment for which is being developed the software product.

This means that software engineers have enough experience in requirement elicitation area. This is extrapolated and equivalent to knowledge elicitation.

On the other hand in knowledge management field there is no a cataloging of knowledge elicitation techniques, so this work is going to approach on identifying of the requirement elicitation techniques coming from the software engineering field and that can be applied on knowledge management field as well as their cataloging based on the applicability and the knowledge creation model phase where these are applied. Furthermore, it is proposed for the selected knowledge elicitation techniques categories, the type of knowledge asset that is can be generate.

So, it will be analyze the different techniques of software engineering applied to knowledge elicitation. The knowledge asset types that exist and the knowledge life cycle phases to conclude with a proposal that combines the three elements previously mentioned, that may be used as discernment element by the time to choose the knowledge elicitation technique type that better adjust in each moment according to a particular situation and the knowledge asset type that is going to elicit.

The article is structured on 4 sections detailed next. Section 2 is dedicated to related works about the knowledge management models and the knowledge assets and elicitation techniques, section 3 describes the proposal of the authors and finally on section 4 the obtained conclusions of this work are presented.

# 2      Related Works

In this section the knowledge management models and the knowledge assets and elicitation techniques applied on the software engineering area are discussed.

## 2.1      Related Works about Knowledge Management Models

It has been analyzed the contributions of different authors that go into the knowledge management models in depth. Next, the works of [21], [8], [19][1] and [15] are described concisely. It is worth mentioning that the analyzed works have choose as a basis the Nonaka's spiral model of knowledge creation owing to this model presents a continuous process of knowledge creation described by phases that facilitates knowledge creation, use and transformation, is a model recognized by many scientific community authors and has been used as a reference in numerous works related on the topic.

*Wiig Model [21]:* This model presents the definition and the establishment of the process of knowledge creation, codification and application for support the knowledge management for the organizations. For this, it determines that a "knowledge vocabulary" has to be built in which the necessary knowledge for the organization is described; the author proposes to create a "knowledge encyclopedia" through information technologies that will help to share, assign and use the collected knowledge.

Although this model directs the creation of a knowledge organization structure, it doesn't differentiate the knowledge dimensions (epistemologic and ontologic), which works against the eduction process and its acquisition.

*Grant Model [8]:* This model argues that knowledge creation is done at individual level and the organization is entrusted with the knowledge coordination, integration and application of its employees in organizational activities. This model proposes the mechanisms of materialized rules in proceedings, design of productive activities like sequences in time, organizational routines and problems resolution groups. These mechanisms support the knowledge integration in the organization. Reliability of this integration is the result of the measures of efficiency, reach and flexibility of the integration.

Even though the model is directed to the efficient integration of individual knowledge, it doesn't consider the existence and importance of other type of knowledge, like the one of organizational environment.

*KPMG Model [19]:* KPMG proposes an organizational learning model centered on the shape that the organizational structure must have for achieving an adequate knowledge management. This model explain some requirements that have to be obtained by the organizational structure for the knowledge and its management being successful and indicates the need of provide adequate mechanisms to obtain the maximum benefit of the creation, raising, storage, transmission and interpretation of the knowledge as people towards organization as organization towards people.

The model emphasizes all its efforts in cultural elements minimizing importance to the management axis, the knowledge.

This model considers factors related to the organizational structure for supporting the learning to the people's levels, work teams and organization, but focus all its efforts in cultural elements minimizing importance to the management axis, the knowledge. The model lacks of distinguish between the epistemological and ontological dimensions of the knowledge.

*Arthur Andersen Model [1]:* This model, from the individual perspective, establishes the personal responsibility of sharing and making explicit the knowledge to the organization and, from the organizational perspective, the responsibility to create the support infrastructure for making effective the individual perspective, contributing to the processes, culture and technology creation.

This model, like the previous one, gives priority to the cultural elements and considers that the time and effort dedicated to build practices communities or developing interaction abilities between persons and teams is more important to manage and improve the knowledge management of the organizations that to invest in technology.

The model presents the weakness of suborder the knowledge management to the clients' recruitment only, so the people that form the organization the knowledge that being adequate with this purpose are important only. Although it provides facilitator elements relevant to this goal, it doesn't consider the epistemological and ontological dimensions of the knowledge.

*Spiral Model of Knowledge Creation [15]:* This work proposes a knowledge creation process through a spiral knowledge generation model, described through knowledge conversion phases. In this work, the knowledge is classified as:

Tacit Knowledge: Knowledge highly informal, personal, un-verbalized, intuitive and derived from experience. This knowledge is applied on specific contexts including cognitive elements (mental models) and technical elements (applicable to specific works).

Explicit Knowledge: It is characterized for being formal and systematic knowledge that can be expressed without ambiguities through writing, mental maps, schematics, databases, etc.

Making use of this classification, the spiral model of knowledge creation [15], is presented as an interactive process between tacit and explicit knowledge that has dynamic and continuous nature making up a permanent spiral of knowledge transformation carried on 4 phases (see Fig. 2).

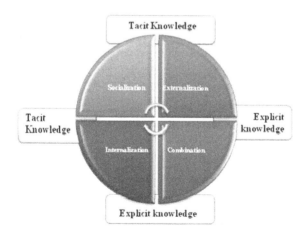

**Fig. 2.** Knowledge Creation Model

*Socialization:* to convert tacit knowledge into tacit knowledge through the knowledge transfer from one person to other by means of social interaction and shared experiences among the members of the organization.

*Externalization*: to convert tacit knowledge into explicit knowledge represented in concepts, models and articulation of best practices or lessons learned.

*Combination*: to convert explicit knowledge into explicit knowledge by means of categorizing, reclassifying and synthesis of explicit existing knowledge.

*Internalization*: to convert tacit knowledge into explicit knowledge, allowing to persons to acquire explicit knowledge and to expand their tacit knowledge, so that new knowledge can be developed.

Although the Knowledge creation model [15] describes knowledge transformation phases, this model does not identify which elicitation techniques can be used for knowledge elicitation in each of the 4 phases.

**Table 1.** Summary of the elicitation techniques / knowledge elicitation

| Techniques | Description | Tacit | Explicit | Process/Activity | Concepts | Type |
|---|---|---|---|---|---|---|
| Card Sorting | It allows to know how the user mentally organizes the information, categories and priorities in his mind. | ◆ | | | ◆ | D |
| Scenarios | It consists in the description of a sequence of actions and events for a specific case in the domain. | ◆ | | ◆ | | I |
| Structured Interview | It consists in interviewing the user with a set of prepared questions | | ◆ | ◆ | | D |
| Critical success factor (CSF) | It is a technique to analyze factors that ensure the success for an organization, and that represent the management area, that must receive special and continual attention to achieve high performance. | | ◆ | | ◆ | D/I |
| Unstructured Interview | It consists in interviewing the user about a specific domain with a set of questions without planning | | ◆ | ◆ | | D |
| Brainstorming | A group of users provide ideas about a specific domain, without emphasis on evaluation. | | ◆ | ◆ | ◆ | I |
| Text analysis | It consists in examining existing and related documentation, contributes with obtaining knowledge, domain requirements, identification of reusable components and concepts. | ◆ | ◆ | | ◆ | I |
| Repertory grid | It consists in asking the user for the applicable attributes to a set of entities and their values. It is an array of attributes. | ◆ | | ◆ | ◆ | D |
| Multi-dimensional scaling | Multidimensional scaling represents a set of statistical techniques used in information visualization for exploring similarities or dissimilarities in data. | ◆ | | ◆ | ◆ | I |
| Concepts mapping | This technique can help to understand the relationships between concepts. It is simple, uses hierarchies, and visual representation. | ◆ | ◆ | | ◆ | D |
| Task analysis | It consists in the observation of the user while he is doing his activities. This technique provides knowledge of the processes, actions and interactions in the real environment. | ◆ | ◆ | ◆ | | D |
| Participant observation | It analyzes the current practice of users in the domain. | ◆ | | ◆ | | D |
| Behavior analysis | The expert analyzes over long periods of time to users in their workplace. The aim is to describe the functional relationships between response classes and classes of stimulus. Explanation of behavior. | ◆ | | ◆ | | D |
| Protocol analysis | The user performs a task and provides detailed information quietly about how it is performed. | ◆ | ◆ | ◆ | | D |
| Prototyping | The user provides information on a prototype of the desired system. | | ◆ | | ◆ | D |

## 2.2    Techniques Contributed by Software Engineering

Next, is presented a summary of the elicitation techniques of requirements and/or knowledge elicitation. These techniques correspond to an important subgroup of the universe of existing techniques. In Table 1, is presented a short description of each technique, the knowledge epistemological dimension that can be obtained through the application of this technique, if the acquired knowledge can be used to describe processes or activities, or to clarify and classify concepts, and finally determines if the knowledge was acquire from direct or indirect source (Direct is denoted with D, Indirect is denoted whit I), this according to the type of interaction with the domain expert.

## 2.3    Knowledge Assets Involved in Knowledge Management

To manage the organizational knowledge in a much more efficient way, its flows, the critical management points and other factors, it is beneficial to divide and classify knowledge as it is proposed in [7]. The method is indicated next. This knowledge assets classification has been chosen due to the existing importance that organizations develop an integrated approach of knowledge management that covers all knowledge potential components and make the most of the particular components in order to reach the strategic aims of business.

Next, it is briefly described the five knowledge assets proposed by [7] and that have been taken as the basis of this research work (see Fig. 3).

**Data** includes the facts summarized in simple values or figures; it is about very explicit knowledge that comes from processes, operations, experiments or polls. As knowledge asset, its importance lies on the ability to be associated inside a context to turn into strategic information and to create value and utility for decisions choosing.

**Experience** is a knowledge way, skill or ability coming from observation, from the facts and events experience and coming from events that happen in person's life. As experts as theirs experiences are source of big knowledge quantity in an organization. Knowledge coming from the experience is highly tacit, related to a specific domain, coming from the experiences, formal education and collaboration.

The **learning lessons** correspond to the knowledge set obtained through analysis and thought about an experience, project, process or situation in an organization. This experience may be positive or negative and it is available for all those interested in explicit knowledge way. To acquire and to document the learning lessons contribute to transform the tacit knowledge into explicit knowledge, which facilitates its spreading to all levels of the organization. This explicit type of knowledge is based on true facts and leads to process and decisions identification that reduces or deletes failures and reinforces the obtaining of a positive result.

The **knowledge documents** represent knowledge codifying in highly explicit way. The source of codifying knowledge may be internal to the organization or may come from external sources. Assets, reports, documented procedures, statistical analysis, process maps or activities are part of these. These assets may have specific structured formats like the case of technical reports, project reports, research reports and other publications. They also may be explicit in an unstructured way like images, diagrams, presentations, multimedia files, on-line handbooks, tutorials, etc.

The **Proceedings and politics** is the knowledge asset that represents the organizational knowledge required for the organization works in efficient and coherent way. The proceedings and politics document collects regulations and work flows of the routine operations of the organization. Clearly and coherence of the proceedings contribute to the learning of the new employees and promote the fulfillment of the operations on the part of the existent employees. The proceedings and politics documents are designed to provide the know-how of a process, they are of instructive type and represent an integration effort of knowledge in the organization. The source of this type of asset may be the tacit aspects of the assets Learned lessons and experience. This asset can be transferred in knowledge way to the employees through the delivery of organization rules, routines, culture, structures and technologies, for helping the learning.

**Fig. 3.** Knowledge Assets

## 3    The Proposal

The performed analysis has allowed to establish the relationship between elicitation techniques provided by software engineering and some key elements of knowledge management methods studied, as well as the identification of the concepts that have enabled the authors to classify the techniques found according to these determinants factors to choose an elicitation technique.  According to this, the authors have established some considerations to guide the user in choosing the technique to be applied as appropriate.

The proposal in this work includes:

- Identification and establishment of the interaction between different types of knowledge assets and the way how may be possible to create and to provide feedback organizational knowledge, on the basis of the spiral model of knowledge creation [15].
- Classification of elicitation techniques that has been analyzed in each phase of the spiral model of knowledge creation that will contribute to the choice of the technique or group of elicitation techniques suggested as the most appropriate for use in each one of the phases according to the type of knowledge asset.

*Interaction between knowledge assets and the Nonaka's Model.*

As it was mentioned before, each knowledge asset must be considered individually and differently according to their phase in the life cycle of it [4]. However, knowledge assets may be take part in the 4 phases of knowledge creation.

It is possible that from a type of knowledge asset a new one can be generated or this asset can be to provide feedback and be expanded, improved or updated through the application of the knowledge elicitation techniques identified and classified for each stage of knowledge conversion.

In Table 2, the first column indicates the types of starting knowledge asset, while the first row indicates the new asset that can be generated or to provide feedback if it is the same type asset. It achieved through the application of the techniques of a particular phase of conversion. The phases are detailed in the squares: S: Socialization, E: Externalization; C: Combination; I: Internalization.

**Table 2.** Relationship between types of knowledge assets and the stages of spiral model of knowledge creation

|  | Expertise | Knowledge Documents | Data | Policies & Procedures | Lessons Learned |
|---|---|---|---|---|---|
| **Expertise** | S/E | E | E | E | S/E |
| **Knowledge Documents** | I |  | C | C | I |
| **Data** | I | C |  | C | I |
| **Policies & Procedures** | I | C | C |  | I |
| **Lessons Learned** | S/E | E | E | E | E/C |

*Classification of Elicitation Techniques in the Nonaka's Model [15]*

Next, a classification of the studied elicitation techniques is introduced. Using this classification, it is possible to establish relationships between these categories and the knowledge conversion phases of [15].

In Table 3, it is shown a summary of some of the most relevant characteristics of the studied techniques. In first column a classification of the requirements elicitation and knowledge elicitation techniques widely used in software engineering in five categories is shown.

Some of these techniques are applied in requirement elicitation, knowledge elicitation, or both areas. For this reason in the Applicability column, is referenced the discipline that used the technique. The knowledge elicitation is denoted by Knowledge E., and requirement elicitation is denoted by Requirement E.

In the same way, in Knowledge creation Phase column is presented the relationship between the categories for elicitation techniques and the knowledge creation model phases [15]. The aim of relationship establishment is to propose a convenient combination between knowledge conversion phases [15] and the suggested techniques by the authors to create or provide feedback for the knowledge assets on each phase (See Table 3). The establish relationship in this work, between the knowledge conversion phases and elicitation techniques is justified under next assumptions:

In first instance, the socialization is applied for unstructured elicitation techniques. Inside this category, techniques as the open interview and the brainstorming make tacit to tacit knowledge conversion easier through the knowledge and experience transference from one person to another, through social interactions.

**Table 3.** Guideline to select knowledge elicitation technique

| Classification | Techniques | Tacit | Explicit | Process/ Activities | Concepts | Type | Applicability | Knowledge creation Phase |
|---|---|---|---|---|---|---|---|---|
| Structured Elicitation Techniques | Card Sorting | ◆ | | | ◆ | D | KE | E I |
| | Scenarios | ◆ | | ◆ | | I | KE/RE | |
| | Structured Interview | | ◆ | ◆ | | D | KE/RE | |
| | Critical success factor | | ◆ | | ◆ | D/I | RE | |
| Unstructured Elicitation Techniques | Unstructured Interview | | ◆ | ◆ | | D | RE | S E I |
| | Brainstorming | | ◆ | ◆ | ◆ | I | RE | |
| Formal Analysis Techniques | Text analysis | ◆ | ◆ | | ◆ | I | KE/RE | C |
| | Repertory grid | ◆ | | ◆ | ◆ | D | KE/RE | |
| Representation techniques | Multi-dimensional scaling | ◆ | | ◆ | ◆ | I | KE | E C |
| | Concepts mapping | ◆ | ◆ | | ◆ | D | RE | |
| Observation-based techniques | Task analysis | ◆ | ◆ | ◆ | | D | KE/RE | S I |
| | Participant observation | ◆ | | ◆ | | D | KE/RE | |
| | Behavior analysis | ◆ | | ◆ | | D | KE | |
| | Protocol analysis | ◆ | ◆ | ◆ | | D | KE | |
| | Prototyping | | ◆ | | ◆ | D | KE/RE | |

In the same way this knowledge conversion type can be carried on through the techniques based on observation, because these facilitate the social interactions between the employees of different levels of the organizational structure (e.g. behaviour analysis in view of particular situations, to discover how the experts solve the problems and to perform their tasks, to provide tacit knowledge to the people that provide feedback about individual knowledge).

The externalization has the purpose to convert tacit to explicit knowledge, for this it is possible to apply the categories of unstructured elicitation techniques, structured elicitation techniques and mapping based techniques. The first two techniques satisfy the need to extract knowledge from the people for each problem domain. The structured elicitation techniques allow knowledge acquisition in tidy way and create scenarios to guide the interviewed person in the answers in presence of certain circumstances; moreover these contribute in concepts clarifying and classification. The mapping based techniques benefit the externalization of the acquired knowledge through the usage of mental maps, correlations establishment, hierarchies and visual representation of knowledge elements.

Combination consists on explicit to explicit knowledge conversion. For this, the usage of mapping based techniques and formal analysis is proposed as elements that allow identifying, analysing and classifying explicit knowledge. In addition to this,

this categories combination facilitates the fusion, categorization and summarized representation of existing knowledge.

The internalization allows to acquire explicit knowledge to the people of the organization and to expand their tacit knowledge. This may be supported in structured elicitation techniques, unstructured elicitation techniques and based on observation techniques. Through structured social interactions formally or informally, the scenario deployment or the brainstorming can be transform and provide feedback to the people knowledge. The same thing happens with the based on observation techniques that allow the person to learn through the observation of others behavior, their answer to particular situations and the task execution way. In the squares Knowledge elicitation: KE, Requirement elicitation: RE, Direct: D, Indirect: I; and the knowledge creation phases are denoted: Socialization: S, Externalization: E, Internalization: I, and Combination: C.

## 4    Conclusions and Future Works

The knowledge elicitation is an active part of knowledge management. It involves the elicitation, acquisition and to transfer the knowledge of experts of a specific domain, to a formal representation that allows understanding, use and reuse such knowledge in a particular domain.

One of the problems presented in knowledge elicitation process is lack that has the knowledge elicitation techniques to capture the tacit and explicit knowledge that covers the 4 phases of the Nonaka's spiral model of knowledge creation as well the epistemological dimensions of knowledge. Therefore, the authors propose a guide to select knowledge elicitation technique. For this, in this paper was presented the interaction between the different knowledge assets and how the organizational knowledge can be created and provided feedback starting from the basis of Nonaka's spiral model of knowledge creation [15], the classification of the elicited techniques analyzed on each one of the Nonaka's spiral model of knowledge creation phases that will provide which elicited technique is more appropriate for use in each one of the phases, and the Proposal of the product patterns as knowledge elicited technique.

The authors are currently working on the definition of an elicitation technique to cover the knowledge creation phases, supported in knowledge management of software development organizations. Also, this technique will provide a strategy for value creation for activities and processes of the organization starting from the use, distribution and preservation of the knowledge because we believe that if we can adequately represent the knowledge about the processes and products of the organization, we will be able to express the maturity of the processes used efficiently by the organization and we can control and reduce the time required for development.

**Acknowledgements.** This work has been partially funded by the Spanish Ministry of Science and Technology through the TIN2009-10700 project and the Spanish Ministry of Industry through projects PPT-430000-2008-54, PPT-430000-2009-0012 and PPT-430000-2009-0013.

# References

[1] Alexander, C.: The Timeless Way of Building. Oxford University Press, Oxford (1979)

[2] Andersen, A.: El Management en el siglo XXI: Herramientas para los desafíos empresariales de la próxima década. Editorial Granica-Buenos Aires (1999) ISBN: 950-641-272-3

[3] Baruch, L., Juergen, D.: The dominance of intangible assets: consequences for enterprise management and corporate reporting. Measuring Business Excellence 8(1), 6–17 (2004)

[4] Birkinshaw, J., Sheehan, T.: Managing the knowledge life cycle. Mit Sloan Management Review 44(1), 75–83 (2002)

[5] Brulé, J., Bount, A.: Knowledge Acquisition. McGraw-Hill, New York (1989)

[6] Debenham, J.: Knowledge System Design. Prentice Hall, Sidney (1989)

[7] Freeze, R., Kulkarni, U.: Knowledge management capability: defining knowledge assets. Journal of Knowledge Management 11(6), 94–109 (2007)

[8] Grant, R.: The Knowledge-Based View of the Firm: Implications for management practice. Long Range Planning 30(3), 450–454 (1997)

[9] Greenwell, M.: Knowledge Engineering for Expert Systems. Ellis Horwood Limited, Chichester (1988)

[10] Huang, Y., Huang, G., Hu, Z., Maqsood, I., Chakma, A.: Development of an expert system for tackling the public's perception to climate-change impacts on petroleum industry. Expert Systems with Applications 29(4), 817–829 (2005), doi:10.1016/j.eswa.2005.06.020, ISSN 0957-4174

[11] Kuhn, O., Abecker, A.: Corporate Memories for Knowledge Management in Industrial Practice: Prospects and Challenges. Journal of Universal Computer Science 3(8), 929–954 (1997)

[12] Mason, D., Pauleen, D.: Perceptions of knowledge management: A qualitative analysis. Journal Knowledge Management 74, 38–48 (2003)

[13] Meyer, M., Booker, J.: Eliciting and Analyzing Expert Judgement. A Practical Guide. Academic Press, Londres (1991)

[14] Nonaka, I., Takeuchi, H.: The Knowledge Creating Company: How Japanese Companies Create the Dynamics of Innovation. Oxford University Press, New York (1995)

[15] Nonaka, I., Takeuchi, H.: The knowledge-creating company. Oxford University Press, Nueva York (1997)

[16] OECD, Measuring Innovation: A New Perspective. Organisation for Economic Cooperation and Development. OECD Publishing (2010) ISBN: 10.1787/9789264059474

[17] Rus, I., Lindvall, M., Sinha, S.: Knowledge Management in Software Engineering, the Data & Analysis Center for Software (DACS) State-of-the-Art-Report (2001)

[18] Snowden, D.: Complex acts of knowing paradox and descriptive self-awareness. J. Knowledge Manage. 6(2), 100–111 (2002) (special issue)

[19] Tejedor, B., Aguirre, A.: Proyecto Logos: Investigación relativa a la Capacidad de Aprender de las Empresas Españolas. Boletín de Estudios Económicos LIII(164), 231–249 (1998)

[20] Webster, E., Jensen, P.: Investment in Intangible Capital: An Enterprise Perspective. Economic Record 82, 82–96 (2006), doi:10.1111/j.1475-4932.2006.00296

[21] Wiig, K.: Management of Knowledge: Perspectives of a New Oportunity. The Wiig Group, Arlington (1988)

# A Review
# on Artificial Intelligence in Special Education

Athanasios S. Drigas and Rodi-Eleni Ioannidou

NCSR DEMOKRITOS,
Institute of Informatics and Telecommunications
Net Media Lab,
Ag. Paraskevi, 15310, Athens, Greece
dr@iit.demokritos.gr,
elena.ioan@hotmail.com

**Abstract.** Innovative educational technologies have started to open new ways of interacting with students with special educational needs (SEN). Amongst the most effective approaches during the last decade (2001-2010) are those based on Artificial Intelligence (A.I.) techniques. The effective application of A.I. methods is seen as a means of improving the quality of life of SEN learners. Hence, a need for introducing A.I. techniques arises in order to develop both diagnosis and intervention processes. This paper presents a brief overview of the most representative studies of the past ten years, used for the above purposes.

**Keywords:** Artificial Intelligence, special educational needs, learning difficulties, diagnosis, intervention.

## 1 Introduction

The constant development in technology has dramatically transformed the world during the past decade and devolved computing power in every aspect of our daily life. One of the most important aspirations of computing science was the quest to understand human intelligence in all forms. This quest for the last fifty years led a large number of researchers to develop the field of Artificial Intelligence (A.I.). A.I. is usually defined as the study and design of intelligence agents which are able to perceive their environment and take actions that increase their possibilities of success [1].

One of the research communities of Artificial Intelligence field deals with the intersection of A.I. and education. The vast majority of scientists and researchers seem to support the idea that A.I. tools can successfully contribute to the educational process [2]. Recently there has been an increasing emphasis on educating all children and ensuring the learning needs of all young people and adults. This fact has reinforced the use of technology as a mean of overcoming barriers to learning. The benefits of A.I. in education have been lauded for many years. Artificial Intelligence methods have long been used to the field of special education as well. The first

M.D. Lytras et al. (Eds.): WSKS 2011, CCIS 278, pp. 385–391, 2013.
© Springer-Verlag Berlin Heidelberg 2013

research tasks mainly applied 'Expert Systems' of which the only aim was to model the behavior of a human expert to achieve an intellectual task [3].

The term 'special educational needs' refers to a wide range of difficulties which cause problems in learning. In addition, it has much to do with the cultural and historical development of research in different countries. Since a term such as 'special educational needs' is very general, for the needs of this paper we decided to use the definition of 'learning difficulties' which is closer to the one of 'learning disabilities', as it is defined in IDEA. The 'Individuals with Disabilities Education Act' (IDEA) defines learning disability as a 'disorder in one or more of the basic psychological processes involved in understanding or in using spoken or written language, which may manifest itself in an imperfect ability to listen, think, speak, read, write, spell or to do mathematical calculations' [3].

Link-up between Artificial Intelligence educational approaches and students with different abilities and needs has opened new eras and trends which require use of specific tools and new methods in order to improve children's life in both school and home settings. During the last decade there have been an important number of studies which address how A.I. computing tools can be used in practice in order to improve the quality of education of students with learning difficulties [4]. In this article we will focus on the most representative Artificial Intelligence techniques of the last decade which have been used for the diagnosis and intervention processes of learners with special educational needs. These assistive tools can be used from school staff, special educators and parents as well. In order for these studies to be classified, this report consists of two main categories. In the first one we introduce applications regarding the identification of learning difficulties and the second section includes intervention based tools.

## 2    Diagnosis

Considering the implicit characteristics of learning difficulties, the diagnosis with A.I. methods of learners with learning difficulties has long been an issue with great debate around it [5]. The variety of symptoms and nature of the special educational needs, the co-occurrence with other disorders, the differences between boys and girls are some of the several issues that arise during the assessment procedure.

Georgopoulos et al., 2003 presented a fuzzy cognitive map approach for differential diagnosis of specific language impairment (SLI). Fuzzy cognitive maps are a soft computing methodology that uses a symbolic representation for the description and modeling of complex systems. The aim of this tool is to provide the specialists with a differential diagnosis of SLI from dyslexia and autism, since in many cases SLI is difficult to be discerned due to its similar symptoms to other disorders. The system has been tested on four clinical cases with promising results [6].

In 2004 Rebolledo-Mendez and Freitas presented the NeuroSky MindSet (MS) which is able to detect attention levels in an assessment exercise by combining performance data with user-generated data, taken from interaction. NeuroSky consists of a headset with three electrodes, which are put beneath the ears and on the forehead. The electrical signals read at the above locations are used as inputs by NeuroSky's algorithms to assess the attention levels. An A.I. driven avatar was also designed to pose questions and have limited conversation with the users. It is a low-cost, non-clinical and easy to use tool designed for leisure. This model was tested on first-year undergraduate students in the following years and the results indicated that there is a positive relation between measured and self-reported levels of attention [7] ,[8].

Arthi and Tamilarasi (2008) introduced a model which helps in the diagnosis of autism in children by applying Artificial Neural Networks (ANN) technique. The model converts the original autistic data into suitable fuzzy membership values and these are given as input to the neural network architecture. Moreover, a pseudo algorithm is created for applying back propagation algorithm in predicting the autistic disorder. This approach is proposed to support apart from medical practitioners, psychologists and special educators. In future the autistic disorder could be predicted using k-nearest neighbor algorithm for a comparative research [9].

Hernández et al., (2009) introduced SEDA ('Sistema Experto de Dificultades para el Aprendizaje' or 'Expert System for Learning Difficulties' in English) a diagnostic tool for Learning Difficulties in children's basic education. It is developed using the Expert Systems design methodologies which include a knowledge base consisting of a series of strategies for Psycopedagogy evaluation; trying to identify the relationships between input variables (e.g. age, sex, educational level) and the output systems (e.g. psychomotor aspect, intellectual aspect). All of the above provides the expert system's users the possibility of acknowledge the psychological profile of the pupil. 80% of the evaluators rated the system as Efficient using an estimation scale of: Poor, Moderately Efficient and Efficient [10], [11].

In the same year Jain et al., (2009) proposed a model called Perceptron based Learning Disability Detector (PLEDDOR). It is an artificial neural network model for identifying difficulties in reading (dyslexia), in writing (dysgraphia) and in mathematics (dyscalculia) using curriculum based test conducted by special educators. This computational diagnostic tool consists of a single input layer with eleven units that correspond to different sections of a conventional test and one output unit. The system was tested on 240 children collected from schools and hospitals in India and was evaluated as simple and easy to replicate in huge volumes, but provides comparable results based on accepted detection measures [12].

Kohli et al., (2010) introduced a systematic approach for identification of dyslexia at an early stage by using artificial neural networks (ANN). This approach is amongst the first attempts which have been made for addressing the dyslexia identification problems with the use of ANN. Moreover, it can be distinguished from other platforms of its kind because it is based on test data, covering the evaluation results of potential dyslexic pupils, between the years 2003 – 2007. These test data consist the input data of the system while the output results classify the students in two categories (dyslexic and non-dyslexic). An error back-propagation algorithm is responsible for mapping college performance to the underlying characteristics. The initial results obtained using test data were fairly accurate and suggest the application of this platform to real data as well [13].

Anuradha et al., (2010) developed a platform for a more accurate and less time consuming diagnosis of Attention Deficit Hyperactivity Disorder (ADHD). They used one well-known Artificial Intelligence technique, the SVM algorithm. According to the authors, this is the first attempt at identifying ADHD using SVM algorithm.

Support vector machines (SVMs) are a set supervised learning techniques suitable for classification and regression. A data-set which was verified by a doctor including the results of a questionnaire used by the doctors to diagnose the disorder was given to the SVM module. After that the data-set was introduced and afterwards returned to the SVM module, which finally provides us with the diagnosis. The most important advantage of applying the SVM algorithm is that it can control the complexity of the diagnostic process. This method was tested on children between the ages six to eleven years old and the results indicated a percentage of 88,674% success in diagnosing [14].

## 3     Intervention

A reliable and valid diagnosis is the first step in order to help a child overcome his or her difficulties. The second step is the intervention process. An important number of studies are currently addressing the use of Artificial Intelligence systems in the education of students with learning difficulties.

Melis et al., (2001) introduced ActiveMath, a web-based intelligent tutoring system for mathematics. ActiveMath is an Intelligence Tutoring System (ITS), which allows the students to learn in their own environment whenever it is convenient for them. It uses a number of Artificial Intelligence techniques to realize adaptive course generation, student modeling, feedback, interactive exercises and a knowledge representation which is appropriate for the semantic Web. In ActiveMath the user starts his/her own student model by self-assessment of his/her mastering level of concepts and later chooses learning goals and scenario, for instance, the preparation for an exam. The capabilities of the student are adapted in course generation and in the suggestion mechanism as well. Moreover, a "poor man's eye-tracker" is designed which is able to trace child's attention and reading time in detail. This application has reported many positive outcomes in the following years by a large number of studies, all of them supporting the effect of this ITS during the learning process [15], [16], [17].

Schipor et al., (2003) attempted to create a Computer Based Speech Therapy (CBST) system using a fuzzy expert system for helping learners with speech disorders. They designed an improved CBST system, called LOGOMON (Logopedics Monitor) and developed its classical architecture with a fuzzy expert system. The aim of this approach is to suggest optimal therapeutic actions for every pupil based on the information selected. The evaluation of this system indicates that by using an expert system, the learner is provided with more therapy time, predictability and the explanation of results [18].

In 2007 Riedl et al, designed a platform which can aid adolescents with High Functioning Autistic Spectrum Disorders (HFASD) rehearse and learn social skills with reduced help from parents, teachers, and therapists.. A social scenario game is presented – for example going to a movie theater- which challenges learners with HFASD to role-play and complete tasks involving social situations. Artificial Intelligence is used to assist the above groups with the authoring of tailored social scenarios. An A.I. system automatically examines the causal form of the narrative plan, searching for points at which a student's actions can undo causal relationships.

The alternative narrative scenario is a branch developed for handling the contingency of the learner's action. This Artificial Intelligence tool embed in this particular platform decreases the manual authoring burden where application of intervention strategies can be handled by specialists. This social scenario intervention approach is complete and currently undergoing evaluation with promising results [19].

In 2008 Drigas et al., presented 'Dedalos' project which deals with the teaching of the English language as a second language to hearing impaired people, whose mother language is the Greek sign language. In an educational e-content adapted to the needs of every user, the whole procedure consists of audits and evaluation of the linguistic abilities of the e-learners. The system uses an intelligence taxonomy system which is developed for the evaluation of the pupil and the setting of pedagogic material. The approach promotes a complete support system for the education of hearing impaired Greek students while at the same time opens the way for their inclusion [20].

Gonzalez et al, (2010) designed an automatic platform for the detection and analysis of errors in mathematical problems to support the personalized feedback of pupils. This method is referred to all students and particularly to students with special educational needs such as those with Down syndrome, who exhibit difficulties in the arithmetic operations of addition and subtraction. An error detection algorithm was developed which is able to analyze the data gathered as a result of the interaction between the students and the platform, while afterwards the output of the error is available to the teachers about the specific difficulties and to allow them to personalize the instruction. Moreover, they designed a model which returns the set of errors made by the pupils in the corrected exercises so as the students can learn from their own mistakes. The system was tested on a group of students with Down syndrome and the results confirm that the module exhibits the proper behavior [21].

In the same year Baschera and Gross introduced an adaptive spelling training system which can be used from all students who exhibit spelling difficulties. This platform is based on an inference algorithm designed to manage unclassified input with multiple errors defined by independent mal-rules. The inference algorithm based on a Poisson regression with a linear link function, estimates the pupil's difficulties with each individual mal-rule, based on the observed error behavior. This knowledge representation was implemented in a student model for spelling training such as optimized word selection and lessons for individual mal-rules to pupil adjusted repetition of erroneously spelled words. This system was tested on a two large-scale user studies and showed an important increase in the learner's performance, induced by the student adapted training actions [22].

## 4    Conclusions

Artificial Intelligence techniques have successfully been applied to solve problems in the field of special education. There is a general consensus amongst scientists that Artificial Intelligence methods are able to integrate the freedom of action of the user and lead him or her toward personnel learning goals. This study has reported some of the most representative articles over the last decade which introduced diagnostic and intervention approaches based on Artificial Intelligence techniques. These educational tools are specifically oriented to assisting students with learning difficulties as well as teachers, parents, special educators and therapists. The identification of students with learning difficulties using A.I. techniques can provide us a valid and accurate diagnosis which later can help us choose the most appropriate intervention method. However there are still several issues which demand further research such as the lack of the offered A.I. intervention tools and the lack of nationally regulated standards regarding the A.I. diagnostic methods. Moreover, the future studies should include a larger sample of pupils and also groups of pupils with other learning difficulties. Research studies regarding the use of Artificial Intelligence technology are very promising and can ensure a better quality of the life of special educational needs students and all the people around them.

# References

1. Russell, S.J., Norvig, P.: Artificial Intelligence: A Modern Approach, 2nd edn., New Jersey (2003)
2. Lanzilotti, R., Roselli, T.: An Experimental Evaluation of Logiocando, an Intelligent Tutoring Hypermedia System. International Journal of Artificial Intelligence in Education 17, 41–56 (2007)
3. Wu, T.K., Meng, Y.R., Huang, S.C.: Application of Artificial Neural Network to the Identification of Students with Learning Disabilities. In: International Conference on Artificial Intelligence, pp. 162–168 (2006)
4. Public Law, Individuals with Disabilities Education Act (IDEA), USA, pp. 101–476 (1990)
5. Nanni, L., Lumini, A.: Ensemble generation and feature selection for the identification of students with learning disabilities. Expert Systems with Applications 36, 3896–3900 (2008)
6. Georgopoulos, V.C., Malandraki, G.A., Stylios, C.D.: A fuzzy cognitive map approach to differential diagnosis of specific language impairment. Artificial Intelligence in Medicine 29, 261–278 (2003)
7. Rebolledo-Mendez, G., De Freitas, S.: Attention modeling using inputs from a Brain Computer Interface and user-generated data in Second Life. In: The Tenth International Conference on Multimodal Interfaces (ICMI 2008), Crete, Greece (2008)
8. Rebolledo-Mendez, G., Dunwell, I., Martínez-Mirón, E.A., Vargas-Cerdán, M.D., de Freitas, S., Liarokapis, F., García-Gaona, A.R.: Assessing NeuroSky's Usability to Detect Attention Levels in an Assessment Exercise. In: Jacko, J.A. (ed.) HCI International 2009, Part I. LNCS, vol. 5610, pp. 149–158. Springer, Heidelberg (2009)
9. Arthi, K., Tamilarasi, A.: Prediction of autistic disorder using neuro fuzzy system by applying ANN technique. International Journal of Developmental Neuroscience 26, 699–704 (2008)
10. Hernadez, J., Mousalli, G., Rivas, F.: Expert System for the Diagnosis of Learning Difficulties in Children's Basic Education. In: Proceedings of the 8th WSEAS International Conference on Applied Computer and Applied Computational Science, Italy (2008)
11. Hernadez, J., Mousalli, G., Rivas, F.: Learning Difficulties Diagnosis for Children's Basic Education using Expert Systems. WSEAS Transactions on Information Science and Applications 7(6) (2009)

12. Jain, K., Manghirmalani, P., Dongardive, J., Abraham, S.: Computational Diagnosis of Learning Disability. International Journal of Recent Trends in Engineering 2(3) (2009)
13. Kohli, M., Prasad, T.V.: Identifying Dyslexic Students by Using Artificial Neural Networks. In: Proceedings of the World Congress on Engineering, London, U.K, vol. 1 (2010)
14. Anuradha, J., Tisha, Ramachandran, V., Arulalan, K.V., Tripathy, B.K.: Diagnosis of ADHD using SVM algorithm. In: Proceedings of the Third Annual ACM Bangalore Conference (2010)
15. Melis, E., Andres, E., Budenbender, J., Frischauf, A., Goguadze, G., Libbrecht, P., Pollet, M., Ullrich, C.: ACTIVEMATH, A Generic and Adaptive Web-Based Learning Environment. International Journal of Artificial Intelligence 24(4), 1–25 (2001)
16. Libbrecht, P., Melis, E.: Methods to Access and Retrieve Mathematical Content in ACTIVEMATH. In: Iglesias, A., Takayama, N. (eds.) ICMS 2006. LNCS, vol. 4151, pp. 331–342. Springer, Heidelberg (2006)
17. Melis, E., Siekmann, J.: ACTIVEMATH: An Intelligent Tutoring System for Mathematics. In: Rutkowski, L., Siekmann, J.H., Tadeusiewicz, R., Zadeh, L.A. (eds.) ICAISC 2004. LNCS (LNAI), vol. 3070, pp. 91–101. Springer, Heidelberg (2004)
18. Schipor, O.A., Pentiuc, S.G., Schipor, M.D.: Improving computer based speech therapy using a fuzzy expert system. Computing and Informatics 22, 1001–1016 (2003)
19. Riedl, M., Arriaga, R., Boujarwah, F., Hong, H., Isbell, J., Heflin, L.J.: Graphical Social Scenarios: Toward Intervention and Authoring for Adolescents with High Functioning Autism. In: Virtual Healthcare Interaction, Papers from the AAAI Fall Symposium (2007)
20. Drigas, A.S., Kouremenos, D., Vrettaros, J.: Teaching of English to Hearing Impaired Individuals Whose Mother Language Is the Sign Language. In: Lytras, M.D., Damiani, E., Tennyson, R.D. (eds.) WSKS 2008. LNCS (LNAI), vol. 5288, pp. 263–270. Springer, Heidelberg (2008)
21. Gonzalez, C.S., Guerra, D., Sanabria, H., Moreno, L., Noda, M.A., Bruno, A.: Automatic system for the detection and analysis of errors to support the personalized feedback. Expert Systems with Applications 37, 140–148 (2010)
22. Baschera, G.M., Gross, M.: Poisson-Based Inference for Perturbation Models in Adaptive Spelling Training. International Journal of Artificial Intelligence in Education 20, 1–31 (2010)

# Open Source Application in Multimodal Biometry

Bojan Kezele, Ivan Milenkovic, Miloš Milovanović, Miroslav Minović,
and Dusan Starcevic

Faculty of Organizational Sciences, Jove Ilica 154, Belgrade, Serbia
{bojan.kezele,ivan.milenkovic,milos.milovanovic,
miroslav.minovic,dusan.starcevic}@mmklab.org

**Abstract.** This paper describes MBARK (Multimodal Biometric Application Resource Kit) software, developed by American National institute for standards and technology, NIST. MBARK is designed to acquire different biometric data and to work with different biometric sensors. Biometric client configuration is described. Software's advantages and disadvantages are shown, as well as possibilities for further development and use.

**Keywords:** multimodal biometry, biometric system, biometric data acquisition, MBARK.

## 1    Introduction

Passwords are short phrases which are used for identification purposes. Although using passwords is one of the oldest identification methods, it is also one that is the most insecure. The reason for this is that passwords have to be memorized. If the password is short and easy to memorize, it is also susceptible to password cracking. In order to enhance password security, a *strong password policy* is usually used, enforcing minimum password length, use of both upper and lower-case letters, numbers and special characters. When all of these security measures are enforced, the resulting password is really difficult to crack, but also difficult to memorize.

A possible solution to the password problem could be the use of token-based identification methods. Token-based identification methods use "something that you have" to make a personal identification, such as RFID cards (with or without PIN code), USB sticks with appropriate software, etc. The successful use of such solutions solve password memorizing problem, but also suffers from several disadvantages: tokens may be lost, stolen or misplaced. In order to overcome such problems, a better solution, different from knowledge-based or token-based identification methods is needed.

The answer could lie in using biometrics. Everybody possesses unique physiological or behavioral characteristics which could be used for personal identification. When using biometrics, there is no need for users to remember passwords and there are no tokens that can be lost or stolen. Nevertheless, the person can be identified anywhere, and if needed, not only by single biometric characteristic.

M.D. Lytras et al. (Eds.): WSKS 2011, CCIS 278, pp. 392–397, 2013.

## 2    Biometric System

A biometric system uses biometric characteristics of its users for identification purposes. The nature of biometric system can be active or passive, depending on which way user interacts with the system.

User's biometric data can be acquired from distance, even without requiring an active participation or the knowledge of the user (passive mode). Otherwise, user is required to place his or her hand on the palm-scanner or use the retina scanner (active mode). Depending on the application context, a biometric system may operate either in *verification* mode (for example, user uses an identification token to claim his identity and system is used to verify if that claim is true or false) or in *identification* mode (system conducts an one-to-many comparison to establish an user's identity using his biometric characteristics ) [1].

Two key phases of biometrics system usage are enrollment phase and test phase. Enrollment phase is critical for biometric system because successful matching of stored templates and system input depends on the quality of the enrolled data.

Acquisition of biometric data can very often cause different kinds of problems. Users are not always willing to cooperate, sometimes they simply feel uncomfortable, or on other occasions the whole system seems too complicated for them. Needed time for biometric data acquisition should also be considered. In the ideal case, biometric data acquisition is easy to accomplish. However, in real world applications, biometric data is very often damaged, corrupted, or simply doesn't contain enough information for interpretation. Therefore, unimodal biometric systems can sometimes be unreliable.

Multimodal biometrics system implies using multiple biometric characteristics during enrollment and test phases. Practically, it means that system user will have to not only lean their finger on the fingerprint scanner, but also have to access retina scanner and maybe say a passphrase in order to be recognized by the system. There are several reasons for such approach. First, in certain situations some of the biometric characteristics are simply unusable. For example, unfavorable illumination conditions may significantly affect the face images acquired from an individual, no matter how the camera is positioned. Similarly, a scar can change a subject's fingerprint, consequently downgrading the match result. Secondly, a multimodal biometric system is way more difficult to spoof, because an intruder has to simultaneously spoof multiple biometric traits of a legitimate user, which is more difficult than spoofing just one biometric characteristic.

It was already mentioned that users may find using biometric scanners unpleasant. In multimodal approach that problem is even more present, because system users can feel discomfort while using more than one sensor. The application designers are responsible for finding different ways to solve this problem, in order to make the biometric system more user-friendly and more acceptable for users.

## 3    MBARK

Multimodal Biometric Application Resource Kit (MBARK) developed by National Institute for Standards and Technology (NIST) reduces the complexity and costs of developing biometric applications. Incorporating the MBARK libraries can yield a variety of enhancements critical for the success of any real-world system. MBARK provides operators means to quickly recover from both minor mistakes and major hardware failures. In addition, the use of Extensible Markup Language (XML) facilitates true sensor interoperability via plug-ins and allows for changes in workflow on-the-fly.

MBARK is open-source software and is publicly available.

Biometric systems change interfaces depending on which sensors are being used. MBARK, however, provides a consistent and user-centered interface, reducing errors and minimizing the need to retrain users as vendors develop new sensors and software. User-centered design is a formal process that helps ensure the efficiency, effectiveness, and user-satisfaction of a system throughout the system's lifecycle.

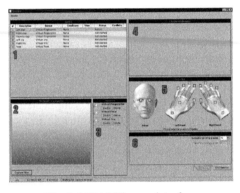

**Fig. 1.** MBARK's user interface

MBARK user interface, as shown on Fig. 1, is divided in six sections. In section one are shown actions that are about to happen. Section two serves to show scanner data during reading session. Middle section (section three) shows which scanner is currently active. In section four scanning results are shown. Section five is used to mark the injuries, in order to notify system to expect corrupted input. Section six is used to state if there are special recording conditions, such as user wearing spectacles.

It is important to mention about MBARK user interface the fact that it remains unchanged regardless of which sensor is currently active. Consequently, it is easier to work with multiple sensors and the system is more user-friendly.

According to [2] MBARK offers following features: *consistent user interface, fast and easy exception recovery, flexible user configuration, adjusts workflow automatically, multitasking and sensor interoperability.*

### 3.1 Installation and Architecture

MBARK installation is not simple and requires a lot of effort, in order for software to work properly. Necessary requirements are Windows XP, Visual Studio 2008, and .NET framework 3.51.SP1. Specific version of ANTLR has to be used, while the references to the Syncfusion libraries have to be added in a special way [2].

*ANother Tool for Language Recognition, ANTLR,* is a language tool that provides a framework for constructing recognizers, interpreters, compilers, and translators from grammatical descriptions containing actions in a variety of target languages. ANTLR takes as input a grammar that specifies a language and generates as output source code for a recognizer for that language. Put in the simple words, it is a program that writes other programs. If code snippets are added, recognizer can become compiler or interpreter. ANTLR provides excellent support for tree construction, tree walking, translation, error recovery, and error reporting [3].

*Syncfusion Essential Studio* is a Syncfusion Inc. product. It contains components and controls written in .NET framework for work with Windows Forms,WPF, ASP.NET, ASP.NET MVC and Silverlight.

MBARK uses following libraries from *Essential Studio User Interface Edition*: *Essential Grid, Essential Tools, Core* and *Shared* libraries [4] and [5].

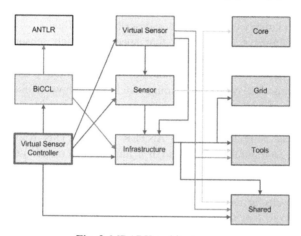

**Fig. 2.** MBARK architecture

MBARK architecture is quite complicated, and is shown on Fig. 2. MBARK is a domain specific program, so it works only on Windows operating systems.

To make things even more complicated, a project written in C# is used for biometric client configuration (green), user interface is written in Visual Basic (blue) , Syncfusion libraries are necessary for proper functioning of user interface and for compiling biometric client configuration (red), and ANTLR, a project written in Java is used (black). Also, MBARK uses XML for proper system configuration and memorizing program state. VirtualSensorController project is used for system management. This project is also used as a system entry and contains program forms. Sensor, VirtualSensor and Infrastructure projects contain necessary libraries for work with sensors. These projects rely upon Syncfusion libraries from *Essential Studio User Interface Edition.*

### 3.2    Biometric Client Configuration

Essential part of MBARK is *Biometric Client Configuration Language* (BiCCL). It is written in C#, and uses ANTLR for compiling its syntax into the MBARK XML configuration files.

Semantically, BiCCL is designed to directly reflect the desired workflow. A biometric workflow needs to use obvious and simply structured logic. For example, users need to be able to easily describe logic such as "if the subject is carrying glasses, take one picture with glasses on, and one with glasses off. Otherwise, just take two pictures." The internal representation of this construct is irrelevant from the user's point of view.

Syntactically, language authors desired a language that was directly editable in a standard text editor. Therefore, the DSL was designed to take on a 'C'-like syntax. A disadvantage of this approach is that standard XML tools cannot be used to parse or transform BiCCL files.

In order to satisfy semantic and syntactic constraints, language authors decided that BiCCL should be a domain specific language (DSL), rather than a markup language such as XML. The basic syntax for BiCCL files is fairly simple, and almost anybody could relatively easy understood described workflow.

Each task references a definition that specifies which sensor it uses, desired parameters for that sensor, and other information. The result is that end users can very easily copy and paste a workflow into another BiCCL file that uses the same sensors. Furthermore, with this syntax it is immediately clear how to reorder tasks - just reorder the lines of text, without any concern where the sensors are defined or how they are implemented.

BiCCL file is compiled via the ANTLR project. This results in generating according XML configuration file. Also, it is important to mention that XML files are much larger than BiCCL files. More details about BiCCL can be found in [6].

The BiCCL file is split into eight main blocks, which may appear in any order. Each of the blocks is required. Blocks are: *localization*, *experimentalConditions*, *equivalenceClasses*, *sensors*, *configurations*, *tasks*, *initialState*, *workflow*.

A complete BiCCL file example and more details about organization structure of these file blocks can be found in [6] and [7].

MBARK offers a limited sensor support. Some of the most often used sensors are supported, while for other programmers have to implement their own support classes.

## 4     Conclusion

MBARK's main advantage is the fact that it is an open-source and publicly available project. Because of that, programmers can freely re-implement existing and add new functionalities.

Another advantage of this solution is its layered architecture, complete isolation of logical entities and modular approach. Most credits for this advantage should go to BiCCL, because it enables easy and fast system modifications without any need for modifying other system parts or software recompilation.

However, MBARK has some weaknesses. As first, it is a domain specific software solution, connected with Miscrosoft Visual Studio and .NET platform. Although Microsoft operating systems have a large market share, most security experts prefer Linux based systems. Because of that, MBARK's usability is somewhat crippled.

Aside from being domain specific solution, there is another relevant problem. Three different programming languages are used, two from .NET platform (C# and Visual Basic) and Java as third. Although Java project (ANTLR) is only referenced and used as finished project, eventual future modifications could cause problems.

Another important issue is lack of documentation. There is not a single paper which explains what some part of source code does or what is the purpose of each class. Because of large number of classes, the lack of documentation presents a serious challenge for any programmer. Therefore, programmers have to dedicate a lot of time for source code analysis.

Also, it is important to mention that MBARK is software for *biometric data acquisition*. It does not have built in matching algorithms, so it can be considered as an incomplete solution.

Surely MBARK can be used as good foundation for developing biometrics system, but it is necessary to have a well prepared team of programmers in order to successfully deal with all of MBARK's challenges.

**Acknowledgments.** This work is a part of project Multimodal biometry in identity management, funded by Ministry of Science and Technological development, contract no TR-32013.

# References

1. Li, S.Z.: Li: Encyclopedia of Biometrics. Springer, Heidelberg (2009)
2. Biometric Clients Group, Image Group, Information Access Division, Information Technology Lab: MBARK brochure. National Institute of Standards and Technology, U.S. Department of Commerce (2009)
3. ANTLR, http://www.antlr.org/
4. Syncfusion Inc.: Syncfusion – Deliver innovation with ease, brochure, Syncfusion Inc. (2010)
5. Syncfusion Inc., http://www.syncfusion.com/
6. Aronoff, M., Michaels, R.J.: The Biometric Client Configuration Language. National Institute of Standards and Technology, U.S. Department of Commerce (2008)
7. Bojan, K.: Open source application in multimodal biometry, BSc thesis. Faculty of Organizational Sciences, University of Belgrade, Serbia (2010)
8. Aleksandar, J.: Using MBARK in multimodal biometry, MSc thesis. Faculty of Organizational Sciences, University of Belgrade, Serbia (2011)

# Applying IT-Governance Frameworks for SOA and Cloud Governance

Vladimir Stantchev[1,2] and Lubomira Stantcheva[3]

[1] Berlin Institute of Technology, Berlin, Germany
stantchev@computer.org
[2] Hochschule für Oekonomie und Management (FOM), Berlin, Germany
[3] Asperado GmbH, Germany

**Abstract.** Service-oriented architecture (SOA) in the enterprise was one of the key enablers for cloud computing. Therefore, it can serve as a natural fit for bringing traditional IT governance approaches forward to the challenges of cloud governance. In this work we present an approach for mapping IT governance mindsets to the aspects of SOA governance. It allows an IT organisation the adaptation and the continuous usage of already established governance models during the adoption of cloud computing solutions. We also present an application case study where we demonstrate the feasibility of the approach in real-life scenarios in the context of an international telecommunication provider.

**Keywords:** SOA governance, ITIL, IT management frameworks.

## 1 Introduction

The rapid technological improvement and innovation in the last couple of decades and increasing globalization and competition across all industry branches have also forced the IT field to improve itself. Managing the enterprise information more effectively than the competitors became the critical success factor in order to gain a competitive advantage and to increase the value of the organization.

Especially in terms of service providing, new concepts and trends like the Internet of services and devices [1,2,3], which are driven by the vision of providing world-wide distributed applications and increased functionality, and cloud computing, which aims to provide an unlimited flexibility of resources by being able to combine own and outsourced software, platform and infrastructure elements strategically, require improved management capabilities to govern the more complex information structure driven by those concepts. The trend towards service-oriented computing (SOC) and service-oriented architecture (SOA) [4], as well as the availability of cloud computing offerings make the governance of IT even more complex and challenging.

Specific approaches can look at different architectural levels to address governance requirements [5,6,7] or focus at project portfolio aspects of the problem [8]. Other approaches focus on the performance evaluation peculiarities of cloud computing offerings [9].

M.D. Lytras et al. (Eds.): WSKS 2011, CCIS 278, pp. 398–407, 2013.

An interesting idea is to try to extend existing IT governance approaches such as ITIL [10] and COBIT [11] to the world of SOA [12] – a more viable approach compared to the introduction of purely SOA/cloud-based governance frameworks. Such developments gain currently even more traction with the emergence of COBIT V.5.

In this work we extend this approach. After analyzing the similarities and differences, strengths and weaknesses of ITIL and COBIT, the support that they can give to better implement the service oriented architecture and the combination of ITIL and COBIT to combine their power, implement SOA better and achieve the full range of IT management, will be examined. The domains and processes of both frameworks will be mapped to each other in this context to create a basic guideline for organizations, which are looking forward to integrate and implement both frameworks.

The rest of this work is structured as follows: Section 2 presents a short overview of IT governance frameworks and the terminology we use. In Section 3 we give an overview of our proposed mapping of such frameworks for the governance of SOA and cloud computing. In Section 4 we describe a specific mapping process that we have assessed within an industry case study with an international telecommunications provider. Section 5 contains a summary of our results and outlook on our future research activities.

## 2   Preliminaries

In this section we introduce briefly common frameworks for IT governance and provide the terminology that we need throughout the work.

### 2.1   IT Governance Frameworks

IT governance frameworks aim to define standardized processes and control metrics for IT provision. Commonly applied frameworks in this area include the IT Infrastructure Library (ITIL) [10] and the Control Objectives for Information and Related Technology (COBIT) [11]. They typically provide best practices for measurement and control of IT-specific indicators. These indicators can be generally divided into two groups – key performance indicators (KPIs) and key goal indicators (KGIs). KPIs measure how well a process is performing and are expressed in precisely measurable terms. KGIs represent a description of the outcome of the process, often have a customer and financial focus and can be typically measured after the fact has occurred [13]. While KGIs specify what should be achieved KPIs specify how it should be achieved.

## 3   Mapping of IT Governance Framework to SOA

### 3.1   The SOA Lifecycle

The SOA life cycle is an iterative process model that integrates software engineering and business process management approaches to deliver a holistic view of service creation, deployment and management [14]. It consists of two general phases – the preproduction phase and the production phase. The preproduction phase includes two stages – the Model stage and the Assemble stage. In the first stage the business model of an organization is created. It includes business processes and business metrics (KPIs) that relate to them. A formalized business model is the starting point for the Assemble stage where the artifacts of the future information system (IS) that implements the business model are assembled. The use of the verb assembled rather than developed reveals the strong focus on reuse in a service-based system - needed functionality should be provided by existing services as far as possible. This includes functions of legacy applications that can be integrated (e.g., via Web Service wrappers).

## 3.2  Mapping ITIL to the SOA Lifecycle

This mapping is the further elaboration of an idea we presented in [12]. In general, ITIL includes the required processes and good practices to build and manage the service lifecycle. Service management deals with services of a service provider across the service lifecycle and defines all processes and practices, which are critical to systematically and successfully manage every domain of the lifecycle - strategy, design, transition, operation and continual improvement. As mentioned above, the concern of SOA is not primarily about the technology anymore. The technology supporting the new service oriented application concept of SOA already exists. In fact, the risk awaiting the service providers, which intend to apply SOA to their organization, are the management issues of SOA. The technological perspective of SOA has driven a new management concept, which needs to cover additional management and governance practices and processes to handle the complex architecture enabled by SOA. Here is where exactly IT service management and ITIL come into play. They address some of the specific requirements of SOA and assist the management in how to handle the single stages of the lifecycle, as well as how to integrate them, including concrete policies, processes and practices. ITIL is a supporting tool for the management, enlightening the way to proper SOA. Most of the management requirements of SOA shown in Figure 1 are covered by ITIL framework, with Change Management, Availability Management and Service Level Management being the most critical ones. It is necessary to map the lifecycle domains of ITIL to the domains of SOA in order to create a link between them, which directly connects ITIL processes and practices to SOA domains. The mapping should show clearly, that ITIL domains are parallel to SOA domains, and the processes and good practices fully support main SOA goals and match SOA governance requirements.

The concept of continual service improvement is not addressed as a domain in SOA lifecycle, but the included processes, activities, roles and responsibilities are covered within the other domains of the lifecycle. The processes of ITIL continual service improvement domain require the integration and involvement of all other domains and parties anyway. Therefore, the continual service improvement as a domain can be excluded from the mapping, as long as the related processes are covered and implemented by other domains.

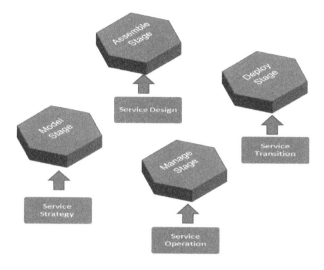

**Fig. 1.** An Overview of ITIL to SOA Lifecycle Mapping

### 3.3 Mapping COBIT to the SOA Lifecycle

To use a high level framework such as COBIT for effective SOA governance can provide great help for the service provider in order to achieve a higher level perspective by monitoring, controlling and evaluating processes and activities, defined by ITIL for example, and ensuring that the IT architecture and information systems actually contribute to the business objectives. As mentioned before SOA is not mainly about the technology today, but it is about the governance aspects to manage the components and information enabled by technology and challenging requirements of SOA. Business focus is the primary concern of CO-BIT and its primary objective is to ensure that every lower level goal contributes to the correspondent higher level goal, so that the main IT goals contribute to the overall business goals. COBIT framework will ensure the service provider during the implementation of SOA not to get lost in details and lose the track of certain activities and processes and their impact on business goals and objectives. COBIT also covers some of the governance requirements of SOA such as the compliance to standards, internal and external regulations.

COBIT lifecycle domains along with the processes will now be mapped to SOA domains to create a clear link between them. However, one should keep it in mind that COBIT is not primarily about defining processes for implementing SOA, but it is rather designed for delivering control objectives, performance measurement metrics and maturity evaluation practices for the processes defined by lower level frameworks such as ITIL. Still, the mapping will show that COBIT and SOA lifecycles and domains are parallel to each other and a combination with a framework such as ITIL in order to support a full range of SOA governance is possible and desirable.

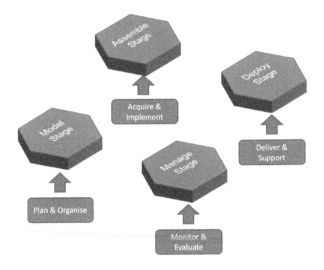

**Fig. 2.** An Overview of CObIT to SOA Lifecycle Mapping

# 4 Case Study: Mapping IT Governance to the SOA Lifecycle

In this case study we describe the application of our approach in an enterprise IT organization that has already introduced ITIL and COBIT as management and governance frameworks accordingly.

## 4.1 Application in the Area of ITIL

**Service Strategy – Model.** The first step of the mapping is to link the Service Strategy domain of ITIL to Model stage of SOA. Modeling is the first step triggering the SOA service lifecycle. It is the process of encoding and transcribing all business activities of an organization into a written form, called the business design. The business design should project the overall objectives of the business, all business processes, decision criteria, policies and assumptions of the organization to reach these business objectives. Service strategy domain supports that objective by providing a long term strategy for the service provider, which needs to consider the overall culture and vision of the organization, be aware of the competitive environment surrounding the service provider and include strategies, tactics and plans that should leverage a competitive advantage and provide value for the organization. Besides, ITIL includes the process of service portfolio management, answering the management requirement of SOA to effectively define and reuse services. Financial management, furthermore, is also a critical process for SOA to manage the budgeting and accounting of the IT service provider. The services of the provider, the underlying service management capabilities and strategic assets of the organization need to be approached from a financial perspective, so that concrete financial values are assigned to providers' services. Key performance indicators, however, which are critical measurement parameters indicating how well the business design is performing its business, are handled in Service Design domain of ITIL framework under the best practice Design Measurement Systems, Methods and Metrics.

**Service Design – Assemble.** Assemble phase of the SOA lifecycle is about transforming the business design items in IT language and to realize and automate the services and other IT components, such as applications and infrastructure. It is essential for SOA that the required services and service components are searched in the application library first, which archives all the legacy applications of an IT organization used in the past, to reuse services that already match the needs of the business without having to create them all over. ITIL's main goal of Service Design stage, to conceptualize and design innovative IT services and the environment that those services need to operate derived from the service strategy, match with SOA objectives and the processes that ITIL offers provide the management with the ability to assemble and develop service components in terms of SOA.

ITIL framework includes service level management process, which is vital for SOA governance to derive the required outcome level for a service from the business strategy, reflecting the customer needs and opportunities for a particular service to shape the optimal service and compare it to the demanded level. Service catalogue management supports business IT alignment by providing a single reliable source for the business as an overview of the status and description of all services of the service providers, leveraging transparency and allowing the business to understand the value of their services. Furthermore, ITIL addresses availability, security and continuity issues in service design stage with its processes and fulfill all SOA expectations in regard to transform the business design into IT terms and language and keep IT synchronized with the business objectives.

**Service Transition – Deploy.** In the third step of mapping the Service Transition stage is mapped to Deploy stage of SOA, which is about the deployment of the IT design by creating a hosting infrastructure for those applications designed in Assemble phase and fulfillment of the quality of service concerns such as availability, reliability, integrity, efficiency and service ability. ITIL Service Transition goals, practices and processes support Deploy stage of SOA by transitioning the service between design and strategy, managing change and focusing on the actual implementation of the designed services into operational use. One of the biggest challenges for managing SOA properly is the implementation of effective and systematic change management and change control practices. Although change is a key concept for today's organizations to sustain their business value and survive in the competition, only a few organizations can manage to define and implement a change control system, which is the balance between regular and emergency change and provides visibility and understanding for the need of change.

ITIL supports continual change with its processes Change Management, Service Asset and Configuration Management, Validation and Testing Management and Release Management, creating a cycle of change within the overall service lifecycle, that systematically identifies the need for change, tests and implements it, reconfigures the system considering that change is now applied and achieves a new state. Thanks to this approach the improvised change is eliminated, so that the change based risk remains limited and under control. Furthermore, ITIL Service Transition includes practices to predict unexpected situations and incidents, which can possibly imply changes in the service design or strategy, thus integrating all lifecycle domains to gather feedback in order to improve the quality of decisions concerning change. Service Transition stage of ITIL include processes and practices, which are vital for implementing SOA effectively and can contribute to governance capabilities and maturity of an IT organization.

**Service Operation – Manage.** In the final step of the mapping ITIL Service Operation domain is mapped to Manage domain of SOA. Manage domain is about maintaining the optimal state of IT during the actual delivery of the services to the customers. The performance of IT to deliver its services should continuously be monitored, system logs need to be analyzed to detect problems in various service components, problems should be solved, and services affected by those problems should be corrected. Accordingly, the responsibility of Service Operation stage is to actually deliver the services to customers on a continual level as planned and ensure that the applications, technology infrastructure, information and people are managed and utilized optimally.

SOA requires continual monitoring and evaluation of the service request and response performances to understand if the services are actually delivered to customers as planned. ITIL framework delivers critical success factors and measurement techniques within its framework and can improve the organization's ability to apply these techniques as an everyday practice and remain cost efficient. Besides, the processes Incident Management, Problem Management and Event Management focus on detecting, avoiding and solving incidents, as well as applying and documenting solutions and changes. The experience gained through repeated exercise of operating these ITIL processes will mostly improve the organization's management ability to deliver SOA enabled services. Finally, Service Desk function along with Request Fulfillment and Access Management processes provide a common interface for every user and use the data they gather to organize and prioritize information across the organization according to the business design and contribute to business IT alignment as requested by SOA.

### 4.2   Application in the Area of COBIT

**Plan and Organize – Model.** The Model domain is the first step of the SOA lifecycle and is about leveraging the business design of the organization, which projects the overall objectives of the business, all business processes, decision criteria, policies and assumptions of the organization to reach these business objectives. Plan and Organize domain matches with this domain perfectly by focusing on the strategy and tactics of how IT can best contribute to the accomplishment of business goals. The business requirements for IT need to be derived from the enterprise strategy and the optimal IT architecture needs to be planned, so that the IT remains aligned with business objectives. Control objectives such as IT value management, business IT alignment, IT strategic plan, IT tactical plan and IT portfolio management delivered within the process Define a Strategic IT Plan will ensure the service provider to know what needs to be done to achieve successful business IT integration, which lies at the core of both SOA governance and COBIT framework. Control objectives concerning the IT architecture, technological direction, resource management and investment management are also delivered within COBIT framework and could be very helpful to consider when planning SOA. COBIT also deals with the communication of the goals and objectives throughout the enterprise and identifying risks threatening the achievement of business goals, thus providing a control mechanism and high level business perspective for the service provider to model the SOA enabled IT components.

**Acquire and Implement – Assemble.** In the second step of the mapping Acquire and Implement stage is mapped to Assemble domain of SOA. Like Assemble domain described above Acquire and Implement is also about realization of the IT strategy planned in the previous domain through concrete IT solutions in this domain. Automated solutions and applications need to be identified, assembled, improved and integrated with the existing system and business needs. New IT projects need to be developed and changes need to be applied in order to improve the existing system with due regard to the business strategy and time or economical constraints.

Acquire and Implement domain also includes the actual deployment of the hosting infrastructure, what extends the borders of the Assemble stage and can better be mapped to the Deploy stage of SOA. Control objectives delivered within the process Identify Automated Solutions, such as Definition and Maintenance of Business Functional and Technical Requirements, Risk Analysis Report and Feasibility Study and Formulation of Alternative Courses of Action, for example reflect the critical activities and best practices, which need to be considered and controlled to achieve high quality of automated solutions that are effective, efficient and fit for purpose. Application software, technology infrastructure development and changes applied to those can be controlled accordingly via the control objectives delivered by COBIT.

**Deliver and Support – Deploy.** In the third phase of the mapping the Deliver and Support domain is mapped to the Deploy domain. Deliver and Support domain is responsible for the successful delivery of IT services that have been planned and acquired in previous domains. COBIT's objective of this domain is to fulfill the quality of service concerns such as availability, reliability, integrity, efficiency and service ability, and thus it supports the SOA objective of Deploy domain to ensure a low margin of error by providing the services of the business. COBIT processes supporting that objective can be summarized as Manage Performance and Capacity, Ensure Continuous Service, Ensure Systems Security, Manage Problems, Manage Service Desk and Incidents. However, The SOA requirement of creating and deploying a hosting infrastructure for those applications implemented in the Assemble phase is covered in the Acquire and Implement domain of COBIT lifecycle and not considered in Deliver and Support. Additionally, service level management, configuration management, educating and training users and identifying and allocating costs are also covered in Deliver and Support domain and the control objectives defined within these processes will help the management to understand and communicate the objectives of this domain and will support the implementation of SOA. Maturity models will provide the opportunity for the management to objectively judge themselves in how good they are in delivering high quality services fulfilling the business requirements from IT and sense the need for improvement.

**Monitor and Evaluate – Manage.** In the last step of the mapping Monitor and Evaluate domain is mapped to Manage domain. Monitor and Evaluate domain is responsible for evaluating the performance of IT services, checking if the IT supports the business goals as planned before and implying changes if not. The purpose and concerns of the domains match majorly and can be mapped perfectly to each other. COBIT delivers measurement metrics such as outcome and performance indicators, which will help the service provider to efficiently evaluate the performance of their services. Through the hierarchical goal relationship structure of COBIT these metrics can enable success predictions on higher level goals and enable the management to take early actions. This ability to be measurement oriented is vital for the successful SOA governance. Furthermore, Monitor and Evaluate domain ensures that the IT stays aligned with the business by controlling the compliance issues with internal and external regulations and supports the continual improvement of the IT system by checking the adequacy of the internal control objectives to reflect the business requirements from IT. All processes of this domain can be mapped successfully to the Manage domain of SOA and are vital for the proper management of the SOA lifecycle and achieving superior IT governance.

## 5   Conclusion and Outlook

In this work we proposed a detailed approach for mapping activities from IT governance frameworks such as ITIL and COBIT to SOA governance processes. The case study demonstrated the feasibility of our approach as a hands-on possibility for IT organizations to move to SOA and Cloud Governance based on their existing governance methodologies. Furthermore, our work is a specific example of the extension and reuse of IT-specific knowledge and learning objects, processes, strategies, systems, and performance as defined in [15].

## References

1. Stantchev, V., Hoang, T.D., Schulz, T., Ratchinski, I.: Optimizing clinical processes with position-sensing. IT Professional 10(2), 31–37 (2008)

2. Stantchev, V.: Enhancing Health Care Services with Mixed Reality Systems. Springer, Berlin (2009)
3. Stantchev, V.: Intelligent Systems for Optimized Operating Rooms. In: Damiani, E., Jeong, J., Howlett, R.J., Jain, L.C. (eds.) New Directions in Intelligent Interactive Multimedia Systems and Services - 2. SCI, vol. 226, pp. 443–453. Springer, Heidelberg (2009)
4. Stantchev, V., Malek, M.: Architectural Translucency in Service-oriented Architectures. IEE Proceedings - Software 153(1), 31–37 (2006)
5. Stantchev, V., Schröpfer, C.: Negotiating and Enforcing QoS and SLAs in Grid and Cloud Computing. In: Abdennadher, N., Petcu, D. (eds.) GPC 2009. LNCS, vol. 5529, pp. 25–35. Springer, Heidelberg (2009)
6. Stantchev, V., Schröpfer, C.: Service level enforcement in web-services based systems. International Journal on Web and Grid Services 5(2), 130–154 (2009)
7. Stantchev, V., Malek, M.: Addressing Web Service Performance by Replication at the Operating System Level. In: ICIW 2008: Proceedings of the 2008 Third International Conference on Internet and Web Applications and Services, pp. 696–701. IEEE Computer Society, Los Alamitos (2008)
8. Stantchev, V., Franke, M.R.: Managing Project Landscapes in Knowledge-Based Enterprises. In: Lytras, M.D., Ordonez de Pablos, P., Damiani, E., Avison, D., Naeve, A., Horner, D.G. (eds.) WSKS 2009. CCIS, vol. 49, pp. 208–215. Springer, Heidelberg (2009)
9. Stantchev, V.: Performance evaluation of cloud computing offerings. In: Third International Conference on Advanced Engineering Computing and Applications in Sciences, ADVCOMP 2009, pp. 187–192 (October 2009)
10. Van Bon, J.: Foundations of IT service management based on ITIL V3. Van Haren (2008)
11. Lainhart IV, J.W.: COBIT: A Methodology for Managing and Controlling Information and Information Technology Risks and Vulnerabilities. Journal of Information Systems 14, 21 (2000)
12. Stantchev, V., Tamm, G.: Addressing non-functional properties of services in it service management. In: Non-Functional Properties in Service Oriented Architecture: Requirements, Models and Methods, pp. 324–334. IGI Global, Hershey (2011)
13. Van Grembergen, W. (ed.): Strategies for Information Technology Governance. IGI Publishing, Hershey (2003)
14. Stantchev, V., Malek, M.: Addressing dependability throughout the soa life cycle. IEEE Transactions on Services Computing 99(PrePrints) (2010)
15. Lytras, M.D., Sicilia, M.A.: The Knowledge Society: a manifesto for knowledge and learning. International Journal of Knowledge and Learning 1(1/2), 1–11 (2005)

# Students' Active Role on the Assessment of Learning Results in Blended-Learning Environments in Engineering in Spain

Mª José Rodríguez-Conde[1], Susana Olmos-Miguéláñez[1], Blanca García-Riaza[1],
Ana Belén González- Rogado[2], and Francisco José García-Peñalvo[2]

[1] University Institute of Educational Sciences, University of Salamanca,
Paseo de Canalejas, 169. 37008 Salamanca, Spain
[2] Computer Sciences and Automatics Department, University of Salamanca,
Higher Polytechnic School of Zamora, Campus Viriato, Avda.
Requejo, 33. 49022 Zamora, Spain
{mjrconde,solmos,bgr,abgr,fgarcia}@usal.es

**Abstract.** In this paper we present an assessment experience with students, based on the use on Information and Communication Technologies (Hereafter ICTs). This process has been developed in the framework of the Research project I+D+i EDU2009-08758, in which one of the main research areas is that of assessing learning in university context, and, more specifically, in the field of Engineering degrees in Spain. The main objective is that of systematize the assessment process carried out in the subject of Computing Systems, already adapted to the European Space for Higher Education guidelines. For this purpose, we have used EvalCOMIX tool, implementing with it several assessment scales that systematize evaluation processes, make students get involved in the process and provide with necessary feedback when required.

**Keywords:** Alternative Assessment, Engineering, E-assessment.

## 1 Introduction

In the process to adapt educative systems to the European Space for Higher Education in Spain, *assessment methods* get a special significance due to the fact that they will have to both guide and motivate students in the learning process. De Miguel et al (2006) [5] point out that, once competences to reach and their corresponding results have been set, these become the centre of the learning process, but it is also necessary to set adequate teaching-learning modalities and methodologies, together with *criteria and assessment procedures* that allow us to test if they have been actually acquired. Gairín et al [7] indicate that the use of competences entails four different interactive components:

"*Competence description, description of activities where competence will be shown, instruments or means to assess competence and criteria or standards to judge competence*" highlighting that traditional assessment procedures do not meet the

M.D. Lytras et al. (Eds.): WSKS 2011, CCIS 278, pp. 408–415, 2013.
© Springer-Verlag Berlin Heidelberg 2013

requirements demanded by the assessment of new contents and the new role of students in university learning processes. In this sense, Calatayud [3] points out that it is not possible to innovate in the teaching-learning process without a parallel innovation in assessment procedures, since students will not change the way they learn if the assessment system is not adapted to their learning as well. Calatayud [3] also emphasizes that assessment is a process that must be done in a continuous way, not being and end in itself, but having as aim the improvement of a learning process which will be conditioned by the information relevant in each case. Information taken from the assessment process can be interpreted and translated into value judgments to propose improvement plans and take decisions. Therefore, assessment is a good opportunity to boost students' learning process ([12], p. 3).

To promote assessment, different adequate assessment systems have to be used to boost a fruitful long-term learning ([8], p.10). Pérez Pueyo et al ([14], p. 439), indicate as adequate ones the *feedback* during the learning process, which enables an improvement; self-assessment and peer-assessment, together with a serious reflection on the process.

As a consequence, the *participation of students in the assessment of their learning* is given much more importance. Their participation will contribute to promote three requisites for any good assessment process: to be motivating, continuous and formative ([2], p. 201). Peer-assessment will also contribute to the self-regulation of the learning process, to the development of critical thinking among students and varied strategies to solve problems, as well as the capacity of students to negotiate, discuss be organized and self-confident in the development of their tasks, facilitating lifelong learning ([11]).

## 1.1    Learning-Oriented e-assessment

The generation of new learning procedures entails as well that new assessment processes have to be born. Santos, Martinez and López [15] point out that we need to overcome the so-called 'exam-culture' and start the way towards an 'assessment culture', oriented more to the improvement of learning than to a final summative measurement of the process. We thus get new concepts around assessment: learning-oriented assessment, authentic assessment, alternative assessment ([1], [13]).

The three main purposes of learning-oriented assessment are: performance measurement, standards maintenance and learning promotion, which complement each other and contribute to a continuous assessment of the effort, perseverance and interest on results shown by students. Assessment, in this way conceived, is aimed at achieving competences equally set for all students, besides enabling them to develop a professional activity in future and promoting their lifelong learning. In this sense, learning-oriented assessment can be defined as a constant interaction between three different elements: *retrospective feedback, assessment tasks as learning tasks, and students as evaluators.* It is thus expected that students get involved in their own assessment process and become professionals able to self-regulate and update their knowledge, putting it into practice in the development of their professional career by implementing the use of competences [18].

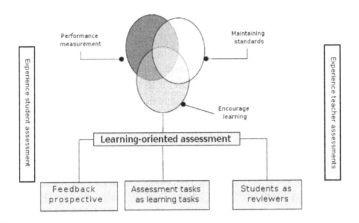

**Fig. 1.** Conceptual framework of learning-oriented assessment [4]

## 1.2 Assessment through Learning Management Systems (LMS)

At the same time, *Learning Management System* (LMS) platforms have turned into essential tools for learning-management in university nowadays context [9]. They facilitate information storage, sharing and the interaction trough the development of tasks and activities. At the University of Salamanca has been put forward a virtual learning space, using Moodle platform, which serves as support to in-class teaching. Using this space, and through a research Project leaded by the University of Cádiz[1], access has been granted to EvalCOMIX, a tool which allows competence assessment in a blended learning context. In this sense, teachers can design and create different assessment tools as, for example, control lists assessment scales and rubrics. As a consequence, not only can the teacher assess students' performance, but also enables students to be an active participant in the process, both in oneself assessment (self-assessment) and in peer-assessment that makes students acquire more autonomy and responsibility in the educational process.

## 2 Empirical Study: Methodology

The *objective* of this experience is to systematize the assessment process of students in a basic subject (Computing Systems) in the field of Engineering and Architecture at the University of Salamanca Computing Engineering and Information Systems Degree) [16]. In this study, 17 students out of the 21 enrolled in the subject, actively participated. In-class sessions are used to present basic concepts of the syllabus, using material explanations as support to motivate and make students be more interested. To boost their participation in the learning process, and at the beginning of the academic year, a series of questions to answer in the virtual campus were planned. Questions

[1] Research Project Re-Evalúa: Re-Evalúa (Re-engineering e-assessment, Technologies and Competence Development of University Teachers and Students), sponsored by Universites, Research and Technologies General Treasury of Andalucía Regional Government (ref. P08-SEJ-03502).

were mainly related to the historical evolution of Computing Sciences, and they were uploaded to the platform together with weekly tasks and objective tests to self-assess the knowledge of students of the contents dealt with in class. In a parallel way, we planned group work, which aims to boost the competence *"to do things with others"* and is considered to be basic tools to change students' mentality and make them involve in the learning process. The final aim was to get an *"active"* student who decides about his/her own learning process.

Tasks were mainly addressed to reading and commenting articles and bibliography related to the field, thus motivating their interest on the subject, or to preparing a report on a specific topic, what implies a bibliographical search.

Tasks were carried out in groups of three or four students, and each group was suggested four different ones. Each task entails an oral presentation and has associated to it a different assessment instrument.

The involvement of students in the learning process will help them to control their own learning in a lifelong process. Therefore, in two out of four tasks, assessment tools were used by students to carry out self-assessment and peer-assessment processes [6].

Taking into account that systematizing assessment facilitates and gives coherence to the process, and using EvalCOMIX tool [10] we created assessment tools for the different tasks that students carried out in this subject, also guided by a coherent assessment procedure [17]. More specifically, we built assessment scales and control lists for the assessment process.

## 3    Results

In respect to the *performance achieved by students* through teachers' assessment, both peer and self-assessment, results show evidences on the responsibility with which peer-assessment was carried out, although it was hard for them to carry out their self-assessment. Nevertheless, it is necessary to emphasize that none of them reflected in their time estimation the period devoted to assessment. As an example, we show marks got in task number 4.

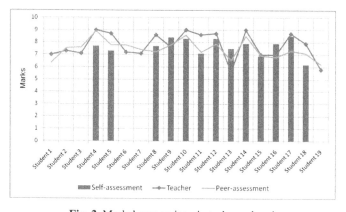

**Fig. 2.** Marks' comparison in task number 4

We assume that these results answer to the fact that they did not take this assessment process as a relevant part of the subject, partially due to the use of a new platform, that of Cadiz University platform. This hypothesis can be tested in items 29 and 30 in the satisfaction survey (Table 1), where we can observe that what has been less valued in the subject has been learning through self-assessment.

**Table 1.** Assessment in the subject (1-5 scale)

| Assessment in the subject | 2010/2011 (n=17) | |
|---|---|---|
| | $\overline{X}$ | $S_x$ |
| 26. Group work | 4,47 | ,624 |
| 27. Research and search learning | 4,25 | ,447 |
| 28. Oral presentations learning | 3,94 | ,443 |
| 29. Self-assessment learning | 3,35 | ,702 |
| 30. Peer-assessment learning | 3,41 | ,618 |

It will therefore be necessary to insist, explain or modify the process in this sense, as we thing that it is relevant for students to get benefit from the assessment carried out among peers, what will help, for example, to develop critical thinking.

From the point of view of the teaching team, we think that learning results of students have been satisfactory, and the involvement of all educational members in the learning process has been facilitated.

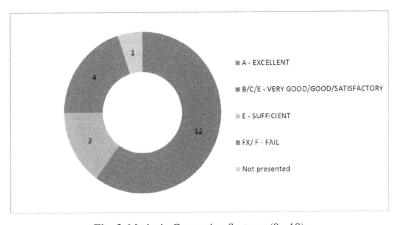

**Fig. 3.** Marks in Computing Systems (0 - 10)

Through a questionnaire, we tested the *satisfaction of students* towards the formative process. Once dealt with the activities, we wanted to know the value that students assigned to experience, know how they worked, their assessment on the methodology used, and moreover, we asked them for an estimation on the number of hours devoted to the subject. For this purpose, the questionnaire was organized in seven dimensions: *a) Personal work methodology of students, b) Depth in the study of the subject, c)Perception of the methodology used, d) General satisfaction about the experience    e)Usefulness degree of several resources used for the subject f) Assessment of educational resources used in the subject  and g) Rough estimate of the number of theoretical/practical hours devoted to studying along the semester.*

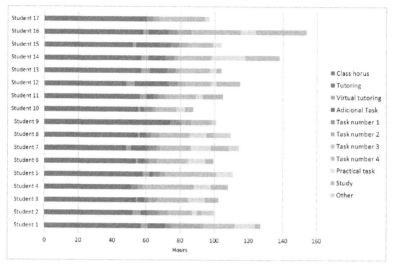

**Fig. 4.** Estimation of students on the number of hours devoted to the subject

The analysis of data has given us the following results: firstly, the overall sensation of work excess which is not a reality, but a perception of students derived to the change of attitude and methodology entailed by the European Space for Higher Education. Computing Systems is a 6 credits, 150 work hours subject, but, on the contrary, estimation data provided by students are always under that quantity (media 110,44; deviation 16,16). Therefore, we think that it is not necessary to delete tasks that have been regarded as appropriate, although it might be necessary to carry out a time redistribution and a higher coordination among subjects, relieving as much as possible that overload sensation.

Secondly,  regarding the valuation carried out by students on the methodology used, and as it had happened in previous years, students think that the methodology used is a good one (over 3 in a scale 1-5), and their satisfaction level is also high (over 4,1 in a 1-5 scale).

Besides being the teachers those who value learning results, it is also relevant for students to perceive that they have accomplished those achievements. In this case, the questionnaire reflects that students think they have understood the subject's objectives, which will be useful ($\overline{X}$ = 4,18; $S_x$= 0,529) and that attending class has been relevant to understand the subject ($\overline{X}$ = 4,69; $S_x$= 0,602), emphasizing the usefulness of the virtual campus (over 3.35 in a scale 1-5), although they have worked with two different virtual campuses at the same time.

## 4     Conclusions and Prospective Research Lines

Conclusions drawn from this study have been extracted from the whole process of design, implementation and assessment of a specific subject in the field of Engineering and Architecture Degrees in Spain, more specifically, at the University of Salamanca. We consider that the systematization of assessment will help students in the learning process, as it can allow them to access their mark quickly (both that of the teacher and the peers' one), as well as his/her colleagues' marks. This will also give them feedback that helps them to enhance their work and stimulates them to continue their learning process.

Regarding EvalCOMIX, and taken as an instrument to create assessment tools, it presents light problems that get the already complex process of assessment, even more complicated. Among the difficulties spotted, we would emphasize that *Moodle* does not allow the creation of work groups, and that hampers the assessment of each of the students, as the mark is collective even if the oral presentation has been carried our individually. We estimate, as possible handicap for the use of assessment systematizing tools, that of getting the teacher to rely on the tool. In this line, we propose as a suggestion that EvalCOMIX be configured not to allow the modification of instruments that have already been employed by users (students/teachers), and to permit a visualization mode that does not alter percentages assigned.

The process developed in this subject, Computing Systems, has been only an approach to the systematization of the assessment process, but, in any case, we consider that the experience has been positive. We also think that it is necessary to go on deepening in the implementation of competence-assessment processes more technical and polished in such a way that we can, as teachers, test that the procedure used has been valid and reliable, and that it counts on a high level of satisfaction of students.

**Acknowledgements.** National Project I+D+i: Key Competences Assessment and Teacher Training in Secondary Education: TIC, ALFIN and School coexistence (EF-TALCO). Ref.: EDU2009-08753.

## References

[1] Boud, D., Falchikov, N.: Aligning assessment with long-term learning. Assessment & Evaluation in Higher Education 31(4), 399–413 (2006)

[2] Bretones, A.: Participación del alumnado de educación superior en su evaluación. Revista de Educación 347, 181–202 (2008)

[3] Calatayud, M.A.: La evaluación como instrumento de aprendizaje y mejora. Una luz a fondo. In: Calatayud, M. (ed.) La Evaluación Como Instrumento de Aprendizaje. Técnicas y Estrategias, pp. 9–54. Ministerio de Educación y Ciencia, Madrid (2007)

[4] Carless, D., Joughin, G., Liu, N.F.: How Assessment supports learning: learning oriented assessment in action. Hong Kong University Press, Hong Kong (2006)

[5] De Miguel Díaz, M., et al.: Metodologías de enseñanza y aprendizaje para el desarrollo de competencias. Orientaciones para el profesorado universitario ante el espacio europeo de educación superior. In: Metodologías de enseñanza y aprendizaje para el desarrollo de competencias. Orientaciones para el profesorado universitario ante el espacio europeo de educación superior. Alianza Editorial, Madrid (2006)

[6] Dochy, F., Segers, M., Sluijsmans, D.: The Use of Self-, Peer and Co-assessment in Higher Education: a review. Studies in Higher Education 24(3), 331–350 (1999)

[7] Gairín, J., et al.: La evaluación por competencias en la universidad: posibilidades y limitaciones (ref. EA2008-0086). Proyecto elaborado dentro del Programa de Estudios y Análisis de la Dirección General de Universidades, MEC (2008),
http://82.223.210.121/mec/ayudas/repositorio/20090709162246 Memoria%20EA%202008-0086%20J%20Gairin.pdf
(accessed November 10, 2010)

[8] Gibbs, G., Simpson, C.: Condiciones para una evaluación continuada favorecedora del aprendizaje. ICE y Ediciones Octaedro, S.L., Barcelona (2009),
http://www.octaedro.com/ice/pdf/13CUADERNO.pdf (accessed July 6, 2011)

[9] Rego, H., Moreira, T., García Peñalvo, J.F.: AHKME eLearning Information System: A 3.0 Approach. IJKSR 2(2), 71–79 (2011)

[10] Ibarra Sáiz, M.S., et al.: EvalCOMIX en Moodle: Un medio para favorecer la participación de los estudiantes en la e-Evaluación. RED, Revista de Educación a Distancia. Special number - SPDECE (2010),
http://www.um.es/ead/red/24/Ibarra_Cabeza.pdf (accessed March 19, 2011)

[11] Ibarra, M.S., Rodríguez, G., Gómez, M.A.: La evaluación entre iguales: beneficios y estrategias para su práctica en la universidad. Revista de Educación, 359. MEC, Madrid (September-December 2012) (2012, en prensa),
http://www.revistaeducacion.mec.es/doi/359_092.pdf (accessed February 08, 2011)

[12] López, V.M., Martínez, L.F., Julián, J. A.: La Red Nacional de Evaluación Formativa, Docencia Universitaria y Espacio Europeo de Educación Superior (EEES). Presentación del proyecto, grado de desarrollo y primeros resultados. Revista de Docencia Universitaria. Red-U, 2 1, 1–19 (2007)

[13] Padilla, M.T., Gil, J.: La evaluación orientada al aprendizaje en la Educación Superior: condiciones y estrategias para su aplicación en la docencia universitaria. Revista Española de Pedagogía 241, 447–466 (2008)

[14] Pérez, A., Tabernero, B., López, V.M., Ureña, N., Ruiz, E., Caplloch, M., González, N., Castejón, F.J.: Evaluación formativa y compartida en la docencia universitaria y el espacio europeo de educación superior: cuestiones clave para su puesta en práctica. Revista de Educación 347, 435–451 (2008),
http://www.revistaeducacion.mec.es/re347/re347_20.pdf (accessed July 06, 2011)

[15] Santos, M.L., Martínez, L.F., López, V.M.: La innovación docente en el EEES. Editorial Universidad de Almería, Almería (2009)

[16] González Rogado, A.B., Rodríguez Conde, M.J., Olmos Miguelañez, S., García Riaza, B., García Peñalvo, F.J.: Assessment of a blended-learning methodology in engineering. International Journal of Technology Enhanced Learning 2(4), 347–357 (2010)

[17] Rodríguez, G., Ibarra, M.S.: La sistematización de la evaluación: los procedimientos de evaluación. Unidad III. In: Apuntes Inéditos del Programa de Formación, Dentro del Proyecto Re-evalúa. Grupo de investigación Evalfor, Cádiz (2010)

[18] Ibarra Sáiz, M.S., et al.: Integration of EVALCOMIX 1.0 into e-learning systems. In: Méndez Vilas, A., Solano Martín, A., Mesa González, J., Mesa González, J.A. (eds.) Research, Reflections and Innovations in Integrating ICT in Education, vol. 2, Formatex, Lisboa (2009),
http://www.formatex.org/micte2009/book/965-968.pdf

# Social Networking in Higher Education: A Knowledge Convergence Platform

Vladlena Benson, Stephanie Morgan, and Hemamali Tennakoon

Kingston Business School
Kingston Hill
Kingston Upon Thames, KT2 7LB
v.benson@kingston.ac.uk

**Abstract.** With the increasing infiltration of online social networking into the everyday life of the younger generation, higher education appears to be a lucrative platform for deploying social networks in an academic context. This paper suggests research questions and opens a discussion in relation to managing knowledge on online social networking in academic settings and beyond. Extant research provides a useful lens into the applications of social networking sites in learning and teaching or at the stages of employability and career management in student life. A limited consideration in current research has been given to exploring capabilities of social networking for lifelong learning and its role in the entire student lifecycle. The potential opened by online social networking in the area of knowledge accumulation and knowledge sharing is yet to be properly addressed by researchers. Therefore more attention is needed to identify the overarching issues of social networking applications in Higher Education (HE) settings. Based on a broad literature review this paper draws attention to some implications for HE institutions of exploiting knowledge resources with online social networks.

**Keywords:** Knowledge management, online social networking, social capital, student lifecycle, educational technology, employability.

## 1    Introduction

The advent of online social networking has had a significant impact on how people stay in touch and communicate, this is especially relevant to younger individuals who are increasingly comfortable with information and communication technology, familiar with a wide variety of communication and computing devices and lead an active social life enriched by means of online social networking services [Pr09]. So high is the proliferation of online social network activity amongst young people that many academics find the possibility of connecting students online through social networking services rather promising. Learning and teaching have naturally attracted greater attention from academics. There even has been suggestions of an emergence of a new Web 2.0 pedagogy which harnesses networking capabilities [Al08] Using

M.D. Lytras et al. (Eds.): WSKS 2011, CCIS 278, pp. 416–425, 2013.
© Springer-Verlag Berlin Heidelberg 2013

social technologies and media allows learners to communicate and collaborate across national and cultural boundaries, generate academic content and become active participants and contributors in the learning process. As student life is multifaceted a number of areas of social networking applications have been explored in recent literature [ESL07].     Student recruitment and marketing, alumni relations and entrepreneurship are only a few areas where higher education institutions endeavour to harness benefits of social networking connectivity [BFM10]. Knowledge generation and meaningful exploitation of resources embedded in relationships in HE settings has attracted significant attention [Al08]. However, the question of the changing nature of knowledge in the age of social networking [Pr09] and mass connectivity remains yet to be answered.

The paper is structured as follows. Having introduced the notion of social networking, the article continues the discussion of the exiting definitions of knowledge, leading to the question of what and how we are attempting to accumulate, manage and share knowledge resources through applications of online social networking in Higher Education. Section four considers stages in a student lifecycle and relates competencies and skills essential at each stage. Subsequent sections of the paper propose a framework for knowledge management through social networking in HE settings and beyond. The final section presents some practical implications of applications of social networks in student lifecycle and summaries some open questions for further research.

## 2     Definition of 'knowledge': Theory Grounding

The term 'knowledge' has attracted research attention from a variety of disciplines. The term 'knowledge' has a history dating back to the time of the Greek philosophers. Questions such as 'what do we know?', 'what can be known?', and 'what does it mean to say that someone knows something?' discussed in philosophical literature [Fa03] remain topical and perhaps unanswered by the contemporary research. Understanding the meaning of 'knowledge' is an important process, as a multifaceted, intangible nature of 'knowledge' lead to a wide array of its definitions.

Wilson defines knowledge as 'what a person knows' and states that, 'knowledge involves the mental processes of comprehension, understanding and learning that go on in the mind and only in the mind'[Wi02]. A similar definition was introduced by Chen as an 'intangible asset' or 'intellectual capital' (IC) which is 'an activity not a commodity' [Ch08]. This definition, confirms Wilson's view that knowledge is more of a mental process rather than a physical object that could be 'managed'. Nonaka and Takeuchi argue in their highly acclaimed paper 'The Knowledge-Creating Company' that knowledge is the result of interaction between 'explicit' and 'tacit' knowledge [NT95]. In other words, this takes us a step forward from the previous definitions by including both the tangible and intangible elements of knowledge. However, this definition has been criticised by scholars [Go06] as a misleading statement since in a previous article Nonaka has defined knowledge as a "personal belief" [No94]. Klein calls it as a "true, warranted belief" [Kl98], while Dewey and Bentley describe it as "vague words" which we are bound to use at times [DB49]. 'Processed information' is the term Myers uses to define knowledge [My96] and a broader description is given by [Da98] when they explain it as "information combined with experience, context, interpretation and reflection" or in other words, as a richer form of information.

Last but not the least of the definitions defines knowledge as "objects" [Ga02] which can be found entrenched in the form of documents, routines in organizations, "physical structure of the work place" of the work place [AI00].The latter definition is summed up in an equation by McShane and Von Glinow which gives the summation of 'Human Capital', 'Structural Capital' and 'Relationship Capital' as equivalent to 'Intellectual Capital'[MVG00]. Table 1 attempts to summarise some existing definitions of the terms 'knowledge'. The meaning of knowledge today has changes considerably giving more value to it and promoting it into the category of an 'asset' to individuals and organisations.

**Table 1.** Knowledge: An elusive concept

| Source | Definition |
|---|---|
| McShane and Von Glinow [MVG00] | Equivalent of 'Human Capital', 'Structural Capital' and 'Relationship Capital' |
| Garavelli et al [Ga02] | "objects" which can be found entrenched in various forms within an organsation |
| Argote and Ingram [AI00] | Exists in the form of documents, routines in organizations, "physical structure of the work place" of the work place |
| Nonaka and Takeuchi [NT95] | the result of interaction between 'explicit' and 'tacit' knowledge |
| Klein [Kl98] | a "true, warranted belief" |
| Myers [My96] | "Processed information" |
| Chen [Ch08] | an 'intangible asset' or 'intellectual capital' (IC) which is 'an activity not a commodity' |
| Davenport et al. [Da98] | "information combined with experience, context, interpretation and reflection" |
| Willson [Wi02] | "what a person knows" and states that, "knowledge involves the mental processes of comprehension, understanding and learning that go on in the mind and only in the mind" |

The many definitions of knowledge help to gain an insight into the concept of knowledge management discussed later in this section. The different types of knowledge such as explicit and tacit knowledge coming from various sources such as from the individuals in the organization, various organisational systems and physical structure of the workplace, etc. need to be captured, organised and managed in such a way so that eventually, they can be used in a productive manner. Knowledge management (KM) is therefore, defined as "the installation of purposeful management processes that enable to capture personal and contextual knowledge" [Br98] with a similar definition given by [Da98]. Sociologists use the term 'knowledge-based societies' [St94], 'knowledge workers', 'knowledge technologies' [Ga02] etc. to discuss related areas that use the theory of knowledge in a narrower perspective. The discussion so far brings to the surface the underlying value of knowledge as a product of learning produced collectively. This leads us to the discussion about the position of online social networks as a tool offering the potential to collectively accumulate, structure, exploit and share knowledge in HE settings.

## 3    Knowledge and the Student Lifecycle

In the context of HE the student lifecycle has been depicted in a number of ways, usually with seven or eight stages [BMF10]. Student life does not start at on the first day of classes and does not end when they pass their last exam. Student lifecycle in its broadest sense means from the first point of contact with potential students to graduation and lifelong learning and career management for graduates [QES07]. The first point of contact can precede the application process considerably and comprise of awareness and aspiration rising stage. Moving on to the application and recruitment and pr-entry support, the student lifecycle process then transits to induction, on-course support, learning, teaching and assessment. Final stages of the lifecycle involve career management and life-long learning. Recent literature draws attention to the potential of online networking services while studying at the university (e.g. [ESL07]). However, little research attention has been drawn to the significance of social networks in the student lifecycle in its entirety [BF10]. This is especially important as the stages of employability management and life-long learning take a centre stage in managing student expectations and influencing their decision of taking up places at which university. As shown in table 2, stages involved in the student lifecycle can include: awareness; application & pre-entry; on-course support; learning, teaching & assessment; employability; alumni support and lifelong learning.    Knowledge management dimension is explored (as suggested in table 2) along the skills and competencies required from individuals at different stages in student lifecycle. As insightfully noted by [FK08] processing of information and generation of knowledge is replaced by the development of networks of trusted people, content and tools while the task of knowing is passed on to the network.

The three areas of academic/learning literacy, information literacy and ICT skills are addressed by schools and universities while students study there. Academics have developed established cultures and frameworks for sharing professional practice in these three areas. Focus on learners as individuals, with their own preferred approaches to study and particular needs have been central to professional best practice. Extant literature points to the fact that instructors work in a relative isolation sometimes unaware of practices of bridging the competencies gap in learners across departments. Where there is an institution-wide policy of assessing and progressing learners' skills, academic support is integrated most effectively.

**Table 2.** Framework for component competencies for student lifecycle stages

| Lifecycle stages | High level terms | Component competencies | Process Objectives |
|---|---|---|---|
| Awareness | Information literacy | Identification, accession , interpretation | Ensure that potential entrants into HE whether currently at school, in HE, in the community or in the workplace are engaged with by the university to raise their awareness of undergraduate, postgraduate and CPD opportunities |
| Application and pre-entry | Informed decision making | Research, synthesis application self-evaluation self-organisation | Prove increased opportunities for students from more diverse backgrounds to enter university |
| On-course support | Engagement | Participation Self-direction Exploration Problem-solving | Support students in fully engaging with their courses and the broader learning community |
| Learning, teaching and assessment | Communication and collaboration skills | Teamwork, networking, project management, problem-solving | Ensure that students have the best possible learning experience |
| | Academic practice, metacognition | Synthesis Argumentation Interpretation Research skills | |
| Employability and career management | Employability skills | Business awareness Networking Communications kills Entrepreneurship awareness innovation | Continually improve the employability of students; Equip students with employability skills; Support their transition into the workplace or further study |
| Alumni management | Identity resources | Participation and engagement citizenship | Alumni network management and engagement |
| Lifelong learning | Personal and professional skills | Self-awareness Strategic planning Self-evaluation, self-analysis | Continually improve and develop personal and professional skills, engage with communities of best practice; development of career management skills |

# 4     Knowledge Management in Higher Education and beyond: A Framework for Social Networking Applications

Online social networks reinforce and help re-enact social links between individuals, connecting people into groups and communities. According to a popular saying 'it isn't what you know, but who you know, that counts'. The concept of social relationships that serve as a resource is not new and has been a focus for scholarly debate across a range of disciplines. Through ties and social connections goal unachievable to an individual become achievable by a community, whilst individuals and groups cooperate to attain objectives otherwise beyond their reach [Ki01]. Through sharing of values and bonds online communities are capable to develop strong bonds and a high level of trust between community members [Be95]. Partnership and collaboration in social networks serve as a platform to bring together individual capacities and the range of knowledge sharing opportunities enhance the network capacity [So98]. Social connections and network membership can explain why networked groups can take advantage of mobilising and combining human capital `and enable individual members to exploit, develop and contribute knowledge to the network. An understanding of the process of how knowledge is built, accessed and exploited in online social networks is significant if knowledge management is to be used as an analytical framework in higher education settings and beyond. [Ki01] argue that interactions in social networks help operationalise (access) and develop knowledge as a resource within communities. Falk and Kilpatrick [FK00] distinguish between two kinds of resources used in interpersonal interactions: *knowledge resources,* i.e. knowledge of who, when and where to go for advice, resources and knowledge of how to get things done, and *identity resources*, i.e. willingness to act for the benefit of the group and individual members. For example, self confidence and reciprocity shared between parties in a network constitute identity resources. Authors further conclude that knowledge and identity resources enable individual network members to coalesce their knowledge and skills with the resources of the community as a whole. Being able to combine diverse talents and skills and other assets in a network has been shown as advantageous in situations requiring problem solving [KM93]. In summary there are two types of benefits generated by the networking and social interactions in a community: positive outcome for the group as a whole when members cooperate and act for the benefit of the community, and the building and maximising of knowledge and identity resources through networking, increasing confidence to act for the communal benefit and build commitment to the network. According to [Ki01] education contributes towards building of knowledge resources and strengthening identity resources, increasing stocks of social capital overall. Stanton –Salazar [SS98] concurs that education positively impacts the breadth and richness of networks and develops personal and interpersonal skills, such as self-confidence, ability to make friends and resolve conflicts. Findings by Stanton-Salazar show that the impact of educational attainment is even more significant among working-class communities as their networks are smaller and bounded, with much less penetration into institutional and professional networks. Higher education experience contributes positively to building various knowledge and identity resources, and social capital variables overall, as shown by Glaeser [Ga10] such as membership in organisations and trust for the benefit of individuals and community as a whole.

To summarise the arguments above in the context of social networking in Higher Education settings, social interactions contribute to knowledge construction and sharing throughout the entire student's lifecycle and provide benefits at individual, group, community and organisational levels. Individuals connected into a social network at the stage of awareness, for example, can draw from the factual knowledge about higher education institutions available from the social networking sites for those institutions as well as engage in interactions with people also looking for University places in order to enrich their own knowledge resources (know who to ask for help and advice). As individuals become engaged in social interactions with the higher institution of their choice they are likely to develop a sense of belonging to the university community and trust long before their studies begin. In the later stages of the student lifecycle individuals can actively participate in knowledge creation and sharing. Another area rapidly gaining attention is career management and exploitation of social capital embedded in social relations. Social networking with future employers, presence on business oriented services and keeping in touch with alumni can open up wider career opportunities for graduates.

In the case of small groups, for example academic learning groups and project teams, social networking services can facilitate communication between group members, help students engage in learning and keep up regular study sessions with group members. Social networks have the capability to replace face to face interactions in completion of group coursework and act as a virtual repository for individual contributions. Group membership can scale to module size, year of study, level of study, programme wide or faculty wide. Tapping into cross disciplinary skills and resources opens even wider capabilities for building and exploiting knowledge assets in a networked higher education institution.

At the next level of social networking granularity stand organisations institution-wide and specialised networks. They play an essential role in acting as entities of university wide knowledge repositories, while specialised organisations, such as support services, societies and interest-based communities help students leverage knowledge resources across multiple network levels and in specialised areas. Finally, the discussion of the social networking potential will be incomplete without the consideration of its role in lifelong learning. Decisions to pursue further education, work-based learning and personal and professional development can be positively influenced by networking and drawing on the experience of other members. Access to the resources of tacit and factual knowledge (how can I progress in my career? What skills I need to compete against others in a tough job market? Which course to apply to suit my work schedule and lifestyle, how to be successful in scholarship application for further education, etc.) can be greatly facilitated through membership in relevant social networks. The argument of this article is that better connected people enjoy better returns. We would like to extend this statement through the student lifecycle stages and argue that better connected individuals enjoy better returns from higher education with the support of social networking services as a knowledge convergence platform.

# 5    Implications, Limitations and Concluding Remarks

There are a number of implications for HE institutions that can be proposed from the above discussion. These are as follows:

*Incorporate SN into home and international recruitment processes* - A number of universities have started to use social networking at the initial stage (awareness) to generate interest in potential students and encourage applications. There is also an increase in the use of social networks to aid admissions (see [HRW09]), and to help students learn about their college, such as location, academic staff and fellow students through the pre-entry stage. Concerns remain regarding the extent of access a student should be allowed before enrolment, and therefore access is often restricted to specific forms of information.

*Integrate SN into student services and administration* - The use of electronic libraries as means of support is now commonplace, however the use of social networks for general student support is in its infancy, and research is needed to assess adequacy. Examples on current networking sites include administrative FAQ's and information about faculty events.

*Include SN into learning and teaching* - Social networks for learning, teaching and assessment are still untapped in many areas. They are more popular in computer courses and, for example, ergonomics. Traditional ideas of privacy and tutor-conduct can create problems [Fo09] and certainly require consideration with students on appropriate use and ethical behaviour. The University of Hong Kong is one example where learning support which encourages sharing and collaboration between students and tutors with similar interests has proven useful [Ch09].

*Incorporate SN into work placement, graduate recruitments and entrepreneurship schemes.* Employability and social networking is a two-edged sword. Employers are increasingly trying to engage students before graduation through social networks, but are also using these to assess suitability. Those students who leave information on their pages that indicate inappropriate behaviour are unlikely to be shortlisted [DF08]. Review and evaluation happens on social networks whether the education provider is supportive or not.

*Maintain Alumni Relations through SN* - The use of social networks after graduation, to support alumni through facilitating ongoing learning and job-search, is also likely to increase. By offering information and expanding the educational experience post graduation Universities can maintain contact with alumni and increase the possibility of referrals. Daley argues that overlaps between subjects in which users participate for employment and leisure will increase [Da09], and Universities may be able to tap into this phenomenon to generate a knowledge based alumni.

*Support Higher Education/Further Education Partnerships, Employers, Stakeholders through SN* – the social aspect and high interconnectivity of the organisations external to HE institutions is likely to increase. Manage career path, learning path and professional development can be strengthened through meaningful relations management. SN can help engage employers and other stakeholders in effective dialogue and review of the purposes of the curriculum, addressing the needs of graduate employers and improving  employability in a challenging social and economic landscape. This dialogue enabled through SN services facilitates continual improvement and development of personal and professional skills, engagement with communities of best practice.

To summarise, students can gather a great deal of information from social networking linked to their education throughout the student lifecycle, some controlled by the University, some not. However the extent to which this information becomes knowledge can be questioned, and requires a conceptual framework to facilitate correct use of this information to generate knowledge. The nature of knowledge is shifting in terms of what is considered useful knowledge, the ability to represent knowledge in digital form increasingly biases knowledge accumulation towards digital content and tacit knowledge and identity resources remain overlooked. Knowledge management becomes increasingly dependent on data processed and shared through information technology. As the data processing techniques progress value of learning and knowledge acquisition become less certain.  Through the networked society the products of intellectual work are easily accessible moving towards openness and collective knowledge bases.  Conflicts over intellectual property, access and licensing are likely to become more critical. Operationalisation of knowledge assets accumulated throughout higher education experience can be effectively enabled through their use appropriate for individual Universities. This article argues that more research is needed to help transform the old cliché 'it isn't what you know, but who you know, that counts' and help knowledge gained through higher education act as a true life-long asset. The online social networking services have the potential to work as a platform for connecting students and graduates beyond university walls.

# References

[Al08]    Alexander, B.: Social Networking in Higher Education. In: Katz, R. (ed.) The Tower and the Cloud, EduCause (2008),
          http://www.educause.edu/thetowerandthecloud
[AI00]    Argote, L., Ingram, P.: Knowledge transfer: a basis for competitive advantage in firms. Organizational Behavior and Human Decision Processes 82(1), 150–169 (2000)
[BFM10]   Benson, V., Filippaios, F., Morgan, S.: Changing the Face of Business Education and Career Planning. International Journal of eBusiness Management 4(1), 20–33 (2010)
[BF10]    Benson, V., Filippaios, F.: Effects of Digital Footprint on Career Management: Evidence from Social Media in Business Education. In: Lytras, M.D., Ordonez De Pablos, P., Ziderman, A., Roulstone, A., Maurer, H., Imber, J.B. (eds.) WSKS 2010. CCIS, vol. 111, pp. 480–486. Springer, Heidelberg (2010)
[Br98]    Broadbent, M.: The phenomenon of knowledge management: what does it mean to the information profession? Information Outlook, 23–31 (1998),
          http://www.sla.org/pubs/serial/io/1998/may98/broad ben.html (retrieved October 26, 2010)

[Ch08]   Chen, C.A.: Linking the knowledge creation process to organizational theories: A macro view of organization-environment change. Journal of Organizational Change 21(3), 259–279 (2008)

[DLB98]  Davenport, T.H., De Long, D.W., Beers, M.C.: Successful knowledge management projects'. Sloan Management Review, 43–57 (Winter 1998)

[DB49]   Dewey, J., Bentley, A.F.: Knowing and the Known. The Beacon Press, Boston (1949)

[ESL07]  Ellison, N., Steinfield, C., Lampe: The benefits of Facebook "friends": Exploring the relationship between college students' use of online social networks and social capital. Journal of Computer-Mediated Communication 12(3) (2007)

[Fa03]   Fagin, R., et al.: Reasoning about knowledge, Paper Back edition. MIT Press (2003)

[GGS02]  Garavelli, A.C., Gorgoglione, M., Scozzi, B.: Managing knowledge transfer by knowledge technologies. Technovation 22, 269–279 (2002)

[Go06]   Gourlay, S.: Conceptualizing Knowledge Creation: A Critique of Nonaka's Theory. Journal of Management Studies 43(7) (2006)

[HRW09]  Hayes, T., Ruschman, D., Walker, M.: Social Networking as an Admission Tool: A Case Study in Success. Journal of Marketing for Higher Education 19(2), 109–124 (2009)

[Kl98]   Klein, P.D.: Knowledge, concept of. In: Craig, E. (ed.) Routledge Encyclopaedia of Philosophy, pp. 266–276. Routledge, London (1998)

[MV08]   McShane, S.L., Von Glinow, M.A.: Organizational Behavior, 2nd edn. McGraw-Hill Higher Education (2008)

[My96]   Myers, P.S.: Knowledge Management and Organizational Design. Butterworth-Heinemann, Boston (1996)

[No94]   Nonaka, I.: A dynamic theory of organizational knowledge creation. Organization Science 5(1), 14–37 (1994)

[NLG05]  Nicol, D.J., Littlejohn, A., Grierson, H.: The importance of structuring information and resources within shared workspaces during collaborative design learning. Open Learning: The Journal of Open and Distance Learning 20(1), 31–49 (2005)

[NT95]   Nonaka, I., Takeuchi, H.: The knowledge creating company: how Japanese companies create the dynasties of innovation. Oxford University Press, Oxford (1995)

[Pr09]   Prensky, M.: H. Sapiens Digital: From digital immigrants and digital natives to digital wisdom. Journal of Online Education 5(3) (2009)

[St94]   Stehr, N.: Knowledge Societies. SAGE Publications, London (1994)

[WA04]   Walton, M., Archer, A.: The Web and information literacy: scaffolding the use of web resources in a project-based curriculum. British Journal of Educational Technology 35(2), 173–186 (2004)

[Wi02]   Wilson, T.D.: The nonsense of 'knowledge management'. Information Research 8(1)     (2002),     http://InformationR.net/ir/8-1/paper144.html (retrieved October 26, 2010)

[YK06]   Yorke, M., Knight, P.T.: Embedding Employability in the Curriculum. Learning and Employability. Higher Education Academy, York (2006)

# An Ontology-Driven Case Study for the Knowledge Representation of Management Information Systems

Jose A. Asensio, Nicolás Padilla, and Luis Iribarne

Applied Computing Group, University of Almería, Spain
{jacortes,npadilla,luis.iribarne}@ual.es

**Abstract.** Web-based Management Information Systems (MIS) require the use of standardized methods and techniques for their design and development. The two most used resources are Model Driven Architectures (MDA) and Ontology Driven Architectures (ODA). The MDA perspective allows us to separate the specification issues from the system architecture as well as the details from its implementation. On the other hand, ODA provides the semantic representation of knowledge domain, also independently of its implementation. This paper presents the use of ODA in the SOLERES system, an information system for environmental management (EMIS).

**Keywords:** Management Information Systems, Ontology-Driven Architecture.

## 1 Introduction

Nowadays, *Web-based Management Information Systems* (WMIS) require the use of standardized methods and techniques for their design and development [8]. The two most used resources are *Model Driven Architectures* (MDA) and Ontology Driven Architectures (ODA). While MDA allows us to separate, on the one hand, the specification from the system architecture and, on the other hand, details from its implementation, ODA provides the semantic representation of knowledge domain also independently of its implementation. Thus, combined use of both resources turns out to be very powerful for the design and development of this kind of systems. Both MDA and ODA have been used in SOLERES. SOLERES is an *Environmental Management Information System* (EMIS) based on WMIS, which is built by using the *Multi-Agent Systems* (MAS) technology. This paper is focused on the use of ODA in SOLERES, particularly on its knowledge representation subsystem called SOLERES-KRS. In this subsystem, the ontologies have been used in two very different contexts. On the one hand, they describe the information domain knowledge in the system; on the other hand, they model the processes and communications between different system components. The content of this article is structured as follows: Section 2 examines the ontologies used in EMIS; Section 3 presents the SOLERES-KRS case study regarding the use of ontologies; finally, Section 4 shows the conclusions.

M.D. Lytras et al. (Eds.): WSKS 2011, CCIS 278, pp. 426–432, 2013.

## 2    Background: EMIS Ontologies

It is obvious the advance of the new technologies in WMIS. Ontology is an example of these advances. Ontology was designed to be used in applications that need to manage the information semantic. In [4], the authors present an environmental decision-support system called *OntoWEDSS* for wastewater management. In this system, ontology is used to model the wastewater treatment process, to provide a common vocabulary, and an explicit conceptualization that describes the semantic of the data. Another example may be found in [5], an air quality monitoring system which uses an ontology to define messages and communications concisely and unambiguously. In [3], the authors present *Ecolingua*, an *EngMath* family ontology to represent quantitative ecological data. These examples show the use of ontologies to build models that describe the entities in the given domain and characterize the relationships and constraints associated with these entities. In [13], the authors present an ontology to represent geographic data and functions related to them. To meet the need for interoperable *Geographic Information System* (GIS), in [1] the authors propose a *Geo Ontology* model design to integrate geographical information. We have also explored an ontological application in the field of geographical information retrieval [11]. A different use appears in [7], where we can find an *Ontology Web Language* (OWL) extension with new primitives for modeling spatial location and spatial relationships with a geographic ontology. Extensions of existing ontologies have also appeared in this knowledge domain. In [10], the authors propose a geographic ontology based on *Geographic Markup Language* (GML) [6], and the OWL-S profile is extended to form geographic profiles. Another case is an extension of *NASAs SemanticWeb for Earth and Environmental Terminology* (SWEET) ontologies that include part of the hydrogeology domain [12].

## 3    The SOLERES-Knowledge Representation System Ontology

The SOLERES system is an information system for environmental management. The general idea of the system is the study of a framework for the integration of the aforesaid disciplines using the "Environmental information" as the application domain, specifically in ecology. SOLERES-KRS is a subsystem used to manage environmental information. Given the magnitude of the information available in the information system, and given that this information may be provided by different sources, at different times or even by different people, the environmental information can be distributed, consulted, and geographically located in different places, called *Environmental Process Units* (EPU). The EPU manages two local repositories of environmental information. One of them contains metadata on the information in the domain itself (i.e., basically information related to ecological and satellite image classifications): *Environmental Information Map* (EIM) data, or EIM documents. This information is extracted from external databases. The EIM documents have been specified by the use of an ontology in OWL [2][9], and they represent the first level of information in the KRS subsystem. The second repository contains meta-metadata:

*Environmental Information metaData* (EID), or EID documents. These documents contain the most important metadata of the EIM documents that could be used in an information recovering service, and further, incorporate other new metadata necessary for agent management itself. To a certain extent, an EID document represents a "template" with the basic EIM document data (the meta-metadata). The EID documents have also been specified by an ontology and represent the second level of information in the KRS subsystem. Each EPU keeps its own set of EID documents locally and also registers them to a *Web Trading Agent* (WTA). In this way, the WTA has an overall repository with all EID documents of all EPUs in order to offer an information search service. Ontology is used in another context, too. It allows us to make the definitions of behavior and interaction protocols between the system agents. When a system agent needs another agent to perform a specific action, he builds a message where he describes such an action through an ontology and sends it to the second agent. The latter, once the message has been received, extracts the content from the ontology, performs the appropriate action and uses the same ontology to show the action result to the former. This methodology is repeated with all actions among the system agents. In next subsections, data and process ontologies used by KRS subsystem will be described. They are written in OWL notation and we formalize them through UML class diagrams.

### 3.1   Data Ontologies

KRS subsystem uses two data ontologies: EIM and EID ontologies. The first one contains metadata on the information in the domain itself. This ontology has widely been described in [2] and [9], so that it will not be described in this paper. The EID ontology contains meta-metadata from EIM documents. Figure 1 shows it. The ecological information domain (one type of environmental information) is related to cartographical maps and satellite images. A cartographical map stores its information in layers (*Layer*), each of which is identified by a set of variables (*Variable*). For instance, in our project we are using cartographical maps classified into 4 layers (climatology, litology, geomorphology and soils) having more than a hundred of variables (i.e., scrubland surface, among others). Something similar happens with satellite images. The information is also stored in layers, but they are called *Bands* here. An example of satellite image is the LANDSAT images, which have 7 bands (and no variables stored in this case). Finally, both the cartographical and satellite classification have geographical information associated and this one (*Classification*) is carried out at a given time (*Time*) by a technician or group of technicians (*Technician*).

### 3.2   Process Ontologies

Process ontologies have been modeled to make the definitions of behavior and interaction protocols between system agents, as indicated in Section 3.

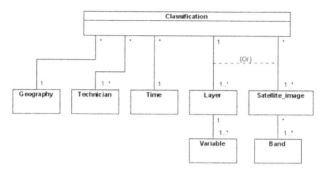

**Fig. 1.** EID ontology

All ontologies have been designed in terms of concepts (domain entities), actions performed in the domain (actions that affect concepts) and predicates (expressions connected with concepts).

The *Admin Ontology* can refer to actions that modify the main parameters of configuration of the trading service. For instance, this ontology allows us to modify the maximum number of results obtained after a query has been executed. This ontology will be used by both *IMI Agent* and *Trading Agent*. Figure 2 represents the structure of this ontology.

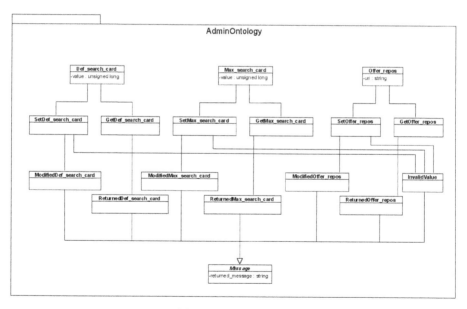

**Fig. 2.** Admin ontology

This defines three pairs of actions: *SetDef_search_card/GetDef_search_card* allows us to establish/get the number of registers to be located by default in a search and uses the *Def_search_card* concept to store such information. On the other hand, *SetMax_search_card/GetMax_search_card* allows us to establish/get the maximum number of registers to be located in a search and uses the *Max_search_card* concept to store such information. Finally, *SetOffer_repos/GetOffer_repos* can establish/get the address (in URL) of the file that stores the repository with the data registers used by the Trading service. The *Offer_repos* concept is used to store the address.

The *Register Ontology* can refer to the management actions (creation, elimination, modification and query) about EIM and EID documents. This ontology is used in communication messages that certain agents exchange with each other: *IMI Agent* with *Resource Agent* and *Resource Agent* with *Trading Agent*. For instance, when a *Resource Agent* adds a new EID to his local repository, he directly registers it in the global repository of his associated *Trading Agent* through the use of this ontology. Figure 3 represents the structure of the *Register Ontology*. This ontology considers actions such as *Export, Modify, Withdraw* and *Describe*. The *Export* action inserts a data register previously stored in the *Offer* concept. The data register can be an EIM Document or an EID Document. The *Modify* action represents the modification of a register and uses the *Offer* concept to refer to a new register with the modified data and *OfferId* concept to represent the identifier of the data register to be modified. Lastly, the *Withdraw* and *Describe* actions represent the elimination and query of a particular data register specified in the *OfferId* concept.

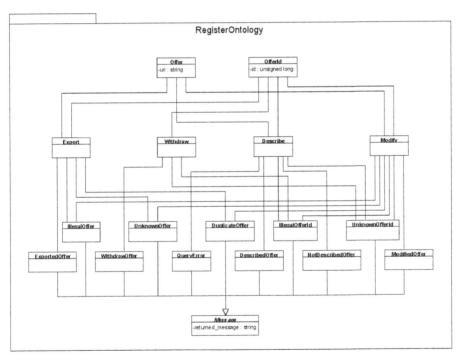

**Fig. 3.** Register ontology

Finally, the *Lookup Ontology* can refer to the search action in a repository under previously established criteria. The data query would be carried out under a specific repository according to previously established policies. This action can be requested by different agents: *IMI Agent, Query Agent, Trading Agent* and *Resource Agent*. For example, *Query Agent* can communicate with a *Resource Agent* to ask for information about an EIM document. Similarly, when an agent solves a query, he sends the right response by using the same *Lookup ontology*. Figure 4 represents the structure of the *Lookup Ontology*. The *Query* action uses *QueryForm* and *PolicySeq* concepts. The *QueryForm* concept represents a query expressed in a specific language, whereas the *PolicySeq* concept represents a set of *Policies* that can be established to make a query.

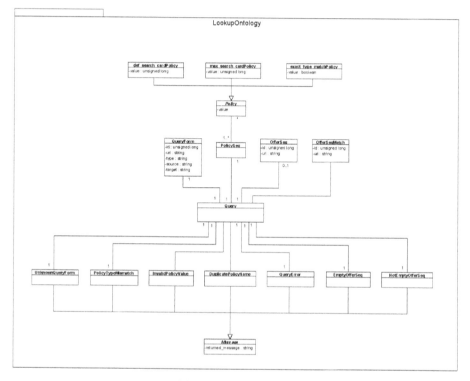

**Fig. 4.** Lookup ontology

## 4    Conclusions

The Ontology-Driven Architecture (ODA) provides the semantic representation for the knowledge domain in information systems. This paper has presented the use of ODA in SOLERES-KRS. This architecture uses ontology in two different contexts: (a) for representing the domain information, and (b) for defining the behavior and interaction protocols between system components (software agents). In order to represent the domain information, the EIM and EID ontologies have been developed. They represent metadata and meta-metadata from environmental information, respectively. On the other hand, three process-ontology documents (Lookup, Register and Admin) have been developed, used by agents for their cooperative activities.

**Acknowledgments.** This work has been supported by the EU (FEDER) and the Spanish Ministry MICINN under grant of the TIN2010-15588 and TRA2009-0309 projects, and the JUNTA de ANDALUCÍA (proyecto de excelencia) under grant TIC-6114 project, http://www.ual.es/acg/soleres.

# References

1. An, Y., Zhao, B.: Geo Ontology Design and Comparison in Geographic Information Integration. In: Fourth International Conference on Fuzzy Systems and Knowledge Discovery, FSKD 2007, vol. 4 (2007)
2. Asensio, J., Padilla, N., Iribarne, L., Muñoz, F., Ayala, R., Cruz, M., Menenti, M.: A MDEbased Satellite Ontology for Environmental Management Systems. Information Technology, Information Systems and Knowledge Management (in press)
3. Brilhante, V.: An Ontology for Quantities in Ecology. In: Bazzan, A.L.C., Labidi, S. (eds.) SBIA 2004. LNCS (LNAI), vol. 3171, pp. 144–153. Springer, Heidelberg (2004)
4. Ceccaroni, L., Cortés, U., Sanchez-Marre, M.: OntoWEDSS: Augmenting Environmental Decision-Support Systems with Ontologies. Environmental Modelling and Software 19(9), 785–797 (2004)
5. Di Lecce, V., Pasquale, C., Piuri, V.: A Basic Ontology for Multi Agent System Communication in an Environmental Monitoring System. In: 2004 IEEE International Conference on Computational Intelligence for Measurement Systems and Applications, CIMSA 2004, pp. 45–50 (2004)
6. GML/OCG: Geography Markup Language. Open Geospatial Consortium, inc. Tech. rep. (2007), http://www.opengeospatial.org/standards/gml/
7. Huang, M.: A New Method to Formal Description of Spatial Ontology. Information Technology and Environmental System Sciences 3, 417–421 (2008)
8. Lytras, M.: Semantic Web and Information Systems: An Agenda Based on Discourse with Community Leaders. International Journal of Semantic Web and Information Systems 1(1) (2005)
9. Padilla, N., Iribarne, L., Asensio, J.A., Muñoz, F.J., Ayala, R.: Modelling an Environmental Knowledge-Representation System. In: Lytras, M.D., Damiani, E., Tennyson, R.D. (eds.) WSKS 2008. LNCS (LNAI), vol. 5288, pp. 70–78. Springer, Heidelberg (2008)
10. Shen, J., Krishna, A., Yuan, S., Cai, K., Qin, Y.: A Pragmatic GIS-Oriented Ontology for Location Based Services. In: 19th Australian Conference on Software Engineering, ASWEC 2008, pp. 562–569 (2008)
11. Song, J., Zhu, Y., Wang, J.: A Study of Semantic Retrieval System Based on Geo-ontology with Spatio-Temporal Characteristic. In: Proc. of International Symposium on Distributed Computing and Applications to Business, Engineering and Science (DCABES 2007), vol. I-II, pp. 1029–1034 (2007)
12. Tripathi, A., Babaie, H.: Developing a Modular Hydrogeology Ontology by Extending the SWEET Upper-Level Ontologies. Computers and Geosciences 34(9), 1022–1033 (2008)
13. Zhan, Q., Li, D., Shao, Z.: An Architecture for Ontology-Based Geographic Information Semantic Grid Service. In: Proceedings of SPIE, vol. 6754, p. 67541U (2007)

# A Survey on eLearning Content Standardization

Ricardo Queirós[1] and José Paulo Leal[2]

[1] CRACS/INESC-Porto & DI/ESEIG/IPP, Porto, Portugal
ricardo.queiros@eu.ipp.pt
[2] CRACS/INESC-Porto & DCC/FCUP, University of Porto, Portugal
zp@dcc.fc.up.pt

**Abstract.** eLearning has been evolved in a gradual and consistent way. Along with this evolution several specialized and disparate systems appeared to fulfill the needs of teachers and students such as repositories of learning objects, intelligent tutors, or automatic evaluators. This heterogeneity poses issues that are necessary to address in order to promote interoperability among systems. Based on this fact, the standardization of content takes a leading role in the eLearning realm. This article presents a survey on current eLearning content standards. It gathers information on the most emergent standards and categorizes them according three distinct facets: metadata, content packaging and educational design.

**Keywords:** eLearning, standards, interoperability.

## 1 Introduction

In the last two decades we are witnessing to an impressive evolution of eLearning. Several types of eLearning systems appeared, from monolithic architectures to service oriented services aiming to cover all the needs of their users (e.g. staff, teachers, content authors, students) regarding academic, student or course management. One such system type is the Learning Management Systems (LMS) used to manage learning and track students' progress. This proliferation and heterogeneity of eLearning systems poses interoperability issues which are being considered by practitioners and educational institutions. In this context, these organizations have been creating standards and specifications to uniformize learning content and to develop interoperable tools and services [1].

The ultimate goal of this paper is to gather information on eLearning standards. For this study we selected several eLearning content standards and categorizes them based on three facets: metadata, content packaging and educational design. The first facet focuses on the description of learning resources. The second facet focuses on the organization and package of those resources for dissemination. The third facet deals with pedagogical issues in the presentation of those resources (e.g. design and sequence).

M.D. Lytras et al. (Eds.): WSKS 2011, CCIS 278, pp. 433–438, 2013.
© Springer-Verlag Berlin Heidelberg 2013

## 2    eLearning Standards

The evolution of eLearning can be summarized by the transition of the early
monolithic systems developed for specific learning domains to the new systems that
can invoke specialized services and be plugged in any eLearning environments. These
types of systems evolved from Content Management Systems (CMS). The CMS was
introduced in the mid-1990s mostly by the online publishing industry. This type of
system can be defined as a data repository that also includes tools for authoring,
aggregating and sequencing content in order to simplify the creation, administration
and access to online content [2]. The content is organized in small self-contained
pieces of information to improve reusability at the content component level. These
content components when used in the learning domain are called "learning objects"
(LO) and the systems that manage them are called Learning Content Management
Systems (LCMS) [3]. LO are context independent, transportable and reusable pieces
of instruction that are digitally managed and delivered [4]. There are other definitions
for Learning Objects (LO). Rehak & Mason [4] define a learning object as: "a
digitized entity which can be used, reused or referenced during technology supported
learning".

In the eLearning context, standards are generally developed for the purposes of
ensuring interoperability and reusability in systems and of the content and meta-data
they manage. In this context, several organizations (IEEE, AICC, IMS, ADL) have
been developed standards and specifications (Figure 1) [5] regarding the creation of
standards, specifications, guidelines, best practices on the description and use of
eLearning content.

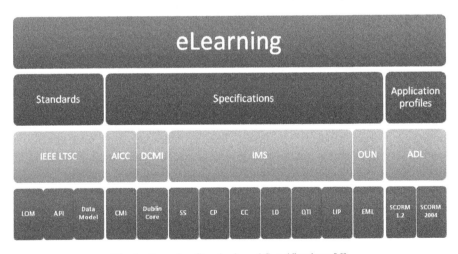

**Fig. 1.** eLearning Standards and Specifications [6]

In this study dozens of specifications were found. For the sake of readability we
detail only the most prominent [7] organized in three facets: metadata, content
package and educational design.

## 2.1    Metadata

A learning object is composed by one or more educational resources. These resources are described by metadata. The most used metadata standard is the Learning Object Metadata (LOM). LOM is a double IEEE and IMS standard data model, usually encoded in XML, used to describe a learning object. LOM was a reaction to Dublin Core used by many repositories (e.g. DSpace). Dublin Core was judged to be too simple for adequately describing learning resources. The purpose of LOM is to support the reusability of learning objects, to aid discoverability, and to facilitate their interoperability, usually in the context of online learning management systems. LOM is integrated in a well known content packaging standard called IMS Content Packaging (IMS CP). The data model is organized in nine categories. The following table enumerates these categories based on a previous study [8].

**Table 1.** LOM data model categories

| Category | Description |
| --- | --- |
| General | Describe the learning object as a whole. This category includes elements such as identifier, title, language, keywords. |
| Lifecycle | Describe features related to the history and current state of the LO such as version, status, and contributors. |
| Metametadata | Group information about the metadata such as identifier, contributors and language used in the metadata. |
| Technical | Describe the technical requirements and characteristics of the LO such as MIME type, size, required software/hardware. |
| Educational | Describe educational and pedagogic characteristics of the LO such as interactivity type, learning resource type, interactivity level, semantic density, educational context, typical age range. |
| Rights | Describe the intellectual property rights and conditions of use for the LO (whether or not any cost is involved, and whether copyright and other restrictions apply). |
| Relation | Describe features that define the relationship between this LO and others ('based on', 'part of', etc.). |
| Annotation | Provide comments on the use of the LO and information on when and by whom the comments were created. |
| Classification | Describe where the LO can be classified within a particular classification system. |

These categories cover many facets of a LO. However, LOM was designed for general LO and does not to meet the requirements of specialized domains. Fortunately, it was designed to be straightforward to extend it. Next, we enumerate four ways that have been used [9] to extend the LOM model:

- combining the LOM elements with elements from other specifications;
- defining extensions to LOM elements while preserving its set of categories;
- simplifying LOM, reducing the number of LOM elements and its choices;
- extending and reducing simultaneously the number of LOM elements.

Based on the previous extension approaches, the IMS GLC created the Question & Test Interoperability (QTI) specification. The IMS QTI specification describes a data model for the representation of questions (e.g. multiple choice, multiple response, fill-in-the-blanks and short text questions) and tests data and their corresponding results reports. It extends the LOM with its own meta-data vocabulary as specified in the *Meta-data and Usage Data* document that describes a LOM profile suitable for use with assessment items and a separate data model for representing usage data (i.e., item statistics).

There are other metadata specifications, such as, the Dublin Core Metadata, which provides a simpler set of elements useful for sharing metadata across heterogeneous systems. At the present, the Dublin Education Working Group is extending the Dublin Core for the specific needs of the education community.

## 2.2   Content Package

Packaging is crucial to store eLearning material and reuse it in different systems. The most widely used content packaging format is the IMS Content Packaging (IMS CP). An IMS CP learning object assembles resources and meta-data into a distribution medium, typically an archive in ZIP format, with its content described in a manifest file in the root level. The manifest file - named imsmanifest.xml -adheres to the IMS CP schema and contains the following sections: Metadata - describes the package as a whole; Organizations - describes the organization of the content within a manifest; Resources - contains references to resources (files) needed for the manifest and metadata describing these resources; and Sub-manifests - defines sub packages.

The manifest uses the LOM standard to describe the learning resources included in the package. Recently, IMS Global Learning Consortium proposed the IMS Common Cartridge that adds support for several standards (e.g. IEEE LOM, IMS CP, IMS QTI, IMS Authorization Web Service) and its main goal is to shape the future regarding the organization and distribution of digital learning content. The latest revised version (1.1) was released in May 2011. The IMS CC manifest (Figure 2) includes references for two types of resources:

- Web Content Resources (WCR): static web resources that are supported on the Web such as HTML files, GIF/JPEG images, PDF documents, etc.
- Learning Application Objects (LAO): special resource types that require additional processing before they can be imported and represented within the target system. Physically, a LAO consists of a directory in the content package containing a descriptor file and optionally additional files used exclusively by that LAO. Examples of Learning Application Objects include QTI assessments, Discussion Forums, Web links, Basic LTI descriptors, etc.

There are other package specifications, mostly derived from the previous ones as application profiles. The term Application Profile generally refers to the adaptation, constraint, and/or augmentation of a metadata scheme to suit the needs of a particular community. A well know content packaging specification is SCORM that extends IMS CP with more sophisticated sequencing and Contents-to-LMS communication. These pedagogical contents and activities standards are detailed in the next subsection.

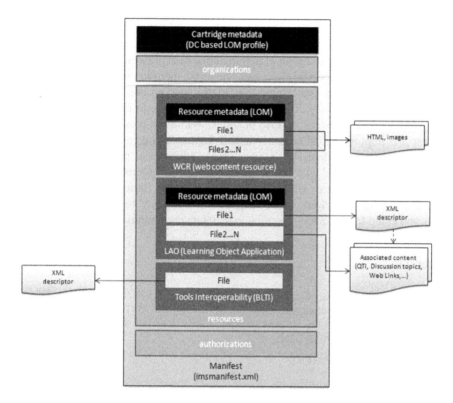

**Fig. 2.** IMS Common Cartridge package

## 2.3    Educational Design

Learning objects can be organized in items and an organization defines a path through those items. The IMS CP specification includes a manifest section called Organizations. This section can be used to design pedagogical activities and articulate the sequencing of instructions. By default, it uses a tree-based organization of learning items pointing to the resources (assets) included in the package. However, other standards could be accommodated in this section, such as IMS Simple Sequencing (IMS SS) and IMS Learning Design (IMS LD). These specifications aims to provide to the teachers mechanisms for coordination of the educational instructions based on students' profile making the instruction more dynamic and flexible.

The **IMS LD** specification is a meta-language for describing pedagogical models and educational goals. Several IMS LD-aware tools are available as players (e.g. CopperCore, .LRN) and authoring/export tools (e.g. Reload, LAMS).

The **IMS SS** is a specification used to describe paths through a collection of learning activities. The specification declares the order in which learning activities are to be presented to a learner and the conditions under which a resource is delivered during an eLearning instruction. Despite all these specifications, the design of more complex adaptive behaviour is still hard to achieve [10].

## 3    Conclusions

In this paper we present a study on eLearning content standards. We select the most prominent standards and specifications and categorize them in three facets. Based on this study we detect two issues that can hinder the proliferation of eLearning: fragmentation and complexity. The former is a typical issue in the technology realm. In this study we found dozens of specifications. While we presented only the most prominent it is important to state that standard fragmentation can reduce the amount of eLearning content available to any user, since educational players must support them. Other issue is related with the complexity of specifications. A good example is the IMS SS that few systems adhere. A modular approach (based on profiles) in the design of these specifications could help in the adequacy to real scenarios and domains and could facilitate the dissemination among communities.

## References

1. Paepcke, A., Chang, C.K., Garcia-Molina, H., Winograd, T.: Interoperability for Digital Libraries Worldwide. Communications of the ACM 41(4), 33–43 (1998)
2. Nichani, M.: LCMS = LMS + CMS [RLOs] – How does this affect the learner? The instructional designer? (April 2009),
   http://www.elearningpsot.com/articles/archives/
   lcms_lms_cms_rlos
3. Leal, J.P., Queirós, R.: From eLearning Systems to Specialised Services. In: Chapter of EduJudge project book called "A New Learning Paradigm: Competition Supported by Technology". Sello Editorial (2010)
4. Rehak, D.R., Mason, R.: Keeping the learning in learning objects. In: Littlejohn, A. (ed.) Reusing Online Resources: a Sustainable Approach to e-Learning, pp. 22–30. Kogan Page, London (2003)
5. Friesen, N.: Interoperability and Learning Objects: An Overview of E-Learning Standardization. Interdisciplinary Journal of Knowledge and Learning Objects (2005)
6. Monroy, F.J.: Estándares en eLearning - Grupo CHICO, E.S. Informática, UCLM
7. Leal, J.P., Queirós, R.: A comparative study on LMS interoperability. In: Babo, R., Azevedo, A. (eds.) Higher Education Institutions and Learning Management Systems: Adoption and Standardization. IGI-Global (2011)
8. Duval, E.: Metadata Standards: What, Who & Why. Journal of Universal Computer Science 7(7), 591–601 (2001)
9. Friesen, N.: Semantic and Syntactic Interoperability for Learning Object Metadata. In: Hillman, D. (ed.) Metadata in Practice, ALA Editions, Chicago (2004),
   http://www.cancore.ca/
   semantic_and_syntactic_interoperability.html (June 11, 2008)
10. Aroyo, L., Dolog, P., Houben, G., Kravcik, M., Naeve, A., Wild, F.: Interoperability in Personalized Adaptive Learning. Educational Tecnhnology & Society (2006)

# A Framework for the Evolutionary Visual Software Analytics Process

Antonio González-Torres, Francisco J. García-Peñalvo, and Roberto Therón

Department of Computer Sciences, University of Salamanca
Plaza de la Merced s/n. 37008, Salamanca, Spain
{agtorres,theron,fgarcia}@usal.es

**Abstract.** Software evolution is made up of changes carried out during software maintenance. Such accumulation of changes produces substantial modifications in software projects and therefore vast amounts of relevant facts that are useful for the understanding and comprehension of the software project for making additional changes. In this scenario, software evolution analysis and software evolution visualization have emerged for aiding software developers and managers. Consequently, the application of visual analytics to software evolution has been an important advancement in the efforts made for assisting the software maintenance community. This paper defines applications of visual analytics as evolutionary visual software analytics and it is aimed to provide a reference framework for researchers in relevant fields, making a special emphasis in the central role played by users.

**Keywords:** Evolutionary Visual Software Analytics, Visual Software Analytics, Visual Analytics, Software Evolution Visualization, Software Visualization, Software Maintenance, Mining Software Repositories.

## 1 Introduction

Visual analytics can be described as the science of analytical reasoning facilitated by interactive visual interfaces [1]. It iteratively collects information, preprocesses data, carries out statistical analysis, performs data mining, and uses machine learning, knowledge representation, user interaction, human cognition, perception, exploration and the human abilities for decision making. The ultimate goal of visual analytics is to provide insight into the problem at hand, described by vast amounts of scientific, forensic or business data from heterogeneous sources [2][3][4]. It combines the advantages of machines with the strengths of humans such as analysis, intuition, problem solving and visual perception. Therefore, the human is at the heart of visual analytics human interaction [5].

Software developers and managers often faced the maintenance of large legacy applications and software projects to which they usually do not provide support, either within their company or a client company. Understanding the evolution of such legacy applications or software projects is a crucial task. Particularly because software maintenance is a process usually compromised due to the lack of proper

M.D. Lytras et al. (Eds.): WSKS 2011, CCIS 278, pp. 439–447, 2013.

system documentation, which frequently is incomplete, outdated or it is not present [6]. The challenge of understanding a software project is to gain insight about the effects produced by changes made to the project during its maintenance. Subsequently, comprehension of the effects caused by changes allows the implementation of the appropriate actions to make additional changes if the quality or functionality of the software project is compromised in the short or long term.

Recently, several studies have been conducted regarding the application of visual analytics to software evolution for supporting software maintenance [7][8]. However, there is no explicit definition for such process. Accordingly, this paper defines the application of visual analytics, and even more specifically of visual software analytics [9][10], to software evolution as evolutionary visual software analytics. Consequently, this paper concerns with the explicit definition of a reference framework to describe the evolutionary visual software analytics and identify the involved research areas, methods and techniques, and the relationships between them. Therefore, the use of a reference framework could make easier to identify the interactions of components and their localization within the reference framework, when used as a location map. The definition of such framework uses the visual analytics mantra as a reference [2][11].

The remainder of this paper introduces software maintenance and evolution (section 2), describes the evolutionary visual software analytics process (section 3), defines the evolutionary visual software analytics framework (section 4), explains the architecture of a tool that has been implemented based on evolutionary visual software analytics (section 5) and finally discusses the conclusions.

## 2     Software Maintenance and Evolution

Software development and maintenance are dynamic tasks that conform to the basis of software evolution. Software maintenance starts from the moment in which a software application has been conceived and its design has started. During software maintenance, project managers and developers necessitate the understanding of the software project structure and its source code, the relationships among software items and software quality metrics for making preventive (for improving source code quality), adaptive (due to software functionality improvements or additional requirements) and corrective changes. In this context, a software item is a source code piece such as a class or interface and the relationships among software items are those defined in the object oriented programming theory as well as other relationships, including the direct and indirect coupling.

Software maintenance is a cyclic process; changes are based on the understanding of the current state of the software project, which is the accumulation of previous changes made by the software maintenance activity. The change process and the tracking of changes are usually managed with the assistance of a Software Configuration Management tool (SCM).

A SCM tool uses revisions for storing details about changes, such as the author who made the change, the date and time of the change, the project structure before and after the change, and the source code and the changes that were carried out on it [12].

A revision identifies the current state of the project at the moment that the change has been committed. Revisions are stored by a software repository under the control of a SCM tool and are associated to a revision number. Consequently, software evolution is an iterative process conformed by the accumulation of changes and revisions during software maintenance and development [13]. Understanding a revision includes the comprehension of the structural characteristics of the project, the relationships among software items, the software quality metrics, source code facts, and the comprehension of the socio-technical relationships derived from the development process. The challenge of understanding the evolution of a software project is to gain insight about the effects produced by changes made to the project. Therefore, comprehension of the effects caused by changes allows the implementation of the appropriate actions to make additional changes if the quality or functionality of the software project is compromised in the short or long term.

## 3    Evolutionary Visual Software Analytics

Understanding the evolution of a software project is a complex process that requires the automatic analysis of the project evolution, the visual representation of such analysis and the active participation of users in the comprehension process by interacting with the visual representation.

The aforementioned analysis takes into consideration the evaluation of individual revisions and the comparison of the output produced by such evaluation for a given number of revisions or all the existing revisions associated to the project. Thereafter, the output of the analysis is visually represented and appropriate interaction techniques are added to the visual representations. The aim is to involve the active participation of users in the discovery process and comprehension of relevant facts regarding the evolution of the software project.

In addition, it is important to consider that the analysis process is very complex because the life cycle of large software projects usually expands through several years, generates thousands and even millions of lines of source code (LOC) [15], hundreds of software components and thousands of revisions [16]. Furthermore, within software projects exists relationships among software items in the form of inheritance, interface implementation, coupling and cohesion. In addition, source code is made up by variables, constants, programming structures, methods and relationships among those elements. Besides logs, communication systems, defect-tracking systems and SCM tools keep records with dates, comments, changes made to software projects and associated users and programmers [17].

Accordingly, the analysis of individual revisions and the comparison of the analysis performed on them are carried out by the mining of software repositories on an evolutionary basis. The data used by software repository mining tools are collected from the source code, the software project structure, communication systems, logs and the metadata records from bug tracking and SCM tools. Thus, an important consideration is that the proposal makes reference to the mining of software repositories on an evolutionary basis as the use of any set of extraction and analysis techniques that have the capability of extracting and analyzing software projects looking to discover patterns and relationships; and calculating software quality metrics and fact extraction from the results of comparing the analysis performed on revisions [16].

Moreover, the datasets produced by mining software repositories on an evolutionary basis are usually overwhelming, due to their large size, and are hard to understand by humans. This makes it necessary to provide a means for allowing software project managers and programmers to get insight and grasp the details of the project evolution. Therefore, information visualization techniques provide such a means with the support of interaction techniques and linked views. However, before visually representing the output generated by the mining of software repositories, such output needs to be transformed into the appropriate data structures that will be used as the input of the visual representations.

A summary of this process is that the evolution of software projects produces a wealth of evolutionary data that is stored in software repositories [17], communication systems, logs and bug tracking databases, which then are mined to discover patterns, relationships and trends [16]. Finally, data are transformed into the appropriate data structures to be turned into an opportunity [3] by means of visual representations.

Hence the application of visual analytics to software systems and related processes, with the aim of supporting the understanding of a software project or an individual revision, is known as visual software analytics [10] [11]. Accordingly, this research defines the process described above as evolutionary visual software analytics.

## 4    Framework

Evolutionary visual software analytics is a specialization of visual software analytics. A practical analogy is that visual software analytics is a movie frame while evolutionary visual software analytics is a movie. Visual software analytics takes into account one revision of the software project whereas evolutionary visual software analytics takes into account all the revisions of the software project. Consequently, both processes share several common techniques but the evolutionary approach could require an extra analysis for comparing the results carried out on individual revisions.

The main components of the visual software analytics process are the knowledge extraction engine, the software facts database, the data transformation engine for visualization models, the software visualization techniques and the user. Figure 1 shows an overview of this process and describes some of the techniques commonly used by each component.

The knowledge extraction engine reads software project associated data from data sources such as software repositories, defect-tracking systems logs, email communications and source code to carry out exhaustive software project analysis for extracting software facts. When the knowledge extraction engine has carried out the analysis, it stores the software facts in its corresponding database. Therefore, the data transformation engine for visualization models transforms the software facts data structures into the appropriate data structures required by software visualizations.

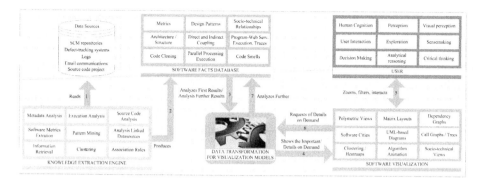

**Fig. 1.** Overview of the visual software analytics process

Finally, the software facts are represented by means of software visualization techniques and the user starts the interaction process looking to understand the software project and get insight of the software project.

The techniques used by the knowledge extraction engine, the software facts that are extracted and the software visualization techniques vary according to the aims of the research or tool design. However, the use of interaction techniques and how visualizations are linked play a relevant role in the knowledge discovery process. Users will make use of human cognition, perception, sense-making, analytical reasoning and critical thinking to find relevant facts and relationships to understand the software project by means of human interaction.

With regards to evolutionary visual software analytics, it allows the understanding of how the project has evolved and provides more details on how software item relationships have been established. Its complexity is higher with respect to visual software analytics because of the additional dimension added by the analysis of evolution and the representation of time (see Figure 2). Therefore, the techniques used by the knowledge extraction engine, the facts stored by the software evolution facts database and the software evolution visualizations take into account the complete evolution of the software project or a given period of time. As a consequence, the design of the visualizations is confronted with the layout of time and space and the user deals with a more complex scenario. Therefore, users become the central component of the understanding process, in which the use of its capabilities and human interaction are the key to disclosing the intricacies of project complexity.

Evolutionary visual software analytics goals usually include software quality assurance, the improvement of the software maintenance process, the forecasting of project related events and assisting software developers in the understanding of the software project and project managers in resource management, including programmer related tasks.

# 5    Tool Architecture

Defining the architecture of software tools is a rather complex task that requires careful analysis. It is a challenge to determine what techniques to use and how these will relate to each other and how these will contribute to the research or the tool design goals. This paper is aimed to provide a reference framework to novel researchers and those designing tool architectures in scenarios where visual analytics is applied to software evolution. Previous sections have discussed so far how evolutionary visual software analytics contributes to software maintenance and the definition of a framework for the evolutionary visual software analytics process. This section takes as reference the framework presented in Section 4 for defining the architecture of a tool that supports the understanding and comprehension of software projects during software maintenance.

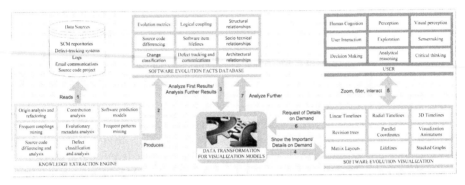

**Fig. 2.** Evolutionary visual software analytics process

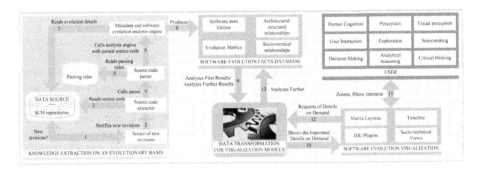

**Fig. 3.** A tool architecture based on the evolutionary visual software analytics process

The tool architecture is shown in Figure 3 and its implementation has been carried in Java. Such architecture has been tested on several open source software projects such as jEdit, JabRef, Jmol and JFreechart. The knowledge extraction engine on an evolutionary basis supports the addition of modules for supporting new software configuration management systems (SCM) and allows configuring connections to several different projects and software repositories for extracting evolutionary details and carrying out software evolution analysis. Its components monitor new revisions, the source code extractor, the source code parser and the metadata and software evolution analysis engine. The monitor of new revisions is a process that continuously monitors the addition of new revisions to software projects and notifies about new revisions to the source code extractor. Then, the source code extractor starts extracting source code from the software repository and invokes the source code parser for collecting details about the software project structure, the hierarchy of classes, the coupling relationships and the source code and metrics raw data for calculating metrics for classes and methods. Finally, the metadata and software evolution analysis engine takes the outcomes produced by the source code parser and query additional details from the software repository. Then, it applies an exhaustive software evolution analysis and stores the results in the software evolution facts database.

The software evolution facts that have been taken into account for the visualizations presented in the next section are the software item lifelines, the evolution metrics, the socio-technical relationships and some architectural/structural relationships such as inheritance, interface implementation and the correlation of structural data with metrics. Therefore, the data transformation engine for visualization models transforms the data software evolution facts data structures into the appropriate data structures that are used by software evolution visualizations. Therefore, the visualizations included in the tool are embedded into an Eclipse plugin and make use of a matrix layout, a timeline and socio-technical views that are supported by a social-network graph and the use of colors for representing programmer's contributions.

The knowledge extraction engine and the software evolution facts database are server side components with a graphical interface. While the data transformation engine is a middleware process that is configured using a graphical interface, it is executed automatically when it detects new additions to the software evolution facts database.

## 6    Conclusions

Visual analytics is an emerging discipline that it is applied to many human knowledge fields. Its application to software evolution is aimed to assist software developers and managers. The main contribution of this paper is to define such processes as evolutionary visual software analytics and its reference framework, which application has been validated through the implementation of a tool using it as reference. Such validation has proven the feasibility of the application of the framework to research and tools design.

The definition of a reference framework can support the understanding of evolutionary visual software analytics through the use of a common language. In addition, the definition of roles, borders and relationships among research areas, methods and techniques can be planned and carried out taking into account the overall process. Furthermore, the elements of the reference framework can be considered as components; where each component has to support the function of other components and produce an output that can be used as the input of other components. Therefore, the benefits of defining a reference framework also apply to visual software analytics and evolutionary visual software analytics, due to the absence of a reference framework definition for these research fields. This could be of great value for novel researches and tool designers.

**Acknowledgements.** This work was supported by Spanish Government project TIN2010-21695-C02-01, by the Castile and Lion Regional Government through GR47 and also by the Ministerio de Ciencia e Innovación of Spain under project FI2010-16234.

# References

1. James, J.T., Kristin, A.C.: Illuminating the Path: The Research and Development Agenda for Visual Analytics. National Visualization and Analytics Center, p. 4, 28 (2005)
2. Keim, D.A., Andrienko, G., Fekete, J.-D., Görg, C., Kohlhammer, J., Melançon, G.: Visual Analytics: Definition, Process, and Challenges. In: Kerren, A., Stasko, J.T., Fekete, J.-D., North, C. (eds.) Information Visualization. LNCS, vol. 4950, pp. 154–175. Springer, Heidelberg (2008)
3. Keim, D.A., Mansmann, F., Schneidewind, J., Ziegler, H.: Challenges in visual data analysis. In: Proceedings of the conference on Information Visualization, IV 2006, pp. 9–16. IEEE Computer Society, Washington, DC (2006)
4. Llorá, X., Sastry, K., Alías, F., Goldberg, D.E., Welge, M.: Analyzing active interactive genetic algorithms using visual analytics. In: Proceedings of the 8th Annual Conference on Genetic and Evolutionary Computation, GECCO 2006, pp. 1417–1418. ACM, New York (2006)
5. Dix, A., Pohl, M., Ellis, G.: Perception and Cognitive Aspects. In: Mastering the Information Age Solving Problems with Visual Analytics, pp. 109–130. Eurographics Association (2010)
6. Murphy, G.C., Notkin, D.: Reengineering with reflection models: A case study. IEEE Computer 30(8), 29–36 (1997)
7. García, J., González Torres, A., Gómez Aguilar, D.A., Therón, R., García Peñalvo, F.J.: A Visual Analytics Tool for Software Project Structure and Relationships among Classes. In: Butz, A., Fisher, B., Christie, M., Krüger, A., Olivier, P., Therón, R. (eds.) SG 2009. LNCS, vol. 5531, pp. 203–212. Springer, Heidelberg (2009)
8. Telea, A., Voinea, L.: Visual Analytics for Understanding the Evolution of Large Software Projects. In: Proc. BENEVOL. Univ. of Eindhoven, The Netherlands (2008)
9. van den Brand, M., Roubtsov, S., Serebrenik, A.: Squavisit: A flexible tool for visual software analytics. In: Proceedings of the European Conference on Software Maintenance and Reengineering, CRMR 2009, pp. 331–332 (2009)
10. Anslow, C., Noble, J., Marshall, S., Tempero, E.: Towards visual software analytics. In: Proceedings of the Australasian Computing Doctoral Consortium (ACDC), Wellington, New Zealand (2009)
11. Puolamäki, K., Bertone, A., Therón, R., Huisman, O., Johansson, J., Miksch, S., Papapetrou, P., Rinzivillo, S.: Data Mining. In: Mastering the Information Age Solving Problems with Visual Analytics, pp. 39–56. Eurographics Association (2010)
12. Estublier, J.: Software configuration management: A roadmap. In: Proceedings of the Conference on The Future of Software Engineering (ICSE 2000), pp. 279–289. ACM, New York (2000)

13. Fernandez-Ramil, J., Lozano, A., Wermelinger, M., Capiluppi, A.: Empirical Studies of Open Source Evolution. In: Software Evolution, pp. 263–288 (2008)
14. Tamai, T., Torimitsu, Y.: Software lifetime and its evolution process over generations. In: Proceedings of 1992 Conference on Software Maintenance, pp. 63–69. IEEE (1992)
15. Kagdi, H., Collard, M., Maletic, J.: A survey and taxonomy of approaches for mining software repositories in the context of software evolution. Journal of Software Maintenance and Evolution: Research and Practice 19(2) (2007)
16. D'Ambros, M., Lanza, M.: Visual software evolution reconstruction. Journal of Software Maintenance and Evolution: Research and Practice 21(3), 217–232 (2009)
17. Hassan, A.E.: Mining software repositories to assist developers and support managers, Ph.D. dissertation, Waterloo, Ont., Canada (2005)

# A Study of a Wireless Smart Sensor Platform for Practical Training

Min Jou[1], Jaw-Kuen Shiau[2], and Kuo-Wei Lee[3]

[1] Department of Industrial Education, National Taiwan Normal University,
Taipei, Taiwan
[2] Department of Aerospace Engineering, Tamkang University,
New Taipei City, Taiwan
[3] National Taiwan Normal University, Taiwan
joum@ntnu.edu.tw

**Abstract.** In order to overcome the obstacles in traditional experimenting and practical training courses, as well as in enhancing the functions of the present e-learning system, the study took sensor network technology as the foundation in developing a web services system. The system will be able to make presentations of the students 'operations and results on an immediate basis, allowing the students to be guided adequately as they face problems during experiment and practical training.

## 1 Introduction

With recent advances in micro-electro-mechanical systems (MEMS) and wireless communication technologies, wireless sensor networks have been produced out of laboratories and transforming our lives. Wireless sensor networks are more attractive and useful than traditional wired sensing systems for their ad-hoc and easy deployment. This new technology expands our sensing capabilities by connecting the physical world to the communication networks and enables a broad range of applications (Akyildiz, Su, Sankarasubramaniam, and Cayirci, 2002). Sensor networks are the integration of sensor techniques, distributed computation, and wireless communication techniques. The network can be embedded in our physical environment and used for sensing, collecting data, processing information of monitored objects, and transferring the processed information to users. The architecture of the sensor node's hardware consists of five components: the sensing hardware, the processor, the memory, the power supply, and the transceiver (Tubaishat, Madria, 2003). For many applications, a sensor network operates in three phases. In the first phase, sensors take measurements that form a snapshot of the signal field at a particular time. The measurements are stored locally. In the second phase, information retrieval takes place where data are collected from individual sensors. In the last phase is where information is processed in which data from sensors are processed centrally with a specific performance metric (Dong, Tong, and Sadler 2007). Such a network is composed of many tiny low-power nodes, with each consisting of actuators, sensing devices, a wireless transceiver, and possibly a

M.D. Lytras et al. (Eds.): WSKS 2011, CCIS 278, pp. 448–453, 2013.
© Springer-Verlag Berlin Heidelberg 2013

mobilize (2002). These sensor nodes are massively deployed in a region of interest to gather and process environmental information. Meanwhile, ubiquitous (or mobile) technology and its applications have spawned an extensive programme of research because of the rapid growth in wireless sensor networks (Chan, Hwang, Yang, Chen, and Huang, 2009).

The higher capital cost of acquiring MEMS's equipment within each university presents a considerable financial challenge. Much time and cost are used in teaching these techniques. Particularly, computerized machines are continuously increasing in use. The development of educating engineers on computerized machines becomes much more difficult than on traditional machines, and this is because of the limitation of the extremely expensive cost of teaching; the quality and quantity of teaching cannot always be promoted in this respect since the traditional teaching methods do not respond well to the needs of the future. Most of technology education relies on "cookbook"-oriented experiments that provide students with a technical question, the procedure to address the question, the expected results of the experiment, and even an interpretation of those results. By contrast, self-directed learning is to encourage students to learn inductively with the help of teaching systems. This method gives students more freedom to come up with their own questions to investigate, devise an experimental procedure, and decide on their own terms for how to interpret the results. Long pointed out that there are at least six kinds of cognitive skills appear to be particularly important in successful self-directed learning, and they are goal setting skills, processing skills, other cognitive skills, some competence or aptitude in the topic or a closely related area, decision making skills, and self-awareness. Effective, or successful, self-directed learning depends on information gathering, information monitoring, students' processing and other cognitive activities, and in the way they react to information. The evolution of computer and Internet technologies has made it easy to access learning contents from virtually anywhere, anytime, and at each individual user's own pace. Students make their own meaning of what they are learning by relying on mental models of the world. Using the user interaction data and direct questioning techniques, this intelligent tutor helps students understand complex technical phenomena by constructing mental models that reflect reality as perceived by acknowledged experts while minimizing models containing significant misconceptions (Miller et al., 1998; Shin et al., 2002).

Even though self-directed e-learning focuses on the independent learner who engages in education at his own pace and free from curricular obligations, the appropriate individual instructions are given by understanding the state of understanding of a student. The intelligent means of tutoring, i.e. the wireless sensor networks, provides information necessary in realizing appropriate tutoring (Matsubara et al., 2002). A number of tools, some purposefully and others serendipitously, have become key enablers of this learning paradigm. For example, tools such as Google Scholar, CiteSeer Research Index, etc. make it possible to conduct literature searches without stepping out of one's room (Desikan, DeLong, Beemanapalli, Bose, and Srivastava). The advance in the optical-fiber network makes real-time transmission of a large amount of data possible between two or more remote places (such as three-dimensional models or video images). In particular, by connecting virtual environments through the broadband network (Paquette, Ricciardi-Rigault, Paquin, Liegeois, Bleicher, 1996), a three-dimensional virtual world can be shared between remote places. The field oú virtual reality (VR) initially focused on immersive viewing via expensive equipment, rapidly expands and includes a growing variety of systems for interacting with 3D computer models in real-time (Sung & Ou, 2003). The various applications in the different fields including education, training, entertainment, medicine, and industry have been developing, while even more areas will gain benefits from using VR-enabled technoloogies (Craig, Sherman, 2003). In the past few years, a number of interactive VR systems have been developed, for instance, an educational virtual environment (Bouras, Philopoulos, Tsiatsos, 2001) is such a special case where the emphasis is more on education and collaboration than on simulation.

## 2    Development of Sensor Network Environment

The new technology of wireless sensor network allows sensing capabilities to be expanded by connecting the physical world to the communication networks existing in cyber space. In order to support self-directed learning in MEMS technology, many sensor devices need to be deployed in the laboratory to collect real-time information of students' motion and machine operation conditions. The Zigbee modules were used to build a wireless sensor network in this research. The proposed architecture of the sensor network system is shown in Figure 1. The overall system architecture consists of a Web camera, a Zigbee dongle (base node), a server, and wireless sensor nodes. The wireless sensor nodes consist of two key parts, referred to as the static and the mobile nodes. The static sensor nodes are scattered in the laboratory and they form a multi-hop mesh networking topology. A key role of the static node is to transfer all the data packets coming from the mobile node back to the dongle. The other key role of the static node is to provide a sufficient number of anchor points for the localization. Each of these sensor nodes has the capability of collecting data and routing data peer-to-peer to the Zigbee dongle. The Zigbee dongle is used to bridge the sensor network to the Internet in that it provides a serial interface and a wireless connection for node programming and data transfer. The server is connected to the Internet to enable remote users to access the laboratory monitoring system. The mobile node, comprised of an accelerometer worn by students, is for monitoring student motion and position in an indoor environment.

During the process of experiment and practice, the students almost always have the need to operate machines and adjust machining parameters manually, in addition , there are some machines also requiring students to step on pedals and have the machining parameters adjusted that way. Therefore, the study intends to incorporate ultra-thin force sensing unit (0.127mm) into a Zigbee node, making flexible force sensors, and then install handles and pedals. "Are students able to use tools correctly?" is the necessary matter of subject that needs to be discussed during experiment and practice. Therefore, the study plans to connect the Zigbee node with the PIR325 infrared sensing unit to make wireless infrared sensor and have it installed in the tool box. The Zigbee node will be connected with a three-axis micro electro-mechanical system (MEMS)-based accelerometer so that a wireless accelerometer can be created, which is a device measuring proper acceleration that will be available to detect the magnitude and the direction of the acceleration as a vector quantity.   When the sensor is worn by the students, it can not only detect their motions inside the laboratory but also record their activities at the same time.

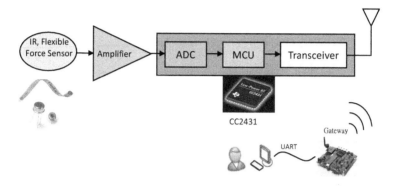

**Fig. 1.** Architecture of the wireless sensor system

# 3    Implementation

A graphical user interface (GUI) was designed for remote users to carry out the desired operations such as sending commands and parameters to drive the sensor nodes and visualizing the measurement results. The thesis use ASP.NET and Microsoft Visual C# to write an internet program in order to achieve the goal of quick and convenient processing of information. Figure 2 shows the Web GUI when a user is monitoring the laboratory environment at the remote client side. A remote user is able to adjust the view angle of camera to get required video data by clicking the mouse.

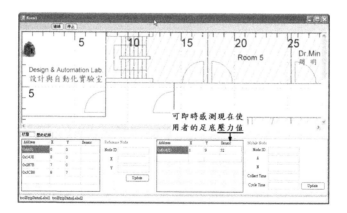

**Fig. 2.** Real time monitoring of force sensor at the remote client side

This interface accepts remote client side to get information about which node he or she wants to monitor by clicking on the buttons and the checkboxes on the panels. After that, clicking the sensor which has been installed on the node and observe the sensors' signal. The data of selected sensors are collected and sent to the Web GUI at fixed time intervals. In Figure 2, the down-left corner is the information measured by force sensor as time changes. In Figure 3, the down-left corner is the information measured by the IR sensor and as time changes, top-left corner shows the student's current motions in the laboratory.

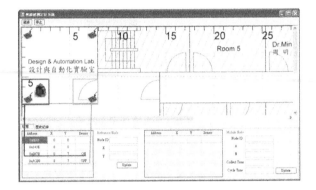

**Fig. 3.** Real time monitoring of IR sensor at the remote client side

# 4    Conclusions

Practical training is the important teaching strategy to improve students' industrial technology competence. Intelligent tutoring systems provide their own learning environment and place the student within it (Butz et al, 2006). The study uses sensor network technology to develop learning and teaching web services environment for industrial technology education that is ubiquitous in presence. The developed system was applied to the course of MENS manufacturing, and according to related data the teacher conveyed high satisfaction to the application of this system. Comparing to manufacturing course offered in the previous years, the average time of practical training for each student has been shortened considerably, and the usage of material has been lowered as well. This indicates that even when practicing in the clean room of a factory, the teacher is aware of problems faced by the students during the process of practice through the system developed by this research and can therefore appropriately provide the students with guidance to avoid mistakes from being made on a repeated basis.

**Acknowledgment.** The authors gratefully acknowledge the partial support of this study by the National Science Council of Taiwan, under the Grant No. NSC99-2511-S-003-034-MY3.

# References

1. Akyildiz, I.F., Su, W., Sankarasubramaniam, Y., Cayirci, E.: A survey on sensor networks. IEEE Communications Magazine 40(8), 102–114 (2002)
2. Tubaishat, M., Madria, S.: Sensor networks: An overview. IEEE Potentials 22(2), 20–23 (2003)
3. Dong, M., Tong, L., Sadler, B.M.: Information Retrieval and Processing in Sensor Networks: Deterministic Scheduling Versus Random Access. IEEE Transactions on Signal Processing 55(12), 5806–5820 (2007)
4. Long, H.B.: Skills for Self-Directed Learning, `http://faculty-staff.ou.edu/L/Huey.B.Long-1/articles.html` (retrieved December 15)
5. Desikan, P., DeLong, C., Beemanapalli, K., Bose, A., Srivastava, J.: Web Mining For Self Directed E-Learning. In: Data Mining for E-Learning. WIT Press (also available as AHPCRC Technical Report –TR # 2005-030)
6. Paquette, G., Ricciardi-Rigault, C., Paquin, C., Liegeois, S., Bleicher, E.: Developing the Virtual Campus Environment. In: Proceedings of Ed-Media, pp. 244–249 (1996)
7. Sung, W.T., Ou, S.C.: Using Virtual Reality Technologies for Manufacturing Applications. Int J. Com. Applications Tech. 17(4), 213–219 (2003)
8. Craig, A.B., Sherman, W.R.: Understanding Virtual Reality – Interface, Application, and Design. Elsevier Science, Morgan Kaufmann Publishers, Calif., USA (2003)
9. Bouras, C., Philopoulos, A., Tsiatsos, T.: E-learning through distributed virtual environments. J. Netw. Comput. Appl. 24(3), 175–199 (2001)
10. Matsubara, Y., Tominaga, H., Furukawa, Z., Yamasaki, T., Nagamachi, M.: Development of Virtual Learning Environment for Discovery Learning in School Education. Systems and Computers in Japan J83-D-I(10), 1109–1119 (2002)
11. Miller, R.L., Ely, J.F., Baldwin, R.M., Olds, B.M.: High-order Thinking in the Unit Operations Laboratory. Chemical Engineering Education 32(2), 146–151 (1998)
12. Shin, D., Yoon, E.S., Lee, K.Y., Lee, E.S.: A Web-based, Interactive Virtual Laboratory System for Unit Operations and Process Systems Engineering Education: Issues, Design, and Implementation. Computers and Chemical Engineering 26, 319–330 (2002)
13. Butz, B., Duarte, M., Miller, S.: An Intelligent Tutoring System for Circuit Analysis. IEEE Transactions on Education 49(2), 216–223 (2006)

# ONTOSPREAD: A Framework for Supporting the Activation of Concepts in Graph-Based Structures through the Spreading Activation Technique

José María Álvarez Rodríguez[1], José Emilio Labra Gayo[1],
and Patricia Ordóñez De Pablos[2]

[1] Department of Computer Science, University of Oviedo, Spain
{josem.alvarez,jelabra}@weso.es
[2] Department of Business Management, University of Oviedo, Spain
patriop@uniovi.es

**Abstract.** The present paper[1] introduces the ONTOSPREAD framework for the development, configuration, customization and execution of
the Spreading Activation technique over graph-based structures, more
specifically over RDF graphs and ontologies arising from the Semantic
Web area. This technique has been used to the efficient exploration and
querying of large and heterogeneous knowledge bases based on semantic
networks in the Information and Document Retrieval domains. ONTO-
SPREAD implements the double process of activation and spreading of
concepts in ontologies applying different restrictions of the original model
like weight degradation according to the distance or others coming from
the extension of this technique like the converging paths reward. This
technique provide a whole framework to ease the information access,
common required feature in the exploitation of the current Web of Data.
Moreover, it is considered to be relevant to support the recommendation
of concepts in different fields liked e-health, e-procurement or e-tourism
with the objective of getting a set of ranked resources. Finally an evaluation methodology and two examples using ontologies from different
domains are provided to validate the goodness, the improvement and
the capabilities of this framework applied to digital libraries.

**Keywords:** recommending and tagging systems, information and document retrieval, decision-support systems, algorithms, api.

**Category:** K.4, K.4.1, D.2, D.2.2

## 1 Introduction

The Spreading Activation technique (hereafter SA) introduced by [5], in the
field of psycho linguistics and semantic priming, proposes a model in which all

---

[1] This is the short version of the paper, some sections have been dropped in order to
adjust the contents to 6 pages. The extended version will again include them.

M.D. Lytras et al. (Eds.): WSKS 2011, CCIS 278, pp. 454–459, 2013.
© Springer-Verlag Berlin Heidelberg 2013

relevant information is mapped on a graph as nodes with a certain "activation value". Relations between two concepts are represented by a weighted edge. If a node is activated their activation value is spread to their neighbor nodes. This technique was adopted by the computer science community and applied to the resolution of different problems, see Sect. 2, and it is relevant to the the digital libraries field in the scope of: 1) construction of hybrid semantic search engines and 2) ranking of information resources according to an input set of weighted resources. Thus this technique eases the information access providing a connectionist method to retrieve data like brain can do. Although SA is widely used, more specifically in recent years has been successfully applied to ontologies, a common and standard framework is missing and each third party interested in its application must to implement its own version [20] of SA.

Taking into account the new information realm and the leading features of putting together the SA technique and the Semantic Web and Linked Data initiatives, new enriched services of searching, matchmaking, recommendation or contextualization can be implemented to fulfill the requirements of access information in digital libraries of different trending scopes like legal document databases [1], e-procurement, e-tourism or e-health.

The proposed work aims to afford a framework for SA to ease the configuration, customization and execution over graph-based structures and more specifically over RDF graphs and ontologies. It is relevant to digital libraries access and interoperability due to the fact that this technique provides a set of proven algorithms for retrieving and recommending information resources in large knowledge bases. Following the specific contributions of this work are listed: 1) study and revision of the classical constrained SA; 2) study and definition of new restrictions for SA applied to RDF graphs and ontologies; 3) implementation of a whole and extensible framework (called ONTOSPREAD) to customize and perform the SA based; 4) outlining of a methodology to configure and refine the execution of SA and 5) an example of configuration and refinement applying SA over a well-known ontology, the Galen ontology.

## 2   Related Work

Since SA was introduced by [5] in the field of psycho linguistics and semantic priming it has been applied to the resolution of problems trying to simulate the behavior of the brain using a connectionist method to provide an "intelligent" way to retrieve information and data.

The use of SA was motivated due to the research on graph exploration [15]. Nevertheless the success of this technique is specially relevant to the fields of Document [10] and Information Retrieval [4]. It has been also demonstrated its application to extract correlations between query terms and documents analyzing user logs [6] and to retrieve resources amongst multiple systems [18] in which ontologies are used to link and annotate resources.

In recent years and regarding the emerging use of ontologies in the Semantic Web area new applications of SA have appeared to explore concepts [16,3] addressing the two important issues: 1) the selection and 2) the weighting of additional search terms and to measure conceptual similarity [9]. On the other hand, there are works [11] exploring the application of the SA on ontologies in order to create context inference models.The semi-automatically extension and refinement of ontologies [13] is other trending topic to apply SA in combination with other techniques based on natural language processing. Data mining, more specifically mining socio-semantic networks[21], and applications to collaborative filtering (community detection based on tag recommendations, expertise location, etc.) are other potential scenarios to apply the SA theory due to the high performance and high scalability of the technique. In particular, annotation and tagging [12] services to gather meta-data [8] from the Web or to predict social annotation [2] and recommending systems based on the combination of ontologies and SA [7] are taken advantage of using SA technique. Also the semantic search [19] is a highlight area to apply SA following hybrid approaches [1,17] or user query expansion [14] combining metadata and user information.

Although this technique is widely accepted and applied to different fields open implementations[2], are missing. Moreover the Apache Mahout [3] project, a recent scalable machine learning library that supports large data sets, does not include an implementation of SA instead of providing algorithms for the classification, clustering, pattern mining, recommendation and collaborative filtering of resources in which SA should be representative.

# 3    ONTOSPREAD Framework

## 3.1    Constrained Spreading Activation

One of the leading features of SA technique is its flexibility to fit to the resolution of different kind of problems. From the configuration point of view some constraints presented in [4] have been customized to improve the expected outcomes of the execution according to the domain problem.

**Distance:** nodes far from an activated node should be penalized due to the number of needed steps to reach and activate them.

**Path:** the activation path is built by the activation process from a node to other and this process can be guided according to the weights of relations (edges).

**Multiple outputs (Fan-Out):** "highly connected" nodes can guide to a misleading situation in which activated and spread nodes are not representative, these nodes should be skipped or penalized by the algorithm.

**Threshold activation:** a node $n_i$ will be spread $iif$ its activation value, $I_i$, is greater than a threshold activation constant $\jmath$.

The aforementioned theoretical model is an excellent start point to design a framework for $SA$ but from the domain expert point of view some configuration

---

[2]  Texai company (http://texai.org/) offers a proprietary implementation of SA.

[3]  http://mahout.apache.org/

requirements to apply this technique to ontologies are missing. That is why a set of extensions are proposed to deal with the specific features of RDF graphs and ontologies.

**Context of activation** $\mathbb{D}_{com}$**:** the framework is able to manage some ontologies at the same time and concepts can be defined in different ontologies identified by a context URI (or namespace). The double process of activation and spreading will only be performed in the set of active contexts $\mathbb{D}_{com}$.

> **Definition 1.** *Let $\mathbb{D}_{com}$ an active domain, if a concept $c_i$ is activated o spread then $c_i \in \mathbb{D}_{com}$.*

**Minimum activation value** $N_{min}$ **:** only concepts with an activation value $N_k$ greater than $N_{min}$ will be spread. This constraint comes from the theoretical model of $SA$.

**Maximum number of spread concepts** $\mathbb{M}$ **:** the process of activation and spreading will be performed, at the most, until $\mathbb{M}$ concepts had been spread.

**Minimum number of spread concepts** $\mathbb{M}_{min}$ **:** the process of activation and spreading will be performed, at least, $\mathbb{M}_{min}$ concepts had been spread.

**Time of activation** $t$**:** the process of activation and spreading will be performed, at the most, during $t$ units of time.

**Output Degradation** $O_j$**:** one of the keypoints to improve and customize the algorithm is to define a function $h$ that penalizes the output value $O_j$ of a concept $c_j$.

1. Generic customization: $h$ calculates the output of a concept $c_j$ according to its degradation level.

$$O_j = h(I_j) \tag{1}$$

Basic case: if $h_0 = id$, the output value $O_j$ takes the level of the activated concept $c_j$ as its value.

$$O_j = h_0(I_j) = I_j \tag{2}$$

2. Customization using **distance**: $h_1$ calculates the level activation of the concept $c_j$ according to the distance from the initial concept $c_l \in \Phi^4$ to the node that has activated it. The activation value should decrease if the distance from $\Phi$ grows thus the algorithm follows a path from $c_l$ to $c_j$: $I_l > I_j$.

The function $h_1$ penalizes the output of concepts (decreasing their rank) far from the "activation core" and rewards closed concepts. Thus, let $d_j$, where $d_j = min\{d_{lj} : \forall n_l \in \Phi\}$:

$$O_j = h_1(I_j, d_j) = \frac{I_j}{d_j} \tag{3}$$

---

[4] Set of initial concepts.

3. Customization using **beats**: the function $h_2$ calculates the degradation of the concept using the number of iterations $k$:

$$O_j = h_2(I_j, k) = (1 + \frac{I_j}{k}) \exp(-\frac{I_j}{k}). \tag{4}$$

## 4   Conclusions and Future Work

This work provides a configurable and extensible framework to support the SA technique. It allows the configuration of restrictions and their combination to get the most accurate set of output concepts. One of the features that turns SA to a widely accepted algorithm lies in its flexibility but some disadvantages are also presented: the adjusting and refinement of restrictions and weights of the relations, the selection of the degradation function and the use of reward functions. This framework minimizes these advantages with an extensible library that can be applied to different scenarios like digital libraries, in particular biomedicine, e-procurement, e-health, etc. providing enriched services of annotation, searching or recommendation.

The main improvement in the algorithm consists on the flexibility of the refinement methodology. An automatic learning algorithm to create SA configurations according to ontologies should be developed. Thus, the training stage of SA could generate the best configuration for a specific domain. The algorithm could optimize the selection of input parameters like the weights of the relations, the degradation functions or the combination of restrictions. Beside new measures related to instances such as 'Cluster Measure", "Specifity Measure" or both could be used in the process of activation/spreading. Also the selection of the next node to spread is based on a "first better" strategy (if two nodes have the same activation value) because of this fact other selection strategies should be implemented. Finally a new version of the SA is being specified and developed following the Map/Reduce[5] programming model with the objective of getting a distributed version of this technique for processing large data sets.

## References

1. Berrueta, D., Labra, J., Polo, L.: Searching over Public Administration Legal Documents Using Ontologies. In: Proc. of JCKBSE 2006, pp. 167–175 (2006)
2. Chen, A., Chen, H.-H., Huang, P.: Predicting Social Annotation by Spreading Activation. In: Goh, D.H.-L., Cao, T.H., Sølvberg, I.T., Rasmussen, E. (eds.) ICADL 2007. LNCS, vol. 4822, pp. 277–286. Springer, Heidelberg (2007)
3. Chen, H., Ng, T.: An Algorithmic Approach to Concept Exploration in a Large Knowledge Network (automatic thesaurus consultation): Symbolic Branch-and-Bound search vs. connectionist Hopfield net activation. J. Am. Soc. Inf. Sci. 46(5), 348–369 (1995)
4. Cohen, P., Kjeldsen, R.: Information Retrieval by Constrained Spreading Activation in Semantic Networks. Inf. Process. Manage. 23(4), 255–268 (1987)

---

[5] http://labs.google.com/papers/mapreduce.html

5. Collins, A., Loftus, E.: A spreading activation theory of semantic processing. Psychological Review 82(6), 407–428 (1975)
6. Cui, H., Wen, J., Nie, J., Ma, W.: Query Expansion by Mining User Logs. IEEE Transaction on Knowledge and Data Engineering 15(4), 829–839 (2003)
7. Gao, Q., Yan, J., Liu, M.: A Semantic Approach to Recommendation System Based on User Ontology and Spreading Activation Model. In: NPC 2008: Proc. of the 2008 IFIP, pp. 488–492. IEEE Computer Society, Washington, DC (2008)
8. Gelgi, F., Vadrevu, S., Davulcu, H.: Improving Web Data Annotations with Spreading Activation. In: Ngu, A.H.H., Kitsuregawa, M., Neuhold, E.J., Chung, J.-Y., Sheng, Q.Z. (eds.) WISE 2005. LNCS, vol. 3806, pp. 95–106. Springer, Heidelberg (2005)
9. Gouws, S., Rooyen, G.-J.V., Engelbrecht, H.: Measuring Conceptual Similarity by Spreading Activation over Wikipedia's Hyperlink Structure. In: Proceedings of the 2nd Workshop on The People's Web Meets NLP: Collaboratively Constructed Semantic Resources, Beijing, China, pp. 46–54 (August 2010)
10. Turtle, H.R.: Inference Networks for Document Retrieval. PhD thesis, University Illinois, Urbana, IL, USA (1991)
11. Katifori, A., Vassilakis, C., Dix, A.: Ontologies and the brain: Using spreading activation through ontologies to support personal interaction. Cognitive Systems Research 11(1), 25–41 (2010)
12. Labra, J., Ordoñez, P., Cueva, J.: Combining Collaborative Tagging and Ontologies in Image Retrieval Systems (2007)
13. Liu, W., Weichselbraun, A., Scharl, A., Chang, E.: Semi-Automatic Ontology Extension Using Spreading Activation. Universal Knowledge Management (1), 50–58 (2005)
14. Nie, J.-Y.: Query Expansion and Query Translation as Logical Inference. J. Am. Soc. Inf. Sci. Technol. 54(4), 335–346 (2003)
15. Preece, S.: A Spreading Activation Network Model for Information Retrieval. PhD thesis, University Illinois, Urbana, IL, USA (1981)
16. Qiu, Y., Frei, H.: Concept-based query expansion. In: Proceedings of SIGIR 1993, Pittsburgh, US, pp. 160–169 (1993)
17. Rocha, C., Schwabe, D., de Aragão, M.: A Hybrid Approach for Searching in the Semantic Web. In: WWW, pp. 374–383 (2004)
18. Schumacher, K., Sintek, M., Sauermann, L.: Combining Fact and Document Retrieval with Spreading Activation for Semantic Desktop Search. In: Bechhofer, S., Hauswirth, M., Hoffmann, J., Koubarakis, M. (eds.) ESWC 2008. LNCS, vol. 5021, pp. 569–583. Springer, Heidelberg (2008)
19. Suchal, J.: On finding power method in spreading activation search. In: Geffert, V., Karhumäki, J., Bertoni, A., Preneel, B., Návrat, P., Bieliková, M. (eds.) SOFSEM (2), pp. 124–130. Safarik University, Slovakia (2008)
20. Todorova, P., Kiryakov, A., Ognyanoff, D., Peikov, I., Velkov, R., Tashev, Z.: D2.4.1 Spreading Activation Components (v1). Technical report, LarKC FP7 project–215535 (2009)
21. Troussov, A., Sogrin, M., Judge, J., Botvich, D.: Mining Socio-Semantic Networks Using Spreading Activation Technique (2008)

# Integrating Knowledge Engineering and Data Mining in e-commerce Fraud Prediction

Timo Polman and Marco Spruit

Institute of Information and Computing Sciences, Utrecht University,
Utrecht, The Netherlands
tppolman@gmail.com, m.r.spruit@uu.nl

**Abstract.** The number of merchants and consumers that participate in b2c e-commerce is still growing. Overall fraud rates have stabilized in recent years but for post-payment transactions in the Netherlands the fraud percentage remains unacceptably high. Companies often have a great deal of knowledge about fraudulent orders, and how to recognize them. Fraud prevention is often aided by automated recognition systems that are created through data mining. There have been few studies examining the combination of explicit domain knowledge and data mining. This study analyses the incorporation of domain knowledge in data mining for fraud prediction based on a historical dataset of 5,661 post-payment orders.

**Keywords:** Data mining, knowledge discovery in databases, knowledge engineering, automated fraud detection.

## 1 Introduction

*Data mining* and the broader *knowledge discovery in databases* or KDD have made a transition from an academic discipline to that of applied science, with usage in almost every field. Particularly interesting are the *predictive* data mining methods that are able to classify new data after being trained with historical data. Often, researchers try to gain knowledge exclusively from data, while in many domains there also is a great deal of relevant domain knowledge available. It has been pointed out quite early that incorporating domain knowledge in data mining might yield better results [1].

Many KDD and data mining publications [2-9] stress the importance of knowledge (engineering) in the process of knowledge discovery but not as an *explicit part of the classification itself*. This has been done in some more recent case studies including genes-disease associations [5], medical diagnosis [2], and indirect lending [9]. However, no such study has yet been performed in the e-commerce fraud prevention domain. While data mining is often used in e-commerce fraud detection [10-12], the incorporation of domain knowledge has yet to be examined for this domain. This research aims to fill this gap by examining the following research question:

*"What improvements in e-commerce fraud prediction rates are possible when integrating expert domain knowledge and data mining techniques?".*

M.D. Lytras et al. (Eds.): WSKS 2011, CCIS 278, pp. 460–466, 2013.
© Springer-Verlag Berlin Heidelberg 2013

# 2     Case Study

E-commerce merchants often suffer from fraud. Payment fraud – where the fraudster evades payment – is the best known and most practiced type of fraud. A payment method with a very high fraud rate is payment-on-credit. Customers then receive their package with an invoice inside it. The invoice can be posted or a regular (online) bank transfer can be used. The payment method is also popular because payment for the customer is postponed until approximately two weeks after delivery. The main problem associated with this payment method is that fraudsters can fake (a part of) their identity when purchasing. The goods are received but never paid for. The faked identity makes tracing afterwards very difficult and cost-ineffective. An undesired consequence is that customers who have honest intentions at the moment of purchase, default because they have run out of cash.

A medium sized online merchant in the Netherlands has provided us with a dataset of 5,661 post payment orders and the expert knowledge they possessed. Too many pay-on-credit orders in the past year have become uncollectible. For the payment method to remain feasible, an increase in fraud detection rates is necessary.

# 3     Methodology

## 3.1     Modeling the Knowledge System

The knowledge system will be classifying an order in terms of *suspicious* or *not suspicious* based on its set of attributes. A knowledge system is formed from domain knowledge, in our case possessed by two experts. As described by Schreiber et al. [13], this knowledge has to be *elicited* in order to be usable in a knowledge system. Furthermore, Shreiber et al. describe various methods for knowledge elicitation of which we will use structured and unstructured interviews.

Through analysis of the unstructured interviews performed we have identified the task template *classification*. A classification task takes object features as input, and gives an object class as output, *suspicious* or *not suspicious* in our case.

We have assembled structured interviews in order to gain insight in the experts' decision making process. These interviews have enabled us to form 13 rules, together forming a knowledge base. The rules apply to order characteristics, both already saved by the e-commerce software, for example *total order amount,* and new ones, to be deducted from the available data, for example *free email address.* We would present the experts with the rules already formed and ask them what rules were missing. This method was adapted from Schweickert et al. [14].

The classification will be performed by evaluating these rules.

Example of a classification rule as described above.

```
if (free_email_address and risk_products)
then score = score + 5
```

This rule will add a score of 5 to an order if the email address used originates from a list of known free email providers e.g. (hotmail, live, gmail), and one or more of the products ordered belongs to a list of products that are relatively more often bought by fraudsters. The sum of the scores generated by all the rules will decide which label will be assigned to the order.

### 3.2    Modeling the Data Mining Classifiers

The data mining will also be performing a classification task. Data mining classifiers are generated by *learning algorithms* that use training data. Different classification techniques employ different *learning algorithms* [15]. The input of an algorithm is the prepared input dataset, and its output is a model that can "predict the class labels of records it has never seen before" [15]. We will be evaluating eight different algorithms because the knowledge enhancement might perform differently over classifiers – as shown in a previous study [9].

We want to prevent *model over-fitting*; that is, if a generated model fits *noise*; "pays attention to parts of the data that are irrelevant" [16] or ". . . [fits] to data by chance" [17]. There are multiple techniques to avoid over-fitting, for example splitting the dataset into a test set and a training set. The classifier algorithm will train on the training set and can be validated on the test set. We will use cross-validation, a technique to split up the dataset multiple times in different training and test sets, to minimize the loss of using a smaller training set. More specifically we will use the *K-fold cross-validation* variant [15, 18].

### 3.3    Integrating KE in KDD and Data Mining

We will incorporate the *suspicious* classification from the knowledge system as a field in the training dataset, together with all the other order characteristics, and evaluate the performance of all eight classifiers – i.e. algorithms – with and without this variable.

## 4    Evaluation Methods

### 4.1    Measuring Classifier Performance

In order to answer our research question, we must know how to measure classifier performance. A classifiers performance can be ranked in *true positives* (correctly classified as positive), *true negatives* (correctly classified as negative), *false positives* (classified as positive while negative) and *false negatives* (classified as negative while positive). We will evaluate the performance of the different classifiers in the following measures deducted from these numbers; *area under the ROC curve* and *total cost*.

**Area Under the Curve (AUC).** A sophisticated measurement based on receiver operating characteristic (ROC) graphs. Recently, data mining studies have been using this method, originating from signal detection theory [19] in measuring classifier performance, for example [9, 20]. "The AUC of a classifier is equivalent to the probability that the classifier will rank a randomly chosen positive instance higher than a randomly chosen negative instance." [21]

**Misclassification Costs.** The costs of false positives and false negatives are good indicators. The use of misclassification costs has since long been applied within the medical domain [22], and increasingly more authors stress the importance of applying misclassification costs [23, 24] in data mining. The most relevant measure for our case company is *total costs* involved with a certain model choice.

## 4.2   Statistical Evaluation

Statistical evaluation of classifier performance over multiple datasets poses some problems in estimating the variance [25] and significance. According to a study [26], research in machine learning often assesses a significant difference in the wrong way. We will use the non-parametric *Wilcoxon Signed-Ranks Test* as proposed in [26] instead of the paired t-test. This test ranks the differences between pairs and then compares sum of the ranks for the positive and negative differences. With this test, we will try to reject our null hypothesis:

$H_0$: *The incorporation of domain knowledge through an attribute added to the dataset yields no difference in AUC outcomes.*

We will reject $H_0$ if the observed difference exceeds the 95% confidence interval.

# 5    Results

## 5.1   Overview

**Table 1** shows the AUC and the standard deviation (SD) for the three best performing classifiers. Seven out of eight classifiers tested showed an increase when the knowledge-induced attribute was added.

**Table 1.** Area Under the Curve (AUC)

|  | No Domain Knowledge | | Domain Knowledge | |
|---|---|---|---|---|
| Classifier | AUC | SD | AUC | SD |
| Naïve Bayes | 0.717 | 0.033 | 0.727 | 0.033 |
| Logistic Regression | 0.728 | 0.033 | 0.738 | 0.032 |
| AdaBoost | 0.683 | 0.031 | 0.701 | 0.028 |
| Average[1] | 0.649 | | 0.658 | |

## 5.2   Statistics

We have statistically evaluated the performance of all eight classifiers combined using the Wilcoxon Signed-Rank Test (1).

$$Z = -1.542, P = 0.123, \alpha = 0.05 \tag{1}$$

P is not equal to, or smaller than our chosen level of significance, which means we cannot reject our null hypothesis. We do not observe a statistically significant difference in data mining classifiers performance when incorporating knowledge engineering.

---

[1] The averages are calculated based upon all eight classifiers as listed above.

### 5.3 Case Study Results

For our case study company the most important performance indicator is cost. In a previous case study [27], false positive and false negative costs were calculated.

For each classifier we have calculated the total fraud related costs with and without incorporating the domain knowledge attribute. The estimated fraud cost decrease as a percentage of the turnover was 6.68% on average, for all eight classifiers. When applying the Wilcoxon Signed-Rank Test (2) we observe a significant increase.

$$Z = -2.100, P = .036, \alpha = .05 \qquad (2)$$

### 5.4 Explanation of Results

Why did we fail to find statistical valid improvements when comparing the AUC of the different methods? First, our evaluation methods, both the classifier performance indicator we have chosen and the statistical test are very robust. This also implicates that a significant improvement is less likely to observe.

Second, as explained in our case description, an unknown part of the instances classified as fraud were *unintentional*. Domain knowledge about fraud is mostly unable to distinguish these from paying customers.

## 6 Conclusion and Discussion

**Research Question.** *What improvements in e-commerce fraud prediction rates are possible when integrating expert domain knowledge and data mining techniques?*

We did not observe a significant increase when comparing the AUC of all our classifiers. For the case-relevant measure, total costs, we have calculated that the cost reduction by integrating domain knowledge for the eight classifiers we have chosen could be 6.68 % on average, a significant decrease.

**Discussion.** The addition of knowledge engineering in data mining as a research topic poses some difficulties. The integration of domain knowledge however is often only applicable in a very specific area, and its associated costs are relatively high, since the process of knowledge elicitation is highly time-consuming. Also, it can be difficult to determine whether a (lack of) performance increase originates from the nature of the data, or the quality of the knowledge system created.

**Further Research Directions.** This issue deserves further empirical study; we are especially interested in the performance of our method when applied to other datasets and domains. Also, another promising line of research would be examining different types of knowledge systems and machine learning integration.

**Acknowledgements.** We would like to thank Total Internet Group for providing sample data, their domain knowledge and a great deal of support. Especially Joost Schildwacht and Joachim de Boer at TIG have been very helpful, both on the scientific and practical domains.

# References

1. Pazzani, M., Kibler, D.: The Utility of Knowledge in Inductive Learning. Machine Learning 9, 57–94 (1992)
2. Alonso, F., Caraça-Valente, J.P., González, A.L., Montes, C.: Combining expert knowledge and data mining in a medical diagnosis domain. Expert Systems with Applications 23, 367–375 (2002)
3. Chapman, P., Clinton, J., Kerber, R., Khabaza, T., Reinartz, T., Shearer, C., Wirth, R.: CRISP-DM 1.0 Step-by-step data mining guide (1999), http://www.crisp-dm.org/CRISPWP-0800.pdf
4. Daniëls, H.A.M., Feelders, A.J.: Integrating Economic Knowledge in Data Mining Algorithms. Tilburg University, Center for Economic Research (2001)
5. Dinu, V., Zhao, H., Miller, P.L.: Integrating domain knowledge with statistical and data mining methods for high-density genomic SNP disease association analysis. Journal of Biomedical Informatics 40, 750–760 (2007)
6. Fayyad, U., Piatetsky-Shapiro, G., Smyth, P.: The KDD process for extracting useful knowledge from volumes of data. Commun. ACM. 39, 27–34 (1996)
7. Kopanas, I., Avouris, N., Daskalaki, S.: The Role of Domain Knowledge in a Large Scale Data Mining Project. In: Vlahavas, I.P., Spyropoulos, C.D. (eds.) SETN 2002. LNCS (LNAI), vol. 2308, pp. 288–299. Springer, Heidelberg (2002)
8. Langseth, H., Nielsen, T.D.: Fusion of Domain Knowledge with Data for Structural Learning in Object Oriented Domains. Journal of Machine Learning Research 4, 339–368 (2003)
9. Sinha, A.P., Zhao, H.: Incorporating domain knowledge into data mining classifiers: An application in indirect lending. Decision Support Systems 46, 287–299 (2008)
10. Chan, P.K., Wei Fan, A.L., Stolfo, J.: Distributed Data Mining in Credit Card Fraud Detection. IEEE Intelligent Systems and Their Applications 1094, 67–74 (1999)
11. Quah, J.T.S., Sriganesh, M.: Real-time credit card fraud detection using computational intelligence. Expert Systems with Applications 35, 1721–1732 (2008)
12. Sánchez, D., Vila, M.A., Cerda, L., Serrano, J.M.: Association rules applied to credit card fraud detection. Expert Systems with Applications 36, 3630–3640 (2009)
13. Schreiber, G., Akkermans, H., Anjewierden, A., de Hoog, R., Shadbolt, N., Van de Velde, W., Wielinga, B.: Knowledge engineering and management. MIT Press, London (2000)
14. Schweickert, R., Burton, A.M., Taylor, N.K., Corlett, E.N., Shadbolt, N.R., Hedgecock, A.P.: Comparing knowledge elicitation techniques: a case study. Artif. Intell. Rev. 1, 245–253 (1987)
15. Pang-Ning, T., Steinbach, M., Kumar, V.: Classification: Alternative Techniques. Data Mining, ch. 5, pp. 207–326. Addison Wesley (2005)
16. Moore, A.: Decision Trees Tutorial Slides (2005), http://www.autonlab.org/tutorials/dtree.html
17. Fayyad, U., Stolorz, P.: Data mining and KDD: Promise and challenges. Future Generation Computer Systems 13, 99–115 (1997)
18. Kirkos, E., Spathis, C., Manolopoulos, Y.: Data Mining techniques for the detection of fraudulent financial statements. Expert Systems with Applications 32, 995–1003 (2007)
19. Provost, F., Fawcett, T.: Analysis and visualization of classifier performance: Comparison under imprecise class and cost distributions. Presented at the Proceedings of the Third International Conference on Knowledge Discovery and Data Mining (1997)
20. Provost, F., Domingos, P.: Tree Induction for Probability-Based Ranking. Machine Learning 52, 199–215 (2003)

21. Fawcett, T.: An introduction to ROC analysis. Pattern Recognition Letters 27, 861–874 (2006)
22. Ambrosino, R., Buchanan, B.G.: The use of physician domain knowledge to improve the learning of rule-based models for decision-support. In: Proc. AMIA Symp., pp. 192–196 (1999)
23. Phua, C., Lee, V., Smith, K., Gayler, R.: A comprehensive survey of data mining-based fraud detection research. Artificial Intelligence Review (2005)
24. Weiss, G., Provost, F.: The effect of class distribution on classifier learning: an empirical study. Rutgers Univ. (2001)
25. Nadeau, C., Bengio, Y.: Inference for the Generalization Error. Machine Learning 52, 239–281 (2003)
26. Demšar, J.: Statistical comparisons of classifiers over multiple data sets. The Journal of Machine Learning Research 7, 30 (2006)
27. Stolte, V.: Onderzoek naar een e-commerce fraudedetectie strategie (2009)

# A Tool for Agent Based Modeling – A Land Market Case Study

Umar Manzoor[1,2], Mati Ullah[1], Arshad Ali[1], Janita Irfan[2], and Muhammad Murtaza[3]

[1] Department of Computer Science, National University of Computer and Emerging Sciences, Islamabad, Pakistan
[2] School of Computing, Science and Engineering, The University of Salford, Salford, UK
[3] Caledonian Business School, Glasgow Caledonian University, Glasgow, UK
{umarmanzoor,matiullah85}@gmail.com,
arshad.ali@nu.edu.pk, janita_irfan@yahoo.com,
mmurta10@caledonian.ac.uk

**Abstract.** Multi-Agent paradigm has become a promising paradigm for developing real world applications and gaining popularity especially in ecological and environmental modeling. Multi-agents are modeled using Agent Unified Modeling Language (AUML) as Unified Modeling Language (UML) notations are not enough to express agent properties / behaviours. In this paper, we have proposed A Tool for Agent Based Modeling to help designer in building rapid multi-agent based applications. The purpose of this toolkit is to make life of a developer easier and to save his time by not reinventing an agent that is already developed.

**Keywords:** Agent-based Modeling, Multi-Agent Rapid Development, Agent Reusability, Land market mechanisms, AUML to Java Code.

## 1    Introduction

In the last decade, computer based environmental modeling has gained attention of researchers all over the world because it is convenient to make computer model of complex environmental problem(s) and analyze the effects of various factors on the environment rather than physically going out in the environment, performing the results again and again to measure these effects. In the last decade, agent paradigm has become a promising paradigm for developing real world applications and has been used by researchers in diverse areas because of their tremendous capabilities [9, 13]. Human-Environment interaction modeling is one area among these areas and agent based modeling is gaining popularity in this area especially in ecological and environmental modeling [8, 10].

Agent can be described as a computer program which acts autonomously in some environment on behalf of the user to fulfill its design objectives [2]. Multi-agents are modeled using Agent Unified Modeling Language (AUML) [1, 3] as Unified Modeling Language (UML) notations are not enough to express agent properties/behaviours etc [5, 6]. Designing and implementing agent based models for

M.D. Lytras et al. (Eds.): WSKS 2011, CCIS 278, pp. 467–472, 2013.

complex problems (such as ecological and environmental problem) can be a demanding task as even a simplest of agent-based model can demonstrate complex behavior [12]. Currently, various toolkits for agent based modeling are being used however, designer has to create/implement the model from scratch even if the same problem is modeled/implemented by some other researcher/designer. The tool we proposed in this paper aims at reducing the effort required for developing an agent based model for complex distributed problem (such as land market modeling [11]) by using already existing agent(s) from the agent repository.

## 2    Background

Researchers in the last decade have used different concepts for modeling of multi-agent systems. Volker Grimm et al in [9] proposed a standard protocol ODD (Overview, Design concepts, and Details) for agent based modeling of ecological problems. According to the authors, full UML requires software engineering knowledge and is complex to understand for ecologists where as ODD can easily be written and understood by ecologists. However, our proposed uses agent interaction protocol for modeling which is very simple to understand and does not require deep knowledge of software engineering. Therefore, researchers of diverse fields can design agent based models with little or no coding and get fully working JAVA code. Mike Livermore in [13] proposed MR. POTATOHEAD framework for agent based modeling of complex human-environment. The proposed framework provides user friendly environment for modeling and designer can model wide range of collaborative models. ODD and MR. POTATOHEAD framework are designed specifically for environmental and ecological modeling whereas our proposed tool can be used in diverse fields.

## 3    System Design

The purpose of A Tool for Agent Based Modeling is to facilitate the designer in modeling/designing of multi-agent based applications [4, 7]. The detailed architecture of system is based on the Subsumption or Layered architecture, aim of this architecture is to decompose the complicated intelligent behavior into several simple modules. The system architecture consists of the following agents:

- GUI Agent
- Agent Handler
- Agent Verifier
- Agent Code Generator

### 3.1    GUI Agent

GUI Agent is the main agent of the system as it initializes the system and interacts with the designer. In initialization GUI agent loads the system configuration XML file which contains designer working path, agent repository path, and last five project paths. GUI Agent is responsible for the creation and initialization of Agent Handler, Agent Verifier, and Agent Code Generator. After system initialization, the responsibility of GUI agent is to interact with the designer, manage GUI panels (i.e. drag and drop facility, drawing, interaction etc), and monitor other agents.

## 3.2    Agent Handler

After initialization Agent Handler, monitors which agents are used in the project by the designer and report it to GUI agent. It also helps designer in adding/modifying/deleting the behaviors/methods of built-in agents. If the designer adds/modify/delete method or behavior in any agent, agent handler passes the changes to agent verifier for validation, if successful the changes are made else appropriate error message is shown to the designer.

## 3.3    Agent Verifier

The responsibility of agent verifier is to validate the changes (i.e. add/delete/modify methods or behaviors) made to the agent by the designer and to validate the compatibility of new agent(s) added by the designer. After initialization Agent Verifier waits for the task from Agent handler, based on the task Agent Verifier either validate the changes or the compatibility and returns the result to agent handler.

## 3.4    Agent Code Generator

Agent Code Generator is responsible for converting Agent Unified Modeling Language model into the JAVA source code. After initialization, Agent code generator waits for the task from GUI agent, on receiving the task it converts AUML model into code and saves it in the folder. The code generated by Agent code generator can be imported to any JAVA editor and designer can edit / modify the code if needed.

# 4    Test Cases

A Tool for Agent Based Modeling has been evaluated using many scenarios; one scenario is described in this section.  Test case 1 shown in figure 1 shows the modeling and interaction of land selling-buying scenario using multi-agents; Seller, Property dealer, Buyer and LandDept (Land Department) agents. Seller agent purpose is to sell the land in good price (i.e. which maximizes its profit) whereas buyer agents' purpose is to buy item in the most reasonable price. Seller, Buyer, Property dealer, and LandDept agents were developed and assigned methods/behaviors to achieve certain goals and usually all the methods/behaviors exhibited are not utilized in one scenario, only the required/essential behaviors are used.Seller agent purpose is to sell product(s) and selling usually requires advertising the land, giving Property dealer agent the details of the land, negotiating price, accepting the conditions of agreement, land paper transfer (if case of deal), returning advance payment (if case of problem with land papers), Transfer the ownership and pay commission to the Property dealer agent. In scenario 1, the following behaviors of Merchant agent are used:

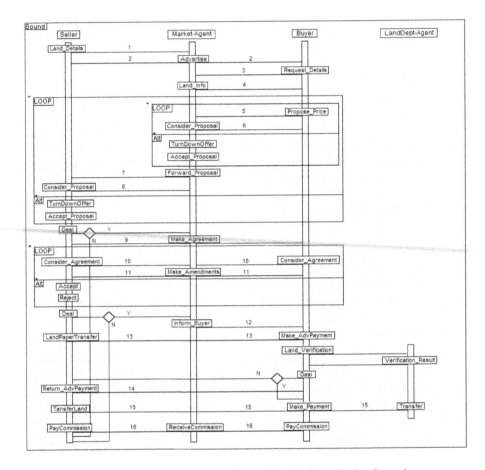

**Fig. 1.** Multi-Agent AUML Modeling of Land Selling-Buying Scenario

1) Land Details: Convey land details and demand to the market by informing the property dealer agent.

2) Consider Proposal: Checks the proposal offered by the buying agent and forwarded by property dealer agent, with the minimum price it can accept. If the price offered is less than the minimum price, it will reply to property dealer agent to increase the proposed price which forwards the message to buyer agent.

3) Accept Proposal: If the price offered by the buyer agents meets the minimum criteria, Seller agent terminates negotiation and calls the Deal method.

4) Turndown Offer: If the negotiation is not successful (i.e. the price offered by the buyer agent does not meet the minimum criteria), Seller agent terminate negotiation and calls the Deal method.

5) Deal: Sends the decision (accept or reject) to property dealer agent which forwards the decision to the buyer agent.

6) Consider Agreement: Checks the agreement conditions, if the agreement conditions violate any of its criteria, it will reply to property dealer agent to make necessary amendments.

7)  Accept: If the agreement offered by the property dealer agent meets all the criteria, Seller agent calls the Deal method.

8)  Reject: If the agreement offered by the property dealer agent violates any of its criteria, it terminates the deal and calls the Deal method.

9)  Land Paper Transfer: It accepts the adv. Payment from buyer agent and gives the copy of land documents to the buyer agent for verification purpose.

10) Return Adv. Payment: In case any allegation is reported by the land department on the land documents, buyer agent terminates the deal and seller agent returns the adv. payment.

11) TransferLand: Seller agent transfers the ownership rights to the buyer agent and receives the remaining payment.

12) Pay Commission: After successfully transferring the ownership rights, Seller agent pays the commission to the property dealer agent.

Buyer agent purpose is to buy land and buying usually requires find the required land, negotiating price (maximum bargain/minimum price), accepting the conditions of agreement, make advance payment, land document verification, make payment and pay commission. In scenario 1, the following behaviors of Buyer agent are used:

1)  Request Details: Request details of the land (i.e. land information, demand, payment time etc) from the property dealer agent.

2)  Propose Price: Proposes price for the land and waits for the response from property dealer agent. If the response is negative and the proposed bid is less than the maximum bid it can offer, it revises the bid and sends it again until the property dealer agent agrees to the proposed bid or the maximum bid is achieved.

3)  Consider Agreement: Checks the agreement conditions, if the agreement conditions violate any of its criteria, it will reply to property dealer agent to make necessary amendments.

4)  Make Adv. Payment: Make advance payment to the Seller agent for the land and gets the copy of the land documents in return.

5)  Land Verification: Verifies the land documents with the land department, in case any allegation is reported, Buyer agent terminates the deal and calls the Deal method.

6)  Deal: Sends the decision (accept or reject) to seller agent.

7)  Make Payment: Makes payment to the seller agent and gets the land ownership in return.

8)  Pay Commission: After successfully purchasing the land, Buyer agent pays the commission to the property dealer agent.

Property dealer agent purpose is to facilitate both seller/buyer in buying/selling of land and acts as middle man. It has the following methods. 1) Advertise (It advertises land for sale on newspapers or websites for potential buyer's information). 2) Land_Info (provides land information to the potential buyer). 3) Consider_Proposal (Checks the proposal offered by the buying agent, if the price offered is less than the minimum price conveyed by seller, it will reply to buyer agent to increase the proposed price). 4) Make_Agreement. 5) Make_Amendments (amend the agreement). 6. Receive Commission etc. Similarly LandDept agent two methods (verification and Transfer) are used in this scenario. The above model can be extended by other developers for modeling fraud detection in land sale/purchase or sale/purchase of motor-vehicle etc; all the developer has to do is to introduce/modify few agent methods.

## 5    Conclusion

In this paper, we have proposed A Tool for Agent Based Modeling to help designer in developing rapid multi-agent based applications by providing built-in agent repository along with the designing interface for developing AUML model. The tool provides drag-drop facility; all the designer has to do is drag-drop agents on the drawing area and built AUML model using AUML notations and after completing the model, designer can convert the AUML into working Java code by a single click.

## References

1. Weib, G.: Agent orientation in software engineering. The Knowledge Engineering Review 16, 349–373 (2001)
2. Manzoor, U., Nefti, S.: Quiet: A Methodology for Autonomous Software Deployment using Mobile Agents. Journal of Network and Computer Applications (2010), http://dx.doi.org/10.1016/j.jnca.2010.03.015
3. Agent Unified Modeling Language Tools (2010), http://www.auml.org/auml/tools/main.shtml (last accessed: June 8, 2010)
4. Manzoor, U., Nefti, S.: An agent based system for activity monitoring on network – ABSAMN. Expert Systems with Applications 36(8), 10987–10994 (2009)
5. Wooldridge, M.J., Ciancarini, P.: Agent-Oriented Software Engineering: The State of the Art. In: Ciancarini, P., Wooldridge, M.J. (eds.) AOSE 2000. LNCS(LNAI), vol. 1957, pp. 1–28. Springer, Heidelberg (2001)
6. Jennings, N.R., Wooldridge, M.: Agent-oriented software engineering. In: Bradshaw, J. (ed.) Handbook of Agent Technology. AAAI/MIT Press (2002)
7. Manzoor, U., Nefti, S.: Autonomous Agents: Smart Network Installer and Tester (SNIT). Expert System with Application (2010), http://dx.doi.org/10.1016/j.eswa.2010.07.066
8. Thiele, J.C., Grimm, V.: NetLogo meets R: Linking agent-based models with a toolbox for their analysis. Environmental Modelling & Software 25, 972–974 (2010)
9. Grimma, V.: A standard protocol for describing individual-based and agent-based models. Ecological Modelling 198, 115–126 (2006)
10. Bousquet, F., Barreteau, O., Le Page, C., Mullon, C., Weber, J.: An environmental modelling approach. The use of Multi-agent Simulations. In: Advances in Environmental and Ecological Modelling, pp. 113–122. Elsevier, Paris (1999)
11. Filatova, T., Voinov, A., van der Veen, A.: Land market mechanisms for preservation of space for coastal ecosystems: An agent-based analysis. Environmental Modelling & Software 26(2), 179–190 (2011)
12. Grimm, V.: Individual-based models. In: Jørgensen, S.E. (ed.) Ecological Models, pp. 1959–1968. Elsevier, Oxford (2008)
13. MR POTATOHEAD Framework – A Software Tool for Collaborative Land-Use Change Modeling. In: Swayne, D.A., Yang, W., Voinov, A.A., Rizzoli, A., Filatova, T. (eds.) International Congress on Environmental Modelling and Software, Modelling for Environment's Sake, Fifth Biennial Meeting, Ottawa, Canada

# Discovery and Learning in a Semantic Framework

Antonella Carbonaro

Department of Computer Science, University of Bologna,
Mura Anteo Zamboni, 7, Bologna, Italy
`antonella.carbonaro@unibo.it`

**Abstract.** The paper presents a web based system that aims to improve Web exploration by enabling users to discover knowledge associated to his need. Indeed, in exploratory search, the user is willing not only to find documents relevant with respect to his query but he is also interested in learning, discovering and understanding knowledge on complex and sometimes unknown topics. We rely on DBpedia to explore the semantics of keywords thus suggesting potentially interesting related topics or keywords to the user and enabling user-friendly and intelligent content discovery.

**Keywords:** Semantic Web Discovery, Exploratory Search, Data Web.

## 1 Introduction

The Semantic Web offers a generic infrastructure for interchange, integration and creative reuse of structured data, which can help to cross some of the boundaries that Web 2.0 is facing. Currently, Web 2.0 offers poor query possibilities apart from searching by keywords or tags. There has been a great deal of interest in the development of semantic-based systems to facilitate knowledge representation and extraction and content integration [1], [2]. Semantic-based approach to retrieving relevant material can be useful to address issues like trying to determine the type or the quality of the information suggested from a personalized environment. In this context, standard keyword search has a very limited effectiveness. For example, it cannot filter for the type of information, the level of information or the quality of information.

Potentially, one of the biggest application areas of content-based exploration might be personalized searching framework (e.g., [3],[4]). Whereas today's search engines provide largely anonymous information, new framework might highlight or recommend web pages or content related to key concepts. We can consider semantic information representation as an important step towards a wide efficient manipulation and discovery of information [5], [6], [7]. In the digital library community a flat list of attribute/value pairs is often assumed to be available. In the Semantic Web community, annotations are often assumed to be an instance of an ontology. Through the ontologies the system will express key entities and relationships describing

M.D. Lytras et al. (Eds.): WSKS 2011, CCIS 278, pp. 473–478, 2013.
© Springer-Verlag Berlin Heidelberg 2013

resources in a formal machine-processable representation. An ontology-based knowledge representation could be used for content analysis and object recognition, for reasoning processes and for enabling user-friendly and intelligent multimedia content exploration and retrieval.

The paper presents a web based system that aims to improve Web exploration by enabling users to discover knowledge associated to his need. Indeed, in exploratory search [8], the user is willing not only to find documents relevant with respect to his query but he is also interested in learning, discovering and understanding knowledge on complex and sometimes unknown topics.

## 2    Semantic Framework

Traditional approaches to personalization include both content-based and user-based techniques. If, on one hand, a content-based approach allows to define and maintain an accurate user profile (for example, the user may provides the system with a list of keywords reflecting him/her initial interests and the profiles could be stored in form of weighted keyword vectors and updated on the basis of explicit relevance feedback), which is particularly valuable whenever a user encounters new content, on the other hand it has the limitation of concerning only the significant features describing the content of an item. Differently, in a user-based approach, resources are processed according to the rating of other users of the system with similar interests. Since there is no analysis of the item content, these information management techniques can deal with any kind of item, being not just limited to textual content. In such a way, users can receive items with content that is different from that one received in the past. On the other hand, since a user-based technique works well if several users evaluate each one of them, new items cannot be handled until some users have taken the time to evaluate them and new users cannot receive references until the system has acquired some information about the new user in order to make personalized predictions. These limitations often refer to as the sparsity and start-up problems. By adopting a hybrid approach, a personalization system is able to effectively filter relevant resources from a wide heterogeneous environment like the Web, taking advantage of common interests of the users and also maintaining the benefits provided by content analysis. A hybrid approach maintains another drawback: the difficulty to capture semantic knowledge of the application domain, i.e. concepts, relationships among different concepts, inherent properties associated with the concepts, axioms or other rules, etc [9].

In this context, standard keyword search is of very limited effectiveness. For example, it does not allow users and the system to search, handle or read concepts of interest, and it doesn't consider synonymy and hyponymy that could reveal hidden similarities potentially leading to better retrieval. The advantages of a concept-based document and user representations can be summarized as follows: (i) ambiguous terms inside a resource are disambiguated, allowing their correct interpretation and, consequently, a better precision in the user model construction (e.g., if a user is interested in computer science resources, a document containing the word 'bank' as it is meant in the financial context could not be relevant); (ii) synonymous words belonging to the same meaning can contribute to the resource model definition (for example, both 'mouse' and 'display' brings evidences for computer science documents, improving the coverage of the document retrieval); (iii) synonymous words belonging to the same meaning can contribute to the user model matching, which is required in recommendation process (for example, if two users have the same interests, but these are expressed using different terms, they will considered overlapping); (iv) finally, classification, recommendation and sharing phases take advantage of the word senses in order to classify, retrieve and suggest documents with high semantic relevance with respect to the user and resource models.

For example, the system could support Computer Science last-year students during their activities in courseware like Bio Computing, Internet Programming or Machine Learning. In fact, for these kinds of courses it is necessary an active involvement of the student in the acquisition of the didactical material that should integrate the lecture notes specified and released by the teacher. Basically, the level of integration depends both on the student's prior knowledge in that particular subject and on the comprehension level he wants to acquire. Furthermore, for the mentioned courses, it is necessary to continuously update the acquired knowledge by integrating recent information available from any remote digital library.

In this paper, we investigate how explorative search, initialized by choosing a keyword, can be enhanced with automatically produced context information so that search results better fit to the actual information needs of the users. In the Semantic Web, the idea is to give the discovery engine designers more to work with than producing results based on keyword frequency and number of pages linked to a document, offering new possibilities that go well beyond finding documents by way of keyword search.

## 3    Web of Data

The idea behind Linked Data [10] is using the Web to allow exposing, connecting and sharing linking data through dereferenceable URIs on the Web. The goal is to extend the Web by publishing various open datasets as RDF triples and by setting RDF links between data items from several data sources. Using URIs, everything can be referred to and looked up both by people and by software agents. In this paper we focus on DBpedia [11], that is one of the main clouds of the Linked Data graph. DBpedia extracts structured content from Wikipedia and makes this information available on the Web; it uses the RDF to represent the extracted information. It is possible to query relationships and properties associated with Wikipedia resources (through its SPARQL endpoint), and link other data sets on the web to DBpedia data.

The whole knowledge base consists of over one billion triples. DBpedia labels and abstracts of resources are stored in more than 95 different languages. The graph is highly connected to other RDF dataset of the Linked Data cloud. Each resource in DBpedia is referred by its own URI, allowing to precisely get a resource with no ambiguity. The DBpedia knowledge base is served as Linked Data on the Web.

Actually, various data providers have started to set RDF links from their data sets to DBpedia, making DBpedia one of the central interlinking-hubs of the emerging Web of Data.

Compared to other ontological hierarchies and taxonomies, DBpedia has the advantage that each term or resource is enhanced with a rich description including a textual abstract. Another advantage is that DBpedia automatically evolves as Wikipedia changes. Hence, problems such as domain coverage, content freshness, machine-understandability can be addressed more easily when considering DBpedia. Moreover, it covers different areas of the human knowledge (geographic information, people, films, music, books, …); it represents real community agreement and it is truly multilingual.

The implemented system shows a pop-up window every time the user selects in his browser a word to have its lookup. The word can be selected from all web pages. The showed window is composed by four different areas: the Quote box displays the selected word; the Result box shows the result labels coming from the lookup and allows the user to open a new DBpedia page related to label; the Definition Box holds an iframe showing the chosen result description; the Class box shows radio buttons corresponding to DBpedia classes, the user can refine the search specifying the desired class and performing a more specific discovery section.

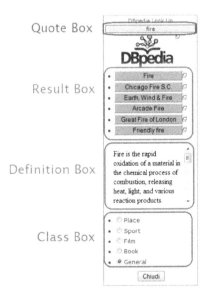

The pop-up window can be activated in every web page just selecting a word. For example, the following Figure shows a Wikipedia page in which the user selects the word "ice" and corresponding results.

To show the actual description in the Definition box we perform a control to delete the old iframe content avoiding to adding several descriptions.

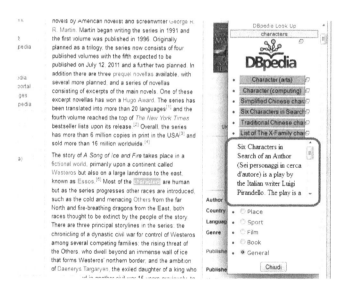

## 4    Considerations

The work described in this paper represents some initial steps in exploring semantic based search framework. It could be considered as one possible instance of a more general concept concerning the transition from the Document Web to the Document/Data Web and the consequent managing of these immense volumes of data. Indeed, advances in search need to do more than simply improve the syntactic keyword matching process and can be used, for example, in new search scenarios, including when the users are (a) unfamiliar with a domain and its terminology, (b) unfamiliar with a system and it's capabilities, or (c) unfamiliar with the full detail of their task or goal.

While the initial results are encouraging, much remains to be explored. For example, many search strategies with specific advantages are available, so designers now have the possibility of deciding which new features to include in order to support them, but it is particularly difficult to distinguish the benefits of each advance that have often been shown independent of others.

# References

1. Henze, N., Dolog, P., Nejdl, W.: Reasoning and Ontologies for Personalized E-Learning in the Semantic Web. Educational Technology & Society 7(4), 82–97 (2004)
2. Bighini, C., Carbonaro, A.: InLinx: Intelligent Agents for Personalized Classification, Sharing and Recommendation. International Journal of Computational Intelligence. International Computational Intelligence Society 2(1) (2004)
3. Pickens, J., Golovchinsky, G., Shah, C., Qvarfordt, P., Back, M.: Algorithmic Mediation for Collaborative Exploratory Search. In: To appear in Proceedings of SIGIR
4. Freyne, J., Smyth, B.: Collaborative Search: Deployment Experiences. In: The 24th SGAI International Conference on Innovative Techniques and Applications of Artificial Intelligence, Cambridge, UK, pp. 121–134 (2004)
5. Calic, J., Campbell, N., Dasiopoulou, S., Kompatsiaris, Y.: A Survey on Multimodal Video Representation for Semantic Retrieval. In: The Third International Conference on Computer as a Tool. IEEE (2005)
6. Carbonaro, A.: Defining Personalized Learning Views of Relevant Learning Objects in a Collaborative Bookmark Management System. In: Ma, Z. (ed.) Web-based Intelligent ELearning Systems: Technologies and Applications, pp. 139–155. Information Science Publishing, Hershey (2006)
7. Bloehdorn, S., Petridis, K., Simou, N., Tzouvaras, V., Avrithis, Y., Handschuh, S., Kompatsiaris, Y., Staab, S., Strintzis, M.G.: Knowledge Representation for Semantic Multimedia Content Analysis and Reasoning. In: Proceedings of the European Workshop on the Integration of Knowledge, Semantics and Digital Media Technology (2004)
8. White, R.W., Roth, R.: Exploratory Search: Beyond the Query-Response Paradigm. Morgan & Claypool (2009)
9. Carbonaro, A., Ferrini, R.: Considering semantic abilities to improve a Web-Based Distance Learning System. In: ACM International Workshop on Combining Intelligent and Adaptive Hypermedia Methods/Techniques in Web-based Education Systems (2005)
10. Bizer, C., Heath, T., Berners-Lee, T.: Linked data - the story so far. International Journal on Semantic Web and Information Systems 5(3), 1 (2009)
11. Bizer, C., Lehmann, J., Kobilarov, G., Auer, S., Becker, C., Cyganiak, R., Hellmann, S.: Dbpedia – a crystallization point for the web of data. In: Web Semantics: Science, Services and Agents on the World Wide Web (2009)

# A Computational Model for Dealing with Narratives

Gian Piero Zarri

Sorbonne University, LaLIC/STIH Laboratory,
Maison de la Recherche, 28 rue Serpente, 75006 Paris, France
zarri@noos.fr, gian_piero.zarri@paris-sorbonne.fr

**Abstract.** In this paper, we provide some details about NKRL (Narrative Knowledge Representation Language), which is both a conceptual language – based on the use of two different ontologies, a 'standard' ontology and an 'event-oriented' one – and a querying/inference environment. NKRL has been expressly specified and implemented for an 'intelligent' representation and management of narratives and event information.

**Keywords:** Knowledge representation, narratives, inference techniques.

## 1   Introduction

The 'pervasive' nature of *narratives* is a well-known 'observable' phenomenon. We can mention, in this context, the first three sentences of the leaflet prepared for the recent AAAI Fall Symposium on Computational Models of Narratives, see [1]: "Narratives are ubiquitous. We use them to educate, communicate, convince, explain, and entertain. As far as we know every society has narratives, which suggests … that narratives *do* something for us. It is clear that, to fully explain human intelligence, beliefs, and behaviors, we will have to understand and explain narratives".

These last years – thanks mainly to several EC-financed projects – a conceptual 'language' called NKRL ("Narrative Knowledge Representation Language") has been expressly designed to represent and manage, in a normalized way, the 'meaning' of complex narrative sources. A complete description of the language can be found in [2]. NKRL is, at the same time, a knowledge representation system, a powerful querying/inference framework and a wholly implemented software environment. Some information in this context will be supplied in the following Sections.

## 2   General Background

### 2.1   "Narratives" and "Elementary Events"

We can note that, in an NKRL context, we are mainly concerned with "*non-fictional narratives*", like those embodied into corporate memory documents, news stories, legal texts, medical records, actuality photos, etc. – even if nothing (apart from considerations of time, appropriateness, amount of code etc.) might prevent us from dealing with a whole "*fictional-narrative*" novel according to an NKRL approach.

Independently from any fictional or non-fictional consideration, we assume that narratives correspond essentially to the "*fabula layer*" introduced by Mieke Bal [3] in

M.D. Lytras et al. (Eds.): WSKS 2011, CCIS 278, pp. 479–487, 2013.

her seminal work on the structures of narrative phenomena. Accordingly, a narrative can be seen *informally* as a *series of logically and chronologically related events (a "stream of elementary events") that describe the activities or the experiences of given characters.* From the above and other work in a "narratology" framework – see [4] for an introduction to this domain – we can infer some important characteristics of narratives, see also [2: 2-13] for more details in this context:

- One of the features defining the *connected* character of the elementary events of the stream concerns the fact that these last are *chronologically related*, i.e., narratives *extend over time* (a narrative normally has a *beginning*, an *end* and some *form of development*).
- *Space* is also very important, given that *the elementary events of the stream occur generally in well defined 'locations'*, real or imaginary ones. The connected events that constitute a narrative are then both *temporally and spatially bounded.*
- A simple chronological succession of elementary events cannot, however, be defined as "narrative" without some sort of *'semantic coherence'* and *'uniqueness of the theme'* of the elementary events of the stream. If this *logical coherence* is lacking, these events pertain to different narratives: a narrative can also be represented by a single "elementary event".
- When the elementary events of a narrative are *verbalized*, their *'coherence'* is expressed through syntactic constructions like causality, goal, indirect speech, co-ordination and subordination, etc. In NKRL, we use the term "*connectivity phenomena*" to denote this sort of syntactic/semantic coherence clues.
- Eventually, *characters* that have a *'leading role'* in the global narrative are not necessarily human beings see, e.g., the description the vicissitudes in the journey of a nuclear submarine (the 'hero', 'central character', 'protagonist' etc.), or the various avatars in the life of a commercial product.

## 2.2    Formalizing Narratives and Elementary Events

Defining, however, a narrative as a "*spatio-temporally bound stream of elementary events*" would be of a scarce utility without being able to specify what an "*elementary event*" is. The formal (*n*-ary) model used in NKRL in this context can be denoted as:

$$(L_i (P_j (R_1 \ a_1) (R_2 \ a_2) \dots (R_n \ a_n))) \ . \tag{1}$$

In Eq. 1, $L_i$ is the "*symbolic label*" identifying ('reifying') the particular structural description a specific elementary event, $P_j$ is a "*conceptual predicate*", $R_k$ is a generic "*functional role*" and $a_k$ the corresponding "*predicate arguments*". In the representation of a simple elementary event like "Bill gives a book to Mary", the predicate $P_j$ (of the GIVE or MOVE type) will then introduce its *three* arguments $a_k$ – i.e., the "individuals" (instances of "concepts") JOHN_, MARY_ and BOOK_1 – through *three functional relationships* ($R_k$ roles) as SUBJECT (or AGENT), BENEFICIARY and OBJECT, the whole *n*-ary construction being *reified through the symbolic label $L_i$ and necessarily managed as a coherent block at the same time.*

Similarities between Eq. 1 and the Davidsonian [5] and neo-Davidsonian representations of elementary events – see, e.g., [6] – are evident. However, some important differences exist given that, in NKRL, both the (unique) conceptual predicate of Eq. 1 and the associated functional roles are "*primitives*". Predicates $P_j$

pertain to the set {BEHAVE, EXIST, EXPERIENCE, MOVE, OWN, PRODUCE, RECEIVE}, and the functional roles $R_k$ to the set {SUBJ(ect), OBJ(ect), SOURCE, BEN(e)F(iciary), MODAL(ity), TOPIC, CONTEXT} – see [7] about the reasons for choosing this particular set of functional roles and for the opposition between "functional" and "semantic roles". The NKRL representation of *specific elementary events* – obtained by producing *concrete instantiations* (called *"predicative occurrences"* according to NKRL's terminology) of structures in the style of Eq. 1, see the next Section – is then, *at least partly*, a sort of *canonical representation*. Note, however, that the $a_i$ terms (the predicate's arguments) in Eq. 1 *are not primitives* and pertain *indirectly*, see the next Section, to an "open", *standard ontology of concepts*.

Several predicative occurrences – denoted by their symbolic labels $L_i$ – can be assembled within the scope of second order structures called *"binding occurrences"*, i.e., labeled lists made of a "binding operator $Bn$" with its arguments. The $Bn$ operators are used to deal with the "connectivity phenomena" mentioned above: they are: ALTERN(ative), COORD(ination), ENUM(eration), CAUSE, REFER(ence) – the "weak causality operator" – GOAL, MOTIV(ation) – the "weak intentionality operator" – COND(ition), see for the details [2: 91-98]. The general expression of a binding occurrence is then:

$$(Bn_k \ \text{arg}_1 \ \text{arg}_2 \ ... \ \text{arg}_n) \ . \tag{2}$$

Eq. 2 coincides in particular – in agreement with the intuitive definition given in Section 2.1 above – *with the formal representation of a (whole) narrative*. The arguments $\text{arg}_i$ of Eq. 2 can, in fact, i) correspond directly to $L_i$ labels – i.e., they can denote simply the presence of particular elementary events represented formally as predicative occurrences and logically/semantically correlated according to the particular $Bn_i$ used – or ii) correspond recursively to sets of labeled lists in Eq. 2 format, i.e., to complex combinations of CAUSE, GOAL, COND etc. clauses.

# 3    Some Implementation Details

## 3.1    The Knowledge Representation Aspects

NKRL adds to the usual *"ontology of concepts"* – called HClass (hierarchy of classes) in NKRL's terms, and used to define the $a_i$ terms of Eq. 1 above – an *"ontology of elementary events"*. This last is *a new sort of hierarchical organization – called HTemp, hierarchy of templates – where the nodes consist of* n-ary structures built *around the basic formal core represented by Eq. 1*, see also Table 1 below. Templates can be conceived as the *canonical representation of generic classes of elementary events* like "move a physical object", "be present in a place", "produce a service", "send/receive a message", etc. More than 150 templates are permanently inserted into HTemp, which corresponds then to a sort of *'catalogue' of narrative formal structures*, very easy to extend and customize.

When a *specific elementary event* must be represented, the corresponding *predicative occurrence* is then derived by instantiating the appropriate HTemp template. To represent a simple elementary event like: "British Telecom will offer its customers a pay-as-you-go (payg) Internet service in autumn 1998", we must then select firstly in HTemp the template corresponding to "supply a service to someone", see the upper part of Table 1.

As it can be seen from this table in the complete, formal representation of the templates, the arguments of the predicate (corresponding to the $a_k$ terms in Eq. 1) are represented concretely *by variables with associated constraints.* These last *are expressed in turn as HClass concepts or combinations of concepts,* i.e., in NKRL, the two ontologies, HTemp (events) and HClass (concepts), *are strictly intermingled.* In a *predicative occurrence* like **c1** in Table 1, the role fillers *must obviously conform to the constraints of their father-template.* For example, BRITISH_TELECOM is an individual, instance of the HClass concept company_ that is, in turn, a specialization of human_being_or_social_body; payg_internet_service is a specialization of service_, etc.

The meaning of the expression "BENF (SPECIF customer_ BRITISH_TELECOM)" is: the beneficiaries (role BENF) of the service are the customers of – SPECIF(ication) – British Telecom. The *"attributive operator"*, SPECIF, is one of the *four operators that make up the AECS sub-language,* used for the set up of the *structured arguments (expansions)*; apart from SPECIF(ication) = S, AECS includes also the disjunctive operator ALTERN(ative) = A, the distributive operator ENUM(eration) = E and the collective operator COORD(ination) = C. The interweaving of the four operators within an expansion is controlled by the so-called *"precedence rule"*. In the occurrences, the two operators **date-1** and **date-2** – that can be assimilated to specific functional roles – materialize *the temporal interval normally linked to an elementary event*; see, e.g., [2: 76-86, 194-201] for a complete description of the formal system utilized by NKRL to deal with temporal information.

**Table 1.** Deriving a predicative occurrence from a template

---

*name*:  Move:TransferOfServiceToSomeone
*father*:  Move:TransferToSomeone
*position*:  4.11
*natural language description*: "Transfer or Supply a Service to Someone"

| MOVE | SUBJ | *var1*: [*var2*] |
|------|------|------------------|
|      | OBJ  | *var3* |
|      | [SOURCE | *var4*: [*var5*]] |
|      | BENF | *var6*: [*var7*] |
|      | [MODAL | *var8*] |
|      | [TOPIC | *var9*] |
|      | [CONTEXT | *var10*] |
|      | {[modulators]} | |

| *var1* | = | human_being_or_social_body |
|--------|---|----------------------------|
| *var3* | = | service_ |
| *var4* | = | human_being_or_social_body |
| *var6* | = | human_being_or_social_body |
| *var8* | = | process_, sector_specific_activity |
| *var9* | = | sortal_concept |
| *var10* | = | situation_ |
| *var2*, *var5*, *var7* | = | geographical_location |

| c1) | MOVE | SUBJ | BRITISH_TELECOM |
|-----|------|------|-----------------|
|     |      | OBJ  | payg_internet_service |
|     |      | BENF | (SPECIF customer_ BRITISH_TELECOM) |
|     |      | date-1: | after-1-september-1998 |
|     |      | date-2: | |

---

To supply now an at least intuitive idea of how a *complete narrative* is represented in NKRL, and returning to the Table 1 example, let us suppose we would now state that: "We can note that, on March 2008, British Telecom *plans to offer* to its customers, in autumn 1998, a pay-as-you-go (payg) Internet service...", where the specific elementary event corresponding to the offer is still represented by occurrence c1 in Table 1. We must then introduce first an *additional predicative occurrence* labeled as c2, see Table 2, meaning that: "at the specific date associated with c2 (March 1998), it can be noticed, modulator obs(erve), that British Telecom *is planning* to act in some way". "*Modulators*", see [2: 71-75], are NKRL operators that can be applied to a *full template or occurrence* to *particularize* their meaning according to the modulators used: in particular, obs(erve) is a "*temporal modulator*" used to identify a *specific timestamp* within the temporal interval of validity of an elementary event (predicative occurrence). We will then add a *binding occurrence* c3 labeled with GOAL – a *Bn* operator, see above – and used to link together the conceptual labels c2 (the planning activity) and c1 (the intended result). The global meaning of the (quite simple) c3 "narrative" can then be verbalized as: "The activity described in c2 is focalized towards (GOAL) the realization of c1".

**Table 2.** Binding and predicative occurrences

```
c2)    BEHAVE    SUBJ     BRITISH_TELECOM
                 MODAL    planning_
                 { obs }
                 date1:   march-1998
                 date2:

Behave:ActExplicitly (1.12)

c1)    MOVE      SUBJ     BRITISH_TELECOM
                 OBJ      payg_internet_service
                 BENF     (SPECIF customer_ BRITISH_TELECOM)
                 date-1:  after-1-september-1998
                 date-2:

Move:TransferOfServiceToSomeone (4.11)

c3)    (GOAL  c2  c1)
```

## 3.2    The Querying/Inference Aspects

*Reasoning* in NKRL ranges from the *direct questioning* of a knowledge base of narratives represented in NKRL format – by means of *search patterns* $p_i$ (formal queries) that unify information in the base thanks to the use of a *Filtering Unification Module* (*Fum*), see [2: 183-201] – to *high-level inference procedures*. Making use of a powerful *InferenceEngine*, these last utilize the richness of the representation to, e.g., set up *new relationships* among the narrative items stored in the base.

Search patterns $p_i$ are particularly important in an NKRL context given that – apart from offering to the user the possibility of posing *directly*, in an information-retrieval style, some questions to an NKRL knowledge base of predicative occurrence – they are also *automatically* generated by *InferenceEngine* as the final forms of the different *reasoning steps* that make up a high-level inference procedure. Formally, these patterns correspond to *specialized/partially instantiated templates* pertaining to the HTemp hierarchy, where the *"explicit variables"* that characterize the templates (*var_i*, see Table 1a above) *have been replaced by concepts/individuals compatible with the constraints imposed on these variables in the original templates*. In a search pattern, the concepts are used then as *"implicit variables"*. When trying to unify a search pattern $p_i$ – manually built up from the user or automatically created by *InferenceEngine* – with the predicative occurrences $c_j$ of the knowledge base, a $p_i$ concept can *match* i) the $c_j$ individuals representing *its own instances*, and ii) all its $c_j$ *subsumed concepts* in HClass along with *their own instances*.

The NKRL high-level inference procedures concern *mainly* two classes of rules, "transformations" and "hypotheses", see [2: 201-239].

Let us consider, e.g., the "transformations". These rules try to *'adapt'*, from a *semantic* point of view, a search pattern $p_i$ that *'failed'* (that was unable to find a unification within the knowledge base) to the *real contents* of this base making use of a sort of *analogical reasoning*. Transformations attempt then to *automatically 'transform'* $p_i$ into one or more *different* $p_1, p_2 \dots p_n$ that *are not strictly 'equivalent' but only 'semantically close'* (analogical reasoning) to the original one.

**Table 3.** An example of transformation rule

---

*t11: "working noise/condition" transformation*

**antecedent:**

| OWN | SUBJ | var1 |
|-----|------|------|
|     | OBJ  | property_ |
|     | TOPIC | running_ |

var1 = consumer_electronics, hardware_, surgical_tool, diagnostic_tool/system, small_portable_equipment, technical/industrial_tool

**first consequent schema (*conseq1*):**

| EXPERIENCE | SUBJ | var2 |
|------------|------|------|
|            | OBJ  | evidence_ |
|            | TOPIC | (SPECIF var3 var1) |

var2 = individual_person
var3 = working_noise, working_condition

**second consequent schema (*conseq2*):**

| BEHAVE | SUBJ | var2 |
|--------|------|------|
|        | MODAL | industrial_site_operator |

*Being unable to demonstrate directly that an industrial apparatus is running, the fact that an operator hears its working noise or notes its working aspect can be a proof of its running status.*

---

A transformation rule is made of a *left-hand side*, the *"antecedent"* – i.e. the formulation, in search pattern format, of the 'query' to be transformed – and of one or more *right-hand sides*, the *"consequent(s)"* – the representation(s) of one or more search patterns to be substituted for the given one. Denoting with *A* the antecedent and with *Cs_i* all the possible consequents, these rules can be expressed as:

$$A(var_i) \implies Cs_i(var_j), \quad var_i \subseteq var_j \tag{3}$$

Let us now see a concrete example, which concerns a recent NKRL application about the 'intelligent' management of "storyboards" in the oil/gas industry, see [8]. We want ask whether, in a knowledge base where are stored all the elementary and complex events (narratives) related to the activation of a gas turbine, we can retrieve the information that a given oil extractor is running. In the absence of a direct answer we can reply by supplying, thanks to a rule like t11 of Table 3, other related events stored in the knowledge base, e.g., *information stating that the site leader has heard the working noise of the oil extractor*. Expressed in natural language, this last result could be paraphrased as: "The system cannot assert that the oil extractor is running, but it can certify that the site leader has heard the working noise of this extractor".

With respect now to the *hypothesis rules*, these allow us to build up automatically a sort of *'causal explanation'* for an event (predicative occurrence) retrieved within a NKRL knowledge base. These rules can be expressed as *biconditionals* of the type:

$$X \text{ iff } Y_1 \text{ and } Y_2 \ldots \text{ and } Y_n , \tag{4}$$

where the 'head' $X$ of the rule corresponds to a predicative occurrence $c_j$ to be 'explained' and the 'reasoning steps' $Y_i$ – called "condition schemata" in a hypothesis context – *must all be satisfied*. This means that, *for each of them*, at least one *'successful'* search patterns $p_i$ must be (automatically) derived by *InferenceEngine* in order to find, using *Fum* (see above), a *successful unification* with some information of the base. *In this case, the set of* $c_1, c_2 \ldots c_n$ *predicative occurrences retrieved by the condition schemata* $Y_i$ *thanks to their conversion into* $p_i$ *can be interpreted as a context/causal explanation of the original occurrence* $c_j (X)$.

To mention a well-known NKRL example, let us suppose we have directly retrieved, in a querying-answering mode, the information: "Pharmacopeia, an USA biotechnology company, has received 64,000,000 dollars from the German company Schering in connection with an R&D activity"; this information corresponds then to $c_j$ ($X$). We can then be able to automatically construct, using a "hypothesis" rule, a sort of 'causal explanation' for this event by retrieving in the knowledge base information like: i) "Pharmacopeia and Schering have signed an agreement concerning the production by Pharmacopeia of a new compound", $c_1 (Y_1)$ and ii) "in the framework of this agreement, Pharmacopeia has actually produced the new compound", $c_2 (Y_2)$.

Note that – as usual in an 'hypothesis' context – the explication proposed by the rule expressed informally above *corresponds to only one of all the possible reasons that can be interpreted as the 'cause' of the original event*: a particular hypothesis rule must always be conceived as a member of a 'family' of possible explications.

An interesting development of NKRL concerns the possibility of using the two modalities of inference *in an 'integrated' way*, see [2: 216-234]: this means that *it is possible to make use of "transformations" when working in a "hypothesis" context*. Therefore, whenever a search pattern $p_i$ is derived from a condition schema $Y_i$ of a hypothesis to implement a step of the reasoning process, we can use it *'as it is'* – i.e., as it was been originally built up by *InferenceEngine* from its 'father' condition schema – but also in *a 'transformed' form if the appropriate transformation rules exist*. In this way, a hypothesis that was deemed to fail because of the impossibility of deriving a 'successful' $p_i$ from one of its condition schemata *can now continue* if a new $p_i$, obtained using a transformation rule, will find a successful unification within the base, getting then new values for the hypothesis variables. This strategy can also be used to discover all the possible *implicit* relationships among the stored data.

We will now limit us to supply an informal example, see again [8]. Using the hypothesis of Table 4 we would then try to explain, see the "premise", why an operator has activated a (particularly costly and critical) "piping segment isolation procedure" in the context of, e.g., a gas leakage. The explication proposed is based on: i) a previous 'milder' maintenance procedure has been executed (*cond1*), but this was unsuccessful (*cond2*); ii) the accident is a serious one (*cond5*). In the absence of some occurrences corresponding exactly this last condition, the $p_i$ derived from *cond5* *can be transformed* to obtain *indirect* confirmations of the gravity of the accident, getting then information in the style of, e.g. "The gas leakage has a gas cloud shape" or "An alarm situation has been validated (*conseq1*) *and* the level of this alarm is 30% LEL, Low Explosion Level (*conseq2*)", see the last lines of Table 4.

**Table 4.** Gas/oil hypothesis in the presence of transformations

| | |
|---|---|
| (*premise*) | An individual has carried out an "isolation" procedure in the context of an industrial accident. |
| (*cond1*) | A different individual had carried out previously a (milder) "corrective maintenance" procedure. |
| (*cond2*) | This second individual has experienced a failure in this corrective maintenance context. |
| (*cond3*) | The first individual was a control room operator. |
| (*cond4*) | The second individual was a field operator. |
| (*cond5*) | The industrial accident is considered as a serious one. |

  – (**Rule t6, Consequent**) *The leakage has a gas cloud shape …*
  – (**Rule t8, Consequent**) *A growth of the risk level has been discovered …*
  – (**Rule t9, Conseq1**) *An alarm situation has been validated,* **and**
  – (**Rule t8, Conseq2**) *the level of this alarm is 30% LEL.*

## 4    Conclusion

In this paper, we have evoked first the *ubiquity* and the *importance* of the so-called "non-fictional narratives". These are information resources of a high economical importance that concern, e.g., corporate knowledge documents, news stories, medical records, surveillance videos or visitor logs, etc. We have then supplied some information about a conceptual language, NKRL, expressly specified and implemented to deal with the description and management of (non-fictional) narratives making use, among other things, of *n*-ary and second order knowledge representation structures. One of its main characteristics concerns the addition of an *ontology of (elementary) events* to the usual *ontology of concepts*. Its inference solutions employ advanced causal- and analogical-based reasoning techniques to cope with the entities mentioned in the narratives and their possible relationships.

## References

1. Finlayson, M.A., Gervás, P., Mueller, E., Narayanan, S., Winston, P. (eds.): Computational Models of Narratives – Papers from the AAAI 2010 Fall Symposium (TR FS-10-04). AAAI Press, Menlo Park (2010)

2. Zarri, G.P.: Representation and Management of Narrative Information, Theoretical Principles and Implementation. Springer, London (2009)
3. Bal, M.: Narratology: Introduction to the Theory of Narrative, 2nd edn. University of Toronto Press (1997)
4. Jahn, M.: Narratology: A Guide to the Theory of Narrative (version 1.8). English Department of the Cologne University (2005),
   http://www.uni-koeln.de/~ame02/pppn.html
5. Davidson, D.: The Logical Form of Action Sentences. In: The Logic of Decision and Action, pp. 81–95. University Press, Pittsburgh (1967)
6. Parsons, T.: Events in the Semantics of English: A Study of Subatomic Semantics. The MIT Press, Cambridge (1990)
7. Zarri, G.P.: Differentiating Between 'Functional' and 'Semantic' Roles in a High-Level Conceptual Data Modeling Language. In: Proc. of the 24th Int. Florida Artificial Intelligence Research Society Conference, FLAIRS-24, pp. 75–80. AAAI Press, Menlo Park (2011)
8. Zarri, G.P.: Knowledge Representation and Inference Techniques to Improve the Management of Gas and Oil Facilities. Knowledge-Based Systems 24, 989–1003 (2011)

# The Influence of 'Insideness' and 'Outsideness' on Learning in Collective Intelligence Systems

Craig Deed[1] and Anthony Edwards[2]

[1] Faculty of Education, La Trobe University, Australia
c.deed@latrobe.edu.au
[2] Faculty of Education, Liverpool Hope University, UK

**Abstract.** The knowledge society and social networking in particular has created affordances for learning through collective intelligence systems. However the learning preferences and approaches of neo-millennial students are both similar and different to traditional models of top-down education. In this conceptual paper, the metaphors of insideness and outsideness are used as an explanatory framework to identify these new affordances and to determine tensions and questions emerging in relation to individual agency.

**Keywords:** Collective intelligence; agency; insideness; outsideness; higher education; learning.

## 1 Introduction

The knowledge society sits upon the pillars of uncertainty, complexity, and contestability. The facet of modern life that typically characterizes these forces is social networking. Recent events and discussion about the role of social media in the so-called Arab Spring; the advantages it provided for Barak Obama during the 2008 US Presidential election; and the grieving and support networks generated after natural disasters, are examples of the representation, communication and data generation possibilities of our wired world.

These possibilities are also apparent in higher education, as students use social networking skills to disrupt and subvert expected individual exploratory learning processes through informal idea and experience sharing and peer support and collusion. As an example Dede [1] argues that the learning styles and preferences of neo-millennial students include fluency in multiple forms of media, social and active learning in virtual environments, non-linear multi-modal representation, and a tendency to seek and create personalized learning experiences. Speaking generally, these emerging student characteristics are likely to place significant pressure on traditional text- and classroom-based learning routines in higher education classrooms.

The principal purpose of this conceptual paper is to identify questions, dilemmas and future trends in higher education student agency in relation to learning in collective intelligence systems. This paper is concerned with higher education student

M.D. Lytras et al. (Eds.): WSKS 2011, CCIS 278, pp. 488–493, 2013.
© Springer-Verlag Berlin Heidelberg 2013

use of social media as part of a collective intelligence model of learning. Meta-concepts such as social media, learning, agency and collective intelligence are each defined below through a focused literature review, leading to a discussion about the emerging questions and directions for future strategizing and research.

## 2    Collective Intelligence

Levy [3] defined collective intelligence as "a form of universally distributed intelligence, constantly enhanced, coordinated in real time, and resulting in the effective mobilization of skills." Collective intelligence remains an abstract concept, hard to define but easy to recognise in the interactive practices used in wikis and blogs, hyper-linking, Rich Site Summary (RSS) and Google [4]. It remains important to explore this concept as a means of improving understanding of knowledge building in contemporary learning environments.

Gruber [5] identified the main elements of collective knowledge systems as (a) user-generated content through participative social interaction; and (b) a synergy between people – the source of experience and ideas - and computers – providing a means of linking people and storing searchable data - resulting in a rapid increase in the volume of information being constructed online.

Collective intelligence structures are evident in multiple variants within education settings, including students interacting with known and unknown peers, sharing ideas and hyperlinks to useful resources and ideas, generating and exploring ideas - learning using collaborative knowledge construction in digital contexts. Students send each other thoughts, ideas, drafts and hyperlinks, as well as pose questions and comment on each other's postings; as well as organise contact with each other in public or private spaces.

Table 1 offers a perspective about the disruptive and contestable elements of collective intelligence models of learning, as compared to a more traditional hierarchical model. In practice it is difficult to simply identify a traditional classroom, as there are many educational settings that can be identified as progressive or innovative in their pedagogical approach. This somewhat black-and-white model is offered here as a basis for continuing dialogue concerning conceptual differences in models of learning.

The comparison has been deliberately constructed to show how each individual has responsibility for seeking, translating and judging information in order to construct knowledge in a collective intelligence system. The principal means of comparison between the traditional and emergent learning models is the use of academic conversation to engage with ideas.

The affordances outlined in Table 1 are explained in the following section on outsideness. The main affordances outlined are the accessing and interplay of a variety of ideas, where questioning and imagining multiple possible interpretations and applications, raise questions and doubt about the ideas being discovered and examined. The extensions noted in Table 1 refer to variants afforded by the use of online social media to expand the possible learning strategies available to students. While traditional models of education and learning remain in use, they are perhaps distorted by student inter-activity through collective intelligence systems.

**Table 1.** Extensions and affordances of a collective intelligence model of learning

| Traditional learning model | Collective intelligence | |
|---|---|---|
| | Extensions | Affordances |
| Centrality of expert; critique; sensorial; prescriptive | Open; distributed expertise; creativity; disruptive | Representation and communication of ideas to distant peers |
| Respect for expertise | Expertise questioned | Learning perceived as dynamic, involving formal and informal sources |
| Formal; structured; defensible ideas | A mix of formal and informal; ideas are of varying quality | Progressively cycling through sharing, explanation and |
| Expert structures and formally presents ideas | Individual must locate, interpret, interact with, and assess usability of information | questioning, based on a sense of doubt in order to make sense of new ideas and experiences |
| Expert models of interrogation | Individual conducts analytical and evaluative processes | Purposeful sharing, building and exploring ideas |
| Academic; largely text based | Multi-modal | Deliberately seeking outside ideas and diverse |
| Procedural within set time and space e.g. classroom | Individual opts in and out; varying intensity of effort | perspectives |

# 3     'Insideness' and 'Outsideness'

Collective intelligence systems have always been a component of education, but technology has enabled a diffused and globalized adaptation to become accessible. This has created a refined set of affordances. Here, these are explicated through the metaphor of outsideness. In a technologically-infused social networking context outsideness refers to an individual's sense of geographic, experiential or cultural differences among peers as a stimulus for a rich, interactive and complex learning conversation.

Outsideness is coherent with Engestrom's [5] extensive writing about expansive learning. In relation to collective intelligence, expansive learning involves co-construction of ideas as an adaptive and dynamic production of knowledge, with no definitive end-point. This affords opportunity for engaging with varied loosely bound communities of practice through access to multi-disciplinary teams and expert knowledge. While the purpose of collaboration in a formal system may be to devise new knowledge, Engestrom et al. [6] argue that the driving influence in expansive learning is disturbance, unexpected events and a lack of coordination. Adding to the complexity of academic conversation in virtual spaces is that the nature of communication is usually through text. Emig [7] asserted that "writing is more readily a form and source of learning than talking". Yet, when a person writes they simultaneously project multiple meanings and different levels of understanding by using past, current and future interpretations of experience. Thus, conversation through social networking media is required to sort through and determine meaning.

In contrast, insideness refers to interactions with local peers who share the same language, education and cultural context and strategic orientation to learning. In addition to using social networking to share and comment on ideas, groups are also able to meet face-to-face. Insideness means a sense of control can be added to collaborative ventures, as all members are likely to have the same purpose and awareness of end-point requirements. Participants who restrict their interactivity to inside peers may perceive outsiders as alien and thus place a low value on different perspectives.

A key idea employed in collective intelligence (regardless of whether this involves only insiders, or a mix of insiders and outsiders) is moving from brief and informal text-messaging type communication to the inherent complexity of academic conversation. The main affordances are the interplay of ideas, and emerging from doubt - questioning and imagining multiple possible interpretations and applications. Social learning tasks using technology employ multi-pathway dialogue, where participants present, comment on and compare ideas; seek and provide feedback; generate or resolve questions; reflect on experience; and adapt practice [8].

# 4    Agency – Tensions and Questions

The concept of agency is introduced here to account for tensions created by students who balance, switch between and blend learning in traditional classroom contexts with collective intelligence systems.

In simple terms agency refers to an individual's capacity to take action. "Agency is an elemental basis of power. It is the capability to do otherwise and that is the basis of power" [9]. Agents are assumed to be knowledgeable about their own experiences and to make strategic choices about current and future actions. Here, agency is examined in relation to adaptive capacity to enact academic conversation in online social networking contexts. Academic conversation is defined here as purposeful and intense interaction starting with comments, ideas and asking questions of peers or educators, adapting explanations or ideas in response to feedback, rigorous peer-based discussion, representation of collective ideas and personal and critical reflection on the experience.

Three fundamental tensions emerge from this literature review and resulting conceptualization of agency in collective intelligence systems:

- Although the application of the metaphor of outsideness provides sound arguments for student learning agency, it does not account for those students who find the use of social networking to be alienating, dispassionate or do not value different perspectives.
- The responsibility of individuals in collective intelligence systems is to seek, make sense of, and extract useful ideas, information and data. This may be problematic in communities of practice where participants construe ideas, problems and purposes of collaborating differently and require an outcome specific to their own context [10]. There may be a tendency for social networking practices to disaggregate ideas and information into disparate individual pockets, depending on the capacity of individual participants to reassert meaning over the fragments. This raises the question of individual capacity to engage in knowledge construction in these off-map contexts.

- Knowledge may be generated by an individual through a collective intelligence system, yet what processes of critique are used or can be employed to validate these ideas as appropriate and credible within an academic context.
- While collective intelligence may be thought of as merely an extension of conventional academic conversation, perhaps new means of interactivity, connectedness and exploration of ideas are emerging.

These emerging tensions have implications for student learning. Thus, while academic conversation may include interactions that are informal and reactive, the generation and exploration of ideas to a coherent and credible end-point remains a fundamental although complex part of academic conversation. Several questions can be identified for fruitful investigation, as part of ongoing discourse about the capacity of students to use collective intelligence systems for academic learning:

- What constraints influence the capacity of learners to represent and communicate ideas using social networking technologies, including language and cultural understanding?
- What strategies are used by learners in formal and informal learning spaces as part of an integrated collective intelligence system?
- What strategies for making sense of inside and outside generation of ideas are used already by learners, and what other strategies can be taught and practiced in order to improve efficiency and effectiveness of learning?
- What prompts, guidelines or boundaries can be placed on student activity to afford the sharing, building and exploring of ideas?
- How to 'force' students to seek outside ideas and diverse perspectives as part of the mechanics of academic conversational?

These questions focus on a process that is already occurring – the extension of traditional learning models into virtual collective intelligence systems. While the mechanism may for this extension may be social networking technology, students are engaging with a range of affordances that are simultaneously influenced by what we have characterised using the metaphor of insideness and outsideness. The principal question that requires an investment of thinking and strategizing relates to Emirbayer and Mische's [11] claim that agents engage and disengage with "different contextual environments" and experience situations that require "imagination, choice and conscious purpose". In effect, how are learners in higher education engaging with emerging learning spaces. The answers may challenge and question our traditional teaching approaches, but this question is being asked by our students as well, and we need to learn from each others' experiences.

# References

1. Dede, C.: Determining, developing and assessing the capabilities of 'future-ready' students (2009), http://www.fi.ncsu.edu/assets/research_papers/brown-bag/determining-developing-and-assessing-the-capabilities-of-future-ready-students.pdf

2. Levy, P.: Collective Intelligence: Mankind's Emerging World in Cyberspace. Plenum, New York (1997)
3. O'Reilly, T.: What is Web 2.0: Design patterns and business models for the next generation of software. Communications & Strategies 65, 17–37 (2007)
4. Gruber, T.: Collective Knowledge Systems. In: 5th International Semantic Web Conference (2007)
5. Engestrom, Y.: Learning by expanding: An activity-theoretical approach to developmental research. Orienta-Konsultit, Helsinki (1987)
6. Engestrom, Y., et al.: Coordination, cooperation and communication in the courts: Expansive transitions in legal work. In: Cole, M., Engestrom, Y., Vasquez, T. (eds.) Mind, Culture and Activity: Seminal Papers from the Laboratory of Comparative Human Cognition. Cambridge University Press, Cambridge (1997)
7. Emig, J.: Writing as a mode of learning. College Composition and Communication 28, 122–128 (1977)
8. Laurillard, D.: The pedagogical challenges to collaborative technologies. Computer-Supported Collaborative Learning 4, 5–20 (2009)
9. Giddens, A., Pierson, C.: Conversations with Anthony Giddens: making sense of modernity. Polity Press, Cambridge (1998)
10. Kangasoja, J.: Complex design problems: An impetus for learning and knotworking (2002), http://www.edu.helsinki.fi/activity/publications/files/47/ICLS2002_Kangasoja.pdf (cited May 21, 2011)
11. Emirbayer, M., Mische, A.: What is agency? The American Journal of Sociology 103, 962–1023 (1998)

# Effectiveness of Person-Centered Learning in the Age of the Internet

Renate Motschnig-Pitrik

University of Vienna, Faculty of Computer Science
renate.motschnig@univie.ac.at

**Abstract.** Extensive research has confirmed the effectiveness of the Person-Centered Approach in face-to-face education. More recently, advances in web-technology have opened up new dimensions of searching: Is person-centered learning effective along the application of modern technology in education? In this contribution I reflect 10 years of research at the University of Vienna, Austria. Essentially, we found that, given learners perceive the facilitators' person-centered attitudes and courses employ a thoughtful blend of face-to-face and online elements, these courses tend to be perceived by students as carrying value far beyond just cognitive gains: For example, students indicate that they are motivated to engage in active, self-initiated learning, they improve their interpersonal relationships and team skills, become better listeners and learn significantly from the multiple perspectives they perceive.

## 1 Introduction

Numerous studies (see e.g. Barrett-Lennard, 1998; Cornelius-White and Harbaugh, 2010; Rogers, 1983) and a metastudy (Cornelius-White, 2007) confirmed the effectiveness of the Person-Centered Approach (PCA) in education. So, "have we arrived" and "just" need to incorporate the findings into practice? While I certainly agree that putting into practice, living, and passing on the person-centered value base /Rogers, 1961) is what education in our modern times needs most urgently, I also feel a deep interest in contributing to the transfer of the Person-Centered Approach to the modern world of which internet-based communication, teamwork, and diversity have become essential assets. This new context throws up questions such as:

- How can online communication and web-based environments be exploited such as to be most beneficial for significant learning of persons and any groupings such as teams, partnerships, groups, communities that, at times, are distributed?
- How does an effective blending of face-to-face and online-elements look like in various contexts and how can it be facilitated?
- Under what circumstances and conditions can added value arise when technology is introduced into learning?
- What/where are the new opportunities as well as challenges and risks emerging in the dynamically evolving socio-technical field?
- How can the competencies needed for facilitating significant learning in the age of the Internet best be acquired and developed?

M.D. Lytras et al. (Eds.): WSKS 2011, CCIS 278, pp. 494–499, 2013.
© Springer-Verlag Berlin Heidelberg 2013

Before starting the review let me share some personal perceptions and statements that might clarify the journey and directions taken to entering the "virtual world" with as much openness, sensitivity and presence as possible

I consider it essential to base research on person-centered technology enhanced learning (PCeL) on one's, in this case the facilitator's concrete experience. So far, a theory on how to effectively integrate web-based technology into person-centered learning does not exist, although the related model of learner-centered instruction has successfully been combined with the use of learning technology (Cornelius-White and Harbaugh, 2010).

The field is extremely complex, dynamic and open, with new, improved technology being developed in short cycles, digital-literacy and media-competence rising faster in the young than in older generations, ICT (information and communication technology) becoming more easily available and increasingly impacting our lives and work processes, new demands and changes of all kinds arriving at a faster rate, etc.

Consequently, strictly controlled, classical research procedures do not appear to provide adequate, timely responses to the questions raised above. Rather, triangulations of qualitative and quantitative methods embedded into action research (Motschnig-Pitrik, 2006), case studies (Bauer, 2010) and design-based research procedures (Kabicher, 2010) appear to shed illuminating light on regularities and tendencies in the field.

Ethically, to me, providing students with the one course design that I believe is (or, better, we as a course community come about thinking to be) most effective under the given constraints has always been the highest priority. Just using or not using some technological tool only to have a control group for the sake of research has never been an option to me. At times students could choose to fulfill a task with or without web-support, but it has always been their own choice which way they decided to go (Motschnig-Pitrik, 2005).

As examples of thorough, innovative research let me point to four PhD Theses (published as books), in which the Person-Centered Approach has served as the value base:

- Derntl (2006) derived of design patterns for person-centered elearning and empirically studied their effects on various features of students' learning
- Figl (2009) conducted several empirical studies on team development, skills and attitudes in academic, technology-enhanced, person-centered courses.
- Bauer (2010) conducted case-studies investigating facilitative activities, motivation, and peer reviews in technology enhanced environments. Bauer (2009) conducted case-studies investigating facilitative activities, motivation, and peer reviews in technology enhanced environments.
- Kabicher (2010) identified strategic patterns for curriculum (re-)design based on a truly democratic approach including multiple stakeholders (such as students, staff, industry, government, EU-policies) and maximizing transparency.

## 2    Selected "Responses" from Researching PCeL Effectiveness

In which ways can person-centered education enter a growthful, symbiotic relationship with web-based technology? The initial hypothesis that has been confirmed in several studies -- mainly action research and case studies, complemented by online-questionnaires and semi-structured interviews to capture students' perceptions on learning – is: In the case that computer support can take over significant parts of the administration and transfer of intellectual information, more room will be left for significant learning (i. e. whole-person learning emphasizing the integration of cognitions, intuitions/feelings, and skills) and face-to-face interactions in a facilitative climate.

There is initial qualitative evidence that person-centered technology-enhanced learning (PCeL) based on communicating person-centered attitudes while integrating face-to-face with online sessions is perceived as more motivating and promoting of significant learning than traditional course designs. This is because the resourceful, not-imposing, self-initiation encouraging style of the Person-Centered Approach – its essential "feeling and trust" basis – once established – is well supported by a rich repertoire of resources and tools promoting communication (Derntl, 2006). The consequent learning is of several kinds, inherent, explicit, often transformative and typically open-ended, turning on learners' innate curiosity and desire to know more deeply (Motschnig-Pitrik, 2005). We have observed that straight forward availability of material eases the facilitator's task of organizing material and gives (advanced) students still more opportunities to satisfy their curiosity by finding sources that suit their interest and style. If left with a choice, students tend to search the Internet and integrate self-found resources into their project work rather than strictly keeping to the reading lists provided by facilitators, given the students' self-initiative is acknowledged (Figl, 2009).

A collection of practices and underlying research can be found in (Bauer et al. 2006; Motschnig-Pitrik, 2005). A more comprehensive collection of visually modeled patterns for PCeL is the published dissertation (Derntl, 2006). Selected case-studies are documented in the dissertation (Bauer, 2010).

**Learning on three levels.** In order to emphasize that PCeL means more than an accumulation of facts and procedures, we have didactically distinguished three levels of learning: knowledge or intellect, skills, and attitudes, feelings, personality. At the end of several PCeL courses, students were asked to estimate how much they had learned on each of the levels in that particular course and how much they tended to learn in comparable traditional courses. A general response pattern – across various courses –could be identified that shows that students indicate that they learn about the same at the level of intellect, but significantly more at the level of skills and the level of attitudes. For publications regarding the learning on three levels in various courses see (Derntl and Motschnig-Pitrik, 2007; Motschnig-Pitrik and Dernt, 2008).

**Motivation.** It could be confirmed that facilitators who are perceived as being highly congruent, respectful, empathically understanding and competent in the subject area, can motivate students more strongly than educators who are rated lower on these dimensions. - Empirical evaluations indicated that students' most significant motives for participating in PCeL style courses are the increase of professional competence, the experiencing of a constructive atmosphere, the collegial cooperation with peers, and interest in the subject matter. Interestingly, these top motives each address one of the three levels of learning and the differences in mean values of these top motives are statistically not significant (Motschnig-Pitrik and Mallich, 2004).

**Profitable elements.** In various PCeL courses of the computer science curriculum we asked students to estimate how much they benefited from various features of the course. From 24 features those that students indicated to benefit most from and that were rated to be present in person-centered classrooms significantly more strongly than in traditional courses were: active participation in the course; exchange and discussion with peers and instructor; the opportunity of bringing in personal interests and contributions; and the support via a web-based platform (Derntl and Motschnig-Pitrik, 2007, Motschnig-Pitrik, 2006; Motschnig-Pitrik and Derntl, 2008).

**Online-learning contracts.** Web-based tools help to administer learning contracts and to expose deliverables to peers for commenting and evaluation. This practically enables new forms of assessment even in other than very small classes. When asked how much they learned from employing learning contracts, the vast majority of students responded that they had learned more or much more than through learning for traditional exams. Students also tended to indicate that they had spent more time with fulfilling the learning contracts than with learning for traditional exams (Motschnig-Pitrik et al., 2008; Motschnig-Pitrik and Derntl, 2005).

**Creativity.** In a recent, theoretical investigation, several aspects of promoting a person-centered perspective of creativity by interpersonal qualities and web-based tools have been identified (Motschnig-Pitrik and Pitner, 2009).

**Feeling of community.** In order to find out whether students who attended a person-centered course felt more like a community, they were asked to fill out the community questionnaire by Barrett-Lennard (2005) at the end of the course. From the 14 features, the most significant increases tended to happen in "Attentive listening to others", "climate of respect, caring, trust", and "experience of connectedness and community", across all courses. Features like "experiencing being heard" and "communication owned feelings and meanings" were evaluated particularly highly in courses that included encounter-group-like phases. (Motschnig-Pitrik and Figl, 2008).

**Team competencies, team orientation.** Intensive research on the development of team competences in person-centered courses showed that although students experience a significant rise in team skills, their team orientation and team attitudes do not change statistically significantly as the result of attending one person-centered course. Still, semi-structured interviews indicate that students feel they have improved their teamwork competencies as a result of person-centered courses more than when attending traditional courses that included teamwork. The research is most comprehensibly documented in Kathrin Figl's PhD Thesis (Figl, 2009). Individual studies can be found in (Figl and Motschnig-Pitrik, 2008; Motschnig-Pitrik, 2006).

**Interpersonal Relationships.** In courses such as Person-Centered Communication, Project Management Soft Skills, Organizational Development that were facilitated in a person-centered way, the majority of students indicated that their interpersonal relationships had improved as a result of attending the course. This was not only the case for relationships with class mates but also with family, partners, and work colleagues (Motschnig-Pitrik, 2006; 2008; Motschnig-Pitrik and Figl, 2008)).

## 3    Conclusions and Open Questions to Explore

As in pure face-to-face settings, person-centered attitudes are essential in technology enhanced environments. Using web-based technology as an ally to providing resourceful learning environments has proved highly worthwhile, if the integration complements rather than substitutes the rich presence in face-to-face encounter. Online support allows for sharing and following up communication between face-to-face meetings, such that the sharing can continue anytime at each person's own pace and with each person having equal "voice" in the virtual world. A "healthy" mix of face-to-face and online elements – will tend to combine the advantages of each medium and enhance the potentialities of person-centered education.

Further research should confirm the experienced added value of PCeL by conducting more long-term studies. In fact, *long-term perceptions* are likely to capture the sustained, meaningful learning outcomes unfolding form person-centered settings well. A further area to be explored concerns the *development of competencies and skills through blended learning*. While we know that competencies like communication and team skills developed in face-to-face situations are helpful in the online-context as well, it is an open question in how far competencies developed online might be fruitful for face-to-face situations. For example, could "active listening" competencies – better "active/exact reading and writing" competencies developed online make persons better listeners in face-to-face contact? Last but not least the effectiveness of person-centered learning across cultures and in *multi-cultural environments* needs to be confirmed. Multinational projects, in particular, need to establish clear understanding between participants who often belong to different cultures. Finally, transparent communication and understanding appear to be at the core of constructive problem solving in our interconnected, complex world.

## References

1. Barrett-Lennard, G.T.: Carl Rogers' Helping System – Journey and Substance. Sage Publications, London (1998)
2. Barrett-Lennard, G.T.: Relationship at the Centre - Healing in a Troubled World. Whurr Publishers, Philadelphia (2005)
3. Bauer, C.: Promotive Activities in Technology-Enhanced Learning. P. Lang, Frankfurt (2010)
4. Bauer, C., Derntl, M., Motschnig-Pitrik, R., Tausch, R.: Promotive Activities in Face-to-Face and Technology-Enhanced Learning Environments. The Person-Centered Journal 13(1-2), 12–37 (2006); ADPCA, ISSN 1932-4920
5. Cornelius-White, J.H., Harbaugh, A.P.: Learner-Centered Instruction: Building Relationships for Student Success. Sage Publications, Thousand Oaks (2010)
6. Derntl, M.: Patterns for Person-Centered e-Learning. Aka Verlag, Berlin (2006)

7. Derntl, M., Motschnig-Pitrik, R.: The Role of Structure, Patterns, and People in Blended Learning. The Internet and Higher Education 8(2), 111–130 (2005)

8. Derntl, M., Motschnig-Pitrik, R.: Inclusive Universal Access in Engineering Education. In: Proc. of 37th Frontiers in Education Conference (FIE). IEEE, Milwaukee (2007)

9. Figl, K.: Team and Media Competences in Information Systems. Oldenbourg, München (2009)

10. Figl, K., Motschnig-Pitrik, R.: Researching the Development of Team Competencies in Computer Science Courses. In: Proceedings of 38th ASEE/IEEE Frontiers in Education Conference, Saratoga Springs, pp. S3F-1–S3F-6. IEEE, NY (2008)

11. Figl, K., Motschnig-Pitrik, R.: Developing Team Competence in Technology Enhanced Courses. In: Proceedings of World Conference on Educational Multimedia, Hypermedia & Telecommunications (ED-MEDIA). AACE, Vancouver (2007)

12. Kabicher, S.: Processes and Patterns for (Re)Designing Modular Curricula. Dissertation: University of Vienna, Austria. CS Didactics and Learning Research Center (2010)

13. Motschnig-Pitrik, R.: Person-Centered e-Learning in Action: Can Technology help to manifest Person-centered Values in Academic Environments? Journal of Humanistic Psychology 45(4), 503–530 (2005)

14. Motschnig-Pitrik, R.: Two Technology-Enhanced Courses Aimed at Developing Interpersonal Attitudes and Soft Skills in Project Management. In: Nejdl, W., Tochtermann, K. (eds.) EC-TEL 2006. LNCS, vol. 4227, pp. 331–346. Springer, Heidelberg (2006)

15. Motschnig-Pitrik, R.: Can Person Centered Encounter Groups Contribute to Improve Relationships and Learning in Academic Environments? In: Behr, M., Cornelius-White, J.H.D. (eds.) Development and Interpersonal Relation - Person-Centered Work. PCCS Books (2008)

16. Motschnig, R., Derntl, M., Figl, K., Kabicher, S.: Towards Learner-Centered Learning Goals based on the Person-Centered Approach. In: Proceedings of 38th ASEE/IEEE Frontiers in Education Conference, Saratoga Springs, pp. F4A-9 - F4A-14. IEEE, NY (2008)

17. Motschnig-Pitrik, R., Derntl, M.: Three Scenarios on Enhancing Learning by Providing Universal Access. Universal Access in the Information Society 7(4) (2008)

18. Motschnig-Pitrik, R., Figl, K.: Developing Team Competence as Part of a Person Centered Learning Course on Communication and Soft Skills in Project Management. In: Proceedings of 37th Frontiers in Education Conference (FIE). IEEE, Milwaukee (2007)

19. Motschnig-Pitrik, R., Figl, K.: The Effects of Person Centered Education on Communication and Community Building. In: Proc. of World Conference on Educational Multimedia, Hypermedia and Telecommunications, pp. 3843–3852. AACE, Vienna (2008)

20. Motschnig-Pitrik, R., Mallich, K.: Effects of Person-Centered Attitudes on Professional and Social Competence in a Blended Learning Paradigm. Journal of Educational Technology & Society 7(4), 176–192 (2004)

21. Motschnig, R., Pitner, T.: Promoting a Humanistic Perspective of Creativity by Interpersonal Qualities and Web-Based Tools. In: Lytras, M.D., Damiani, E., Carroll, J.M., Tennyson, R.D., Avison, D., Naeve, A., Dale, A., Lefrere, P., Tan, F., Sipior, J., Vossen, G. (eds.) WSKS 2009. LNCS, vol. 5736, pp. 1–12. Springer, Heidelberg (2009)

22. Rogers, C.R.: On Becoming a Person - A Psychotherapists View of Psychotherapy. Constable, London (1961)

23. Rogers, C.R.: Freedom to Learn for the 80's. Charles E. Merrill Publishing Company, Columbus (1983)

# Towards Merging Models of Information Spreading and Dynamic Phenomena in Social Networks

Erick Stattner, Martine Collard, and Nicolas Vidot

LAMIA Laboratory
University of the French West Indies and Guiana, France
{estattne,mcollard,nvidot}@univ-ag.fr

**Abstract.** While the impact of network properties on information spreading is now widely studied, influence of network dynamics is very little known. In this paper, we study how evolution mechanisms traditionally observed within social networks can affect information diffusion. We present an approach that merges two models: model of information diffusion through social networks and model of network evolution. Since epidemics provide a reference in application domains of information spreading, we measure the impact of basic network structure changes on epidemic peak value and timing. Then we investigate observed trends in terms of changes appearing in the network structure. Our results provide promising results on how and why network dynamics is a strong parameter to integrate in requirements for information spreading modelling.

## 1 Introduction

Network analysis has been the subject of an active domain, so-called "Science of Networks" [2,4], an emerging scientific discipline that encompasses the whole diversity of researches on interconnected entities. Intensive effort has been done to study the structure of networks, especially with the emergence of Social Network Analysis ($SNA$) and its applications in various fields such as sociology [17], biology [14], ethology [9] or computer science [3].

In this paper, we address the issue of information dissemination through social networks, a field that has recently been explored with a focus on network modeling [16,21]. *Information* is here considered with a wide meaning and may represent either knowledge, rumor or viruses for instance. It has been argued in several works that the nature of the information does not make much difference for the modeling principles of diffusion [4,10,12]. Whatever can be the kind of information, it is now well admitted that the main concern for modeling the diffusion is the impact of social contacts of individuals [15,6].

However although the effect of social network properties on spreading is currently studied [20,6], the impact of network changes is an emerging field [19,7]. Some solutions have been proposed to model evolution processes leading to specific structural features observed on real world networks [18,11]. It is interesting to note that the issues of *dynamics of networks* (network evolution) and

M.D. Lytras et al. (Eds.): WSKS 2011, CCIS 278, pp. 500–508, 2013.
© Springer-Verlag Berlin Heidelberg 2013

*dynamics through networks* (dissemination) are still independent fields. In the latter, the mathematical approach of Gross et al. [13] models the impact of links deletion on spreading. Read et al. [19] show how changes in the frequency of encounters between individuals may impact the dissemination. More recently, Christensen et al. [7] measured the effect of changes in demographic attributes within population on the disease transmission.

Nevertheless, to the best of our knowledge, it seems that no empirical or even comparative study was proposed to explain the impact of network dynamics on the information dissemination process. In this work we focus on the impact of network dynamics by comparing effect of several evolution mechanisms on incidence curves. We show that the dynamics of links plays an important role in spreading through the network, and therefore is a strong requirement to consider for modeling the behavior of information diffusion in real world networks. A concrete example that motivates this study is provided by intervention strategies that are currently proposed in epidemiology and are generally focused on node-based measures. For example, the intervention strategy that gives best results is to vaccinate individuals (nodes) with a highest degree. However, it is obvious that individuals with highest degree at time $t$ will probably not be in the same state at time $(t + 1)$, due to changes that occur in the network. Therefore, dynamic appears to have a strong and real impact on spreading, and have to be taken into account.

As said above, models of information diffusion are very much similar whatever can be the nature of the information. Mathematical approach of compartment models for epidemics modeling like the standard $SIR$ ($Susceptible - Infected - Recovered$) model perfectly fits other cases such as knowledge or rumor spreading. These models consider that individuals moves from a state to another with a given probability. The transitions "Susceptible to Infected" and "Infected to Recovered" defined for epidemics are obviously analogous to "Innovator to Incubator" and "Incubator to Adopter" transitions in knowledge diffusion as underlined by Borner et al. [4]. Network models have extended compartment models more appropriately to understand diffusion process since they involve individuals (nodes) and contact links (vertices) among them [8,5,21]. They are able to match various kinds of information too.

In this work, we experiment the approach on the epidemics field since it is well studied and it provides references and resources such as training networks. We propose an approach that merges two models: model of information diffusion through the social network and network dynamics model. The paper is organized in four sections. Section 2 details our approach and Section 3 presents experiments and results. We conclude in Section 4.

## 2    Proposed Approach

Networks are alive and animated objects, in which nodes can appear and disappear, links can be created, removed, or can even evolve. Complex networks such as human sexual contact often do not have an engineered architecture but instead-of are self-organized by the actions of a large number of individuals. In the network paradigm, these actions are often modeled as a set of rules, that create or delete links leading to particular topological features.

Thus, we compare effects of four well known basic evolution models, accepted in the literature as reproducing changes observed in real world networks [11,18,4]. In this preliminary work, we have deliberately chosen simple evolution mechanisms that are restricted to link creation only:

- **Random** ($R$): random creation of a link between two nodes.
- **Triadic Closure** ($TC$): a node creates links with neighbors of its neighbors i.e "friends of my friends become my friends".
- **Global Connection** ($GC$): a node creates links with other nodes outside of its local neighborhood i.e. beyond friends of its friends.
- **Preferential Attachment** ($PA$): a node is more likely to connect to one with high degree i.e. "rich get richer".

To address the problem of diffusion in evolving networks, we integrate a dynamic layer into the diffusion (epidemic) model. Thus, we measure the impact of evolution strategies on the diffusion process by introducing the information (a disease) in an evolving network. We assume, as is often the case in real life, that individuals behavior does not change with the occurrence of the disease, i.e. the network still follows to the same evolution strategy.

The two models of evolution are concerning: **(1)** the network that is evolving and **(2)** the disease that is spreading into this evolving network. In the commonly used $SIR$ model of disease spreading, parameters are the $\beta$ probability of transmission per contact and the $\gamma$ probability of recover. We assume that a susceptible individual $i$ has a probability $1 - (1 - \beta)^{k_t^i}$ to become infected, where $k_t^i$ is the number of infected neighbors of the node $i$ at time $t$. Incidence curves of $SIR$ epidemics spread are illustrated in Figure 1. According to this model, the epidemic is dependent on the initial infected population size and on probabilities $\beta$ and $\gamma$. For instance it is demonstrated that for high values of $\beta$ and low values of $\gamma$, the diffusion is improved as depicted on Figure 1.

Our approach to merge both spreading and dynamics models is illustrated in Figure 3. Let $N$ be the number of individuals within the network. We denote $G_t$ the state of the network at time $t$, $L$ the infection list that stores the percentage of infected nodes at each time $t$, $W$ the network evolution model ($R$, $TC$, $GC$ or

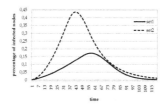

**Fig. 1.** Example of incidence curves obtained by $SIR$ with two sets of parameters: set1 ($\beta = 0.55$ and $\gamma = 0.1$) and set2 ($\beta = 0.775$ and $\gamma = 0.05$)

|  | N1 | N2 |
|---|---|---|
| **Origine** | Generated | Portland |
| **#nodes** | 3233 | 4829 |
| **#links** | 5154 | 7455 |
| **Density** | 0.000986 | 0.0006395 |
| **Avg Degree** | 3.188 | 3.087 |
| **Max Degree** | 118 | 17 |
| **Distribution Degree** | 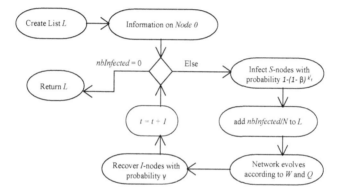 | |
| **Clust. Coeff.** | 0.00427 | 0.60880 |

**Fig. 2.** Main features of seed networks

**Fig. 3.** Proposed approach to merge dynamics and diffusion

$PA$) and $Q$ the evolution speed (number of links created at each iteration). We use two seed networks (see Fig. 2) and the classic $SIR$ model and we introduce evolution mechanisms and measure their effects on each network. $N1$ is a kind of networks most commonly observed in real world, such as the Internet, telephone calls networks, sexual networks or friendship networks known as scale-free networks. In was generated with the BarabasiAlbert model [1]. $N2$ is a synthetic network extracted from $EpiSims$, an epidemiological simulation system prior to $EpiSimdemics$ [3].

Both networks $N1$ and $N2$ are appropriate candidates for applying the dynamic models $R$, $TC$, $GC$ and $PA$ that add new links. And indeed, in real world networks such as scale free networks or random networks like $N1$ and $N2$, link updates are mostly creations and link removing is rare.

Thus the approach was to experiment the resulting spreading-dynamic model and to observe how the network evolution may have an impact on spreading.

## 3    Experiment and Results

In this section, the approach is first experimented to analyze effects of evolution models $(R, TC, GC, PA)$ on the epidemic strength in terms of value and in occurrence time. Afterwards, we investigate explanations on network properties.

### 3.1    Effects on Spreading

Disease behavior depends on many parameters such as the number of initial infected individuals, the probability of transmission or the probability of recover. However, changes in these parameters often influence only the virulence of the epidemic and are quite well known. In the issue we address, the most relevant parameter seems to be the evolution speed of the network. Thus to study the impact of this parameter on the disease behavior, we trained the two networks, evolution models and different evolution speeds.

The data collection was done over a period of 120 iterations. The probability of transmission was set to 0.1 and the probability of recover was set to 0.2, i.e. $\beta = 0.1$ and $\gamma = 0.2$. Each test was performed upon 100 runs and the average was computed.

On Figures 4 and 5, we compare the results obtained for each model. As a first analysis, with Figure 4, one can compare the **incidence curves** obtained with two arbitrary speeds 50 and 150. This first test allows us to make several observations on the evolution of the epidemic peak. For a more complete analysis, Figure 5 presents **summary results** on the evolution of the epidemic peak by focusing on its value and its occurrence in time.

On Figure 4, the percentage of infected nodes at each iteration is plotted according to the kind of network and evolution speed ($x$-axis). The incidence curve obtained without any evolution mechanism is plotted as a reference. We can observe that although all evolution strategies generate an epidemic peak

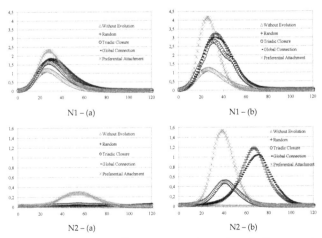

**Fig. 4.** Incidence curves according to networks and evolution speeds ($x$-axis)

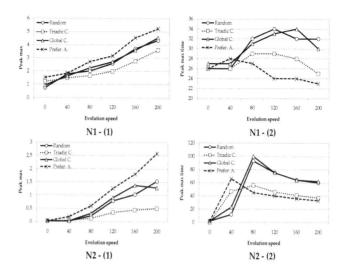

**Fig. 5.** Synthetic results for $N1$, $N2$ according to speed: (1) values of peak maximum, (2) peak maximum occurrence time

on $N1$ at speed 50, the difference between strategies remain very low for this speed. In the case of network $N2$ a speed of 50 links per iteration is not sufficient to generate an epidemic expect with $PA$ the only strategy able to generate an epidemic on this network.

Globally, two main observations can be made. Dynamics has an obvious impact on the epidemic virulence, since peaks values increase with the speed with a different range from one evolution model to another. Dynamics has also an impact on the epidemic timing, since when the evolution speed increases, the epidemic peak appears more or less early according to the evolution model.

These results suggest the direct impact of the network evolution speed on: **(1)** the peak value, and **(2)** its occurrence time. Figure 5 shows how these two indices behave when the speed is varying. Figure 5**(1)** (resp. **(2)**) gives the peak value (resp. the occurrence time).

Common trends appear for the two networks. $PA$ tends to give an epidemic curve with a peak that is systematically higher than in the other three strategies. It induces the earliest occurrence of the epidemic. The peak obtained by $TC$ is always the lowest and is the second to appear in time. $R$ and $GC$ give very similar curves: the peak occurs later than for $PA$ and $TC$.

## 3.2   Changes in Networks Properties

To explain the observed trends, we can investigate what happens at the network level. For this, we focus on changes that occur on network structure, by studying the evolution of main network properties. As shown in Figure 4, there is a strong observable difference between strategies with speed 150. Thus we have compared changes occurred on network features according to each strategy $R, TC, GC$ and

| | | min degree | avg degree | max degree | Clust. C. |
|---|---|---|---|---|---|
| N1 | R | 1.0 | 5.673 | 120.27 | 0.0045 |
| | Tria. C. | 1.0 | 5.367 | 146.04 | 0.3036 |
| | Glo. C. | 1.0 | 5.546 | 119.82 | 0.0020 |
| | Pre. A. | 1.0 | 5.540 | 142.65 | 0.0142 |
| N2 | R | 1.0 | 4.54 | 18.88 | 0.3882 |
| | Tria. C. | 1.0 | 3.95 | 23.40 | 0.6204 |
| | Glo. C. | 1.0 | 4.58 | 18.77 | 0.3763 |
| | Pre. A. | 1.0 | 4.25 | 33.31 | 0.4588 |

**Fig. 6.** Changes in main properties of $N1$ and $N2$ with each evolution model after epidemics with speed 150

$PA$, after an epidemic diffusion with speed 150. Results are shown in Figure 6, and were obtained by averaging 100 runs.

To understand effects on these evolution mechanisms on spreading, the analysis should be conducted at two levels. *(1)* Comparing network properties before and after evolution (see Fig. 2 *VS* Fig. 6). *(2)* Comparing properties resulting from different evolution models (see Fig. 6).

**Preferential Attachment** reinforces links of the most connected nodes. This can be observed on the growth of max degree. For example, max degree of $N2$ is 17 against 18.88 for $R$, 23.40 for $TC$, 18.77 for $GC$ and 33.31 for $PA$ after evolution. $PA$ enables rapidly the emergence of individuals sufficiently connected to result in a strong and fast transmission of disease within the network. The virulence and earliest occurrence of the epidemic peak are thus explained.

**Triadic Closure** strengthens links within groups of nodes to result in a significant increase in the overall clustering coefficient: from 0.00427 to 0.3036 for $N1$ and from 0.60880 to 0.6204 for $N2$. It is interesting to note that other models may even reduce the clustering coefficient. While the strategy $TC$ allows the emergence of highly connected nodes, it also generates network with a high clustering coefficient. So the epidemic appears relatively early and is less virulent, since the transmission occurs mainly within a same community.

**Random** and **Global Connection** both tend to shorten the range of degree value. However, $GC$ allows a node to connect only with any node outside its immediate community. This explains that, except for clustering coefficient, observed properties with $R$ and $GC$ strategies are very close. $GC$ does not allow creating *triangles* while $R$ is likely to do it. $R$ and $GC$ provide very similar results on spreading, since their effects on network properties prove to be very similar.

## 4   Conclusion

Dynamics is an intrinsic property of real world networks. This work tackles the emerging and fundamental issue of spreading in evolving networks. We have addressed here this issue by comparing effects of various dynamics models on incidence curves in epidemic spreading. As currently admitted, the nature of the information spread through social networks (rumor, knowledge, virus, disease...) does not make much difference. Our work has highlighted a set of trends related to evolution mechanisms and provides an interesting view about the way a disease spreads through an evolving network.

In this preliminary work, the evolution strategies have been restricted to link creation and we have shown that network properties are differently modified from one strategy to another. These promising results have highlighted the impact of the network dynamics upon diffusion. They should be useful to define requirements that cannot be ignored to control and model spreading phenomena. We are currently investigating more complex dynamics model in a similar approach.

# References

1. Albert, R., Barabasi, A.L.: Statistical mechanics of complex networks. Reviews of Modern Physics 74, 51 (2002)
2. Barabasi, A.L.: Linked: The New Science of Networks. Perseus Books (2002)
3. Barrett, C.L., Bisset, K.R., Eubank, S.G., Feng, X., Marathe, M.V.: Episimdemics: an efficient algorithm for simulating the spread of infectious disease over large realistic social networks. In: ACM/IEEE Conference on Supercomputing (2008)
4. Borner, K., Sanyal, S., Vespignani, A.: Network science. In: Cronin, B. (ed.) Annual Review of Information Science & Technology, vol. 41, pp. 537–607 (2007)
5. Chen, Y., Tseng, C., King, C., Wu, T., Chen, H.: Incorporating geographical contacts into social network analysis for contact tracing in epidemiology: a study on taiwan sars data. In: Conference on Intelligence and Security Informatics (2007)
6. Christakis, N.A., Fowler, J.H.: Social network sensors for early detection of contagious outbreaks. PloS One 5(9) (2010)
7. Christensen, C., Albert, I., Grenfell, B., Albert, R.: Disease dynamics in a dynamic social network. Physica A: Statistical Mechanics and its Applications 389(13), 2663–2674 (2010)
8. Christley, R.M., Pinchbeck, G.L., Bowers, R.G., Clancy, D., French, N.P., Bennett, R., Turner, J.: Infection in social networks: Using network analysis to identify high-risk individuals. American Journal of Epidemiology 162(10), 1024–1031 (2005)
9. Croft, D.P., James, R., Krause, J.: Exploring Animals Social Networks. Princeton University Press (2008)
10. De, P., Das, S.K.: Epidemic Models, Algorithms, and Protocols in Wireless Sensor and Ad Hoc Networks, pp. 51–75. John Wiley & Sons, Inc. (2008)
11. Dorogovtsev, S.N., Mendes, J.F.F.: Evolution of networks. Adv. Phys. (2002)
12. Eubank, S., Anil Kumar, V.S., Marathe, M.: Epidemiology and Wireless Communication: Tight Analogy or Loose Metaphor? In: Liò, P., Yoneki, E., Crowcroft, J., Verma, D.C. (eds.) BIOWIRE 2007. LNCS, vol. 5151, pp. 91–104. Springer, Heidelberg (2008)
13. Gross, T., D'Lima, C.J., Blasius, B.: Epidemic dynamics on an adaptive network. Physical Review Letters 96(20) (2006)
14. Jeong, H., Tombor, B., Albert, R., Oltvai, Z.N., Barabási, A.-L.: The large-scale organization of metabolic networks. Nature 407, 651–654 (2000)
15. Klovdahl, A.S.: Social networks and the spread of infectious diseases: the aids example. Soc. Sci. Med. 21(11), 1203–1216 (1985)

16. Lopezpintado, D.: Diffusion in complex social networks. Games and Economic Behavior 62(2), 573–590 (2008)
17. Milgram, S.: The small world problem. Psychology Today 1, 61–67 (1967)
18. Newman, M.E.J.: The structure and function of complex networks. Siam Review 45, 167–256 (2003)
19. Read, J.M., Eames, K.T.D., Edmunds, W.J.: Dynamic social networks and the implications for the spread of infectious disease. J. R. Soc. Interface 5(26) (2008)
20. Salathe, M., Jones, J.H.: Dynamics and control of diseases in networks with community structure. PLoS Comput Biol. 6(4) (2010)
21. Tripathy, R.M., Bagchi, A., Mehta, S.: A study of rumor control strategies on social networks. In: 19th ACM International Conference on Information and Knowledge Management, pp. 1817–1820 (2010)

# A Semantic P2P Platform for Sharing Documents in eGovernment Domains

Manuel Jose Fernández Iglesias, Luis M. Álvarez Sabucedo,
Juan M. Santos Gago, and Luis E. Anido Rifón

Telematics Engineering Department, Universidade de Vigo, Spain
{Manuel.Fernandez,Luis.Sabucedo,
Juan.Santos,Luis.Anido}@det.uvigo.es

**Abstract.** One of the obligations in any modern administration is to provide complete and on-time information about its own services to the citizens. This task is sometimes overlooked and may suffer from many barriers such as not-so-simple mechanisms to locate the desired piece of information or problems on the access related to insufficient bandwidth or others. This papers present an original mechanism to locate and download this information taking advantage of semantics (for the discovery) and P2P networks (for the actual downloading of information). The combination of both technologies turn out to offer a number of advantages and a scalable manner to deploy the proposal, as shown on the paper. Authors also present some conclusions for future attempts on the domain.

## 1 Introduction

Providing solutions in the domain of eGovernment tackles a wide range of features that must be properly addressed. In the present moment, we are experiencing a transition from a paper-based approach to a environment that can be actually referred to as a fully transactional stage. According to the ONU classification[1], this would be the networked stage of eGovernment, the stage were all services are interconnected and citizens can access services to fulfill all their needs in the net. In this long-term development, several milestones must be reached. The community involved in the development of eGovernment, including both the academic part and the official part, are paying attention to the support the access to documentation from Public Agencies and Public Administrations (hereafter PAs). This is illustrated in initiatives such as the Open eGovernment Initiative[2] from the White House. This initiative is aimed to make the government actually open by make available on the Internet of all documents that can be of interest for the people.

In line with that concept, this paper presents an original contribution to facilitate the distribution and spread of this data among all possible citizen interested on documents from PAs. This involves documents with forms to fulfill different services but also documents with information from PAs regarding any particular purpose ranging budgets to statistical information. In this paper is presented

M.D. Lytras et al. (Eds.): WSKS 2011, CCIS 278, pp. 509–514, 2013.
© Springer-Verlag Berlin Heidelberg 2013

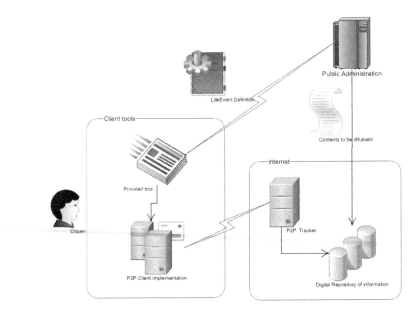

**Fig. 1.** General schema of the model

an approach to locate and retrieve these documents in P2P semantically annotated environment. Also, taking advantage of distributed P2P networks, an entire software architecture is presented.

This architecture (check Figure 1) shows how the citizen may request one or several documents that may be of his/her interest. These documents are, usually, related to a particular service he/she is interested at. This request is mapped into a semantic model and accessed in a P2P network. In the context of this work, it is implicit the use of a centralized P2P network[3] where a tracker is provided that can handle the request and is included in the proposal.

To properly describe the entire system, this article presents firstly how the contents are actually represented (check Section 2). On the basis of this model of information, the contents are accessed from user agents, as described on Section 3. Finally, some conclusions are presented to the reader on Section 4.

## 2   Describing Contents

In order to describe the knowledge in the system, the use of an ontological support is the most convenient tool. In the current case, former works in the area, in particular, the ontological support presented in [4] will be taken as a starting point. This contribution proposes the use of annotations based on a fully developed ontology to describe the domain of eGovernment (an excerpt is shown on Figure 2).

This semantic information involves a large amount of information about the modeling of the business model implicit in the problem and its aim is to take into

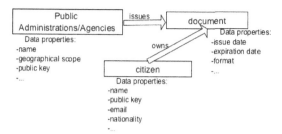

**Fig. 2.** Simplified model of the ontology to define the business model

account all relevant features for PAs. However, in the present approach this level of semantic information could exceed actual requirements of the system. Besides, it could be difficult for normal users or even civil servants to generate the full set of information related to these semantic descriptions. To keep a balance between the complexity of the system and its simplicity of use, some restrictions were put on the semantic model to make it fit the proposal of microformats. Therefore, the solution is just concerned with modeling ASs, and for its definition, a number of relevant fields were identified taking the ontological model in Fig. 2 as a basis:

- name: name of the service itself.
- description: brief description of the service.
- PA: public entity in charge for the service.
- Input Document: name of the documents required to invoke the service.
- Output Document: name of the documents generated as output for the service.
- MaxSpan: maximum delay in the execution of the service, expressed in days.
- Areas: Areas of interest for the AS.

Within this model, information can be translated from OWL to a microformat model and the other way round. This is quite useful in order to store and recover the information in the most convenient manner for each case.

## 3   Distributing Contents

As already mentioned, the aim for this paper is the provision of a simple and cost-efficient mechanism to distribute information, i.e., official documents, from PAs to citizen. To make that possible, it will be taken advantage of semantic technologies and P2P networks. As mentioned previously, this sort of bets must be considered in the long term and a key factor for success in this context is achieving the critical mass required to that end. Therefore, we suggest a two-way approach to fit on both, solutions with a low level of integration and those more technologically evolved.

Firstly, it is introduced an approach that does not require any change on currently available systems in PAs. With a minimum effort it is possible to take full advantage of the proposed approach (check Section 3.1). As systems evolve and the proposed concepts are included in the design of PAs, a more sophisticated approach is suggested (check Section 3.2). Thus, it is possible to provide a path toward a *connected solution* using current solutions as the starting point.

### 3.1   Short Term Approach

To develop a simple-to-use mechanism to access contents for citizen, it is proposed a schema based on the publication of contents using semantics and a *ad-hoc* client software. Within this approach, PAs are requested to provide an OWL file containing the definition of the services provided. These files will be downloaded by the citizen and imported into the client agent created as a proof-of-concept.

Using the provided feature to import contents via a HTTP connection included in this tool, users, i.e., citizens, can access the information from a PA. Taking advantage of the semantic wrapper for data, the software can analyze the contents within the file and add the new information into the local pool of services. The tool will discover the new services included in the file and support the download of documents related to these services.

From the point of the user, once the file is imported into the system, he/she just needs to select the right PA among the possible ones in the local pool. Afterwards, the droplist for LEs/ASs is updated and the desired service can be selected. Once the PA and the LE or AS is selected, the tool will know the URL of torrent file containing the required data. This information is not generated on the client but, on the contrary, will be included in the original file downloaded from the PA in the very first step.

Of course, several files can be downloaded and inserted into the local pool of PAs and LEs. The software provided will just manage them as a local ontology that is loaded in memory when required. At this point, the tool will make use of the P2P network support. The file attach to each service a torrent file for the set of required documents. This torrent file can be operated with any of the current available torrent clients. Contents to be downloaded will be distributed along the net but it is put on the corresponding PA the installation and/or maintenance of the tracker for the contents to be published. Reader should note that the key point is accessing to the URL where contents are referenced by means of a torrent file.

### 3.2   Long Term Approach

In the in-so-far projects, the issue of locating contents is solved by means of an URL, a Uniform Resource Locator, pointing to the actual content. Nevertheless, this option poses some drawbacks: it is required a particular host always online and aware of the exact location of the resource on that address. In our case, we are prone to use a scheme based on the content itself rather that on its location. Bearing this idea on mind, it was decided to use Magnet URI scheme[5].

This is an open standard still in a draft stage that makes possible the location of a resource using information about it, usually, the hash value of the content. In our case, we will take advantage of additional information to actually provide a description of it. In this approach a URN will be created using the ontology gathered. This URN is expected to be processed by a particular application, not a browser necessarily, that will be in charge for actually downloading the content. Using the current version of this standard, some parameters are on clear usage in this proposal:

- $kt$ Keywords
- $dn$ Display name

Additionally to those parameters accepted in the standard, magnet links include an extension on the protocol to extend its possibilities: the supplement format ($x$.). Using this a basis the following addition are used:

- $x.pa$. Public Administration
- $x.kd$. Public service name
- $x.dt$. Date of publication

Using these fields, it is possible to refer to the documentation desired. The following link is an example to catch documentation for the LE involving the payment of taxes from the IRS office:

```
magnet:?kt=Taxes&dn=Form%20%To%20Pay%Taxes&x.pa=IRS&x.kd=Paying%
20Taxes&x.dt=01/06/2011
```

After parsing and analyzing this URN, the tracker can locate the actual content and the download of these pieces of information may begin. The reader can note the use of the semantic annotations for gathering the content from the net. Actually, the tracker is the key element now in this approach, as it will have to gather the actual content using the above mentioned schema. With these pieces of the information, the tracker will have to locate the requested content and initiate its download.

## 4    Conclusion

The management of information, on paper or on a digital format, in Public Administration drives all the workflows in the daily routine. The modernization of the document management is a primary goal for all Governments engaged in the advent of eGovernment. This issue is not related only to internal procedures in Public Administrations but also involves changes in the way citizen can interact with its administrators. In line with those ideas, this paper presents a novel approach to the delivery of documents from Public Administrations to their citizens. It must be borne in mind that Public Administrations are a source of huge amount of data that may of interest for citizens, ranging from instructions to deal with the last epidemic to new legal regulations that impact of citizens' life.

In order to provide an up-to-date and feasible mechanism to distribute this contents, this paper proposes a novel approach based on the use of semantics and P2P networks. Within the frame of this proposal, it is suggested to describe contents using a metadata based approach and, afterwards, publish contents on P2P networks. From the use of semantics, it is derived a set of services to locate and identify documents that may interest the client of the system, i.e., the citizen. The use of P2P offers a powerful way to redistribute contents on the Internet with quite little resources. The combination of those features turned out the proposed solution into a simple a effective manner to disseminate information on the network. This approach is especially suitable for contents highly demanded such as new laws or forms to apply for a popular services. Nevertheless, due to the proposed architecture it is clear that Public Administrations must be responsible for the tracker. Besides they must store all contents possible in the system.

A consequence of this approach is that citizens do not need to explore different website or check on different repositories. As all the documents are available on the tracker, it is possible to locate any document with just one search avoiding problems related to sessions on the access to official websites or documents accessible by means of POST methods, i.e., without a valid URL to access them.

**Acknowledgment.** The authors would like to thank Spanish Ministerio de Ciencia e Innovación for their partial support to this work under grants "Methodologies, Architectures and Standards for adaptive and accessible e-learning (Adapt2Learn)" (TIN2010-21735-C02-01) and Xunta de Galicia, Consellería de Innovación e Industria through project "SEGREL: Semántica para un eGov Reutilizable en Entornos Locais" (08SIN006322PR).

# References

1. United Nations: Un e-government survey 2008: From e-government to connected governance. Web available (2008), http://unpan1.un.org/intradoc/groups/public/documents/UN/UNPAN028607.pdf
2. The White House: Open government initiative. Web available (2009), http://www.whitehouse.gov/Open/
3. Liu, Z., Yu, H., Kundur, D., Merabti, M.: On peer-to-peer multimedia content access and distribution. In: 2006 IEEE International Conference on Multimedia and Expo., pp. 557–560 (July 2006)
4. Álvarez Sabucedo, L., Anido Rifón, L., Corradini, F., Polzonetti, A., Re, B.: Knowledge-based platform for egovernment agents: A web-based solution using semantic technologies. Expert Systems with Application, 1–10 (2009) ISSN 0957-4174
5. Magnet-uri project. Web available (2011), http://magnet-uri.sourceforge.net/

# A Recommender System for Learning Goals

Nicola Capuano[1], Roberto Iannone[1], Matteo Gaeta[1,2], Sergio Miranda[2],
Pierluigi Ritrovato[2], and Saverio Salerno[1,2]

[1] CRMPA, Centro di Ricerca in Matematica Pura ed Applicata,
Via Ponte don Melillo, 84084 Fisciano (SA), Italy
{capuano,gaeta,iannone}@crmpa.unisa.it
[2] Dipartimento di Ingengeria Elettronica e Ingegneria Informatica, Università di Salerno,
via Ponte Don Melillo 84084 Fisciano (SA), Italy
{mgaeta,smiranda,pritrovato,salerno}@unisa.it

**Abstract.** The aim of a recommender system is to estimate the utility of a set of
objects belonging to a given domain, starting from the information available
about users and objects. Adaptive e-learning systems are able to automatically
generate personalized learning experiences starting from a learner profile and a
set of target learning goals. Starting form research results of these fields we
defined a methodology to recommend learning goals and to generate learning
experiences for learners of an adaptive e-learning system.

**Keywords:** e-learning, recommender systems, intelligent tutoring systems.

## 1 Introduction

A significant educational action able to guide the learner in a comprehensive learning
process is not only focused on learning (cognition level) but also on fostering a
correct learning behavior that empowers learners to achieve their learning goals in a
controlled and directed way (metacognition level) [1].

Starting from this principle we defined and developed an e-learning system able to
build personalized learning experiences starting from a set of target concepts selected
on an ontology-based domain model [2]. We then extended such system in order to
allow course generation form an explicit request in terms of needs to be satisfied and
expressed by the learner in natural language [3].

The work presented in this paper deals with the definition of a further process of
course building starting from an implicit request rather than from an explicit one. In
other words, a methodology to recommend learning goals based on the analysis of a
learner' profile (including known topics) and on the comparison of this profile with
profiles of similar learners is defined.

The proposed methodology upholds the social presence while supporting the
development of self-regulated learning. Educational recommendations serves as a
pedagogical advanced organizer for the learners, as it anticipates and spreads needs,
knowledge and learning paths. Furthermore it also supports help seeking processes
improving the students' control over learning.

M.D. Lytras et al. (Eds.): WSKS 2011, CCIS 278, pp. 515–521, 2013.

The paper is organized in this way: the section 2 introduces some background about recommender systems and presents some existing application of such systems in e-learning; the section 3 briefly introduces the starting point of our research i.e. the learning system IWT; the section 4 describes the proposed methodology; eventually the section 5 describes conclusions and planned future work.

## 2    Background and Related Work

Recommender Systems (RS) are aimed at providing personalized recommendations on the utility of a set of objects belonging to a given domain, starting from the information available about users and objects.

A formal definition of the recommendation problem can be expressed in these terms [4]: $C$ is the set of users of the system, $I$ the set of objects that can be recommended, $R$ a totally ordered set whose values represent the utility of an object for a user and $u$: $C \times I \rightarrow R$ a utility function that measures how a given object $i \in I$ is useful for a particular user $c \in C$. The purpose of the system is to recommend to each user $c$ the object $i$ that maximizes the utility function so that:

$$i'_c = \arg\max_{i \in I} u(c,i).$$

(1)

The central problem of the recommendations is that the function $u$ is not completely defined on the space $C \times I$ in fact, in typical applications of such systems, a user never expresses preferences on each object of the available catalog. A RS shall then be able to estimate the values of the utility function also in the space of data where it is not defined, extrapolating from the points of $C \times I$ where it is known.

Several approaches to recommendation exist in the literature. They are usually classified in three categories: *content-based approaches* recommend to a user objects similar to those that he have positively rated in the past; *collaborative approaches* recommend to a user those objects that are liked by other people with similar tastes; *hybrid approaches* combine the two previous approaches.

Several **RS for e-Learning** have been introduced to select and propose learning resources to users. One of the first systems, based on a collaborative approach, has been Altered Vista [5]. Its goal was to explore how to collect user-made evaluations of learning resources and to propagate them in the form of recommendations about the qualities of the resources. A Similar system is RACOFI [6] that integrates a collaborative RS with a rule-based inference engine.

QSIA [7] is a RS for learning resources sharing, assessing and recommendation in online communities. CYCLADES [8] uses a collaborative approach with user-based ratings, but does applies the technique to several communities at the same time. A related system is CoFind [9]: it uses digital resources that are freely available and applies for the first time folksonomies for recommendations.

Shen and Shen [10] developed a recommender system for learning objects that is based on sequencing rules that help users be guided through the concepts of an ontology of topics. A similar sequencing system is LSRS [11] that analyzes group-learning experiences to predict and provide a personal list for each learner by tracking others' learning patterns regarding certain topics.

In ReMashed [12] learners can rate information from an emerging amount of Web 2.0 information of a Learning Network and train a recommender system for their particular needs. The CourseRank system [13] uses instead a hybrid recommendation approach and is used as an unofficial course guide for Stanford University students. In the APOSDLE project [14] a contextual recommendations is offered to the employees of large organizations in the context of a knowledge-sharing environment.

## 3     The Starting Point

In this section we introduce a learning system named **IWT** (Intelligent Web Teacher) that we adopted as a basis to apply models and methodologies hereafter defined. As described in [2] IWT allows to generate personalized learning experiences and relies on four interacting models as described below.

The *domain model* describes the knowledge that is object of teaching through a set of concepts (representing topics to be taught) and a set of relations between concepts. A set of *teaching preferences* can be added to the domain model to define feasible teaching strategies that may be applied for each available concept.

The *learner model* represents a learner and is composed by a *cognitive state* that measures the knowledge reached by him at a given time and by a set of *learning preferences* that provide an evaluation of which learning strategies are more feasible for him. Both components are automatically assessed by IWT by analysing results of testing activities and the learner behaviour during the learning experience.

The *learning resource model* is a metadata representing a learning resource and is based on the application of the IEEE LOM standard [15]. It includes the set of concepts that are covered by the learning resource and an additional set of didactical properties representing learning strategies applied by the learning resource.

The *unit of learning model* represents a sequence of learning resources needed for a learner in order to understand a set of target concepts in a given domain.

In [2] we have described the process to generate a unit of learning starting from a set of a target concepts and from a learner model. The process generates a feasible sequence of domain concepts able to teach the target concepts. Then it removes domain concepts already known by the target learner by looking at his/her cognitive state. Eventually it associates to each remaining concept the best matching learning resources taking into account teaching and learning preferences.

To simplify user interactions with the system, IWT also implements an alternative method for the expression of a learning need through **Upper Level Learning Goals** (ULLG). An ULLG is a meaningful set of target concepts on a given domain model with a connected textual description [3]. ULLGs can be built either by teachers and by learners and are accessed through a search engine.

The learner can so specify a learning need in natural language and let the system find the list of best matching ULLGs basing on the similarity between the expressed need and the textual descriptions connected to ULLGs. Then the learner can select a

ULLG and let the system build a personalized unit of learning starting from the connected set of target concepts and from his/her learner model.

# 4    The Proposed Approach

This paper deals with the integration in IWT of a new process of course building based on ULLG but starting from an implicit request rather than from an explicit one. In other words, a methodology to recommend ULLGs based on the analysis of a learner' cognitive state and on the comparison of this cognitive state with cognitive states of similar learners is provided. In order to do so we will adapt and extend a user-to-user collaborative recommendation algorithm.

The algorithm consists of the following steps: concept mapping, concept utility estimation and ULLG utility estimation each described in one of the following sub-sections. Once the utility of each ULLG is estimated for a learner, the ULLGs with the greater utility can be suggested to him.

## 4.1    Concept Mapping

Given a set of concepts $C$ and a set of learners $L$, the *cognitive state* of a learner $l \in L$ (as reported in section 3 and detailed in [2]), describes the knowledge reached by $l$ at a given time and it is represented as an application $CS_l: C \rightarrow [0, 10]$. Given a concept $c$, with $CS_l(c)$ we indicate the degree of knowledge (or grade) reached by the learner $l$ for $c$. If such grade is greater then a threshold $\theta$ then $c$ is considered as known by $l$, otherwise it is considered as unknown.

At a given time a learner can be enrolled to one or more units of learning. As reported in 3 (and detailed in [2]), a unit of learning represents a sequence of learning resources needed by a learner in order to understand a set of target concepts in a given domain. Among the components of a unit of learning there is the learning path $LPath = (c_1, \ldots, c_n)$: an ordered sequence of concepts that must be taught to a specific learner in order to let him/her complete the unit of learning.

Starting from that, we can define the set $COT_l$ of all concepts that are object of teaching for a given learner as the union of all learning paths $LPath$ corresponding to the units of learning the learner is enrolled in. Then we can define the **concept mapping function** that is a Boolean function $CMF: L \times C \rightarrow \{0, 1\}$ that can be defined as follows:

$$CMF(l,c) = \begin{cases} 1 \text{ if } CS_l(c) > \theta \text{ or } c \in COT_l \\ 0 \text{ otherwise} \end{cases}. \tag{2}$$

So, given a leaner $l$, $CMF(l,c) = 1$ for all concepts $c$ that are already known by $l$ plus all concepts $c$ that are currently object of teaching for him/her. It is equal to 0 for any other concepts.

## 4.2    Concept Utility Estimation

The utility $u(l,c)$ of a concept $c$ for a learner $l$ can be estimated starting from the concept mapping function. The utility of a known concept or of a concept that will be known soon is equal to 0. So $CMF(l,c) = 1 \rightarrow u(l,c) = 0$. Conversely, to estimate the utility of remaining concepts, a collaborative recommendation algorithm is used.

We can estimate the unknown utility of a given concept $c$ for a learner $l$ by aggregating, through a weighted sum, ratings for the concept $c$, included in the concept mapping function, coming from learners that are similar to $l$. The estimation can be done through the following formula:

$$u(l,c) = \frac{\sum_{l' \in L'} CMF(l',c) \cdot sim(l,l')}{\sum_{l' \in L'} |sim(l,l')|} \tag{3}$$

where $L'$ is the set of the $n$ learners most similar to $l$ while $sim(l,l')$ is the similarity degree between $l$ and $l'$ obtained though similarity measures like the *cosine similarity* or the *Pearson correlation coefficient* [4] calculated on *CMF*.

From the algorithmic point of view, to estimate the concept utility function, we start from the concept mapping matrix where each element $CMF(l,c)$ is defined with (2). This matrix is built the first time by considering every cognitive state and every course available on the system. Each time a learner starts, terminates or abandons a course then the row corresponding to this learner is updated, again, through (2).

Starting from the concept mapping matrix, the user-to-user similarity matrix is calculated. Each element $sim(l,l')$ of this matrix is obtained through a similarity measure between the rows of the concept mapping matrix corresponding to users $l$ and $l'$. Once the similarity matrix is calculated, to estimate an undefined $u(l,c)$ for a given learner $l$, it is necessary to isolate and combine, by applying (3), the utility expressed for $c$ by the $n$ learners more similar to $l$.

## 4.3     ULLG Utility Estimation

An *ULLG* can be formally defined as a tuple $ULLG_i = (D_i, TC_{i1}, \ldots, TC_{in})$ where $D_i$ is a text describing the learning objective in natural language, while $TC_1, \ldots, TC_n$ is the list of target concepts that have to be mastered by a learner in order to reach such learning objective. A learning need $LN$ is a textual sentence (like "to learn Java programming" or "how to repair a bicycle" etc.) expressed by a learner in order to start the unit of learning building process.

Through the unit of learning generation algorithm introduced in section 3 (and detailed in [2]) IWT is able to generate a learning path starting from a set of target concepts. By applying the algorithm described there, it is possible to determine, for each existing upper level learning goal $ULLG_i$, the corresponding learning path $LPath_i$ starting from the connected list of target concepts.

Once determined learning paths associated to available ULLGs, it is possible to estimate the **aggregated utility** $au(l, ULLG_i)$ of each of them for a learner $l$ with the following formula:

$$au(l, ULLG_i) = \sum_{c \in LPath_i} \frac{u(l,c)}{|LPath_i|}. \tag{4}$$

The calculus of the aggregated utility takes into account the utility of all concepts explained by the ULLG. This means that, if the learning path connected with the ULLG includes many concepts already known by the learner, its aggregate utility can be low even if the utility of remaining concepts is high. To take into account this information we introduce the concept of **marginal utility** $mu(l,ULLG_i)$ of $ULLG_i$ for a learner $l$ that can be obtained with the following formula:

$$mu(l,ULLG_i) = \frac{\sum_{c \in LPath_i} u(l,c)(1-CMF(l,c))}{\sum_{c \in LPath_i} (1-CMF(l,c))}. \tag{5}$$

Thus the utility of an ULLG for a given learner can be obtained by combining aggregated and marginal utilities through a weighted sum with the following formula:

$$u(l,ULLG_i) = \alpha\; au(l,ULLG_i) + (1-\alpha)\; mu(l,ULLG_i). \tag{6}$$

where $\alpha$ is the hybridization coefficient that is a real number between 0 (highest priority to the marginal utility) to 1 (highest priority to the aggregated utility). The choice for $\alpha$ will be done empirically basing on experimentation results. Low values for $\alpha$ privileges novelty while high values privilege accuracy of suggestions given by the recommender system.

## 5    Conclusions and Future Work

We defined in this paper a methodology to recommend learning goals and to generate learning experiences that will be integrated in IWT: an already existing adaptive e-learning system. The next step is to design and develop software components able to implement the defined methodology. An experimentation phase will follow to provide comments and suggestions to be used for models and methodologies improvement.

In addition to comments coming from experimentation, some improvement can be already foreseen. The application of *matrix factorisation techniques* [16] able to transform the concept mapping matrix that is an huge sparse matrix in a product of smaller dense matrixes can be applied to optimize recommender performances. In addition, the possibility for learners to rate ULLGs created by other teachers or learners will be explored. This rating can be exploited by recommender algorithms as explicit feedback to improve recommendations.

**Acknowledgements.** The research reported in this paper is partially supported by the European Commission under the Collaborative Project ALICE [17] "Adaptive Learning via an Intuitive, interactive, Collaborative, Emotional system", VII Framework Program, Theme ICT-2009.4.2, Grant Agreement n. 257639.

## References

1. Mangione, G.R., Gaeta, M., Orciuoli, F., Salerno, S.: A Semantic Metacognitive Learning Environment. In: Cognitive and Metacognitive Educational Systems, AAAI Fall Symposium (2010)
2. Capuano, N., Gaeta, M., Marengo, A., Miranda, S., Orciuoli, F., Ritrovato, P.: LIA: an Intelligent Advisor for e-Learning. Interactive Learning Environments 17(3), 221–239 (2009)

3. Capuano, N., Gaeta, M., Orciuoli, F., Ritrovato, P.: On-Demand Construction of Personalized Learning Experiences Using Semantic Web and Web 2.0 Techniques. In: 9th IEEE International Conference on Advanced Learning Technologies, pp. 484–488 (2009)
4. Adomavicius, G., Tuzhilin, A.: Toward the next generation of recommender systems: a survey of the state-of-the-art and possible extensions. IEEE Transactions on Knowledge and Data Engineerin 17(6), 734–749 (2005)
5. Recker, M.M., Wiley, D.A.: A non-authoritative educational metadata ontology for filtering and recommending learning objects. Interactive Learning Environments 9(3), 255–271 (2001)
6. Anderson, M., Ball, M., Boley, H., Greene, S., Howse, N., Lemire, D., McGrath, S.: RACOFI: A Rule-Applying Collaborative Filtering System. In: IEEE/WIC COLA 2003 (2003)
7. Rafaeli, S., Barak, M., Dan-Gur, Y., Toch, E.: QSIA-a Web-based environment for learning, assessing and knowledge sharing in communities. Computers, Education 43(3), 273–289 (2004)
8. Avancini, H., Straccia, U.: User recommendation for collaborative and personalised digital archives. International Journal of Web Based Communities 1(2), 163–175 (2005)
9. Dron, J., Mitchell, R., Boyne, C., Siviter, P.: CoFIND: steps towards a self-organising learning environment. In: World Conference on the WWW and Internet (WebNet 2000), pp. 146–151. AACE, USA (2000)
10. Shen, L., Shen, R.: Learning content recommendation service based-on simple sequencing specification. In: Liu, W. et al. (eds), LNCS, pp. 363–370, Springer (2004)
11. Huang, Y.M., Huang, T.C., Wang, K.T., Hwang, W.Y.: A Markov-based Recommendation Model for Exploring the Transfer of Learning on the Web. Educational Technology & Society 12(2), 144–162 (2009)
12. Drachsler, H., Pecceu, D., Arts, T., Hutten, E., Rutledge, L., van Rosmalen, P., Hummel, H., Koper, R.: ReMashed – Recommendations for Mash-Up Personal Learning Environments. In: Cress, U., Dimitrova, V., Specht, M. (eds.) EC-TEL 2009. LNCS, vol. 5794, pp. 788–793. Springer, Heidelberg (2009)
13. Bercovitz, B., Kaliszan, F., Koutrika, G., Liou, H., Zadeh, Z.M., Garcia-Molina, H.: CourseRank: a social system for course planning. In: 35th SIGMOD International Conference on Management of Data. ACM (2009)
14. APOSDLE Advanced Process- Oriented Self- Directed Learning Environment. EU-project, http://www.aposdle.tugraz.at
15. IMS Global Learning Consortium. IMS Meta-data Best Practice Guide for IEEE 1484.12.1-2002 Standard for Learning Object Metadata (2006)
16. Rendle, S., Schmidt-Thieme, L.: Online-updating regularized kernel matrix factorization models for large-scale recommender systems. In: The 2008 ACM Conference on Recommender Systems, RecSys 2008. ACM (2008)
17. ALICE Adaptive Learning via an Intuitive, interactive, Collaborative, Emotional system. EU-project, http://www.aliceproject.org

# A Semantic Web Vocabulary Supporting Brainstorming for Research Communities

Luca Dell'Angelo[2], Matteo Gaeta[1], Giuseppe Laria[2],
Giuseppina Rita Mangione[2], Francesco Orciuoli[1], and Pierluigi Ritrovato[1]

[1] Dipartimento di Ingegneria Elettronica e Ingegneria Informatica
University of Salerno,
Fisciano, Salerno, Italy
{mgaeta,forciuoli,pritrovato}@unisa.it
[2] Centro di Ricerca in Matematica Pura e Applicata (CRMPA)
University of Salerno,
Fisciano, Salerno, Italy
{dellangelo,iannone,laria,mangione}@crmpa.unisa.it

**Abstract.** The e-Brainstorming tools represent plausible solutions to improve the e-research community activities with respect to processes regarding idea generation and idea selection. However, the existing e-Brainstorming systems show methodological and technological limitations. The present work proposes a brainstorming model that aims at overcoming the aforementioned limitations by exploiting Social Web and Semantic Web technologies and practices sustaining on-line social dimension, application interoperability, knowledge representation, knowledge sharing and correlation discovery.

**Keywords:** Semantic Web, Brainstorming, Social Network, Research Communities.

## 1 Introduction

The *e-research*, i.e. the set of collaborative activities combining abilities and resources of distributed groups of researchers in order to achieve research goals, evolves concurrently to the development of models and methods able to sustain ubiquitous networking processes and activities. Researchers joint a community with the aim to execute innovative and challenging research activities also by means of suitable digital environments. Moreover, the social dimension and the context (i.e. the set of relationships raising within a group) significantly impact on the behaviour of each individual and of the collective. The *e-Brainstorming* tool represents a plausible solution to improve the e-research community activities. Existing Group Support Systems (GSS), that support on-line brainstorming sessions, show mehodological and technological limits. From the methodological point of view, GSSs are based on the assumption that if people generate more ideas, then they will produce more good ideas (Osborn's conjecture). Hence, these systems do not take care of the process transforming the quantity into

M.D. Lytras et al. (Eds.): WSKS 2011, CCIS 278, pp. 522–527, 2013.

quality with respect to the generation of ideas [5]. From the technological point of view the GSSs do not guarantee interoperability among different applications and are limited with respect to the possibility to simply and rapidly correlate and share knowledge among people and software agents. In this work, a brainstorming model (section 2) and its Semantic Web-based representation (section 3) are provided. Furthermore, in section 4, the contextualisation of BrainSIOC within research communities is illustrated. The model provides a solution to overcome the Osborn's conjecture by exploiting the Bounded Ideation Theory [1] by means of Social Web tools. The representation, by exploiting the Semantic Web technologies and practices, provides a solution to the interoperability and knowledge sharing issues and fosters the correlation discovery (among different pieces of knowledge) by means of the linked data approach, standard query languages (e.g. SPARQL[1]) and inference languages (both rule-based and ontology-based). Conclusions are presented in section 5.

## 2   The BrainSIOC Model

Unlike other recent brainstorming models [4], BrainSIOC, firstly introduced in [3] and subsequently detailed in the present work, mainly focuses on defining a brainstorming model and structuring it by means og Semantic Web vocabularies like SIOC[2]. In the BrainSIOC approach a brainstorming session is composed by three phases and prefigures the presence of a *moderator* while the other *participants* have no specific roles.

In the first phase, namely *Activation* or *Idea Generation*, the issue, on which the discussion has to take place, is presented and the participants have the possibility to socialize. In this phase, the focus is to produce the greatest number of ideas, which is initially more important than their quality, especially because the greater the number of ideas, the greater the chance of finding some useful. The topic of discussion has not be completely defined in order to unleash the power of idea generation. The ideas have to be freely expressed in the initial phase assuming that quantity is more important than quality at this stage.

In the second phase, namely *Production* or *Knowledge Construction*, the moderator asks participants to speak freely on the subject, urges them to be active, asks questions, rewords questions. The participants freely express ideas, thoughts, opinions. Ideas are not subjected to criticism during the meeting, in fact the adverse judgement of ideas must be withheld until the next phase (deferring judgement [6]). In this phase, which is the more challenging phase of a brainstorming session, ideas should be evaluated, in relation to their effectiveness, selected and developed further.

In the third phase, namely *Synthesis* or *Revision Circle*, the moderator summarizes the generated ideas, uses various criteria to stimulate participants to assess and select the best ideas. In addition, participants should suggest how the ideas of others can be turned into better ideas or how two ideas can be merged into new one.

---

[1] http://www.w3.org/TR/rdf-sparql-query/
[2] http://sioc-project.org/

In order to define a digital environment able to support brainstorming sessions as we have defined them above, the *Knowledge Forum* [2] can be exploited to support the creation and the continuous improvement of knowledge and modelled by extending SIOC (see section 3).

## 3    BrainSIOC Ontology Description

First of all, the BrainSIOC ontology considers two roles for the brainstorming activity, i.e. the generic participant and the moderator. In order to model the first one we need to define the `bsioc:Participant` class and the `bsioc:Moderator` class as subclasses of `sioc:Role`. An instance of `sioc:UserAccount` is linked to a specific role by using the `sioc:funcion_of` property. The link between a moderator and a specific container (e.g. a forum) can be also asserted by using the `sioc:has_moderator` property with domain `sioc:Forum` and range `sioc:UserAccount`. Furthermore a brainstorming session is modelled by subclassing the `sioc:Forum` class and defining the `bsioc:Brainstorming` in order to reuse all the properties defined for `sioc:Forum`.

In SIOC, there exist several properties that are useful to link instances of `sioc:Item` (and hence of `sioc:Post`) to each other.

In particular, the `sioc:related_to` property is extended in the BrainSIOC in order to define other properties able to correlate different types of posts (e.g. `bsioc:hasIdea`, `bsioc:advances`, `bsioc:accepts`, etc.). Another useful SIOC property is `sioc:next_version` that can be used to link two different versions of the same item. In the end, the `sioc:content` property (with domain `sioc:Item` and range `rdfs:Literal`) is used to store the text representing ideas, questions, answers and so on.

Fig. 1 focuses on how the `sioc:Post` class is extending in order to support the three brainstorming session phases defined in the section 2. In particular,

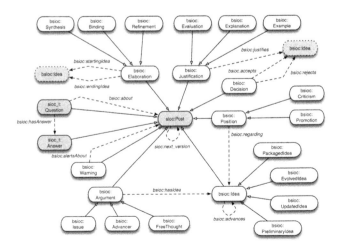

**Fig. 1.** Extending the `sioc:Post` class

during the *Idea Generation* phase, a new problem or argument can be introduced using an instance of `bsioc:Argument` or an instance of its subclasses: `bsioc:Issue` (i.e. the issue proposed by the moderator to be discussed in the current brainstorming session), `bsioc:Advancer` (i.e. a message anticipating problems or providing additional information that should guide the discussion) and `bsioc:FreeThought` (i.e. thoughts expressed by the participants in order to share intuitions, opinions, insights, etc. that cannot be formulated as ideas at the current stage). Ideas to solve a problem can be proposed by instantiating the `bsioc:Idea` class or one of its subclasses: `bsioc:PackagedIdea` (i.e. detailed description of an idea that has been selected and accepted during the *Revision Circle* phase), `bsioc:EvolvedIdea` (i.e. description of the evolution of a previously introduced idea during the *Knowledge Construction* phase), `bsioc:UpdatedIdea` (i.e. a modified description of a previously introduced idea during the *Idea Generation* and *Knowledge Construction* phases) and `bsioc:PreliminaryIdea` (i.e. description of a preliminary idea proposed by a participant during the *Idea Generation* phase). An argument (or problem) and its solution (idea) can be related by using the property `bsioc:hasIdea` (domain `bsioc:Argument` and range `bsioc:Idea`). Two ideas, for instance an evolved idea and a preliminary idea are linked by using the property `bsioc:advances`. BrainSIOC provides furher classes to track the rationale of the manipulation of ideas. For instance, if a new idea raises from the synthesis among three previously defined ideas it is possibile to use an instance of the `bsioc:Synthesis` (a subclass of `bsioc:Elaboration` class) and the properties `bsioc:startingIdea` and `bsioc:endingIdea`. Other subclasses of the `bsioc:Elaboration` class are `bsioc:Refinement` (in order to provide a refinement to a proposed idea) and `bsioc:Binding` (in order to motivate a correlation among several ideas). During the *Revision Circle* phases, promotions and criticisms about ideas can be provided by using the instances of `bsioc:Promotion` and `Criticism` classes. During the same phase, the moderator can accept or reject an idea by using an instance of the `bsioc:Decision` class and the properties `bsioc:accepts` and `bsioc:rejects`. Instances of `sioc_t:Question` and `sioc_t:Answer` are used during the *Idea Generation* and *Knowledge Construction* phases in order to ask for clarification or further deepening and to answers to the aforementioned requests. During the *Knowledge Construction* phase, instances of `bsioc:Warning` (i.e. an alert launched by the moderator with respect to an idea, a correlation between two ideas, and so on), `bsioc:Evaluation` (i.e. a judjment provided by a participant in order to evaluate a preliminary or an updated idea), `bsioc:Example` (i.e. a real world example about an idea in order to demonstrate its feasibility) and `bsioc:Explanation` (i.e. further explanation about an idea, a question, an answer, etc.).

# 4 Linking BrainSIOC with SWRC

Lorenzo et al.[4] and Gaeta et al. [3] propose the harmonization of brainstorming vocabularies with of FOAF, Review RDF, SKOS, Tag Ontology (SCOT/MOAT) to empower their models with social networking, reviewing, rating tagging and

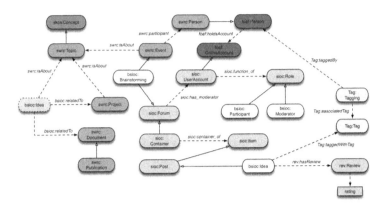

**Fig. 2.** Harmonization of BrainSIOC with SWRC and other vocabularies

classification features. Furthermore, Lorenzo et al. also use the Event Ontology [3] and provide new classes and properties[4] to model the objective and the duration of a brainstorming session. The core of this section is to insert BrainSIOC in the context of the research communities by linking BrainSIOC with SWRC (Semantic Web Research Community Ontology)[5] and by exploiting the aforementioned results.

The SWRC vocabulary models key entities in a typical research community and proposes six top level concepts: `Person`, `Publication`, `Event`, `Organization`, `Topic` and `Project`. The harmonization among BrainSIOC, SWRC and other existing vocabularies is illustrated in Fig. 2 where top level concepts and their relations are provided.

In particular, SWRC has been related to BrainSIOC by means of `swrc:Event` that subsumes `bsioc:Brainstorming`. The brainstorming participants and moderators have been related to `swrc:Person` and the `swrc:Topic` class has been related to `bsioc:Idea` by means of `swrc:isAbout` property in order to link ideas to specific topics. Moreover, in the present proposal `swrc:Topic` is a sublass of `skos:Concept` in order to foster knowledge sharing among applications, agents, sessions, etc. It's important to underline alos the introduction of the `bsioc:relatedTo` property (domain `bsioc:Idea` and domain `swrc:Project`) that is able to link ideas with projects and documents (e.g. publications). The aforementioned links enable to share knowledge about the applicability of an idea to solve a problem in the context of a specific project, the discussion of an idea within a publication, and so on. In order to achieve the best result for the `bsioc:relatedTo` property, it is needed to define subproperties: `bsioc:applicableIn`, `bsioc:discussedIn`, etc.

In the end, some features (objective and duration of the brainstorming event) of the Brainstorming Ontology presented in [4] could be exploited to enrich the vocabulary provided in Fig. 2.

---

[3] http://motools.sourceforge.net/event/event.html

[4] http://vocab.deri.ie/br

[5] http://ontoware.org/swrc/

# 5   Conclusions

In this paper Semantic Web-based languages and vocabularies are exploited in order to define an ontology to structure the brainstorming activities within research communities. In particular, a brainstorming model is defined and represented by means of a Semantic Web-based vocabulary, namely BrainSIOC. The BrainSIOC vocabulary, extending the SIOC ontology and linking to SWRC ontology, simplifies interoperability and knowledge sharing among people and applications and fosters innovation within research communities.

**Acknowledgement.** This research is partially supported by the EC under the Project ARISTOTELE "Personalised Learning & Collaborative Working Environments Fostering Social Creativity and Innovations Inside the Organisations", VII FP, Theme ICT-2009.4.2 (Technology-Enhanced Learning), Grant Agreement n. 257886.

# References

1. Briggs, R., Reinig, B.: Bounded Ideation Theory: A New Model of the Relationship Between Ideaquantity and Idea-quality during Ideation. In: 40th Annual Hawaii International Conference on System Sciences HICSS 2007, p. 16. IEEE (2007)
2. Chen, B., Chuy, M., Resendes, M., Scardamalia, M.: "Big Ideas Tool" as a New Feature of Knowledge Forum. In: 2010 Knowledge Building Summer Institute, Toronto, Canada (2010)
3. Gaeta, M., Loia, V., Mangione, G.R., Orciuoli, F., Ritrovato, P.: Social semantic web fostering idea brainstorming. In: International Workshop on Semantic Adaptive Social Web in Connection with UMAP 2011 (2011)
4. Lorenzo, L., Lizarralde, O., Santos, I., Passant, A.: Structuring e-brainstorming to better support innovation processes. In: Workshop on Social Innovation and Social Media (2011)
5. Reinig, B.A., Briggs, R.O.: On The Relationship Between Idea-Quantity and Idea-Quality During Ideation. Group Decision and Negotiation 17(5), 403–420 (2008)
6. Yuan, S.T., Chen, Y.C.: Semantic Ideation Learning for Agent-Based E-Brainstorming. IEEE Transactions on Knowledge and Data Engineering 20(2), 261–275 (2008)

# An Approach to Automatic Generation of Fuzzy Membership Functions Using Popularity Metrics

Aitor Almeida[1], Pablo Orduña[1], Eduardo Castillejo[1], Diego López-de-Ipiña[1],
and Marcos Sacristán[2]

[1] Deusto Institute of Technology - DeustoTech
University of Deusto. Bilbao, Spain
{aitor.almeida,pablo.orduna,eduardo.castillejo,dipina}@deusto.es
[2] Treelogic. Llanera, Spain
marcos.sacristan@treelogic.com

**Abstract.** Creating membership functions for fuzzy system can be a difficult task for non-expert developers. This is even more difficult when the information available about the specific domain is limited. In our case, we wanted to create membership functions that model the different characteristics of mobile devices. Due to the lack of public data about the mobile phones sales it is difficult to estimate the market share of each device. To tackle this problem we have developed a mechanism that uses popularity metrics to estimate the market share and generate the membership functions. In this paper we describe the used algorithm and discuss the obtained results.

**Keywords:** fuzzy, mobile devices, characterization, membership functions, google trends, popularity, WURFL.

## 1    Introduction

While developing the Imhotep framework [1] for the creation of adaptive user interfaces, one of our design goals was to simplify the development cycle as much as possible. As part of the framework, developers can use preprocessor directives to guide the interface adaptation. These directives employ the device characteristics (screen size, CPU, RAM memory, supported formats, codecs…) to decide how the interface adaptation should be done. One problem we identified during the development of the framework was that developers without extensive experience usually do not have the required knowledge to identify the exact values to be used in the preprocessor directives. For example a developer might want to know if a processor is "fast" or a screen is "big", without having to deal with specific values. Working with values closer to natural language eases the use of preprocessor directives. We encountered initially several problems with this approach. Obviously one screen is big when we compare it with the other screens in the market. To have an accurate concept of what is "big" we have to know the market share of the devices to identify the distribution of the screen sizes. Also, the concept "big" will change over time. What was considered a big screen in 2004 nowadays would be considered normal or small. Finally, it will also change with the location; a big screen in Europe

M.D. Lytras et al. (Eds.): WSKS 2011, CCIS 278, pp. 528–533, 2013.

probably is not so big in Japan. To be able to create fuzzy membership functions that model the device characteristics accurately we would have needed the market share data of all the existing devices. Being this option completely unfeasible we adopted another approach: the use of popularity metrics to infer the device adoption rate. To do this we have used two different tools. First we have used WURFL, an XML mobile device database, to compile an exhaustive list of the existing devices and their characteristics. With that list we have retrieved the popularity metrics of those devices from Google Trends.

Using this data we have developed a process to automatically generate membership functions. We will describe this process in the following paper. In Section 2 we will analyze the related work, in Section 3 we will explain how the generation process works. Finally in Section 4 we will expose the conclusions and future work.

## 2    Related Work

Google Trends has been used to model different domains and scenarios. In [2] authors use data from Google Trends and Google Insights to make short-term economic predictions. This approach has also been used to predict private consumption [3]. Another domain where Google Trends has been used is epidemiological research, studying influenza epidemics [4] or the expansion of Lyme disease [5]. In [6] authors present a web tool for disease outbreak surveillance based on Google Trends. Finally in [7] the trend data is used to track diseases. As can be seen the information contained in Google Trends is an interesting pool of data that can be used to model and infer the behavior of the users.

Automatic membership function generation has already been addressed by several authors. This problem has been tackled using different approaches. In [8] and [9] authors describe a method to generate membership functions using genetic algorithms. Authors in [10] propose the use of inductive reasoning for the construction of membership functions. Finally in [11] authors use an ad-hoc method to generate the membership functions.

## 3    The Characterization Process

There are situations where the crisp values of device characteristics are not suitable to be used directly. For example, the developer may want to show certain video only if the screen of the device is "big" or to use a certain reasoning engine only if the processor capabilities are "high". The main problem with this scenario is that the concept "big" is not directly related to one value and is a relative value (which implies that what is a big screen today probably won't be big in 2 years). The goal of our system is to identify new capabilities using the already existing ones and to fuzzyfy them. To do this we have defined a set of fuzzy rules that take as input numeric values from the existing capabilities and create symbolic values for the new ones. An example for the reasoning that takes place in this stage would be: "If the resolution is big and the screen size is big the video suitability is very high". This reasoning will be modelled with fuzzy rules. The main problem we have encountered using fuzzy rules is that we need to fuzzify the crisp variables encountered in the databases (in our case WURFL). This raises some challenging questions. What do we consider a "big" screen size? How can we identify what characteristics are inherent of the average mobile device? These concepts are relative to the values of other device models. One screen is big if its height and width are larger than the average values of the other models. To answer these questions we would have to know the actual distribution of the market. Our proposed solution is to use popularity metrics to estimate the market share of the devices (in our case, we use Google Trends). Besides, all the device models can not have the same weight in the calculation, not all the device models have sold the same number of units. This is why the most popular models should have more weight during this calculation. In order to calculate the popularity of one device we have to adjust it with its "age". Popularity fades with the passing of time. Users tend to change their mobile phones frequently, drastically altering the perception of what is a big screen from one year to another. While this number does not represent the sale volume, it is often used as an indicator of the interest shown by the consumers in a specific model [12]. Due to the lack of data regarding the real sale volume for most mobile devices, it is one of the few available indicators. This trend value can change drastically from one location to another; the most popular devices are not the same in Japan and Europe. To tackle this problem we support the geolocation of the results to filter them according to the needs of the developers.

The device characterization process can be divided en three different steps: the initial data retrieval, the decay process and the automatic membership function generation. The first step consists on retrieving and formatting all the necessary data. This means to parse the WURFL database and to retrieve the Google Trends data for all the devices. This is a tedious process (it takes days to gather all the data) due to the IP address and account restrictions of Google Trends and must be done in a distributed way. The final result is a database with all the records of the trends for each device taking into account the geolocation.

```
function createBaseUniverse
Inputs:
    TRENDS is an association of key-value pairs where the keys are each distinct value of the target
    device feature, and the associated value is the summation of the trends
    for the devices with that feature value. The keys are ordered incrementally.
    NUM_OF_TERMS is the number of desired linguistic terms
Outputs:
    REGION_LIMITS is the location of the regions in the base universe

TOTAL_TRENDS ← Σᵢ₌₀ VALUES(TREND)

NUM_OF_REGIONS ← NUM_OF_TERMS - 1
IDEAL_TREND ← TOTAL_TRENDS / NUM_OF_REGIONS
ACCUMULATED_TREND ← 0
REGION_LIMITS ← empty set
CURRENT_VALUE ← first feature value in TRENDS

for CURRENT_REGION = 1 to NUM_OF_REGIONS do
    while ACCUMULATED_TREND <= CURRENT_REGION * IDEAL_TREND do
        CURRENT_TREND ← associated trend in TRENDS to CURRENT_VALUE
        ACCUMULATED_TREND += CURRENT_TREND
        CURRENT_VALUE ← next feature value in TRENDS
    end while
    add CURRENT_VALUE to REGION_LIMITS
end for
return REGION_LIMITS
```

**Algorithm 1.** Calculation of the base universe

Once we have all the data the next step is to process the trend values to take into account their "age". Older trend values have less weight in the accumulated trend value of each device, reflecting the transitory nature of the mobile device market. We have implemented two different strategies for the decay: LogarithmicDecay and ModelDecay. The first one uses a logarithmic function to calculate the decay. The value taken for logarithm base is the point where the trends will no longer have any weight in the calculation (5 years in our case) and while the function returns negative values no decay will be applied. Using this decay strategy, five year old trends will not be taken into account and the newer trends will not have any penalty.

The second strategy takes into account the phone plans of the principal telecommunication companies to try to model the mobile phone change cycle among users. We acknowledge that every user does not change its mobile phone at the end of the acquired mobile plan. We use the following values to calculate the decay: for the latest 15 months we take into account the 100% of the trend value.From 16 to 24 months we take into account the 90% of the trend value. From 25 to 36 months we take into account the 40% of the trend value. From 37 to 60 months we take into account the 10% of the trend value. More than 60 months we take into account the 5% of the trend value. We would like to use a more robust model to calculate the decay, but we have found that this is a good approximation. Once we have the processed data and the desired linguistic terms we can automatically generate the membership functions for those terms. The first step is to divide the data in regions (see Algorithm 1) that will mark the point where each membership function will have its highest value. While creating the regions the algorithm seeks to equally distribute the total trend value contained in each membership function, but usually this goal is not achieved in the first iteration.

```
function findBestUniverse
Inputs:
  REGION_LIMITS is the location of the regions in the base universe
Outputs:
  BEST_UNIVERSE is the universe with the best fitness

ALL_UNIVERSES ← every possible permutation generated by moving one step the limits contained in
REGION_LIMITS

for each PERMUTATION in ALL_UNIVERSES do
    if first region of PERMUTATION does not start in 0 then
        remove PERMUTATION from ALL_UNIVERSES
    for each REGION in PERMUTATION do
        if left limit of REGION > right limit of REGION then
            remove PERMUTATION from ALL_UNIVERSES
        elif left limit of REGION < right limit of previous REGION then
            remove PERMUTATION from ALL_UNIVERSES
    end for each
end for each

UNIVERSE_FITNESSES ← empty set

for each PERMUTATION in ALL_UNIVERSES
    PERMUTATION_FITNESS ← Σ_regions∈PERMUTATION |IDEAL_TREND − Σ_trends∈region trend |
    add PERMUTATION_FITNESS, PERMUTATION to UNIVERSE_FITNESSES
end for each
BEST_UNIVERSE ← first PERMUTATION in UNIVERSE_FITNESSES with lowest
PERMUTATION_FITNESS

return BEST_UNIVERSE
```

**Algorithm 2.** Calculation of the best possible universe

To solve this problem we generate every possible permutation by moving each of the initial region boundary one step to each side. For each universe we calculate its deviation from the ideal one (see Algorithm 2). First we discard inconsistent universes following these rules: A) If the first region in the universe does not start in the 0 point, then that universe is discarded. B) If the left boundary of a region in the universe starts after the right boundary, then that universe is discarded. C)If the left boundary of a region starts before the right boundary of a previous region, then that universe is discarded.

The second step is to calculate the deviation of each remaining universe. What we seek is to minimize the deviation from the ideal universe, thus, we select the universe with the lowest deviation. Once we have found the best universe we can finally build the membership functions for each linguistic term (see Algorithm 3). To do this we take into account that: A) The region boundaries mark the inflexion point from the ascending and descending curves of a linguistic term. B)The first linguistic term will only have a descending curve that will start in the left boundary of the first region and will end in the right boundary of the first region. C) The last linguistic term will only have an ascending curve that will start in the first boundary of the last region and will end in the right boundary of the last region. D) The ascending curves are calculated accumulating the trend values in a region. E) The descending curves are symmetrical to the ascending curves: $dc(x) = 1 - ac(x)$, where ac is the ascending curve and dc the descending curve.

```
function calculateMembershipFunctions
Inputs:
    BEST_UNIVERSE is the universe with the best fitness
Outputs:
    MEMBERSHIP_FUCTIONS the membership functions for the linguistic terms

LAST_CURVE ← empty set
MEMBERSHIP_FUNCTIONS ← empty set
for each REGION in BEST_UNIVERSE do
    ASCENDING_CURVE ← ac(x) = Σⁱ_{i=left_limit} TREND_i | x ∈ feature values in REGION
    DESCENDING_CURVE ← dc(x) = 1 - ac(x) | x ∈ feature values in REGION
    CURRENT_CURVE ← LAST_CURVE + DESCENDING_CURVE
    add CURRENT_CURVE to MEMBERSHIP_FUNCTIONS
    LAST_CURVE ← ASCENDING_CURVE
end for

add LAST_CURVE to MEMBERSHIP_FUNCTIONS

return MEMBERSHIP_FUNCTIONS
```

**Algorithm 3.** Calculation of the membership functions

# 4    Conclusions

In this paper we have presented a mechanism to automatically create membership functions using popularity metrics. We have also shown the results of this process, comparing the results of different mobile phones and different locations, and showing how the passing of time changes the relative perception of the characteristics of the devices. As future work we would like to implement some new decay functions and compare the results with the existing ones. We will also implement a new version of the membership function generation mechanism that will allow users to specify the percentage of the trends contained in each linguistic term.

**Acknowlegment.** This work has been supported by project grant TSI-020301-2008-2 (PIRAmIDE), funded by the Spanish Ministerio de Industria, Turismo y Comercio. We would like to thank the members of our laboratory that helped us recovering the trend data.

# References

[1]  Almeida, A., Orduña, P., Castillejo, E., Lopez-de-Ipiña, D., Sacristan, M.: Imhotep: an approach to user and device conscious mobile applications. Personal and Ubiquitous Computing (Journal) 15(4), 419–429 (2011), doi:10.1007/s00779-010-0359-8, ISSN: 1617-4909

[2]  Varian, H.R., Choi, H.: Predicting the Present with Google Trends. Google Research Blog (April 2, 2009),
     `http://googleresearch.blogspot.com/2009/04/predicting-present-with-google-trends.html`, available at SSRN:
     `http://ssrn.com/abstract=1659302`

[3]  Schmidt, T., Vosen, S.: Forecasting Private Consumption: Survey Based Indicators Vs. Google Trends. RUB, Dep. of Economics (2009)

[4]  Ginsberg, J.: Detecting influenza epidemics using search engine query data. Nature 457(7232), 1012–1014 (2008)

[5]  Seifter, A., Schwarzwalder, A., Geis, K., Aucott, J.: The utility of "Google Trends" for epidemiological research: Lyme disease as an example. Geospatial Health 4(2), 135–137 (2010)

[6]  Carneiro, H.A., Mylonakis, E.: Google trends: a web-based tool for real-time surveillance of disease outbreaks. Clinical Infectious Diseases 49(10), 1557 (2009)

[7]  Valdivia, A., Monge-Corella, S.: Diseases Tracked by Using Google Trends, Spain. Emerging Infectious Disease 16(1), 168 (2010)

[8]  Homaifar, A., McCormick, E.: Simultaneous design of membership functions and rule sets for fuzzy controllers using genetic algorithms. IEEE Transactions on Fuzzy Systems 3(2), 129–139 (1995)

[9]  Shimojima, K., Fukuda, T., Hasegawa, Y.: Self-tuning fuzzy modeling with adaptive membership function, rules, and hierarchical structure based on genetic algorithm. Fuzzy Sets and Systems 71(3), 295–309 (1995)

[10] Kim, C.J., Russell, B.D.: Automatic generation of membership function and fuzzy rule using inductive reasoning. In: Third International Conference on Industrial Fuzzy Control and Intelligent Systems, IFIS 1993, pp. 93–96 (1993)

[11] Nieradka, G., Butkiewicz, B.S.: A Method for Automatic Membership Function Estimation Based on Fuzzy Measures. In: Melin, P., Castillo, O., Aguilar, L.T., Kacprzyk, J., Pedrycz, W. (eds.) IFSA 2007. LNCS (LNAI), vol. 4529, pp. 451–460. Springer, Heidelberg (2007)

[12] Xu, K., et al.: Predict Market Share with Users' Online Activities Data: An Initial Study on Market Share and Search Index of Mobile Phone. In: PACIS 2010 Proceedings, Paper 30 (2010)

# A Social-Empowered Platform for Gathering Semantic Information

Angel Esteban-Gil[1], Francisco García-Sanchez[2], Rafael Valencia-García[3], and Jesualdo Tomás Fernández-Breis[3]

[1] Fundación para la Formación e Investigación Sanitarias de la Región de Murcia
C/Luis Fontes, 9 30003 Murcia (Murcia), Spain
`angel.esteban@ffis.es`
[2] Escola Tècnica Superior d'Enginyeria, Universitat de València,
46100, Burjassot (Valencia), Spain
`Francisco.Garcia-Sanchez@uv.es`
[3] Dpto. Informática y Sistemas, Facultad de Informática, Universidad de Murcia,
30100, Espinardo (Murcia), Spain
`{valencia,jfernand}@um.es`

**Abstract.** Social Networks constitute the key ingredient for the huge success of the so called Social Web or Web 2.0. In social networks, a user has the possibility to interact with other users without the need of meeting them. The value of social applications benefit from the network effect, which states that the value of a service to a user arises from the number of people using the service. However, the associated semantics for this kind of applications, delivered through tagging, is generally scarce, thus narrowing the range of permissible operations for exploiting these data. In this paper, we present a semantic-based social platform that incorporates the benefits of semantic Web technologies into traditional social environments. The value of the proposed framework is two-fold. First, the interaction of the users with the system gives rise to semantic content that can populate a knowledge base. Then, the social-side of the platform is improved by taking advantage of the captured semantics.

**Keywords:** Social Web, Semantic Web, Web 3.0, Social Networks.

## 1 Introduction

A common feature in most Web 2.0 [5] applications is the establishment of ties or linkages between the users of such applications, constituting social networks. The synergies between the users in a social network is a critical factor for the success of the Social Web. Unfortunately, the associated semantics for Web 2.0 applications, delivered through tagging, is generally scarce [4] and this lack of semantic data descriptions on Web 2.0 limits the complexity that these sites can achieve. The goal in the formulation of the Semantic Web [1] is markedly different. It aims at adding semantics to the data published on the Web (i.e., establish the meaning of the data), so that machines are able to process these data in a similar way a human can do.

M.D. Lytras et al. (Eds.): WSKS 2011, CCIS 278, pp. 534–539, 2013.
© Springer-Verlag Berlin Heidelberg 2013

In distinctive ways, the technologies of both Web 2.0 and the Semantic Web address the fundamental concept of socially shared meaning. In the last few years, it has become clear that the Semantic Web and Web 2.0 are natural complements of each other [2]. The combination of Semantic Web technologies with Web 2.0 application design patterns has given rise to the social-semantic Web, also referred to as Web 3.0. In line with this idea, in this paper we present a software platform that successfully combines both Web 2.0 concepts and Semantic Web technologies. Our framework combines a series of semantic-based software modules in a fully-fledged social application with the objective of capturing semantics at the point of data entry.

The rest of this paper is organized as follows. In Section 2, the fundamentals of the technologies employed in our research are described and different related research studies analyzed. The general framework that allows to gather semantic information with the assistance of social techniques is formulated in Section 3. Finally, conclusions and future work are put forward in Section 4.

## 2  Background

The focus of our work lies in the intersection between the research domains of knowledge capture and management, and collaborative and social Web applications. Ontologies and the Semantic Web constitute two key topics within the former research field. The Semantic Web can be seen as an extension of the current Web, in which information is given well-defined meaning, better enabling computers and people to work in cooperation [1]. Ontology learning and population are some of the main drawbacks for the success of the Semantic Web vision, which partly motivates this work. Web 2.0 and Social Networks are of paramount importance for the research on collaborative systems. The term "Web 2.0" is commonly associated with a cluster of technologies and design patterns that assist in developing Web applications that facilitate interactive information sharing, interoperability and collaboration on the World Wide Web [5]. The social networking construct is critical to the success of Web 2.0 applications [4]. The value of social applications benefit from the network effect, which states that the value of a service to a user arises from the number of people using the service [4]. However, the associated semantics for this kind of applications, delivered through tagging, is generally scarce, thus narrowing the range of permissible operations for exploiting these data.

In the last few years, it has become clear that the Semantic Web and Web 2.0 are natural complements to each other. The combination of Semantic Web technologies with Web 2.0 application design patterns has given rise to the social-semantic Web, also referred to as Web 3.0 [2]. The synergies between these two technological advances are bidirectional. The shortcomings of manual ontology building can be overcome by exploiting the collective intelligence of Web 2.0 applications, and the limitations of Web 2.0 applications associated with the lack of semantics in tagging can be surmounted by applying Semantic Web-based techniques.

The work presented here is inspired by Gruber's ideas [3]. The author distinguishes between "collected intelligence" and "collective intelligence". The Web 2.0 trend enables the collected intelligence, i.e., the mere pooling of contributions from individual users. Adding Semantic Web technology would allow to reach collective intelligence, i.e., a higher level of understanding constituted by answers, discoveries and other results not found in the original contributions. For this, semantic technologies can contribute in two ways: by adding structure to user data and by connecting the existing silos of data that characterize the Web 2.0 landscape. To succeed in the achievement of the social-semantic Web in general, and collective intelligence in particular, the challenge is partly a matter of the user interface [4]. In particular, the approach taken in our research is to capture semantics at the point of data entry, thus exploiting the interaction of users with the social network to gather the knowledge generated by them.

## 3   A Social Semantic Platform

The interaction between users and the vast majority of social platforms is through free-text fields, and the only way to structure data and organize the content is by means of tags. However, while tags in collaborative tagging systems serve primarily an indexing purpose, facilitating search and navigation of resources, it is the use of the same tags by more than one individual what have an impact on a collective classification schema. Besides, these tags are not usually based on formal models and lack in well defined semantics. The work presented here aims at facilitating the generation of shared and formal knowledge entities from the information introduced by users in their interaction with social applications. From the Semantic Web viewpoint, the ultimate goal is to be able to integrate the captured semantic information with an existing knowledge base augmenting the overall semantic resources available. From the Social Web perspective, the semantically-enhanced information gathered serves to improve the interactions between individuals within the collaborative environment by providing a richer understanding of their needs and motives and enabling the alignment of their common interests. With all, the proposed system architecture is divided into five interconnected functional modules (see Figure 1): knowledge manager, content manager, social network manager, recommender subsystem and social semantic platform. Next, each of these modules is described in detail.

### 3.1   Knowledge Manager

At the bottom of Figure 1 it is possible to appreciate that the whole system is sustained by a hybrid architecture that integrates an ontology-based knowledge base and a traditional relational database management system. While the users' registration information and other related data are stored in the relational database, the impact of the proposed platform lies on the use of a knowledge base to store all the information concerned with the application domain. Having such formalized data will empower the system to improve the way the contents generated by users are managed, providing added-value functionality to end users.

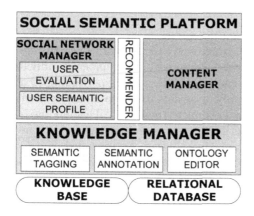

**Fig. 1.** Modules Architecture

The Knowledge Manager is responsible for facilitating the communication between the social platform and the knowledge base. This module is comprised of two main components, namely, the Semantic Tagging tool and the Semantic Annotation tool. These tools provide the means to classify and structure the contents as expected by the knowledge base. A further component form part of the Knowledge Manager module, the Ontology Editor. This tool enables users to increase and expand the knowledge in the knowledge base by adding concepts and instances not previously anticipated. Thus, the Knowledge Manager as a whole allows to both automate the semantic classification process and properly exploit the formalized content available.

### 3.2   Content Manager

Contents constitute one of the most important pieces in a social platform. Generally, these contents are directly generated by the users of the platform in the form of blog entries or comments. However, in a social semantic environment such as the one described here, the contents can also come from domain experts or even external data sources. Besides, in contrast to traditional social platforms, in a social semantic application most data items are stored in a knowledge base. Accordingly, in the proposed architecture (see Figure 1), the Content Manager lies directly on top of the Knowledge Manager layer. This represents the fact that the Content Manager exploits the tools of the Knowledge Manager module. In particular, it profits from the functioning of these tools in three ways: (i) the efficient storage of contents, (ii) the efficient recovery of information, and (iii) the generation of new knowledge through reasoning processes.

The Content Manager module is responsible for the intelligent management of the platform contents, a key factor for the successful achievement of the desired goals.

### 3.3  Social Network Manager

This module contains the logic to manage the social side of the platform. In particular, the elements necessary to deal with social groups are included in this module. A social group is comprised of a number of individuals with shared interests that interact with each other. Users pertaining to a group can generate private data that is only accessible to group members, which are the only ones allowed to evaluate and comment these data. This module is also concerned with other social-related utilities such as the management of favorites (authors, entries, tags, etc.) or the rating of users. An extended model of SIOC is employed to store social groups information. In particular, we have added into the SIOC specification the *"sioc:Evaluation"* class, which allows to store the evaluation given to the qualifiable elements of the platform, as well as the following properties: (i) *"sioc:has-favourite"* to express whether a content, user or tag has been chosen as favorite by a user, (ii) *"sioc:has-evaluate"* to represent the evaluation given by a user to other users or users' contents, and (iii) *"sioc:is-shared"* to indicate whether the content generated by a group of users is to be shared with other groups, or it is private. Additionally, the users in each social group are represented using the FOAF specification.

### 3.4  Recommender Subsystem

The Recommender module is placed on top of the Knowledge Manager, but also takes advantage of the contents generated in the Social Network Manager and the Content Manager modules. In fact, three main elements are considered when defining a recommendation: (i) the semantic classification of the information supplied by the users, (ii) the users' semantic profile, and (iii) the users' evaluation score, which aggregates the evaluation of the entries produced by them. Two types of recommendations are distinguished as follows:

– **Contents recommendation.** The user profile represents a high level description of the main topics of interests for a given user. Through the contents recommendation, the system informs users automatically when new content is available in the platform that can be valuable to them.
– **Users recommendation.** The gist of social applications is the possibility to build social networks. The proposed platform includes a users recommendation tool that allows the creation of social groups on the basis of the compatibility between the users' semantic profiles.

### 3.5  Social Semantic Platform

The Social Semantic Platform lies in the upper tier of the architecture and uses all the features that are provided by the modules in the lower layers of the picture. It constitutes the front-end of the application, what the end user sees and interacts with. As for other components of the architecture, the Social Semantic Platform must be customized to meet the requirements of the domain in which the tool is going to be applied.

# 4    Conclusions

Web 2.0 and the Semantic Web can be seen as two different approaches to improve the current Web and overcome its limitations. Besides, their combination can give rise to a new evolution of the Web named the social-semantic Web: *"in a social-semantic web, certain formally representable parts of human meaning can be encoded and reasoned about via the tools of the semantic web, but can also be curated and maintained via the social, community-oriented techniques of Web 2.0"* [2]. The framework proposed here represents a further step toward the integration of the Social and the Semantic Web and the achievement of the social-semantic Web. It combines a social platform with a ontology-based knowledge repository in order to manage the information inputted by the users of a social network at the knowledge level. If we return our attention to our original goal of reaching the "collective intelligence" conceived by Gruber, the use of controlled natural language interfaces and natural language processing techniques to capture semantically-enhanced information at the point of data entry leads to a system having the means to provide added-value services to users. This approach allows the system to enact more powerful and precise searches, and assists in providing a more sophisticated, knowledge-based recommender system.

**Acknowledgments.** This work has been partially supported by the Spanish Ministry for Science and Innovation through project TIN2010-18650.

# References

1. Berners-Lee, T., Hendler, J., Lassila, O.: The semantic web. Scientific American, 34–43 (May 2001)
2. Greaves, M., Mika, P.: Semantic web and web 2.0. Journal of Web Semantics 6(1), 1–3 (2008)
3. Gruber, T.: Collective knowledge systems: Where the social web meets the semantic web. Journal of Web Semantics 6(1), 4–13 (2008)
4. Hendler, J.A., Golbeck, J.: Metcalfe's law, web 2.0, and the semantic web. Journal of Web Semantics 6(1), 14–20 (2008)
5. O'Reilly, T.: What is web 2.0: Design patterns and business models for the next generation of software (September 2005), http://oreilly.com/web2/archive/what-is-web-20.html

# Recommendation of Personalized Learning Contents Supported by Semantic Web Technologies

Jesualdo Tomás Fernández-Breis[1], Francisco Frutos-Morales[1],
Angel Esteban Gil[2], Dagoberto Castellanos-Nieves[3], Rafael Valencia-García[1],
Francisco García-Sánchez[1], and María del Mar Sánchez-Vera[4]

[1] Facultad de Informática, Universidad de Murcia, 30100 Murcia, Spain
jfernand@um.es, ffm98973@um.es, valencia@um.es, frgarcia@um.es
[2] Fundación para la Formación e Investigación Sanitaria, 30003 Murcia, Spain
angel.esteban@carm.es
[3] Grupo MODO, Universidad de Granada, 18071 Granada, Spain
dcastellanos@ugr.es
[4] Grupo GITE, Universidad de Murcia, 30100 Murcia, Spain
mmarsanchez@um.es

**Abstract.** Information and Communication Technologies are changing educational processes in several ways and making possible new options for longlife learning. One important issue is to provide mechanisms for the design of contents adapted to the needs and preferences of individuals, that is, providing personalized courses. In this paper we present a recommendation module based on semantic web technologies that combines the semantic modelling of both learning objects and learning objectives. We also describe how the recommendation module has been included in two eLearning systems developed by our research group, for the recommending reinforcement contents and supporting the design of on-demand courses.

**Keywords:** eLearning, Semantic Web, Ontology, Recommendation.

## 1 Introduction

Information and Communication Technologies (ICT) are producing a revolution in social behaviour. ICTs allow to improve many traditional processes, making possible the automation of repetitive tasks and enabling the access to services from anywhere and at anytime. The development of ICTs has also affected the educational sector with the development of eLearning. The main properties of eLearning are: the physical separation of the learner and the teacher in most of the educational process, the use of technical media that enables the communication between learner and teacher, as well as the exchange of educational contents, and the significant cognitive and instrumental interactivity.

The current educational, social and economic context requires eLearning solutions to facilitate longlife learning. In Higher Education, undergraduate studies

M.D. Lytras et al. (Eds.): WSKS 2011, CCIS 278, pp. 540–545, 2013.
© Springer-Verlag Berlin Heidelberg 2013

tend to provide general skills, whereas specialized ones are acquired through postgraduate degrees. Besides, professionals need to get involved in training programmes in order to adapt their skills to changes in the requirements of their companies. Since such professionals do not usually have time to attend on-site courses, eLearning-based solutions become fundamental. On the other hand, such professionals have acquired a series of skills through their previous learning activities and such skills are likely to be different for two people working for the same company or playing a similar role in different ones. Moreover, due to personal preferences and the needs of the company, the skills to be acquired may be different. This means that there is not only a need for eLearning solutions but each worker might need a different course.

In this paper we describe an approach for recommending learning contents adapted to the needs and preferences of individuals. This approach uses semantic web technologies [1], which meet the requirements for the devevelopment of eLearning systems [7] and that have been applied in Education with different purposes [3]. This approach is based on the semantic modelling of learning objects and the semantic modelling of the learning objectives of individuals.

## 2    The Recommendation Approach

In this section, we describe the method used for recommending contents. First, we will describe the learning objects that will be used. Then, the approach for modelling preferences will be presented. Finally, the algorithm used for making the recommendations will be described.

### 2.1    The Semantic Learning Objects Repository

SICARA [4] is a semantic repository of learning contents. The contents are represented in SICARA as learning objects, which are any entity, digital or non-digital, that may be used for learning, education or training[6]. The semantic representation of SCORM objects was enabled by a semantic extension done to the SCORM standard by our research group. SICARA permits the annotation of both the metadata and the text fields of the learning objects. For this purpose, SICARA makes use of domain ontologies implemented in the Web Ontology Language (OWL[1]). Such ontologies must represent knowledge about domains for which the learning objects have been defined. An annotation in SICARA consists then in associating a class of an ontology to a metadata or to a piece of text. The repository of such semantic annotations will play a very important role in this approach, since those annotated learning objects will be the ones used for the recommendations.

### 2.2    Representation of the Learning Preferences

The design of the personalized contents will be based on the preferences of the individuals, which will be the search criteria. Such preferences are series of

---

[1] http://www.w3.org/TR/owl-ref/

concepts from existing ontologies. In this context, a preference means a knowledge area of learning interest. We have developed an ontology that models the learning preferences of an individual. The formal model permits to represent, store and exploit the learning preferences in a semantic way so that both the objects and the preferences will be managed in the same technological space. This ontology is simple and permits the modelling of the relation between invividuals and domain concepts through preferences. In this sense, a person may have preferences, and each preference consists of a concept that belongs to a domain ontology and each learning preference has a priority. Such concepts represent knowledge areas of interest for the person.

## 2.3    The Recommendation Algorithm

The input to the recommendation algorithm is both the semantic repository and the semantic representation of the preferences of an individual and the output is a set of recommended learning objects. The algorithm returns the set of learning objects that provides the best coverage for the set of preferences. This algorithm (see Figure 1) makes use of a similarity function [2] that compares the concepts included in the preferences with the annotations of the learning objects.

```
select_objects (preferences: PR, objects: R, real: threshold)
{ for each element(i) in PR
    for each element(j) in R
        annotations(j) = getAnnotation(R(j))
            for each element(k) in annotations(j)
                if (similarity (PR(i),annotations(j,k))>= threshold) then
                    selected_objects.add(R(j))
    return selected_objects)}
```

**Fig. 1.** The recommendation algorithm

The similarity function (see Figure 2) returns a value between 0(least similar) and 1(most similar) for each pair of concepts. This function permits the comparison of concepts from the same ontology, so that it will return 0 for concepts from different ones. In order to compare the similarity between two concepts, the function uses the taxonomic distance of both concepts in the ontology, the similarity between their labels and how similar their respective sets of properties are. Moreover, the value of the parameters cp1, cp2 and cp3 is between 0 and 1 and cp1+cp2+cp3=1. Such parameters permit to adjust the function according to the desired similarity policy.

```
concept_similarity(c1,c2)=
    cp1*tax_distance(c1, c2) + cp2*prop_sim(c1, c2) +cp3*linguistic_sim(c1, c2)
```

**Fig. 2.** The similarity function

Thus, the recommendation method consists on searching for those objects annotated with the preferences of the individual. For each concept included in the set of preferences, we will obtain the most similar concept from the annotations of the learning object. If such similarity is greater than the similarity threshold, then the concept is considered similar to the preference and that learning object is included in the recommendation list. Once the set of objects of interest has been identified, the individual may select the ones she prefers to create the course with.

# 3   Applications of the Recommendation Module

The algorithm described in the previous section has been implemented in Java and as a result we have obtained the SELCOR library. In this section, we describe how such module has been integrated into previously developed eLearning tools with different purposes.

## 3.1   Recommendation of Reinforcement Contents

The Ontology eLearning Evaluation (OeLE) platform [2,5] proposes semantic methods for supporting assessment. Technologically speaking, the platform uses ontologies, semantic annotations and state-of-the-art semantic similarity functions in order to calculate such similarity. In OeLE, each semantic annotation consists on associating one or more elements of a domain ontology to the question or to the student's answer. For the implementation of the ontologies, OeLE uses OWL. The OeLE platform is able to mark exams and generating semantic feedback to the students. The feedback consists on the list of knowlege items that have been acquired and not acquired by the students. However, OeLE was not able to include reinforcement contents in its feedback (see Figure 3).

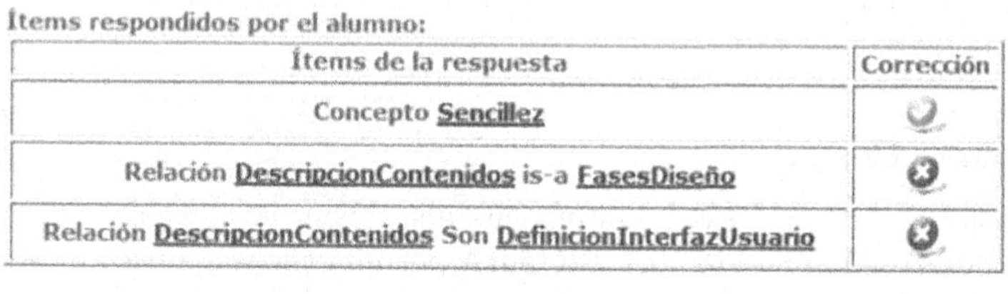

**Fig. 3.** Example of original feedback in OeLE, showing the right and wrong answers of the student

In order to integrate the recommendation module into OeLE we had to look for equivalencies between the entities managed by OeLE and SELCOR. Given that SELCOR requires a set of learning preferences and given that the feedback generated by OeLE includes a set of non-acquired knowledge entities, which correspond to concepts of domain ontologies, we developed a middleware that transforms the non-acquired entities into learning preferences. Therefore, useful queries over the semantic learning object repository can be issued.

An example of such enriched feedback is shown in Figure 4. There, we can see that a series of pdf files are recommended to one particular student. For each learning object, its associated annotations are also displayed. For example, the file "DiseñodeMateriales.pdf" is useful for reinforcing the concepts phases of design("FasesDiseño"), bases of design("BasesDiseño") and design of concepts(DiseñoContenidos"), which had been previously identified as not acquired by the student. By proceeding in this way, the student knows the learning purpose of each recommended object.

Objetos a consultar:

| Nombre Objeto | Anotaciones |
|---|---|
| DiseñoDeMateriales.pdf | Concepto: **FasesDiseño** Concepto: **BasesDiseño** Concepto: **DiseñoContenidos** |
| FasesDeDiseño.pdf | Concepto: **FasesDiseño** Concepto: **Fuentes** |
| Herramientas.pdf | Concepto: **Herramientas** |
| GuiasDeUso.pdf | Concepto: **Recomendaciones** Concepto: **Fuentes** |

**Fig. 4.** Example of reinforcement contents suggested by SELCOR in OeLE

**Fig. 5.** (left) defining preferences in SICARA; (right) example of recommended learning objects

## 3.2  Course Design

An extension to the SICARA system has also been performed in this research work. As described in Section 2.1, SICARA permits the semantic annotation and management of SCORM learning objects. The original system provided search facilities based on free text, guided by the SCORM ontology or guided by the domain ontologies available in the system. Such search options would return the learning objects that matched a particular query, but SICARA was not able to recommend objects for a particular user profile. This new extension permits users to define their learning preferences (see the left part of Figure 5) by selecting the desired concepts from the ontologies available in the system.

Once the preferences have been defined, the SELCOR module looks for the appropriate contents and returns a set of learning objects (see the right part of Figure 5). Then, the user selects through the "new course" tab which ones must be part of her course. Finally, SICARA generates a new SCORM course that contains the selected learning objects, that is, the personalized course.

# 4 Conclusions

The current social and economic context requires highly trained workers, but such workers cannot follow traditional presential learning programmes given their limited availability of time. In addition to this, such workers are likely to be interested in parts of existing courses since they must have acquired some knowledge and skills of such courses through previous courses or professional experience. Consequently, approaches for facilitating personalized longlife learning have become crucial. In this paper, we have presented an approach that addresses such problems and provides a solution based on Semantic Web technologies. This approach represents both the learning preferences and the learning objects in a semantic way, so algorithms based on semantics that recommend suitable learning objects from existing courses to the individuals can be proposed. As a result of this work, the SELCOR library has been obtained and integrated into two existing systems, thus enabling the recommendation of reinforcement tests as part of students' feedback, and the design of personalized courses.

**Acknowledgement.** This work has been possible thanks to the Seneca Foundation, through grants 08756/PI/08 and 15295/PI/10.

# References

1. Berners-Lee, T., Hendler, J., Lassila, O.: The Semantic Web. Scientific American, 34–43 (May 2001)
2. Castellanos-Nieves, D., Fernández-Breis, J.T., Valencia-García, R., Martínez-Béjar, R., Iniesta, M.: Semantic Web Technologies for Supporting Learning Assessment. Information Sciences 181(9), 1517–1537 (2011)
3. Devedzic, V.: Semantic Web and Education. Springer, Heidelberg (2006)
4. Esteban-Gil, A., Fernández-Breis, J., Castellanos-Nieves, D., Valencia-García, R., García-Sanchez, F.: Semantic enrichment of SCORM metadata for efficient management of educative contents. Procedia - Social and Behavioral Sciences 1(1), 927–932 (2009)
5. Frutos-Morales, F., Sánchez-Vera, M., Castellanos-Nieves, D., Esteban-Gil, A., Cruz-Corona, C., Prendes-Espinosa, M., Fernández-Breis, J.: An extension of the OeLE platform for generating semantic feedback for students and teachers. Procedia - Social and Behavioral Sciences 2(2), 527–531 (2010)
6. Learning Technology Standards Committee: IEEE Standard for Learning Object Metadata (2002), http://ltsc.ieee.org/wg12/par1484-12-1.html
7. Stojanovic, L., Staab, S., Studer, R.: Elearning based on the Semantic Web. In: WebNet 2001 - World Conference on the WWW and Internet, pp. 23–27 (2001)

# The Role of ICT in the New (Virtual) Working Space

## An Empirical Investigation on Enterprise 2.0

Mariano Corso[1], Luca Gastaldi[1], and Antonella Martini[2]

[1] Polytechnic of Milano, P.zza Leonardo da Vinci 32,
20133 Milano, Italy
{Mariano.Corso,Luca.Gastaldi}@polimi.it
[2] University of Pisa, Via Diotisalvi 2,
56100 Pisa, Italy
A.Martini@ing.unipi.it

**Purpose.** The article explores how ICT supports the open enterprise approach, which is emerging empirically as one of Enterprise 2.0 model. More specifically, it explores (1) the applications characteristics - in terms of drivers and barriers - adopted by companies to support E2.0, and (2) the different ways of integrating applications in the E2.0.

**Design/methodology/approach.** The article is based on evidence from 52 case studies. In addition, an online community (Enterprise20.it) was developed in order to promptly receive cues and suggestions to refine the research.

**Findings.** Four application areas for the E2.0 have been identified and explored in details, in terms of the main sponsors of the initiatives, the motivations and the barriers to introduction of E2.0. For each area, different levels of maturity have been identified, and explicative variables discussed. Four different levels of integration of the approaches to E2.0 emerged, each representing a different integrating path.

**Practical implications.** The article provides empirically grounded and actionable knowledge (guidelines) for companies to design and implement new ICT-enabled (virtual) working environments able to extend the boundaries of their knowledge creation to their mobile workers, customers and suppliers.

**Originality/value.** The article, which is based on evidence from the E2.0 Observatory in Italy, reports an extensive empirical investigation of the phenomenon during three years and proposes a framework to interpret the E2.0. It breaks up the open box, highlighting the role of ICT in terms of processes and governance approaches.

**Keywords:** ICT-driven innovation; enterprise 2.0; case studies.

## 1 Introduction

The term Enterprise 2.0 derives from Web 2.0 and is often used to indicate the introduction and implementation of social software inside a company and the social and organisational changes associated with it. The term was coined by Andrew McAfee, a Professor at Harvard Business School, to refer to simple, free platforms for self-expression (McAfee`s blog, 24 March 2006). He soon followed up with a refined

M.D. Lytras et al. (Eds.): WSKS 2011, CCIS 278, pp. 546–556, 2013.

definition: Enterprise 2.0 is the use of emergent social software platforms within companies, or between companies and their partners or customers (McAfee's blog, 27 May 2006).

Since then, it has been given different definitions by scholars and practitioners (Hinchcliffe, 2006). We think that E2.0 calls for a broader vision of either organisational and technological model evolution, which includes the design of an adaptive architecture (SOA and BPM), Web 2.0 collaboration tools and the virtual workspace as enabling platforms for connections and processes:

> *E2.0 is a set of organizational and technological approaches steered to enable new organization models, based on open involvement, emergent collaboration, knowledge sharing, internal/external social network development and exploitation.*
> (Corso, Martini and Giacobbe, 2008)

The emerging needs (Davenport, 2005; Tapscott and Williams, 2006) that E2.0 tries to respond to can be divided according to six key dimensions (Corso et al., 2008b):

- *Open belonging*: people increasingly feel (and actually are) as members of extended dynamic networks rather than single organisations
- *Social networking*: people increasingly need to develop and maintain these dynamic networks of relations, which are progressively becoming important assets to develop (Cross et al., 2005; Surowiecki, 2004)
- *Knowledge networks*: to prevent their knowledge and skills from being surpassed workers must be able to build their own network to have access to knowledge and information from different sources, both explicit and implicit (Dearstyne, 2007)
- *Emergent collaboration*: in an increasingly fast and unpredictable competitive scenario, people need to create cooperative settings in a fast, flexible way, even outside formal organisational patterns
- *Adaptive reconfigurability*: in response to the endless changes taking place in corporate policies and strategies, and people need to quickly reconfigure their own processes and activities
- *Global mobility*: people spend an increasingly large share of their time far from the workplace and often in a state of mobility. New ICTs enable them to be connected in any place and at any time of day through their own network of tools, thus making their workspace and working time more flexible

This article intends to explore the following research questions:

- RQ1. what are the applications adopted by companies to support the E2.0?
- RQ2. are there different ways of integrating applications? Can a developmental path towards complete integration be identified?

## 2    Methodology

52 case studies were carried out during 2009-2010 period through a questionnaire and direct interviews to the management of medium/large-sized Italian companies (manufacturing, banking, PA, assurance, pharmaceutical, services).

In order to ensure comparable results, the case study protocol was structured in three sections, namely strategy, organization and technology, with a total numer of 71 questions. The comprehensibility and completeness of the questionnaires were tested in advance in pilot interviews. The interviews, of approximately one and a half hours, were carried out (after returning the questionnaires) either by telephone or face-to-face. All the interviews were recorded and transcribed; subsequently, a report was prepared. Preliminary results have been discussed and validated through the Enterprise20.it, the online community created for the participating firms, vendors and experts.

# 3    The Application Areas for the Enterprise 2.0 (RQ1)

The analysis pointed out four application areas for E2.0. For each area, the specific drivers and barriers enhancing and limiting the effectiveness of E2.0 tools have been identified. The four areas are:

- *Social Network & Community (SN&C):* support in managing and creating relationships between individuals through tools promoting discussion, the exchange of ideas and involvement in networks of extended acquaintances, including those beyond company borders (blogs, forums, social network tools, expert research, advanced user profiles, etc.);
- *Unified Communication & Collaboration* (UC&C): support in managing each type of communication and collaboration, both within and outside the company, uniformly and independently of the media adopted to transmit contents (web, landlines, mobile, TV) through specific infrastructures and tools (audio/web/videoconferencing, instant messaging, VoIP, etc.);
- *Enterprise Content Management* (ECM): support in managing contents and documents within and outside an organization through tools that improve accuracy, accessibility and integrity (Web content management, document management, record management, enterprise search, etc.);
- *Adaptive Enterprise Architecture* (AEA): support of process flexibility and reconfigurability consistent with strategic organizational changes using advanced and flexible process management tools and technologies (BPM – Business Process Management), the construction and management of application architecture services (SOA – Service Oriented Architecture and mash-up) and the use of application services delivered by third parties (SaaS – Software as a Service).

These 4 application areas go beyond simply responding to immediate needs, and enable models and organizational rationales that answer the longer term needs of individuals and organizations that are at the foundation of the E2.0 phenomenon. Traditionally, these areas have not been a part of *"main stream"* ICT investments, and even now represent only average levels of investment, lower in comparison to overall ICT spending.

## 3.1    Social Network and Community

By Social Network & Community, we mean all the initiatives whose goal is to promote relationships within and outside the company. In fact, individuals have an in increasingly greater need to develop and maintain a network of relationships, which represents an increasingly important asset for their professional effectiveness.

Through more consolidated tools (like forums), as well as through much more "innovative" ones (like social network platforms, social voting mechanisms, etc), it is possible to promote the creation and management of relationships, helping individuals to find and contact colleagues and experts within and outside the organization and to keep their profiles up to date regarding interests, competences and roles.

Influenced by the media hype of phenomena like Facebook or LinkedIn, many companies are considering the potential and the possibility of transferring the use of tools and trends originating from the Web into strictly professional areas as well. As previously reported, predictions made by CIOs offer values much higher than the growth the percentages of the last three years. In contrast to the 10% of "pioneer" CIOs who have always felt that these initiatives are important, nearly half (41%) of "converted" CIOs now see the future role of these initiatives as increasingly important. However, a fairly significant number still appear skeptical, maintaining that in the future as well, Social & Networking Communities will have a marginal role (49%).

Alongside the ICT Dept, the departments of Human Resources and Communication (27%) and Marketing and Sales (25%) are the biggest supporters of Social Network & Community initiatives. In many cases, the Top Management (22%) are the first to offer their support - though theirs is typically an inconsistent commitment concentrated mainly in the initial phases of project launching.

Many of the Social Network & Community initiatives are not limited to the confines of a single company, but also involve external players from a perspective of open membership: in 28% of companies surveyed, the initiative involved clients directly, and in 13% secure and selective access to suppliers was guaranteed for a richer and more effective experience. Finally, these tools are used more and more for the sales force (22%), thanks to the strong sponsorship by the Marketing and Sales department.

The motivations driving the introduction of Social Network & Community tools and paradigms are respectively, the increased need to feel a sense of belonging and an improvement in company climate (37%), the increased need for collaborative support (37%) and the increased need for improved customer relations (29%). The impacts on organizational services like efficiency and cost reduction are mainly indirect, tied to the creation of a social and organizational "infrastructure" acting as a catalyst in making relationships more flexible, with significant impacts in terms of adaptability toward change (15%) and timeliness of processes and decisions (18%).

As might be expected in light of the low level of maturity in these initiatives, the main barriers to their diffusion are the poor awareness of their potential (45%) and the resulting difficulty identifying and assessing the direct economic benefits (50%). Though time and costs can be fairly contained, the difficulties specifying and quantifying the benefits of the investment represent a fairly significant barrier, confirmed by the fact that, where these initiatives are adopted, the underlying motivations are related to the need to support organizational and strategic changes, rather to economic efficiency.

## 3.2    Unified Communication and Collaboration

By Unified Communication & Collaboration we mean those initiatives supporting the management of all types of communication, both within and outside the company, in a uniform way, which is independent from the means adopted to transmit contents through infrastructures and integrated tools.

In a progressively open and unpredictable competitive context, organizations must respond to the needs of the individual to create virtual environments for fast and flexible collaboration, even outside of the formal organizational frameworks. The technologies that we include under the name of Unified Communication & Collaboration offer the possibility for richer and faster interaction - both synchronous as well as synchronous. What's more, people are spending an increasing amount of their time in mobility and the current technologies offer the possibility to connect anywhere, giving greater flexibility as to where and when work takes place.

The applications for Unified Communication & Collaboration, conceived separately and as such fairly consolidated, are today brought together in an application suite which, thanks to integration, gives the user the ability of managing different communication channels and tools in a very flexible and uniform way. Moreover, from the company point of view, the convergence on IP networks of all the communication channels offers significant advantages in terms of management simplification and new service set-up and start times. The perception of CIOs is that the important role already played by these initiatives wil grow in the next three years. It is precisely the ability to respond to concrete needs that makes Unified Communication & Collaboration one of the most important areas for company investments. While 9% of CIOs are skeptical and continue to feel that the Unified Communication & Collaboration initiatives are of little importance now and in the future, the majority (91% overall) of CIOs are completely convinced of the importance of these initiatives.

There are many sponsors of these initiatives, ranging from Top Management (25%), to the Marketing & Sales Department (22%) and the Human Resources and Communication Department (21%), but it is also interesting to note that in a fairly significant number of cases, the request of adoption is coming directly from the final users.

As already observed with Social Network & Community initiatives, Unified Communication & Collaboration tools as well often extend beyond the borders of a single company, involving external players from a perspective of open "belonging". In 46% of cases, for example, the initiative involves clients directly, whereas 56% of companies surveyed guarantee suppliers access to information, documents and processes for a richer and more effective interaction. But it is in the management of the sales force that these innovative collaboration and communication rationales are increasingly more utilized (over 63%), thanks once again to the strong support from the Marketing and Sales Department.

Unified Communication & Collaboration responds first to the need to support collaboration (60%), efficiency and cost reduction (54%) and timeliness of processes and decisions (43%).

Once introduced, the greatest benefits in terms of productivity come from factors like the increased exploitation of flexible forms of work independent of the work place, or the reduction of trips or "business trip" expenses which can now be effectively substituted by other forms of communication or by videoconferencing services.

Though not as easily measured or immediately perceived, the benefits brought on by the introduction of new forms of relationships and transversal collaboration strategies are still very high.

The main barrier to Unified Communication & Collaboration is the level of investment and costs required to make effective the relative initiatives (37%).

### 3.3    Enterprise Content Management

By Enterprise Content Management we mean the initiatives supporting the management of informational assets, both inside and outside of the organization, through tools that improve accuracy, accessibility and integrity in the management of documents and contents in general. The growing attention to these tools derives from the increasingly intense need of individuals to have access to increasingly complex and variegated information both in terms of format and sources. Organizations find themselves having to promote rapid and flexible access, but at the same time secure access, to increasing volumes of unstructured content, which for their size and importance, today represent a value equal, if not superior to that of structured data coming from traditional transaction systems.

As previously noted, the perception of CIOs is that these initiatives have played an important role and will to an even greater extent in the next few years. The ability to respond to the concrete and immediate needs of individuals, and at the same time, to contribute to creating innovative organizational strategies makes Enterprise Content Management one of the areas in which - even in this period of crisis - companies are continuing to invest. Whereas 12% of CIOs remain skeptical as to the present and future importance of Enterprise Content Management initiatives, 88% overall are fully convinced of the future importance of these initiatives.

It is stressed the transversal support of Enterprise Content Management projects and their inclusion of *lines of business* as well, like the *Operation and Supply Chain department* (23%) amongst which the need is felt for a more systematic management of unstructured information. In this case the Human Resources and Communication Department (19%) and Top Management (21%) have an important sponsorship role.

As would be logically expected, these initiatives systematically involve suppliers and partners (67%) in an effort to go beyond company borders. There is a high level of openness towards clients (59%) and the sales force (50%).

The needs driving the adoption of Enterprise Content Management technologies are mainly operational and immediate in nature, like efficiency and cost reduction (51%); but important longer term needs include the support of knowledge management (50%), effectiveness in decision-making processes (35%) and innovation of products and services (18%).

Despite the progressive reduction of costs of application suites and the diffusion of Open Source platforms, the main perceived barrier to the diffusion of Enterprise Content Management remains the level of investment and costs required (49%). Criticalities are represented by the need for organizational changes (31%) and the resistance of final users to its use (28%), confirming the profound impact that these initiatives have on organizational behaviors.

Enterprise Content Management systems are amongst the first to have attempted to take on the hot topic of company knowledge management, in particular moving towards the centralization and retrievability of company documents. These tools have a good record and are now seen as an integral part of company information systems, as they have been able to clearly demonstrate their value. For this reason, it is possible even in the current context, to justify further internal changes, driven by varied maturity levels and the promise of eliminating the barriers obstructing their effective adoption within the company.

### 3.4    Adaptive Enterprise Architecture

In response to the continued changes in company polices and strategies, organizations and individuals feel the growing need to quickly reengineer work processes and environments: by   Adaptive Enterprise Architecture we intend all the initiatives aimed at responding to these needs, rendering company information systems more flexible and adaptable.

The Adaptive Enterprise Architecture initiatives analyzed are based on the application of new tools for process management (BPM), the creation and management of services for application architectures (SOA and mash-up) and the use of application services delivered by third parties (SaaS). In fact, these new technologies allow companies and in some cases the users themselves, to redefine and adapt processes with a dynamism, flexibility and customization not easily obtained with traditional technologies.

In the past, the Adaptive Enterprise Architecture initiatives were considered merely infrastructural investments. Today however, a growing number of CIOs give greater weight to the potential impact on the organization.

Beyond the understanding and strong commitment required by the ICT Department, the support of Top Management (26%) seems to be one of the fundamental requisites for the success of a project. From the business point of view, the realization of an Adaptive Enterprise Architecture means creating an organization able to support processes in increasingly flexible and customizable ways.

In many cases, Adaptive Enterprise Architecture initiatives are realized for the integrability of their IS with other external information systems in the management of value chain processes and transactions involving suppliers and partners (38%), clients (30%) and sales channels 38%.

The main needs driving the introduction of Adaptive Enterprise Architecture tools and strategies are: flexibility to change (46%), efficiency and cost reduction (44%) and effectiveness and timeliness of processes and decisions (34%).

The main barriers to Adaptive Enterprise Architecture are the level of investment necessary (39%), the poor knowledge of its potentials (27%), the difficulty evaluating economic benefits (25%) and the need for organizational change (28%).

The initiatives tied to Adaptive Enterprise Architecture are considered fundamental by a growing number of CIOs. The first steps often taken are the virtualization of infrastructures, the componentization of application portfolios and the creation of standard basic services common to all (like information for Single Sign-On, uniform search engines and document environments). But today the most radical interventions are often slowed down since they are difficultly justifiable from an economic viewpoint. There is instead a tendency to use a more incremental strategy: an increasing number of CIOs try to take the path of Adaptive Enterprise Architecture by small, evolutionary steps, taking into consideration alternative offer models like those of Cloud Computing and Software as a Service.

# 4    The Maturity Levels and Paths to Full Integration (RQ2)

## 4.1    Maturity Levels for the Areas

In order to better understand if there are different integration paths to be taken for the 4 application areas of E2.0, the level of adoption of these environments has been mapped out, distinguishing between the following five growing levels of maturity of the initiatives:

- *absence*: no tools are present in the company;
- *experimentation*: few tools are present and used in the testing phase;
- *emerging development*: there are some tools that are not used to their fullest and integrated (like   Social Network & Community tools that are little integrated into the management system of company knowledge and relations, Unified Communication & Collaboration tools used as stand-alone);
- *uniform development*: there are many tools integrated amongst each other and used effectively in each environment;
- *strategic development*: the tools present, besides being used effectively and integrated amongst each other with specific objectives, are also integrated with processes and other company business applications.

The comparison between the various initiatives (Figure 1) highlights how yet again Enterprise Content Management and Unified Communication & Collaboration are the most mature areas of the four, with nearly 40% of companies currently involved in a unified or strategic Enterprise Content Management initiative, and  26% in Unified Communication & Collaboration. The picture is slightly different for Adaptive Enterprise Architecture and above all for Social Network & Community, as 21% and 8% of companies respectively are actually moving forward with these important initiatives. The adoption of these initiatives represents the exception more than the rule, as in the majority of cases companies have no active projects underway.

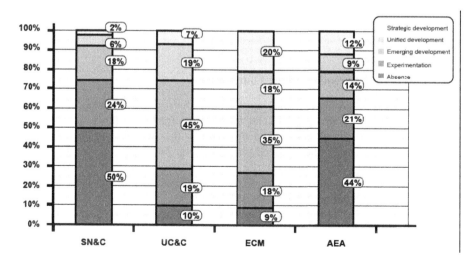

**Fig. 1.** The maturity levels of the initiatives in the various areas

The level of maturity in the various areas is often attributable to governance choices as well. One of the most frequently cited barriers is the necessity for organizational change, which should be managed through the creation of specific roles or procedures. In order to strategically manage these initiatives, dedicated budgets, explicit development plans and systems of governance must be available to allow their coherent and integrated management.

The increased presence of development plans with at least annual horizons in particular in Unified Communication & Collaboration and Enterprise Content Management (nearly 70%) is a first sign of organizational maturity, along with the more than 30% of cases, and the mechanisms established for the management of initiatives. On the other hand, Adaptive Enterprise Architectures and even more so, Social Networking & Community are still experiencing delays both in the definition of development and budget plans, as well as in the creation of standard governance systems.

In the majority of cases (51%), the ICT Department plays a key role in anticipating and soliciting needs and in promoting and implementing the different initiatives along with the *lines* and suppliers involved. In order to create greater understanding regarding the potential strategic impacts of Enterprise 2.0 on business, participation in internal work tables on particular topics or the creation of programs that promote greater awareness are among the most effective strategies cited. Only in a mere 13% of cases, the department has no current role in the initiatives that are simply left to the proactivity of the single business lines and suppliers. The remaining 36% respond reactively, guaranteeing operational support in the implementation of the lines or suppliers, or supporting standards chosen to guarantee continuity and coherence with existing infrastructures.

Another interesting aspect involves the role of suppliers in the development of this type of initiative. From the CIO perspective, the average supplier contribution especially for more advanced and less consolidated topics is still of little significance and for the most part reactive, especially in the case of Social Network & Community, where consolidated offer models are missing. Even for the more mature Enterprise Content Management environment, the percentage of suppliers considered proactive remains low.

## 4.2    Adoption Approaches in the Four Areas

We tried to understand the company approach on the path toward Enterprise 2.0. In this analysis, for each of the cases, all the projects related to the four areas were considered. Four different paths have emerges as the one able to lead to a full ICT-based integration of organizational processes (Fig. 2):

- *Embryonic model (40%):* there are either few experimental services or the services are not integrated with each other;
- *Focused model (36%):* there is an integrated and strategic development, but only in one area;
- *Composite model (21%):* there is elevated development of two areas;
- *Complete model (3%):* most of the areas are characterized by an advanced level of unified and strategic development.

The majority of companies are still in the embryonic stage or at most the focused stage (76%). Among the focused companies, the ECM model is the most widely applied (16%), followed by UCC (13%) and AEA (7%). It is important to point out the current absence of a focused model based solely on the Social Network & Community area.

The next developmental step, i.e. expansion in another environment, will lead to a sharp increase in organizational and infrastructural complexity, but on the other hand, will offer new synergies between the single environments. An analysis of various composite models (21%) shows a strict correlation between the two specific areas of Unified Communication & Collaboration and Enterprise Content Management. In 7% of cases, in fact, companies are moving forward with initiatives in coordinated fashion in precisely these two areas. The other viable combinations analyzed involve Enterprise Content Management paired with Adaptive Enterprise Architecture (8%) and Enterprise Content Management with Social Network & Community (4%). Similar combinations with Unified Communication & Collaboration are less common – counting 1% each for Adaptive Enterprise Architecture and for Social Network & Community. Lastly, still few companies appear to have adopted a complete model (3%).

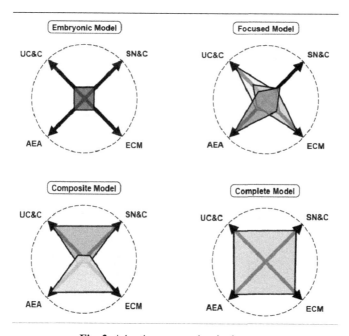

**Fig. 2.** Adoption approaches in the areas

# References

Anderson, C.: The Long Tail: Why the Future of Business Is Selling Less of More. Hyperion, New York (2006)

Benkler, Y.: The Wealth of Networks: How Social Production Transforms Markets and Freedom. Yale University Press (2006)

Chesbrough, H.: Open Innovation: The New Imperative for Creating and Profiting from Technology. Harvard Business School Press, Boston (2003)

Corso, M., Martini, A., Pesoli, A.: Enterprise 2.0: What Models are Emerging? Results from a 70 case-based research. International Journal of Knowledge and Learning 4(6), 595–612 (2008) ISSN 1741-1009

Corso, M., Giacobbe, A., Martini, A.: Rethinking Knowledge Management: the Role of ICT and the Rise of the Virtual Workspace. International Journal of Learning and Intellectual Capital 5(4) (2008)

Corso, M., Martini, A., Pesoli, A.: Evolving from 1.0 to Enterprise 2.0: an Interpretative Review. Empirical Stages and Approaches to the New (Virtual) Working Environment. In: Litras, M., Damiani, E., Ordoñez-de-Pablo, P. (eds.) Web 2.0: the Business Models, pp. 201–236. Springer, US (2009) ISBN 978-0-387-85894-4

Cross, R., Liedtka, J., Weiss, L.: A practical guide to social networks. Harvard Business Review 83, 124–132 (2005)

Davenport, T.H.: Thinking for a living: how to get better performances and results from knowledge workers. Harvard Business School Press, Boston (2005)

Dearstyne, B.W.: Blogs, mashups, & wikis. Oh, my! Information Management Journal 41, 24–33 (2007)

Hinchcliffe, D.: Web 2.0 for the enterprise? Enterprise web 2.0 blog entry (2006), http://blogs.zdnet.com/Hinchcliffe/?p=3 (accessed March 27, 2007)

McAfee, A.P.: Enterprise 2.0: The dawn of emergent collaboration. MIT Sloan Management Review 47, 21–28 (2006)

McKinsey: How business are using Web 2.0: a McKinsey global survey. McKinsey Quarterly (2007), http://www.mckinseyquarterly.com/How_businesses_are_using_Web _20_A_McKinsey_Global_Survey_1913_abstract (accessed April 29, 2008)

Surowiecki, J.: The wisdom of crowds: why the many are smarter than the few and how collective wisdom shapes business, economics, societies and nations (2004)

Tapscott, D., Williams, A.D.: Wikinomics: how mass collaboration changes everything. Portfolio Penguin Group, New York (2006)

Tyndale, P.: A taxonomy of knowledge management software tools: origins and applications. Evaluation and Programm Planning 25, 183–190 (2002)

# How the User Behavior Is Affected by the Use of Secondary Screens on Interactive Television: An Affective Usability Dimension

Javier Burón Fernández[1], Beatriz Sainz De Abajo[2], José Miguel Ramirez[1], Enrique García Salcines[1], and Carlos de Castro Lozano[1]

[1] Department of Computer Science, University of Córdoba, Campus of Rabanales Madrid-Cádiz Road, km.396-A, Albert Einstein Building, 14071 Córdoba, Spain
{egsalcines,jburon,ma1caloc}@uco.es,josemiguel@cpmti.es
[2] Department of Communications and Signal Theory and Telematics Engineering, Higher Technical School of Telecommunications Engineering, University of Valladolid, Campus Miguel Delibes, Paseo de Belén nº 15, 47011 Valladolid, Spain
{beasai}@tel.uva.es

**Abstract.** Television (TV) has deeply influenced on human behavior so far, however Internet is changing the way that people interact with TV. One important change has been leveraged by the wide adoption of small and powerful mobile computers, such as smartphones and tablets. It has raised the opportunity to employ them in multi-user and multi-device interactive television (iTV) scenarios. Two important research questions are: Do these devices compete or cooperate for the attention and the benefit of the user? Most notably, how multi-device interaction is appreciated in multi-user scenarios? Previous research has raised and considered the above research issues and questions for dual screen set-ups in the work environment. Broadly it is explored multi-device user interface configurations in the context of a leisure environment and for entertainment applications. Our objective is to measure the affective usability dimension in the field of iTV and how this kind of new conceptual interaction can change the user behavior. In this paper, a system to control and share the TV content with a smartphone or tablet is defined and the methodology to evaluate this system is presented.

**Keywords:** Interactive Television, iTV, user experience, user behaviour.

## 1 Introduction

Internet and new interfaces are changing the way that people interact with TV. Dan O'Sullivan defines the iTV: *"Interactive Television is an oxymoron. On the other hand, television provides the most common ground in our culture for ordinary conversation, which is arguably the most enjoyable interaction a person has. We should try to leverage the power of television while creating some channel back from the audience to provide content, control or just a little conversation."* [1] The evolution of this oxymoron is difficult to guess but first commercial approaches are

M.D. Lytras et al. (Eds.): WSKS 2011, CCIS 278, pp. 557–562, 2013.
© Springer-Verlag Berlin Heidelberg 2013

bringing PC and Mobile applications to TV with a "face cleaning" to be controlled with a classic remote controller [2,3]. However the wide adoption of small and powerful mobile computers, such as smartphones and tablets, has leveraged the opportunity of employing them for interact with iTV in simple and multi-user scenarios [4,5].

One of the main objectives of this research is to measure the affective usability dimension [6] over multi-device interaction concepts to control and share content in iTV simple and multi-user scenarios to answer some important research questions like: How and Why the devices compete or cooperate for the affect of the user when he/she interacts with iTV in a leisure environment? This study tries to tackle this question thorough the evaluation.

Multi-device & ubiquity scenarios are coming to our extended living room. Consider the following scenario: "Peter goes back home by walking after a hard day of work. In the way, he is watching a boring video on his smartphone and suddenly he received a phone call. It is her girlfriend Sarah, from her parent's house, she is watching a really interesting video on her TV and she wants Peter to watch it too, so she 'transfers' her content to Peter's smartphone to watch the content together and to be able to comment it as they go via videoconference. Someone steps into Peter to ask him for a location, before answering, Peter pauses the video and automatically the Sarah's video is paused too. When Peter arrives at home he 'transfers' the content to TV, he can still control it with his smartphone and now his girlfriend and he can watch the TV together (via videoconference) but delocalized".

Many new concepts of sharing and controlling iTV [7] appear in this scenario. Our old living room has been extended and people not only watch TV wherever but also can share and control it wherever thank Internet. It is hard to assert that scenarios like these have negative or positive impacts on human behaviors, but definitely they will influence people moods [6].

TV has changed the everyday life of people's behavior [8]. But now TV is changing transcendentally, and new changes will affect people again in some factors. But which are these changes? Mainly in three areas: control, editing and sharing content all of them turn around two key issues [7]:

1. Interaction with TV, that it was almost inexistence so far [7] [9].
2. Secondary screens as a remote controller for advance actions. [10]

The next section describes previous work that has used dual displays and how usability has been measured on iTV applications. While there is research that evaluates the usability or performance of the independent displays as a single continuously addressable space, there is also research that employs two synchronized screen devices. Both areas of study are of great interest and influence in our research for both the evaluation of its use and for the development of our prototypes.

## 2    Related Work

Almost all of research in dual-screen set-ups has been focused on the effects of increased screen real-estate, which has been considered as a quantitative parameter in performing user tasks. Indeed, some studies have been developed in a work setting, which lends itself to performance measurements as efficiency. On the other hand, there are few research efforts in leisure environments that have considered the qualitative effects of secondary screens [4,5].

Since the advent of the PDAs there have been some studies to replace the remote control in the interaction with interactive television. One of the most influential researches for this work is the Robertson one [11,12], which proposes a prototype for real estate searching by a PDA bidirectionally communicated with interactive television. The author proposes a design guide remarking the importance of distributing information through appropriate devices. So the right information for display on PDA's is text and some icons, but television is suitable for displaying large images, video or audio. So the nature and quantity of information determines how to display and on which device.

Another way to interact is proposed by Yang et al. [13]. In this case a second screen is attached to the mouse showing helpful and contextual information to interact with a PC. Although the interaction is done with a PC (different to a TV in terms of use), the paradigm is quite similar in which the main screen is extended with an Interactive Touch Display. Also some released products as RedEye[14] that lets the user interacts with TV through a second screen to do some basic operations of content controlling.

In the study area of multiple-screens we should emphasize the study of Hutchings [15] where is compared the general use of a single with multiple monitors (2 or 3). To do this, is evaluated how 31 people use different windows on Windows XP operating system. To carry out the evaluation is used a monitoring tool. As highlight features we can observe that the activation of additional screens arises as a consequence of the desire to hide information in the main screen display. Besides it is important to highlight that is not usually interact with the various windows of the same program.

Another study to really consider is from Grundin [16]. It shows that the users do not treat the second monitor as an additional space, so not establish a single window across multiple monitors. In addition users will typically set a monitor for the primary task and other tasks related to but not synchronized. Like other studies confirm the increased usability of multiple monitors in achieving greater satisfaction of users and more productivity [17]. Besides, user satisfaction and efficiency, it is still an open research question whether coupled screens could also facilitate enjoyment. Early examples in the video-game industry have been well received (e.g., Nintendo link between GameBoy Advance and GameCube)[18], but there are no published reports on user behavior in the context of leisure activities.

On the field of iTV, some recent researches have limited their studies testing qualitatively their prototypes were likeable via surveys [19]. Some usability test suggested not adjusting to usability principles. This is the case of Drucker who demonstrated that user satisfaction was higher for the UI that required more time, more clicks and had the highest error rate. In other words, the most efficient UI was not the most likeable one. This result is contrary to the assumptions of the efficiency as a main principle of usability [20].

On the other hand numerous researching the ability of the TV to change the people mood [8][6]. This research represents a practical translation of all the researches done in psychology and communication about how TV affects the moods of the people over new iTV interaction concepts. To get these answers, an architecture have been developed to support the communication between multiple output/input devices in a simple and localized and delocalized multiuser iTV scenario [5]. Based on this architecture a totally functional prototype has been developed to test different interaction concepts in order to measure the affective usability dimension.

## 3     Methodology

Due to ITV applications serve entertainment aspirations in a leisure context and for a wide diversity of users, there is a need to extend the universal access toolset so that it considers the affective quality of an ITV UI taking in consideration that the user is now a viewer who searches entertainment or relaxation in his/her leisure time representing an affective state and expressing emotions [6].

In [6], Konstantinos et al. develops a UI evaluation framework for ITV applications that combine techniques for measuring emotional responses to TV content and techniques for assessing the affective quality of a UI. In this paper is adopted this framework but with some additions and modifications.

To evaluate the prototypes developed four scenarios of iTV interaction have been developed and tested:

1. To interact with iTV using a remote controller: In this case, user interacts with iTV using remote controller. To control the content there is a play/pause button and two arrows, right and left, to select the next or the previous video. The Menu button is used to show the information related to the video and the next video on the list.
2. To interact with iTV using a tablet as remote controller: In this case, all the overlay information shown in the first scenario is displayed in the tablet cleaning the first screen of interactive information so it wouldn't disturb other users.
3. To interact with iTV using a tablet as remote controller: In this case, all the overlay information is displayed in the TV.
4. iTV inside the  tablet and a screen shared: This scenario suppose that user is watching the iTV in the tablet and there is a TV shared.. The user can "fly out" or expand what he is watching in the TV shared. This scenario is the most interesting one. The user can extend what they are watching to other shared screen and also retrieves or "fly in" any video that is being watched in the TV.

A video-demo explaining how the prototypes work can be downloaded in http://www.uco.es/~i02bufef/euroitv2011/demoshortvideo.ipad.mp4 . The prototypes are totally functional and they are based on architecture defined in [5].

Two different kinds of evaluation have been carried on depending on the amount of users: 1 or more than one.  Both are similar so for space reasons multiusers evaluation evaluating the 4th scenario is detailed:. For it, two or three people of the same family are invited to "watch a list of video clips of music" (the type of content is also a research issue [6] but not in this paper) in their living room (the prototypes are totally installed and functional on their living room). Before go into the living room, the tester explains them that there are three touchable remote controllers on the table (remote controllers are changed randomly), and all of them can control and extend the content of the TV and the content of the tablet or smartphone and if they feel uncomfortable, they can abandon the test. There are two cameras recording to the people in front of them "camouflaged" for not feeling observed. Also, the content shown on the TV is recorded and all the interactions are logged.

While the evaluation happens, data is collected using different techniques. Earlier research has developed many techniques for measuring emotion, which go from physiological measures to iconographic scales [6]. The analysis of the interactivity logs and self-reports can detect the emotional response at the behavioral level. Lastly, retrospective questionnaires can measure the attitudes.

In this study we have used the following quantitative data derived from observation and logs: average number of interactions, number of changes of looking at different screens, time looking at the tablet or smartphone, time looking at the TV, number of changes the position of the user, time of reaction (time from the reaction to the action of press a button). On the other hand qualitative information has been acquired via self-reports, questionaries' and scales have been used to measure qualitatively emotional responses for pleasure and arousal, involvement, liking, feeling states, engagement and hedonic quality [6].

## 4    Early Results and Conclusions

Pilot tests are clearly shown how the engagement of the user increases considerably due to the social interactions. There are more conversations around the content and because of this more feeling states, frequently aligned with energetic and tension states, almost never with calmness. Anyway these data are not relevant because of most of these pilot tests were carried on the usability laboratory where the atmosphere is not suitable to measure how the affective usability affect to the behavior of people. Currently a 40 people evaluation is being carried on.

To sum up, we are motivated by the adoption of small and powerful mobile computers, such as smartphones and tablets. The latter has raised the opportunity of employing them into multi-device scenarios and blending the distinction between input and output. In particular, we are addressing the research issues about how advanced visual interfaces compete or cooperate for the attention and the benefit of the user and how coupled-display visual interfaces are appreciated in multi-user scenarios. It is expected that the case study of TV users and TV content could provide complementary evidence for the design of coupled display interfaces in general.

## References

1. Dan O'Sullivan Projects (September 2011),
   http://itp.nyu.edu/~dbo3/proj/index.html
2. Cesar, P., Chorianopoulos, K.: The Evolution of TV Systems, Content, and Users Towards Interactivity. Foundations and Trends in Human–Computer Interaction 2(4), 279–374 (2008)

3. Jensen, J.F.: Interactive Television - A Brief Media History. In: Tscheligi, M., Obrist, M., Lugmayr, A. (eds.) EuroITV 2008. LNCS, vol. 5066, pp. 1–10. Springer, Heidelberg (2008)
4. Chorianopoulos, K., Burón, F.J., Salcines, E.G., de Castro Lozano, C.: Delegating the visual interface between a tablet and a TV. In: Santucci, G. (ed.) Proceedings of the International Conference on Advanced Visual Interfaces, Roma, Italy, May 26-28, p. 418. ACM, New York (2010)
5. Burón, F.J., et al.: New Approaches on iTV: Usability and Mobility Issues. In: Advances in Dynamic and Static Media for Interactive Systems: Communicability, Computer Science and Design (2011)
6. Chorianopoulos, K., Spinellis, D.: User interface evaluation of interactive TV: a media studies perspective. Universal Access in the Information Society 5(2), 209–218 (2006)
7. Cesar, P., Chorianopoulos, K.: The Evolution of TV Systems, Content, and Users Toward Interactivity. Foundations and Trends in Human–Computer Interaction 2(4), 279–374 (2009)
8. Silverston, R.: Television and everyday life. Roudledge (1994)
9. Cooper, W.: The interactive television user experience so far. In: Proceeding of the International Conference on Designing Interactive User Experiences for TV and Video (UXTV), pp. 133–142 (2008)
10. Cesar, P., Bulterman, D.C., Geerts, D., Jansen, J., Knoche, H., Seager, W.: Enhancing social sharing of videos: fragment, annotate, enrich, and share. In: Proceeding of the 16th ACM International Conference on Multimedia MM 2008, pp. 11–20. ACM, New York (2008)
11. Robertson, S., Wharton, C., Ashworth, C., Franzke, M.: Dual device user interface design: PDAs and interactive television. In: Proceedings of the SIGCHI Conference on Human Factors in Computing Systems, CHI 1996, pp. 79–86. ACM, New York (1996)
12. Fallahkhair, S., Pembertom, L., Griffiths, R.: Dual Device User Interface Design for Ubiquitous Language Learning: Mobile Phone and Interactive Television (iTV). In: Wireless and Mobile Technologies in Education, pp. 85–92 (2005)
13. Yang, X., Mak, E., McCallum, D., Irani, P., Cao, X., Izadi, S.: LensMouse: Augmenting the Mouse with an Interactive. In: CHI 2010: Displays Where You Least Expect Them, pp. 10–15 (2010)
14. RedEye (September 2011), http://thinkflood.com/products/redeye/
15. Hutchings, D.R., Smith, G., Meyers, B., Czerwinski, M., Robertson, G.: Display space usage and window management operation comparisons between single monitor and multiple monitor users. In: Proceedings of the Working Conference on Advanced, Visual Interfaces, AVI 2004, pp. 32–39. ACM, New York (2004)
16. Grudin, J.: Partitioning digital worlds: focal and peripheral awareness in multiple monitor use. In: Proceedings of the SIGCHI Conference on Human Factors in Computing Systems, CHI 2001, pp. 458–465. ACM, New York (2001)
17. Slay, H., Thomas, B.: Interaction and Visualization across Multiple Displays in Ubiquitous Computing Environments. In: AFRIGRAPH 2006, Cape Town, South Africa, pp. 25–27 (2006)
18. Nintendo (September 2011), http://nintendo.com
19. Cesar, P., Bulterman, D.C.A., Jansen, J.: Leveraging the User Impact: An Architecture for Secondary Screens Usage in an Interactive Television Environment. Springer/ACM Multimedia Systems Journal (MSJ) 15(3), 127–142 (2009)
20. Drucker, S.M., Glatzer, A., Mar, S.D., Wong, C.: Smartskip: consumer level browsing and skipping of digital video content. In: Proceedings of the SIGCHI Conference on Human Factors in Computing Systems, pp. 219–226 (2002)

# An Investigation on the Effectiveness of Computer-Aided Simulation in Assisting Student Learning of Manufacturing Technology

Min Jou and Din-Wu Wu

Department of Industrial Education,
National Taiwan Normal University, Taipei, Taiwan
joum@ntnu.edu.tw

**Abstract.** The use of computer-aided Simulation to teach engineering-related courses is rapidly expanding in most universities. Yet the effects of computer-aided Simulation on students' performance and motivation are not yet fully known. We compared the impacts of computer-aided Simulation to college students from academic and vocational high schools.

Universities in Taiwan fall into two educational systems: the comprehensive universities and the technological universities. In the field of engineering, the students of comprehensive universities are recruited from academic high schools and the students of technological universities are recruited from vocational high schools. The purpose of this research is to study the differences in learning outcomes between college students with academic backgrounds and those with vocational backgrounds.

**Keywords:** computer-aided Simulation, comprehensive university, technological university.

## 1 Research Motivation

Taiwan is a country that relies heavily on its manufacturing industries; therefore, it needs an enormous pool of skilled labor. This is the main reason behind Taiwan's development of an extensive technological education system. In the past, there have been more people enrolled in vocational education than in academic education; however, the number of enrollment in vocational education has been in obvious decline due to the upgrading and the transformation that the industries have witnessed in recent years. This change has caused the number of students arriving at university from academic high schools and those who arrive from vocational schools to become equal. The students advance to higher education in different ways.

In the past, due to stringent recruiting regulations, comprehensive universities only recruited students from academic high schools, while technological universities only recruited students from vocational high schools. Fortunately, recruiting regulations in Taiwan have since been lax and the students from vocational schools are able to

M.D. Lytras et al. (Eds.): WSKS 2011, CCIS 278, pp. 563–566, 2013.
© Springer-Verlag Berlin Heidelberg 2013

attend comprehensive universities, and vice versa. Nevertheless, it remains a fact that the majority of the students at the comprehensive universities are recruited from academic high schools, as the majority of the students at the technological universities are recruited from vocational high schools. In comprehensive universities, 18 % of the students (approximately 87,000 students) choose engineering as their major (2009), and in technological universities, 26 % of the students (approximately 80,000) choose engineering as their major, in other words, the number of the students from these two different scholastic backgrounds is almost equal. Furthermore, in terms of professional skills, such as those required in manufacturing technology, regardless of the type of universities that the students have been recruited from, their learning needs will be the same. In addition, since it is becoming more of a commonplace that the vocational high school students are attending comprehensive universities and vice versa, it is thus necessary to analyze the differences in the learning efficacies of the college students with the two different scholastic backgrounds. This research project investigated cognition, skills, and the related topics in the students that attended a manufacturing technology course. The results of this study shall provide a valuable reference point for future educational innovations, course designing, and academic counseling.

## 2      Develop a Competence Scale

Many researchers have discussed how to design manufacturing courses and the learning activities in order to have the interest in learning manufacturing knowledge and skills strengthened in students. However, only a few researchers have performed skill assessments for manufcturing technology, hence this study aims to develop a competence scale to evaluate manufcturing skills of students based upon E. J. Simpson's educational theory of the seven levels of taxonomy.

To thrive in a global marketplace that is highly competitive requires the commercialization of knowledge and technology to produce faster, more flexible, intelligent, and multi-functional products at the lowest price possible. Engineers involved in product realization processes must master technology as it develops and quickly integrate it into products well ahead of the competition. Manufacturing technology, being an interdisciplinary engineering subject that studies the holistic design process through which intelligent machines are created in order to develop efficient and complex processes and products, plays an important role to achieving this goal. It integrates mechanics, electronics, and computing to achieve control and automation and has become a recurring theme in engineering education, for instance, CAS provide an excellent teaching tool for introducing students to the burgeoning field of manufacturing technology.

Educational manufacturing activities are developed not only so that learners can acquire manufacturing skills, but also demultiplicative, strategic, and dynamic skills. The dynamic competencies are related to motivation. The strategic competencies are concerned with metacognition (i.e., problem solving). The demultiplicative competencies enable the learner to obtain information by him/herself and to acquire more specific competencies (Leclercq, 1987; Denis and Hubert, 1999).

Many researchers have discussed how to design manufacturing technology courses and the learning activities in order to have the interest in learning manufacturing technology and manufacturing knowledge and skills strengthened in students. However, only a few researchers have performed skill assessments for manufacturing technology, hence this study aims to develop a competence scale to evaluate manufacturing skills of students based upon E. J. Simpson's educational theory of the seven levels of taxonomy.

Various researchers have examined this taxonomy with the intention of identifying or developing improved learning delivery systems for students. Simpson introduced the concept of taxonomy levels in 1966. He has provided the best discussion of the psychomotor domain, and her psychomotor objective classification system is the most widely accepted (Gordon, 2002). In the psychomotor domain there are a series of seven sequential steps that a learner follows while acquiring new knowledge, which involves physical tasks of some kind (Lynch, 2002).

# 3    Research Setting

The curriculum contains a series of formal lectures and laboratory sessions. A manufacturing technology course had been developed and was offered to students. Besides the fundamental scientific and technology subjects presented in the classroom, the students were required to complete practical work designed based on the CAS approaches. The practical work aimed at improving the theoretical understanding of the subjects taught and the development of practical skills applied in manufacturing technology.

This study utilizes CAS to enhance motivation in students and academic achievements delivered in the course. The implementation of CAS enables students to explore the essential integrity of a design and manufacturing technologies. The findings have revealed that the CAS is contributive to advancing cognition in students. However, there are no apparent differences between the two groups of students, perhaps due to the fact that the Computer-Aided Simulation require the students to learn in a condition where strict specifications are being placed in effect. Though learning effectiveness actually increased during the experiment, students may not appreciate the transformations in the long haul.

The results of path analysis show that student satisfaction and pre-course cognition did not display any significant correlation to technical skills, though there were some specific correlations found between post-course cognition and manufacturing skills. The main difference between the college students with academic high school background and those with vocational high school background was the correlation of post-course cognition and manufacturing skills. There was more positive correlation found in the students with vocational high school backgrounds while there was no such correlation found in those with academic high school backgrounds. The students with vocational high school backgrounds got higher average grades for post-course cognition, as they also got higher average grades for manufacturing skills. This indicates that students with vocational school backgrounds are more capable of applying knowledge to practical tasks.

## 4     Conclusion

Differing from other countries, technological education is a legitimate educational system in Taiwan, where the proportion of students with vocational schooling backgrounds is fairly high. The students with vocational school backgrounds were better than students with academic school backgrounds in terms of comprehension skills and had better abilities at applying knowledge to practical tasks, according to both the radar chart and the results of the path analysis.

## References

Gordon, D.: The design phase: objectives. University of Nevada, Reno (2002), http://www.scs.unr.edu/~dpg/develop.html (retrieved March 20, 2010)

Leclercq, D.: L'ordinateur et les defis de l'apprentissage, in Horizon, 13 (November 1987)

Lynch, M.M.: The online educator: A guide to creating the virtual classroom. Routledge Falmer, London (2002)

Monthly Report on the Manufacturing Sector, Industrial Development Bureau, Ministry of Economic Affairs, Taiwan (2008)

Phillips, H.K.: Teaching kids to sing. In: The Psychomotor Process, ch. 2 (1996), http://www.bsu.edu/web/srberry/portfolio/psyp.html (retrieved March 20, 2010)

Simpson, E.: What People Will Need to Know in the 80s and Beyond to Be Intelligent Consumers and Effective Homemakers. National Institution of Education, NIE-P-80-044 (1981)

Simpson, E.: The Home as a Learning Center for Vocational Development. Occasional Paper No. 16. Ohio State University (1976)

Simpson, E.: The Classification of Educational Objectives, Psychomotor Domain. U.S. Department of Education, BR-5-0090 (1966)

Simpson, E.: Advice in the Teen Magazines. Illinois Teacher of Home Economics (1964)

Simpson, E.: Educating for the Future in Family Life. Information Series No. 228 (1960)

Statistics in University and College, Ministry of Education, Taiwan (2009), http://www.edu.tw/files/site_content/b0013/97_student.xls (retrieved February 28, 2010)

# Designing a Web-Based VR Machine for Learning of Packaging and Testing Skills

Min Jou[1] and Yu-Shiang Wu[2]

[1] Department of Industrial Education, National Taiwan Normal University, Taipei, Taiwan
[2] China University of Science and Technology
joum@ntnu.edu.tw

**Abstract.** This research designed and implemented an interactive learning system to support self-directed learning of microfabrication technology from both technical and functional viewpoints, along with end-user evaluation results. The current study applied virtual technology to design virtual machines with online interaction, to acquaint students with microfabrication facilities, learn how to operate machines, and practice the microfabrication process through the internet. This study incorporated the microfabrication technology courses with the developed web-based learning system.

**Keywords:** virtual reality environments, interactive learning system, technical skills.

## 1    Introduction

Microsystems, often referred to as microelectromechanical systems (MEMS), are miniaturized mechanical and electrical systems with a dimensional range within a few micrometers. These include a wide range of applications in the automotive (Caliano, et al., 1995; Barbour, et al., 1997; Gripton, 2002), communications, biomedical industries, and in process control. Some current applications include crash sensors for airbag systems, ink jet print heads, and pressure sensors. Several industrial surveys have shown sales growth of microsystem-based technologies at a rate of 16% per year and are expected to reach more than $25 billion by the year 2009 (EXUS MST/MEMS Market Analysis III, 005-2009).

The demand for microsystems is increasing; however, the university system is not sufficient for training to be conducted in order to have microsystems built because it cannot fulfill the qualitative or quantitative needs of the industry. The traditional technique enhances teaching effectiveness by increasing equipments utilities, spaces needed, and teaching time, whereas experimental and practical training require expensive teaching equipments (eg. MEMS), along with a proper teaching environment (eg. clean room). The current teaching method for microfabrication technology relies on "cookbook" oriented experiments that present students with a technical question, the procedures to address the question, the expected results of the experiment, and an interpretation of the results produced. Due to the limitation of

M.D. Lytras et al. (Eds.): WSKS 2011, CCIS 278, pp. 567–573, 2013.

facilities, space, cost of materials, and teaching time, it is difficult to re-examine the operation base of student mistakes from experiments. This is a major pedagogical challenge in learning microfabrication, and the main hindrance to improving teaching quality or quantity.

This study therefore developed a web-based system to support self-directed learning of microfabrication technology so that the students are enabled to learn microfabrication and related facilities using a web-based system to build a basic concept of microfabrication technology. The web-based system allows students to practice on the Internet and familiarize themselves with microfabrication technology to decrease error rates and increase learning effectiveness. Self-directed learning encourages students to learn inductively with the aid of teaching systems.

The self-directed learning approach encourages students to learn inductively with the assistance of teaching systems. This method empowers the students to investigate freely, devises an experimental procedure, and decides on how the results could be interpreted. Long (2010) pointed out at least six types of cognitive skills particularly important to successful self-directed learning, and they are goal setting, processing, cognition, competence or aptitude in the topic or a closely related area, decision-making, and self-awareness. Effective self-directed learning depends on gathering information to monitor student processing and other cognitive activities and how learners react to information. The evolution of computer and internet technologies has enabled effortless access to learning contents from almost anywhere, anytime, and at each individual's own pace. Self-directed e-learning focuses on the independent learner that engages in education at his own pace and that is free from curricular obligation. Several tools have become key enablers of this learning paradigm. Tools such as Google Scholar, CiteSeer Research Index, etc. make it possible to search the literature in any location (Desikan). Researchers have recently attempted to apply e-learning technology to the self-directed learning process. Idros, S.N.S., et al., (2010) sought to reignite enthusiasm in students to enhance self-directed learning skills through a system called "e-SOLMS.", for instance, Liu, M. (2009) built a web-based course for self-directed learning in psychology. One of the common points of these two research papers is the major capability of this system to present course contents (i.e., audio files, video files, and text files) to students. Another common point is their introduction of self-directed learning (SDL) into the curricula using the student-centered approach. However, this approach is not appropriate for some courses that focus on experiment and practice. Recent technological development of virtual reality (VR) has provided a chance to teach some subjects through a three-dimensional (3-D) model. Especially, the advance in optical-fiber networks has made real-time transmission of a large amount of data possible, such as 3-D models or video images, between remote places. Remote places can now share a three-dimensional virtual world by connecting virtual environments through the broadband network (Paquette, Ricciardi-Rigault, Paquin, Liegeois, Bleicher, 1996). The field of virtual reality (VR), which initially focused on immersive viewing via expensive equipment, is rapidly expanding, and includes a growing variety of systems for interacting with 3-D computer models in real-time (Sung, Ou, 2003). Various applications in the fields include education, training, entertainment, medicine, and industry have been developing, and increasingly more areas will benefit from using VR (Craig, Sherman, 2003). Several interactive VR systems have recently been developed. An educational virtual environment (Bouras, Philopoulos, Tsiatsos, 2001) is a special case of a VR system that emphasizes more on education and collaboration than on simulation.

Although these studies have already provided a basic technique support for self-directed learning, they still lack the self-reflective learning mechanism in the system. For experimental and practical training, the system is limited to assist students because experiments and practical training needs a self-reflective function for students to correct mistakes after the experiment has been conducted, to revise the wrong selection of process parameters and process planning, and finally, to explore microfabrication technology. Abdullah (2001) and Garrison (1997) suggested providing environments where students can self-monitor, revise their work, and reflect on their own cognition and learning processes to foster self-directed learning. Hence, the current study developed a web-based and self-directed learning system with a self-reflective function based on wireless sensor networks to support microfabrication technological education.

## 2    Web-Based Self-directed Learning Environment

This system employs Web2.0, VR, and sensor network technology. The application tier is consisted of a web server and a Java application server, while the presentation tier is consisted of a client-side terminal that comprises the HTML, XML, and 3-D web player plug-in. The client, which runs in a web browser, provides a student interface that handles input and output (displaying results, simulation). The web server performs actions and computations based on student input using XML and JSP languages. The application server reads and writes to the databases by JavaBean and interfaces with external software packages. Web pages written in HTML mainly present the course content. Standardized definitions for course structures are necessary in order to move courses from one system to another, and to extract and/or perform automated processing on the documents. To meet the requirements, Extensible Markup Language (XML) is used to develop course structures, and to acquire cross-platform applications, JAVA language is used in programming to develop interactive web pages.

The main facilities for operating the microfabrication process include a crucible for crystal growth, coating, an optical microscope, an exposure machine, packaging, and inspection. This study designed on-line virtual machines for these facilities to become a microfabrication virtual laboratory through organizing. Figures 1-3 show snapshots of the developed virtual machines. To engage students in this virtual laboratory, this research implemented multiple interactive functions such as path design, parameter selection, view angle, and animation, while zoom, pan, rotation, machine, and working table navigation functions for the purposes of exploring 3-D simulations. Students have access to a variety of options before they trigger an event, animation, or simulation, and they can repeat the selection process to study microfabrication processes. The intention here is to emulate the operations of microfabrication machines in the VR environment. Adaptive selection simulation stimulates experimental learning through observations made of manufacturing processes using a sequence of events: trigger an event → observations of the manufacturing process → interpretation → assimilation. Students are able to operate VR machines and simulate the development of micro products. The learning content of the microfabrication processes will be extracted from the database based on the group technology approaches. The appropriate microfabrication procedures are displayed for students to learn the principles of manufacturing process planning. The manufacturing method for each of the microfabrication features is delivered to students by virtual laboratory once he/she has selected the microfabrication features.

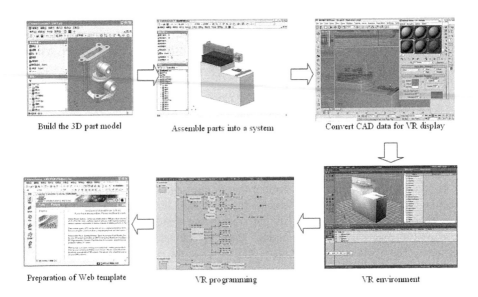

Build the 3D part model          Assemble parts into a system          Convert CAD data for VR display

Preparation of Web template          VR programming          VR environment

**Fig. 1.** Building virtual environments in six steps

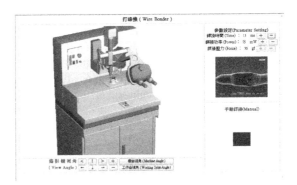

**Fig. 2.** Screenshot of online interactive wire binding

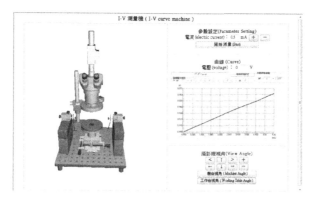

**Fig. 3.** Developed interactive testing system

## 3 Conclusions

The developed system provides students opportunities for self-monitor, self-correct, revisions of work, and self-reflections made on the research project, as well as on their learning process. Courses with concentrations on experimentations and practical training are notably difficult to teach via the Internet because of the need for physical spaces such as laboratories, and how engineering education can be offered without being confined by the physical limitations and via the Internet with quality, scale, and breadth instead deserves more attention for that the endeavor would encourage online engineering education to become more widely accepted and employed in the future.

**Acknowledgment.** The authors gratefully acknowledge the support of this study by the National Science Council of Taiwan, under the Grant No. NSC98-2511-S-003-015-MY2 and NSC98-2511-S-003-017-MY2.

## References

Abdullah, M.H.: Self-directed learning [ERIC digest No. 169]. ERIC Clearinghouse on Reading, English, and Communication (ERIC Document Reproduction Service No. ED459458), Bloomington, IN (2001)

Akyildiz, I.F., Su, W., Sankarasubramaniam, Y., Cayirci, E.: A survey on sensor networks. IEEE Communications Magazine 40(8), 102–114 (2002)

Barbour, N., Brown, E., Connelly, J., Dowdle, J., Brand, G., Nelson, J., O'Bannon: Micromachined Inertial Sensors for Vehicles. In: IEEE Conference on Intelligent Transportation System, ITSC 1997, November 9-12, pp. 1058–1063 (1997)

Bhaskar, A.K., Menaka, S.: The state of MEMS in automation (2007),
http://www.isa.org/ (retrieved May 20, 2010)

Borkholder, D.A.: Cell-Based Biosensors using Microelectrodes. Ph.D. Thesis, Electrical Engineering Department, Stanford University, Stanford, CA (1998)

Bouras, C., Philopoulos, A., Tsiatsos, T.: E-learning through distributed virtual environments. J. Netw. Comput. Appl. 24(3), 175–199 (2001)

Caliano, G., Lamberti, N., Iula, A., Pappalardo, M.: A piezoelectric bimorph static pressure sensor. Sensors and Actuators A 46-47, 176–178 (1995)

Craig, A.B., Sherman, W.R.: Understanding Virtual Reality – Interface, Application, and Design. Elsevier Science, Morgan Kaufmann Publishers, Calif., USA (2003)

Creswell, J.W.: Research design: Qualitative and Quantitative Approaches. Sage Publication, California (1994)

Desikan, P., DeLong, C., Beemanapalli, K., Bose, A., Srivastava, J.: Web Mining For Self Directed E-Learning. In: Data Mining for E-Learning. WIT Press (also available as AHPCRC Technical Report –TR # 2005-030)

Dong, M., Tong, L., Sadler, B.M.: Information Retrieval and Processing in Sensor Networks: Deterministic Scheduling Versus Random Access. IEEE Transactions on Signal Processing 55(12), 5806–5820 (2007)

Elliott, J.: Action Research for Education Change. Open University Press, Philadelphia (1991)

Garrison, D.R.: Self-directed Learning: Toward a comprehensive model. Adult Education Quarterly 48(1), 18–33 (1997)

Grayson, A.C.R., Shawgo, R.S., Johnson, A.M., Flynn, N.T., Li, Y., Cima, M.J., Langer, R.: A BioMEMS Review: MEMS Technology for Physiologically Integrated Devices. Proc of the IEEE 92(1), 6–21 (2004)

Gripton, A.: The application and future development of a MEMS SiVS/spl reg/ for commercial vehicles. In: Position Location and Navigation Symposium, April 15-18. IEEE (2002)

Huang, L.H., Lee, S.S., Motamedi, S.S., Wu, E., Kim, C.J.: MEMS packaging for micro mirror switches. In: 48th IEEE Electronic Components and Technology Conference, May 25-28, pp. 592–597 (1998)

Idros, S.N.S., Mohamed, A.R., Esa, N., Samsudin, M.A., Daud, K.A.M.: Enhancing self-directed learning skills through e-SOLMS for Malaysian learners. Procedia Social and Behavioral Sciences 2, 698–706 (2010)

Long, H.B.: Skills for self-directed learning (2010),
http://faculty-staff.ou.edu/L/Huey.B.Long-1/articles.html
(retrieved May 20, 2010)

Lott, G.W.: The effect of inquiry teaching and advance organizers upon student outcomes in science education. Journal of Research in Science Teaching 20(5), 437 (1983)

NEXUS MST/MEMS Market Analysis III (2005-2009),
http://www.enablingmnt.com/html/nexus_market_report.html
(retrieved May 20, 2010)

Okandan, M., Galambos, P., Mani, S., Jakubczak: BioMEMS and microfluidics applications of surface micromachining technology. In: Microelectromechanical Systems Conference, pp. 1–3 (August 2001)

Paquette, G., Ricciardi-Rigault, C., Paquin, C., Liegeois, S., Bleicher, E.: Developing the Virtual Campus Environment. In: Proceedings of Ed-Media, pp. 244–249 (1996)

Paris, S.G., Ayres, L.R.: Becoming Reflective Students and Teaching. American Psychological Association (1994)

Pardo, F., Simon, M.E.: Design for reliability of MEMS/MOEMS for lightwave telecommunications. In: The 15th Annual Meeting of the IEEE Lasers and Electro-Optics Society, LEOS 2002, November 10-14, vol. 2, pp. 418–419 (2002)

Shea, H.R., Arney, S., Gasparyan, A., Haueis, M., Aksyuk, V.A., Bolle, C.A., Frahm, R.E., Goyal, S., Stieve, H.: Sensors of Biological Organisms-Biological Transducers. Sensors and Actuators 4(4), 689–704 (1983)

Sung, W.T., Ou, S.C.: Using Virtual Reality Technologies for Manufacturing Applications. Int. J. Com. Applications Tech. 17(4), 213–219 (2003)

Shymansky, J., Hedges, L., Woodworth, G.: A reassessment of the effects of inquiry-based science curricula of the 60's on student performance. Journal of Research in Science Teaching 27(2), 127–144 (1990)

Shymansky, J., Kyle, W., Alport, J.: The effects of new science curricula on student performance. Journal of Research in Science Teaching 20(5), 387–404 (1983)

Tseng, F.G., Linder, C., Kim, C.J., Ho, C.M.: Control of Mixing with Micro Injectors for Combustion Application¡. In: 1996 ASME IMECE, Micro-Electro-Mechanical Systems (MEMS), DSC, Atlanta, vol. 59, pp. 183–187 (1996)

Tubaishat, M., Madria, S.: Sensor networks: An overview. IEEE Potentials 22(2), 20–23 (2003)

Turunen, H., Taskinen, H., Voutilainen, U., Tossavainen, K., Sinkkonen, S.: Nursing and social work students' initial orientation towards their studies. Nurse Education Today 17, 67–71 (1997)

Wu, M.C., Solgaard, O., Ford, J.E.: Optical MEMS for Lightwave Communication. J. of Lightwave Tech. 24(12) (2006)

# TvCSL: An XML-Based Language for the Specification of TV-Component Applications

Jesús Vallecillos[2], Antonio Jesús Fernández-García[2], Javier Criado[1], and Luis Iribarne[1]

[1] Applied Computing Group, University of Almería, Spain
{javi.criado,luis.iribarne}@ual.es
[2] Ingenieros Alborada IDi Almería, Spain
{jesus.vallecillos,ajfernandez}@ingenierosalborada.es

**Abstract.** The world implementation of *Interactive Digital Television* (iDTV) has led to the emergence of technologies that offer the concept of new business models. There aren't currently any private/public repositories for an imminent market of software components for Digital Television industry, or any techniques providing registration and discovery of services at runtime. This paper presents a standard XLM-based language for software components specification running for digital television. Such language is part of a methodology and a set of tools for the deployment of a trading service and repositories of TV services being developed by the company Alborada Engineers IDI.

**Keywords:** Component Specification Language (CSL), Interactive Digital Television (iDTV), XML-based documentation.

## 1 Introduction

The audio visual world and specifically the television industry have a big impact on today's society. This has involved, in view of the power of this medium, the implementation of new software applications for television. The world implementation of *Interactive Digital Television* (iDTV) not only allows higher quality of transmission and more digital channels but also has led to the emergence of technologies that offer the concept of new business models. Moreover, a strong increase in both technologies and methodologies in Interactive Digital Television (iDTV) is expected in the coming years. Some of these new business models within the TV are the implementation of software applications. Once developed and using the appropriate hardware, these applications have access to the Internet, which makes them really useful. This enables to use the television almost like a computer without having to get up off the couch. Standards such as MHP [6] and DASE [7] have been developed in order to define television applications, but due to several factors they haven't had the impact it was expected. That's why some big companies are currently developing their own technology to get this market. Some of the companies involved are Google, Sony, Samsung, Yahoo and Microsoft among others, which have created proprietary technologies such

M.D. Lytras et al. (Eds.): WSKS 2011, CCIS 278, pp. 574–580, 2013.
© Springer-Verlag Berlin Heidelberg 2013

as GoogleTV [1], Bravia TV Applications [2], SmartTV [3], Yahoo TV Widget [4] and MicrosoftTV [5] to cover the TV application market.

In the large niche market we're referring to, a trading service of component for TV (TDTrader) doesn't exist yet [13]. Therefore, we'll try to define a trading service to exploit centralized and registered Tv software components, regardless of the platform on which it has been developed or by whom it has been developed. Nevertheless, in order to create a trading service for software components of TV (TDTrader) [12], we first need to define a TV component specification language. That is the goal of this work, a description and discussion of the main parts of such component. We'll be able to specify the parts of the component and to describe the instances managed by the trading service [14]. The rest of the paper is organized as follows. Section 2 presents some related work, and Section 3 explains the TV Component Specification Language. Section 4 presents a simple case study. Finally, Section 5 contains some conclusions and outlines future work.

## 2    Related Work

Nowadays there are different proposals related to software component specification. In [8] the authors define a COTS component description language. Such description has been divided into four main parts. Firstly, they made a functional description of the component, including the syntactic and semantic information. Secondly, they defined non-functional information related to COTS component properties. Thirdly, they described packaging information giving details of component deployment and implementation. Finally, there is a marketing section with non technical and business information. The authors used XML[1] as a language to document components and defined XML grammar by using the XML-Schema notation[2]. For their proposal they gave a simple example for the component documentation. They showed a framework of the component description where we can clearly see the four part component. However, we go one step beyond. Our TV component description needs to have registered not only the functional and non-functional information, related to packaging and marketing, but also the data associated with the software and hardware requirements necessary for the component.

In [9] the authors defined an XML-based model for a iDTV component description. Like the previous one, its grammar is defined through XMLSchema. This model is divided into four main groups. They are as follows: attributes (listing functional characteristics), dependences (identifying other required components), properties (expressing non-functional requirements) and ports (defining provided ports and established connections among ports). We'll expand on the group of dependences. As regards the group of ports, [9] is included in the description to be defined within the group of interfaces.

Another related work [10] that shows a component at a model and service level is the work about some concepts less specific than those being developed.

---

[1] http://www.w3c.org/XML
[2] http://www.w3c.org/XML/Schema

Similarly, [11] defines a software component and its parts, described in general and for any type of component; however, it's necessary to develop something more specific for the problem we're trying to sort out.

## 3   TV Component Specification Language

Before discussing the TV component specification language, let's locate the instances within the trading service (Trader) to be developed. As seen in Figure 1, the structure of the trader is divided into six main parts formed by *Offer Repository Data*, *Service Type Repository*, *Offer Repository*, *Interface Repository* and

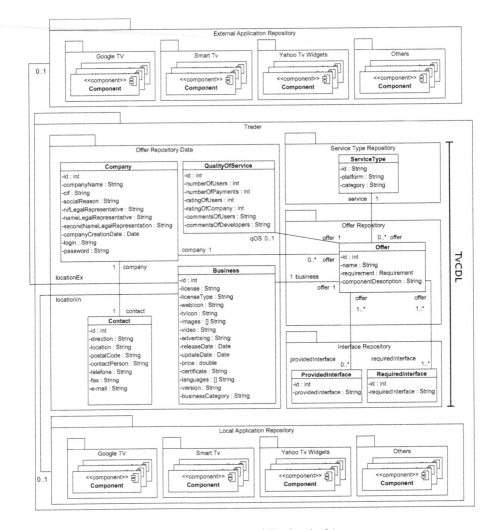

**Fig. 1.** Class Diagram of Trader Architecture

*Local Application Repository* [12]. The *Trader* can also refer to other external application repositories where users store components. Let's see the contents of each repository:

- *Offer Repository* contain the TV components to be offered.
- Service Type Repository specify the service that a TV component offers.
- *Interface Repository* is formed by the provided and required interfaces of a component.
- *Offer Repository Data* stores the company information related to the television component.
- *External Application Repository* and *Internal Application Repository* store the TV physical components.

Therefore, a TvCSL instance will be stored by sections within the Trader's repositories, that is, the service type repository, offer repository and interface repository, as shown in Figure 1. The section related to the platform and category of the TvCSL will be stored in the table "Service" of the service type repository. The section related to the component name, description and requirements will be stored in the table "Offer" of the offer repository. The last section related to the provided and required interfaces will be stored in the interfaces repository within the tables "ProvidedInterfaces" and "RequiredInterfaces", respectively. Keeping on with the Trader architecture regarding the offer repository data, we can observe that one instance will be related to an element from the table "Company", in turn with an assigned contact from the table "Contact". Each instance is also related to the business information from table "Business" and optionally to the quality of service information from "QualityOfService". Each instance of the TV component specification language will have a physical component associated, stored in an internal or external repository with regard to our Trader. Such association is found in table "Business", through the `locationIn` and `locationEx` references.

Let's now see the TV component specification language (TvCSL) in Table 1. The XML-Schema is the encoding used to define the XML grammar. As seen in the XML-Schema associated to the TV component description language, an instance has an attribute with the component "name" and a sequence of elements

**Table 1.** A piece of the XML template for describing TV component applications

```
1:  <xs:element name="TvCSL">
2:    <xs:complexType>
3:      <xs:sequence>
4:        <xs:element name="platform" type="xs:string"/>
5:        <xs:element name="componentDescription" type="xs:string" minOccurs="0"/>
6:        <xs:element name="requirements" type="requiremType" minOccurs="0" maxOccurs="1"/>
7:        <xs:element name="category" minOccurs="0"> ... </xs:element>
8:        <xs:element name="interfaces" type="interfaceType"/>
9:      </xs:sequence>
10:     <xs:attribute name="name" type="xs:string" use="required"/>
11:   </xs:complexType>
12: </xs:element>
```

describing it. Such elements are the following: a "platform" related to the TV component, a description of the component, the "requirements" of the component, a "category" and "interfaces" of the component. The "platform" determines which tv software development platform the component is related to. The "description of the component" colloquially defines the component functionality and what it's used for. The "requirements" of the component are used for defining which elements are necessary and what environment the component should be located in to run. This section is detailed within the "requirementsType". Here we defined the software system to which set-box, Tv, component size, implementation language and component update address is assigned. "Category" will determine for what the developed component is set aside, thus creating the category "Graphics" for graphic components, "Connection" for components devoted to establish connections with data or other components, "Process" for components sorting out tasks, "I/O" for components that interact with input/output elements and "Others" for components required for other purposes. The "interfaces" define the provided and required interfaces of the component.

## 4   A Case Study

Let's suppose we're going to develop a TvCSL instance of the graphic component from Figure 4 (a). Such graphic component intends to visualize a "user login" action in the application and show the message exchange between users. In order to define the instance in the Trader, we'd have to fill in the template shown in

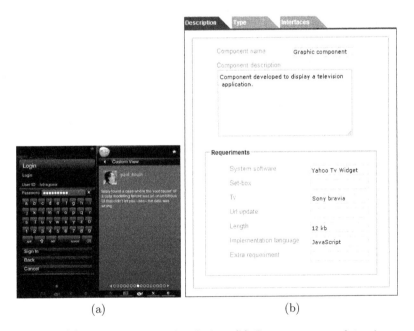

(a)                                    (b)

**Fig. 2.** (a) Component' graphical view; (b) Component template view

**Table 2.** Instance of TV Components Specification Language

```
 1:  <?xml version="1.0" encoding="UTF-8"?>
 2:  <TvCSL xmlns:xsi="http://www.w3.org/2001/XMLSchema-instance"
 3:          xsi:noNamespaceSchemaLocation="..." name="Graphic component">
 4:   <platform>YahooTvWidget</platform>
 5:   <componentDescription>
 6:      Component developed to display a television application.
 7:   </componentDescription>
 8:   <requirements>
 9:       <system_software></system_software>
10:      <tv>Sony Bravia</tv>
11:      <length>12 kb</length>
12:      <implementationLanguage>JavaScript</implementationLanguage>
13:   </requirements>
14:   <category>Graphics</category>
15:   <interfaces>
16:      <requiredInterfaces> ... </requiredInterfaces>
17:   </interfaces>
18: </TvCSL>
```

Figure 4 (b). Such template can be filled with some information describing the component such as its name, description and requirements. We can also determine the type of component through the category definition of component and platform within the tab "Type" as well as the provided and required component interfaces within the tab "Interfaces". Once this has been done, we'll create an instance as shown in Table 2.

As it can be observed, the fields filled in the template appear now inside the instance in XML. In "Type" we specified that our component was for Yahoo TV Widget platform [4] and it had the Graphics category. In the instance we can see how it appears in XML within the tab "platform" and "category". Inside the "Description" section of the component template, we defined the component name, description and requirements such as software system, TV, component size and implementation language. All these elements can already be seen in the instance. Similarly, once the interfaces have been defined in the template when creating an instance, they can be seen in XML within the tab "Interfaces".

## 5    Conclusion and Future Work

The iDTV software component development is a new market that is emerging. Therefore, the management of these components is necessary. Thus, the creation of a trading service [14] would help to manage them. This is why this work has focused on a development of TV component specification language crucial to carry out such trading model. As future work we'll need a repository model of component templates where we'll have to define the repository structure as well as the use and administration policy. We'll also have to determine a query language for the repository where the tv component templates are stored. This repository model will have to be adapted by the trading model (TDTrader) [13]. Then, we'll have to define the adapted model (TDTrader) [12] for this kind of software components. Once these basic models have been defined, we'll study how to implement a trading service in collaboration with other services in a system in Internet, which will lead to an implementation methodology. Moreover, this methodology is expected to be validated with a proprietary framework. Then, we'll have to carry out trials on the implementations previously developed. There will be trial prototypes to validate the proposed models and a utility trial package for the methodology implementation. The trials will be either individual, that is, carried out by developers or collective, that is, carried out by third-parts, though supervised by developers.

**Acknowledgments.** This work has been supported by Ingenieros Alborada (http://www.ingenierosalborada.es/), the EU (FEDER) and the Spanish Ministry MICINN under grants of the TRA2009-0309 and TIN2010-15588 projects, and JUNTA ANDALUCIA ref. TIC-6114. http://www.ual.es/tdtrader.

# References

1. Google TV Projects, http://www.google.com/tv
2. Applicats Bravia Widgets, http://www.braviawidgets.com
3. Smart TV, http://www.samsung.com/mx/smarttv/
4. Yahoo TV Widgets, http://www.connecttv.yahoo.com
5. Microsoft TV, http://www.microsoft.com/tv
6. EBU/ETSI. Digital Video Broadcast (DVB) Multimedia Home Platform (MHP) Specification v 1.1 (2001)
7. ATSC Standard A/100: DTV Application Software Environment, DASE (2003)
8. Iribarne, L., Troya, J.M., Vallecillo, A.: A Trading service for COTS components. Computer Journal 4(3), 342–357 (2004)
9. Borelli, F., Lopes, A., Elias, G.: An XML-based Component Specification Model for an Adaptive Middleware of Interactive Digital Television Systems. In: AINA 2004, pp. 457–462. IEEE (2004)
10. Weinreich, R., Sametinger, J.: Component Models and Component Service: Concepts and Principles. In: Component-Based Software Engineering: Putting the Pieces Together, pp. 33–48. Addison Wesley (2001)
11. Councill, B., Heineman, G.T.: Definition of a Software Component and Its Elements. In: Component-Based Software Engineering: Putting the Pieces Together, pp. 5–19. Addison Wesley (2001)
12. Maturana, C., Fernández-García, A.J., Iribarne, L.: An Implementation of a Trading Service for Building Open and Interoperable DT Component Applications. In: Corchado, J.M., Pérez, J.B., Hallenborg, K., Golinska, P., Corchuelo, R. (eds.) Trends in Practical Applications of Agents and Multiagent Systems. AISC, vol. 90, pp. 127–135. Springer, Heidelberg (2011)
13. Fernández-García, A.J., Iribarne, L.: TDTrader: A methodology for the interoperability of DT-Web Services based on MHPCOSTS software components, repositories and trading models. In: IWAAL 2010, pp. 83–88 (2010)
14. Iribarne, L., Troya, J.M., Vallecillo, A.: A Trading Service for COTS Components. The Computer Journal 47(3), 342–357 (2004)

# Constructivism Based Blended Learning in Higher Education

Ahmad Al-Huneidi and Jeanne Schreurs

Hasselt University, Hasselt, Belgium

**Abstract.** This paper explains how to apply Constructivism and Conversation theories in Blended Learning environment in order to increase learning outcomes and quality. Some scenarios of Constructivism based blended learning activities are presented in this paper. In addition, a Constructivism Based Blended Learning model for "ICT Management" course, a compulsory course in Master of Management Information Systems program at Hasselt University, is proposed. The proposed model applies and combines Constructivism and Conversation theories in Blended Learning environment, in which the student is an active maker of knowledge. In the proposed model a variety of learning activities and scenarios, differentiated for working students and regular students are applied, supported by innovative ICT tools, which facilitate applying Constructivism and Conversation theories and increase the level of communication and interaction between students; as a result, learning quality, experience and outcomes are increased effectively.

**Keywords:** Blended Learning, E-Learning, Constructivism Theory, Conversation Theory, Higher Education.

## 1    Introduction

Face-to-face learning has some advantages such as learning in a social interaction environment, which facilitate an exchange of ideas, and lower the possibility of misunderstanding. However face-to-face learning allows very limited room for self-directed learning and student-centered learning, limits the possibilities for customizing the course content to reflect learners' skills [1].

The experience gained from first generation e-learning, often riddled with long sequences of 'page-turner' content and pointed-click quizzes, is giving rise to the realization that a single mode of instructional delivery may not provide sufficient choices, engagement, social contact, relevance, and context needed to facilitate successful learning and performance [2]. Although of the advantages gained from e-learning, such as possibility of learning at anytime and from anywhere, which reduced the cost, faster learning delivery, and servicing unlimited number of learners, there are a few disadvantages of e-learning, which include low motivation to complete courses, lower learner satisfaction, lack interaction with teachers and peers, difficult to use real tools, and high initial costs for developing courses [1].

M.D. Lytras et al. (Eds.): WSKS 2011, CCIS 278, pp. 581–591, 2013.
© Springer-Verlag Berlin Heidelberg 2013

Blended Learning arose to overcome the disadvantages of traditional learning and to obviate the failure of e-learning by providing a combination of various learning strategies or models. It mixes various event-based learning activities, including face-to-face class room, live e-learning, student-centered learning, and self-paced learning, which increases learning quality, social contents, and learners' interactivity. Blended Learning is an evolution of e-learning; it provides the best mix of traditional learning and e-learning.

## 2    Constructivism and Conversation Theories

One of the harshest criticisms of Blended Learning is that it focuses on the teacher for creating the knowledge, rather than on the student [7]. To overcome this drawback, Constructivism theory may applied in Blended Learning environment, which increases students' interactivity and focuses on the student to construct new knowledge based on his/her previous experience.

Constructivism theory is based on the idea that people construct their own knowledge through their personal experience. The effectiveness of Constructivism is that it prepares students for problem solving in complex environment [3]. In Constructivism theory; students are more active in building and creating knowledge, individually and socially, based on their experiences and interpretations.

Teacher's role is essential and important in learning process. The role of the teacher in Constructivism theory is to try to understand how students interpret knowledge and to guide and help them to refine their understanding and interpretations to correct any misconception arises between students at an early stage and improve learned knowledge quality.

In addition, Conversation theory supports Constructivism theory. Conversation theory is based on discussion of the learning system. It believes that the interaction and collaboration between students and teachers play an important and essential role in learning process. It focuses on continued and ongoing interaction between students and teachers. In this sense, Conversation theory of learning fits into the constructivist framework, since the emphasis is on student as an active maker of knowledge.

## 3    Constructivism and Conversation Theories in Blended Learning Environment

In Blended Learning environment, teachers should use a variety of ICT tools such as synchronous and asynchronous learning technologies to facilitate and encourage collaboration, interaction, communication, and knowledge construction and sharing among the students.

Blended Learning environment has the characteristics to adapt, support, and facilitate applying Constructivism and Conversation theories in learning process (see Fig. 1). Blended Learning environment facilitates and improves discussion, communication, and knowledge construction processes as discussed later in this paper.

**Table 1.** Constructivism Characteristics and their Correspondent Learning Activities and ICT Support Tools.

| Constructivism Characteristics | Learning Activities | ICT support Tools |
|---|---|---|
| Personalization/Customization | Reading about a selected topic on the internet and discuss it with other students and with the teacher. | - Online chat system.<br>- Internet access. |
| Responsibility | -   Conducting an interview with one of the business people, followed by a presentation and discussion about the interview outcomes to the whole class.<br>- Self reading followed by whole class discussion.<br>- Attending an online conference with a selected business people, followed by a report requested from each student about what he/she learned and an online discussion. | -   Online Whiteboard system to present the power point presentation to the whole class in addition to the discussion.<br>-   Online discussion forum.<br>-   Online conference system. |
| Critical Thinking | Presenting a real life problem and asking the each group of students to solve it and make a report of their solution, followed by a discussion of the proposed solution. | -   Online discussion forum.<br>- Online meeting system or interactive whiteboard system. |
| Self and Collaborative Assessment | Group preparation of a report about selected topic, followed by exchanging the reports among students to assess each others' reports and then send them to the teacher. | Email System. |

Table 1 illustrates various Constructivism characteristics and their correspondent learning activities and ICT support tools to gain a better understanding of applying Constructivism characteristics in learning process. Moreover, by applying Conversation theory beside Constructivism theory in Blended Learning environment, the students have the opportunity to interact with the teacher; in addition, the teacher has the opportunity to guide and assess students' learning and knowledge construction at an early stage and take any needed correction action if there is any misconception. Conversation theory supports Constructivism theory by facilitating collaboration, communication, interaction, and knowledge construction and sharing amongst the students, which improves learning outcomes and quality more effectively.

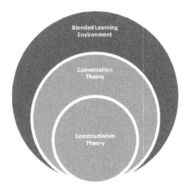

**Fig. 1.** Adapting Conversation and Constructivism Theories in Blended Learning Environment

To apply Constructivist theory, a learning environment should be designed, implemented, and then guided through the process of collaboration and interaction between students, so that learning is constructed by the group, rather than just the individual [4].

The effectiveness of collaboration in a live or synchronous learning environment depends on dynamic and active communication between students that fosters knowledge construction and sharing [5]. Synchronous discussions are very beneficial and important for students who might not participate actively and collaboratively within face-to-face classroom. Moreover, synchronous discussions facilitate fast and efficient exchanges of ideas [6]. On the contrary, in face-to-face classroom; participation of all students in discussion process is often difficult due to time constraints or students' nervousness or shyness.

# 4    Constructivism Based Blended Learning Best Practices [8], [9]

## 4.1    Introduction

As teachers, on course level, we have to define the course specific competencies and linked it with the content of the course. The learning content of the course is structured as a set of topics or modules.

In this phase the intended learning level for each module has to be identified. For some modules the learning process can be limited to only a traditional classroom session and for the learner being informed about the topic. Though for more important topics the learning process will include more participation of the learner in various learning activities, in which constructivism based learning is applied [10].

## 4.2    Knowledge Management Course Module

This is a generic two part, two-week module on the knowledge management (KM) topic. The learning activities include both individual and collaborative activities.

Part 1: In this part each student has to visit the online university's library and search for a real-world example about a selected topic, and write a brief explanation of his/her findings. Thereafter, based on his/her previous knowledge and experience, the student has to write a 300 to 400-word-essay regarding his/her thoughts and reactions about the topic.

Part 2: Students are formed into various teams of 3 to 5 individuals and each team will read all their colleagues' postings from part 1. Each team will choose three of their colleagues' postings that they agree to evaluate and assess.

The team will write a 400 – 500-word essay that includes:

- A brief explanation of the three postings;
- Their interpretation and understandings;
- And their thoughts, advice, and reaction.

The part 1 of this module begins with exploration, in which each individual has to choose a real-world example. In addition, knowledge construction takes place in individual contexts, in which each individual presents his/her reaction based on his/her previous knowledge. In Part 2, collaborative learning and assessment among students is promoted. Knowledge construction takes place through social negotiation, collaboration and experience. At all times, the instructor evaluate students and acts as a coach, a mentor, and/or a guide to provide his/her feedback to students and to correct any mistaken understanding that may appear between students in an early stage.

## 4.3     Human Computer Interaction (HCI) Course Module

This module is seven weeks in duration. The learning activity is an HCI journal activity. It requires students to keep a human-computer interface (HCI) journal for the next six weeks and provide a summary of their report. The journal will include: Student's daily experiences and observations using devices and products with human-computer interfaces.

The students have to write a 15 page report that includes:

- A chronological log of dates that provide a clear narrative of student observations/experiences;
- Entries that contain a description of students experience;
- And one to two pages summarizing what a student has learned from this experience and how it relates to his/her own previous knowledge.

On the first day of Week 3 each student is required to post, on the discussion board, a description of his/her experience, how usable the interface was and what changes he/she would make for improvement. Thereafter, and during the same week every student must read all his/her classmates' postings and respond (providing reactions and/or viewpoints about the experience) to any of them. At the end of the six week period, students are required to post, on the discussion board, a summary of what they have learned and how their experiences relate to their previous knowledge.

During week 7 every student must read all his/her classmates' postings and respond (providing reactions and/or viewpoints about the experience) to any of them and the instructor has to guide, evaluate, read all postings and provide his/her feedback.

In this module, students document their experiences of HCI and identify the changes that could be made to improve the interface based on their previous knowledge (Problem-solving and higher-order/critical thinking skills). In addition, active participation on the discussion board promotes and encourages collaborative learning among students and multiple perspectives. For all activities, the instructor guiding, evaluating, and providing his/her feedback on the assessment to students. Moreover, collaborative assessment takes place during week 7, in which every student must read all his/her classmates' postings and evaluate them.

### 4.4    Strategic Information Management Course Module

In this module, the students are requested to make a project on corporate performance management (CPM) and information systems in small and medium enterprises (SME) and it takes 10 weeks in duration and includes three parts.

Part1: Theoretical concepts and methodology of CPM (Week 1 – 3)
Each student will visit the online university's library and search for an article that includes a real world example, then he/she should write a 700 - 800-word essay, which contains a summary of the article's findings and student's explanation of  his/her thoughts and reactions based on his/her previous experience. This task will be submitted at the end of Week 3.

Part 2: CPM in SME (Week 4)
Students must read all their colleagues' postings and form questions based on their readings to be asked from a CPM expert.

Moreover, in this part the instructor will schedule an asynchronous session on the discussion board with a CPM expert within a real company to answer students' questions.

Based on colleagues' postings and the discussion between students and the CPM expert, each student has to write a 500 – 600-word essay about his/her thoughts, reaction, and/or viewpoints.

Part 3: Information System supporting CPM (Week 5 – 10)
Students will participate in a demonstration session that includes a real-world best practice CPM in a real company. The session will be scheduled by the instructor.  The instructor will then schedule an asynchronous Q&A session with an expert within the company to further explore and examine the CPM within the company. Based on the acquired experience, students will develop a set of quality criteria that can be used in the selection process of CPM using a balanced scorecard (BSC).

The learning activities in this module starts with exploration, in which students search for a real-world example. The activities are both individual and collaborative, in which a high level of interaction takes place among students, expert consultants and the instructor.

Knowledge construction takes place in individual contexts and through social negotiation, collaboration and experience. At all times the instructor guides, provides feedback to students and assesses their learning (Facilitator's assessment).

### 4.5    Programming Assignment

This Assignment is 3 weeks in duration. The class will be divided into small teams of three to five students, in which individuals on each team will search the Internet for a simple mortgage calculator and share a description of the calculator on the team's assigned discussion board. Then, as a group, the team will create a Java program with functionality similar to what was found in the calculator on the Internet. This module consists of three parts:

In part 1, each student has to use the Internet to find a Web site that includes a mortgage payment calculator, run the calculator with a set of realistic values, and post the following on his/her team's discussion board: A link to the calculator, a description of the values that he/she input, and a description of the value(s) that the calculator generated.

In part 2, each group of students has to create a Java program that is a mortgage calculator. All codes and discussion should be posted on the discussion board. In this part, it is expected that every individual will contribute to this program and its discussion. The team's last entry in the discussion board should be the complete program. In part 3 the project is completed and each student has to submit the following paragraphs:

- A reflection on the benefits and obstacles to programming in a team environment.
- Comment on how well he/she contributed to the programming process.
- A reflection on what he/she would have done differently if he/she could do this assignment again as a team (200 to 300 words).

This assignment starts with exploration as well, in which students search for a real-world example. In addition, it supports collaborative learning, in which knowledge construction takes place in social negotiation. Students construct the new knowledge based on their previous programming knowledge and interchange it with their classmates. Furthermore, all assessment elements (Team assessment, self assessment, and instructor assessment) are included in this assignment.

# 5    Applying Constructivism Based Blended Learning to "ICT Management" Course at Hasselt University

"Information and Communication Technology (ICT) Management" is a compulsory course in Master of Management Information Systems program at Hasselt University. Part of the course description is as follows: "ICT management is responsible for ICT project management including the development and implementation of ICT solutions for the company. ICT management is organizing the ICT services enterprise-wide, supporting the business processes and the management decision making". The course consists of two modules; in the first module, the foundation of the theory and an overview of the content is presented to the students, and in the second module, a project based learning activities take place, in which constructivism characteristics are applied.

By applying Constructivism Based Blended Learning to "ICT Management" course, the lecture component will evolve from a fairly traditional teacher-centered learning to a much more interactive student-centered learning, in which Blended Learning environment and ICT tools will be utilized to facilitate and adapt Constructivism and Conversation theories in learning process.

The proposed Constructivism Blended Learning model consists of a variety of face-to-face classrooms and online learning activities. The learning process starts with a face to face lecture to give an overview of the course, discuss the most significant knowledge that will be taught, and learning strategies and tools that will be used. In this model a variety of online and face-to-face learning activities are differentiated for working students and regular students, in which Constructivism and Conversational theories are applied. These activities include collaboration, communication, and interactions between students themselves, the teacher, and the business people. In the last week of the course, the students attend a face-to-face class to make a written open book exam. Moreover, permanent email system is provided during the semester, in which the students can communicate with the teacher and expect response within 24 hours.

ICT support tools such as synchronous chat system, online conference system, online interactive whiteboard, and discussion forum play a significant role in learning process by facilitating communication, collaboration, interaction, and knowledge construction among the students.

The evaluation method used in this model, is a combination of online assessment and traditional assessment (written exam and project work). The teacher evaluates students' interactivities, participation, and their works in the online activities. In addition, at the last week the teacher evaluate the students based on their projects and their results in the written exam.

Beside the benefits of applying Constructivism and Conversation theories in this model, it takes into consideration working students in designing and implementing learning activities. Therefore it could be applied for both working students and regular students. Fig. 2 illustrates the proposed Constructivism Based Blended Learning Model for ICT Management course.

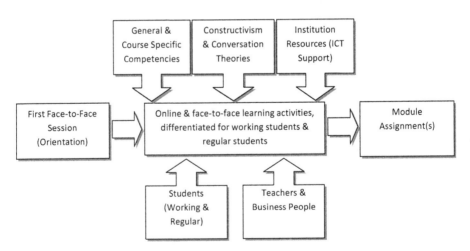

**Fig. 2.** Constructivism Based Blended Learning Model for a Course Module

The proposed learning process consists of 2 modules, in which various scenarios could be applied, as illustrated in Table 2. During these phases the students are building up and constructing the knowledge through a variety of learning activities linked with a continuous evaluation process.

**Table 2.** Constructivism Based Blended Learning process for "ICT Management" Course

| Module No. | Module Description | Period | Scenarios | Main Activities |
|---|---|---|---|---|
| 1. | Presenting the foundation of the theory by the teacher. | Two weeks | One scenario | - Presenting course guidelines, and objectives.<br>- Discussing the most important knowledge to be taught. |
| | Self-paced learning. | One week | One scenario | - Self study of course materials and presentations. |
| 2. | Search for additional knowledge/ expanding the knowledge. | Three weeks | Three scenarios | A. Self reading and asynchronous online discussion. |
| | | | | B. Internet search, preparing a presentation, and making a discussion. |
| | | | | C. Internet search, writing a report, and collaborative assessment. |
| | Link with business practices/ people. | Two weeks | Two scenarios | A. Attending a conference presented by selected business people, preparing a presentation/ summary, and making a discussion about it. |
| | | | | B. Making an interview with one of the business people, preparing a presentation, and making a discussion about it. |
| | Applying learned knowledge. | Three weeks | Four scenarios | A. Writing a report and making a video presentation about it. |
| | | | | B. Making a research about the last theory or technology in a selected topic, preparing a presentation, and making a discussion about it. |
| | | | | C. Preparing a presentation about the challenges and future trends of a selected topic and making a discussion about it. |
| | | | | D. Proposing a solution for a real life problem, selected by the teacher, and making a discussion about the proposed solutions. |
| | Written exam. | One session | One scenario | Open-book written exam. |

## 6    Conclusion

There are many benefits which make teachers choose Blended Learning over other learning strategies, such as extending the reach, increasing flexibility, pedagogical richness, reusable patterns (reusable contents and functionality), optimizing development cost, social interaction, and easy to revision and customization.

However, Blended Learning system tends to focus on the teacher for creating knowledge rather than on the student [7]. Therefore, there is a need to improve Blended Learning environment in order to apply student-centered learning methodology to increase learning outcomes, which has been achieved by applying Constructivism and Conversation theories.

Constructivism theory tends to focus on the student to construct new knowledge based on his/her experience, which increases and improves learning outcomes. Blended Learning environment and strategies has the characteristics to facilitate adapting and employing Constructivism theory's principles and elements in learning process, which improves students' critical thinking, analyzing, problem solving skills, knowledge construction, and collaborative working, through its variety of learning strategies and ICT support tools.

There are a variety of scenarios and best practices for applying Constructivism Based Blended Learning program in academic institutions, which some of them are stated in this paper in order to acquire familiarity in employing them to improve learning outcomes.

In order to increase learning outcomes and improve learning quality more effectively, we employed Conversation theory beside Constructivism theory in Blended Learning environment model for "ICT Management" course, which is a compulsory course in Master of Management Information Systems program at Hasselt University. Since Conversation theory supports Constructivism theory by facilitating collaboration, communication, interaction, and knowledge construction and sharing amongst the students.

By applying Conversation theory beside Constructivism theory in Blended Learning environment, the students have the opportunity to interact with the teacher; in addition, the teacher has the opportunity to guide and assess students' learning and knowledge construction at an early stage and take any needed correction action if there is any misconception.

Furthermore, we applied a variety of innovative ICT support tools which play a significant role in Constructivism Based Blended Learning environment, since employing an effective and interactive ICT tools, such as online interactive whiteboard, chat system, online conference system, and discussion forum, in implementing and executing learning activities, facilitates and increases collaboration, cooperation, interaction, communication, and knowledge construction and sharing among the students, which improves learning outcomes and quality.

The proposed model has many benefits and characteristics such as Self-paced learning, Constructivism based learning, collaborative assessment, independent problem-solving skills, critical thinking, collaboration, communication, interactivity, knowledge sharing, and flexibility.

Further research remains to be done on different levels and wider scope, such as designing and implementing a more customized, dynamic, and flexible learning models, and utilizing more innovative ICT tools and strategies, such as social media, in learning process. Moreover, future research should focus on primary education and how to design and implement a Constructivism Based Blended Learning model for primary levels. The new generation of students in primary levels is more familiar with ICT tools and able to learn new ICT skills more quickly, which can be employed to design and implement a Constructivism Based Blended Learning model for primary levels to increase and improve learning outcomes and experience.

# References

1. Mackay, S., Stockport, G.J.: Blended Learning, Classroom and E-Learning. The Business Review 5(1), 82–88 (2006)
2. Singh, H.: Building Effective Blended Learning Programs. Issue of Educational Technology 43(6), 51–54 (2003)
3. Schuman, L.: Perspectives on instruction (1996)
   http://edweb.sdsu.edu/courses/edtec540/Perspectives/
   Perspectives.html (retrieved July 05, 2010)
4. Alonso, F., Manrique, G.L.D., Vines, J.M.: An instructional model for web-based e-learning education with a blended learning process approach. British Journal of Educational Technology 36(219) (2005)
5. Singh, H.: Building effective blended learning programs. Educational Technology 43(6), 51–54 (2003),
   http://www.bookstoread.com/framework/blended-learning.pdf
   (retrieved July 09, 2010)
6. Bremer, C.: Design of a Group Oriented. Virtual Learning Environment (1998),
   http://www.bremer.cx/paper1/ (retrieved July 09, 2010)
7. Carbonaro, M., King, S., Taylor, E., Satzinger, F., Snart, F., Drummond, J.: Integration of e-learning technologies in an interprofessional health science course. University of Alberta, Canada (2008)
8. Koohang, A., Riley, L., Smith, T., Schreurs, J.: E-Learning and Constructivism: From Theory to Application. Hasselt University, Belgium (2009)
9. Al-Huneidi, A.: Constructivism Based Blended Learning in Higher Education. Master thesis, Hasselt University, Belgium (2011)
10. Schreurs, J., Al-Huneidi, A.: Development of a learner-centered learning process for a course. Case: The course Business Information Systems in Hasselt University. In: Techeducation 2011 Conference, Corfu, Greece, May 18-20 (2011)

# The Relevance of Context in Trust Networks

Vincenza Carchiolo, Alessandro Longheu, Michele Malgeri,
and Giuseppe Mangioni

Dipartimento di Ingegneria Elettrica Elettronica ed Informatica
Facoltà di Ingegneria - Università degli Studi di Catania - Italy

**Abstract.** The increasing use of Internet in real world activities such as e-commerce, blogs, wikies and several others makes the question of trust a critical issue. However, everyone can push information on line, so it is not easy to get knowledge about trust from centralized authorities. Moreover, discovering trusted entities often stricly depends on what context that entity is related to or it is actually exploited for. We address this issue by presenting an approach of searching for a "guru" user (expert in a specific context) using local, context-dependent information within the Epinions.com recommendation network. Results show that context-based search can be used to significantly reduce the number of nodes (users) to query with a limited loss of "guru" nodes.

## 1  Introduction

The evolution of hardware and software technologies together with the ubiquitous high–speed connectivity determined an unthinkable amount of services based on the interactions among Internet users. As a consequence, more and more human interactions have been transposed into the virtual world of e-commerce, file sharing, on-line communities, blogs, wikies and p2p networks, to cite some [1]. In such a scenario, the role of trust and recommender systems has been consolidated as a way of selecting valid (trusted) persons and/or valid (recommended) items, somehow mitigating the lack of a physical counterpart in virtual interactions.

Trust is a broad research topic that spanned different areas in addition to computer science, as sociology, psychology and economics [2,3,4,5,6]. On the other hand, the recommendation is an information filtering technique that generally exploits users' profiles to rank interesting items; most important algorithms for recommendation are referred as *collaborative filtering* [7,8].

Often recommender systems leverage trust, allowing to select the items recommended by trusted users. According to this vision, several authors proposed algorithms that associate each user with a trustworthiness index used to rank the items according to users' recommendation [9,10,11,12,13,14].

Most approaches however do not consider the context (area of interest) where trust is assigned. For instance, it is reasonable that in real life I trust a lot the

M.D. Lytras et al. (Eds.): WSKS 2011, CCIS 278, pp. 592–600, 2013.

mechanic I used to go anytime my car is broken down, but this does not imply that I will trust him enough to put my children in his hands, thus I assign him a high trustworthiness in the "car repairing" context and a low one in the "baby sitting" context. The concept of context-dependent trust is sometimes referred to as *expertise* [15,16], although trust and expertise are sometimes considered distinct concepts [17]; in the rest of paper, we will use the term expertise.

The context can be used to improve the quality of recommendations by selecting those provided by users not generally *trusted* but *expert* in the same context those recommendations are about. For instance, when searching for a new car the opinion of a good mechanic or a professional driver should be considered more relevant than others. In this paper we explore the relevance of context in trust networks, showing how the search for a trusted user can be more efficient when context is exploited, i.e. when trust become expertise. We adopt the Epinions.com recommendation network [18] as a working scenario, using a dataset extracted from the site to illustrate how product categories (i.e., contexts) can be effectively used to improve the search of an expert user's recommendations, in particular minimizing the number of nodes to query in the network.

In section 2 we describe the logic behind the Epinions website and how the dataset has been extracted. Our proposal is introduced in section 3 and in section 4 simulations of effective context-based searches are shown. Section 5 presents our conclusions and future works.

## 2   The Working Dataset

As described in the introduction, our goal is to show that searching for an expert user's recommendations can be more efficient if biased by the context. The scenario where this can be applied is a recommendation network (in the following, it will be referred to as the *dataset*). The dataset can be synthesized according to a given structure or it can be derived from a (virtual) social network. The use of a synthesized dataset allows to impose specific properties - for instance, the network topology - but it is quite difficult to achieve a trust distribution faithful to real world. On the other hand, the use of a real dataset is usually more complex due to the difficulty to find an adequate example that tailors to our needs. To work on a real distribution we chose a dataset extracted from the Epinions.com website.

Epinions (http://www.epinions.com) is a recommendation system that *"helps people make informed buying decisions"*[18]. This goal is achieved through unbiased advices, personalized recommendations, and comparative shopping. Epinions allows registered users to rate products writing a review in order to provide visitors with opinions; a review can be represented as a numeric value plus a text comment about the product. Registered users also rate the reviews thus establishing whether they were useful or not in evaluating the product. We use the Epinions dataset to validate our approach because it is a large and real dataset and although it is mainly a recommendation network, the product reviews' rating mechanism can be easily interpreted as an user expertise assessment, where the expertise is inferred from the rates users assigned to authors of products reviews within a given context (the category that product falls into).

In particular, we started by considering an user $w$ writing a review on a product belonging to a given category, and another user $v$ that can provide a rank to $w$'s review, considering it *useful* or not; $w$ can provide several reviews on products belonging to different categories, and $v$ can rate all of them.

Based on such information, we then build the expertise assessment relationship $(v,w)$ and label it with a set of pairs $\{(c_i, x_i)\}$, where we associate each context to exactly one products category $i$, and the expertise $x_i$ with the rate $v$ provided about $w$'s review for the product belonging to the category $c_i$; note that in the case $w$ reviewed more products belonging to the same category, we evaluate the normalized average rate provided by $v$ over all these products, so that $x_i$ is within the $[0,1]$ range. Of course, we discard all users that did not provide any review, which is however a limited set since the nature of Epinions is to endorse users in writing reviews.

In summary, the network is modeled as a directed edge-labeled graph $\mathcal{G}(\mathcal{V}, \mathcal{E})$ on which is defined the vertex labeling function $\mathcal{F}_{\mathcal{L}} : \mathcal{E} \rightarrow \mathcal{L}$, where $\mathcal{L}$ is the set of pairs $\{(c_i, x_i)\}$ described above. Each $e \in \mathcal{E}$ is the relationship between two users $v$ and $w$, and is mapped by $\mathcal{F}_{\mathcal{L}}$ to one or more pairs $((c_i, x_i) \in \mathcal{L})$, depending on how many context were involved when $v$ rated $w$'s reviews.

Note that the set of contexts $\mathcal{C}=\{c_i\}$ corresponds to the set of product categories inside Epinions, hence we did not considered different contexts vocabulary, e.g. based on external ontologies. Moreover, categories in Epinions are arranged into a hierarchy with general entries (e.g., Electronics) that embed specific subcategories (e.g. cameras, dvd players etc.); in this first work however, we did not exploit categories semantic relationships as synonymity or hypernonymity that could be inferred from the hierarchy. Moreover, in according to the Epinions review rating scale, an expertise rate $x_i$ can assume one value in the set $\{1, ..., 5\}$, where 1 means the review was not helpful and 5 means "most helpful". Finally, table 1 summarizes the characteristics of the dataset extracted from Epinions website we used in our experiments.

**Table 1.** Characteristics of the dataset extracted from Epinions website

| Dataset extracted from www.epinions.com | |
| --- | --- |
| # users | 196 000 |
| # contexts | 114 000 |
| # rated reviews | 13 670 000 |

## 3    Exploiting Context in Searching Expert Nodes

The goal of this paper is to propose an algorithm aiming at finding a set of expert users using context and inferred expertise information, minimizing the computational cost needed to explore the expertise network. The search strategy we applied to the dataset described in the previous section is based on the following criteria:

- the deepness of the search must be limited in order to avoid an overuse of network resources. An idea is to use average path length to limit the deepness of the visit. We implemented this by simply counting the number of *hops* from the source (searching) user.
- expertise level must be as high as possible during the network search. Usually lower expertise diminish the impact of the response up to drop results, therefore the search stops when the expertise of encountered users (in the meaningfully context) is less than a given threshold.
- we prefer users that are expert in the searched context, or in some others *similar* to the involved context. The question of context similarity (e.g. *TVs* category is intuitively much more related to *electronics* than *wellness and beauty*) is not a trivial matter and requires a specific metric. Measuring the semantic distance $sim(c_i, c_j)$ between terms $c_i$ and $c_j$ (here, contexts) has been considered in literature [19,20,21]), however in this first work the implementation we provided for $sim(c_i, c_j)$ is the equality (i.e., $sim(c_i, c_j)=1$ if and only if $c_i=c_j$ and 0 otherwise).

---

**Algorithm 1.** local behaviour

---

**Require:** setOfNeighbours, i.e. set of edge starting from the local node $l$ ($l$=sourceNode at first step)
**Require:** the minimum expertise level required $\tau$
**Require:** the desired context $\bar{c}$
**Require:** the desired context similarity $\bar{s}$
  **loop**
    **wait for** a search request (if this node is the starting node, the request is local, otherwise is remote)
    {searching for users with expertise greater or equal to $\tau$ within the context $\bar{c}$}
    **for all** $userId \in$ setOfNeighbours **do**
      {finding expert users}
      **if** in the set of pairs $(c_i, x_i)$ labelling the expertise relationship $(l, userId)$ there exists at least $c_i=\bar{c}$ and the corresponding $x_i$ is greater than or equal to $\tau$ **then**
        send to sourceNode the $userId$
      **end if**
      {search propagation}
      **if** in the set $\{(c_i, x_i)\}$ labelling $(l, userId)$ there exists at least $c_i$: $sim(c_i, \bar{c}) \geq \bar{s}$ and $x_i \geq \tau$ **then**
        forward to $userId$ the request
      **end if**
    **end for**
  **end loop**

---

The algorithm 1 is performed by each user and needs only local knowledge according with the hypothesis of a fully distributed system. Also note that here $\bar{s}=1$.

Once sourceNode collects enough responses he needs to rank them according to their properties in order to provide an effective response. We assign a score to each found user (target) according to *the best path* joining sourceNode with the target; to calculate the best path we use a proper cost function (here omitted) that takes into account both expertise and context. Therefore, the score assigned to each target also depends on the lenght of the path because the longer is the path the lower is the expertise level.

## 4   Simulations

The goal of the simulation is to assess the effectiveness and the efficiency of the algorithm proposed in the previous section. As discussed above we performed the simulations using a dataset extracted from a the Epinions recommendation network.

All simulations refer to 100 sets of 10 000 users randomly extracted from the original dataset in order to reduce the biasing due to the network topology and users. For a sake of simplicity, the system has been simulated globally, without any loss of generality, using the algorithm 2. This algorithm has a global behaviour that is equivalent to the distributed version discussed in the previous section, but is easier to implement and analyze since it does not need to tackle users communication matters.

The first simulation shows the search of nodes expert in a given context analizing all neighbours along the network, starting from the node that issued the search query. The path lenght has been limited up to 50 hops and the minimum expertise level of nodes we are searching is 3. This comes from the observation of the Epinions dataset. As in most trust networks indeed, users tend to assigns rating to reviews only if they found them useful, so the rate is either absent or present with high values. In our Epinions dataset, the 85% of ratings falls within the 3...5 range, whereas only the remaining 15% is 1 or 2. Our assumption is that reviews rating are used to infer the expertise levels, so it assumes high values (3 or more) too; this is the reason for which 3 is the reasonable minimum expertise level.

The figure 1 shows the results obtained averaging on 100 simulation sessions on different sets of 10 000 users. The number of target is calculated (for each session) at 5, 10, 30 and 50 hops in order to highlight the evolution of the search during the network crawling. In figure 1 (a) the expertise threshold $\tau$ introduced in algorithm 2 is 1, i.e., we removed the rating constraint on searched nodes in order to find all targets (this is why the figure is labelled "unlimited"). In the "limited" experiment in figure 1 (b), we introduced the constraint on the rating of the final target at 3; compared with the previous experiment, slightly less targets have been found but with a lower network traffic. In both figures 1 (a) and (b) refer to simulations where contexts have not been considered in search propagation.

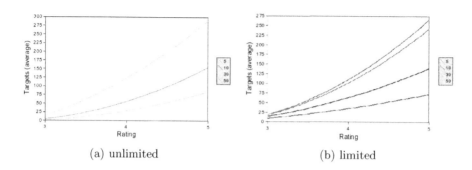

(a) unlimited                    (b) limited

**Fig. 1.** Searching experts without using context information

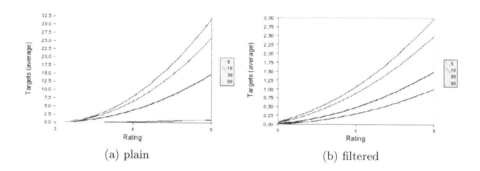

(a) plain                    (b) filtered

**Fig. 2.** Searching experts using 100 contexts

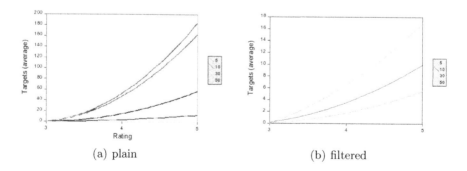

(a) plain                    (b) filtered

**Fig. 3.** Searching experts using 1000 contexts

**Algorithm 2.** Centralized Algorithm

---

**Require:** sourceNode
**Require:** maxDeepness
**Require:** expertiseThreshold $\tau$
**Require:** setOfContexts (desired contexts)
**Require:** the desired context similarity $\bar{s}$
  $currentUser$ = sourceNode
  **while** maxDeepness $> 0$ **do**
    **for all** $userId \in currentUser's\,Neighbours$ **do**
      **if** in the set of pairs $(c_i, x_i)$ labelling $(currentUser, userId)$ there exists at least a $c_i \in setOfContexts$ **then**
        push(userId)
      **else**
        **if** there exists at least a $c_i \in \{(c_i, x_i)\}$ labelling $(currentUser, userId)$ and a $c_j \in setOfContexts : sim(c_i, c_j) \geq \bar{s}$ AND $x_i \geq \tau$ **then**
          push(userId)
        **end if**
      **end if**
    **end for**
    currentUser = pop()
  **end while**

---

In the next simulations we introduced contexts to forward the query (as stated in the algorithm 2): only users expert in the searched context will be asked for targets. Rather than using a single desired context $\bar{c}$, here we introduced a $setOfContexts$, which is a set of 100 (figure 2) and 1000 (figure 3) different contexts randomly chosen among the 114 000 our dataset exposes. Each result is first presented for $\tau=1$ (referred to as "plain" and shown at the left in figures 2 and 3 ), and then with $\tau=3$ (referred to as "filtered" and shown at the right of the same figures ); this constraint is applied at each step, i.e. for each neighbour that receives and forwards the query.

Simulations show that the more contexts are considered, the better is the result since more contexts implies that more paths can be explored. On the other hand, filtered results are always worst than the corresponding unfiltered since the constraint on the expertise level prunes away all not expert nodes during the search. [1]

Finally, we provided some measure concerning the efficiency of our proposal, in particular we considered the search space, strongly related with bandwidth. Fig 4 clearly shows that users involved in a context-aware search are much less than user involved in a plain flooding (first row), in conclusion confirming that the proposed approach, although appearing to be less effective in finding expert users, is able to save a lot of computational resources.

---

[1] Ho cercato di seguire l'impostazione data da michele, ma mi e' venuto piuttosto complesso, anche rileggendo la tesi, vedete se tutto il discorso quadra.

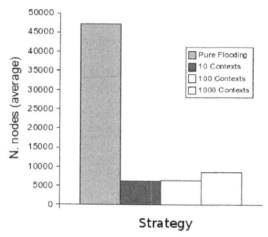

**Fig. 4.** Search space comparison (efficiency)

## 5    Conclusions

In this paper we presented an approach of searching for a "guru" user (expert node in a specific context) using context-dependent and expertise information within the Epinions.com recommendation network. Results shown that the proposed context-based search, although appearing to be less effective in finding expert users, is able to save a lot of computational resources since it significantly reduces the number of nodes (users) to query.

Future works include the possibility of exploiting categories semantic relationships as synonymity or hypernonymity that could be inferred from the hierarchy, or even the adoption of some external reference ontology. Moreover, the semantic similarity function deserves a major attention since its implementation could significantly affect the search. Finally, other large dataset in addition to that of Epinions should be used to validate our proposal.

## References

1. Wellman, B.: Computer networks as social networks. Science 293(5537), 2031–2034 (2001)
2. Dunn, J.: The Concept of Trust in the Politics of John Locke. In: Philosophy in History. Cambridge University Press (1984)
3. McKnight, D.H., Chervany, N.L.: The meanings of trust. Technical report, Minneapolis, USA (1996)
4. Misztal, B.: Trust in Modern Societies. Polity Press (1996)
5. Golbeck, J.: Trust and nuanced profile similarity in online social networks. ACM Transactions on the Web (2008) (to appear)
6. Abdul-Rahman, A., Hailes, S.: Supporting trust in virtual communities. In: HICSS 2000: Proceedings of the 33rd Hawaii International Conference on System Sciences, vol. 6, p. 6007. IEEE Computer Society, Washington, DC (2000)

7. Goldberg, D., Nichols, D., Oki, B.M., Terry, D.: Using collaborative filtering to weave an information tapestry. Communications of the ACM 35(12), 61–70 (1992)

8. Su, X., Khoshgoftaar, T.M.: A survey of collaborative filtering techniques. Advances in Artificial Intelligence, 1–20 (2009)

9. Walter, F.E., Battiston, S., Schweitzer, F.: A model of a trust-based recommendation system on a social network. Journal of Autonomous Agents and Multi-Agent Systems 16, 57 (2008)

10. Marti, S., Garcia-Molina, H.: Limited reputation sharing in P2P systems. In: EC 2004: Proceedings of the 5th ACM Conference on Electronic Commerce, pp. 91–101. ACM Press, New York (2004)

11. Kamvar, S. D., Schlosser, M.T., Garcia-Molina, H.:The eigentrust algorithm for reputation management in P2P networks. In: Proceedings of the Twelfth International World Wide Web Conference (2003)

12. Zhou, R., Hwang, K.: Powertrust: A robust and scalable reputation system for trusted peer-to-peer computing. IEEE Trans. Parallel Distrib. Syst. 18(4), 460–473 (2007)

13. Zhou, R., Hwang, K., Cai, M.: Gossiptrust for fast reputation aggregation in peer-to-peer networks. IEEE Trans. on Knowl. and Data Eng. 20(9), 1282–1295 (2008)

14. Carchiolo, V., Longheu, A., Malgeri, M., Mangioni, G., Nicosia, V.: Applying Social Behaviours to Model Trusting. In: Badica, C., Paprzycki, M. (eds.) IDC 2008. SCI, vol. 78, pp. 105–114. Springer, Heidelberg (2008)

15. Grandison, T., Sloman, M.: A survey of trust in internet application. IEEE Communication Surveys and Tutorials 4(4), 2–16 (2000)

16. Freeman, J., Stacy, W., MacMillan, J., Levchuk, G.: Capturing and Building Expertise in Virtual Worlds. In: Schmorrow, D.D., Estabrooke, I.V., Grootjen, M. (eds.) FAC 2009. LNCS, vol. 5638, pp. 148–154. Springer, Heidelberg (2009)

17. Artz, D., Gil, Y.: A survey of trust in computer science and the semantic web. Web Semantics: Science, Services and Agents on the World Wide Web 5(2), 58–71 (2007)

18. Shopping.com Network: Epinions.com © (1999-2010), http://www.epinion.com

19. Salton, G., Wong, A., Yang, C.S.: A vector space model for automatic indexing. Communications of ACM 18(11), 613–620 (1975)

20. Resnik, P.: Using information content to evaluate semantic similarity in a taxonomy. In: IJCAI, pp. 448–453 (1995)

21. Banerjee, S., Pedersen, T.: An adapted lesk algorithm for word sense disambiguation using wordnet. Computational Linguistics and Intelligent Text Processing, 117–171 (2002)

# Applying MapReduce to Spreading Activation Algorithm on Large RDF Graphs

Jorge González Lorenzo[1] , José Emilio Labra Gayo[2],
and José María Álvarez Rodríguez[3]

[1] Universidad de Oviedo
jorgonlor@gmail.com
[2] Universidad de Oviedo
labra@uniovi.es
[3] Universidad de Oviedo
josem.alvarez@weso.es

**Abstract.** Over the recent years, the Semantic Web has experienced a considerable growth. Governments and organizations are putting major efforts in making information publicly available using Semantic Web formats. Algorithms such as spreading activation have effectively been used for finding relevant and related information on Semantic Web datasets. But, as the Semantic Web grows, these datasets quickly outgrow the computational capacity of a single machine. The same computational problems found in the past in the traditional web arise. On the other hand, computational frameworks like MapReduce have proven successful resolving problems that handle large amounts of data. We introduce an implementation of the spreading activation algorithm using MapReduce paradigm, discussing the problems of applying this paradigm to graph problems and proposing solutions. Hereby, a concrete experiment with real data is presented to illustrate the algorithm performance and scalability.

**Keywords:** Spreading Activation, MapReduce, Semantic Web, RDF.

## 1   Introduction

The Semantic Web [1] is considered as an extension of the World Wide Web, adding metadata understandable by machines; and the same issues about size addressed in the traditional web are present. The Semantic Web data is expressed using RDF triples, each consisting of a subject, a predicate and an object. A set of such triples is called an RDF graph. If data is modeled through a graph, then we can use graph algorithms to explore this data. One of these algorithms is the spreading activation algorithm [2]. But, if we take into account that the whole Semantic Web has billions of triples, it is obvious that the generated graph would be very large to fit into one single machine. Fortunately, this kind of size issues has been solved before in the traditional web by using parallel and distributed computing approaches. One of the most successfully applied framework for parallel and distributed processing is MapReduce[3]. MapReduce has proven to be efficient resolving problems involving big data, whereas low latency is not required.

M.D. Lytras et al. (Eds.): WSKS 2011, CCIS 278, pp. 601–611, 2013.

The main motivation of our research if providing a way of reducing the amount of time needed for processing large RDF datasets. In this article, an implementation of the spreading activation algorithm using the MapReduce programming model is presented. The spreading activation algorithm is used to find out related concepts starting from a set of activated nodes. The algorithm propagates this activation through the graph vertices, and, at the end, the related concepts are the ones with highest activation level. First, we describe the main problems of solving graph problems with MapReduce, and then the decisions and details about the final implementation of the algorithm are shown. Finally, a result section is presented to demonstrate the scalability of the implementation.

## 2     Previous Work

### 2.1     MapReduce

MapReduce is a framework introduced by Google in 2004 for processing huge datasets using a large number of machines in a parallel and distributed way [3]. MapReduce framework transparently handles system-level details, such as scheduling, fault tolerance or synchronization. The main advantages of the framework is the simplicity of the map and reduce operations, that allow a high degree of parallelism with little overhead, at the cost of writing programs in a way that fits this programming model. MapReduce has proven to be efficient and is used by Google internally for processing petabyte order datasets. This success has motivated the apparition of the open source initiative Hadoop[1], which is an Apache project mainly developed and supported by Yahoo.

MapReduce handles all the information using tuples of the form *<key, value>*. Every job consists of two phases: a map phase and a reduce phase. The map phase process the input tuples and produce some others intermediate tuples. Input tuples are divided in groups, each of them processed by a map function running in a single machine. Then, these intermediate tuples are grouped together according to their key value forming a group. Finally, each group is processed by the reduce function, producing a set of output tuples.

### 2.2     Spreading Activation

The spreading activation algorithm (SA) was introduced as an approach for modeling the human memory and its cognitive processes by following its low-level structure [2]. It takes advantage of the similarity between neural networks and graph models, so the same ideas behind the spreading activations mechanisms can be applied to graphs modeled problems. The algorithm has been successfully applied to problems like categorization, information retrieval and search engine ranking [4, 5, 6, 7, 9]. The SA process starts with the activation of an initial set of vertices of the graph. An initial activation value is assigned to these vertices and then this activation is propagated to the connected vertices, taking into account the weight of the edges that join these vertices. This operation is repeated in an iterative process which uses a decay factor to

---

[1] http://hadoop.apache.org

model the idea of the energy of the activation dying out. The process stops after a predetermined number of iterations. Nodes with an activation level over a certain threshold are considered active. The inactive nodes are filtered out and the selection ends up with a sub-graph representing the nodes most related to the initial ones.

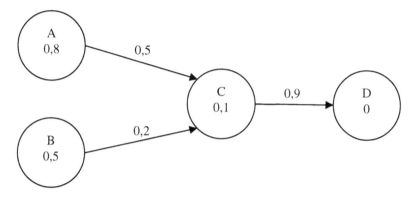

**Fig. 1.** Spreading activation graph example

The illustration (Fig. 1) shows a basic example of semantic graph with four vertices (A, B, C and D) and three edges connecting them. Vertices have an activation level and edges have a weight. At a given time, activation levels are the one shown in fig. 1, and we set a firing threshold of 0,4. In order to calculate activation levels for next iteration, we should propagate the activation of vertex A and B to vertex C, given that A and B are the only vertices with activation level over the threshold, using the formula:

$$A_j = A_j + \sum_i A_i \cdot w_{ij} \cdot D \tag{1}$$

Activation level of vertex C is calculated as the sum of incoming-connected vertices activation (A and B in the example), considering edge weight and a decay factor $D$. In the next iteration, vertex C is supposed to have activation over the threshold so it will propagate activation to vertex D, and so on.

## 3    Spreading Activation and MapReduce

### 3.1    Graph Problems and MapReduce

In order to apply MapReduce to solve a SA problem we need to take into account some considerations. Since the SA algorithm resolution is ultimately a graph problem, we will need a MapReduce algorithm that also operates on a graph. This will bring some disadvantages. Due to the large size of the datasets, this graph is also expected to be very large, and therefore impossible to fit into one single machine. For example, a foaf graph can span millions of vertices and edges, making very difficult to analyze it. Representing the graph as a matrix and trying to solve it using matrix operations is neither a valid solution for the same reason, matrix would be too big. We need to divide data and parallelize calculations in order to be processed independently using many machines at the same time. The key idea for this implementation is to consider the graph as a group of smaller graphs each of which can be processed individually in a single node, not requiring data from other nodes. The RDF data graph can be represented as a set of connections, each one comprising two nodes (subject and object) and an edge (predicate). Each machine of the cluster will have only a small set of connections and perform operations on this piece of data knowing nothing about other parts of the graph. Using this approach we solve another problem: the input is not ordered. For a given vertex, some ingoing or outgoing edges will be found at some point of a file, and some other edges of the same vertex will be in other point. With this approach we don't need to have all the edges of a node at the same time in order to make calculations. But if we need so, the MapReduce framework will do this for us in the shuffle phase. In other words, for a given vertex, calculations that don't need all the information of that vertex at the same time will be done in the *mapper* function, while calculations that need all the information about a vertex will be performed in the *reducer* function. This approach has proved to be successful in similar algorithms such as Pagerank [8].

### 3.2    Applying MapReduce to the Spreading Activation Algorithm

The SA resolution can be seen as an iterative process. At a given time we have some vertices with an activation level over a certain threshold, others below the threshold and others not activated at all. Vertices activated over the threshold propagate activation to the outgoing edges. Therefore, vertices receiving activation need to know all the incoming values of their incoming edges in order to calculate their final activation value for a given iteration. So we can identify two phases here. The first one iterating on all the vertices of the graph, checking if activation is over the threshold and, if so, propagating activation to vertices connected by outgoing edges. This phase can be performed independently on each vertex of the graph not needing any other information, so we will carry out these calculations in the *mapper* function. The other phase would be, for each node, sum all the incoming activations in order to calculate the final activation of the vertex at the end of this step. This will require grouping all the data involving a given vertex; fortunately the MapReduce framework will do this for us. MapReduce group the pairs before the reduce phase attending to the key value. In the map phase, for a given vertex, if we emit pairs pointing out in the key the identifier of the outgoing-connected vertex and in the value the activation provided by the current vertex, the framework will group all the ingoing activation values for a given node in the reducer function. Then, we will only need to sum these values inside the reducer function. At this point, current iteration would be finished, and pairs emitted in the reduce phase are used as input in next iteration. This iterative process can finish on different conditions, like a fixed number of iterations.

### 3.3    Iterative Graph Problems and MapReduce

There is a disadvantage on using MapReduce for solving iterative graph problems: graph structure must be available at the end of every iteration. In our case, if we just emit pairs of activated vertices, all the other ones will be missed in the next iteration.

This issue is commonly resolved passing along the graph structure from the *mappers* to the *reducers* [14]. In other words: the *mapper* do normal algorithm calculations, emits a pair for every edge of an activated vertex, but also emits a pair for every node and its connections, no matters if that node is activated or not. We will denote these vertices as network vertices. Note that this is already done at the end of the *mapper* function. A special flag indicating if the pair is a network structure pair is necessary and is used in the *reducer* to distinguish between network pairs and activation pairs. The *reducer* combines, not only all the incoming activated edges but the network structure pairs in order to obtain at the end of the iteration the whole graph again. In other words, for a given vertex, network pairs provide the outgoing edges of the vertex, and not network pairs are used to calculate the activation level of that vertex.

# 4     System Architecture

We divide the full processing in three stages. The pre-processing phase imports data and set initial values. Then the spreading phase, computes activation and spread it over the graph iteratively. Finally the post-processing phase retrieves relevant information from the output. Each of these stages are implemented as a MapReduce job.

## 4.1     Pre-processing

In this stage, initial activation levels of vertices and weights of edges are set to a specific value. This phase is executed only once, before the spreading phase. The number of edges and vertices in the RDF graph can be very large, therefore it can be interesting the use of methods like default values or regular expressions, and specify individual activations and weights only for a small set of elements.

## 4.2     Spreading: Mapper function

The mapper function receives pairs of the form *<key, value>* where key is the vertex identifier, and value is a structure that contains the current activation value of the vertex, and a list of outgoing edges, one for each outgoing connection with other vertex. This connection info will be composed of a vertex identifier and a weight. The mapper function then checks, for the current pair, if the vertex is activated and if so, spread the activation to the connected vertices. In order to spread the activation, it has to iterate over all the vertex outgoing connections, and emit a pair where key is the identifier of the outgoing vertex, and the value is the source vertex activation value multiplied by the edge weight and a decay factor.

```
map(key, value)
    if value.activation > threshold and not value.visited
        value.visited = true
        for connection in value.connections
```

```
        output.activation = value.activation *
          connection.weight * decay_factor
        output.network = false
        emit(connection.node_id, output)
    end
  end
  value.network = true
  emit(key, value)
end
```

[Map function pseudo code]

Following the example illustrated in fig. 1, the only vertices activated are *A* and *B*, they both have vertex *C* as destination. Therefore two pairs would be emitted *<C, 0.4>* and *<C, 0.1>*. Key value is *C* in both cases, corresponding to the destination vertex of *A* and *B*, and the float value is vertex activation level multiplied by edge weight. A pair for network reconstruction is also emitted, one for each edge of the graph. The need of these pairs is explained in the section "Iterative Graphs Problems and MapReduce".

### 4.3    Spreading: Reducer function

The reducer function receives a key and a tuple of values, where key is the vertex identifier and each value is a structure containing an activation value provided by each incoming-connected vertex. Previously, the framework has grouped all the pairs with same value, so in each call to the reduce function we have all the incoming activation levels for a given node. In order to calculate the total activation of this vertex, all activations values must be added together. Finally, a pair with the node identifier used as key, and a value structure with the total activation level and connections is emitted. It is also necessary to distinguish between normal vertex info and network info, the first ones contain only activation values the second ones contain also connection information.

```
reduce(key, iterator values)
  total_activation = 0
  network_activation = 0
  visited = false
  for node_info in values
    if not node_info.network
      output.activation += node_info.activation
    else
      output.connections += node_info.connections
      network_activation = node_info.activation
      visited = node_info.visited
    end
```

```
  end
  if not visited
    output.activation = network_activation
  end
emit(key, output)
end
```

[Reduce function pseudo code]

Continuing with the map example, we have pairs *<C, 0.4>* and *<C, 0.1>* that had been emitted before. Now, the framework would group these two pairs, since both have the same key. So these two pairs will be processed in the same reduce call. A pair with key *C* and a list of activations as value would be received *<C, [0.4, 0.1]>*.

The reducer function should now sum all the activations values in order to calculate the final activation of *C* at the end of this iteration. Edges going out from C must also be emitted as value in order to have available the network topology in next iteration.

These special pairs are emitted by the map function, and combined here in the reduce with the activation information (see section "Iterative Graphs Problems and MapReduce" for further details). The final emitted pair would be *<C, [0.5 D]>*, containing the node identifier as key, and the final activation and reachable vertices, in this case *0.5* and *D* respectively.

### 4.4    Post-processing

This phase consists in retrieving results from the output. Since the algorithm is an iterative process, the results are the output of the last iteration. This task can be different depending on the kind of problem we are solving and the results we want to extract. Usually, output is so large that another MapReduce job is advisable for parsing the data. Some common tasks in this phase are ordering and normalization.

## 5    Results

For the evaluation of our implementation we have set up a cluster comprising 16 nodes and a 10/100 MB connection. Each node is equipped with a Pentium 4 dual core processor, 1GB RAM and a 160GB hard disk. We have used the open source implementation Hadoop, version 0.20.203, latest stable version to date.

The experiment program consists of a configuration of the algorithm for finding related people using *foaf* data. The chosen dataset is the one used in the Billion Triple Change[2] in the year 2009 , which is real-world data crawled from many different semantic search engines. We set up a high activation value to one o more specific individuals for those who we want to find out related people, and weighting the

---

[2] http://challenge.semanticweb.org

*foaf:knows* relation over the rest. Then, we run the program on the cluster and, after the execution finishes, we obtain a sorted list of related people. In order to make calculations over the whole input and avoiding discarding most of the RDF graph, we set up a default activation value and a default weight for every vertex and edge in the net, so every vertex is processed and all the connections are used as a part of the calculations. We configured the algorithm to execute four iterations.

We made two different experiments using this program, in order to obtain two different measures. The first one for proving algorithm scalability as data grows, and the second one to measure how execution time behaves when more nodes are added to the cluster. Every test has been repeated three times in order to obtain average measures.

We report in figure 2 the result of the first experiment varying input data size and maintaining the number of nodes in the cluster to a fixed value. For this experiment we have used 16 nodes in the cluster.

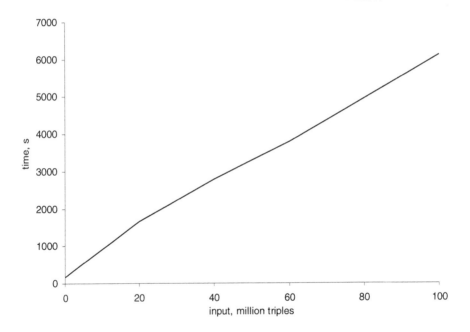

**Fig. 1.** Scalability with different input size

A linear correspondence between execution time and input size can be observed, proving that the algorithm scales well as data grows.

The other experiment keeps a fixed input data size and changed the amount of nodes in the cluster. The same program for finding related people, with exactly the same configuration has also been used for this experiment. We started with a single node configuration, and repeated the experiment with 2, 4, 8 and 16 nodes. Results of this experiment are shown in figure 3.

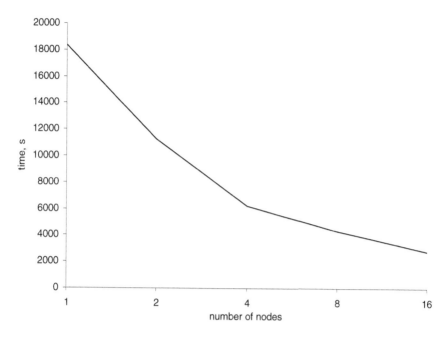

**Fig. 2.** Scalability with different nodes

In figure 3 we can observe how execution time reduces as more nodes are added to the cluster. This is the expected result and means that the algorithm scales well as more computing units are used, something essential for a MapReduce program. However, performance does not increase linearly as more nodes are added. If we take a look at execution time in figure 3, we can see that there is not a linear correspondence between time and number of nodes. This is because of the overhead introduced by the framework. A fragment of time is lost in setting up machines and communication between the different nodes in the cluster. If too many nodes are used, and input is not big enough, then overhead time becomes significant compared with computation time. We can conclude that, for a fixed input size, there is an amount of nodes above which is not worth adding more. Also, there are other framework configuration parameters, such as splits size that can dramatically affect performance, as has been stated by Kambatla et al [10].

## 6    Related Work

Jimmy Lin and Chris Dyer [8] have studied the application of MapReduce to text processing problems in the context of natural language processing, information retrieval and machine learning. More specifically, they have used MapReduce on graph problems, like the calculation of Pagerank. They have also stated common mistakes, proposed design patterns and strategies for solving graph problems using

MapReduce. Some of the issues presented in their research were found during the development of our implementation, especially graph structure problems.

Alexander Schätzle et al [11, 12] have applied MapReduce to many different problems related to the Semantic Web and RDF graphs. They have worked on mapping SPARQL to Pig Latin, and done some research on processing large RDF graphs using MapReduce. Their work is focused on performing path queries on very large graphs.

Alan Dix et al [14] describe a collection of methods to allow SA to be used on web-scale information resources. In their work, they use custom methods and procedures to manage semantic data, with special emphasis on RDF repositories and data caching.

Jose María Álvarez Rodrigues et al [4] have applied successfully the Spreading Activation algorithm in medical ontologies for recommending concepts.

Jacopo Urbani et al [16] have developed a distributed reasoner using MapReduce that works on web scale input data. They describe the problem of very large scale reasoning and propose a Hadoop implementation that outperforms all existing solutions.

## 7    Conclusions and Future Work

Due to the enormous quantities of data generated in the Semantic Web, parallel and distributed computing paradigms are more crucial than ever. Our purpose was to take advantage of the widely used framework MapReduce and apply it in the Semantic Web context. We have introduced an implementation of the spreading activation algorithm, widely used on RDF datasets, applying the MapReduce programming paradigm. Algorithm scalability has been evaluated on a 16 nodes cluster using real-world data. This implementation has proved to manage large amounts of data and scale out by using more machines simultaneously. It has also proved to scale linearly as data grows. Future research will attempt to find specific uses of the algorithm on large datasets.

Jacopo Urbani et al [11] have proved that dictionary encoding can improve overall performance of text processing MapReduce jobs despite the overhead that it introduces. In their work, they prove that a MapReduce algorithm can efficiently compress and decompress large amounts of data, and also scale linearly as input grows. Dictionary encoding is a technique that would probably improve our SA implementation, avoiding passing along large URI strings.

## References

1. Berners-Lee, T., Hendler, J., Lassila, O.: The Semantic Web. Scientific American 284(5), 34–43 (2001)
2. Todorova, P., Kiryakov, A., Ognyanoff, D., Peikov, I., Velkov, R., Tashev, Z.: Spreading activation components

3. Dean, J., Ghemawat, S.: Mapreduce: Simplified data processing on large clusters. In: Proceedings of the USENIX Symposium on Operating Systems Design & Implementation, OSDI 2004 (2004)
4. Alvarez, J.M., Polo, L., Abella, P., Jiménez, W., Labra, J.E.: Application of the Spreading Activation Technique for Recommending Concepts of well-known Ontologies in Medical Systems (2011)
5. Crestani, F.: Application of Spreading Activation Techniques in Information Retrieval. Artificial Intelligence Review 11, 453–482 (1997)
6. Troussov, A., Sogrin, M., Judge, J., Botvich, D.: Mining sociosemantic networks using spreading activation technique. In: Proceedings of IMEDIA 2008, and I-KNOW 2008, JUCS 2008 (2008)
7. Ziegler, C.-N., Lausen, G.: Spreading Activation Models for Trust Propagation. In: Proceedings of the IEEE International Conference on e-Technology, e-Commerce, and e-Service, EEE 2004, Taipei (March 2004)
8. Lin, J., Dyer, C. (2009), Data-intensive text processing with MapReduce. In: Proceedings of Human Language Technologies (2009)
9. Berrueta, D., Gayo, J.E.L., Polo, L.: Searching over Public Administration Legal Documents Using Ontologies. In: Proceedings of Joint Conference on Knowledge-Based Software Engineering (2006)
10. Kambatla, K., Pathak, A., Pucha, H.: Towards Optimizing Hadoop Provisioning in the Cloud. In: Proceedings of the Conference on Hot Topics in Cloud Computing, HotCloud 2009 (2009)
11. Urbani, J., Maaseen, J., Bal, H.: Massive Semantic Web data compression with MapReduce. In: Proceedings of the MapReduce Workshop at HPDC (2010)
12. Schätzle, A., Przyjaciel-Zablocki, M., Lausen, G.: PigSPARQL: Mapping SPARQL to Pig Latin. In: Proceedings of 3rd International Workshop on Semantic Web Information Management, SWIM (2011)
13. Przyjaciel-Zablocki, M., Schätzle, A., Hornung, T., Lausen, G.: RDFPath: Path Query Processing on Large RDF Graphs with MapReduce. In: 1st Workshop on High-Performance Computing for the Semantic Web, HPCSW 2011 (2011)
14. Lin, J., Schatz, M.: Design Patterns for Efficient Graph Algorithms in MapReduce. In: Proceedings of the Eighth Workshop on Mining and Learning with Graphs, MLG 2010 (2010)
15. Dix, A., Katifori, A., Lepouras, G., Vassilakis, C., Shabir, N.: Spreading Activation Over Ontology-Based Resources: From Personal Context To Web Scale Reasoning. International Journal of Semantic Computing (2010)
16. Urbani, J., Kotoulas, S., Maassen, J., Drost, N., Seinstra, F., Van Harmelen, F., Bal, H.: WebPie: A Web-Scale Parallel Inference Engine. In: Proceedings of the Third IEEE International Scalable Computing Challenge, SCALE 2010 (2010)

# How Sure Are You? Impact of the Degree of Certainty Shared Display in Collaborative Computer-Based Decision Making Task

Margarida Romero

ESADE Business and Law School,
Universitat Ramon Llull, Av. de Pedralbes, 60-62 E-08034 Barcelona, Spain
margarida.romero@esade.edu

**Abstract.** The Collaborative Decision Making (CDM) process is affected by the individual traits of the group members but also by the interaction process they develop. The group members involved in the CDM could have varying levels of expertise affecting the quality of their contribution to the CDM. The evaluation of the own knowledge and the other team-mates' knowledge are essential for an effective CDM. The challenge of evaluating the team-mates' knowledge appears when the group members doesn't know each others' knowledge and should perform together the task. Aiming to facilitate the process of developing an awareness of the team-mates' knowledge, we designed a Computer-Aided Collaborative Decision Making (CA-CDM) where the students declare their knowledge in terms of the Degree of Certainty (DC) they have before submitting their answer. The effect of the DC elicitation is analysed in a quasi-experimental situation, where 19 dyads uses the CA-CDM based in the DC elicitation and 16 dyads are considered as control groups. The dyads are required to reach a consensus in a three phase activity, including a first phase where the students' answer individually, a second phase where the learners' should evaluate their peers' knowledge and a third phase where the CMD is produced by the dyad. Results show a significant effect of the CA-CDM in the peers' evaluation phase of the CDM, but there are not differences observed in the quality of the CDM.

**Keywords:** Knowledge Management, Collaborative Decision Making, Computer-Aided Collaborative Decision Making, Information Systems, Computer Supported Collaborative Learning, Degree of Certainty.

## 1    Introduction

Effective Collaborative Decision Making (CDM) requires a certain level of collaboration and consensus building (Jankowski et al., 1997) among a group of persons that could have different levels of knowledge and different ways to interact in the context of a group. The quality of the decisions in CDM could be affected by individual traits or behaviours of the group members at the individual members but also by the group interaction process during the CDM. Reaching a consensus could be then affected not only by the knowledge of the group members individually, the quality of the information (Cabrerizo et al, 2010), but also by the knowledge each of

M.D. Lytras et al. (Eds.): WSKS 2011, CCIS 278, pp. 612–617, 2013.

the team-mates' have about their team-mates' knowledge and their capacity to collaborate in the CDM. In some cases the groups are having difficulties to reach a consensus, but in the other, some other groups are reaching a groupthink where the alternatives decisions has not been correctly evaluated leading to a premature consensus (Burnett, 1993). Among the different factors that are related to the efficiency of CDM, we focus our study on the different levels of knowledge of the team-mates', their Degree of Certainty (DC) and the effect of the DC elicitation in the CDM.

## 2     Diversity of Group Members' Knowledge in CDM

The knowledge level in the teams is generally diverse, and this difference of knowledge could affect the CDM. Considering this diversity in a context of interdependence where the level of interdependence is high in terms of the task performance and grading, the team as whole, and each of the individuals, should try to identify, organize and maximize the knowledge of each of the members of the group to achieve the group objectives. Each of the members should consider the other team-mates' expertise in order to weight the relevance and reliability of their contribution, before considering it in CDM. In educational contexts, where the group is graded as a whole for their CDM quality, students' should consider not only their own knowledge but also the team-mates' knowledge. In interdependent learning situations is important that the students share their ideas and argumentations to the other members of the group in an elicited way (Lehtinen, 2003). The team-mates' could also share their degree of expertise in order to facilitate the process of co-regulation and identifying the more knowledgeable members to help the less knowledgeable ones. The individual contributions of the team members could be put in relation to the Degree of Certainty (DC) they declare in association to their knowledge. This DC could be assumed in different ways, but it can be also made elicit inviting the students to declare their DC at the moment they share their answers in a Computer Learning Environment (CLE). Displaying a common visualisation of the team-mates' DC elicitation, could permit the team-mates' to develop a more accurate evaluation of their team-mates' knowledge, of Feeling of Anothers' Knowledge (FOAK, Brennan & Williams, 1995). The FOAK refers to the evaluation of a correspondent DC in a collective situation. Some conversational aspects of the interactions could help to develop the FOAK within a pair or group of persons. In addition to the conversational aspects introduced by Brennan and Williams, we consider an elicitation mechanism to display in a shared display each of the team-mates' DC. We discuss this shared visualisation of the DC in a Computer Learning Environment (CLE) as a Computer Aided Collaborative Decision Making (CA-CDM) in the next section.

## 3     DC Elicitation in a CA-CDM

In collaboration tasks, the small groups composed from 2 to 5 peers could benefit from cognitive tools (Dillenbourg, 1999), which could help the students represent what they know  (Kirschner & Erkens, 2006) and facilitate critical thinking, deep learning and transformation of information into knowledge. According to these authors, these tools can be semi-structured, as conversations between peers, or structured; *ad hoc* tools specifically designed to facilitate knowledge declarations. Shared visualisation of personal knowledge is divided into displaying (showing the DC associate to the knowledge) and monitoring (becoming aware of peer's DC, Buder 2010). Monitoring can be shown to all the participants leading to an interpersonal comparability of performances and knowledge (Janssen, Erkens, Kirschner, & Kanselaar, 2010).

### 3.1   Research Questions and Hypotheses

The aim of the study presented in this paper was to investigate whether the elicitation in a Computer Aided Collaborative Decision Making (CA-CDM) task could enhance the CDM. We consider two possible stages for the effect of the DC elicitation in the CDM. The first hypothesis is the effect of the DC elicitation in the peer evaluation of the decision making. The second hypothesis is the impact on the CDM performance.

## 4     Method

In order to test these two hypotheses, we design a quasi experimental study where 35 dyads collaborate together in a CDM task in finance. Among them, 19 dyads are required to make elicit their DC for each answer and could see their partners DC in the collaborative phase. We describe thereinafter the CDM finance task; the participants and the CA-DCM intended to support the elicitation and collaborative sharing of the DC among the students.

### 4.1   Task

We designed an activity including three phases, for analysing the impact of the DC in a first individual phase, in a second peer assessment phase and in a final phase of CDM phase where the students are also allowed to discuss their answers before submitting them. We expect the DC elicitation to increase the performance in the peer evaluation and CDM phases, and by allowing the students to consider the DC of the individuals before taking a collaborative decision. In this study, we test these hypotheses considering a quasi experimental situation where 35 dyads collaborating together in a finance task where they should reach a consensus in their answers as a result of their CDM. The collaborative finance task proposes each of the dyads' members to answer the questions individually in a first phase. In the second phase the dyad could modify their answers after considering his partner answers and they discuss together. Among them, 19 dyads are required to make elicit their DC for each answer and could see their partners DC in the collaborative phase.

The DCM task is based on a classification test in the field of finance. The activity is introduced to the students as a game because each of the dyads compete against the other dyads, promoting in this way a competitive situation where each of the dyad has an internal challenge to perform better than the other dyads. The DCM task consists in two panels with 12 basic financial concepts that have to be correctly classified by members of dyad teams. Content goals are focused on management terms as assets and liabilities; students should up by understanding and be able to determine whether a financial item is an asset or as a liability. The computer environment proposes each of the dyads' members to answer the questions individually in a first phase.

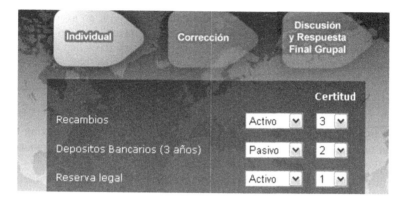

**Fig. 1.** Individual phase of the task

In the second phase the dyad could modify their answers after considering his partner answers and they discuss together.

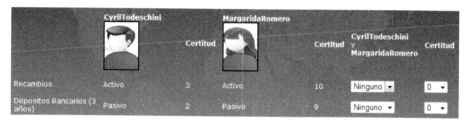

**Fig. 2.** Collaborative phase of the task

Researchers have also designed an *ad hoc* tool for the elicitation of the DC. The DC declaration allows the student to choose among 10 different grades grade of DC. Only groups in the experimental condition could use this functionality that aims to support the elicitation and collaborative sharing of the students' DC.

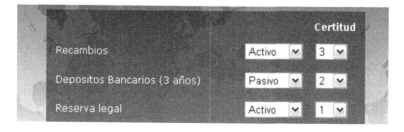

**Fig. 3.** DC elicitation

## 4.2    Participants

The CDM finance task is used as a face to face activity in Esade Business School.

Participants (n = 70) were adult learners in the introductory course of finance of Esade Executive Education during the 2nd semester of the academic year 2010-2011.

The students were composed by 27 women and 43 men with an average age of 31 years (SD=8,37). The dyads were created trying to maximize the heterogeneity among women and men. The students participated on a voluntary basis and receive neither remuneration nor a grade for their work.

## 5     Results

The first hypothesis (H1) aims a better performance of the students having the DC system at the collective phase of the game. Here we observe a positive impact of the dyads in the experimental condition ($F_{(1,68)}. = 4.81, p=0.032$).

The second hypothesis (H2) assumed a increase of the DC accuracy across the different stages in the DC explicitness group. The ANOVA test failed to reveal a significant impact of the DC in the number of comments shared by the students ($F_{(1,68)}. = 2.28, p=0.135$).

## 6     Discussion

We have observed a CDM task in the field of finance with a high level of interdependence, where the performance is evaluated in the team level after the CDM. In this context, we have considered that the group members of the team considers their own knowledge but also their team-mates' knowledge in order to maximize the performance at the team level. In this cases, the groups could develop strategies to evaluate their team-mates' knowledge with different degrees of efficiency. We have hypothesized the elicitation of the DC to have a positive effect in the CDM by the improvement of the students' awareness of the other team-mates' knowledge.

The result of the quasi-experimental situation allows us to observe an improvement of the students' awareness of the other team-mates' knowledge in the second phase of the CDM task, where the experimental groups considered in a more accurate way their teammates' knowledge in a significant way. However, we do not observe significant differences in the CDM in this finance task, despite the better awareness of the group members about their team-mates' knowledge. This lack of significant differences in the CDM could be related to the informal interactions the students' produced during the third phase of the CDM task, allowing both control and experimental dyads to interact together before choosing their CDM. Further studies should control these interactions in order to analyze their possible impact in the results of the CDM.

**Acknowledgement.** We acknowledge financial support from the Network of Excellence Games and Learning Alliance (Cooperation - ICT, Technology Enhanced Learning).

## References

Brennan, S.E., Williams, W.: The feeling of another's knowing: Prosody and filled pauses as cues to listeners about the metacognitive states of speakers. Journal of Memory and Language 34, 383–398 (1995)

Buder, J.: Group awareness tools for learning: Current and future directions. Computers in Human Behavior 27(3), 1114–1117 (2010)

Burnett, R.E.: Conflict in collaborative decision-making. In: Blyler, N.R., Thralls, C. (eds.) Professional Communication: The Social Perspective, pp. 144–162 (1993)

Cabrerizo, F.J., López-Gijón, J., Ruíz-Rodríguez, A.A., Herrera-Viedma, E.: A Model Based on Fuzzy Linguistic Information to Evaluate the Quality of Digital Libraries. International Journal of Information Technology & Decision Making 9(3), 455–472 (2010)

Dillenbourg, P.: What do you mean by collaborative learning? In: Dillenbourg, P. (ed.) Collaborative-Learning: Cognitive and Computational Approaches, pp. 1–19. Elsevier, Oxford (1999)

Jankowski, P., Nyerges, T.L., Smith, A., Moore, T.J., Horvath, E.: Spatial group choice: a SDSS tool for collaborative spatial decision-making. International Journal of Geographical Information Science 11(6), 577–602 (1997)

Janssen, J., Erkens, G., Kirschner, P.A., Kanselaar, G.: Influence of group member familiarity on online collaborative learning. Computers in Human Behavior 25, 161–170 (2009)

Kirschner, P.A., Erkens, G.: Cognitive tools and mindtools for collaborative learning. Journal of Educational Computing Research 35, 199–209 (2006)

Lehtinen, E.: Computer-supported collaborative learning: an approach to powerful learning environments. In: De Corte, E., Verschaffel, L., Entwistle, N., Van Merriëboer, J. (eds.) Unravelling Basic Componets and Dimensions of Powerful Learning Environments. Elsevier (2003)

# The Role of Deficient Self-regulation in Facebook Habit Formation

Dimple Thadani

dimple.thadani@gmail.com

**Abstract.** With the proliferation of new social media technologies (e.g. Facebook), there has been a rising concern over the problem of technology dependency. Recognizing that deficiency in self-regulation is a necessary condition for the dependency to take place, this study aims to examine the role of deficient self-regulation in habit formation in the context of online social networking sites (SNSs). The findings of an empirical study of 406 Facebook users indicate that deficient self-regulation plays a role in augmenting SNS users' perceptions, which indirectly influences habit. Our theoretical model of habit formation explains 43.7% of the variance. Implications of the findings are discussed.

**Keywords:** Deficient self-regulation, Habit, Social Networking Sites, Facebook.

## 1    Introduction

The reasons users employ information system (IS) have long intrigued the IS research community. Over the years, the focus of this line of research has been shift from adoption decisions [1] to IS continuance [2] where habit plays a role. In general, IS researchers agree that if individuals are habitually performing a particular behavior (e.g., using an information system), the future behavior (the continued use) will be largely in an automatic fashion with minimal conscious control [3].

In this regard, habitual behaviors require minimal cognitive processing and deliberate control. The concept is often confused with another related concept "technology dependency" which conscious self-regulation is difficult. There have been recent calls for further studying of technology dependency [4] [5].

Technology dependency is a form of behavioral non-substance dependency which includes excessive interaction with information technologies (i.e., both the technology and the content it provides) under conditions of psychological dependency [6]. Technology dependents lack ability in consciously self-regulating their thoughts and behaviors. Deficient self-regulation is considered to be a necessary condition for the dependency to take place. Prior research indicates that technology dependency is usually accompanied with a number of psychobiological and psychological processes distorting user's perceptions of internal and external factors [7], [8], [9]. With the distorted perceptions, users' affective responses (e.g. satisfaction) towards the

M.D. Lytras et al. (Eds.): WSKS 2011, CCIS 278, pp. 618–629, 2013.

technology could be further distorted because system perceptions are key antecedents of affective variables (e.g. [10]).

In that sense, deficient self-regulation, a process in which perceptions are distorted, is believed to play a role in habit formation. A significant precondition for the development of habit is that the behavior in question should be performed repetitively [11]. Satisfaction, an affective variable which is directly affected by perceptions, influences one's tendency of repetitive uses and in turn impacts habit formation.

Thus, the motivations of this paper are twofold. First, research on habits remain new in the field of information systems (IS). We notice that little theoretical and empirical attention has been given to the formation of IS habit. We believe that there is a need to further elaborate the concept of IS habit and derive a theoretical model examining the antecedents of IS habit. Second, it is important to understand the relationship between habit and technology dependency. Particularly, we build on social cognitive theory of self-regulation, and propose that deficient self-regulation plays a role in distorting the perceptions of technology. As such, deficient self-regulation moderates the relationship between system perceptions and satisfaction, indirectly influencing habit formation.

Online social networking site (SNS) was chosen to be the context for this study because we believe that online social networking is perhaps the biggest phenomenon of the Internet. According to a report published by Nielsen Company [12] in year 2010, internet users spend nearly a quarter of their time on social networking sites (SNSs), dominating all forms of online activities. In the social network category alone, an overwhelming 84.8 percent share of all online activities went to Facebook.

Relevant literature in the fields of psychology, telecommunication/media, and IS is reviewed. A theoretical model on habit formation is developed and tested in the context of Facebook. We hope this study could enrich our understanding of the formation of habit and thus equips users to defend themselves when unconscious processes can lead to negative outcomes.

The rest of the paper is structured as follows. First, we address the theoretical background and propose a theoretical model of IS habit formation in social networking sites. Then, we describe a survey of study of users of a social networking site (i.e., Facebook). Next, we discuss the findings of our empirical study. Finally, we conclude the paper by discussing the implications for both research and practice.

## 2     Theoretical Background

### 2.1     Online Social Network (OSN) Dependency

Online Social network dependency (OSN dependency) is a form of deficiency in self-regulation with which an individual is unable to effectively regulate one's dependency on social networking sites. LaRose [13] built on social cognitive theory of self-regulation [14], [15] and conceptualized media dependency as a deficiency in self-regulation. Deficient self-regulation is not an all-or-nothing condition, in which one is either classified as "normal" or "addicted" [13]. Rather, it is possible to have varying degrees of deficient self-regulation.

Social cognitive theory of self-regulation [14], [15] highlights the self-regulatory mechanism through which individual observe their own behavior (Self-observation), judge it in relation to personal and social standards (Judgmental process), and adjust their own behavior to environment (self-reaction). Empirically, deficient self-regulation breaks down into two dimensions: deficient self-observation and deficient self-reaction.

It is believed that users who suffer from online social network dependency (OSN dependency) demonstrate deficiency in self-regulation. The OSN dependent fails to provide oneself with accurate self-diagnostic information required for the judgmental process. Distorted perceptions and beliefs on the system at hand would be resulted [16], [17]. OSN dependents may see SNSs as the only place they could socialize and maintain connectivity. They might have conditioned their mind with the benefits of using SNSs. Caplan [18] believed that deficient self-regulation may take the form of preoccupied thoughts in the cognitive aspects and compulsive use in the behavioral aspects. .

Consistent with other kinds of behavioral dependency [19], OSN dependency may be manifested through a number of symptoms including (1) *Tolerance*: engaging in the activity to achieve or maintain the desired positive emotion; (2) *Salience*: dominating user's thoughts and behavior; (3) *Withdrawal*: cessation of the activity leads to occurrence of unpleasant emotions or physical effects; (4) *Relief*: engaging in the activity offers relief ; (5) *Relapse and reinstatement:* inability to voluntarily reduce the engagement in the activity; (6) *Conflict*: engaging in the activity leads to conflict with other or oneself ; (7) *Euphoria*: engaging in the activity offers thrill or heightened emotion.

## 2.2   Habit

In the context of IS, habit is defined as "the extent to which using a particular IS has become automatic in response to certain situations" [20].Habit is not considered as a behavior but a mind-set that enhances the perceptual readiness for habit-related cues [20], [21]. These habit-related cues could be both external (e.g. highly socialized online environment) emphasized by context-dependent position and internal (e.g. goal-related cognition primed by internal states) emphasized by goal-dependent approach [22].

Habit is learnt through repetition of behavior in the stable context in response to stimulus or cues [23]. In a stable context, contextual cues and relevant goals of individuals are similar or the same across consecutive situations [20]. Thus, during the initial adoption of a technology, individuals are most likely involved in cognitive processing in determining their behaviors. Once a habit is established, conscious attention diminishes [24]; behavior is performed automatically [25], [26]. Habitual behaviors require minimal cognitive processing and deliberate control which are both effortless and efficient [27].

## 3   Research Model and Hypotheses

Figure 1 depicts the research model in which the hypothesized relationships are illustrated.

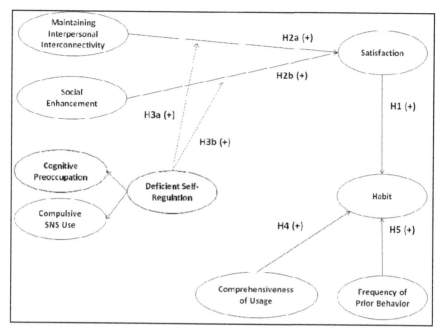

**Fig. 1.** Research Model

## 3.1    Satisfaction

In the context of social networking sites, satisfaction refers to one's feeling of pleasure with the use of SNSs. Users are likely to repeat SNSs use once they have their needs fulfilled consistently. The positive feelings associated with fulfilling one's needs, reinforce the level of satisfaction along the repeated use of SNSs. Satisfactory experiences thus increase one's tendency to repeat the use of SNSs. We believe that the higher the level of satisfaction, the stronger the habit strength. Thus, with this notion, we propose that:

*Hypothesis 1: The level of satisfaction in using SNSs is positively related to Habit.*

Uses and gratifications (U & G) framework suggest that individuals are goal-oriented and aware of their needs [28].They are motivated to choose a medium which could fulfill their needs. In the context of virtual communities, five key values (or needs) including purposive value, self-discovery value, maintaining interpersonal interconnectivity, social enhancement and entertainment value are widely adopted to determine the use of virtual communities [29].

   SNSs are designed to allow users meet other users online, maintain connection with friends, reconnect with old friends, and interact with them virtually. Research found that individuals who use SNSs are likely to possess needs in relation to maintaining interpersonal interconnectivity as well as enhancing social status [30]. Thus, the present study only focus in examining the social related value, "maintaining interpersonal interconnectivity" and "social enhancement", instead of all of the five values found in social communities.

As SNSs are embedded with social features that contribute in fulfilling users' social related needs, satisfaction is likely to be resulted along with the SNSs use. Thus, we propose:

*Hypothesis 2a: The level of maintaining interpersonal interconnectivity of using SNSs is positively related to the level of satisfaction in using SNSs.*
*Hypothesis 2b: The level of social enhancement of using SNSs is positively related to the level of satisfaction in using SNSs.*

## 3.2    Deficient Self-regulation

Deficiency in self-regulation is a necessary condition for OSN dependency to take place. Individuals who possess deficient self-regulation are unable to effectively regulate their dependence on SNSs in both cognitive and behavioral aspects.

Referring to the social cognitive theory of self-regulation, self-regulation is done through three processes – self-observation process, judgmental process, and self-reaction process [14], [15].

An individual with deficiency in self-regulation lacks ability to effectively self-observe in the self-observation process. S/he is likely to provide himself / herself with poor self-diagnostic information. As a result, s/he is likely to come up with a biased judgment in the judgmental process. In the cognitive aspects, Caplan [18] found that an individual who is unable to self-regulate effectively demonstrates "salience" symptom associated with OSN dependency.    Specifically, OSN dependents are consciously preoccupied with thoughts about social networking sites. They are unable to get their mind off the issue.

Prior research empirically showed that dependency are often accompanied by a number of psychological processes which are responsible for forming cognitive bias which affects and distorts user's perceptions of external and internal factors[7], [8]. Often, dependents' perception is distorted to an extent in which they might impair their views of reality so as to justify their own behaviors [17], [31]. The cognitive bias, which takes the form of preoccupation, exerts a positive "framing effect" on the benefit they could obtain from using the social networking sites. Individuals with deficient self-regulation are only able to see the positive side of using the system but ignore or minimize the negative views.

As mentioned in the prior section, maintaining interpersonal interconnectivity and social enhancement are two significant values perceived by individuals in using the SNSs [30], [32]. Individuals with deficiency in self-regulation are very likely to overstate the values they could obtain from using the SNSs. Thus, we propose that

*Hypothesis 3a: The level of deficient self-regulation positively moderates the relationship between the level of maintaining interpersonal interconnectivity and the satisfaction in using SNSs.*
*Hypothesis 3b: The level of deficient self-regulation positively moderates the relationship between the level of social enhancement and the satisfaction in using SNSs.*

### 3.3    Comprehensiveness of Usage

Limayem et al. [20] defined Comprehensiveness of Usage as "the extent to which an individual makes use of the various applications offered under the umbrella of a single IS system". It is a relatively new concept in IS research which extends the concept of deep usage [33], [34] and feature-centric view of technology [35]. Comprehensiveness of usage has been considered irrelevant in prior habit literature until Limayem et al. [20] modeled and empirically validated its relationship with habit in the context of information systems usage.

We believe that comprehensiveness of usage is relevant and applicable to the SNS context. Most of the social networking sites such as Facebook are multifunctional systems in which user can choose among many different applications. For example, Facebook users can play social games or chat with their friends on their walls. Extensive use of the SNSs fosters user's familiarity with the site which, in general, should positively influence the formation of habit. Thus, we propose

*Hypothesis 4: The level of comprehensiveness of usage in SNSs has a positive direct effect on the habit in using SNSs.*

### 3.4    Frequency of Prior Behavior

Aforementioned, a significant precondition for the development of habit is that the behavior in question should be performed repetitively [11]. In fact, with sufficient repetition, individual gains adequate practice and learning of the particular behavior. The increased familiarity through practice decreases the cognitive efforts one needs on performing that behavior [20]. Therefore, the more often one performs the behavior, the more likely that the behavior will become a habit [36], [37]. Apart from this, the strength of habit was empirically found to be directly related to the frequency with which the behavior is performed [38]. In line with these empirical evidences, we propose that

*Hypothesis 5: The frequency of using SNSs in the past has a positive direct effect on the habit in using the SNSs.*

## 4    Study Design and Method

Facebook (www.facebook.com), an online social networking site, was used in this study. We believe that Facebook is appropriate for the current study due to the surge of its popularity globally. Facebook has surpassed MySpace and become the most popular social networking site.

Web-based field survey was used to test and validate the conceptual model. A convenience sample of Facebook users were created by inviting volunteers to participate in our study. An invitation message with the URL to the online questionnaire was posted on a number of platforms including Facebook, MySpace, MSN, and weblogs. A screening question was used to ensure that the respondents were current active users of Facebook. A total of 406 usable questionnaires were collected. Among the respondents, 50.2 percent were female. Over 70 percent of the respondents aged between 21 and 30.

## 4.1    Measurement

Measurements in this study were based on validated seven-point Likert scales. We modified the wordings of the questionnaire to fit the social networking site context. Deficient self-regulation was measured by two sub-constructs: (1) Cognitive preoccupation and (2) Relapse and Reinstatement. Items for both sub-constructs were adapted from Caplan [18]. Habit was assessed using the measures from Limayem and Hirt [39]. Items for satisfaction were adapted from Bhattacherjee [40]. The scale for comprehensive of usage and frequency of prior behavior includes items adapted from Limayem et al. [20]. Items for maintaining interpersonal connectivity and social enhancement were adapted from Dholakia et al. [41].

# 5    Data Analysis and Results

The data analysis was performed in a holistic manner using partial least square (PLS) path modeling. PLS technique is chosen because of its ability to model latent constructs under conditions of non-normality and in small-to medium sized samples [42], [43]. It allows one to both specify the relationships among the conceptual factors of interest and the measures underlying each constructs, resulting in a simultaneous analysis of the measurement model and structural model. The item product items approach, as suggested by Chin et al. [44], was used to test the moderating effect of online social network dependency. SmartPLS version 2.0 was used. Factors such as self-regulation ability, self-efficacy and gender that are suspected to infer the results have been controlled.

## 5.1    Assessment of the Measurement Model

As we modeled deficient self-regulation as a second-order construct, we first analyze the measurement properties of the reflective construct and sub-constructs of the instrument. Then we replaced first-order reflective constructs with their latent variable scores, as suggested by Wang and Benbasat [45]. This allowed us to test for the validity of the second-order construct and the analysis of the structural paths.

Convergent validity is shown when each measurement items correlates strongly with its assumed theoretical construct. It can be examined by using composite reliability (CR) and the average variance extracted (AVE). The critical values for CR and AVE are 0.7 and 0.5, respectively [46]. As shown in table 1, all the values of CR and AVE are considered satisfactory, with CR at 0.760 or above and AVE at 0.535 or above. In addition, all items have significant path loadings at the o.o1 level.

Discriminant validity involves checking whether the items of a scale measure the construct in question or other related constructs. Discriminant validity was verified with the squared root of the average variance extracted for each construct higher than the correlations between it and all other constructs [46]. We found that each construct shares greater variance with its own block of measures than with the other constructs representing a different block of measure.

**Table 1.** Psychometric properties of measures

|  | CR | AVE |
|---|---|---|
| **Second Order Construct:** | | |
| -  **Deficient Self-regulation (DEF)** | 0.928 | 0.867 |
| **First Order Construct:** | | |
| -  **Cognitive Preoccupation (CP)** | 0.942 | 0.766 |
| -  **Relapse and Reinstatement (RR)** | 0.927 | 0.761 |
| -  **Maintaining Interpersonal Interconnectivity (MII)** | 0.850 | 0.739 |
| -  **Social Enhancement (SE)** | 0.736 | 0.590 |
| -  **Frequency of Prior behavior (FREQ)** | 0.860 | 0.754 |
| -  **Comprehensiveness of Usage (UCOMP)** | 0.882 | 0.535 |
| -  **Satisfaction (SAT)** | 0.916 | 0.733 |
| -  **Habit (HAB)** | 0.970 | 0.800 |

## 5.2    Assessment of the Structural Model

Figure 2 shows the results of testing of our research model with overall explanatory powers, estimated path coefficients (all significant paths are indicated with an asterisk), and associated t-value of the paths. Test of significant of all path were performed with using the bootstrap resampling procedures.

This model accounts for 22.4 percent of variance in satisfaction and 43.7.percent of the variance in habit. All Hypothesized paths except H3b in the research model were found statistically significant. The result of the study indicated that deficient self-regulation has exerted indirect effect on habit. Deficient self-regulation positively moderates the relationship between maintaining interpersonal connectivity and satisfaction, impacting habit via satisfaction. Satisfaction was the most significant exogenous variables of habit with a path coefficient of 0.366 and t-value of 7.901. Then followed by comprehensiveness of usage ($\beta$= 0.330, t=7.398). Frequency of prior behavior was the least significant variable with a path coefficient of 0.191 and t-value of 5.131. Deficient self-regulation only demonstrates a significant moderating effect on the relationship between maintaining interpersonal interconnectivity and satisfaction, supporting H3a, but not H3b.

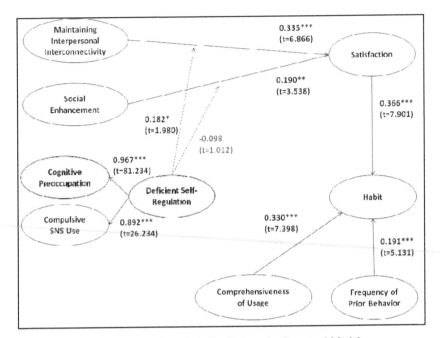

**Fig. 2.** Standardized Path Coefficients for Structural Model

# 6    Discussion and Conclusion

The main objectives of this study are to identify the key antecedents of habit, as well as to investigate the moderating role of deficient self-regulation in habit formation. Our results are consistent with prior research on habit [20]. Frequency of prior behavior, comprehensiveness of usage and satisfaction are found to be significant antecedents of habit in the context of online social networking sites. Though frequency of prior behavior is found to be the most widely studied factor of habit formation, our results show that it has the least impact on habit formation, compared with the other two antecedent variables (satisfaction and comprehensiveness of usage).

Building on social cognitive theory of self-regulation, we empirically illustrate that deficient self-regulation exhibits a significant moderating effect on the relationship between maintaining interpersonal connectivity and satisfaction, and affects habit indirectly via satisfaction. Our research model explains 43.7 percent of the variance of habit formation.

## 6.1    Theoretical and Practical Implications

This study is one of the very first studies which attempt to understand the formation for habit. To date, little theoretical and empirical attention has been given to the formation of habit in the IS context. Adding deficient self-regulation to the habit model allows us to better understand the process of habit formation. Compared with prior IS habit studies [20], the explanatory power of our habit model has also been significantly improved. As habit is an important factor in IS continuance study, further elaboration on habit help enriching the IS continuance studies.

Additionally, this study adheres to the calls by American Medical Association as well as Serenko et al. [16] to further investigate the concept of dependency and its consequences. Our results highlight the important of this line of inquiry and have introduced potential link to new theory.

This study enriches our understanding of the formation of habit and thus equips users to defend themselves when unconscious processes can lead to negative outcomes. Moreover, a better understanding of the habit formation process is crucial to guide the further development of effective training programs. By recognizing the process in which users' perceptions are distorted, educational or other intervention programs could be better designed to promote good habit such as sports, and reading.

### 6.2    Theoretical and Practical Implications

While this study focused on dependency to a single technology – social networking sites, it is certainly plausible that similar links exist in other technology settings such as mobile technology. Besides, we only focus on one condition of OSN dependency – deficient self-regulation in current study. Future research may further exam other conditions. Lastly, we believe that habit involves different stages of formation; spurious case-effect inferences may be presented. A longitudinal design is needed in the future.

## References

1. Davis, F.: Perceived usefulness, perceived ease of use, and user acceptance of information technology. MIS Quarterly 13(3), 319–340 (1989)
2. Bhattacherjee, A.: Understanding Information Systems Continuance: An Expectation Confirmation Model. MIS Quarterly 25(3), 351–370 (2001)
3. Limayem, M., Hirt, S., Cheung, C.: How habit limits the predictive power of intentions: the case of IS continuance. MIS Quarterly 31(4), 705–737 (2007)
4. Turel, O., Serenko, A., Giles, P.: Integrating technology addiction and use: An empirical investigation of online auction users. MIS Quarterly (forthcoming)
5. American Medical Association, http://www.ama-assn.org/
6. Griffiths, M.: Internet addiction: Fact or fiction? The Psychologist 12(5), 246–250 (1999)
7. Perl, E., Shufman, E., Vas, A., Luger, S., Steiner, J.E.: Taste and odor-reactivity in heroin addicts. Israel Journal of Psychiatry and Related Sciences 34(4), 290–299 (1997)
8. Greenfield, T.K., Rogers, J.D.: Alcoholic beverage choice, risk perception and self-reported drunk driving: Effects of measurement on risk analysis. Addiction 94(11), 1735–1743 (1999)
9. Serenko, A., Turel, O., Giles, P.: Integrating technology addiction and adoption: an empirical investigation of online auction websites. In: AMCIS, San Francisco, California (2009)

10. Cenfetelli, R.: Inhibitors and Enablers as Dual Factor Concepts in Technology Usage. Journal of AIS 5(11-12), 472–492 (2004)
11. Kim, S.S., Malhotra, N.K., Narasimham, S.: Two competing perspectives on automatic use: a theoretical and empirical comparison. Information Systems Research 16(4), 418–432 (2005)
12. Neilsen Company,
    `http://blog.nielsen.com/nielsenwire/online_mobile/`
    `what-americans-do-online-social-media-and-games-dominate-`
    `activity/`
13. LaRose, R., Lin, C.A., Eastin, M.S.: Unregulated Internet Usage: Addiction, Habit, or Deficient Self-Regulation? Media Psychology. Media Psychology (3), 225–253 (2003)
14. Bandura, A.: Self-Regulation of Motivation through Anticipatory and Self-Regulatory Mechanisms. In: Dienstbier, R.A. (ed.) Perspectives on Motivation: Nebraska Symposium on Motivation, vol. 38, pp. 69–164. University of Nebraska Press, Lincoln (1991)
15. Bandura, A.: Social cognitive theory: an agentic perspective. Annu. Rev. Psychol. 52, 1–26 (2001)
16. Serenko, A., Turel, O., Giles, P.: Integrating technology addiction and adoption: an empirical investigation of online auction websites. In: AMCIS, San Francisco, California (2009)
17. Turel, O., Serenko, A., Giles, P.: Integrating technology addiction and use: An empirical investigation of online auction users. MIS Quarterly (forthcoming)
18. Caplan, S.E.: Theory and measurement of generalized problematic internet use: A two-step approach. Computers in Human Behavior 26(5), 1089–1097 (2010)
19. Brown, R.: A theoretical model of the behavioral addictions - applied to offending. In: Hodge, J.E. (ed.) Addicted to Crime. Wiley, Chichester (1997)
20. Limayem, M., Hirt, S., Cheung, C.: How habit limits the predictive power of intentions: the case of IS continuance. MIS Quarterly 31(4), 705–737 (2007)
21. Verplanken, B., Aarts, H., van Knippenberg, A., Moonen, A.: Habit Versus Planned Behaviour: A Field Experiment. British Journal of Social Psychology 37(1), 111–128 (1998)
22. Verplanken, B., Wood, W.: Interventions to break and create consumer habits. Journal of Public Policy and Marketing 25, 90–103 (2006)
23. Verplanken, B., Aarts, H.: Habit, attitude, and planned behaviour: Is habit an empty construct or an interesting case of goal-directed automaticity? European Review of Social Psychology 10(1), 101–134 (1999)
24. James, W.: The Principles of Psychology. Henry Holt & Co., New York (1890)
25. Orbell, S., Blair, C., Sherlock, K., Conner, M.: The Theory of Planned Behavior and Ecstasy Use: Roles for Habit and Perceived Control over Taking Versus Obtaining Substances. Journal of Applied Social Psychology 31(1), 31–47 (2001)
26. Triandis, H.C.: Values, Attitudes, and Interpersonal Behavior. In: Page (ed.) Nebraska Symposium on Motivation, 1979: Beliefs, Attitudes, and Values, pp. 195–259. University of Nebraska Press, Lincoln (1979)
27. Lindbladh, E., Lyttkens, C.H.: Habit versus choice: the process of decision making in health related behavior. Social Science and Medicine 451–465 (2002)
28. Katz, E.: Mass communication research and the study of popular culture: An editorial note on a possible future for this journal. Studies in Public (1959)
29. Cheung, C., Lee, M.: Understanding the sustainability of a virtual community: Model development and empirical test. Journal of Information Science 35(3), 279–298 (2009)

30. Valenzuela, S., Park, N., Kee, K.F.: Is there social capital in a social network site?: Facebook use and college students' life satisfaction, trust, and participation. Journal of Computer-Mediated Communication 14(4), 875–901 (2009)
31. Coombs, R.: Addiction counseling review: Preparing for comprehensive, certification, and licensing examinations. Taylor & Francis, New York (2004)
32. Na, S., Lee, M., Cheung, C., Chen, H.P.: The Continuance of Online Social Networks: How to Keep People Using Facebook. In: Proceedings of Hawaii International Conference on System Sciences Kauai, Hawaii, USA (January 2010)
33. Chin, W.W., Marcolin, B.L.: The future of diffusion research. The Data Base for Advances in Information Systems 32(3), 7–12 (2001)
34. Schwarz, A., Chin, W.: Looking forward: Toward an Understanding of the Nature and Definition of IT Acceptance. Journal of the Association for Information Systems 8(4), 230–243 (2007)
35. Jasperson, J., et al.: A comprehensive conceptualization of post-adoptive behaviors associated with information technology enabled work systems. MIS Quarterly 29(3), 525–557 (2005)
36. Charng, H.W., Piliavin, J.A., Callero, P.L.: Role Identity and Reasoned Action in the Prediction of Repeated Behavior. Social Psychology Quarterly 51(4), 303–317 (1998)
37. Wittenbraker, J., Gibbs, B.L., Kahle, L.R.: Seat Belt Attitudes, Habits, and Behaviors: An Adaptive Amendment to the Fishbein Model. Journal of Applied Social Psychology 13(5), 406–421 (1983)
38. Aarts, H., Dijksterhuis, A.: The Automatic Activation of Goal-Directed Behaviour: The Case of Travel Habit. Journal of Environmental Psychology 20(1), 75–82 (2000)
39. Limayem, M., Hirt, S.G.: Force of Habit and Information Systems Usage: Theory and Initial Validation. Journal of the Association for Information Systems (4), 65–97 (2003)
40. Bhattacherjee, A.: An Empirical Analysis of the Antecedents of Electronic Commerce Service Continuance. Decision Support Systems 32(2), 201–214 (2001)
41. Dholakia, U.M., Bagozzi, R., Pearo, L.K.: A social influence model of consumer participation in network- and small group-based virtual communities. Internat. J. Res. Marketing 21(3), 241–263 (2004)
42. Chin, W.W.: The Partial Least Squares Approach for Structural Equation Modeling. In: Marcoulides, G.A. (ed.) Modern Methods for Business Research, pp. 295–336. Lawrence Erlbaum Associates, Hillsdale (1998)
43. Chin, W.W., Gopal, A.: Adoption Intention in GSS: Relative Importance of Beliefs. DATABASE for Advances in Information Systems 26(2), 42–64 (1995)
44. Chin, W.W., Marcolin, B.L., Newsted, P.R.: A partial least squares latent variable modeling approach for measuring interaction effects: Results from a Monte Carlo simulation study and an electronic mail emotion/adoption study. Information Systems Research 14(2), 189–217 (2003)
45. Wang, W., Benbasat, I.: Trust and adoption of online recommendation agents. Journal of the AIS 6(3), 72–101 (2005)
46. Fornell, C., Larcker, D.F.: Evaluating structural equation models with unobservable variables and measurement error. Journal of Marketing Research 48, 39–50 (1981)

# Importance of the Task Visibility on KS-Reward Relationship: An Explorative Investigation

Xi Zhang[1,2]

[1] Institute of Policy and Management, Chinese Academy of Sciences
[2] Center for Innovation and Development, Chinese Academy of Sciences,
Zhongguancun Beiyitiao No 15, Beijing, P.R.China
xizhang@casipm.ac.cn

**Abstract.** Knowledge sharing (KS) literature offers inconsistent findings on the moderating effects of employee's exchange ideology (EI) on the relationship between organizational reward (ER) and employee's KS behavior within organizations. This study contributes to the literature by examining how interaction effect of EI and individual perceived organizational reward depends on the organizational environment variable, i.e., knowledge sharing visibility (KSV). The data were collected from 159 respondents in an innovative service Chinese company. The results show that KSV×EI×ER had a significant interaction in the prediction of employee's knowledge sharing behaviours in the organization. Specially, in the work environment of high KSV, the positive relationship between Reward and KS is stronger when the employee's EI is higher. In the environment of low KSV, Reward is unrelated to KS regardless of the level of individuals' EI. Theoretical and practical implications are discussed in the end.

**Keywords:** Knowledge sharing, organizational reward, exchange ideology, knowledge sharing visibility.

## 1    Introduction

Knowledge sharing is a critical step in the knowledge management [1], as it can enable organizations to leverage their most valuable asset of employees sharing their knowledge with others. Without effective knowledge sharing, organizations might not integrate experts' critical knowledge, skills and abilities (KSAs) to accomplish the complex and innovation work [2]. Thus, how to encourage employees' knowledge sharing behaviour is the important research issue in the knowledge management (KM) field.

Knowledge sharing has been characterized as an exchange involving the provision of personal experience and knowledge in return for economic and social benefits [3]. In the literature, economic exchange has been represented by organizational reward, reflecting the explicit benefits of knowledge contribution. Organizational reward (ER) involves explicit and enforceable terms which organizations can provide directly (e.g., improved pay, conditions, and benefits). Thus, many organizations have provided reward systems as critical KM strategies to encourage employees' knowledge sharing

M.D. Lytras et al. (Eds.): WSKS 2011, CCIS 278, pp. 630–640, 2013.

behaviours, such as a knowledge market in Infosys [4], and a point redemption system in Samsung [5]. However, a review of knowledge sharing literature shows organizational reward affects employees' knowledge sharing behaviours at dissimilar levels: none [5], positive [3, 6] and even negative [7, 8]. Subsequently, to explain the inconsistent findings, researchers draw on contingency perspective to explore moderated variables that might interact with organizational reward.

According to social exchange theory (SET), the employee-organization exchange relationship is also influenced by individual exchange orientation [9]. In various variables measuring individual exchange orientation, exchange ideology (EI) is considered to be a critical moderator, referring to the strength of a participant's belief that work effort (e.g., effort on sharing knowledge) depends on treatment by the organization [10-12]. High EI individuals are calculative and rational [12]. Previous studies have confirmed significant moderating effects of EI on social exchange relationships in organizations [10, 12, 13].

Since KS has come to be considered as an exchange process, recent studies have examined the moderator effect of EI on the reward-KS relationship [14, 15]. Unfortunately, related empirical studies have reported ambiguous results of the moderating effects of EI again [10, 12, 13, 15]. Some previous studies have confirmed positive moderating effects of EI; however, other studies show EI to have significantly negative moderating effects. High EI employees may, especially, have strong incentives to shirk or engage in social loafing, showing no incentive to share knowledge unless the task condition allows employees to demonstrate discrete performance. Redman et al. [15] suggested that to the extent by which employees will repay their organization in an organization-employee exchange relationship may depend on different organizational contexts. Therefore, it is expected that the interaction effect of EI and organizational reward may be conditional upon a third-level contextual variable.

The social loafing theory (SLT) identifies series of contextual factors that may attenuate the positive effects of collective reward on rational employees' repayment behaviour, such as organizational structure, division of labour, group size, and task characteristics [16]. Individuals with high social loafing tendency may respond organizational reward with little repayment [17]. From the perspective of social loafing theory (SLT), one of the most important contextual variables is task visibility [18]. As KS behavior is the special task in the current research, we use "knowledge sharing visibility" (KSV) to refer to employees' effort (e.g. sharing knowledge with co-workers) on their jobs being identifiable [19]. Task visibility (i.e., KSV) will reduce the intention of social loafing for rational employees [18]. Under high KSV, high EI individuals believe that gaining organizational rewards is due to their previous effort. To obtain more anticipated benefits, they will be more likely to respond to organizational rewards with more repayment, such as contributing knowledge. Under low KSV, high EI individuals deem that gaining organizational rewards is unrelated to their previous knowledge contribution, and they will accept these rewards without any KS behavior. Thus, the interaction effect of organizational rewards and employees' EI might be dependent on employees' perceived KSV.

So far, rare studies examined a three-way interaction that perceived KSV regulates the interaction between organizational reward and employees' EI. To bridge up this gap, this study aimed to move beyond a two-way interaction and examine a three-way interaction in which knowledge sharing visibility moderates the interaction effect of organizational reward and employees' exchange ideology on employees' knowledge sharing behaviour.

## 2    Literature Review and Hypotheses

### 2.1    Knowledge Sharing Visibility

Social loafing theory (SLT) posits that productivity losses in group work are due to the social loafing phenomenon [20, 21]. According to SLT, individuals will reduce their contribution in group work when their individual performance and effort cannot be evaluated [22, 23]. The perspective of social loafing has been widely adopted to understand productivity losses in several types of groups in the fields of organizational behavior, such as work group [24, 25], and large organizations [18]. As the knowledge has been seen to be the public good, and the performance of knowledge sharing are difficult to evaluate, SLT can be applied to understand the productivity losses in KS.

According to SLT, task visibility is a critical organizational environmental factor which is negatively associated with social loafing behaviour in organizations [26, 27]. Task visibility refers to the extent to which employees' effort in their jobs can be identified [19]. When the task visibility of a group is low, individuals' work effort cannot be identified and evaluated by other colleagues and organizations. In this study, KS is the critical task. Thus, we can recognize knowledge sharing visibility (KSV) which originated from the definition of task visibility [16]. KSV is defined as the extent to which employees' KS behavior can be identified and monitored by other participants (e.g., their supervisors and peer knowledge reviewers).

In the research stream on social loafing, some studies have adopted KSV to explain reward-KS relationship within organizations. They have found reward to be positive to individual KS in the environment where individual performance can be evaluated (i.e., high KSV) [5]. They explain that the positive effects of reward on KS due to individual social loafing are reduced in that environment. However, the two-way interaction model of KSV and reward may not sufficiently explain the reward-KS relationship in KMS. One core assumption of SLT is that actors are rational. Based on this assumption, in the low KSV environment, individuals may have low performance-outcome expectancy, and have a high social loafing tendency. However, when actors have no self-interest and no intrinsic motivation, their performance-outcome expectancy may not increase when the environment is task visible. For these participants with a low level of self-interest, the effects of reward cannot be explained from the social loafing perspective. Few studies have considered the rationality of participants in extending two-way interaction model of KSV and reward. In order to better understanding the effects of organizational reward systems on KS in the KMS, it is important to investigate the three-way interactions of EI, KSV and reward.

### 2.2    Research Model and Hypotheses

Empirical evidence shows that task visibility is negatively associated with social loafing behavior in organizations [19, 27]. In the context of KS, KSV suggests that individuals' various efforts on jobs are identifiable, including knowledge contribution [19]. It is expected that high KSV will be related to high KS.

Although, the main effect of task visibility has been widely examined, little is known about the moderating effect of task visibility in an exchange relationship, especially under the context of KS. When task visibility (i.e., KSV) is high, knowledge shared by individuals is highly identifiable. Individuals will tend to regard organizational reward as a incentive for their previous KS. Therefore, employees with high EI, who wish to maximize their anticipated benefits, will be more likely to respond to organizational reward with KS. However, for employees with low EI, who place little importance on extrinsic rewards, the organizational instrumental will not affect their KS in KMS.

In contrast, when KSV is low, individuals' KS is not identified. Employees will deem organizational reward as a collective incentive rather than a reward to their knowledge contribution. High EI individuals have a social loafing tendency to maximize their own net benefits, and respond to organizational reward with little knowledge contribution behavior. Low EI employees, for whom moral reasons or obligation induces their KS, organizational reward will not affect their KS.

Therefore, it is expected that the interactive effect of EI and reward is dependent on KSV. The above argument is captured by the following hypotheses. The conceptual model of three-way interaction of knowledge sharing visibility, exchange ideology and organizational reward is illustrated in Figure 1.

**Hypothesis 1:** There will be a three-way interaction of organizational reward, exchange ideology, and knowledge sharing visibility on employees' knowledge sharing behavior (KS) with orgainzations.

**Hypothesis 2:** Organizational reward will be unrelated to KS under the condition of low knowledge sharing visibility, regardless of the level of individuals' exchange ideology.

**Hypothesis 3:** For employees with high perceived knowledge sharing visibility, the positive relationship between organizational reward and KS is stronger when exchange ideology is high compared to when it is low.

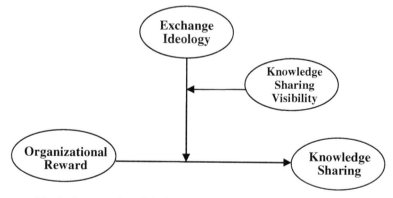

**Fig. 1.** Conceptual model of three-way interaction of KSV, EI and Reward

# 3    Methodology

## 3.1    Operationalization of Constructs

In this study, a cross-sectional survey instrument was also designed to get information on the variables. The formal definition of each construct is given in Table 1.

**Table 1.** Definition of Constructs

| Heading level | Example | Font size and style |
|---|---|---|
| Perceived Organizational Reward (ER) | Employees' perceptions of the material benefits that organization will bring them. | Sverke et al. [28] |
| Exchange Ideology (EI) | The strength of an employee's belief that work effort should depend on treatment by the organization. | Eisenberger et al. [29] |
| Perceived Knowledge Sharing Visibility (KSV) | Employees' beliefs about the extent to which KM group or their supervisors are aware of how much effort they exerted on the knowledge sharing. | George [26] |
| Knowledge Sharing Behaviour (KS) | Individual sharing work relevant experiences and information within organizations. | Lee [30] |

We adapted existing scales to enhance validity [31]. Some questions were modified to match the background of this study. One construct for knowledge sharing behavior was measured through seven-point Likert scales by the frequency of "never" to "very frequently." All other constructs were measured through seven-point Likert scales anchored from "strongly disagree" to "strongly agree." As mentioned, since the survey was executed in China, we used backward translation to ensure consistency between the Chinese and the original English version of the instrument [32].

## 3.2    Respondent and Procedure

The field study was conducted in ASG (Xuan Cheng Division (XC)) in Mainland China, over a period of about one month in 2009. To avoid selection bias, the criterion of identifying knowledge contributors was based on their knowledge sharing behaviors in knowledge management system (KMS) of ASG, rather than face-to-face knowledge sharing behaviors. In this way, we could ensure that data was collected from knowledge workers who had experience in sharing knowledge in KMS. This was done since employees sharing knowledge in their work place would not mean that they would share knowledge in KMS.

We distributed 210 questionnaires in 7 sub-divisions of ASG (XC). In the end, a total of 179 questionnaires were collected. Among them, 12 responses were not completely filled, and 8 responses were not filled out seriously (e.g., all the items were filled out as "7"). These 20 observations were excluded from further data analysis. Thus, the 159 successfully completed questionnaires represent a response rate of 75.7%, which is higher than the threshold of 70% response rate [33].

# 4    Result

## 4.1    Measurement Model

### 4.1.1    Descriptive Statistics and Reliability

Table 2 presents means, standard deviations, and correlations of study variables. We assessed reliabilities of all independent variables by calculating Cronbach's alpha at individual level. As shown in table 3, all the Cronbach's alpha values were found to be greater than 0.7, the threshold suggested by Nunnally [34].

**Table 2.**  Descriptive Statistics

| Constructs | Mean | Std. Deviation | KS | ER | EI | KSV |
|---|---|---|---|---|---|---|
| KS | 5.72 | 1.00 | (0.927) | | | |
| ER | 4.63 | 1.38 | 0.122 | (0.933) | | |
| EI | 3.74 | 1.86 | 0.202* | 0.389*** | (0.960) | |
| KSV | 4.90 | 1.13 | 0.159* | 0.256** | 0.438*** | (0.735) |

$^+$ P <0.1;   * P<0.05;   ** P<0.01;   *** P<0.001

### 4.1.2    Convergent and Discriminant Validity

The items were tested for validity using factor analysis with principle components analysis and varimax rotation. Convergent validity was assessed by checking loadings to see if items within the same construct correlated highly amongst themselves. Discriminant validity was assessed by examining the factor loadings to see if questions loaded more highly on their intended constructs than on other constructs [35]. Tabachnick and Fidell [36] suggest that loadings should be at least 0.32, and loadings from 0.45 to 0.54 are considered fair, 0.55 to 0.62 are considered good, 0.63 to 0.70 are considered very good and above 0.71 are considered excellent.

## 4.2    Hierarchical Multiple Regression Results

To test the hypothesized three-way interaction, four-step hierarchical linear regression model was examined for knowledge sharing behavior [37]. Following Aiken and West [37], the independent variables were mean-centered before forming the interaction terms. A set of demographic factors (i.e., department size, position) was controlled, because previous research has identified them as predictors of knowledge sharing [17, 38]. In the first step, the control variables were entered into the regression. In the second step, the three main effects of organizational reward (ER), exchange ideology (EI) and knowledge sharing visibility (KSV) were entered. In the third step, three two-way interactions were included, and in the fourth step, the three-way interaction was included.

As shown in Table 3, in step 1, no variables were significantly related to KS behavior. In step 2, EI was significantly positively related to KS behavior, and explained 4.9% of the variance ($\Delta R2=0.049$, $\Delta F (3, 151) = 2.608$, $P<0.05$). The main effects of reward and KSV were not predictive for KS behavior. In step 3, the two-way interaction of reward and exchange ideology (ER×EI) was significantly positively related to knowledge sharing behavior, and explained 5.7% ($\Delta R2=0.057$, $\Delta F (3, 148) = 3.165$, $P<0.05$). All the other two-way interactions showed no significant effects on employees' KS behavior. Finally, in step 4, the focal three-way interaction reached high significance, and explained 2.3% of the variance in employee's KS behavior ($\Delta R2=0.023$, $\Delta F (1, 147) = 12.1$, $P<0.05$). Therefore, hypothesis 1 (the same with study 2) was confirmed.

**Table 3.** Results of Hierarchical Multiple Regression

| Constructs | Knowledge Sharing | | |
|---|---|---|---|
| Independent Variable | Standardized Coefficients | $\Delta R2$ | R2 (adj.) |
| Step 1: Control Variables | | | |
| Position | 0.023 | | |
| Team Size | 0.024 | | |
| | | | |
| Step 2: Main Effects | | | |
| Reward (ER) | 0.022 | | |
| Exchange Ideology (EI) | 0.177+ | | |
| Knowledge Sharing Visibility (KSV) | 0.064 | 0.05* | 0.05(0.05) |
| | | | |
| Step 3: Two-way Interactions | | | |
| ER×EI | 0.257* | | |
| EI×KSV | 0.077 | | |
| ER×KSV | -0.099 | 0.06* | 0.11(0.03) |
| | | | |
| Step 4: Three-way Interactions | | | |
| ER×EI×KSV | 0.244* | 0.02* | 0.13(0.05) |

$^+$ P <0.1; * P<0.05; ** P<0.01; *** P<0.001

To evaluate our hypothesis 2 and 3, we plotted the interaction and examined the simple slopes according to Aiken and West's [37] procedure. The three-way interaction patterns were plotted in a two-step procedure. In the first step, we plotted the three separated two-way interaction figures of ER×EI, ER×KSV, and EI×KSV. We found ER×EI has positive interaction effect on knowledge sharing. ER×KSV and EI×KSV are not significant.

In the second step, we plotted the three-way interaction of ER×EI×KSV (See Figure 2). The results show that organizational reward does not have significant relationship with KS behavior under the conditions of low KSV environment of KMS in this case, regardless of the level of individual exchange ideology (EI). In H2, we hypothesized that organizational reward will be unrelated to KS under the condition of low knowledge sharing visibility. Therefore, the interactive effect fully confirms hypothesis 2.

Under the conditions of high KSV, organizational reward has a positive and significant relationship with knowledge sharing behavior at high levels of both KSV and individual EI (p<0.01). Furthermore, organizational reward has a negative significant relationship with knowledge sharing behavior under the conditions of high KSV and low EI (p<0.01). The interactive effect is in support of hypothesis 3 that under high KSV, the positive relationship between reward and KS is stronger when employees' EI is high than when it is low.

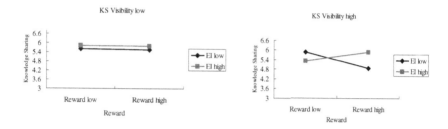

**Fig. 2.** Three-way Interaction Patterns of Study 3 (Quantitative)

The summary of three-way interaction effects on KS is illustrated in Table 4. For the employees with high perceptions of KSV and high EI, the relationship between reward and KS is positive. For employees with high perceptions of KSV and low EI, the relationship between reward and KS is negative. For the employees with low perceptions of KSV, the relationship between reward and KS is non-significant.

**Table 4.** Summary of Three-way Interaction Effects

| High KSV | | Low KSV | |
|---|---|---|---|
| High EI | Low EI | High EI | Low EI |
| Reward-KS relationship is Positive | Reward-KS relationship is Negative | Reward-KS relationship is Non-significant | Reward-KS relationship is Non-significant |

## 5 Discussion

This study has several implications for theory. First, this study contributes to knowledge management literature with a more complete understanding of reward-KS relationships within organizations. Past research has found that an employee's EI has moderating effects in the relationship between organizational reward and KS behavior [11, 14, 15]. However, the moderating effects have been inconsistent. Some findings suggest the positive effects, while others suggest absent or negative effects. Our findings unite and begin to clarify these past findings by investigating KSV as the third-level moderator. Second, this study presents an important step in building a theory to understand reward-KS relationship by integrating the individual level SET perspective with the organizational environment level SLT perspective. The three-way interaction model of this study was adapted and integrated from social exchange theory (SET) and social loafing theory (SLT), which helps to understand under which task conditions, and for which employees, the reward system is effective. This three-way interaction model explains 13% of the variance in the cross-organizational sample, compared with the explanatory power of 11% in the two-way interaction models. Our results suggest that the integration of SET and SLT in a single model can help to predict KS behavior.

The practical implication of our findings seems to be clear. Organizational reward aimed at increasing employees' knowledge sharing behaviours should consider task conditions (i.e., KSV) and individual difference (i.e., EI). First, it is suggested that organizations should establish an individual performance evaluation process for reviewing individuals' knowledge sharing to increase the KSV within organizations. This "knowledge reviewing" strategy is also useful to help organization to establish a knowledge sharing culture which may positively influence KS in the long term [40]. Second, organizations should encourage individual employees treating KS as one important task in their work, and provide guidelines to help employees to complete KS tasks systematically and structurally. Our third suggestion is that organizations should consider "different strokes for different folks". In the other words, organizations should provide a portfolio of incentives different individuals for everyone favouring the outcomes of their sharing effort.

This study also has some potential limitations, i.e., common method variance may bias our findings to some degree. However, findings concerning the direction of interaction effects may be less susceptible to common method bias than are those concerning the significance of main effects [41].

# References

1. Wasko, M.M., Faraj, S.: Why Should I Share? Examing Social Capital and Knowledge Contribution in Electronic Networks of Practice. MIS Quarterly 29, 35–57 (2005)
2. Breu, K., Hemingway, C.J.: Making organizations virtual: the hidden cost of distributed teams. Journal of Information Technology 19, 191–202 (2004)
3. Kankanhalli, A., Tan, B., Wei, K.K.: Contributing Knowledge to Electronic Knowledge Repositories: An Emprical Investigation. MIS Quarterly 29, 113–143 (2005)
4. Garud, R., Kumaraswamy, A.: Vicious and Virtuous Circles in the Management of Knowledge: The Case of Infosys Technologies. MIS Quarterly 29, 9–33 (2005)
5. Moon, H.K., Park, M.S.: Effective Reward Systems for Knowledge Sharing: Facilitating Knowledge Flow at Samsung Life Insurance. Knowledge Management Review 4, 22–25 (2002)
6. Lin, H.F.: Effects of extrinsic and intrinsic motivation on employee knowledge sharing intentions. Journal of Information Science 33, 135–149 (2007)
7. Bock, G.W., Kim, Y.G.: Breaking the Myths of Rewards: An Exploratory Study of Attitudes about Knowledge Sharing. Information Resources Management Journal 15, 14–21 (2002)

8. Bock, G.W., Zmud, R.W., Kim, Y.G., Lee, J.N.: Behavioral Intention Formation in Knowledge Sharing: Examining the Roles of Extrinsic Motivators, Social-Psychological Forces, and Organizational Climate. MIS Quarterly 29, 87–111 (2005)
9. Cropanzano, R., Mitchell, M.S.: Social Exchange Theory: A Interdisciplinary Review. Journal of Management 31, 874–900 (2005)
10. Eisenberger, R., Huntington, R., Hutchison, S., Sowa, D.: Perceived Organizational Support. Journal of Applied Psychology 71, 500–507 (1986)
11. Sinclair, R.R., Tetrick, L.E.: Social Exchange and Union Commitment: A Comparison of Union Instrumentality and Union Support Perceptions. Journal of Organizational Behavior 16, 669–680 (1995)
12. Witt, L.A.: Exchange Ideology as a Moderator of Job Attitudes-Organizational Citizenship Behaviors Relationships. Journal of Applied Social Psychology 21, 1490–1501 (1991)
13. Witt, A.: Equal opportunity perceptions and job attitudes. Journal of Social Psychology 131, 431–433 (1991)
14. Lin, C.P.: To share or not to share: modeling knowledge sharing using exchange ideology as a moderator. Personel Review 36, 457–475 (2007)
15. Redman, T., Snape, E.: Exchange Ideology and Member-Union Relationships: An Evaluation of Moderation Effects. Journal of Applied Psychology 90, 765–773 (2005)
16. Jones, G.R.: Task Visibility, Free Riding, and Shirking: Explaining the Effect of Structure and Technology on Employee Behavior. Academy of Management Review 9, 684–695 (1984)
17. Albanese, R., Fleet, D.D.V.: Rational Behavior in Groups: The Free-Riding Tendency. Academy of Mangement Review 10, 244–255 (1985)
18. Liden, R.C., Wayne, S.J., Jaworski, R.A., Bennett, N.: Social Loafing: A Field Investigation. Journal of Management 30, 285–304 (2004)
19. George, J.: Extrinsic and Intrinsic Origins of Perceived Social Loafing in Organizations. Academy of Management Journal 35, 191–202 (1992)
20. George, J.: Extrinsic and Intrinsic Origins of Perceived Social Loafing in Organizations. Academy of Managment Journal 35, 191–202 (1992)
21. Karau, S.J., Williams, K.D.: Social Loafing: A Meta-Analytic Review and Theoretical Integration. Journal of Personality and Social Psychology 65, 681–706 (1993)
22. Chidambaram, L., Tung, L.L.: Is Out of Sight, Out of Mind? An Empirical Study of Social Loafing in Technology-Supported Groups. Information Systems Research 16, 149–168 (2005)
23. Karau, S.J., Williams, K.D.: Social Loafing: Research Findings, Implications, and Future Directions. Current Directions in Psychological Science 4, 134–139 (1995)
24. Karau, S.J., Williams, K.D.: The Effects of Group Cohesion on Social Loafing and Social Compensation. Group Dynamics: Theory, Research, and Practice 1, 156–168 (1997)
25. Lin, T.C., Huang, C.C.: Understanding Social Loafing in Knowledge Contribution from the Perspective of Justice and Trust. Expert Systems with Applications 36, 6156–6163 (2009)
26. George, J.M.: Extrinsic and Intrinsic Origins of Perceived Social Loafing in Organizations. Academy of Management Journal 35, 191–202 (1992)
27. Price, K.H.: Decision Responsibility, Task Responsibility, Identifiability, and Social Loafing. Organizational Behavior and Human Decision Processes 40, 330–345 (1987)
28. Sverke, M., Kuruvilla, S.: A new conceptualization of union commitment: Development and test of an integrated theory. Journal of Organizational Behavior 16, 505–532 (1995)
29. Eisenberger, R., Armeli, S., Rexwinkel, B., Lynch, P.D., Rhoades, L.: Reciprocation of perceived organizational support. Journal of Applied Psychology 86, 42–51 (2001)

30. Lee, J.N.: The impact of knowledge sharing, organizational capability and partnership quality on IS outsourcing success. Information & Management 38, 323–335 (2001)
31. Stone, E.F.: Research Methods in Organizational Behavior. Goodyear, Santa Monica (1978)
32. Singh, J.: Measurement Issues in Cross-National Research. Journal of International Business Studies 26, 597–619 (1995)
33. Leslie, K., Berenson, C.: Mail Surveys and Response Rates: A Literature Review. Journal of Marketing Research 12, 440–453 (1975)
34. Nunally, J.C.: Psychometric Theory. McGraw-Hill, New York (1978)
35. Cook, M., Campbell, D.T.: Quasi-Experimentation: Design and Analysis Issues for Field Settings. Houghton Mifflin, Boston (1979)
36. Tabachnick, B.G., Fidell, L.S.: Using Multivariate Statistics, 4th edn. Allyn & Bacon, Upper Saddle River (2000)
37. Aiken, L.S., West, S.: Multiple Regression:Testing and Interpreting Interactions. Sage, New York (1991)
38. Riege, A.: Three-dozen Knowledge-Sharing Barriers Managers Must Consider. Journal of Knowledge Management 9, 18–35 (2005)
39. Lin, C.P.: To Share or Not to Share: Modeling Knowledge Sharing Using Exchange Ideology as a Moderator. Personnel Review 36, 457–475 (2007)
40. MvDermott, R., Dell, C.O.: Overcoming Cultural Barriers to Sharing Knowledge. Journal of Knowledge Management 5, 76–85 (2001)
41. Podsakoff, P.M., Mackenzie, S.B., Lee, J.Y., Podsakoff, N.P.: Common Method Biases in Behavioral Research: A Critical Review of the Literature and Recommended Remedies. Journal of Applied Psychology 88, 879–903 (2003)

# Specification of Interaction of Digital TV Applications in Converged Scenarios and Using Pre-patterns

Marília Soares Mendes, Clayson S.F. de S. Celes, and Elizabeth Furtado

[1] University of Ceará (UFC), Computer Science Department (MDCC), Campus do Pici - Bloco 910 - Fortaleza, CE, Brazil
mariliamendes@gmail.com
[2] State University of Ceará (UECE), Graduate in Computer Science, – Av. Paranjana - Fortaleza, CE, Brazil
claysonsandro@gmail.com
[3] University of Fortaleza (UNIFOR), Av. Washington Soares, 1321 - Fortaleza, CE, Brazil
elizabet@unifor.br¶

**Abstract.** The possibility of convergence of interactive digital television to other devices enables various usage scenarios. Such scenarios must be studied to assess their viability. This paper aims to present the use of pre-patterns in specification of scenarios of converged applications for interactive digital television in order to validate the usage scenarios and to define their interaction design.

**Categories and Subject Descriptors**
H5.m. Information interfaces and presentation (e.g., HCI): Miscellaneous.

**General Terms**
Design, Human Factors.

**Keywords:** Pre-patterns, Human Computer Interaction, Innovative Systems, interactive Digital Television, Interaction Design.

## 1 Introduction

With the advent of mobile devices and truly networked environments, works [2]; [4]; [6] show that the interactive Digital TeleVision (iDTV) set is becoming increasingly a system of convergence of media. The possibility of convergence of iDTV to other devices enables various usage scenarios, for example: *"If a user interacting with the iDTV has to leave from home, she can continue to interact with content from the web or her mobile device."* In this work, usage scenarios of applications of convergence of media with characteristics of cross-media [6] are called converged scenarios. Cross-media refers to the use of multiple devices seamlessly. The specification of converged scenarios must to describe the user's access to the various forms of contents that will be delivered in the most appropriate device in a specific contextual situation and according to her needs.

M.D. Lytras et al. (Eds.): WSKS 2011, CCIS 278, pp. 641–654, 2013.
© Springer-Verlag Berlin Heidelberg 2013

So that many problems related to ethical, social and environmental factors of system during a transition of content can take place. Some works that deal with mobile iDTV modeling look for answers to the following questions: How will be made the transition from content? What is the use context of the user when interacting with the system? How will she handle privacy issues? These works apply different techniques, as experience prototyping [1] contextual design [9], collaboratorium design [14]. They focus on participatory design.

Designers of software development have become increasingly concerned with reuse in your projects. One way of ensuring reuse is the use of patterns defined from designers' experiences in situations similar to the design being developed. The use of patterns is meant to avoid rework and ensure an effective solution [13]. However, with rapidly changing technology, there are new systems that do not have yet patterns set and tested by their developers. Such systems are called "*Innovative Systems*". Although the development of iDTV applications has grown significantly in recent years, systems in this area are still regarded as innovative.

An innovative system is characterized by the fact that users do not have familiarity with the technology, having difficulty talking about their expectations. In these systems, rather than patterns, pre-patterns can be applied. While patterns provide solutions that have been tested and approved by others, the pre-patterns are patterns emerging and not yet in common use by the design community and end users [5].

At this point, the following question arises: what Pre-patterns can be used in the interaction design of converged scenarios for iDTV? For being an innovative, iDTV systems still do not have pre-patterns defined, therefore, in previous work the authors of this paper [12] defined pre-patterns for the context of iDTV.

The aim of this paper is to present and discuss the results with a case study conducted to support professionals (HCI, designers and engineers of requirements) to use pre-patterns, so on as to assess the potential of these pre-patterns of new ones to inform and support the identifying constraints on contextual factors during the analysis of scenarios.

The system presents scenarios of convergence with the iDTV, in accordance with the concept of media convergence shown in [4]. Specifically, the scenarios refer to the production, distribution and use of multimedia contents through various media such as mobile devices, iDTV and computer (internet), having the iDTV as the main device (communication) of convergence of media.

As mentioned before, we raised some challenges in working with pre-patterns previously, they were:

- Difficulty of linking pre-patterns in the development of any interactive applications;
- Difficulty of adapting a pre-pattern to the context of the problem.

With this paper we try to modestly fill in these gaps by description a methodology for the (re) use of pre-patterns associated with the definition of a model of use. To define the model of use we decided to apply the AMITUDE [7]. The AMITUDE model of use claims that system use can be helpfully modeled as having the aspects: Application type, Modalities, Interaction, Task or other activity, domain User, Device and Environment of use.

This paper is organized as follows: we first presented the pre-patterns. After, we present the application of methodology, followed by results, related works, discuss and conclusion.

## 2    Pre-patterns

The pre-patterns used in this paper, were defined in [8, 9] and focused on a system for creating educational content for iDTV. The process of creating pre-patterns involved contact with the users and the developers of such system. The developers were 8 professionals, including the authors of this paper, and the users were: teachers, who would create educational content using a framework web, and student, who would interact with the content via iDTV Module, Personal Computer (PC) or mobile device module. Content in this system can be classes, exercises or research activities. The methodology was applied during the users' need analysis. They participated in the application of creativity – encouraging techniques, reporting two situations: their routine for getting contents and their hypothetic scenarios using the future system.

The pre-patterns created for the system are organized in a catalog (see Figure 1) in the following categories: A) Accessibility, B) Collaboration, C) Copyright, D) Security, C) Usability, D) Reuse and E) pedagogical [11]. Each category can have more than a pre-pattern associated for letters, for example, "A3" means that it is the third pattern of group A. Some examples of pre-patterns for the system are: A1) Support for accessibility; B1) collaborative content creation; B2) collaborative participation of users of iDTV content; C1) Warnings about the content copyright; C2) Inclusion of credits or references in the content; D1) Message moderation; E1) Location of content in the system; E2) Location of content on the iDTV; F1) Reuse of content; G1) Return of user interaction; G2) Help each system functionality; G3) Environment planning content.

**Fig. 1.** Main categories of pre-patterns

The example (see Board 1) shows the pre-pattern **G1) Return of user interaction** derived from a type of scenario. This pre-pattern enables the system send the user interaction for the teacher. The format of a pre-pattern [5] includes the information described into the following board.

**Board 1.** Pedagogical pre-pattern for the web framework

---

### G1: Return of user interaction

**Synopsis:** The teacher wants to know the student interaction in the content published.

**Background:** The teacher wants to know information about the student interaction in content, for example: the time that the student answered, how many times the student free accessed a certain media. The system will provide these answers to the teacher.

**Problem:** The teacher needs to know the effectiveness of her content in student learning.

**Solution:** The system will provide the return of student interaction for the teacher.

**References:** The system will have an option to send the questions that the student will access and put her questions about the content (see B2). The system saves the students' responses (answered via iDTV) and also the interaction of student. Then, the system provides return channel for the teacher (via web framework).

---

In this article, we intend to focus on the analysis of the interaction of converged scenarios for the same system with developers using these pre-patterns created.

## 3    Methodology of Application of Pre-patterns

The application of pre-patterns was performed by the authors of this paper in group sessions of participatory design. 6 sessions were run at laboratory, one session for each scenario description lasted about 40 minutes. The scenarios have emerged from the users and were described according to techniques described in this section and the use of the following materials: The catalog of pre-patterns, a board and pens. They had the following objectives: the requirements definition and specification of the interaction design for each described scenario.

## Scenarios' Description

A scenario description was initially composed of a textual narrative. The following usage scenarios were defined (see Table 1):

**Table 1.** Textual description of the usage scenarios

| |
| --- |
| **Scenario 1: Preparation of content for iDTV** |
| In this scenario, the teacher uses the Framework web to prepare some educational content for iDTV, specifying media types and target devices. |
| **Scenario 2: Access to the application in the iDTV** |
| In this scenario, the student uses the iDTV module to learn educational content. |
| **Scenario 3: Access extra content by mobile devices during use of the iDTV** |
| While the student accesses content though iDTV, in certain moments, may be exhibited some extra content, which can be viewed by the student on mobile phone. The student makes a transition between devices to gain access to personalized content, so as not to impact the experience of other users. This approach is known as non-intrusive [3]. |
| **Scenario 4: The user still accessing the iDTV content by mobile phone** |
| The scenario begins with the user viewing the content via iDTV. However, at some instant, the student, for any reason needs to leave and no longer view the content on television, but she has the option to continue viewing the contents on mobile phone. In this case, the transition (iDTV to mobile phone) was useful for providing of the content visualization in a mobility scenario. |
| **Scenario 5: User accesses the same iDTV content in the mobile phone** |
| The student accesses the content via mobile phone, exploring the characteristics of mobile digital television. The content is similar to content shown on television, with a few variations. In this scenario, the focus is to show that the content can be accessed anytime and anywhere, although some limitations. |
| **Scenario 6: User sends message to the producer of content through mobile** |
| After concluding the use of content on iDTV, the student can communicate with the producer (teacher) of content even while away from television. To send the message, the student uses a mobile phone and can receive the answer by email (user sees it on the computer) or by SMS (user sees it on mobile phone). |

Then for each scenario, we created a task model to help identify the user actions and the system resources to perform a scenario according to AMITUDE model (see Figure 3). The AMITUDE framework defines a set of aspects that must be analyzed in order to create a usable content. Besides AMITUDE elements, we specified a new one. The C element refers to the content, as education content. Adding this element to a definition of scenario required thinking about the types of cross-media contents.

By this reason, a converged scenario was associated with a level of cross-media defined by Hayes [8]. Hayes categorized into four levels of cross-media concept, where level 1 (pushed): content is distributed partially or entirely to other devices, for example: the same content can be displayed on mobile and iDTV. Level 2 (Extra): the content produced is different from the main content and assumes complementation function. Level 3 (Bridges): the structure of the services direct users to use the content on other devices, for example: there are television shows that after the end of the program provide a link to the user to continue following the issue via Internet. Level 4 (Experiences): It consists of a combination of the three previous levels. The content is distributed to the devices through bridges defined by the users according to their needs.

For reasons of space we present only the task model for scenario 3 because it will be used throughout the paper. This scenario is a scenario of cross-media level 2 (Extra). The task model uses the ConcurTaskTrees Environment [10] (see Figure 2). The task model represents the activities performed in the iDTV environment and mobile environment.

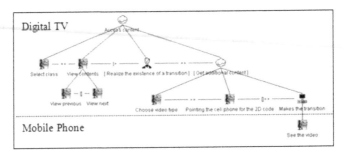

**Fig. 2.** Example of task model to show an additional video (Scenario 3)

### Exploration of Pre-patterns

In this session we show how we link the pre-patterns in the development of the system whenever we found constraints related to contextual factors of use of such system.

As we were dealing with a system categorized as innovator, finding an appropriate solution to its constraints was not so simple. For example, when we came across with some problems, it was complicated to define the best solution, considering various elements such as context, user, device, and so on. Example of problems:

Problem 1: How students with hearing impairments may use the content?
Problem 2: How students can access content on other devices?

Thus, the reuse of pre-existing solutions was an alternative driven by the catalog of pre-patterns. The application of pre-patterns aimed to ease potential problems in defining requirements by thinking about several contextual factors.

Figure 3 shows the board built for the definition of scenario 3. The numbers represent all the elements used in the exploration of pre-patterns. First we put the description of the scenario (1). Then, we separated the board in parts to represent the following possible access environments: iDTV and cell phone. For each environment we made the association of the task model (3) with the AMITUDE model (2). While modeling the tasks (3) we thought about the type of cross-media content (5) according users, modalities and we associated the pre-pattern related (4).

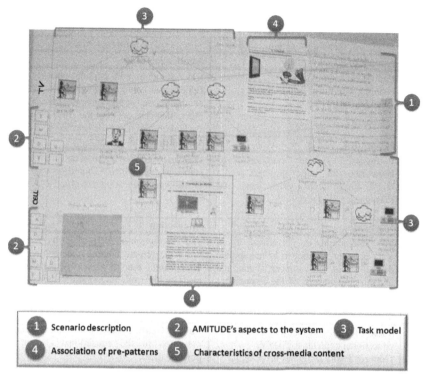

**Fig. 3.** Exploration of pre-patterns for a scenario's description

# 4     Results

The results of these activities were the definition of requisites for the system and the specification of interaction design from some chosen pre-patterns.

## 4.1     The Requirements Organized by Model of Use

In the scenario 1, our aim is to show the vision of the teacher in producing content. In the scenario 2, our aim is to show the vision of the student when using the application in the iDTV and in the scenarios 3, 4, 5 and 6 our goal is to show the vision of student interacting with the content, and by considering the convergence of iDTV with other devices. Thus, we organized the requirements according to these two visions and AMITUDE model of use.

Table 2 specifies the seven elements of AMITUDE framework.

The use of AMITUDE model describes all aspects of use of the system that must be taken into account when developing for its usability. These aspects were used during the definition and validation of scenarios.

**Table 2.** AMITUDE's aspects to the system

| | Teachers' vision | Students' vision |
|---|---|---|
| **A** | **Application type** | **Application type** |
| | Framework web to prepare educational contents with linear or non-linear structure for iDTV. | iDTV module and Mobile phone module. Educational content to Digital TV. The user can be access supplementary/extra content via other devices or see the full educational content on mobile phone (mobile TV). |
| **M** | **Modalities** | **Modalities** |
| | Portuguese spoken notation and keywords. 2D static graphic: media board, image icons, video icons and Portuguese typed text | Portuguese spoken notation and keywords. 2D static graphic: media board, image icons, video icons and Portuguese typed text |
| **I** | **Interaction** | **Interaction** |
| | The interaction is performed by a teacher using the mouse to manipulate digital medias (e.g., images, sound, and text) to content area of the Framework web. | The interaction is performed by a student using the remote control and mobile phone. The content transitions between devices are made with user intervention by transition bridges (e.g., bar code, icon). |
| **T** | **Task** | **Task** |
| | **Task Goal:** (Scenario 1) Create educational contents for iDTV.<br>**Generic Task:** Drag-and-drop digital medias preview and deploy the generated content.<br>**Task analysis:** Create content. Evaluate interaction log. View response from iDTV and mobile phones. View suggestions and doubts. Send message to students. | **Task Goal:** Understand the concepts presented in the educational content and practice them.<br>**Generic Task:** view content and answer questions.<br>**Task analysis:**<br>(Scenario 2: access content, select the class and view contents (View previous and next).<br>(Scenario 3: realize the existence of a transition. Get supplementary contents. Read bar code referenced by contents. See supplementary contents.)<br>(Scenario 4: Similar to Scenario 3, but in this case the user will perform the transition only when he needs to leave the room and need to continue seeing the content on the mobile device while on the move.)<br>(Scenario 5: Access the content via mobile device with a digital television receiver. Navigate in the class. Answer the questions.)<br>(Scenario 6: Access content from digital TV module. End lesson. Send a message to the teacher. Receive the response on the PC or mobile phone.) |
| **U** | **User** | **User** |
| | Portuguese speaking and reading skills; has knowledge basic to manipulate the PC and the Framework web. | 12–16 years old who: has Portuguese speaking and reading skills; has knowledge basic to manipulate the mobile phone and remote control. |

**Table 2.** *(continued)*

| D | Devices | Devices |
|---|---------|---------|
|   | **Input:** mouse, keyboard<br>**Output:** personal computer, digital TV screen | **Input:** remote control, mobile phone keypad<br>**Output:** Digital TV screen, mobile phone screen, loudspeaker |
| E | **Environment of use** | **Environment of use** |
|   | Someplace with computer and Internet access. | Indoor and outdoor environments with digital TV and Internet access. |

## 4.2    Selected Pre-patterns and Interfaces Designed

Table 3 presents the scenarios, problems encountered in each scenario and the pre-pattern adopted as a possible solution.

**Table 3.** Association of pre-patterns in the scenarios

| Scenarios | Problems identified | Pre-pattern adopted |
|-----------|--------------------|--------------------|
| Scenario 1<br>*Preparation of content for iDTV* | • How a teacher can add something important in a content already created without having to create other content with the same subject?<br>• If the teacher publishes a content that does not belongs to him?<br>• The teacher intends to publish a content that is not him, but what he does about copyright?<br>• The teacher creates a lot of content but how she can organize her content without becoming lost?<br>• How teacher reuses a content already created?<br>• How does the teacher know that your content was good enough on student learning?<br>• How to help the teacher who does not know how to make content available to iDTV?<br>• How to help the teacher who doesn't know how to plan and organize your content for iDTV? | B1) collaborative content creation;<br><br>C1) Warnings about the content copyright;<br>C2) Inclusion of credits or references in the content;<br><br>E1) Location of content in the system;<br><br>F1) Reuse of content;<br><br>G1) Return of user interaction;<br><br>G2) Help each system functionality;<br><br>G3) Environment planning content. |
| Scenario 2<br>*Access to the application in the iDTV* | • How to facilitate access for students who have difficulty hearing?<br>• The student accesses a lot of content, but if don't have an indication of the location of the system, how she can access the content without becoming lost? | A1) Support for accessibility;<br><br>E2) Location of content on the iDTV. |

**Table 3.** *(continued)*

| Scenario 3<br>*Access extra content by mobile devices during use of the iDTV* | • How a student accesses an extra content in other media? | H1) Transition of iDTV content to other media. |
|---|---|---|
| Scenario 4<br>*The user still accessing the iDTV content by mobile phone.* | • How a student continues accessing the content of iDTV in other media? | H1) Transition of iDTV content to other media. |
| Scenario 5<br>*User accesses the same iDTV content in the mobile phone* | • How a student accesses the content of iDTV in other media? | H2) Access to the contents of iDTV in other media. |
| Scenario 6<br>*User sends message to the producer of content through mobile* | • How students can send their questions and suggestions for the teacher (content producer)? | B2) collaborative participation of users of iDTV content. |

In scenarios 1, 2 and 6 we reuse the pre-patterns of the catalog. But there was not any pre-pattern for the scenarios 3, 4 and 5. In this moment, we create a new category and named as **H - Device convergence** with the pre-patterns *"H1 - iDTV Transition of content"* and *"H2 - Access to the contents of iDTV in other media"*.

Board 2 shows the pre-pattern used to assist in solving the scenarios 3 and 4 for the transition of iDTV content to other devices.

13 interfaces were created for the 6 scenarios. The interfaces created for iDTV were implemented in Ginga NCL and those created for the mobile application were implemented in J2ME and the web module in PHP.

In this context, we did not intend to evaluate the quality of the final interface design. The interface design depends more on the creative skills and knowledge Ergonomic designer. Our goal was to identify which elements of the interfaces were derived from descriptions of pre-patterns previously associated with a scenario. The elements of the interfaces are graphical objects that communicate to the user the activities she can do when experiencing a converged scenario.

The Figure 4 illustrates the interfaces design to the scenario 3. On left it is the screen of iDTV application, that makes it possible the transition of iDTV content from TV screen to a secondary screen (pre-pattern H1 – allowing the transition of the iDTV content to other media, as cell phone or PC). The secondary screen (on the right) shows the supplementary video from YouTube. The transition is realized with use of QR-Code, the scanned code (on the middle) is directed to the video URL.

The pre-pattern of content transition prompted us to seek a means to convey the content between the media. The QR-Code, located below the video (Figure 4 - on the right) was the solution for the content iDTV transition for the cell.

In a nutshell, the designers, us, felt most confident when had a model that relies. We were reassured to learn that we had a support for our ideas (pre-patterns used).

Board 2. Pre-pattern of Transition of Media for the iDTV framework

### H1: Transition of the iDTV content to other media

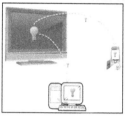

**Synopsis:** The student wants to access iDTV content in other media.

**Background:** Students enter the classroom via iDTV, browsing the content. If she perceives the possibility of transferring content to other media such as mobile phone or Internet, she may request the transition of the desired content.

**Problems:** The student would like to access the content from the iDTV or at later times; the student would like to access the content through another device or even your personal device.

**Solution:** The system will enable the student to access the content of iDTV in other media.

**References:** There are many systems currently available in which access can be done through various media. The *YouTube* is an example of a system in which the user can access it both by computer and by phone via the internet.

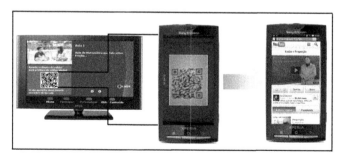

**Fig. 4.** Screen obtained from the pre-pattern H1 – Transition of iDTV content from TV screen to a secondary screen

### 4.3     Implications for Interaction Design

The results of this work for the interaction design are described in three levels:

- Conceptual modeling level. During the scenarios description (see figure 3), we did:
    - The refinement of the library of pre-patterns with the creation of new pre-patterns;
    - The specification of the requirements of the system characteristics of the transitions to access content;
- Problem analysis level. During the identification of a solution (Table 3), we meet and discuss the limitations found in each scenario and did see that the pre-patterns were useful for understanding the limitations (problems) of system.
- Interface design level. During the definition of how content could be accessed on cross–media (figure 4) we did we discuss in order to find a better solution to the problem of transition from the content.

## 5     Related Works and Discussion

Chung et al. [5] create pre-patterns for Ubiquitous Computing design and Saponas et al. [15] worked with pre-patterns for the digital home. Chung, et al. constructed a set of 45 pre-patterns classified into four different categories and performed tests of designers using pre-patterns [5]. Saponas et al. [15] aimed to examine how the use of pre-patterns is useful for designers. The authors defined pre-patterns for the digital home, trying to investigate how they can evaluate empirically whether a design apparatus, such as design patterns, affects early stage design and how do pre-patterns positively affect early stage design. They defined and implemented pre-patterns and thus found that the designers could quickly start using them. We believe pre-patterns are useful to communicate design concepts to others (developers, users), to generate new ideas and get specific information to design. The team must go through a process of understanding the use to define requirements in order to design usable systems. Moreover, even the developers (including designers) have difficulties in defining the features and system constraints. By this reason, we also believe that is important to show how pre-patterns can be explored when several elements must be considered in converged and innovative scenarios.

Our objective was to show a process of application of pre-patterns in definition of usage requirements of a target system. To the interaction design specification of this system, we associated the appropriate pre-patterns.

Indeed, the association of pre-patterns was a goal to solve potential problems in definition of requirements, but also facilitated the definition of requirements and allowed the creation of new pre-patterns. This activity also provided a reflection of the contextual factors and facilitated the transition from specification to access content.

During the application of pre-patterns we faced some challenges:

- Difficulty of linking pre-patterns in the development of interactive applications: some pre-patterns did not fit in proposing that we wanted and we had to create pre-pattern that did not exist yet.
- Adaptation of the pre-pattern to the context of the problem: when we selected in a pre-pattern that was similar to that proposed, we had to adapt it to the context of the system. This made us to realize that we needed to improve the pre-existents patterns in order to make them more generic increasing the range of possibilities of their use.

## 6    Conclusion

In the last year we did the creation process of pre-patterns which greatly helped in defining the system. In this study we observed a faster definition of requirements and consequently development of the system with the use of pre-patterns.

This paper has its importance for the presentation of a methodology of application of pre-patterns and for the association between AMITUDE model of use and aspects of the system. The re (use) of pre-patterns allowed the validation of them, besides facilitating the creation of a new pre-pattern.

## References

[1] Buchenau, M., Suri, J.F.: Experience Prototyping. In: Proceedings of DIS 2000: Designing Interactive Systems: Processes, Practices, Methods, & Techniques, Brooklyn, New York, pp. 424–433 (2000)

[2] Celes, C.S.F.S.: Análise de aplicações convergentes para a televisão digital interativa baseada nos aspectos de sincronismo, portabilidade de conteúdo e da interação do usuário. UECE – Fortaleza, Março de (2011)

[3] Cesar, P., Bulterman, D.C.A., Obrenovic, Z., Ducret, J., Cruz-Lara, S.: An Architecture for Non-intrusive User Interfaces for Interactive Digital Television. In: Cesar, P., Chorianopoulos, K., Jensen, J.F. (eds.) EuroITV 2007. LNCS, vol. 4471, pp. 11–20. Springer, Heidelberg (2007)

[4] Chakaveh, S., Bogen, M.: Media Convergence, an Introduction. In: Jacko, J.A. (ed.) HCI 2007. LNCS, vol. 4552, pp. 811–814. Springer, Heidelberg (2007)

[5] Chung, E.S., Hong, J.I., Lin, J., Prabaker, M.K., Landay, J.A., Liu, A.L.: Development and Evaluation of Emerging Design Patterns for Ubiquitous Computing. In: Proceedings of Designing Interactive Systems, Cambridge, Massachusetts, USA, pp. 233–242 (2004)

[6] Davidson, D.: Cross-Media Communications: an Introduction to the Art of Creating Integrated Media Experiences. ETC Press (2010)

[7] Dybkjaer, L., Bernsen, N.O.: Multimodal Usability. Springer, NY (2009)

[8] Hayes, G.: Social Cross Media – What Audiences Want. Personalizemedia (Novembro 2006),
http://www.personalizemedia.com/cross-media-what-audiences-want/ (accessed: March 21, 2011)

[9] Löwgren, J., Stolterman, E.: Thoughtful interaction design: A design perspective on information technology. MIT Press, Cambridge (2004)

[10]  L'Outil CTT ConcurTaskTrees Environment, http://giove.cnuce.cnr.it/ctte.html (accessed: March 21, 2011)

[11]  Mendes, M.S.: D.F. DIRCE - Design da Interação e levantamento de Requisitos com foco na Comunicação e Exploração de ideias: experiências de uso aplicadas em sistemas de criação de conteúdo para a televisão digital. Dissertação de Mestrado (Mestrado em Informática Aplicada) - Universidade de Fortaleza (UNIFOR), Fortaleza, 176f (2009)

[12]  Mendes, M.S., Furtado, M.E.S.: Uma metodologia para o design da interação utilizando técnicas de Prototipação da Experiência e pre-patterns. In: Fourth Latin American Conference on Human-Computer Interaction (CLIHC 2009), Mérida (2009)

[13]  Ole, N., Dybkjaer: Multimodal Usability. Springer (2009); Mitchell, W.H. (whm): An Introduction to Design Patterns (2003)

[14]  Dow, S., Saponas, T.S., Li, Y., Landay, J.A.: External representations in ubiquitous computing design and the implications for design tools. In: Proceedings of DIS 2006: Designing Interactive Systems: Processes, Practices, Methods, & Techniques, pp. 241–250. University Park, Pennsylvania (2006)

[15]  Saponas, T.S., Prabaker, M.K., Abowd, G.D., Landay, J.A.: The impact of pre-patterns on the design of digital home applications. In: Proceedings of the 6th ACM Conference on Designing Interactive Systems, pp. 189–198. University Park, Pennsylvania (2006)

# Upward Influence Tactics in Virtual Work Settings

Sebastián Steizel[1] and Eva Rimbau-Gilabert[2]

[1] Universidad de San Andrés, Vito Dumas 284
(B1644BID) Buenos Aires, Argentina
ssteizel@udesa.edu.ar
[2] Internet Interdisciplinary Institute (IN3) & Business and Economy Studies
Universitat Oberta de Catalunya (UOC), Av. Tibidabo 39-43, 08035 Barcelona, Spain
erimbau@uoc.edu

**Abstract.** The globalization of work within organizations has generated a greater need for all type of workers to exert interpersonal influence through technology-mediated communication tools. This paper contributes to the analysis of interpersonal relations in virtual environments from a specific perspective: the choice of upward influence tactics. We propose that virtual work settings may impact the upward influence tactic selected, as well as the communication medium used to enact it. In particular, we study whether the types of upward influence strategies found in presence environments, are relevant in a virtual work context. This research also analyzes the link between communication media and influence tactics used. Preliminary results suggest that there is an influence tactic that is specific of virtual work relations, which may be called intermediation and consists of finding a mediator who is well connected with the target and can help in defining the best approach by the agent.

**Keywords:** Influence tactics, upwards influence, virtual communication, virtual relationship.

## 1 Introduction

The globalization of work within organizations is an unavoidable reality in today's business world. We are increasingly dealing with virtual work arrangements in which employees of the same company or different companies must collaborate through technology-mediated communication tools. These new forms of work are associated with the development of new organizational structures that take the form of interconnected, small organizational units, which are marked by lower hierarchical control, and more horizontal relations. In such context, there is greater need for rethinking interpersonal relations in general, and interpersonal influence in particular ([1], [2]).

Although interpersonal influence is a key element in this new organizational reality, it has mostly been studied in traditional or presence environments. This study contributes to the analysis of interpersonal relations in virtual environments from a specific perspective: the choice of upward influence strategies. Within influence

M.D. Lytras et al. (Eds.): WSKS 2011, CCIS 278, pp. 655–660, 2013.

relationships, probably those exercised by employees towards their employers or managers express the purest form of influence. In the absence of any hierarchical authority and prerogatives, employees must often exercise influence over their managers to do their jobs, in search of resources to achieve results. In addition, such influence is nowadays increasingly exerted through the use of electronic media, which probably impact the chosen influence tactics and their effects.

Therefore, the research presented in this paper analyzes the influence tactics used by subordinates working in virtual environments, in pursuing to influence their supervisors. Specifically, we address the following questions: Are the types of upward influence tactics found in presence environments relevant in a virtual work context? Are there certain influence tactics that are specific of virtual work relations? Preliminary results regarding the first question are presented.

## 2    Theoretical Background

Research on influence tactics has covered both its antecedents and its consequences, but it has rarely mentioned ther virtual environment or the mediating technology as variables to be taken into account (for a review see [3], [4]). Only a few studies have analyzed the phenomenon of influence tactics in virtual environments. Elron and Vigoda [5] for example, found that task focus, the centrality of the team, and the familiarity among members were factors that affected the use of influence tactics in virtual teams. Other authors have focused on the process of virtual influence, analyzing this phenomenon as a dynamic process in which the influence strategy is affected by the target perception and their reaction to the influence intent [2]. Dealing specifically with the impact of the communication media, Barry and Bateman [6] suggested that influence tactics and media usage, were influenced by the hierarchical position of the individuals, and by the direction of the influence intent (upwards, downwards or horizontal). The work of Cho et al. [7] is the only one that has specifically focused on upward influence tactics. They found that media choice was affected by personal preference for certain influence tactics, as well as the interpersonal relationship between agent and target. The present study continues this stream of research but takes a different perspective, since it focuses on the impact of the media on the upward influence tactic choice.

We first turn to the question of wheter the types of upward influence strategies found in presence environments, are relevant in virtual work contexts. In a virtual work setting, new communication tools may foster or hinder the use of certain strategies, thus rendering the traditional classification of presence-based influence inapplicable. The logic behind this question is based on the assumptions developed by the Adaptive Structuration Theory (AST). AST provides a model that describes the interplay between advanced information technologies, social structures, and human interaction. DeSanctis and Poole explain that "advanced information technologies trigger adaptive structurational processes which, over time, can lead to changes in the rules and resources that organizations use in social interaction." ([8], pp:142-143). For this reason we expect that as employees assimilate the technologies available, their modes of relation will be affected, not only in altering their already-known forms of influence, but also creating new, emerging forms.

The classification developed by Kipnis et al. [9] is one of the more wide used to assess interpersonal influence. Their taxonomy included the following six tactics:

- *Ingratiation:* using a friendly or helpful behavior to get the other in a good mood.
- *Exchange:* offering an exchange of positive benefits or asking to make a concession or personal sacrifice.
- *Rationality:* use of logical persuasive arguments based on reason.
- *Assertiveness:* making repeated request or use pressure.
- *Upward appeal*: causing additional pressure to conform by invoking the influence of higher levels in the organization
- *Coalition*: using the assistance of others or noting their support to persuade the other to comply with the desired goal.

This scheme has been one the most used by interpersonal influence researchers, and has been empirically and methodologically validated over the years (see [10], [11], [12], and [13]). Although the findings about frequency and use of influence tactics are not always consistent, the data obtained from the main studies shows that the tactics that prevail in presence environments are *rationality* and *ingratiation*, followed by *coalition* ([9], [11]).

Even though this taxonomy is one of the most comprehensive, the virtual work context may provide opportunities to develop new forms of influence tactics or –at least- may change the relative weigh of each tactic as compares to presence settings. The following characteristics of the virtual environment may affect the choice of influence tactics:

- There is a lack of mutual knowledge among the members of the influence dyad, which impacts mutual understanding [14].
- Virtual communication offers less social cues, which also affects the information exchange process [15].
- Virtual teams tend to be more task-focused and less social-focused than traditional teams [16].
- Distance work may involve people from different national cultures, which may affect the influence preferences ([5], [17], [18]).

These structural features of virtual media may impact relationship building and, thus, the upward influence process. As posed by Contractor and Eisenberg (in [19]), the communication structures and the organizational use given to the media shape each other in an emerging pattern of social interaction. Therefore, in interpersonal relations developed in virtual settings, where the primary ways of communication are technology-mediated, we expect to find new upward influence tactics or –at least- different frecuency of tactics use, as compared with presence environments.

# 3    Methodology

The methodology to address these issues combines the use of quantitative and qualitative strategies. We first obtained data from semi-structured interviews with employees of multinational companies who have their supervisors at a distance, asking them about their tactics to influence their supervisor. This step provides information to confirm or change the influence tactics inventories that have been developed for presence settings.

A questionnaire addressed to a wider sample of employees in muntinational corporations will be used to evaluate the frequency of the diverse influence tactics used in virtual environments, and their combination with different technologies. The instrument used to measure influence tactics is an adaptation of that developed by Kipnis et al [9], and updated by Schriescheim and Hinkin [12], called the POIS (Profile of Organizational Influence Strategies).

## 4    Preliminary Findings

Preliminary results from semi-structured interviews suggest that there is a particular set of upward tactics that emerge in a virtual environment. Most of the interviewees highlighted that a task-oriented relationship is built under this kind of work environment. They also underscored that the formal content of such communication interactions affects the way they try to influence their supervisors and the media they select for that purpose. Because of the lack of informal social interaction that could add data about each side's situation, there is not a common understanding of the context under which each member of the influence dyad is talking or listening (country context, physical context, target network, internal power distribution, local organization dynamics, etc.). This weak information about the supervisor's situation leads people to be careful in their intention to influence their supervisors, as explained below.

The tactics that were more frequently mentioned in the interviews are 1) *rationality*; 2) what we have dubbed *intermediation*; and 3) *coalition*. Whit *rationality* tactics, the subordinates' attempt to get something from their supervisors is mainly based on logical argumentation to support their requests. This is the more accepted way to approach the supervisor. The way interviewees use this tactic follows a two-step sequence: they firstly send an electronic mail to brief the supervisor about the request and, after some time, they resort to a call conference to reinforce the arguments and complete the influence intent. This contributes to the notion that workers are particularly careful when trying to influence their distant supervisor.

The second tactic emerged in the interviews, which we have called *intermediation-* adds a new tactic to the aforementioned list by Kipnis *et al.* Many interviewees stated that when they had difficult issues to discuss, and they did not know how their supervisor might react to their request, they looked for someone that is physically or socially close to their supervisor and who could help them to transmit their intentions. The mediator could be a local colleague of the agent, or a local colleague of the target. The main point was to find someone who is proximate to and trusted by the target, was able to understand the target's context, and could then suggest the best way to approach him/her. When the mediator was at the same place than the agent, the selected communitacion medium with him or her was face-to-face interaction. When this person was at a distance, the interviewees tended to prefer the telephone.

The third tactic most frequently mentioned was *coalition*. Before the influence intention, the subordinates tried to build an agreement among their peers to present their request to the target as a collective issue.

The most frequently used tactics in virtual settings (rationality, intermediation and coalition), as compared with those found in presence settings (rationality, ingratiation and coalition), point out to the difficulties of establishing personal bonds between distant subordinate and supervisors, which in turn hinder the use of "soft" influence tactics such as ingratiaion.

# References

1. Fulk, J., DeSanctis, G.: Electronic communication and changing organizational forms. Organization Science 6(4), 337–349 (1995)
2. Barry, B., Fulmer, I.S.: The medium and the message: The adaptive use of communication media in dyadic influence. Academy of Management Review 29(2), 272–292 (2004)
3. Barbuto Jr., J., Moss, J.: Dispositional Effects in Intra-Organizational Influence Tactics: A Meta-Analytic Review. Journal of Leadership & Organizational Studies 12(3), 30–52 (2006)
4. Higgins, C.A., Judge, T.A., Ferris, G.R.: Influence tactics and work outcomes: A meta-analysis. Journal of Organizational Behavior 24, 89–106 (2003)
5. Elron, E., Vigoda-Gadot, E.: Influence and political processes in cyberspace: The case of global virtual teams. International Journal of Cross Cultural Management: CCM 6(3), 295–317 (2006)
6. Barry, B., Bateman, T.: Perceptions of influence in managerial dyads - the role of hierarchy, media, and tactics. Human Relations 45(6), 555–574 (1992)
7. Cho, N., Park, K., Su, C.: Effects of the Upward Influence Strategies on the Communication Media Selection. Contemporary Management Research 4(2), 137–154 (2008)
8. DeSanctis, G., Poole, M.S.: Capturing the complexity in advanced technology use: Adaptive structuration theory. Organization Science 5(2), 121–147 (1994)
9. Kipnis, S., Schmidt, S., Wilkinson, I.: Intraorganizational influence tactics: exploration in getting one's way. Journal of Applied Psychology 65(4), 440–452 (1980)
10. Schilit, W., Locke, E.: A Study of Upward Influence in Organizations. Administrative Science Quarterly 27(2), 304–316 (1982)
11. Yukl, G., Falbe, C.M.: Influence tactics and objectives in upward, downward, and lateral influence attempts. Journal of Applied Psychology 75(2), 132–140 (1990)
12. Schriesheim, C.A., Hinkin, T.R.: Influence tactics used by subordinates: A theoretical and empirical analysis and refinement of the Kipnis, Schmidt, and Wilkinson subscales. Journal of Applied Psychology 75(3), 246–257 (1990)
13. Farmer, S.M., Maslyn, J.M., Fedor, D.B., Goodman, J.S.: Putting Upward Influence Strategies in Context. Journal of Organizational Behavior 18, 17–42 (1997)
14. Cramton, C.D.: The Mutual Knowledge Problem and Its Consequences for Dispersed Collaboration. Organization Science 12(3), 346–371 (2001)
15. Sproull, L., Kiesler, S.: Reducing social context cues: electronic mail in organizational communication. Management Science 32(11), 1492–1512 (1986)

16. Chidambaram, L., Bostrom, R.: Evolution of Group Performance Over Time: A Repeated Measures Study of GDSS Effects. Journal of Organizational Computing 3(4), 443–469 (1993)
17. Hirokawa, R., Miyahara, A.: A Comparison of Influence Strategies Utilized by Managers in American and Japanese Organizations. Communication Quarterly 34(3), 250–265 (1986)
18. Yeh, R.-S.: Downward influence styles in cultural diversity settings. The International Journal of Human Resource Management 6(3), 626–641 (1995)
19. Fulk, J.: Social construction of communication technology. Academy of Management Journal 36(5), 921–950 (1993)

# Exploring the Role of Computer-Aided Work in Men's Interactions with Their Children

David Miyar-Cruz[1] and Eva Rimbau-Gilabert[2]

[1] Internet Interdisciplinary Institute (IN3)
Universitat Oberta de Catalunya (UOC)
C/ Roc Boronat, 117, 7°, 08018 Barcelona. Spain
[2] Av. Tibidabo, 39. 08035 Barcelona. Spain
{dmiyar,erimbau}@uoc.edu

**Abstract.** In an age where the use of wireless technology is increasing in most domains of society, this paper discusses the relations between work arrangements that adopt computer technology as a flexibility-aiding tool on one hand, and the work-life interface on the other. Through in-depth interviews, we explore how men's interactions with their children are shaped under such work arrangements. Early findings would suggest a heterogeneous map of variable usage regarding computer-based tools as work flexibility enablers. Differences in father involvement would be highly explained by work type, housework-load distribution, perceived partner support, actual work-life balance micropolicies and practices in the workplace, and men's personal motivation. While some individuals seem to effectively use ICTs as an aid for their involvement in child rearing, others are as involved regardless of computer usage. A relevant counterintuitive finding is that computer literacy is not necessarily linked to the actual usage of computer tools for work flexibility.

**Keywords:** father involvement, work flexibility, computer-aided work, work-family interface.

## 1 Introduction

It is generally agreed that current societies are experiencing a major shift in work life through the individualization of labor [1]. Furthermore, the mobile network society significantly intensifies such shift due to the pervasiveness of wireless communication devices, which enable individuals to be permanently connected to their work. This permanent, ubiquitous connectivity may affect men and women's work-life balance, and specifically their parenting practices.

Under this background, our paper focuses in identifying if and how computer aided work affects men in coping with the work-family conflict by means of enhanced flexibility. We address a broad research question, *How do computer aided work arrangements affect the involvement of fathers in child rearing?* while pursuing the following objectives:

M.D. Lytras et al. (Eds.): WSKS 2011, CCIS 278, pp. 661–668, 2013.
© Springer-Verlag Berlin Heidelberg 2013

- Explore if and how men use computer aided work arrangements as flexibility enablers for managing work-family conflict.
- Explore if differences in father involvement of men are explained by personal or organizational traits such as personal motivation, perceived partner support or workplace policies and practices

## 1.1 Why Is This Research Relevant?

There are two interrelated justifications for this research. Firstly, ICT-aided forms of work are challenging the conceptual framework of the traditional workplace and positing new social problems to researchers, such as the possibility of "transcending time and space" in social practice, the "office on-the-run" as a working arrangement or the family-life implications of these new contexts [1]. However, existing literature shows either unclear or openly contradictory conclusions when exploring the implications of new ICTs for the work-family interface and the distribution of gender or parenting roles [2, 3]. The paper will contribute to this line of research.

Secondly, in work-family research there is a need to focus on men in general and on fathers in particular. While family-work studies have overwhelmingly explored how the relationships between ICTs, work arrangements and family roles affect women, "the category of 'men'", as highlighted by Jeff Hearn, "is both all-pervasive and strangely invisible" in what Mary O'Brian labeled the "malestream" social science [4]. Additionally, while fatherhood as such has been the object of study by scholars and policy makers throughout the past decades [5], the role of workplace practices and policies upon FI in child rearing has seldom been addressed. Such gap contrasts with the large body of literature focusing on how women's lives are conditioned by their dual role of workers and mothers [6]. Furthermore, the coin of the under-representation of women in strategic labor industries has a flip side in men's lack of contribution to the domestic sphere in general and to informal care in particular, as policy analysts have argued [7]. Therefore, an analytical perspective that includes men as units of analysis seems relevant in order to fill in this research gap as well.

## 1.2 Reconceptualizing the Workplace

This study is based on the key assumption that the working contexts of men affect their involvement in child rearing. It is also apparent that ICTs are changing significantly the way work can be deployed, which has led some scholars to suggest a reconceptualization of the workplace [8] as explained below.

The traditional and implicit image of the workplace is connected to notions of offices, home or factories, as exclusive and permanent locations. In contrast, remote work in its different forms conveys notions of location-based flexibility: home-based telecommuting, satellite offices, hotelling, neighborhood work centers or mobile work [9, 10].

Wirelessly enabled multilocation work in particular allows "any space that they [workers] are able to use/manipulate for work purposes, on however a temporary basis" [8] to potentially become a workplace. This definition conveys a comprehensive and complex notion of telework, whereby workers today have the potential to deploy their duties not just at a distance from the workplace but rather "networked", that is, combining "home, work and field contexts" [11] with variable aid from ICTs.

## 2    Theoretical Framework

This work is based on the now extensive and systematic work–family field literature, fed in turn by the Social Psychology, Sociology of Work and Organization Management fields (see [12]) to address the interactions between working and parenting roles.

### 2.1    Key Definitions

**ICT-Aided Work Arrangements (IFWAs).** We define ICT-aided work arrangements as work contexts that convey "the ability of workers to make choices influencing when, where, and for how long they engage in work-related tasks" [13] with the support of new computer based technology, namely wireless communication devices and widespread broadband access to the Internet. This definition has two significant implications. Firstly, the "choices" referred to are potentially increased when these new ICTs are involved. Secondly, we are assuming the workers' perspective as opposed to the organizational perspective for our analysis.

A crucial assumption of this research, however, is that ICTs are not the only or even necessary causing conditions of flexible work practices. In fact, different authors have identified organizational policies, individual choice or institutional and workplace micropolicies as especially relevant drivers for the adoption of flexible work [11, 14]. Micropolicies can be defined as perceived support from work supervisors and colleagues, regardless of formally existing family-friendly policies [14].

**Father Involvement in Child Rearing (FI).** FI can range from engaging in financial contributions in support of the family [15] to very close emotional and affective support with the children, passing through other historically determined models, such as moral teacher or guide, breadwinner or sex-role model [16]. However, some of these father models contradict each other in terms of time investment or emotional proximity, which become key determinants for different roles; for instance, breadwinning versus child nurturing.

With the rise of the "nurturant father model" [16] Lamb, Pleck, Charnov and Levine introduced in 1987 a conceptualization of FI used in subsequent works, and involving three distinct dimensions that we use for the purposes of this research:

(a) *engagement*, which involves both time spent in direct interaction with children and the affective nature of the interaction;
(b) *accessibility*, which covers being available to the child in close proximity, but not actually interacting on a one-to-one basis; and
(c) *responsibility*, which covers having responsibility for the day-to-day care of a child, taking time off work to care for a sick child, and the extent to which the parent takes direct or sole responsibility for decisions and activities related to the child (quoted in [17]).

## 2.2    Theoretical Perspectives

Considering our specific focus on fathers, a reference to the studies on men is relevant here. Critical studies on men as a specific branch of Gender and Women's Studies use a social constructionist intellectual approach to explore men and masculinities, which are defined, from this view, as gendered constructs. This view criticizes the theoretical poorness of other non-critical or even openly antifeminist views, whereby "Men's Studies" is considered a brand new discipline [4, 18]. While we will take into account the empirical usefulness of the latter when appropriate, this paper uses a critical perspective of men and masculinities.

Regarding the fathering experience. Russell and Hwang [17] suggest that FI is not only conditioned by individual, family and social factors but also by workplace factors, which are considered "significant influencers" and can become a "potential significant barrier and enabler of father involvement" [17]. Few theories, as highlighted by Hill and others [13], address the role that workplace flexibility plays in this. In fact, most of the research focuses strictly on the role of family leave policies in FI, neglecting a more comprehensive perspective.

As for the work-family interface, micro level theories used in previous research have two different focuses: conflicts in role and facilitation. Conflicts in role approaches state that paid work and family life roles are inherently incompatible [19]. Facilitation theories, in contrast, suggest that instances of positive interaction of the work and family interface are possible and actually exist. Such positive interaction is labeled enrichment, positive spill over or enhancement, depending on the perspective and measurement tools used [13, 19]. While this paper initially suggests that computer-based technology may play an important role as facilitator of the involvement of some fathers in child rearing, it also acknowledges the possibility of role overload and role related stress.

## 3    Computer-based Technology as an Enabler of Father Involvement

Previous literature has explored different perspectives on the relations between work arrangements and father involvement in child rearing. This paper is part of a wider research project focused on the role that both flexible work arrangements (FWAs) in particular and the workplace in general play for the involvement of fathers in child rearing (FI). Here we specifically explore the use of a particular form of FWA based in computer aided technology, which we call ICT aided flexible work arrangements or IFWAs, as defined above.

A significant part of the literature revolves around the negative influence of IFWAs for women's work-family balance. Apart from specific problems such as the double shift and obstacles for career advancement, some authors link the absence of staff from the work-site to the loss of the "socializing aspects of work, forms of social support and feedback, and on-site learning" [20]. However, the possibility of combining child-care and work, as noted by Ursula Huws, is one of the few positive benefits that working women have reported in relation to telework [20]. We submit that this latter advantage should also be explored as a potential benefit for men.

Looking at the bigger picture, Russell and Hwang [17] suggest that it is unclear whether the availability and utilization of FWAs is a cause or an effect of FI. They propose that personal motivation should be regarded as the "complex interactive component" [18]) in fathers who make major changes in their work conditions to improve the quality of their family life, such as reduced hours, increased flexibility, and shifting to less demanding positions. Furthermore, the "sense of entitlement" of workers regarding family-friendly options seems to be a driver of workers' willingness to opt for flexible arrangements. Our research includes personal motivation as a key aspect in the study of the relation between IFWAs and FI.

# 4    Methods

Considering that the purpose of this research is exploratory in nature, at this stage we are not (yet) setting out to contrast a predetermined hypothesis on a representative sample that allows for extrapolation, but have selected a diversified sample of eligible men, namely working fathers with different work arrangements. Choosing interviews as a research method is consistent with previous empirical work that focuses in research questions addressing issues similar to those included herein. As Marsh and Musson [6] have noted, interviews "capture subjective narratives that are in themselves constitutive of the formation of people's identities". However, the same authors warn about the risks linked to methodologies that deal with the performances of emotion and identity, as these can become the products of the participant's interactions with us as we exercise our interviewer role. We therefore admit a "specific slant in our data" [6], considering that the guidance inherent to semi-structured interviews may finally direct respondents in their narratives of father and worker identities. This is why our second stage in research will include quantitative methods.

Respondents were interviewed as they were located and became available [21], and were selected through a "snowball" or chain referral sampling procedure. However, at this stage we have not focused exclusively in individuals with an intensive use of ICTs in their work arrangements, but in individuals under all sorts of arrangements, in order precisely to explore if, when and how they are able or unable to use ICTs as work flexibility enablers to cope with the work-life interface. Consistently with other literature, we assume that the formal availability of flexible arrangements through computer technology does not always match actual utilization of such flexible options for the purpose of balancing work roles with family roles.

In order to analyze the different levels of FI in child rearing, respondents' answers are being categorized according to the different themes that emerge from their narratives. We have identified issues connected to men's ideas about their gender roles, work-related determinants and themes linked to their private sphere.

# 5    Initial and Expected Findings

This research is work in progress and our findings are limited and emergent in nature. However, the interviews conducted so far provide useful insights. While perceived partner attitude and micropolicies at the workplace have emerged as determinants of some of our respondents' father role performance, a counterintuitive finding is that individuals with high computer literacy not necessarily make use of all available computer based resources in order to enhance flexibility. To illustrate this let's look at Ramón, a tenured university professor who defined himself as an advanced user of computer technology and very much praised the work flexibility linked to his privileged position at a virtually based higher education institution. At one point, after being asked about how he uses ICTs daily to manage work flexibility, he remarked how annoying it was for him to walk around with a laptop when having to travel around to conferences or meetings for work:

> if I have to move around the city and I have spare time, what I do is I take stuff to read. The laptop actually bothers me a lot. No I don't do it, no... I dislike it. Well, I do it when I need it. So, when I'm out, and I know I'll have extra time I always bring along things to read.[1]

As we proceed through our research, we expect to fine grain these initial findings and expect others to emerge, including personal motivation as a key role in FI under all types of work arrangements, or the fact that IFWAs may be especially suitable in enhancing the 'accessibility' dimension of FI in motivated men. This would be a relevant finding, as motivated fathers who are enrolled in work arrangements other than IFWAs could find barriers to develop this dimension. In turn, non-motivated fathers will arguably remain uninvolved as parents regardless of their work/ICT contexts. Conversely, as compared to traditional work arrangements (TWAs), FWAs will presumably foster a higher level of FI in men who are already motivated.

## 6    Preliminary Conclusions

Early findings seem to suggest a heterogeneous map of usage regarding computer-aided tools as work flexibility enablers. Variability in FI is explained by a set of isolated or interrelated elements: work type, housework-load distribution, perceived partner support, actual work-life balance micropolicies and practices in the workplace, and men's personal motivation. While some individuals effectively use ICTs as an aid for their involvement in child rearing, others seem to be as involved regardless of computer usage. A relevant counterintuitive finding is that computer literacy is not necessarily linked to the actual usage of computer tools for work flexibility.

Considering all that has been said and the contradictory findings of studies exploring the link between FWAs and FI [18], we reasonably expect a final picture whereby IFWAs would not be the single main determinant of FI, thus challenging the popular technologically deterministic assumption that considers ICTs *per se* directly

---

[1] This and all other quotation transcriptions are the authors' translations of vernacular versions of the conducted interviews (from Catalan or Spanish). Following is the Catalan original version of the quoted text: "si vaig fora i tinc temps, el que faig és portar per llegir. Però l'ordinador em molesta molt, no ho faig, no... no m'agrada. O sigui, ho faig quan ho necessito. O sigui, fora, quan tinc fora, i sé que tindré temps lliure porto per llegir sempre."

correlated to enhanced work-family balance. We also expect to confirm initial findings suggesting that computer expertise is not always linked to actual utilization of computer aided flexibility, however unrestricted the availability of such technical tools might be.

# References

1. Castells, M.: Materials for an exploratory theory of the network society. Br. J. Sociol. 51(1), 5–24 (2000)
2. Greenhill, A., Wilson, M.: Haven or hell? Telework, flexibility and family in the e-society: a Marxist analysis. European Journal of Information System 15(4), 379–388 (2006)
3. Wilson, M., Greenhill, A.: Gender and teleworking identities in the risk society: a research agenda. New Technology, Work and Employment 19(3), 207–221 (2004)
4. Hearn, J.: The implications of critical studies on men. NORA - Nordic Journal of Feminist and Gender Research 5(1), 48–60 (1997)
5. Marsiglio, W., Amato, P., Day, R.D., Lamb, M.E.: Scholarship on Fatherhood in the 1990s and beyond. Journal of Marriage and Family 62(4), 1173–1191 (2000)
6. Marsh, K., Musson, G.: Men at Work and at Home: Managing Emotion in Telework. Gender, Work & Organization 15(1), 31–48 (2008)
7. Herman, C., Webster, J.: Taking a lifecycle approach: redefining women returners to science, engineering and technology. International Journal of Gender Science and Technology 2(2), 179–205 (2010)
8. Hislop, D., Axtell, C.: To infinity and beyond?: workspace and the multi-location worker. New Technology, Work and Employment 24(1), 60–75 (2009)
9. Kurland, N.B., Bailey, D.E.: Telework: The Advantages and Challenges of Working Here, There, Anywhere, and Anytime. Organ. Dyn. 28(2), 53–67 (1999)
10. Mann, S., Varey, R., Button, W.: An exploration of the emotional impact of tele-working via computer-mediated communication. Journal of Managerial Psychology 15(7), 668–690 (2000)
11. Garrett, R.K., Danziger, J.N.: Which telework? Defining and testing a taxonomy of technology-mediated work at a distance. Soc. Sci. Comput. Rev. 25(1), 27–47 (2007)
12. Pitt-Catsouphes, M., Kossek, E.E., Sweet, S.A.: The Work and family handbook: multi-disciplinary perspectives and approaches. Lawrence Erlbaum, Mahwah (2006)
13. Hill, E.J., Grzywacz, J.G., Allen, S., Blanchard, V.L., Matz-Costa, C., Shulkin, S., et al.: Defining and conceptualizing workplace flexibility. Community, Work & Family 11(2), 149–163 (2008)
14. Palkovitz, R.J.: Involved fathering and men's adult development: provisional balances. Lawrence Erlbaum Associates, Mahwah (2002)
15. Schindler, H.S.: The Importance of Parenting and Financial Contributions in Promoting Fathers' Psychological Health. Journal of Marriage and Family 72(2), 318–332 (2010)
16. Lamb, M.E.: The history of research on father involvement. Marriage Family Review 29(2), 23–42 (2000)
17. Russell, G., Hwang, C.P.: The impact of workplace practices on father involvement. In: Lamb, M.E. (ed.) The Role of the Father in Child Development, 4th edn., pp. 476–503. John Wiley & Sons, Hobokem (2004)

18. Hearn, J.: Critical Studies on Men in Four Parts of the World (2001)
    http://www.nikk.uio.no/?module=Articles;action=Article.publi
    cShow;ID=419 (accessed September 30, 2010)
19. Hill, E.J., Allen, S., Jacob, J., Bair, A.F., Bikhazi, S.L., Van Langeveld, A., et al.: Work—
    Family Facilitation: Expanding Theoretical Understanding Through Qualitative
    Exploration. Advances in Developing Human Resources 9(4), 507–526 (2007)
20. Haddon, L., Lewis, A.: The experience of teleworking: an annotated review. International
    Journal of Human Resource Management 5(1), 193–223 (1994)
21. Biernacki, P., Waldorf, D.: Snowball sampling. Sociological Methods Research 10(2),
    141–163 (1981)

# Managing Matrixed, Dispersed Advisors in Virtual Universities

Eva Rimbau-Gilabert, María J. Martínez-Argüelles, and Elisabet Ruiz-Dotras

eLearn Center & Internet Interdisciplinary Institute (IN3)
Universitat Oberta de Catalunya (UOC)
Av. Tibidabo 39-43. 08035 Barcelona. Spain
{erimbau,mmartinezarg,eruizd}@uoc.edu

**Abstract.** There is a lack of research about how to manage the advising role in purely virtual universities. This paper highlights the need for virtual universities to coordinate a large, distributed teaching staff through virtual workgroups. In the particular case of academic advising, these groups may function in a virtual, matrix structure –as occurs in the Open University of Catalonia-, thus generating specific coordination challenges. The paper elaborates an Input-Process-Output model that can be used as a guide for researching the effectiveness of matrixed, dispersed advisors.

**Keywords:** Academic advising, virtual universities, virtual advising, advising effectiveness.

## 1    Introduction

With the development of electronic information and communication media, virtual universities have become a widespread reality in the world of higher education. As a result, a large number of articles and books have been published on topics related to online teaching methodologies and evaluation systems, teacher-student and student-student relationships in the virtual university classroom, etc. Additionally, some effort has been devoted to analyze how traditional universities should transform their activities in order to offer online programs. However, there is still a lack of theoretical models and empirical research about how to manage purely virtual universities. This paper contributes to fill in this gap, by concentrating on the factors that contribute to successful academic advising in purely technology-based universities or born-virtual universities.

## 2    Virtual Universities Need Virtual Teams

Virtual universities are "all the higher education institutions that are relying more than any of their predecessors on distance teaching delivery through the new ICTs" [1]. Although these universities deliver their courses through different technologies and are based on diverse organizational infrastructures, they share the goal to provide totally online course delivery through the use of computer networking [2]. Virtual

M.D. Lytras et al. (Eds.): WSKS 2011, CCIS 278, pp. 669–676, 2013.

universities are similar to traditional distance universities in the fact that they are not campus-based. Instead of assembling students from dispersed locations in one place, they reach out to students wherever they live or wish to study [3]. The main difference among distance and virtual universities lies in their educational model. Distance institutions are characterized by an industrial model, based on "teaching large numbers of students by a handful of professors, most of whom do not communicate with the students at all" [4]. In contrast, the e-learning model that characterizes virtual universities requires a close relation between students and teachers [4]. This results in the need to employ large numbers of teaching professionals. ICTs make it possible: just as students in virtual universities do not gather in a physical campus, teachers do not need to travel to a fixed location, but most of the time can work from wherever they are through a virtual campus.

In summary, virtual universities have to coordinate a large, distributed teaching staff to offer educational services to a large, distributed student clientele. Such coordination is required to guarantee the principles of sameness and uniformity in content, teaching quality, assignments and assessment. Thus, educational managers in virtual universities need models to help them coordinate a distributed workforce. To address this issue, little advice is found in educational literature, which has mainly focused on student rather than teacher coordination (see, for example [5]), on presence-based rather than online advising activity [6], or on technology as a support for advising systems rather than for its organization [7]. Thus, this study resorts to literature from the fields of management, organizational psychology and information systems.

This paper is an initial result of a research project undertaken at the Universitat Oberta de Catalunya (UOC, Open University of Catalonia) aimed at designing guidelines for effective management of distributed teachers. The project focuses on two types of teaching figures: *subject tutors*, who ensure students' progress in each subject, and *academic advisors*, who accompany students throughout their academic life in the university, from the moment they show some interest in enrolling in a programme until they receive their diploma. In some universities, the advising role is developed part-time by subject tutors, but at the UOC subject tutoring and advising are developed by different people. This paper focuses on academic advisors, who have specific coordination needs in this institution, as explained below.

## 3    The Virtual Matrix for Academic Advising at the UOC

This section briefly explains the organizational structure used for academic advising at the UOC. This structure, which originates a double line of responsibility, creates a complex setting that demands especial coordination efforts. This explanation is intended to give flesh to the rather abstract concepts used in organizational literature, as well as to help in adapting them to an educational context.

We will use the term *academic advising* to refer to the support that learners receive regarding their operation within the context of an academic program. Students need support to understand the virtual environment where they will be immersed in, to establish relations with their peers, to plan their academic goals and keep striving towards them, to select the subjects they will study each semester, to select extra-academic activities that can improve their learning experience, etc.

According to Pardee [8], models for delivering advising services may be categorized according to advisors' professional definition (professional advisors or counselors, or faculty) and according to where advisors are housed (in academic or administrative units, or both). At the UOC, advisors are professionals who do not teach subjects and who focus exclusively on their advising activities. Although Pardee's second categorization revolves around the physical location of advisors, it points towards a criterion of responsibility: advisors may report to an academic or an administrative supervisor, or to both at the same time. The advisorial structure at the UOC points to this shared responsibility: academic advisors have a double internal dependency, which creates a matrix structure.

On the one hand, they organically depend on the Program Director. The Director selects them, appraises their performance and decides on their continuation. Directors provide training and advice and resolve questions on everything related to the academic aspects of their programs. On the other hand, the advisors functionally depend on the so-called Advisorial Function team, which is transversal to the entire university. This team is responsible for providing training and assistance to advisors so that they can, in turn, train students to take full advantage of their effort. Subsequently, the Advisorial Function monitors such training given by advisors. Similarly, this team offers suggestions and monitors advisors' activity in relation to student motivation and university procedures.

According to the matrix structure adopted, advisors are part of both the Advisorial Function and the Academic Program and have two separate workspaces, one for each dependency line. In the first workspace, communication flows between the Program Director and the advisors. Throughout the semester, the director helps advisors with all possible educational problems that may arise. At the same time, advisors comment upon any significant information they obtain from students. This information is extremely useful for the Program Director, who may use it to detect problems and plan improvements. In the other virtual room, the advisors communicate with the member of the Advisorial Function assigned to a group of programs as well as with the other advisors of those related programs. Obviously, every advisor has also a personal e-mail and can contact directly with the Program Director and the assigned member of the Advisorial Team.

Organizations adopt a matrix structure when the following three conditions converge [9]: pressure for a dual focus, a need to process large amounts of information simultaneously, and pressure for shared resource. In the case of advising at the UOC, the dual focus refers to program specific knowledge (vertical dimension) and horizontal coordination among programs in terms of administrative processes. The different nature of academic and administrative knowledge and the growing numbers of students, explain the other reasons that lead to implement this structure.

In this matrix structure, advisors are part of both the Advisorial Function and the academic program. This generates specific coordination challenges, since the advisors are not only distributed, but they also have to navigate through the potential for conflict that characterizes matrix structures. Thus, the research described in this paper does not only try to learn more about the effectiveness of dispersed advisors, but it also focuses on the specific problems of matrixed, dispersed teams.

## 4    Management of Dispersed, Matrixed Work Groups

**Dispersed or virtual teams** are significantly different from traditional teams. Powell et al. [10] define virtual teams as "groups of geographically, organizationally and/or time dispersed workers brought together by information technologies to accomplish one or more organization tasks". By definition, they are composed of members who rarely, if ever, meet physically [11]. In the proverbial traditional team, the members work next to one another, while in virtual teams they work in different locations. In traditional teams the coordination of tasks is straightforward and performed by the members of the team together; in virtual teams, in contrast, tasks must be much more highly structured. Also, virtual teams rely on electronic communication, as opposed to face-to-face communication in traditional teams [12]. Thus, the challenges for managers are magnified by the introduction of such geographic or temporal distances [11].

Researchers have frequently used an Input-Process-Output model to analyze the factors that intervene in virtual teamwork. The precise elements in each part of the model vary, but in general they all agree in a framework similar to the one depicted in Figure 1 (adapted from [10] and [14]). This paper explains the application of such generic model to the case of matrixed, virtual university advisors (see [11] for generic thoughts on how to manage matrixed, virtual teams).

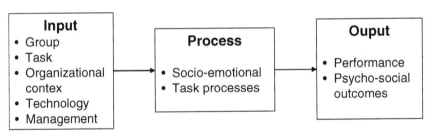

**Fig. 1.** Generic research model of virtual group effectiveness

Turning to **matrix organizational structures**, they combine a vertical structure with an equally strong horizontal overlay. While the vertical structure provides traditional control within functional departments, the horizontal overlay provides coordination across departments to achieve profit goals. This structure has lines of formal authority along two dimensions, such as functional and product or product and region. Thus, matrixed employees report to two bosses simultaneously [15], which adds complexity both for matrixed employees and for the managers of each structural dimension.

Virtual teams share with matrix structures the need for a clear structure in order to be effective. For example, Lurey [14] states that in virtual teams the individual team members' roles and the team's primary objectives must be explicit, not simply assumed. Goold and Campbell [16] suggest that the main problem of a matrix structure is lack of clarity about each matrixed unit's role and responsibilities.

Consequently, the use of a matrix structure with virtual groups needs to be reflected in task definition and management practices. Thus, these aspects will receive closer attention in the proposed research.

# 5 Researching the Effectiveness of Matrixed, Dispersed Advisors

The generic model for the study of virtual teams effectiveness in Figure 1 can be adapted to the situation of matrixed, dispersed academic advising. Every element in the model can be measured through diverse variables, with the aim of assessing their relative impact on advising processes and outcomes.

It is necessary mentioning that the following list does not intend to be exhaustive; it is rather thought as a heuristic guide for researchers. Additionally, not all items have been thought to require equal clarification; specifically, more detailed explanations are given for those elements that may be more affected by a matrix structure.

## 5.1 Input

**Group. Properties of the group and its members.**

- Size. Size does not only impact group processes, but also the manager activity, since coordinating bigger groups normally requires more time devoted to communication and hinders control. In a matrixed structure, team's size can be different for the Program Director and for the Tutorial Function member. Thus, both data have to be considered.
- Advisors' tenure; turnover ratio of advisors in each team.
- Advisors' personal characteristics.
- Advisors professional background and technical expertise. Are the advisors faculty members at a university or do they work in the corporate world? Did they graduate at the university where they serve as advisors? Do advisors have adequate technical expertise to be able to cope with technical problems?
- Advisors' commitment to their activity. It may differ for different types of advisors (faculty vs. professional advisors) and for different work relationships (permanent vs. contingent).

**Task**

- Degree of task-driven interdependence among advisors. The task of advising is often understood as highly individual, whereby each advisor uses the available resources to independently attend to their advisees. However, team models for advising have also been proposed [17], that require high interaction among the separated roles of counselors and instructors.
- Task content, in terms of the time advisors spend on conceptual or behavioral tasks (following [18]), as well as the relative weight of routine, problem solving and creative tasks.

**Organizational Context**

- Organizational culture.
- Human resource practices for advisors: Training, reward systems, type of contract, etc.
- Power balance between the matrix dimensions. The success of a matrix structure depends on the appropriate balance of power attributed to each dimension (vertical and horizontal) [9]. For example, if the academic line of hierarchy dominates, the process and outputs will surely be different that those obtained if the administrative line takes the lead.
- Role clarity for each matrix dimension. Program Directors and the Tutorial Function members need to have a clear vision of their respective responsibilities. They also have to be able to transmit such vision to advisors in order to avoid misunderstandings.

**Technology.** In virtual advising groups, almost all communications will be technologically mediated. However, in a virtual university technology is not only used for communication among people, but also for information retrieval and analysis. All kinds of technology may be classified according to the sphere it is used in:

- Technology used by managers and advisors to communicate and coordinate among themselves.
- Technology that advisors can use, as a means to perform their advising task.

**Management**

- Managers' turnover.
- Management practices. Leadership style, as well as the degree to which Program Directors of Tutorial Function member apply Malhotra et al.'s [19] recommendations for virtual team leadership, may impact advising processes and outcomes.

## 5.2   Process

Virtual team processes include socio-emotional and task-related processes [10].

**Socio-Emotional Processes.** Virtual teams may have specific difficulties to develop positive socio-emotional processes such as relationship building, group cohesion and trust. However, the impact of these factors on the expected outcomes may vary as a function of the structure given to the advising task. In independent advising models such as the one adopted at the UOC, socio-emotional processes may have a limited impact on performance and satisfaction.

**Task Processes.** Task processes are those that occur as all the actors involved in advising work together to accomplish their task or goal.

- Communication. The frequency and predictability of communication among advisors, and between managers and advisors.
- Coordination. Coordination represents the degree of functional articulation and unity of effort between different actors involved in advising, and the

extent to which their work activities are logically consistent and coherent. There may be more significant challenges for coordination in a virtual, matrixed model.

- Task-technology-structure fit. Is there a fit between the various technologies available to virtual advisors and their managers, and the tasks they are called upon to execute?
- Workload. It can be measured through the size of the advisee groups, combined with the attention model adopted (individual vs. group).

## 5.3   Output

**Perfomance.** The idea of performance refers to the effectiveness of advising in terms of the university's goals.

- Students' loyalty: the ratio of students who re-enroll in the university's programs.
- Students' satisfaction with their advisor.
- Ratio of students who reach their graduation.

**Psycho-social outcomes.** These kinds of outcomes include advisors' well-being and their assessment as to whether the virtual group experience has been a worthwhile and productive one, as well as satisfaction [10].

# References

1. Guri-Rosenblit, S.: Virtual Universities: Current Models and Future Trends. Higher Education in Europe XXVI(4), 487–501 (2001)
2. Harasim, L., Hiltz, S., Teles, L., Turoff, M.: Learning Networks: A Field Guide to Teaching and Learning Online. MIT Press, Cambridge (1995)
3. Guri-Rosenblit, S.: Distance and Campus Universities: Tensions and Interactions – A comparative Study of Five Countries. Pergamon Press & The International Association of Universities, Oxford (1999)
4. Guri-Rosenblit, S.: 'Distance Education' and 'e-Learnig': Not the Same Thing. Higher Education 49, 467–493 (2005)
5. Erkens, G., Jaspers, J., Prangsma, M., Kanselaar, G.: Coordination processes in computer supported collaborative writing. Computers in Human Behavior 21, 463–486 (2005)
6. King, N.: Organization of Academic Advising Services. In: Gordon, V.N., Habley, W.R., Grites, T.J. (eds.) Academic Advising: A Comprehensive Handbook, 2nd edn. NACADA, Jossey Bass (2008)
7. Leonard, M.J.: Advising Delivery: Using Technology. In: Gordon, V.N., Habley, W.R., Grites, T.J. (eds.) Academic Advising: A Comprehensive Handbook, 2nd edn. NACADA, Jossey Bass (2008)
8. Pardee, C.F.: Organizational structures for advising. The NACADA Clearinghouse of Academic Advising Resources (2004),
   http://www.nacada.ksu.edu/Clearinghouse/AdvisingIssues/org_m odels.html (retrieved March 01, 2010)
9. Kolodny, H.F.: Managing in a Matrix. Business Horizons 24(2), 14–24 (1981)

10. Powell, A., Piccoli, G., Ives, B.: Virtual teams, a review of current literature and directions for research. The Data Base for Advances in Information Systems 35(1), 6–36 (2004)
11. Cascio, W.F., Shurygailo, S.: E-leadership and virtual teams. Organizational Dynamics 31(4), 362–376 (2003)
12. Ebrahim, N.A., Ahmed, S., Taha, Z.: Virtual Teams: a Literature Review. Australian Journal of Basic and Applied Sciences 3(3), 2653–2669 (2009)
13. Antoni, C., Hertel, G.: Team processes, their antecedents and consequences: Implications for different types of teamwork. European Journal of Work and Organizational Psychology 18(3), 253–266 (2009)
14. Lurey, J.S., Raisinghani, M.S.: An emprirical study of best practices in virtual teams. Information & Management 1914, 1–22 (2000)
15. Anand, N., Daft, R.L.: What is the Right Organization Design? Organizational Dynamics 36(4), 329–344 (2007)
16. Goold, M., Campbell, A.: Making Matrix Structures Work: Creating Clarity on Unit Roles and Responsibility. European Management Journal 21(3), 351–363 (2003)
17. O'Banion, T.: An Academic Advising Model. Junior College Journal 42, 62, 64, 66–69 (1972)
18. Stewart, G.L., Barrick, M.R.: Team structure and performance: Assessing the role of intra-team process and the moderating role of task type. Academy of Management Journal 43, 135–148 (2000)
19. Malhotra, A., Majchrzak, A., Rosen, B.: Leading Virtual Teams. Academy of Management Perspectives 21, 60–70 (2007)

# Integration of Google Docs as a Collaborative Activity within the LMS Using IMS BasicLTI

Marc Alier Forment[1], Maria José Casañ[1], Jordi Piguillem Poch[1], Nikolas Galanis[1], Enric Mayol[1], Miguel Angel Conde[2], and Francisco J. García-Peñalvo[2]

[1] Universitat Politècnica de Catalunya, c/Jordi Girona Salgado 1-3,
08034 Barcelona, Spain
[2] Computer Science Department. Science Education Research Institute (IUCE). GRIAL Research Group. University of Salamanca
{malier,mjcasany,jpiguillem,ngalanis}@essi.upc.edu
{mconde,fgarcia}@usal.es

**Abstract.** Google Docs is a well-known suite of online collaborative tools for document processing, spreadsheets, online presentations, drawing and even quizzes. Google Docs has the potential to become a powerful tool within and LMS course, primarily due to its collaborative qualities. This paper presents an integration that using the IMS BLTI standard turns Google Docs into an engine that powers collaborative learning activities within the Moodle LMS platform.

**Keywords:** VLE, LMS, Interoperability, eLearning, Software as a Service, Cloud Computing, PLEs.

## 1   Introduction

One of the most used acronyms in the world of eLearning is PLE, which stands for Personal Learning Environment. This loose concept shapes a way that long life learners are going to learn: not within a walled garden of the VLE (Virtual Learning Environment or LMS Learning Management System) owned and managed by learning institutions, but as a rather self organized set of sources of information, interaction with peers, learning services, tools, contents and social networks.

This paper presents GDocs-Task, an open source project that embeds the features of Google Docs, as a learning activity within a VLE or LMS course. GDocs-Task works with all the major LMSs in the market, since it is compliant with the interoperability standard IMS BasicLTI.

While this paper is not about PLEs, it has a great deal to do with them. The basic goal of a PLE is how a life long learner should plan, get and organize her learning; she is supposed to learn the necessary knowledge, skills and basic digital competences through her formal learning processes. If these processes only happen within the VLE and the basic set of learning tools implemented on its courses, where content and interaction will remain inside the institution and often will expire shorty after the course is finished, the learner will not be able to keep her learning activities nor learn how to build a PLE.

M.D. Lytras et al. (Eds.): WSKS 2011, CCIS 278, pp. 677–683, 2013.

Let's consider this -not so fictional- scenario: a subgroup of students of a class are using tools like Instant Messaging, Wikis, Wave or are participating in a Social Networking site, while -and sometimes for- doing homework. The students engaged in the usage of all these online tools might get better grades or not - some studies say they most likely will -, but they will also learn important skills and become competent in taking advantage of information technologies to access, share information and collaborate with others. However, their teacher may not know about it, because all the information (feedback) she receives is what appears on the LMS's course's logs, and all the tools she is aware of, are the ones bundled in the LMS.

A number of teachers are experimenting with the use of online tools and information services with their students in and out of class. They learn a lot of lessons both from their success cases and their less successful ones. They blog about it, comment on it at conferences and gatherings, tweet about it, etc. But these best practices are not passed along to the big collective of teachers that will, at best, use just the tools provided out of the box by the LMS installed in the institution [1].Another way of facing this challenge is to find out ways to integrate external tools inside the VLE/LMS. This line of work has to consider three main problems:

1. a technical problem of making learning tools and services interoperable,
2. achieving this in a way that has a pedagogical sense and utility for the learner and
3. convincing LMS and tool developers and vendors to comply with the standards proposed.

## 2    IMS BasicLTI

The IMS Global Learning consortium [2] is a well-known international organization working since 2005 in standards towards interoperability and integration of learning services and systems. Major vendors, open source organizations and learning institutions are present on the IMS board of members and enforce the compliance with the standards proposed. Standards like the widely adopted standard for quizzes QTI.

The IMS Learning Tools Interoperability (LTI), developed under supervision of Dr. Charles Severance (creator and former lead developer of the Sakai [3] LMS), focuses on the process on how a remote online tool is installed on a web based learning system. In other words, LTI solves the problem of how the teacher and the student can reach an external application (tool) from within the LMS.

The basic idea of IMS LTI is that the LMS has a proxy tool that provides an endpoint for an externally hosted tool and makes it appear as if the externally hosted tool is running within the LMS. In a sense this is kind of like a smart tool that can host lots of different content. The proxy tool provides the externally hosted tool with information about the user, course, tool placement, and role within the course. In a sense the Proxy Tool allows a single-sign-on behind the scenes and permits an externally hosted tool to support many different LMS's with a single instance of the tool.

IMS LTI is a work in progress that has not bet made public yet. But the current IMS Common Cartridge v1.1 standard [4] includes support for BasicLTI. BasicLTI contains the core functionalities that LTI aim for, and its consumer is already implemented in the major LMS open source and proprietary (Moodle, Sakai, OLAT, Angel, WebCT and Blackboard). The authors of this paper have implemented the Moodle 1.9 and Moodle 2.0 consumers for Moodle [5] http://code.google.com/p/basiclti4moodle/. (The Moodle 2.0 consumer is awaiting revision of the Moodle community to be included on the official release of Moodle 2.1. http://tracker.moodle.org/browse/MDL-20534).

## 3     Google Docs as a Learning Tool

Google Docs [6] is a sophisticated cloud computing based set of office tools, that implements a collaborative rich environment that provides the mostly used features of the desktop based office suites.

Google enforces Google Docs for educational purposes [7] because it allows learners to create and edit documents from anywhere and collaborate with multiple people at the same time. Documents are saved online and can be accessed from any computer with an Internet connection. It is also a tool of collaboration, since multiple people can work together on the same document. Google Docs saves automatically, on a regular basis. Each change is tracked as a new revision. The user can see exactly what's been revised, by whom, and when.

If a teacher is invited to share a document with the student she can review, comment, and grade their work at any time, while it is hard for students to get away with unwanted practices when the teacher can review their work at all times. Moreover, the documents can be made public to wider audiences, like parents, or even published directly to blogs.

Google Docs implement a document editor, an online spreadsheet, a presentation tool, a drawing tool, and Google Forms, which the teacher can easily use to create self-grading quizzes [7].

Google Docs is primarily a free service, although there is also a paid version that can be a substitute for using an office suite. Using Google Docs, documents become ubiquitous, so the students can access their documents from school and home. Google makes a strong case about the use of Google Docs for education.

## 4     Current Integration of Google Docs in Moodle 2.0, Not Enough

The latest versions of the most popular LMSs, like Moodle, come with integration with Google Docs. But how do these integrations work? What features do they provide?

Moodle 2.0 integrates Google docs through the repository API. This means that when the user wants to upload a document, he can choose Google Docs as a source for this document on Moodle's file picker. So Moodle 2.0 is using Google Docs the same way it uses any other file storage system. Thus we loose all the advantages hinted in section 3: Visibility of the document's creation process, collaboration, possibility for participation by the teacher in the student's document by correcting and hinting at elements, use of quick quizzes created either by the teacher or the students with Forms, tracking and organization of cumulative project data on documents and spreadsheets, and a lot of other, more subtle uses.

## 5    GDocs-Task Overview

The GDocs-Task project aims to develop an interoperable software connector that embeds the functionalities of Google Docs as a LMS native activity within the virtual classroom. Let's consider the most simple use case:

1. The teacher sets up a writing activity inside the LMS course. This writing needs to be done with the Google Docs editor. (Fig 1.)
2. When the student enters in the activity, a Document is created within his Google Docs account. This document is shared with the teacher, so the teacher can observe the student's progression through the "Revision history" view, and also can make contributions to the document.
3. When the student considers the assignment is complete he can "deliver" the document within the activity, creating a PDF copy of the current version and sharing it with the teacher. The student will keep the living version of the document and can, if she whishes to, stop sharing the document with the teacher.
4. The teacher can make assessments of the student's activity and send the grades to the LMS course gradebook.

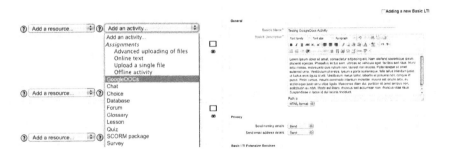

**Fig. 1.** The teacher creates a GoogleDocs activity within Moodle

More complex use cases include the collaborative editing of documents, where a single document is shared by the whole classroom or group; document workflows where a document needs to be revised by a sequence of students; peer reviewing of documents. These cases are yet to be implemented.

**Fig. 2.** The student can access the document within the LMS or directly in her Google Docs account

# 6     Architecture and Security Issues

## 6.1     Architecture

GDocs-task is a java based web application. It implements the BasicLTI protocol performing as Tool *producer*. The LMS needs to implement a BasicLTI *consumer*. Most of the popular LMSs have such a consumer implemented. The LMS consumer allows the creation of activities within the LMS courses that are representing the tools outside the LMS. When a user accesses a BasicLTI based activity the consumer interacts with the tool, sending the necessary data back and forth so the user can interact with the tool as if it were an LMS native activity.

GDocs-task also interacts with the webservices API that Google Docs offers to developers. That's how it can perform tasks such as creating and sharing documents, launching the Google Docs user interface and binding it to the LMS.

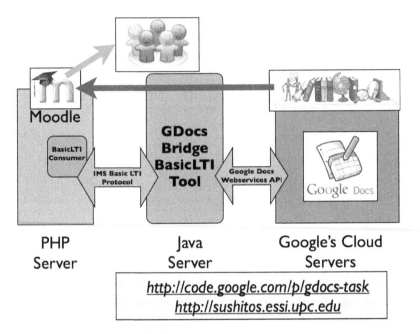

**Fig. 3.** GDocs-Task architecture

## 6.2   Security Issues

Privacy and security are two very important issues in this project. We need to be sure that the student's Google account password is revealed to neither GDocs-task nor the LMS. And we need to be sure that Google does not receive information concerning academic matters. Google just needs to handle the data inside the document within the Google Docs terms of service.

GDocs-task, as every BasicLTI tool, needs to be configured by the LMS administrator. The connection between the LMS and the Tool is signed using OAuth [8]. The IMS BasicLTI consumer takes care of this. Additionally, administrator and teacher can limit the information about the student that the LMS is going to provide to the BasicLTI Tools. In the most restrictive case, the student will only be identified by a number to the tool.

Before editing documents and fully using GDocs-task, the teacher and the student will be asked by Google to authorize the GDocs-task to access its Google Docs service. This is also done using OAuth, and means that the Google account remains a secret between Google and the user.

## 7     Future work and Conclusions

The current implementation of GDocs-task is a first step to integrating the full bundle of Google Docs tools: spreadsheets, presentations, painting tool, forms, etc. We need to start experimenting with different ways of wrapping these tools for different educational purposes. We need to work along with teachers to communicate and teach how to use these tools and to learn how to improve them.

More elaborate uses of the architecture require some additions to the IMS BasicLTI standard in form of extensions. We need to follow the IMS process to push our proposals.

Finally other web 2.0 cloud services can be transformed into learning activities and be included in the toolkit that LMS can offer.

**Acknowledgements.** A Google research award has funded this project. We thank Google for its support and in particular the Googlers Dr. Max Sengues and Julio Merino.

# References

1. Alier, M., Casañ, M.J., Piguillem, J.: Moodle 2.0: Shifting from a Learning Toolkit to a Open Learning Platform. In: Lytras, M.D., Ordonez De Pablos, P., Avison, D., Sipior, J., Jin, Q., Leal, W., Uden, L., Thomas, M., Cervai, S., Horner, D. (eds.) TECH-EDUCATION 2010. CCIS, vol. 73, pp. 1–10. Springer, Heidelberg (2010) ISBN: 978-3-642-13166-0
2. IMS Global Learning Consortium, http://www.imsglobal.org/
3. Sakai Project, http://sakaiproject.org/
4. IMS Common Cartridge v1.1 Specification, http://www.imsglobal.org/cc/
5. Moodle, http://moodle.org/
6. Google Docs, http://docs.google.com
7. Google Tools for Learning, http://sites.google.com/site/ld6edtech/
8. The OAuth 1.0 Protocol RfC, ISSN: 2070-1721, http://tools.ietf.org/html/rfc5849

# Author Index